What GARDEN PEST or DISEASE Is That?

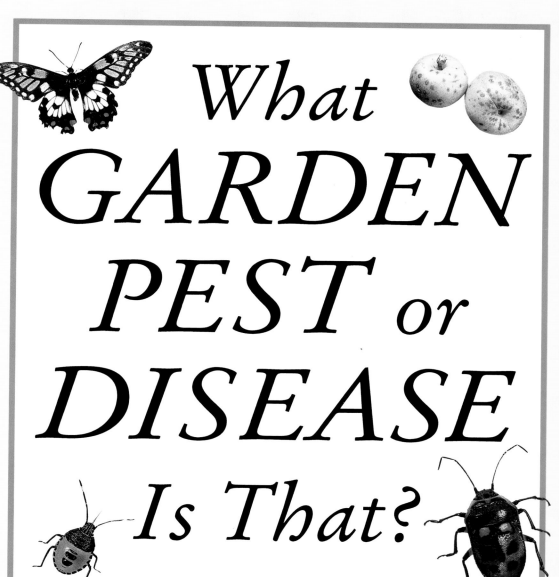

What GARDEN PEST *or* DISEASE *Is That?*

Organic and Chemical
Solutions for Every Garden Problem

JUDY MᶜMAUGH

NEW
HOLLAND

DISCLAIMER

Laws governing pesticide use vary from country to country and from State to State. They may also vary from time to time.

Therefore, irrespective of the recommendations in this book, it is essential that the user follows the registered label instructions on pesticides, and otherwise complies with current local pesticide regulations. The author and publisher are in no way responsible and make no guarantees for the use of the pesticides mentioned.

The omission of certain trade names is inadvertent and should not be seen as an endorsement of the names included.

WARNING

In New South Wales, Australia, it is an offence under the Pesticides Act 1978 to use a pesticide in a way that does not comply with the instructions on the registered label (unless a specific permit has been issued under the Act to do so). Details of regulations in other Australian states, and in New Zealand, can be obtained from the appropriate Government departments.

Published in Australia by
New Holland Publishers (Australia) Pty Ltd
Sydney • Auckland • London • Cape Town

14 Aquatic Drive Frenchs Forest NSW 2086 Australia
218 Lake Road Northcote Auckland New Zealand
86 Edgware Rd London W2 2EA United Kingdom
80 McKenzie Street Cape Town 8001 South Africa

First published by Lansdowne Press in 1985
Reprinted 1986, 1987
Reprinted by Weldon Publishing 1989, 1990
Reprinted by Ure Smith Press 1991
Revised edition published by Lansdowne Publishing Pty Ltd 1994
Reprinted 1996
Reprinted by New Holland Publishers (Australia) Pty Ltd in 2000, 2001, 2003, 2004

National Library of Australia Cataloguing-in-Publication Data:

McMaugh, Judy.
What garden pest or disease is that?: organic and chemical solutions for every garden problem.

Includes index.
ISBN 1 86436 699 0.

1. Plant diseases—Australia. 2. Garden pests—Australia.
3. Gardening—Australia. I. Title.

635.0490994

Revised edition:
Publishing Manager: Deborah Nixon
Production Manager: Sally Stokes
Project Coordinator/Editor: Bronwyn Hilton
Cover design: Kathie Baxter Smith
Interior Design: Bronwyn Hilton
Printer: Phoenix Offset, Hong Kong

CONTENTS

How to Use this Book

This book is intended to help gardeners avoid garden problems and to deal efficiently with any that do occur.

The hundreds of pests and diseases included in this book do not all occur in the same geographic area or in the same season. In fact years may pass before most of them are of serious concern in a particular garden. Some insects have been included only to show that although commonly seen they do very little damage and should be accepted as part of the friendly garden fauna.

Although pesticides have been included it is not intended to urge their use. On the contrary, I hope that all gardeners will minimise the use of pesticides and concentrate on the many other methods of pest and disease control and even learn to live with a little more plant damage.

The Planning and Maintaining Your Garden section discusses general garden procedures and how best to carry them out so that pest and disease problems are lessened. There is also information about a range of organic or non-chemical control measures and how they might be applied.

Each plant pest and disease is listed under a frequently used common name. Common names, however, do vary from place to place and country to country so check the index if the name you use does not appear in the main relevant section.

Scientific names have been included to make the seeking of further information easier. The names of pests, both common and scientific, conform in the main to the CSIRO Publication, *Handbook of Australian Insect Names* (1993) by Ian Naumann.

The A-Z of Plant Care section outlines appropriate culture for a wide range of plants and indicates their most common pest and disease problems. It also suggests some solutions.

More information about most of these problems, together with coloured photographs can be found in the Pest or Disease section.

The letter (P) indicates that further information occurs in the Pest section and the letter (D) indicates that more information can be found in the Diseases section. These two sections are arranged in alphabetical order.

For example, part of the entry for azalea reads:

Brown spots or patches on leaves may be a fungal leaf spot or may be caused by azalea leafminer (P). White circular areas may be powdery mildew (D).

This means that further information about azalea leafminer may be found in the Pest section and that more about powdery mildew can be found in the Disease Section.

Both Organic and non-organic control measures are given for each plant problem and you should read the control recommendations at the beginning of the Pest section and the Disease section.

I hope that using this book will make your gardening easier and more enjoyable.

Judy McMaugh
Sydney, 1994

PLANNING & MAINTAINING
your Garden

*A guide to planning and caring for your garden
so that pest and disease problems
are minimised*

PLANNING TO AVOID GARDEN PROBLEMS

Apart from personal preference there are a number of other factors that should be taken into account when choosing plants for a garden.

Find out about the climate of the general region, and look at the features of the house block you have chosen. Use this information to plan a trouble-free garden: either choose plants that suit the site, or be prepared to alter the site to suit your favourite plants.

Climate

The climate of the region is an important influence on choice of garden plants. Do frosts occur in the area? Droughts? Strong winds? Find out the extremes of temperature recorded in your area and how much rain to expect and when. Your government meteorological service should have some information, and local gardening clubs can help too.

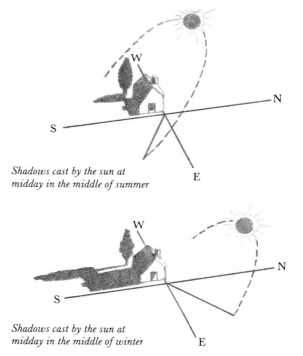

Shadows cast by the sun at midday in the middle of summer

Shadows cast by the sun at midday in the middle of winter

The extent of shade in a garden depends on the time of year and the proximity to the equator. These diagrams compare winter and summer shade in the same garden and show the sun's movement.

Microclimate

As soon as structures such as houses and fences are erected on a piece of land, various different microclimates are created. The first-planted trees and shrubs also alter the environment and may make it a more suitable place for plants that are more demanding. Some areas may be in constant shade, while others may be particularly hot and dry such as the area under the eaves of the house on the western side. Look for these differences in your own garden when choosing plants for particular places.

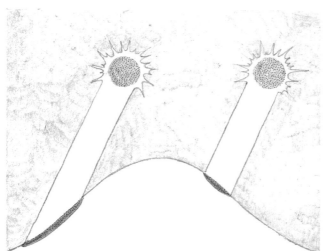

The right-hand side of the hill in this diagram is north-facing. The sun's rays are concentrated into a smaller area than on the south-facing slope (on the left-hand side of the diagram), and therefore give a greater warming effect. The north-facing slope is protected from southerly winds.

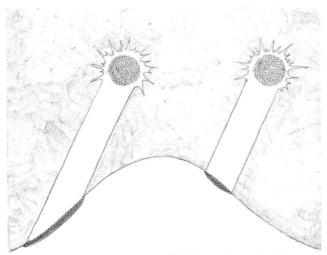

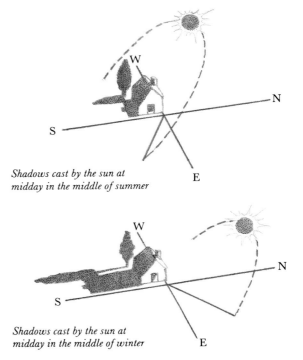

Shadows cast by the sun at midday in the middle of summer

Shadows cast by the sun at midday in the middle of winter

The extent of shade in a garden depends on the time of year and the proximity to the equator. These diagrams compare winter and summer shade in the same garden and show the sun's movement.

Microclimate

As soon as structures such as houses and fences are erected on a piece of land, various different microclimates are created. The first-planted trees and shrubs also alter the environment and may make it a more suitable place for plants that are more demanding. Some areas may be in constant shade, while others may be particularly hot and dry such as the area under the eaves of the house on the western side. Look for these differences in your own garden when choosing plants for particular places.

Soil

Knowing something about the soil in your garden and how to look after it will not only help you to grow better plants but also conserve an important national resource.

Since the dependence of mankind on green plants is absolute, it seems incredibly foolish to destroy by bad management, the substance in which most of them are grown, the soil.

The two most important considerations about soils are fertility and structure. These factors are determined by the nature of the rock (or other parent materials) from which the soil developed, the conditions under which it developed (the climate and vegetation), and the treatment it has received since at the hands of humans.

Soil is in layers and this can be easily seen where a road or railway has been cut deeply into a hill. The uppermost layer is referred to as the topsoil and the layer beneath that as the subsoil. The parent rock may be visible at the bottom.

A trench dug for house foundations on your block of land will help to show you how deep the topsoil is in the garden. The topsoil is the area of greatest fertility and greatest activity of micro-organisms and earthworms. It varies in depth from place to place. It may be only millimetres deep, or more than a metre deep.

The subsoil is likely to be more dense than the layers above and harder to dig. It may be a heavy clay which will make drainage difficult and may slow the growth of plant roots into it.

Soil is made up of particles of rock, sand, clay and silt. It also contains air, water, and organic matter and is the home of billions of micro-organisms.

Sand particles are the largest and range in size from 2 mm to 0.02 mm. They are derived from hard glass-like rocks and are normally the major component of a soil. Silt particles are smaller and cannot be seen with the unaided eye. Sand and silt particles often operate as individual units in a soil.

Clay particles are the smallest but because of their structure they tend to clump together into groups. They also attract and hold large amounts of the nutrients which plants need. Soils with a wide range of particle sizes are more subject to compaction than others.

If the topsoil is very shallow or has been buried under the subsoil during construction work, you may need to buy some soil for the garden. There is an Australian standard for garden soil (AS 2223–1978) which, among other things, restricts the quantity of stones, roots, claylumps and vegetative parts of certain weeds such as oxalis, nut grass and onion weed.

Unfortunately, however, in many cases all that is available for sale is a silty sand from the flood plains of rivers near big cities. Many of these 'garden soils' are worse than the other soils they are brought in to replace or augment.

It is often much better to take the 'on site' soil and improve it by incorporating beneficial components such as compost. This is a slow but sure method. Australian soils are notoriously low in organic matter, so the value to a garden of compost, green manures and animal manures cannot be over-emphasised.

Organic matter consists of pieces of dead plant and animal material in various stages of decay. It is broken down into smaller and smaller particles by the activities of soil organisms and finally becomes humus. During this process nutrients are released. These are used by plants and also by micro-organisms.

Organic matter and humus increase soil water-holding capacity and improve the aeration of most soils by helping to bind soil particles together into crumbs.

Breakdown of organic matter will be very slow if the soil is waterlogged or if it is acid.

Drainage

Water is essential for plant growth, but too much of it can cause serious problems. Adequate drainage is essential for the establishment of a healthy garden. Most popular garden plants will grow poorly and may die if the soil is waterlogged. This is not so much because of the presence of the water itself but rather because of the absence of oxygen.

Plant roots, like the above-ground parts, need oxygen if they are to grow and carry out their functions, such as the uptake of nutrients, satisfactorily. They cannot obtain oxygen if the air in the soil spaces is displaced by water for long periods.

During periods of rain, water drains down through the soil under the influence of gravity but usually not quickly enough to prevent all the spaces being filled with water. This soil is then saturated and plants cannot grow. If this situation continues, damage or death will occur. Different plants tolerate waterlogging for different lengths of time.

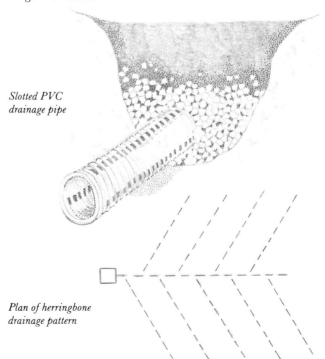

Slotted PVC drainage pipe

Plan of herringbone drainage pattern

Drainage lines should have an even slope to the lowest point so that water flows easily to the soakaway or stormwater drain. The pipes should be surrounded by coarse material such as gravel.

The ability of the roots to take up plant nutrients is decreased if the soil is too wet, and the proportion of nutrients available may be changed. For example, waterlogging may cause phosphorus to be less available and manganese to be more available.

Excess water may have a bad effect on soil structure and interfere with the activities of useful soil micro-organisms and may cause them to produce substances toxic to plants.

Root-rotting organisms such as *Phytophthora* and *Pythium* spread readily if free water is present.

Poorly drained lower soil levels encourage plants to produce most roots near the surface.

Roots need warmth for active growth. Wet soils remain cold for longer than drier ones because it takes more heat to warm them.

All the above factors lead to death of roots, particularly the young ones which take up most nutrients.

Root damage may go unnoticed if the weather is cool and the plants are not losing much water from the leaves. When the weather becomes warmer, perhaps months later, the symptoms will be similar to those produced by mineral deficiency or lack of water. These include leaf yellowing, leaf withering, leaf fall, and dieback of branches. There will be fewer small roots than normal, and if inspected they may be brown to black inside instead of white and the outer layers may readily separate from the inner, more fibrous, layers.

If drainage is not to be improved, plants that tolerate wet soil conditions must be chosen. Consider the development of a bog garden.

Understanding pH
This is a scientific term which describes the amount of acid in a soil. A highly acid soil has a very low pH (e.g. 4). This level may not be low in absolute terms — for example, battery acid would have a pH of about 2.

Soils that lack acidity, or are high in lime, are described as alkaline and may have a pH of about 8. Again this is not high in absolute terms — caustic soda, which is highly alkaline, would have a pH of 13 or 14. A pH of 7 is the neutral point where acidity and alkalinity are in perfect balance. Every step on the pH scale is ten times the value of the previous one, so that a pH of 6 is 10 times more acid than a pH of 7, while a pH of 5 is 100 times more acid than a pH of 7, and a pH of 4 is 1000 times more acid than a pH of 7.

pH controls solubility and therefore the availability to the plant of various plant nutrients. As pH increases — that is, as the soil becomes more alkaline — iron, manganese, zinc, copper and boron become less and less available and eventually deficiency symptoms will appear unless the plants have evolved on alkaline soils.

Phosphorus is less soluble and therefore less available to plants in very acid soils, and this often limits growth. Plants such as some Australian natives that come from areas of acid soils are better at extracting phosphates than are other plants in these circumstances.

The pH may also cause certain elements to be available to the plant in toxic quantities. For example, in very acid soils manganese and aluminium may become toxic.

On the other hand, in acid soils molybdenum may become less available to the plant. It becomes a matter of finding the 'happy medium' for each plant.

You shouldn't worry about the pH of your soil if most plants (the ones you want to grow) perform reasonably well. If they do not grow well then consider pH as one possible reason for this and make investigations into the pH level and how to cope with it.

Nutrient availability

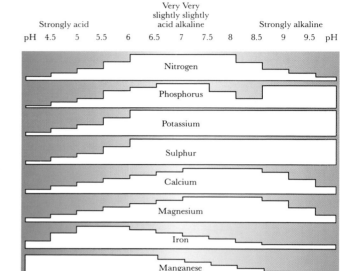

Availability is least at the pH corresponding to the narrowest parts of the band for each element and most at the widest.

To find out the pH of your garden soil, you could buy a small soil testing kit from your nursery. These work with dyes and can be successfully used by home-gardeners. The way the soil is sampled for the test is important — always follow the directions carefully.

If necessary more accurate results can be obtained with more sophisticated equipment such as a meter with a glass electrode. These cost about fifty times as much as a dye kit and need care in their use and maintenance.

Establishing a new garden
If you own the land before building starts, attention to the factors listed below will save trouble later.

Excavations for foundations and levelling procedures on a block of land often result in the subsoil, which is not good for growing plants, being at the top. Try to make sure that the topsoil is scraped up and stockpiled in one area. It can then be spread over the surface when building is finished.

If you want to keep existing trees, try hard to protect their trunks from earth-moving machinery and from

Excavations for a driveway removed half the roots of this tree. It will gradually die and may even blow down in a storm.

thoughtless humans. Altering the level of soil around a tree or compacting the soil with large machines is almost always fatal (see also the introduction to the Trees and shrubs section).

Remove the stumps of unwanted trees and as many roots as possible. A fungal disease called armillaria root rot (D) can spread from these pieces of root to shrubs and trees planted later.

It is important to remove any perennial weeds such as onion weed before planting the garden out.

Be meticulous in the removal of building rubbish and do not allow the builder to bury waste materials on the site. Pick up as much mortar from new brick work as possible; mortar tends to make the soil more alkaline, and many plants grow poorly in such conditions.

Choice of species

Some plants will grow quite well in a wide range of climates including places that seem quite different from where they originated. Such adaptable plants should form the basis of a garden plan and provide a background for others that are shorter-lived or less reliable. Most permanent plants chosen should also suit the native soil. Soil can be modified, but it is a long-term project and will take years to achieve.

The quality and availability of the water to be used is also important. If water is scarce, eliminate flowering annuals and large areas of lawn from the plan. Mulch garden beds and choose trees and shrubs that originated in dry areas.

In certain areas the water is saline, and plants that tolerate this condition must be chosen.

Tree ferns, bird's nest ferns and busy lizzies are ideal for this shady spot and should provide a trouble-free garden.

Buying plants

Get your garden off to a good start by carefully choosing the healthiest possible specimens and planting them promptly. Do not buy a plant of any sort and then leave it for hours in a hot car.

Seedlings that are very tall and spindly have probably been in the shop for a considerable period of time and should be left there. Check that the stems are firm and the same width right to soil level. Any indentations or sunken areas may indicate a collar rot.

Make sure that trees and shrubs do not have many roots growing out through the holes in the pot. This indicates a condition referred to as 'potbound' and it may mean that the plant never grows well from that point onward.

Plants that appear dried out and brittle and in need of a drink should be left in the shop. Do not buy the last scruffy specimen. Look elsewhere.

Planting and placement

Group together the plants that need similar conditions and culture. This applies particularly to the water supply they require.

Space plants so that each can grow without undue competition from others. This applies to both above and below ground level. Soil space has a limit, and if too many roots are crowded close together none of the plants will thrive.

If water is in short supply, plants should be spaced further apart than usual so that the roots of each have a larger area to exploit.

Not only do plants compete for water and nutrients, they also compete for light. Some plants are very poor competitors for light and this is easily seen in grasses; heavily shaded gardens usually have poor lawns because most grasses need open well-lit areas.

Humidity is often high around crowded plants. This may lead to more frequent problems with leaf diseases.

These tall seedlings have been left in the punnet too long.

Never buy plants that are very tall in small pots, particularly if they have roots emerging from the bottom.

These plants should have been repotted long ago. They will never grow satisfactorily after this treatment.

The elm and the eucalypt planted in this garden will soon be competing for space.

The shrubs crowded together here cannot grow to their natural shape and size. Crowding also increases humidity around the plants and makes leaf diseases more likely.

MAINTAINING THE GARDEN

Once the garden has been planned and planted, it requires some care and attention to keep it healthy and thus avoid major problems.

To a certain extent, plants can defend themselves against pests and diseases. They can do this most efficiently and for longer if they are well cared for and growing in a suitable environment.

But plants have a certain life span just like dogs or cats or humans. Some wattles, for example have completed the active growing part of their life after about five years, and gradually become more vulnerable to pests and diseases. Care of mature plants will lengthen the time they remain healthy and beautiful.

The procedures discussed here are all necessary at various times in any garden but will need to be carried out less frequently if you have planned a low-maintenance garden. Read this section in conjunction with the notes on cultural controls (pages 34–40).

Fertiliser

Plants cannot grow and function well unless certain elements are available. Carbon, hydrogen and oxygen are obtained from air or from water in the soil. Nitrogen, phosphorus, potassium, calcium, sulphur and magnesium are obtained from the soil by the roots. Some other elements although essential are needed in very small quantities. These 'trace elements' are boron, chlorine, copper, iron, molybdenum and zinc. They are also taken up by the roots.

Soils rich in clays and organic matter have large reserves of these elements and will normally support plant growth for a long time without fertiliser additions.

In many other soils, limited quantities of some or all of these elements may be present and if plants are grown and harvested (removed) on a regular basis, a replacement programme using fertilisers will be necessary.

Fertilisers may be of mineral composition or they may be organic materials like manures. Most of the former are prepared by industrial processes and are sometimes referred to as chemical fertilisers. As far as the elements themselves are concerned, it makes no difference to a plant whether they come from organic or chemical sources. However, organic fertilisers such as poultry manure, are important sources of trace elements which are necessary to keep soil microbes working properly as well as for plant growth. Also, organic matter helps improve soil structure.

The type of fertiliser required by plants varies with the age of the plant and the purpose for which it is being grown. Germinating seeds and young plants require a higher level of phosphorus than do older plants.

Excessive levels of nitrogen when seed is germinating may lead to a high incidence of damping-off (D) (*pythium* spp.); but plants grown for leaves (e.g. lawns, indoor foliage plants and vegetables such as lettuce) require more nitrogen than other plants.

The correct balance of elements in soils and their availability is just as important as the total quantity present. Soil pH is the dominant controlling factor in keeping nutrients in balance.

If excessive amounts of micro-nutrients are available to the plant, serious damage can result. Symptoms are often difficult to distinguish from those of deficiency problems, and records of fertiliser applications could be a great help in diagnosis. Such toxicities are more likely to be related to pH and availability to the plant than excessive applications of fertiliser.

10% (by weight) of the contents of this bag is nitrogen (N); 4% is phosphorus(P) and 6% is potassium (K).

Major ingredients of fertiliser bags can be seen at a glance.

Lombardy poplar: salt toxicity

Watsonia: damaged by excess nutrients

Grevillea 'Robyn Gordon': nutrient imbalance

The symptoms of nutrient excess or deficiency vary from plant to plant and element to element.

Gardenia: magnesium deficiency

Apricot: manganese deficiency

The application of excessive quantities of fertiliser is wasteful and harmful. The rate at which plants can use fertiliser is related to light and water supply; if these other factors necessary for growth are not completely satisfactory, the fertiliser may be wasted.

Excess nutrients may be washed from the root zone by rain and watering before the plants have a chance to use them, or they may cause leaf and root burn. Leaf burn is typically at tips and edges because excess salts are exuded from hydathodes in guttation water.

Excessive nitrogen causes the production of large soft leaves which are easily damaged by wind and prone to pest and disease attack. There may also be suppression of food storage and limited development of flower, fruit and seed. If plants have been fertilised too much by mistake, several heavy waterings will help to remove the excess nutrients from the root zone. In areas of heavy rainfall, nutrients (particularly nitrogen) are readily leached from the soil, and higher quantities can be applied more frequently than in lower rainfall areas. Nutrients are leached from sandy soil more readily than from those with more clay or organic matter content.

Serious environmental problems can be caused if large amounts of nutrients end up in drainage water and reach creeks, rivers and dams. Gardeners should take the trouble to understand the nutrient requirements of the plants they want to grow and the characteristics of their garden soil so that they can better supply what the plants need with little left over. The likelihood of nutrients causing pollution can be reduced if organic or slow release fertilisers are used. Avoid over-watering.

Root and leaf damage may result if fertiliser is applied in hot weather or when the soil is dry.

If plants have insufficient available nutrients, their growth is abnormal, Unfortunately it is almost impossible to look at a leaf or two and diagnose deficiency diseases accurately unless one is very familiar with that particular crop. Some deficiency diseases have been thoroughly studied, and details will be given later in this book of boron deficiency (D), zinc deficiency (D), manganese deficiency (D), magnesium deficiency (D), iron deficiency (D), chlorosis (D), whiptail of crucifers (D), blossom-ended rot (D) and bitter pit (D).

Chemical analysis of soil may reveal deficiencies, but

sometimes nutrients are unavailable to plants although they are present in the soil.

Leaf analyses are a more accurate way to diagnose deficiency diseases. Information obtained from tests must be related to what is known of conditions in the field. It is not usually possible for home-gardeners to obtain this type of information because tests are expensive and the staff and facilities available to do such tests are limited at Departments of Agriculture.

For home-gardeners it is generally easier to ensure an adequate supply of mirco-nutrients by using a fertiliser containing them once or twice a year, than it is to try to analyse for them.

Fertiliser placement will be discussed in the Trees and Shrubs introduction. See also the Vegetables section.

Crop rotation

Crop rotation involves planting a sequence of different crops in the same area of soil. It is principally designed to make best use of soil nutrients and to reduce the likelihood of damage from soil-borne diseases. It has most use in vegetable and annual flower production and will be discussed further in these sections.

Even if no pests and diseases have been identified in the areas, crop rotation should be practised. It may postpone their arrival indefinitely.

Unfortunately, the wider the range of plants a disease can attack, the more unlikely it is that control can be achieved with crop rotation. Grey mould (D) *Botrytis* sp.)

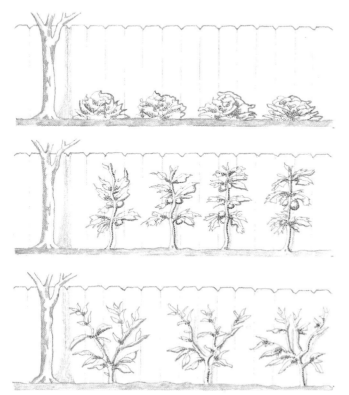

The same area of garden should have vegetables from different groups planted in it each year so that disease problems will be minimised and nutrients will be used efficiently.

is a disease that cannot be minimised using this method. It attacks a wide range of plants and would cause problems with almost any plant chosen for the rotation. It also produces sclerotia, structures that can remain in the soil for years and still infect susceptible plants.

Root knot nematode (D) does attack a wide range of plants, but can be very much reduced in numbers by including a period of fallow in the rotation. The soil must be kept completely free of living plant material, including weeds.

Club root (D) is a disease that attacks only crucifers, and provided crucifers are grown in the one area no more frequently than once in three years, damage should be minimal. The different plants grown in the other years would not be attacked at all.

The number of pests that can be discouraged by the use of crop rotation is rather small. The pest must have a restricted host range — that is, it must be possible to follow a susceptible crop with a crop that the pest does not like. The pest must also have limited mobility — flightless weevils, for example, or moths with inefficient flight. Crop rotation can be successful in the case of tomato russet mite (P).

Companion planting

The term 'companion planting' usually refers to the practice of grouping different plants together in order to discourage pests and diseases or to increase plant growth and production. Companion planting practices are based on the observations of many gardeners over many years and in different locations.

The problem is that if the basis or reason for a certain satisfactory relationship between plants in one situation is not known, then the same success may not necessarily be achieved in another situation. The garden or farm of the original success may differ in some unrecorded respects from others where attempts are made to repeat the practice. Weather, soil type, and other plants and insects in the vicinity are some factors that may affect successful repetition of these methods.

There are several general reasons for good results from companion planting. The diverse plants in such a garden will flower at different times and therefore provide a more continuous nectar supply to feed beneficial insects such as wasps and flies.

The food supply of plant-feeding insects is not as accessible as it would be if the same host plants occurred in row after row.

Strong-smelling herbs included in the garden may make it more difficult for insects to find their food plants, because many insects use the sense of smell to do this.

Different species of plants produce roots of different lengths. A variety of different plants in an area may mean that all can obtain adequate nutrients without competing with one another.

The presence of certain plants, and particularly their root exudates, may adversely affect micro-organisms capable of producing diseases in other plants. As plant roots live and grow, they release into the soil large quantities of organic compounds including sugars and proteins. These released substances are used as a food supply by micro-organisms such as bacteria, and the region around the roots contains large numbers of them. Some produce compounds that stop or slow the growth of other micro-organisms.

The root exudates of one plant may also influence the growth of another more directly. For example, it has been reported that the black walnut (*Juglans nigra*) produces from its roots substances that are toxic to many plants and cause their death. Tall fescue (*Festuca arundinacea*) is known to inhibit the growth of liquidambar seedlings. A similar inhibition of growth occurs around river red gums (*Eucalyptus camaldulensis*). In this case the chemical concerned is exuded by leaves and washed off by rain. These are all examples of a widespread phenomenon termed 'allelopathy'.

More time and money for research on companion planting are necessary before particular combinations of plants can be confidently recommended. The following commonly quoted examples are provided for your interest. There is little scientific evidence to show that they actually work.

Carrots grow well with chives, leeks, onions, peas, lettuce and sage. Cabbage grows well with potatoes and sage (the latter is said to repel cabbage pests). Peas grow well with sweet corn but not with garlic, onions or shallots. Pumpkins grow well with sweet corn but do not grow well with potatoes.

Basil is said to be good for repelling pests and diseases from tomatoes. Nasturtiums are supposed to discourage woolly apple aphid, and chives are supposed to protect apple trees from the disease apple scab (D). Marigolds (*Tagetes* sp.) are said to repel whitefly from tomato plants and to reduce nematode populations.

It is said that although corn earworm (*Helicoverpa armigera*) feeds on both corn and tomatoes, it prefers corn. Thus if corn is planted near tomatoes the latter will be free of infestation even though the corn cobs are damaged.

Basil and marigolds planted near tomatoes are said to repel pests such as whitefly and to reduce nematode populations. This is an example of companion planting.

Cultivation

Digging the soil is not necessarily a beneficial practice. It may destroy the structure of some soils by shattering the soil crumbs. Yet other soils cannot support plant growth unless they are cultivated.

Avoid working with very wet or very dry soil. Digging, rotary hoeing or even walking on wet soil is very likely to damage the soil structure and result in compaction. Rotary hoes used on a regular basis will tend to produce a hard layer where the blades continually pound the soil at the bottom of their sweep.

Cultivation aerates the surface layers. More air causes an increase in microbial activity and thus an increase in organic matter breakdown. Therefore, if fairly large quantities of organic matter are present, cultivation should improve soil structure, and the amount of nitrogen available to the next crop can be increased.

However, the supply of nutrients available to plants will be decreased if the soil is constantly cultivated without the replacement of organic matter or fertiliser.

Mulching

'Mulching' usually refers to the application of an extra layer to the soil surface. Organic materials such as leaf litter, poultry litter and straw are useful because they eventually improve the soil; but pebble mulches and sheets of plastic also have their uses.

Black plastic is convenient under strawberries and similar crops as a barrier between the fruit and the rotting organisms found in the soil. The holes in the plastic made for planting *may* allow the plant to receive enough water but extra holes are often needed. Plants surrounded by plastic mulches must be watered slowly if water penetration is to be satisfactory.

Woven plastic sheeting, which is now available, allows water and air to penetrate more readily. It can be put down over existing weeds and will kill most of them.

The soil should be well prepared and well watered, and perennial weeds should be removed before mulches are applied. However, a thick mulch is an efficient control for most annual weeds.

Avoid organic mulches such as rice husks which may contain seeds that will germinate in the garden. Some wood-chip products contain seed or roots of weeds such as privet. Do not use clippings from a lawn that has been treated with herbicide in the previous four to six weeks.

Most mulches help to keep soil cool. This is an advantage in summer but in winter makes frost damage more likely. It also means that plants grow more slowly in late winter and early spring than unmulched plants.

A black plastic mulch absorbs heat and therefore growth is better in early spring. In summer, however, plant roots may be killed. The heat radiated from pebbles in hot summer weather may burn plant leaves.

It may be possible to change the type of mulch from season to season or use mulch at some times of the year and not others.

Shiny aluminium foil sheeting such as Sisalation® reflects heat and keeps the roots cool. It also helps to confuse flying aphids so that they do not land on nearby plants. Blue plastic is said to have the same effect.

Mulching mat made from wool fibres is now available. It is like felt and is made in several thicknesses. It has good insulating properties and will break down over time, adding nutrients to the soil.

Mulches protect the soil from the pounding of heavy rain or irrigation which destroys soil structure. Water run off is reduced and therefore more water soaks into the soil. The reduction in water splash and runoff can slow the spread of some diseases. Less evaporation occurs from a mulched soil; this is particularly helpful in areas where the water is high in soluble salts.

Wilting may result from suitable mulch management because some mulches such as lawn clippings can form a crust which stops water reaching plant roots.

Mulches may contain toxic substances that damage plants, particularly young ones. Straw should not be spread around seedlings because they may be damaged by chemicals released in the early stages of decomposition. Some sawdusts and barks seems to cause damage when they are fresh and plants are young. When there is a possibility of this problem arising, spread the mulch thinly (say, 30 mm thick). If plants do suffer damage, water heavily to wash toxins below the root zone and possibly also remove the mulch until the plants are older.

It has been suggested in the past that mulching encourages plants to form many surface roots in the moist area just under the mulch and few deeper roots. If this were the case, plants could be more susceptible to periods of low water supply. Experiments have now indicated that mulched plants grow as many large deep roots as unmulched plants, but they; grow more fibrous roots near the surface. These roots enable the plant to take advantage of the greater fertility near the surface.

Organic mulches must be kept away from the trunks of trees and shrubs. Close contact keeps the bark moist and may enable fungi to attack the trunk. Sometimes heavy applications of organic mulches can produce water repellency in soils. The use of a wetting agent such as Wetta Soil ® or Saturaid ® should solve this problem.

Some pests feed on or breed in decaying organic matter. Large areas of mulch may increase problems with animals such as millipedes (P), garden soldier fly (P), springtails (P) and the common slater (P). Small, flat prawn-like creatures which jump when disturbed and are found in damp areas of mulch or around the edges of compost heaps do no harm. They are amphipods belonging to Family Talitridae and related to sea prawns

Composting

Garden compost can be used both as a surface mulch and as a fertiliser. In addition, making compost disposes of large quantities of garden and kitchen rubbish. You can use fruit and vegetable peelings, tea leaves, eggshells and most kitchen scraps, also old cut flowers, lawn clippings, weeds (without seed heads or perennial roots or bulbs), small leafy bits pruned from shrubs, fallen leaves, sawdust, straw, shredded paper, egg cartons, wood ashes, shredded woody prunings, animal manure and pine needles. In fact almost any organic material is suitable. However, do not use plant stems or roots showing signs of disease. Make the heap in a warm, sunny

Straw can be a useful and decorative mulch.

Pebble mulches last indefinitely but can get kicked onto lawns where they damage mowers.

corner of the garden or buy or construct a container.

The work of turning these materials into useful plant nutrients is done by micro-organisms. They need certain conditions to work quickly. A successful combination will be one that supplies a suitable balance of carbon and nitrogen. Carbon is a constituent of all organic materials and there will usually be enough carbon. Nitrogen content is low in sawdust, dried leaves and paper and higher in vegetable scraps and green leafy material. The heap should generally contain more of the latter or have some animal manure added to increase the supply of nitrogen. Aerate the heap by forking it over regularly or by turning it in a rotating drum composter.

The heap should not be too wet — cover it in rainy weather. It should not be too dry — in hot summer weather it may be necessary to sprinkle it with water. More details about composting are to be found in the CSIRO publication *Gardening Down-under* by Kevin Handreck — see Further Reading on page 301.

Weeding

Weeds should be removed from a garden because they compete with wanted plants for water and nutrients. They may also cause shading and reduce air circulation leading to high humidity and an increase in disease problems. Many weeds are hosts for pests and diseases.

They may be removed by surface cultivation using implements such as hoes, but care must be taken not to damage wanted plant roots and stem bases. Care must also be exercised in the use of motorised equipment with a long arm and flexible cord rotating at high speeds. The cord can seriously damage the bark of young trees and shrubs and sever smaller stems of garden plants.

In home gardens, herbicides are used most on grass lawns for the control of broadleafed weeds. The chemical MCPA is suitable for this purpose in many situations, but should the weed population include clover, medics or weeds with taproots then buy a product that includes dicamba as well.

Many garden plants however are very sensitive to this herbicide, and it should be used carefully where there are tree specimens within the lawn or where there are shallow-rooted shrubs such as azaleas very close to the edge of the lawn. In some such instances a product which contains a combination of MCPA and bromoxynl would be a much better choice.

Some vegetables, such as tomatoes and cucurbits, are very susceptible to damage from the hormone-type chemicals used to control most lawn weeds, and great care must be taken while spraying to ensure that no chemical drifts onto wanted plants. Even very small doses can cause plant distortion.

Kikuyu growing around and up shrubs and small trees can seriously damage them by competing for nutrients and excluding light from the leaves.

Weeds can be removed from paths with a herbicide such as amitrole.

Weeds in situations of this kind can be easily controlled.

Hormone herbicide damage on Hibiscus mutabilis

Broadleafed weeds can be removed by hand or by spraying with a herbicide such as MCPA. Some weeds such as clovers may require treatment with MCPP or dicamba.

Growth on tomato deformed because of herbicide drift

If large areas of vegetables are being grown, pre-emergence materials such as propyzamide (e.g. Kerb ®) may be useful to minimise the amount of weeding that has to be done. This is applicable only in situations where seedlings are being transplanted into the treated area and not in situations where seed is being sown direct. Seeds are damaged by any pre-emergent herbicide.

In large gardens the problem of weed control along fence lines, around posts and the bases of trees and shrubs may become a big problem. The use of non-residual, totally systemic poisons such asglyphosate (Glypho ®, Zero ®, Wipeout ®) makes the maintenance of these areas much easier. These products kill a wide range of weeds and have the big advantage of leaving no residues in the soil to adversely affect wanted plants later. It must be kept off the green bark which readily absorbs the poison. Glyphosate can be used on paths, but it kills only the weeds present at time of application. Sometimes a residual total herbicide such as amitrole may be needed if the frequency of spraying with Roundup becomes excessive.

Grasses on waste areas can be killed by spraying with 2,2-DPA or with glyphosate, but grass weeds in a lawn can be removed with glyphosate only if each weed is treated individually with a wick-applicator. If this is not practicable, seek advice from a horticulturalist specialising in weed control.

There are many other occasions when specialist advice is necessary. Accurate identification of the weed may be required, and factors such as its stage of growth and its nutritional status may need to be considered before a control programme is carried out.

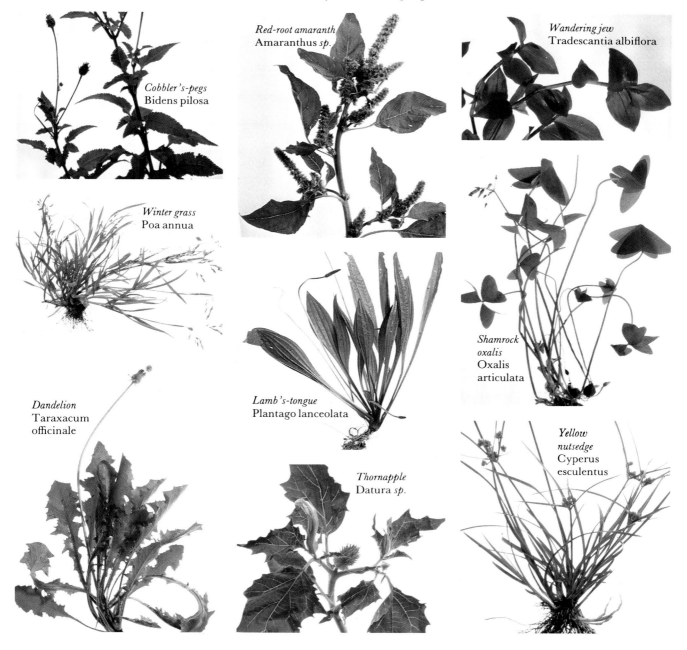

Cobbler's-pegs Bidens pilosa

Red-root amaranth Amaranthus sp.

Wandering jew Tradescantia albiflora

Winter grass Poa annua

Shamrock oxalis Oxalis articulata

Dandelion Taraxacum officinale

Lamb's-tongue Plantago lanceolata

Thornapple Datura sp.

Yellow nutsedge Cyperus esculentus

Watering

Frequent shallow watering means that most roots will develop in the surface layers, which dry out readily if not regularly watered.

Deep watering enables plants to develop an extensive deep root system and survive without constant attention.

Gardeners often apply far too much water; the application of much more water than is needed to wet the root zone is wasteful in most circumstances. However, in areas where the soil or the water contains excessive amounts of salt, application of extra water is accepted practice. This water washes some of the salt to areas below the roots and helps to reduce plant damage. This cannot be achieved unless drainage is good.

Overwatering helps the plant leaves to become soft and flabby and more easily damaged. It also makes conditions favourable for root-rotting organisms.

Once plants have developed in a high water situation, they need to have the water supply gradually (not suddenly) reduced.

If the water available is high in dissolved salts, watering should not be carried out in strong winds or in the middle of the day. The high evaporation rate at these times concentrates the salts on the leaves and leaf burn may occur.

It is a good idea to water in the evening or early morning. Less water is lost by evaporation and therefore more actually gets to the plants.

However, leaves wet by watering in the evening may remain wet for long periods and therefore lengthen the time during which fungal spores can successfully germinate and infect the plant.

Aphids (P) hosed off new shoots are not able to find their way back; and increase in populations of two-spotted mites (P) can be slowed by thoroughly watering infested leaves.

Overhead watering, however, increases humidity and therefore increases the likelihood of leaf diseases. It may also splash bacteria or fungal spores from plant to plant. Working on wet plants makes disease spread more likely, so work first, water second.

Do not expose plant roots by boring holes in the soil with a strong jet of water. Collar rots may occur on trees and shrubs if trunks or stems are kept moist near ground level. If possible adjust sprinklers to avoid this.

Frost protection

Frost damage can be reduced if measures are taken to enable the soil to warm up as much as possible during the day. It should be moist, bare, and have a firm surface. Mulches, lawns, ground covers, weeds and a loose fluffy surface all insulate the soil and limit the heat stored. Dry soil or very wet soil makes frost damage more likely. Look around your garden for barriers to the flow of cold air. If possible, alter plantings to allow movement of cold air further down the slope.

Grow frost sensitive plants near walls that may radiate some heat at night; grow them in the shelter of trees; or cover them with wooden or cardboard boxes, hessian on a frame, or similar materials. Covers must be removed during the day to allow light to reach the plants.

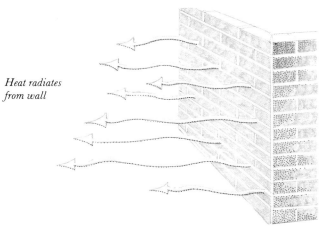

Heat radiates from wall

Solid structures such as brick fences or house walls absorb heat from the sun during the day and lose it again at night. This radiation keeps plants near the wall warmer at night.

Frosts are most likely on still, clear nights particularly if they follow cloudy days when the sun was not shining on the soil.

Frost damage may be lessened if action is taken before the frost has thawed: direct a fine spray of water over the plants and continue until the frost has thawed. Damage will be considerably worse if the plants are thawed quickly because of exposure to the morning sun.

Small trees can be protected from frost by surrounding them with hessian or clear plastic supported on stakes, or by purchasing a cover such as the ones shown here. These have two sections. Stiff wires on the bottom section are pushed into the soil and the top section clips into place. They can be re-used.

Pruning

Pruning should not be considered a routine annual procedure; some plants benefit from pruning, while others may be damaged by it.

Tools such as secateurs and pruners should be the best you can afford. Keep them sharp.

At planting time, the common practice of pruning some top growth off trees sold barerooted or balled, to compensate for roots lost or damaged during digging and transportation, is now considered by several researchers to be harmful. They say that removal of foliage slows down formation of new roots by reducing the food supply to the roots and by reducing the flow of hormones from buds to stimulate the initiation of roots. However, reduction in transpiration is still desirable, and this can be achieved by temporarily sheltering the plant from hot afternoon sun and from wind.

In subsequent years, many deciduous plants can be pruned any time they are dormant, although many general decay fungi produce spores in autumn and gain entry to wounds through pruning cuts. On some trees it has been shown that wounds are slower to callus if made in autumn. Do not prune in autumn, particularly if the weather is showery then, unless there is some other reason of overriding importance.

Pruning stimulates remaining nearby buds to grow. If pruning is carried out before all danger of severe cold weather and frosts is passed, new growth made in mild winter weather may be damaged if temperatures drop again later.

Pruning during the time of vigorous spring growth when bark is soft and the cambium is active will make bark-tearing more likely and therefore attack from pests and diseases more likely.

Correct procedures for branch removal help to avoid problems. The secateurs of most home-gardeners will not cope with branches more than 25 mm in diameter. Use a saw and remove the branch in three stages. Make the first cut in the branch from underneath and 300–600 mm from the trunk. Cut about a quarter through or until it becomes difficult to move the saw. Make the next cut from the top and 25–50 mm further away from the trunk. This procedure will remove the major part of the branch without bark damage. It is easier to make the third and final cut neat and smooth if the weight of the branch has gone.

It has long been the accepted practice to remove branches right at the trunk, leaving no stub. This is now considered to be damaging to the tree and it is recommended that the branch rings and collar be left intact. Branch rings are ridges, folds or bulges in the bark. This area may be darker or rougher than the other bark on the tree. If they cannot be seen clearly, cut so as to leave a small stub of branch.

The painting of wounds with bituminous preparations or water-based paints is now generally thought to be a useless practice, one that may even be detrimental to long-term plant health.

The presence of particular diseases such as silver leaf (D) and bacterial canker (D) will also influence the time at which pruning takes place.

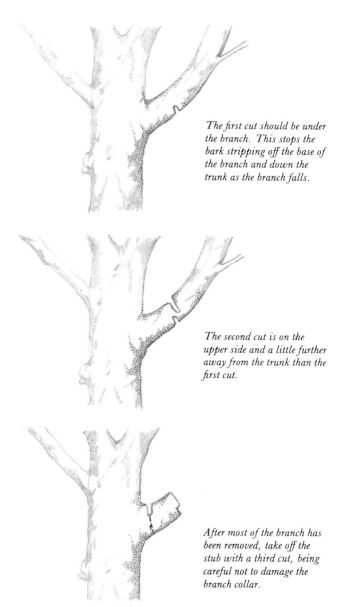

The first cut should be under the branch. This stops the bark stripping off the base of the branch and down the trunk as the branch falls.

The second cut is on the upper side and a little further away from the trunk than the first cut.

After most of the branch has been removed, take off the stub with a third cut, being careful not to damage the branch collar.

Careful removal of damaged branches will help avoid future pest and disease problems and improve the appearance of the tree.

Application of pesticides

This should not be considered a routine procedure. Fungicides and insecticides applied weekly, just in case a problem arises, will probably do more harm than good and cause unnecessary pollution.

There are times, however, when one or two treatments before the problem is expected to occur may avoid many more treatments afterwards. This involves predicting the occurrence of pest or disease by using records from previous years and by taking the prevailing weather into account. Some plants growing in a certain area are known to suffer from the same problems year after year. For example, roses grown in the humid Sydney climate almost invariably suffer from black spot (D) which is more efficiently controlled if spraying begins as soon as warm humid weather prevails.

IDENTIFYING A PROBLEM

Despite time spent in planning and in continuing garden care, problems do arise from time to time.

The first step is to make sure that the 'problem' is a real one. Unless you are familiar with your plants when they are healthy, you may either not realise that something is wrong until long after action should have been taken, or you may mistake normal occurrences for pest and disease problems.

The cases mentioned below are natural events or features that sometimes worry the owners of gardens.

Most people are aware of leaf fall in autumn, but not all deciduous plants show a range of attractive yellow, orange and red leaf colours. Some have leaves that turn yellow and then brown. Sometimes, as with the pin oak (*Quercus palustris*) and the dawn redwoods (*Metasequoia glyptostroboides*), the brown leaves may be held on the plant for a considerable length of time. Someone unfamiliar with the tree could easily believe that it was dead.

The corky outgrowths on twigs of liquidambar (*Liquidambar styraciflua*) and of the English elm (*Ulmus procera*) sometimes alarm the gardener but are quite natural features.

Leaf spots and marks can also cause confusion: Japanese oleaster (*Elaeagnus pungens*) has small brown spots on the leaves, which are a normal feature of the plant. Variegated leaves may be considered desirable, or they may indicate such things as a mineral deficiency, a virus disease or even insect damage.

These examples have been included to emphasise the fact that a knowledge of healthy plants (easily obtained from gardening books) is a great help when considering possible pest and disease problems.

Note that natural features — the lenticels on the Taiwan cherry (*Prunus campanulata*), for example — tend to be evenly distributed.

Once you are fairly sure that the plant is abnormal in some way you should try to find out exactly what the problem is before deciding on particular control measures. If this is not done, time and money may be wasted and the environment polluted.

The lower surfaces of the leaves of these three plants are perfectly normal, but sometimes the spots and colours alarm inexperienced gardeners.

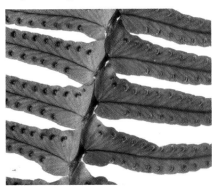

Fishbone fern (Nephrolepis *sp.*)

Southern magnolia (Magnolia grandiflora)

Japanese oleaster (Elaeagnus pungens)

Golden diosma (Coleonema pulchrum *'Sunset Gold'*)

Zucchini

Nasturtium

Naturally variegated plants such as the nasturtium and zucchini pictured are sometimes thought to be diseased, as are golden-foliaged plants. The yellow flecks on the camellia result from the feeding of scale insects under the leaves.

Camellia (Camellia japonica)

Lumps on stems and other plant parts may be normal, like the corking on elm and liquidambar and the lignotuber on eucalypt, or they may indicate pest attack or the presence of a disease.

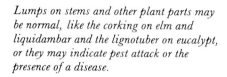

Elm: corking on twigs

Liquidambar: corking on young stem

Eucalypt: lignotuber

Sydney golden wattle (Acacia longifolia)*: galls on flowers caused by a cecidomyiid fly*

Spindle tree (Euonymus japonicus)*: scale insects on stem*

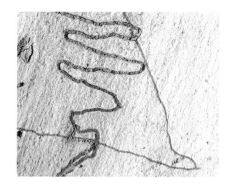

Eucalypt (Eucalyptus haemastoma)

This and a few other eucalypts commonly have the larvae of the scribblygum moth (Ogmograptis scribula) feeding under the bark. The 'scribble', although caused by an insect, does absolutely no damage to the tree.

Diagnosis

How to use this book: Read the cultural notes for the plant in which you are interested, and look for remarks or symptoms that fit with what you know about your own plant. Then check the details of any possible pests and diseases mentioned. The text, and photograph or drawing, may indicate whether you are on the right track. If not, read the details of some other pests and diseases that attack that particular plant and also consult the introductory notes for that group of plants.

In dealing with problems on plants not mentioned in this book, use the checklist given below. This outlines the sort of information it is necessary to gather and think about when solving garden problems.

If some particular plants are not looking their best, consider simple explanations first. It is more likely that some requirement for plant growth has been overlooked than that the plants are suffering from a terrible disease or from pest attack.

On these occasions it is useful to have records of weather and gardening practices to consult. Have you had time to water the garden during a dry spell? Was there a hailstorm last week? Have the local dogs been urinating on your plants? Are your plants suffering from lack of nutrients? Once you are satisfied that growing conditions are not a major factor, then consider pest and disease problems.

A little practice with the checklist will enable you to narrow down the possibilities and to more efficiently seek advice from horticultural consultants or from government agencies such as your local Department of Agriculture or forestry authority.

Potted plants should be inspected regularly for mealybugs and scales. Place them in a bright light and look under the leaves as well as on top. Fluffy material indicates mealybugs. Feel the stems and leaf surfaces for lumps which may be scales.

A checklist for diagnosis

In general, the plant itself, the environment in which it is growing and the treatment it has received are all important, but for any one plant or situation some of the following factors will be more important than others. How much of the following information can you provide for your garden and its plants?

Plant

PLANT NAME Preferably botanical name or at least type, e.g. climber, tree.

AGE AND SIZE Approximate planting date or at least the length of time you have owned the garden.

WHEREABOUTS OF THE PROBLEM On leaves (old or new; both?) in centre? around edges? On buds or flowers or fruit? On stem, bark, trunk . . . or roots?

EXTENT OF THE PROBLEM All over the plant? only on one side? top or bottom? On other similar plants nearby? On other dissimilar plants nearby?

TIMING OF THE PROBLEM When did it start? Has it been going on for long? Has it happened before?

APPEARANCE OF THE PROBLEM Gazing aimlessly at a plant is unlikely to solve the problem. Systematically search every part of the plant. Look at the plant from all directions, not only from above. Move potted plants into a bright light. Insects are usually able to camouflage themselves with particular colour patterns or with shape or simply by remaining absolutely still. Some baby scale insects look like little brown specks on the stems, and many other pests are difficult to see with the unaided eye. Use a hand lens (× 10 or × 20) or a magnifying glass to help you.

Regular inspection means that pests and diseases can be dealt with before too much damage is done.

Also inspect furniture or floor beneath potted plants. The droppings of caterpillars are often easily seen this way and indicate a reason for disappearing leaves. Sticky furniture indicates the presence of insects such as some scales (P), aphids (P) or mealybugs (P).

Many pests and diseases produce symptoms that can be described as spots, patches or streaks. You should observe the colour and whether it is the same for new marks and old marks; and whether it is the same all over—perhaps there is a ring of a different colour around the mark. How big are the marks and are they a particular shape (e.g. oval, round or 'target' spots)? Target spots are like tide marks, or circles within circles. Are the marks flat or raised? Are they firmly attached or able to be removed? Are there any holes? Wilting? Outgrowths? Sawdust? Webs? Furry growth? Stickiness?

LEAVES Look at both sides, because caterpillars often feed beneath. Inspect the junction of the leafstalk and the stem.

STEMS Are there any lumps, or 'twigs' at unusual angles or in unusual places?

BRANCHES Look for splits in the bark, fungal brackets and gum oozing out.

TRUNK Don't forget to inspect the trunk near the ground level and also the surrounding soil.

FLOWERS   Shake the petals and breathe on them gently. Any thrips present will move and therefore be more easily seen.

Symptoms such as stunting, wilting, slow growth and poor performance are not, in themselves, sufficiently characteristic of a particular problem for a diagnosis to be made. They may be the result of a poorly developed root system or one attacked and damaged. The causes of root problems are many and varied. They include insect attack; nematode injury; lack of water or nutrients; fungal damage; and mechanical removal of roots by tools such as spades.

The plant may appear perfectly normal when it is receiving a good water supply but wilt quickly if water is withheld for some reason. This indicates that the smaller root system could cope while it was easy to obtain water but could not supply the top of the plant with enough water at other times.

Further investigations would be necessary in order to pinpoint the problem.

Environment

LOCATION OF THE PLANT   Which suburb or town? This may provide clues as to the climate; soil type; and likelihood of industrial pollution.

POSITION   Indoors or outdoors? If outdoors, where (e.g. south wall, under eaves, in shade of trees, full sun)? Is it in a container or in the garden? If indoors, where? Near window, heater, in hall, in bathroom?

RECENT CHANGES   Have extensions, a pool or paving been added lately?

SOIL   Type—clay, sand, loam? Rock outcrops?

DRAINAGE   Are the garden beds raised? Does the water lie on the ground after rain?

RECENT WEATHER   Heavy rain/frost/hail/heatwave?

ANIMALS   Are there dogs, cats, possums, bandicoots, fruit bats or birds in the area?

Culture

WATER SUPPLY   Town, dam or bore.

WATERING   Frequency and type of water application.

FERTILISING   Type of fertiliser, frequency and method of application.

MULCHING   What with? Grass clippings? Pinebark? Pebbles? Black plastic? Leaf litter?

SPRAYING   What with and when? Could spray drift of herbicides on to wanted plants have occurred?

CULTIVATION   When was it done and what tools were used—e.g. spade or rotary hoe?

The factors listed above may influence the growth of plants and their susceptibility to pest and disease attack. The problems, however, may not show up until after the actual cause has been forgotten, and it is therefore a very good idea to keep some records of what happens in the garden on a weekly or even daily basis if possible.

Record the names of plants in the garden by listing them or sticking the labels into a notebook. It is easy to forget what has been planted. (This information could be passed on with the house if it is sold.) Note also the date of planting and subsequent treatments such as pruning, fertilising and spraying. The quantities of fertiliser and pesticides applied should also be recorded.

Flowering and fruit ripening times may be important in pest and disease control, so note these also.

Frosts, heatwave conditions, drought, and hailstorms may all harm plants directly or predispose them to certain diseases. For example, some fungi are unable to enter undamaged plants but are able to gain access through wounds such as bruises caused by hailstones.

holes in
Norfolk Island
hibiscus leaves

'scabs' on
camellia leaves

mottling on
azalea leaves

spots on
celery leaves

large
spots on
agapanthus
leaves

patches on
camellia leaves

The ability to give a good description of damaged areas will help you to obtain further advice. With reference to the specimens above, you should notice that the celery spots are surrounded by a pale area and that the agapanthus spots have bands of different colours. On the azalea and Norfolk Island hibiscus leaves the damage is evenly distributed, whereas on the agapanthus the spots are on the edge of the leaf.

Specimens should be packed so that they are not broken or squashed in transit. Do not send damp specimens in plastic.

Getting more information

The photographs in this book should facilitate identification of garden problems on most occasions. There will be times, however, when a gardener needs more help and information. This may be obtained from other books such as those listed in the Bibliography. The best procedure, however, is to take (or send) actual specimens of the problem to your local Department of Agriculture or Primary Industries. In some capital cities there are special home-garden advisory services.

It is practically impossible to diagnose pest or disease problems if one leaf is all there is to go on, particularly if the identity of the plant is not known. Specimens of leaves, stems, flowers, fruit and roots are necessary in many cases. With small plants (vegetables or annual flowers), try to take one or more 'problem' plants and one healthy plant. If a shrub or tree is involved, collect samples of as many different parts as possible.

Completely dead and shrivelled material is not very useful. Look for a specimen that shows the problem just beginning and several others that show the problem gradually getting worse.

Shrub or tree leaves should be left attached to a piece of small branch and sent in a dry plastic bag. Leaves and grass specimens may be sent pressed between dry paper and supported by some firm material such as cardboard. A specimen for diagnosis of lawn problems should be a piece of sod cut so that part is healthy and part affected. The sod should be about 100 mm across and 100 mm deep. Wrap so as to keep an air space of at least 25 mm near the grass. Label all specimens with name of plant, name of sender, address and date of despatch. A sample of soil from the root area of the plant may help diagnosis. It can be tested for pH, salinity and for the presence of nematodes. Lightly moisten 0.5–1 kg with water and pack in a strong plastic bag.

Include information about cultural practices and recent weather conditions. Time despatch so that the parcel does not arrive at its destination during a weekend or holiday period.

If an enquiry is to be made by letter or by telephone, look carefully at the problem beforehand and include, or be prepared to provide, as much information as possible. The more information the adviser is given, the more likely it is that a firm diagnosis can be made. Note that a three- or four-minute conversation is rarely sufficient time for a diagnosis.

As well as making your own observations and keeping records, a basic knowledge of insects and disease-causing organisms helps with diagnosis and with efficient control.

Defining a plant disease

It is difficult to produce a definition of plant disease that takes account of every possibility. It is reasonable, however, to say that plant disease is any harmful deviation from normal plant activities.

This means that to identify a diseased plant one needs to be familiar with plants growing normally in a favourable environment. Get to know your own plants. If you look at them closely on a regular basis, you will not only

Diseases caused by fungi

Spindle tree: powdery mildew

Custard apple: black canker (Phomopsis sp.)

Gerbera: powdery mildew damage

Cabbage: leafspot (Alternaria brassicae)

appreciate them more but also find symptoms and signs of diseases (and pests) before much damage has been done. If only a few leaves are abnormal, their removal may prevent further spread of the disease.

Causes of disease

Most plant diseases are caused by fungi. Bacteria, viruses and nematodes also cause many problems. Mycoplasmas, which are a little like bacteria and a little like viruses, will not be discussed in detail. They have been found to be responsible for a number of diseases previously thought to be caused by viruses. Diseases caused by these agencies can be termed infectious diseases. Higher plants, such as dodder (D) and mistletoe (D) can cause serious problems in some circumstances.

Although it seems strange to a layman, plant problems caused by such environmental factors as lack of water, high temperatures, leaking gas mains, hail or insufficient supply of nutrients are also considered to be plant diseases. These may be called non-infectious diseases.

The spread of pathogens

Plant pathogens can be taken from place to place by humans in soil, or in or on plant material such as bulbs, tubers, cuttings and seeds. Soil may be stuck to shoes, or to tools and machinery; or transported in pots or as loads of garden soil. Humans can also spread diseases from plant to plant on their hands or on tools such as secateurs and knives.

Water running over the surface of the ground or in irrigation ditches or creeks can move pathogens quite long distances. Splashing water (rain or overhead irrigation), or even pesticide sprays, can spread pathogens from plant to plant.

Insects may transport disease-causing organisms on their mouthparts or other parts of the body. For example, viruses are commonly spread by aphids, and driedfruit beetles (P) spread brown rot (D) spores. Some pathogens, particularly fungi in the form of spores, can be transported long distances in wind and moved from plant to plant in slight air currents.

Diseases caused by bacteria

Disease caused by virus

Pelargonium: pelargonium mosaic virus

Apricot: bacterial spot (Xanthomonas campestris *pv.* pruni)

Snapdragon: bacterial leafspot (Pseudomonas syringae *pv.* antirrhini)

Diseases caused by environmental factors

Butternut pumpkin: cold damage

Tomato: sunburn

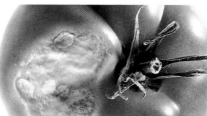

Rhododendron: sunburn

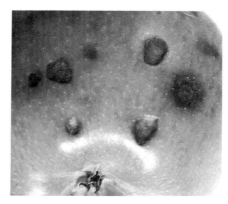

Grape: magnesium deficiency

African violet: water damage

Apple: hail damage

Survival of pathogens

Many crops are grown only once a year. This growing period may be a few months to many months long, but any pathogens that attack the crop must be able to survive during the time between the end of one crop and the beginning of the next.

Many pathogens can attack more than one type of plant. This means that during the non-growing season of one of their hosts there is another living crop on which they can survive.

Poplar rust (D) fungi in the northern hemisphere survive the winter, when there are no leaves on the poplar, growing in various species of conifer. Their spores are spread back to the poplars by wind when there are leaves again in spring. Other fungi have various weeds as alternate hosts.

Many fungi survive the period without a host in the form of spores. For example, the fungus that causes leaf curl of peach can only infect the leaves when they are very small. It is able to survive in the form of spores lodged around buds on the tree between leaf fall and the time new leaves appear in the following spring.

Some fungi, such as *Pythium* spp. and *Rhizoctonia* spp., survive when there is no living plant to attack by obtaining nourishment from dead plant material in the soil. They have a wide host range, and as soon as there are living plants available they usually infect them.

The apple scab (D) fungus survives the winter, when there are no leaves and no apples, in dead leaves on the ground. In spring, the spores that infect the new leaves are produced in the dead leaves and moved up to the tree in air currents.

Bacteria may also survive in pieces of dead host plant.

The formation of resting bodies such as sclerotia enables other fungi to survive without a host. Resting bodies are resistant to drying out and may remain alive for long periods. They are able to infect suitable hosts when the latter are available.

Symptoms and interference with plant functions

There are some plants that certain organisms are unable to enter or in which they cannot establish themselves. Others produce very severe symptoms in reaction to the same organisms. Plant-attacking organisms obtain their food supplies from the plant. The effects of this cannot be seen immediately, but if the plant continues to be interfered with over a few days or a few weeks symptoms such as leaf spots or wilting will appear.

There are probably also cases where the effects of attack are chronic and no spectacular symptoms ever appear on the plant.

Symptoms are an indication that the plant is under attack. They are discussed in more detail in connection with every disease included in the Diseases section.

Early sighting of symptoms increases the chances of stopping their spread with a control programme that acts on the organism responsible.

Note that once symptoms such as galls or splits in the bark have appeared, they cannot be made to disappear by the use of pesticides or by altering cultural practices.

Leaves marked with yellow because of a deficiency may re-green if supplied with the necessary minerals.

Plants can be damaged mechanically by activities such as fungal hyphae growing through them or nematodes jabbing with stylets.

More serious damage may be done, however, when processes such as photosynthesis, respiration and hormone production are interfered with by substances produced when such organisms live and grow. For example, toxic substances commonly cause stomates to close when they would normally be open. This stops photosynthesis, and therefore the sugars necessary to provide energy for plant functions become unavailable.

Entry into a plant and progress of the disease

Pathogens can gain entry to plants in different ways. Many fungi and nematodes are capable of entering plants through a healthy, undamaged epidermis. Some pathogens, however, need some type of wound or opening through which to pass. Even slight damage would be sufficient to allow access.

Damage such as sunburn and mechanical injuries such as pruning wounds, bruises on fruit, or abrasion by wind-driven sand, enable many pathogens to start

Air currents carry many different fungal spores and sometimes these spores are blown onto plants they are capable of infecting.

The spores germinate if conditions are suitable and the fungal threads start to obtain nourishment from the plant.

After a time-lag a few symptoms appear. This is the first indication that the plant is under attack.

If conditions continue to favour the fungus, its activities disrupt plant functions more and more, and symptoms spread.

These decayed beans were infected with the fungus Sclerotinia
sclerotiorum *while in the field. In storage, the fungus continued
to grow and eventually produced the black seed-like structures
which are called 'sclerotia'. Each one of these is a source of
infection for beans and the many other plants the fungus is capable
of attacking.*

growth in a plant. Almost all viruses need wounds
through which to enter plants, and these are usually
those caused by insects or by tools such as secateurs.

Insect damage may also enable bacteria to gain access
to plants. For example, one way the soil-inhabiting
bacterium that causes crown gall (D) can enter plants is
through areas damaged by insects such as white curl
grubs (P) or weevil larvae.

Bacteria also enter plants through natural openings:
the bacteria responsible for black rot of crucifers (D) may
enter leaves through hydathodes; and those that cause
fireblight may enter through nectaries. Lenticels and
stomates are other natural openings through which
pathogens can infect.

Natural wounds such as leaf scars can also allow
pathogens to enter. The fungal disease of camellia,
dieback (D), begins at leaf scars.

Lenticels on Taiwan cherry (Prunus campanulata).
*These structures are made up of parenchyma cells. Gases which
enter through lenticels, are able to move freely through the
intercellular spaces, and thus oxygen can reach the interior of
woody stems. They may also be a point of access for disease-
causing organisms in certain circumstances.*

Damage caused by one pathogen may make it possible
for others to infect the plant. Many other factors
influence the ability of pathogens to get into and successfully attack plants.

Pathogens differ in their ability to attack tissues of
different ages. For example, seedlings are easily attacked
by *Pythium*, a fungus which causes them to collapse at
ground level (damping-off (D)). This fungus, however,
rarely successfully attacks older plants even if environmental conditions are favourable.

On the whole, excessive nitrogen supplied to a plant
makes it more susceptible to disease. Generalisations
cannot be made about supplies of other nutrients as the
effects of excess supplies vary from one type of plant to
another. The balance of nutrients seems to be more important than the actual level of supply of each.

Some diseases never or rarely occur in particular geographic areas because the weather is not suitable there.
In other areas, definite combinations of temperature and
humidity for certain lengths of time may be necessary
before the pathogen can succeed and symptoms appear.
Once these conditions are known for a particular disease,
it is possible to predict when outbreaks will occur and to
reduce the amount of pesticide applied, by spraying only
when disease is likely instead of on a regular schedule,
say, weekly.

Factors such as temperature and humidity also greatly
influence the progress of a disease. If these factors
change to favour the disease-causing organism, the
symptoms will increase in extent and severity. If they
change so that the organisms are put under stress, the
symptoms will probably stop spreading.

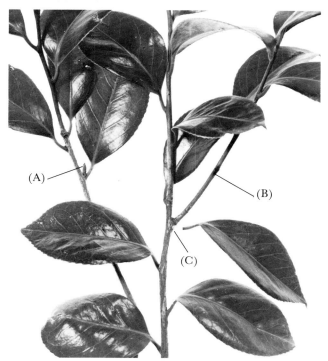

This bud (A) *grows into a shoot such as the one at* (B). *If the
fungus which causes dieback gains entry to the plant through a leaf
scar* (C), *the shoot above can be infected.*

Eggs of a member of Order Hemiptera

Bronze orange bug eggs

Mantid egg capsule

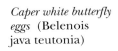

Caper white butterfly eggs (Belenois java teutonia)

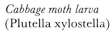

Cabbage moth larva (Plutella xylostella)

Banksia moth (Danima banksiae) larva

Ladybird larvae

Plant-attacking insects

Efficient control depends on a knowledge of insect life cycles and habits.

Most insects begin life in the form of an egg. Insect eggs range in size from less than 0.25 mm to about 3 mm. Small insects like springtails (P) produce very small eggs, and larger insects produce proportionately larger eggs. Considering the small size of eggs and the young insects that hatch from them, it is not surprising that insect infestations are often overlooked until a great deal of damage has been done.

Some insect eggs actually hatch inside the female's body and the young insects are born. This happens with aphids (P) for much of the year.

The eggs of most species hatch a week or two after they are laid, but there are some species whose eggs hatch in a few hours and others where the egg stage occupies months or years. Hatching may be delayed if the prevailing weather conditions are unsuitable for the survival of the young insect.

The eggs vary greatly in shape. For example, codling moth (P) and oriental fruit moth (P) have flat and scale-like eggs while the bronze orange bug (P) has more or less spherical eggs.

Insect eggs may be laid singly or in groups. Green vegetable bug (P) females lay about sixty eggs in rows to form a hexagonal shape nearly 10 mm across.

All the eggs are adapted to the environment in which they are usually deposited, and some may have extra protective coverings. The eggs of some mantids, for example, are enveloped in a foam-like material, and mealybug (P) females produce a mass of waxy threads in which to lay eggs. The structure and composition of insect egg shells also help to protect them from desiccation and from many insecticides. Some eggs are protected because the female inserts them inside part of the plant such as a leaf or stem.

Eggs are usually positioned so that when the young hatch out they have a food supply immediately available. Butterflies and moths lay their eggs on the plants their caterpillars like to eat and hover flies lay eggs near colonies of aphids (P). The act of egg laying may cause plant damage in some cases. Cicadas damage twigs when they insert eggs and so do insects such as gumtree hoppers. When fruit flies (P) lay eggs in fruit, they may introduce fungi which cause rots.

The immature stages of insects with holometabolous life cycles are called larvae and their main function is

Bronze orange
bug nymphs

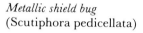

Metallic shield bug
(Scutiphora pedicellata)

Spined citrus bug nymph

Bee hawk moth
(Cephonodes kingii)

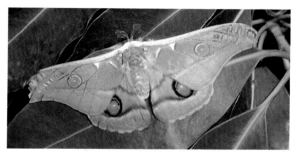

Emperor gum moth
(Opodiphthera eucalypti)

Damage of
gumleaf skeletoniser

eating. Larvae and adults of the same species do not necessarily have the same type of mouthparts or feed on the same material. For example, the caterpillars of large citrus butterfly (P) chew leaves whereas the butterflies themselves suck nectar through a tube; the larvae of whitefringed weevil (P) chew plant roots but the adults chew leaves.

The larvae of some insects have particular common names. The term 'caterpillar' usually refers to larvae of butterflies and moths; the term 'grub' to larvae of some beetles and weevils or bees, wasps and ants; and 'maggot' to fly larvae.

Adult insects are adapted for the tasks of reproduction and dispersal. Once the adult stage is reached the individual cannot increase in size. Sometimes small individual adults occur because the young stages have had only a minimum food supply. Males and females of the one species may be of different sizes and may have different markings. This is most noticeable with butterflies such as the large citrus butterfly (P).

Not all species have males. White wax scales (P) are all female and so are vegetable weevils (P). Insects such as this are capable of producing viable eggs without mating. In other insect species males occur only at certain times of the year. Some adults may live for only a few days but others live for years. This depends on the species and its habits. Adults which do not feed, usually die quickly. Each species takes a more or less set time for the development from egg, through immature stages to the adult. This time varies from hours to several years.

When and where the insect feeds is important. Some caterpillars feed at night and rest during the day; they are often hard to detect under leaves or lying along stems. Others, such as steelblue sawfly (P) larvae, gather in groups during the day and can be easily seen. Insects that feed inside stems or on the root system are often the most difficult to control.

A large number of insects chew their food. Examples are earwigs (P), grasshoppers and of course caterpillars.

Many other insects have mouthparts through which they suck sap. These are generally referred to as 'piercing and sucking' mouthparts and occur on aphids (P) and bugs and all the other insects in the order Hemiptera. If you look at the underside of a bronze orange bug (P) or a cicada, you can easily see the mouthparts which rest between their legs when they are not feeding. The mosquito (Order Diptera) is another insect that has piercing and sucking mouthparts.

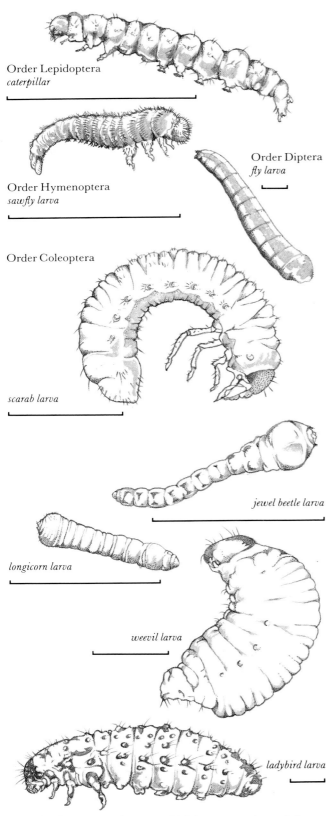

Order Lepidoptera
caterpillar

Order Hymenoptera
sawfly larva

Order Diptera
fly larva

Order Coleoptera

scarab larva

jewel beetle larva

longicorn larva

weevil larva

ladybird larva

It is often important to know to which insect group larvae belong. The drawings show typical shapes for common groups but they are not to the same scale. The bars beside each larvae give a guide to the length of a typical fully grown specimen.

Thrips (P) damage surface cells of plants with what are known as 'rasping and sucking' mouthparts. Mites (P) have similar mouthparts.

Sapsuckers, particularly aphids (P) and leafhoppers are the insects most commonly involved in the spread of virus diseases. In some cases their saliva stimulates the plant to produce extra cells, and galls then develop.

Recently-hatched caterpillars tend to remain in a group and graze on the surface of a leaf. This is called 'skeletonising' because the surface is removed and a network or skeleton of veins is left. Later, when they are bigger, they separate and may chew pieces from the leaf.

Many butterflies and moths do not feed at all. During the time it takes to find a mate and lay eggs in a suitable place, they survive on fat stored in their bodies while they were in the larval stage. The ones that do feed have siphoning mouthparts and usually suck nectar from flowers to a tube which is curled up under their head when not in use and straightened out when the insect wants to feed. A very few moths, such as the fruitpiercing moths (P) can cause damage with the tips of their mouthparts.

One insect species may feed on only one plant species, only on a few closely related plant species or on many unrelated plant species.

Plants can be attacked at any stage of their growth: seed, seedling, cutting, mature plant. They can be damaged both above and below ground.

Insects may feed from the outside of the plant or from the inside and they cause various kinds of damage.

Over the years human activities have created more and more pest problems. Land has been cleared and water flow in creeks altered so that populations of insect eaters like frogs, lizards and birds, have decreased. Farms and gardens provide an easily accessible and well-cared-for food supply for plant-feeding insects. World trade and travel markedly increased the spread of insects.

Some insects are generally harmful wherever they are found, and every year, but some other insects although pests in one area are not pests under the different conditions found in another area. Some insects are pests only occasionally, when weather and other conditions particularly favour them, and others cause spectacular damage to one plant part, such as leaves, but do not harm the part for which the plant is being grown, perhaps the roots.

Many winged insects can fly from one area to another over fairly long distances. Others that are weak fliers or very small like aphids (P) and thrips (P) tend to get carried around in winds and smaller air currents.

Insects may be spread in or on plant material and in products such as grain, timber, hay and soil.

Beneficial insects

Not all insects are pests! A large number cause no damage at all to humans or their food and possessions, and many are helpful in the garden. Ensure that insects seen near damaged plant parts actually did the damage before thinking of killing them.

Insects such as praying mantids, most ladybirds and their larvae, many hover flies and lacewings, and bugs

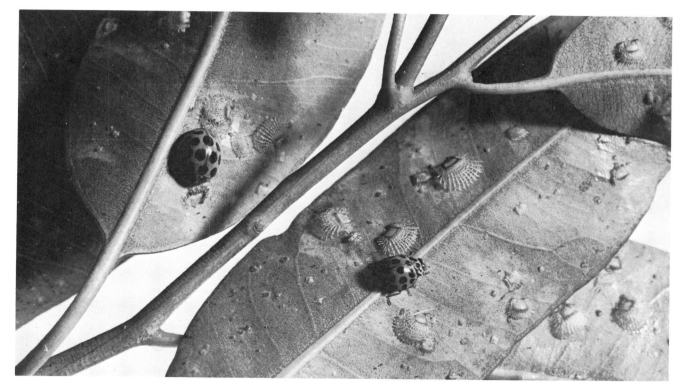

These ladybirds search for and eat small insects such as the brown basket lerps (Cardiaspina fiscella) *scattered on these eucalypt leaves.*

such as the assassins, either eat or suck the juices from other insects—many of which are considered to be pests in a garden.

Almost all ladybirds can be referred to as 'beneficial' because both they and their larvae feed on insects such as aphids, scales and mealybugs. The small, black ladybird (*Stethorus* spp.) feeds on mites and can be an important controlling agent.

Ladybirds with 26 or 28 spots, however, are leaf feeders and can cause serious damage.

Hover flies (so-called because they can 'fly on the spot') lay eggs near colonies of aphids. When their small slug-like larvae hatch from the eggs, they begin feeding on the aphids.

Lacewings and their larvae attack small soft-bodied insects. Some species have larvae called ant-lions which construct small crater-like traps in dry sandy soil. They hide at the bottom and suck the juices from insects that fall into the trap.

Apart from insects (predators) that chew or suck at their prey, there are many other small insects which are termed 'parasites'. These are mostly tiny wasps. They lay eggs in other insects which are killed when the eggs hatch and the wasp larvae feed on them.

Control or not

Once a problem has been diagnosed it is then necessary to decide whether or not control measures are warranted in the circumstances.

Fruit and vegetables may require more care than ornamental plants. Pests or diseases which attack the part of the plant that is to be eaten are often more serious than those which attack other parts. For example, attacks on some pumpkin leaves can be tolerated on a mature plant, but if the fruit, or flowers that will become fruit, are being damaged, action should be taken.

The plant's stage of growth is also important. Two insects chewing on a seedling may kill it, whereas the same two insects chewing on a mature plant may hardly be noticed.

In general, immature plants should be given protection from pests and diseases. If fruit is attacked by pest or disease when it is young and rapidly growing, it will be more distorted than if attacked later when more or less fully formed. This comment also applies to other plant parts which are rapidly growing.

Damage on ornamental plants is generally less serious, but control is definitely important in some cases. There is no point, for example, in caring for rose bushes for months only to have the buds seriously damaged by a bad aphid infestation.

Damaged leaves of an ornamental plant may look ugly, and also they may not be able to satisfactorily fulfil their function of producing food supplies to stock the storage organs such as bulbs, corms and tubers or to keep the plant supplied with sugars for use in day-to-day activities such as respiration.

Problems with a shrub or tree of a formal shape should be taken seriously, because should a part of the plant need to be removed the whole decorative effect may be permanently spoiled.

Chewing insects can be considered natural pruning agents when they remove leaves from a plant—the plant may become more bushy.

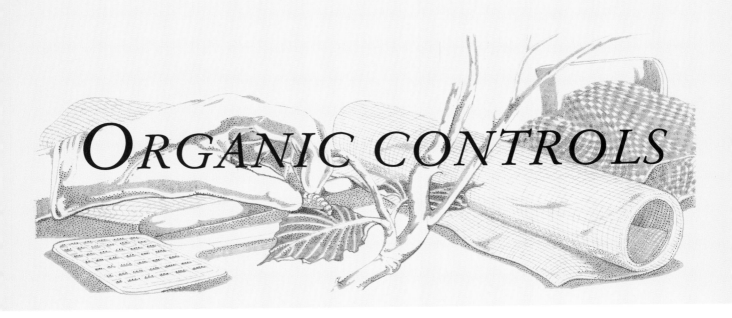

ORGANIC CONTROLS

During the last ten years the realisation that much more care must be taken of the environment in which we all live has increased. We all depend on soil, water and fresh air and it has become clearer that careless actions which destroy and pollute have serious consequences.

Methods of farming and gardening, water management, waste disposal, development of new urban areas and management of natural flora and fauna are under scrutiny and considerable changes are being made.

There is a strong move towards reduced pesticide usage and improved soil management.

These days, most commercial plant growers pay a lot of attention to non-chemical pest and disease controls. They aim to become familiar with the habits and life cycles of pests that attack their crops in order to achieve more efficiently timed pesticide applications, thus reducing the total amount of pesticide used. More often non-chemical methods are part of the overall strategies.

Integrated Pest Management (IPM) is practised more and more. This involves the use of a combination of different procedures during the life of the crop to control pests and diseases and to keep plants growing well. It includes reduced and careful pesticide applications along with biological and cultural methods.

Some farmers and gardeners have decided not to use artificial pesticides or fertilisers at all and have focussed on what have come to be called 'organic' methods.

Organic farming and gardening
Chemicals such as artificial herbicides, insecticides, fungicides, superphosphate and urea are not used in organic farming or gardening. No artificial chemical is used to prepare the soil or grow the plants. See Appendix page 299 for a list of acceptable chemicals.

Gardens and farms where so-called artificial or chemical pesticides and fertilisers have been used cannot claim to be organic until organic methods are used for a period of time. This may be several years. Consumers who buy organically grown food should check that the produce comes from farms certified organic.

Organic gardening and farming are much easier in areas geographically separated in some way from large orchards and farms growing the same crops.

At present some plants cannot be grown satisfactorily in particular areas without the use of 'chemical' pesticides and setting up a truly organic suburban garden surrounded by close neighbours is difficult. Make a start by becoming an environmentally thoughtful gardener.

Learn to accept more blemishes on fruit and vegetables. Compost garden and household wastes and take care not to overwater or overfertilise. If pesticides must be used, mix the smallest possible amount and spot spray only where the problem is. Never spray weekly or where there are no pests and diseases.

Acknowledge that insects and other small animals as well as micro-organisms like fungi and bacteria are part of the world in which we live and always will be.

Don't aim to eliminate insects from the garden — most are beneficial. Instead, create a balance where pests will decrease to a level where little damage occurs.

Creating a balance
Actions taken to solve one problem may create others — a balance has to be attained and this will take time and knowledge. For example, birds encouraged into a garden may control pest numbers but may also eat the fruit. Information about bird species and their feeding preferences would be useful in this case.

Compromises have to be made and control programs are usually geared to minimising the effects of the worst pests and diseases.

Planning and observing
Being familiar with your garden plants and observing them carefully on a regular basis is important in organic gardening. You need to act before problems have developed into major infestations.

Become more aware of plant growth and climatic events such as when first budding and dry spells occur.

Attention to setting up and maintaining the garden as

described in the first two chapters is particularly important because of the restricted range of control measures acceptable in an organic garden.

The selection of plants suitable to the geographic area and to the position in the garden must be emphasised.

In particular, organic gardeners need to apply the principles of crop rotation.

Organic gardening is not a policy of neglect or inaction but rather a system of careful planning and avoidance of problems. You should know and approve the source of any materials imported into your garden including organic matter. It is not acceptable to plunder natural areas in order to enrich your own home garden. Activities such as removal of fallen leaves from forests and seaweed from beaches must be questioned.

Organic growers should be aware that they are required to conform to the same laws about pest, disease and weed control as other growers.

Getting started

Start using the control measures described. Remember, each method is only applicable to some pests or diseases. As you become more familiar with life cycles and habits you will be better at matching control with pest.

Controls must have a direct link with either plant or pest to be effective. Even conventional pesticides are aimed at a particular stage of the pest life cycle and timed carefully for maximum effect.

The A-Z of Plant Care section of this book helps explain why problems occur and the pest and disease sections make suggestions about what action to take.

Timing of planting and harvesting

It is usual to plant a crop on a date that will ensure the most favourable weather conditions. Sometimes a time of high pest numbers or disease prevalence can be avoided by altering this date. For example, in the Sydney area tomato planting should be timed so that the main crops have been harvested by mid-summer. This is because the population of Queensland fruit fly is low in September and gradually builds up to a peak in late January/February. It is often possible to pick good crops of tomatoes up to mid-January without spraying at all. After that time, fruit fly damage would be severe.

But if a change from the normal planting date puts the plants under stress and leads to decreased vigour, they may be more susceptible to problems other than the one which is being avoided.

Particular examples vary from area to area. Keeping records of what pests and diseases occur in your garden and when they are most common may help you to alter planting dates accordingly in subsequent years.

Destruction of crop wastes and weeds

Prompt removal and destruction of infected fruit will help keep pest numbers down. Fruit infested with fruit fly larvae must not be buried as this continues their usual life cycle. The easiest disposal method is to seal the fruit in an undamaged plastic bag and leave it in full sun for at least a week. It can then be added to the compost heap or be buried as the larvae would be dead.

Fruit infected with brown rot (D) should also be destroyed. Later, any mummies remaining must be removed because if this is not done, this dried-out fruit will be a source of spores to infect the next crop.

Burn twigs and branches that have been attacked by citrus gall wasp (P) or diseases such as silver leaf (D).

It may be useful to collect and destroy the diseased leaves of trees or shrubs. The usefulness of this method depends on the life cycle of the pathogen. In the case of apple scab (D) the new leaves in spring are infected by spores which come from old leaves on the ground. The destruction of these old leaves will delay infection but not stop it as spores will eventually blow from further afield. In towns and cities where burning garden waste is prohibited it should be sent to the tip with other household rubbish unless it is suitable for the compost heap.

'Volunteers' are specimens of wanted species which grow by accident here and there in the garden. This may happen if annuals are allowed to go to seed, for example. Unless cared for, they may be a source of pest and disease problems and should be removed. Annuals that have suffered from leaf diseases can also be deeply buried to get rid of fungal spores.

Weeds should not be allowed to grow in a garden, as they are often alternative food sources for pests and may also act as a reservoir of disease organisms and a shelter for snails. The vegetable weevil (P), for example, can exist quite happily on capeweed (*Arctotheca calendula*), mallow (*Malva* spp.) and other weeds. These should be removed as part of the control programme. Two-spotted mites (P) feed on weeds and are also to be found on old bean plants. These should be removed and burnt or dug into the soil as soon as the crop is finished.

Hedges and windbreaks can substantially alter the climate in a garden and make it possible to grow delicate plants.

Weeds and diseased plant parts should not be composted unless care is taken with this procedure. Weed seeds and pathogens would die if they were subjected to about three weeks of temperatures of 55–60°C, but many home-garden compost heaps won't get hot enough.

Organic weed control

It is often suggested that weeds should not be removed from organic gardens because they encourage the presence of beneficial insects. However, there are many other small garden perennials and shrubs that do not have the disadvantages of weed species and will provide nectar and pollen for beneficial insects like wasps.

Excluding weed seeds from the garden is a very important part of weed control. It is hard to ensure that loads of top dressing soil, mulch and animal manure do not contain weed seeds. Store these materials for a month or two; many weed seeds will germinate to be dealt with in the one spot instead of over the whole garden or lawn. Allowing manure to sit for a few weeks in plastic bags in a hot, sunny spot kills many weed seeds.

Take care not to import weeds in plant pots along with the desired plant. Annual weeds are usually easily seen in the pot but perennial weeds — those with bulbous underground parts — are harder to detect.

Perennial weeds are likely to be present where soil from a garden has been used to grow plants for a school fete or similar plant sale or where plants have been dug from the garden of a friend. Perennial weeds would not be found in plants from an established nursery.

It is important to get perennial weeds like oxalis, onion weed and nut grass under control before planting garden beds. Established perennial weeds require patient and repeated digging out to eradicate.

Weeds will colonise bare ground. Groundcover plants grown between shrubs and trees can discourage them.

Mulching with pine bark, wood chips, straw or leaf litter can reduce the germination of weed seeds very effectively or at least make it much easier to handpull or hoe out the weeds that do appear. The mulch should be at least 5 cm deep and can be used alone or over thick layers of newspaper. The latter is quite effective in killing weeds already present as it excludes light and water. If newspaper is used around wanted plants take care to ensure that water reaches the plant roots — it is usually necessary to make some holes.

Once annual weeds are present handpulling or careful hoeing are the most common control methods.

The problem of weeds in lawns can largely be avoided by good management. Mowing should be regular and not too low — set the mower at different heights for different grass species but remove no more than one third of the leaf growth in any one cut. Use enough water and fertiliser to keep the lawn growing reasonably vigorously but not so much that it requires extra cutting.

Small weeds in paths and paving can be killed easily by pouring boiling water on them. Larger weeds with a thick taproot should first be cut off close to the ground and the root damaged with a garden stake or similar implement. Pour the boiling water into the hole.

Weeds will usually grow in the spaces between paving stones if they are not filled with concrete or another plant. The best solution is to encourage a small decorative plant like native violets to grow there instead.

Overall, the best way to control weeds in a garden is to work to a plan. Suppose you have two hours available. Use the first half hour to remove every weed flower and seed head in the garden. Completely remove low, spreading weeds with seeds. Next, remove the most mature weeds — the biggest ones that will be flowering and seeding soon. Next weed one section of the garden thoroughly and mulch the cleared ground. Then weed another section and mulch that immediately and so on.

Follow such a plan every week for a month and you will gradually gain control, decreasing your weeding time markedly. Remember, always remove seed heads first.

Manipulation of air movements

In areas of strong wind, hedges and windbreaks not only lessen drying out of soils and plants and reduce physical damage to young growth, but can also lower the incidence of some pests and diseases.

A dense windbreak or a solid wall creates turbulence on the protected side often causing leaves or insects to drop to the ground. A more permeable windbreak allows some wind to pass through and thrips, aphids and other insects are more likely to remain airborne.

As a general rule, a windbreak will provide some shelter for a distance of 10–15 times its height, but to get maximum benefit each situation should be studied separately and account taken of such things as height of crop to be protected and direction of prevailing winds.

A living windbreak should not include plants that are botanically related to those to be protected as they are likely sources of disease organisms or provide an alternative food supply for pests that also attack the crop. Some unrelated plants may also harbour pests and diseases.

Allocasuarina spp. (she-oaks) can be very useful trees to include in a windbreak. They can be satisfactorily trimmed like a formal hedge if necessary.

The tradition of surrounding large beds of roses with hedges has its disadvantages. In more humid areas, regular air flow around and through the bushes helps to reduce the incidence of leaf diseases.

Similarly, encouraging air circulation through the centre of fruit trees will help avoid fungal diseases.

Windbreaks can be made from polyethylene fabrics supported on poles. These are effective earlier than living windbreaks and do not harbour pests and diseases.

Where space permits, a shelter belt is better than a single line of trees. A shelter belt is a band of trees and shrubs of different sizes, shapes and densities planted in several rows. One advantage is that if any of the individual trees or shrubs dies they can be more easily replaced than they can be in a single line of trees.

Cultivation

Cultivation, as far as pest and disease control is concerned, involves mainly burying things or turning them up to the surface where they dry out and die.

Springtails (P) and root knot nematodes (D) are

among the pests and diseases that will dry out on the soil surface, but this control measure alone would not be sufficient to control nematodes. Weeds, if not bearing seed, can be hoed out and left to dry.

Birds will feed on insect larvae and pupae turned up to the surface. This is a good way to reduce the numbers of African black beetle (P).

If certain insect larvae and pupae, or weeds, are deeply buried they cannot survive to reinfest the next crop. Unfortunately this is probably not possible with usual home-garden equipment.

Turning the soil will also encourage weed seed germination. A second light cultivation while these plants are still small easily kills large numbers of them.

Soil pH change
In a very few cases, changing pH can make a pest or disease problem less serious. Springtail (P) numbers will decrease if soil is limed, and the disease of crucifers, club root (D), will be less severe if acid soils are limed.

Common scab (D) of potatoes, on the other hand, is more likely to cause problems in alkaline soils, so soils should definitely not be limed where this disease occurs.

Manual removal of pests
Manual removal is time-consuming and may be unsatisfactory because it requires practice to find and recognise egg masses and very young (small) stages of an insect species. Pests may also be out of reach.

However, if you are serious about reducing the use of chemical pesticides there is much that can be done.

Aphid numbers can be reduced by hosing them off every few days or by squashing them on the plant stem or around buds. Do so until natural predators build up enough to keep the aphids under control themselves.

Use a stick to knock bronze orange bugs off the tree and into a container of water with a little detergent or kerosene added. These bugs can squirt a corrosive fluid that causes painful damage so protect your eyes by wearing sunglasses or goggles.

Caterpillars can be searched out, squashed or dropped into hot water or the same mixture as the bugs.

Snails can be collected from their hiding places under the rims of pots, in corners of walls or garden edging or under strap leaves of plants like agapanthus.

Wear gardening gloves, insects should not be handled. They may have hairs that break off like small splinters, or they may produce defensive chemicals that have very penetrating smells and could cause rashes.

Some beetles and caterpillars drop quickly from the plant if disturbed and are impossible to find on the garden surface. Hold a folded newspaper or a tray under the foliage as you search.

Pruning
Pruning is often a useful way to reduce pest and disease problems. Dead, diseased and insect-damaged wood should be removed promptly from trees and shrubs so that problems cannot spread to healthy plant parts.

Dead wood is more easily recognised during spring and summer when growth is taking place. Destroy these prunings. Do not leave them lying around nearby.

Removal of diseased or damaged leaves may or may not be helpful. In the case of a virus disease such as apple mosaic (D), the removal of yellow-patterned leaves may improve plant appearance but will not free the tree of infection. The same applies to any virus-infected plant and to any part of the plant. It is possible to spread virus diseases on secateurs. Sterilise secateur blades before pruning each plant by dipping in a solution of household bleach (sodium hypochlorite). Use 150 mL of 4% bleach per litre of water.

Outer leaves, twigs and branches damaged by frost should not be removed in winter. They provide a certain amount of protection for the rest of the plant. Prune only when all likelihood of frost is over.

In hot districts where sun can burn branches and trunks, the pruning method should be adjusted so that foliage will shade the most vulnerable areas during the summer. The fungi which cause wood rots (D) can begin growth in sunburnt areas of bark.

In trees and shrubs prone to leaf diseases, thin out the centre so that air circulation is increased. This reduces humidity and helps lessen the incidence of leaf spots.

Plants can sometimes be saved from leaf-chewing caterpillars by pruning off the branches on which they are feeding. For example, on occasions there are so many paperbark sawfly (P) larvae feeding on a melaleuca that hand-removal would be impractical. Pruning off the smaller twigs where the larvae are concentrated encourages vigour in the plant as well as removing the pest.

Roguing
Roguing, the removal of individual diseased or insect-infested plants from a crop, involves keeping a close watch on the crop to remove plants as soon as they show any signs of abnormality. As each plant is pulled out, it should be put carefully and immediately into a bucket or bag so that the problem is not spread while the search continues through the rest of the crop. The usefulness of this control method for a particular pathogen depends on the type of organism and how it spreads.

Quarantine
It is important for travellers whether interstate or overseas to observe quarantine regulations. These regulations constitute a barrier to the entry of unwanted animals and plants and the associated pests and diseases.

New pests and diseases brought into this country can have a devastating effect on the production of commercial crops and plants in home gardens. They are usually able to increase in numbers and spread easily without the natural enemies found in the country of origin.

Chrysanthemum white rust and western flower thrips are pests and diseases that have recently arrived.

Barriers
These barriers include netting to keep birds from fruit. Small-growing plants such as blueberries are most easily protected but trees can also be enclosed. The netting keeps out fruit bats as well as birds. Woven or knitted polyethylene fabrics used to stop hail or sun injury can

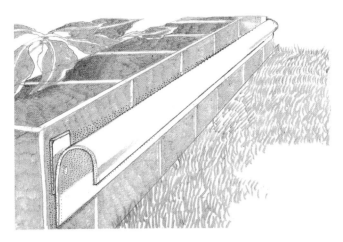

Millipedes can be prevented from entering houses by erecting barriers such as this length of curved galvanised iron.

also protect crops from disease attack because some organisms only gain entry to the plant if it is damaged.

Other possibilities are netting or thick waterproof paper to protect young trees from rabbits; smooth, shiny adhesive tape around the base of house walls to keep millipedes (P) out; projecting metal sheets on top of house foundations to make termites (P) more visible on their way to the timbers above; grease bands to stop ants (P) and weevils walking up tree trunks; and mesh screens on windows to keep flies and mosquitoes out.

Paper cups with the bottom removed are said to stop cutworm (P) damage if pushed firmly into the soil around each seedling.

Snails can be kept out of a garden bed by surrounding it with a 'fence' made from a strip of galvanised iron about 300 mm wide, set about 100 mm into the soil. A flange 100 mm wide, at the top of the strip and projecting outwards at an angle of about 45°, prevents the snails gaining access to the garden.

In dry weather snails and slugs (P) may be deterred by dry materials such as sand, sawdust, ashes or lime being spread in a band around small plants or seedlings.

Paper bags tied around ripening fruits will protect them from fruit fly damage. It may not be practicable to bag a large crop but when trees are young and not yet producing heavily most fruit can be protected this way.

Tree-trunk banding

Bands that are intended to stop insects walking up tree trunks can be made of various materials including thick axle grease, and aluminium foil or other very slippery sheeting which the insects cannot negotiate.

Commercial products to stop insects crawling or walking up plant stems or trunks will soon be more readily available on the home garden market. One of these, a non-drying adhesive, applied 2–3 mm thick around tree trunks in two bands, each 5 mm wide and 50 mm apart, will capture insects such as weevils attempting to walk up the trunk. They stick to it, unable to move further.

Note other routes that insects may take to reach the tree top — trim branches that touch the ground and adjoining plants. Apply the banding material to stakes.

Bands of sacking can be tied around the tree to help control whitestemmed gum moth (P), white cedar moth (P), and codling moth (P). The latter will pupate in sacking or corrugated cardboard, and it can be removed and destroyed. The larvae of the two other moths mentioned will shelter under the sacking during the day and can be destroyed before they spread out on to the foliage to feed during the night. Trunk bands must be inspected regularly. Like other non-chemical methods, banding by itself may not be a sufficiently good control.

Trapping

The term 'trapping' usually applies to situations where insects are attracted to a particular place and later killed when the trap is inspected. Earwigs (P) move under the orange peel 'shells' left over from juicing, and into flowerpots filled with straw or crumpled newspaper. Earwigs, slaters and wireworms move into scooped-out potatoes which can then be destroyed.

Snails and slugs (P) are attracted to beer. Put about half a cup of beer into a jam jar and bury it as shown in the illustration. It has been suggested that they escape less readily from a container with a narrow mouth.

Some traps contain pheromones, chemicals which are produced naturally in insect bodies and many of which can now be synthesised. Pheromones help insects of the one species communicate with one another. For example, ant trails are defined with pheromones and pheromones enable male and female of the one species to find one another for mating. Using pheromones, the target insects can be attracted to the trap and prevented from leaving by a barrier of some sort.

Water pan traps can be made from shallow containers something like 2 litre plastic icecream containers although a bigger surface area would be better. The

Snails and slugs are said to be attracted to beer. Place half to one cup of beer in a glass jar or sturdy plastic container. Bury the container at an angle in the garden near plants you want to protect. Remove dead snails and replenish the beer periodically.

inside should be painted bright yellow. Half fill with water, add a few drops of detergent and place between rows of small plants to attract aphids.

Whiteflies (P), particularly in a greenhouse or any enclosed space, can be attracted to bright orange-yellow boards. These are sometimes available commercially, but they can be easily made at home. They should be about 300 mm square and hung between the plants. Use about four in every 12 square metres. Cover the boards with a sticky substance such as motor oil. Insects fly onto the boards and remain stuck there. Clean and reapply the oil when the boards lose their stickiness.

Light-trapping has potential for crop pest control but requires much more research. An associated electric-grid that electrocutes insects is useful at night. It attracts a wide range of insects including mosquitoes and moths, and so is more successful in reducing the total number of insects than in controlling a particular type.

Heat treatment of seeds, bulbs and soil

Seed bought in home-garden packs are unlikely to need any treatment, but seed saved at home or acquired from friends may need attention.

Heat treatment of seed is carried out in order to kill pathogens inside the seed as well as on the outside. It is most useful against fungi — as most bacteria in seeds survive temperatures so high that the seed would be killed first. Hot water can be used by home-gardeners if the temperature is regulated carefully and accurately.

Some examples are included here, more information is available from your local Department of Agriculture.

The idea is to make the water hot enough for long enough to kill the pathogen but few of the seeds. The instructions should be carefully followed. Use a large quantity of hot water previously heated to the correct temperature and kept at that temperature throughout the procedure. Stir from time to time.

The seed should be treated in small lots tied loosely in an open-weave fabric such as nylon curtaining or muslin. After the set time in hot water, cool the seed quickly in cold water and immediately spread it out to dry on absorbent paper (even newspaper). Do not dry the seed in strong sunlight.

Treated seed is more subject to attack from rotting fungi in the soil than untreated seed, so it is also necessary to dust it with fungicide.

Cabbage seeds should be soaked at 50°C for 25 minutes and other crucifer seed for only 18 minutes. This treatment is completely effective against black rot *(Xanthomonas campestris)* and reduces problems with black leg *(Leptosphaeria maculans)*.

The flowering annual, stock, also gets black rot *(X. campestris)*. This seed should be treated at 56–56.5°C for 10 minutes.

Celery seed treated for 25 minutes at between 47.5 and 48°C will be free of late blight (D) *(Septoria apii)*. Onion seed treated at 50°C for 25 minutes will be free of downy mildew (D) *(Peronospora destructor)*.

For bulb nematode control, the following treatment is recommended. Allow the foliage to die down naturally at the end of the growing season. Lift the bulbs and clip

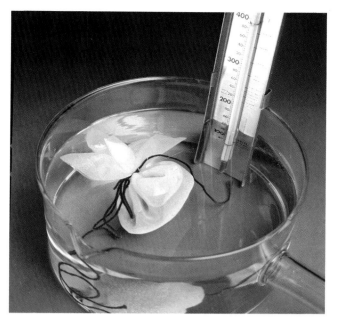

It is possible to treat seeds in hot water for disease control, provided the temperature is controlled accurately and the seeds are cooled and dried promptly.

off the foliage 3–5 cm from the neck. Spread the bulbs out in a cool place and store for several weeks. Clean the bulbs and destroy soft ones. Put them into a wire basket if possible, and treat in hot water at 43°C for 4 hours (up to 4 1/2 hours for large bulbs). The temperature must be accurate. Heat the water to about 49°C initially because when the bulbs are added the temperature will drop. Stir the water from time to time.

Dry heat treatment of soil, such as would be achieved in a domestic convection oven, is undesirable. It breaks down soil structure, and may make nutrients available to

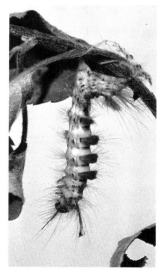

Painted apple moth (Teia anartoides)   *Common anthelid (Anthela acuta)*

These caterpillars were killed by polyhedrosis virus infection.

plants in toxic quantities. It would be possible to devise a system of treatment in a microwave oven but it would be easier to buy good quality potting mix from a nursery or garden centre.

Solarisation
This term is applied to a treatment of soil that kills weed seeds, a range of pathogens and insect larvae. It involves spreading a sheet of thin clear plastic over the soil, securing the edges and leaving it there for about one month. It works best if the soil is moist and in a fairly fine crumbly condition as if seeds were to be sown.

This method is designed for use in very warm to hot summer weather and works best if the ambient temperature reaches 35°C several days during the treatment. If the soil temperature reaches 45°C and above at a depth of 150 mm the treatment will be fairly successful.

Other physical and mechanical methods
Various methods of confusing insects have been developed. For example, sheets of aluminium foil or blue plastic spread between rows of plants is said to discourage flying aphids from coming to feed.

Biological control
Government agencies research, set up and monitor biological control programmes. The aim is to produce a balance that is self-perpetuating.

Individual gardeners cannot initiate biological control programmes, and their involvement is small, but they should be aware of the controls in operation and avoid actions that would disrupt them.

Biological control means keeping a pest species' numbers at a tolerable level by encouraging other organisms to attack it. In most instances, one insect is used to control another, but the term has a much wider application. It can include using diseases to kill insects, using diseases to kill weeds, and using ducks to eat snails.

All of these relationships occur naturally and there are a multitude of examples. From these scientists have, over the years, chosen certain cases that seemed particularly useful. These natural controls have been copied and encouraged in a variety of different situations.

One example of biological control is the control of the woolly aphid (P) *(Eriosoma lanigerum)* by a parasitic wasp *(Aphelinus mali)*. This wasp, which is usually quite active in unsprayed gardens, lays one egg in each aphid body. As the small wasp develops, it uses the aphid body for food. The wasp larva pupates inside the aphid, and when the adult comes out it produces a small exit hole. Aphids that have been parasitised are easily detected because they lose their woolly covering and go black. They are also harder and the exit hole may be visible. Individuals can encourage this particular control by collecting twigs with aphids on them in early winter and storing them so that they can't be attacked by birds and other pests. In early spring these twigs should be placed in trees infested with aphids. The wasps will emerge in September and more aphids will be attacked.

One of the most recent successes with biological methods is the control of two-spotted mites (P) by various predaceous mites. The system is working well in many apple orchards where the predator, *Typhlodromus occidentalis*, destroys all stages of two-spotted mite. Some predaceous mite species can be bought and distributed in a home garden. Successful control will take more than distribution of a single batch but if some care is taken a reasonable level of control can eventually be achieved. The predator mites must have a continuous supply of plant-feeding mites or they will starve to death. The aim is to achieve a balance between the two different mites. This may be possible in a large planting of roses or in a home orchard but it is more difficult where only a few plants are attacked by two-spotted mites.

Diseases can also be used to control insects. For example, the product Dipel®, one of the few biological controls that can be actively used by gardeners, is prepared using bacteria that cause disease in caterpillars.

Various fungi (such as *Entomophthora* spp.) cause disease in insects, particulary aphids (P); and also viruses. A caterpillar which hangs limply in an inverted V-shape has probably been killed by a disease caused by a virus.

Biological control of diseases, mainly root-attacking ones, is being studied and should prove possible in the next few years. Previously, research into biological controls was usually done in relation to problems which could not be solved by the application of pesticides.

In view of increasing environmental awareness and insects and diseases that are resistant to pesticides, much more time and money is spent searching for biological solutions. (See discussion of beneficial insects on page 32.)

Bacillus thuringiensis (B.t.)
This preparation is sprayed on plants to kill insect larvae. B.t. will control more than 150 species of lepidopterous larvae but it kills some more efficiently than others. It is a bacterium found naturally.

It is used successfully against cabbage moth, cabbage white butterfly, grape vine moth, cutworms, Heliothis, loopers, lightbrown apple moth and oriental fruit moth.

It is considered to be non-toxic to mammals, fish, honeybees, beneficial insects and the predators of lepidopterous larvae. It is a stomach poison. When a caterpillar feeds on a sprayed leaf and swallows the B.t. its mouthparts and gut become paralysed. It will stop feeding immediately and die 2-5 days later.

The effect is greatest against very small caterpillars and for best kill it should be applied as eggs start to hatch. If the crop is rapidly growing or a series of eggs is hatching B.t. should be applied every five to seven days. Spray where the small larvae are feeding — for example, early stages of cabbage moth larvae feed under the leaves and B.t. applied to the upper leaf surface will miss the target.

Once mixed with water, use immediately. It has no withholding period — edible crops can be harvested straight after spraying. It is suitable for use in an organic regime.

There is also a strain of B.t. suitable for control of mosquitoes and a very limited range of fly species as well as another for control of some beetle species such as the elm leaf beetle *(Pyrrhalta luteola)*. The latter will be available for sale in the next year or two.

CHEMICAL CONTROLS

Pesticides should be kept for situations when and where they are really necessary. Routine weekly pesticide application, regardless of whether pests and diseases are present, is ridiculous, particularly in a home garden. It wastes time and money, adds to pollution, kills beneficial insects and may not kill any or many targeted pests.

In general, ornamental plants need far fewer pesticide applications than fruit and vegetables; and even on the latter, home-gardeners are able to tolerate higher levels of damage than commercial producers. Immediately before you mix up the spray make a final check that the pest or disease is still active and that no natural controls are operating.

Unsprayed fruit trees in home gardens, however, may be a serious source of infestation for nearby commercial growers, and some pests are considered to be so damaging that governments have legislated to ensure that land-owners, including home-gardeners, spray to control them. These pests vary from place to place but may include some of the fruit flies (P), scales such as San José scale (P), codling moth (P) and citrus gall wasp (P).

The following notes should help you to choose and use pesticides wisely.

BUYING PESTICIDES

Do not assume that the shop assistant is trained to advise on the use of pesticides. Take time to read the labels of various products and make sure you buy one that will control your present pest or disease problems.

Most pesticides are marketed under a registered trade name. The product in each bottle, packet or can is made up of various ingredients. The active ingredient (a.i.) is the one that actually kills the pest, disease or weed. In the product, Bayleton®, the active constituent, is triadimefon. It is the triadimefon that controls the powdery mildews(D), azalea petal blight(D) and lawn dollar spot(D). The other ingredients in the bottle or packet vary according to which form (formulation) the a.i. is in. They include substances to help spread the a.i. over the plant and stick it there. It does not usually matter which manufacturer produces the active ingredient you need. Some products contain more than one active ingredient. This is common on the home-garden market, a manufacturer may include in the same bottle chemicals to kill leaf-chewers, sap-suckers and various fungi.

Except in a few cases, which the label will mention, fungicides kill only fungi and insecticides kill only insects. Some insecticides are better at killing certain insects than others, and some fungicides kill only some fungi. For example, zineb controls downy mildew(D) but is of little use against powdery mildew(D).

Insecticides get into insects by three different routes: through the outer covering, through the mouth, or through the breathing holes or spiracles. These are termed contact poisons, stomach poisons and fumigants.

Insecticides or fungicides referred to as systemics or penetrants enter the plant through the roots or leaves and move about inside the plant. Some move only from upper leaf surface to lower leaf surface but some move more extensively. Movement is usually more efficient in an upward direction. Systemic insecticides all act against the pest when they reach the digestive tract, and some may have contact or fumigant action as well.

Most insects in protected places such as down leaf sheaths or inside leaves should be treated with systemics or penetrants. Spraying a contact poison such as maldison (Malathion®) on to a plant in an attempt to kill insects such as leafminers (P) would not be very efficient as the chemical would never come into contact with the stage of the pest doing the damage.

Fortunately most insecticides have more than one of these modes of action. Once inside the insect, most insecticides disrupt the nervous system in some way. The nervous system of humans and other large animals works on the same basic principle as that of insects, and this means insecticides can also be poisonous to them.

Do not buy pesticides in case you need them one day. Do not buy large quantities planning to use them over several years; even if unopened, some pesticides gradually deteriorate and lose their effectiveness. Select a pesticide that is suitable for use with your equipment.

HOW TO READ A PESTICIDE LABEL

Pesticide label directions should be followed at all times. They show what the product is and how to use it safely and effectively. They usually have the same sections arranged in a similar way.

Always read the label before starting a spraying job.

Even if you have used the product before, you need to remind yourself of the safety directions. If you purchase a new batch, check that the proportion of active ingredient has not changed.

Should poisoning occur, show the label to the medical practitioner in attendance. The word 'anti-cholinesterase' on the label below, for example, would indicate the way the nervous system is affected and what actions should be taken to counteract the poison.

Manufacturer or distributor

Please heed this warning

Trade name

How to use the product safely and what to do if poisoning occurs

Miniumum length of time between the last spray application and harvest so that harmful residues are not eaten with fruit and vegetables

This panel shows how much of this product to add to water to get a suitable spray strength, and when and where to apply it for maximum control

Summary of pests the product will control and plants on which its use is suitable

Active ingredient i.e. the chemical which actually kills the pest

Information about which plants this pesticide may harm — phytotoxicity

STORING PESTICIDES

All pesticides should be stored in a locked cupboard, or locked shed, away from children. Pesticides should be stored in their original containers. On no account use food containers such as lemonade bottles for storing or measuring pesticides. Fatalities have occurred because this rule was not observed.

The storage place must be cool, dry and well-ventilated. It must be possible to light the area well when pesticides are being selected but the containers must not be exposed to sunlight or other sources of heat because the contents will be damaged.

Containers can rot or rust and labels can be destroyed by mould if the area is damp. Prevent insects like silverfish eating the labels and keep lids tightly closed.

Extra information printed on the outer packaging or on sheets inserted inside the packet should be kept in a plastic bag or pocket and pinned up nearby for future use. Display charts or information on first-aid.

Write the date of purchase on the outside of the container so that you can see when it is too old to be of further use. Most pesticides have a limited shelf life (even if unopened) and may be completely useless after one or two years.

Measuring equipment should be clearly marked or disfigured like the spoons in this photograph.

USING PESTICIDES

Equipment

There is a wide range of spray equipment available for application of pesticides.

Choose a sprayer which is a suitable size for your garden. Only gardeners with a home orchard or a large vegetable garden would need anything as large as a knapsack spray (15–20 L capacity). A spray tank which contains from one to five litres should suffice for most other gardeners. Look for durable construction materials such as brass, stainless steel and polypropylene. Avoid roughly made components and cluttered designs. Choose units which are easy to operate, fill and clean. A wide opening on the container allows inspection of the interior and easy filling.

Aerosol containers can be convenient pieces of equipment in very small gardens or for speedy application but they are an expensive way to buy the active ingredient.

Most spray units that attach to a hose (venturi sprayers or hose-proportioners) distribute the active ingredient very unevenly because of varying water pressure. In any case most of the active ingredient runs off the plant in the excess water. These units are not suitable for the application of fungicides but are of some use in lawn situations where penetration of the chemical into the soil is required.

Direct action pump sprayers are capable of distributing the active ingredients evenly. They can be adjusted to produce the fairly fine droplets necessary for application of fungicides. Some deliver spray only on the push stroke and others are designed to operate on both push and pull strokes. Attention is necessary to operate the pump and to aim the nozzle at the same time. In models which draw the spray from a separate container such as a bucket, care must be taken not to knock it over.

Some pesticides available for home garden use.

The legal requirements of pesticide use vary from state to state and country to country. In New South Wales it is an offence under the Pesticides Act 1978 to use a pesticide for a purpose not specified on the registered label or in a way which does not conform to label instructions, unless a permit is obtained.

Always read and follow the label, because approved-use instructions vary from time to time and it is the user's responsibility to comply. The success of pesticide use depends not only on correct choice of the active ingredient but also on suitability and accuracy of application methods.

Some common trade names have been included as examples. The omission of other common trade names is not meant to imply that they are not equally suitable for use.

carbaryl	Bugmaster ® Chewing Insect Spray ®	This contact insecticide is used mostly for the control of moth and butterfly larvae, particularly leaf-feeding species. It is also useful for beetle larvae, some aphids and thrips. Toxicity to pests increases as the temperature rises. It is of relatively low toxicity to humans but highly toxic to bees and is relatively short-lived on plant tissue.
diazinon	Diazamin ® Ant Killer Spray ®	This chemical can kill a wide range of sap-suckers and leaf-chewers but it must come in contact with the pest because it has no systemic action. It can be used against pests such as cabbage white butterfly and cabbage moth, carrot rust fly, bean fly, potato moth, slaters, ants, porina caterpillar and grass grub. It has some effect on mites. Damage has been reported on a number of plant species including a range of houseplants, asters, crepe myrtles, hibiscus, and roses. It also kills ants.
dicofol	Kelthane ®	This miticide can be used to control many different mites, particularly spider mites. It will kill eggs as well as active stages. Mites in many areas are resistant to it. It may damage some plant species, including a range of houseplants, chrysanthemums, gardenias, hibiscus and roses.
dimethoate	Rogor ® Sucking Insect Killer ®	This chemical has contact and penetrant action. It can be successfully used against a range of pests, including aphids, fruit flies, two-spotted mite, European red mite, leafhoppers, leafminers and thrips. It is known to damage some plants, including early-ripening peaches and plums, apricots, Meyer lemons, Seville oranges, cumquats, figs, chrysanthemums, carnations, fuchsias, geraniums, hibiscus, hydrangeas, roses, liquidambars, begonias and gloxinias.
fenamiphos	Lawn Beetle Killer ® Nemacur ®	This systemic chemical has been marketed for control of nematodes and African black beetle in soil; and is known also to have activity against aphids, thrips and mealybugs.
fenthion	Lebaycid ®	This is a contact and stomach poison. It has systemic activity. It moves into the plant and is sucked up by insects such as aphids, thrips and lace bugs. It is useful against eggs or newly hatched fruit fly larve. It has been used against household pests such as fleas. It is particularly toxic to birds.
furalaxyl	Fongarid ®	This fungicide is very efficient for the control of diseases caused by *Phytophthora* and *Pythium*. It also controls downy mildews. It is not suitable for control of diseases caused by *Rhizoctonia, Botrytis* and *Fusarium*. It can be applied as a spray or soil drench or included in the potting mix. It gives protection for 6–10 weeks. Plants which are not badly damaged may recover after treatment. It can be used on a wide range of plants without damage, but injury has been observed on some species. These include some species of banksia, grevilleas and ornamental stonefruit.
maldison	Malathion ® Malathon ® Bug-Aphis ®	This chemical only kills pests with which it comes in contact. It would be an inefficient choice for immobile insects in places well protected from spray. It gives quite good results against a wide range of insects and some mites. It is of relatively low toxicity to humans but is highly toxic to bees. There are reports of damage to a wide range of plants, particularly when the e.c. formulation is used. These include a range of house plants, snapdragons, gerberas, petunias, primulas, stocks, camellias, carnations, chrysanthemums, dahlias, feijoas, figs, fuchsias, gardenias, hydrangeas, roses and *Hibiscus rosa-sinensis.*
mancozeb	Dithane ® mancozeb	This protectant fungicide can be used successfully against a wide range of foliage diseases, including downy mildews. It is toxic to fish.
omethoate	Folimat ®	Omethoate, is a pesticide related to dimethoate with similar action. It is effective against a range of aphids, beetles and caterpillars.
trichlorfon	Dipterex ® Caterpillar Killer ® Lawn Grub Killer ®	This insecticide has contact and stomach action against a wide range of pests. These include armyworm, cabbage moth, cabbage white butterfly, and fruit flies. It has penetrant action and can be useful against some sap-suckers. It has fairly low dermal toxicity to humans and its short withholding period makes it a good choice for fruit or vegetables being regularly harvested.
zineb		This protectant fungicide controls a wide range of fungal diseases reasonably well. These include black spot of rose; rust on plants such as beans, peaches, snapdragons and geraniums; and downy mildews on stocks, cabbages, cucumbers and pumpkins. It can cause irritation to the nose, throat and skin.

Pesticides acceptable to organic gardeners

Gardeners and farmers operating organic systems generally focus on methods such as encouraging natural predators and choosing resistant varieties rather than relying on sprays.

However, from time to time sprays are needed. The following notes include only pesticides that are registered and also fulfil the requirements of organic gardening groups.

Bordeaux mixture		This fungicide has been in use for more than a hundred years. It is very effective against a wide range of diseases and sticks on the plant well. It must be mixed freshly on each ocacsion and used within two hours. Use a plastic bucket or sprayer. The process has three steps: first dissolve 50 g of copper sulphate in a little hot water (the finer the crystals the easier it will be to dissolve) then add cold water to make it up to 5 L; then in a separate plastic container mix 50 g of hydrated lime (not agricultural lime) in 1 L of water and make it up to 5 L; lastly, stirring all the time, add the lime solution to the copper sulphate solution. Do not take short cuts with this process. The strength of the spray can be varied for different purposes — this strength is suitable for grapevines and citrus. Do not mix Bordeaux mixture with any other pesticides in the spray tank. Do not apply within two weeks of a lime-sulphur application. Do not use on delicate leaves.
copper hydroxide	Kocide ® Dry Bordeaux ®	This requires less preparation than Bordeaux mixture. It will not clog nozzles or corrode galvanised spray equipment. The plants must be covered thoroughly and the mixture must be stirred frequently during application. Do not use in hot or frosty weather or when the weather conditions will cause slow drying. The withholding period is one day. It will control a range of fungal and bacterial diseases including leaf curl of stonefruit, black spot of citrus, downy mildew of onions and black spot of apples.
copper oxychloride		This protectant fungicide is useful for a number of fungal diseases, and is also one of the very few chemicals that can help control bacterial diseases. It may injure chrysanthemums and care should be taken with ornamental plants, particularly if foliage is soft. It must be applied thoroughly.
Dipel ®		See *Bacillus thuringiensis* page 40.
Petroleum spray oils (PSOs)		These are produced by refining naturally occurring mineral oils. They are sold as white oils and as clear miscible oils. They are applied diluted in water which runs off the plant leaving a thin film of oil. This controls pests such as scale insects by smothering them. The deposits are broken down within weeks by microorganisms and cause no environmental damage. There is very little harm to beneficial insects and predator mites. These oils have very low toxicity to humans. Plants will rarely be damaged if the products are used as directed. Avoid use in very hot weather and do not apply within four weeks of a sulphur spray. Do not use on plants that are short of water. If no information is available about the effects of oil on a particular plant conduct a test run on one part of the plant only. Application must be thorough using plenty of spray per plant until the spray runs off. The mixture of oil and water must be well stirred before and during spraying.
pyrethrins		These are extracted from the flowers of *Dendranthema cinerariaefolium* and control a range of different insects including aphids and caterpillars. They are contact poisons with a rapid knock down action. They do not last long on the plant — the withholding period is only one day.
rotenone		This is extracted from the roots of *Derris* and *Lonchocarpus* spp. It is a stomach poison and can be sprayed or dusted onto plants. It does not last long on the plant and the withholding period is one day. It is best against caterpillars. It is highly toxic to fish and pigs.
soap sprays	Safer ® Natrasoap ®	Those with a vegetable oil origin are to be preferred. They are generally aimed at the smaller softer bodied insects such as aphids, whiteflies, mealybugs, thrips and spider mites. It is necessary for the spray to contact the insect so it is recommended that a number of applications be made in fairly quick succession so that young that have hatched from eggs since the previous spray can be contacted. Some products contain additional substances, for example Clensel ® contains potassium oleate and citronella oil.
sulphur		This can be applied as a dust or as a spray in water (wettable sulphur). Flowers of sulphur are too coarse to apply as a dust and the raw product must be sieved or treated in some other way. It is used as a contact and protectant miticide and fungicide. It is generally not harmful to plants but users should be cautious and try a few plants at a time in previously untried situations. Do not use on apricots. It must not be used on hot days.
lime-sulphur		This chemical will control many fungal diseases such as powdery mildews on ornamentals; insects such as white louse scale and mites such as grapeleaf blister mite. If used when the plants are actively growing it is likely to cause leaf scorch, and leaf and fruit fall. Do not use on apricots or use within 10 days of oil sprays. It is not compatible with most other pesticides. It may stain nearby structures such as walls and fences.

The small blue respirator is suitable only for nuisance dusts such as those generated by shovelling soil or cleaning bricks. The other respirator has two cartridges attached to the front. Use only the type which absorb agricultural chemicals, and replace them after the time specified by the manufacturer or by health authorities.

The bucket system is particularly difficult on sloping or uneven ground. The bucket should be kept only for use with the spray equipment.

Pressurised or pump-up sprayers can be very efficient but they should have a pressure-limiting valve to ensure that the output of spray continues evenly as the pressure inside drops during use. They are pressurised before spraying starts which means that the operator can concentrate on directing the spray nozzle. Follow carefully the instructions for use and care.

Knapsack sprayers which are carried on the back are usually pressurised as spraying proceeds. Filled with spray they may weigh over 20 kg and many people find them too heavy to wear.

Successful use of spray equipment also depends on the type of nozzle used. Cone-type nozzles, which are the normal type supplied with spray equipment, are really designed for spraying shrubs and trees, rather than lawns. Flat-band spray nozzles arranged on a boom spray are the easiest method of spraying lawns to get the best and most even results.

Spray equipment needs care. All hoses, nozzles, pumps and tanks or buckets should be rinsed twice as soon as spraying is finished, and then washed out with warm water and detergent. Finish with a thorough rinsing in clean water. Pour all the rinsings in an out of the way place such as at the back of a garden bed near a fence.

If herbicides are applied with the same piece of equipment, which is not a good idea, the washing process must be particularly thorough. Herbicides can distort or even kill some plants at very low concentrations.

Clean and oil the operational parts so the unit is ready for use the next time you need it. Pay special attention to washers and hoses. The equipment should not be leaky. Do not store the hose over a nail or peg. This may create kinks in the hose and interfere with its efficient operation.

Nozzles should be checked for wear after a few years, particularly if wettable powders are often used.

Although particles in wettable powders are very fine they will gradually erode nozzles and other equipment parts.

Equipment for measuring concentrates is often provided by the manufacturer either with the packaging or as part of the container. Liquid concentrates may also be measured with a dropper graduated in mL. These can be bought at chemist shops. Pesticides which come in powdered form can be measured with metric spoons (see the measurement chart in the Appendix). Spoons and droppers should be boldly marked or disfigured in some way so that they will not end up in the medicine chest or kitchen.

Choice of a suitable time to spray

If chemical control procedures are unavoidable, choose a suitable day and time to spray. Do not spray if the soil is very dry, and the plant under water stress.

Water the plants to be sprayed the day before or at least allow time for the leaves to dry; spray applied to a wet plant runs off the leaves.

If rain is predicted, delay spraying until another occasion. Sprays need from 12 to 24 hours in order to dry on the plant. Once dry, they are usually not very easily removed by rain.

Spraying should not be carried out in very hot weather. At temperatures above 35°C fruit and leaf damage is very likely. This may be a burn or the fruit and leaves may fall. A temperature well below 35°C is much more desirable. Spraying in cold, frosty weather should also be avoided.

Spraying must not be done on a windy day. This is a dangerous and inefficient practice because most of the spray destined for a particular plant will be blown elsewhere.

The stage of the development of the pest and its whereabouts may also be important. White wax scale (P), for example, is much more easily controlled if sprayed in the very early stages, before the protective waxy covering has developed too far. Insect pests are generally more easily controlled on the above-ground part of the plant than when feeding on the root system.

If plants must be sprayed when in flower, wait till late in the day when bees have returned to the hive.

Read the insecticide label. Ensure that the pesticide you plan to use is suitable for the time of year and the stage of growth of the plant. Winter oils, for example, should be applied to deciduous plants only in winter and should never be applied to evergreen plants.

Some insecticides or fungicides damage particular plants even when applied at the right time and using correct procedures. This is termed 'phytotoxicity'.

Consult the label for details. There is still much that is not known about toxicity to ornamental plants. Toxicity may depend on the formulation of the product.

Safe spray application

Weeding, pruning and other gardening should be done before insecticides are applied, because it is not sensible to work on plants or in areas which have just been sprayed.

Harvest ripe fruit and vegetables before spraying. Make sure that children's toys, garden furniture and the feeding dishes of pets are not sprayed by accident. Organise a time of peace and quiet so that children and pets need not be nearby.

Wear suitable clothing. Cover up as much skin as possible with long-sleeved shirt, trousers and shoes and socks. Wear a washable hat, particularly if you intend to spray tall plants or if you are bald. Leather shoes and rubber boots are to be preferred to sandshoes and sneakers because they are less permeable. Shorts, t-shirts and thongs or sandals are not suitable for this job. Undamaged rubber gloves are a must. Do not wear cotton or leather gloves, because these can become impregnated with poisonous substances which would then make contact with the skin on future occasions.

If spraying in a glasshouse or any enclosed space, or if the job will take more than 10–15 minutes, you should wear a respirator. Take care to purchase one suitable for use with agricultural chemicals.

Read the label and calculate the amount of concentrate required to make up the appropriate quantity of dilute spray. The rate of dilution mentioned on the label should be adhered to. Do not add extra concentrate for good measure — it is wasteful, more hazardous, and it may harm the plants. Dead is dead. Twice as much pesticide cannot make the pest or disease twice as dead.

A small quantity (e.g. 1 or 2 mL) of concentrate per litre of water really is enough to do the job. Believe it!

Note that measuring the concentrate is a more dangerous operation than spraying with the diluted spray. If concentrate is spilt on the skin, the area should be thoroughly washed with soap and water for ten minutes. Start washing immediately the accident occurs.

If concentrate is splashed in eyes, wash in running water for at least 15 minutes. Medical attention should be sought. Clothing on which pesticide has been spilt should be removed immediately and should be hosed thoroughly before washing.

Use the diluted spray immediately. It is not safe to leave lying around, and it will begin to lose its efficacy as soon as it is mixed with water.

Do not smoke or eat while you are spraying or before changing your clothes and washing.

Plan the application of the spray to a tree or shrub so that you have as little contact with wet leaves as possible. Spray the lower, inner parts of a tree first and gradually move upwards and outwards. Aim the spray at the part of the plant where the pest is. Populations of white louse scale(P), for example, concentrate on the trunk so spraying leaves only would be a waste of effort.

Withholding period and frequency of application
When mixed with water and exposed to heat and light on the leaves, the active ingredients of most pesticides change and gradually become harmless to humans and to insects or pathogens. This breakdown influences the frequency of application. Advice to 'apply every 7–14 days' is common on labels. In hot, bright weather the active ingredient breaks down more quickly, plants usually grow quickly and new leaves may not be protected by pesticide already applied.

Insects and pathogens are likely to be favoured by these conditions and it may therefore be necessary to reapply the pesticide in seven days. In cooler weather pesticide applications can often be spaced further apart.

The 'withholding period' or 'waiting time' is the period of time during which it is unsafe to eat sprayed fruit or vegetables. It is indicated on the product label.

Children and pets should be kept away from recently sprayed plants and the family should be made aware that fruit and vegetables must not be picked until the withholding period has elapsed.

Compatibility
On various occasions it would save time and effort if a fungicide and an insecticide were mixed together in the same spray tank. This can be done, but it is essential

A pesticide kit is a good idea for a home garden. Use a plastic bin or bucket to hold essential items so that they are easily and quickly available when a spraying job has to be done. Pesticides are best measured and mixed on a flat surface.

that you read the labels carefully. They will usually indicate if the concentrates are compatible or not.

You may also enquire about compatibility from the manufacturer and from your local Department of Agriculture; or read a compatibility chart. Copies of these may be available from the same sources.

It is not advisable to mix more than two different products. If the products are incompatible, several things can happen: a different chemical which is dangerous to the user or the plant may be produced; one or both of the active ingredients may be rendered useless and so not kill the pest or disease it was intended to kill; or the preparation may block up the spray nozzles. Products from the one manufacturer are more likely to be compatible than products from different manufacturers.

Stir thoroughly when mixing and follow all the label directions carefully.

Wetters, spreaders and stickers

Most pesticides have additives which help to wet plant leaves; to spread the active ingredient over the leaf; and to stick it there. The amount used is enough for an 'average plant'. Some leaves, however, are particularly hard to wet.

This can be demonstrated by dipping a dry (i.e. not wet with rain or dew) cabbage or iris leaf into a basin of clean water. When the leaf is removed it will still be dry. If a drop or two of washing-up detergent is added to the water the leaf will become wet when it is dipped.

If you intend to spray plants with hard-to-wet leaves, add proprietary wetter and spreader according to label directions or about 2 teaspoons of washing-up detergent per litre of water.

Disinfecting tools

Removal of disease-causing organisms from garden tools such as knives can be achieved by using household bleach. Use 150 mL of 4% sodium hypochlorite in one litre of water.

Soil treatments

Disease-causing organisms which are found in the soil can be killed with chemicals. Many of these are too poisonous to be applied in a home garden but can be applied by trained operators from pest control firms in a farm situation.

If the only problem is a small area of soil infested with nematodes, the home-gardener can use fenamiphos granules according to the label directions on the product. This pesticide will not harm plants already growing in the garden.

However, in the case of widespread and large populations of nematodes on a farm, it may be more sensible to employ a reputable firm of pest control operators to fumigate the soil. Soil treatments will not be fully effective if there are large clods of earth, and pieces of undecomposed plant material in the area. The soil should be in seed-bed condition and slightly moist.

Treatment is likely to leave residues in the soil that are toxic to some or all plants for a period of time. Check this with the operator and wait until all traces of the chemical have gone before planting. This may take weeks.

Tree injection

Injection is an alternative treatment if spraying is impossible because of the height of the tree or because of wet or windy weather. Despite advantages over spraying — predators are not usually affected, the insecticide protects the tree for longer and there is no drift of chemicals to other areas where they are unwanted — this method can seriously damage trees even if the correct dosages are applied. The procedure involves inserting insecticide into holes drilled in the sapwood (water-conducting tissue) of the tree at regular intervals around a tree trunk. The insecticide moves upwards in the water to kill sap-sucking or leaf-feeding insects.

The dose of insecticide is calculated on the basis of the size of the tree canopy and the diameter of the trunk. Both the drilling of holes and injecting insecticide damage the tree.

This method does not control insects feeding in the trunk (borers), and it is not suitable for pests that attract trees annually.

Most insect pests have a relatively brief affect on a tree, whereas injection can cause long term problems because the tree can be seriously damaged if it is injected too frequently, if the dosage is calculated incorrectly or if the holes are drilled in the wrong place.

Every case is different. Whether or not an individual tree should be injected, and the placement of the holes, needs careful thought. Consult your local Department of Agriculture or forestry office for more details, or employ a qualified arborist.

Sprays run off some plants unless wetters are added.

A–Z of PLANT CARE

An alphabetical listing of a large range of commonly grown plants, with notes on their care. Information on pests and diseases marked (P) and (D) can be found in the sections on Pests and Diseases.

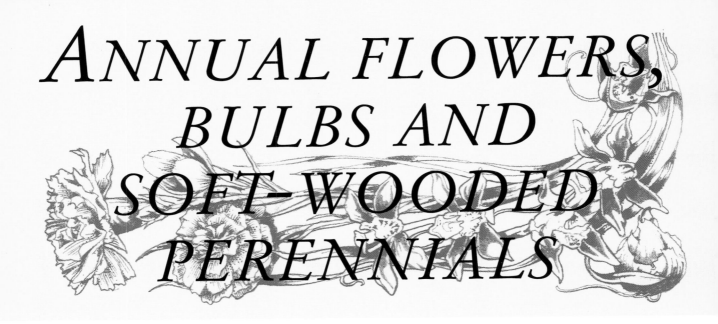

ANNUAL FLOWERS, BULBS AND SOFT-WOODED PERENNIALS

ANNUAL FLOWERS

The term 'annual' refers to plants that grow to their full size, flower, seed and die in one year or less. The following remarks also apply to some short-lived perennials, such as Iceland poppy, snapdragon, stock and wallflower, which are usually used as annuals in areas with mild climates.

Preparation for an attractive and healthy display involves attention to seeds and seedlings and the provision of suitable growing conditions. The work can be very time consuming.

Seeds and seedlings
It is important to begin with healthy seed, so make sure that seed collected in the home garden comes from disease-free plants. Note that sowing the seed too thickly will encourage seed-bed diseases and should be avoided. Some seeds should be sown directly into their final position because the seedlings, if transplanted, either die or never afterwards grow well.

Planting time
Best results will be obtained if sowing times suggested on seed packets are adhered to. Flowering, in many plants, is influenced by day-length. Plants sown out of season may not flower because the days/nights are the wrong length to induce flowering. This effect is termed photoperiodism.

Soil
Many annuals will perform well in a nearly neutral soil (about pH 7) that is well-drained and fertile, with plenty of organic matter. There are exceptions — for example, lupins flower better if grown in rather poor soil. Check that the conditions to be provided suit the particular plants chosen.

Aspect
Some annuals such as livingstone daisy, petunia, portulaca and zinnia do best in hot sunny situations, while others such as cineraria need shady cool situations. Wind protection is desirable for tall-growing and hollow-stemmed plants such as zinnia, unless they are planted in a mass and can support each other.

After the plants are established in suitable conditions, correct cultural practices will help avoid pest and disease problems.

Fertilising
Most annuals benefit from the addition of fertiliser during the growing period, although too much nitrogenous fertiliser near flowering time will encourage the growth of large leaves at the expense of the flowers. For example, nasturtiums, if grown in very fertile soil, produce long leaf stalks and large leaves so that the flowers

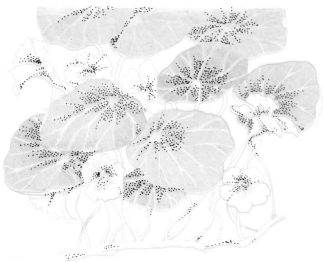

Plants oversupplied with nitrogen may produce leaves that hide the flowers.

are hidden completely. If too much nitrogenous fertiliser is applied, this may also increase susceptibility of the plants to certain diseases.

Watering
Remember that a good soaking of water every few days is more useful than frequent light sprinkling. Avoid watering the leaves late in the day; leaves remain wet for hours during the night, thus increasing the possibility of germination of fungal spores.

Mulching
Mulching is useful to conserve moisture and reduce weed growth, but do not continue the mulch right up to the plant stems or mulch too deeply in the seedling stage. Such practices encourage collar rots. Make sure the mulch does not develop a surface 'crust' that is impervious to water.

Pruning
Many annuals such as phlox, snapdragons, sweet peas and wallflowers benefit from pinching back in the early stages of growth; this encourages a strong, bushy vegetative structure on which flowers can later be produced. Performance will also be improved if flower buds are removed from young plants, and old flowers removed from fully-grown plants. Diseased or eaten plant parts should be removed to improve appearance and reduce spread of disease.

Pests and diseases
Pests and diseases of annual flowers vary from place to place and season to season. Pests such as aphids (P), thrips (P), whiteflies (P) and mites (P) of various sorts should be considered possible problems with any annual flowers. Leaves may be chewed by green loopers (P), cluster caterpillars (P), and caterpillars of the bogong moth (P). Earwigs (P) and black field crickets (P) also cause problems at times. Most small plants need protection from snails and slugs (P).

Roots can be attacked by root knot nematode (D) which causes the plant to wilt easily.

Verticillium wilt (D), fusarium wilt (D), sclerotium stem rot (D), sclerotinia rot (D) and collar rot (D) are all annual flower problems on occasions.

Western flower thrips *(Frankliniella occidentalis)* attack a wide range of ornamental annuals and perennials and many fruit and vegetable crops. As they feed on plant parts they often transmit tomato spotted wilt virus, see spotted wilt (D), causing serious losses in many plants.

These thrips are about 1 mm long and from pale yellow to buff or brown in colour, like many other thrips. With magnification their distinguishing characteristic, long black spines on their 'shoulders', becomes evident.

Feeding occurs in the same way as with other thrips. The cell walls of the surface layer of cells are damaged by rasping with the mouthparts and the insect sucks up the sap. Infested plants show flecking, silvering and deformation of flowers, buds and fruit. It prefers to feed on floral parts but will also attack young leaves and stems.

They cause serious damage in a greenhouse as conditions are usually very favourable for them all year round.

A suitable program for control in home gardens has yet to be established. Control with pesticides is difficult. Programs must concentrate on garden hygiene. Practice weed control. In some circumstances sticky traps may be useful. The yellow commercially available ones could be used although thrips are attracted more to white or blue.

BULBS AND BULBOUS PLANTS

This group includes plants growing from true bulbs (e.g. daffodils and liliums), from corms (e.g. freesia and gladiolus), from tubers (e.g. anemone), from rhizomes (e.g. tall-bearded iris), and from swollen rootstocks (e.g. dahlia). The following information applies to all these plants, although the word 'bulb' will be used for convenience.

Most of these plants are best suited to temperate areas, and considerable extra care is necessary if they are to be grown in tropical or hot dry areas.

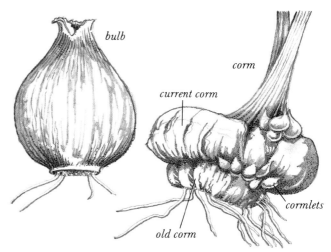

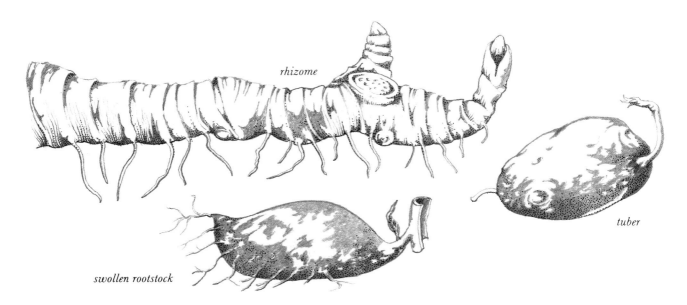

rhizome

tuber

swollen rootstock

In general they need an open sunny situation and well-drained soil, but there are some that thrive in damp or more shady places, so consult gardening books before a final choice is made.

A slightly acid, fertile soil with a high proportion of organic matter will suit most bulbs. Any compost or animal manure used should be well rotted. Bulbs do not require large quantities of fertiliser, and if it is applied it should be high in phosphorus. It must not be allowed to come in direct contact with the bulbs.

Planting depth should be checked for each different bulb, but it is generally two to three times the diameter of the bulb. Constant watering, or cultivation before the leaves appear, may cause the bulb to rot or may damage the growing point. Do not neglect the plant after flowering, because at this time the leaves are producing food supplies to be stored in the bulb and used for next year's flower. This is particularly important in the case of 'true bulbs'. Do not cut the leaves off or lift the bulbs until the foliage begins to yellow and die. Areas where bulbs are left in the soil all year should be watered sparingly or not at all in the non-growing season. Excess moisture may cause the bulbs to rot.

Many bulbous plants are best left undisturbed for several years, whereas others should be lifted annually.

If bulbs are to be lifted, take great care to avoid cuts or bruises, because damaged bulbs are more likely to be attacked by pests and diseases than undamaged ones. Do not leave them out in the sun. Remove rotted parts of rhizomes with a sharp knife, and remove the dry outer leaves from corms. Brush attached soil from the bulbs when it is dry, and store them in a cool, dry, well-ventilated situation in mesh bags or wire-trays. Destroy any bulbs or corms that are spongy or rotted, or have dark marks or scabs.

Buy only bulbs that are plump, rounded, firm and unmarked.

Poor flowering performance may be caused by a variety of factors, such as lack of care after flower production in the previous year, or a position with too much shade. If bulbs become overcrowded they are not able to grow to flowering size because of insufficient space and because nutrients are in short supply. Some, such as tulips, need a period of chilling to stimulate flowering, and in warm temperate areas the weather is not generally cold enough to provide for this.

New bulbs begin flat on one side and gradually become rounder.

True bulbs that are small and flat on one side may be too small to flower. They should be planted and cared for. They will gradually increase in size and be ready to flower next season or the one after.

Some bulbs and tubers flower only once. Tuberose (*Polianthes tuberosa*) is one of these.

Pests and diseases
True bulbs which when cut across have brown rings of rot inside them have probably been attacked by the bulb nematode (D).

Ideally, the bulbs should not be in direct contact with one another in storage. Addition of some dry peat moss, crumpled newspaper or similar material will keep them apart and prevent easy spread of disease. Aphids (P) such as the mangold aphid, the bulb and potato aphid and the tulip bulb aphid (*Dysaphis tulipae*) can feed on stored bulbs and damage them. The latter, a greyish to purple aphid, is often found between the dry outer skins of the bulbs. When the bulbs are producing leaves these aphids move on to them and may cause severe distortion. The bulb mite (P) also attacks stored bulbs.

Check for damaged bulbs again at planting time. These are not likely to produce a good flower crop and may introduce a disease into clean soil. If there is any doubt about their health, they should be grown in a pot for a season and not planted with other bulbs.

Irregular patterns of pale green or yellow on leaves may indicate a virus infection. These plants with their bulbs should probably be destroyed, and should definitely not be used for propagation. Aphids (P), which carry viruses, should be controlled, and further advice should be sought from your local Department of Agriculture.

Rotting near ground level is likely to be bacterial soft rot (D). This usually indicates that conditions have been too wet.

The lesser bulb fly (P) and the bulb mite (P) may cause serious problems. Two-spotted mite (P) and some species of thrips (P) may cause mottling on the leaves, and plague thrips (P) may attack the flowers.

In Europe the onion maggot (P) is known to attack ornamental bulbs.

Millipedes (P), slaters such as the common slater (P), and the very similar pillbugs; snails and slugs (P), springtails (P), and various caterpillars may also damage bulbous plants.

areas with a cool moist summer. Many of them die down to the roots in winter and make new growth in spring.

Pests and diseases
Although their culture is usually relatively easy, they may be attacked by common pests such as aphids (P), thrips (P) and mites (P). Caterpillars such as loopers (P) and budworms (P) chew the leaves or flowers occasionally, and root knot nematode (D) may attack the root

Hostas, the plantain lilies, will thrive in damp soil.

system. Snails and slugs (P) may feed on the leaves of perennials or shelter under them.

If boggy areas of the garden are to be planted, make sure the plants chosen are suitable or root and crown rots will develop.

Some perennials, such as carnations and chrysanthemums, are grown for cut flowers and they demand more cultural attention if good results are to be obtained. These, and a very few others, which are commonly grown and have specific pest and disease problems are included in the following list.

SOFT-WOODED PERENNIALS

Perennials are plants that keep growing and flowering year after year, over a number of years. Strictly speaking this should include groups such as trees and shrubs, but gardeners commonly use the term to describe only shorter-living and less woody plants. There are thousands of these plants, and many are suitable only for

Chrysanthemums are useful for cut flowers and are also grown in pots for use indoors.

African and French marigold
ANNUAL

Tagetes erecta and *T. patula*

Marigolds will perform well in almost any soil. They need a warm sunny position with shelter from wind. African marigolds do not tolerate frosts.

Whiteflies (P) and two-spotted mites (P) may cause problems. Small whitish wandering lines are probably caused by a leafminer (P).

African lily
PERENNIAL

Agapanthus spp.

These plants need a sunny position for best flower production but will grow in the shade. They seem to perform well with a crowded root system and survive heat and drought. The leaves are damaged by frost but the plant will not be killed by this.

Snails and slugs (P) shelter under the strap-like leaves but they do not seem to eat them. Reddish spots and pale brown water-soaked patches are probably leaf scorch (D).

Bedding begonia
ANNUAL

Begonia × *semperflorens-cultorum*

These plants grow well in a warm temperate climate. Tropical or cold areas are not suitable. They perform best in light shade but grow reasonably well in heavy shade. If sited in full sun they must not be allowed to suffer water stress. Hot winds will burn the leaves. Soil type is not critical, but fertilise and water regularly.

Cyclamen mite (P) may cause distortion of new growth.

Calla lily
BULBOUS

Zantedeschia spp.

Plant these in moist soil and protect them from strong sun and hot drying winds. Watch for small, more or less round, grey spots. This may be a leaf spot caused by a fungus such as *Phyllosticta* sp. Remove the affected leaves and destroy them. If no action is taken, large irregular areas of leaf will decay.

A foot rot caused by a *Phytophthora* sp. may also occur. Look for yellow streaks, browning and death of the outer leaves first. Newer leaves and flowers are infected later and, if the plant is pulled up, the root system will appear extensively decayed. Clean the rhizomes and dip them in water at 50°C (122°F) for one hour. Cool and dry. Do not plant back in the same area.

Rotting of leaf stalks near ground level is probably bacterial soft rot (D).

At least two viruses infect calla lilies. Yellow spots and streaks on the leaves probably indicate spotted wilt (D). The spots are smaller and more irregularly spaced than those spots that occur on the golden calla lily (*Zantedeschia elliotiana*).

The leaves of a virus-infected plant may also be wrinkled and distorted. The leaf edges may curl up or down.

The most notable pest is gladiolus thrips (P), but mealybugs (P) can sometimes be a problem.

Carnation
PERENNIAL

Dianthus caryophyllus

Carnations are not a good choice for the tropics or subtropics because the high humidity increases disease incidence and the flowers are comparatively poor. High

temperatures, generally, cause reduction in flower size and stem length. Carnations should have a sunny position sheltered from strong winds. Frost or sudden unseasonable cold weather causes twisted leaves and failure of flower buds to open. Calyx splitting is thought to be caused by sudden and/or great fluctuations in temperature — between day and night, for example.

The ideal soil is a well-drained, slightly acid, medium to sandy loam with plenty of organic matter. Help avoid phytophthora collar rot (D) by planting the crowns just clear of the soil and avoiding plant/mulch contact. Pinch-prune the young plants two or three times to make them bushy, and prune back after each flush of flowers. Pieces of plant material left in the area can make diseases such as grey mould (D) more likely. Pruning and flower gathering should be done carefully with sharp tools so as to avoid ragged cuts, which increase the likelihood of diseases such as fusarium branch blight.

Overhead watering is undesirable because it encourages leaf- and flower-spotting diseases. The fungicides recommended for rust will control most leaf spot diseases.

There are a number of virus diseases of carnations. Symptoms include yellow streaks, leaf malformation, general leaf yellowing and dark-green flecks. These plants should be destroyed. Control aphids, and whenever possible buy cuttings labelled to show that they come from virus-tested stock.

Other diseases and pests of carnations include fusarium wilt (D), sclerotium stem rot (D), rust (D), root knot nematode (D), collar rot (D), aphids (P), two-spotted mite (P), gladiolus thrips (P), and budworms (P). Garden pinks (also *Dianthus* spp.) may have similar problems.

China aster
ANNUAL

Callistephus chinensis

Asters would not be a good choice for a very cold climate because they cannot tolerate frost. They need a sunny position and grow best in sandy loam with plenty of organic matter and good drainage. Water and fertilise regularly. Use mulch to decrease water loss and to keep the roots cool.

Asters may be attacked by general insect pests and diseases. Also look for distorted, green flowers caused by big bud (D); and wilting and death of the growing point which may be caused by broad bean wilt (D).

Chrysanthemum
PERENNIAL

Dendranthema x morifolium

Chrysanthemums will grow well in a wide range of soils but they will not tolerate waterlogging. If drainage is poor or if periods of prolonged wet weather occur, they are likely to suffer from phytophthora root rot (D). The plants, however, must be well-watered to produce flowers of good size with long stems.

An open sunny position is best unless the climate is very hot. Frost will damage flowers. Flower-bearing stems may bend under the weight of the flowers if the plants are not supported by stakes or some other means. Flowers on curved stems are difficult to arrange in a vase.

Dark-brown spots, often on the leaf edge, indicate leaf spot (D); and pale raised spots or dark-brown dust indicate rust (D). White powdery growth on the leaves is probably powdery mildew (D) which is most likely to occur in dry weather. A grey furry growth is grey mould (D) which is most likely in cool moist weather.

Wavy lines on the leaves are probably caused by spotted wilt (D); and almost triangular brown patches are a symptom of leaf nematode (D) attack. Look for this on the lower leaves first.

If lower leaves are purple and hanging down, suspect verticillium wilt (D); and if the plant has a stiff upright appearance, suspect the virus disease called stunt. In both these instances, the plant should be removed and destroyed.

Deep pink spots on the petals are caused by ray blight (D). Buds may be distorted by mites such as the cyclamen mite (P). Chrysanthemum gall midge (P) produces small lumps on the leaves and stems; and flowers can be badly damaged by earwigs (P). Green and distorted flowers are probably caused by big bud (D) which is also referred to as greening or virescence.

Whitish, meandering lines on the leaves are the result of leafminer (P); this leafminer also attacks cinerarias. Chrysanthemums can also be attacked by aphids (P); by earth mites (P) such as blue oat mite; by spider mites such as two-spotted mite (P); and by caterpillars such as budworms (P) and loopers (P).

Watering late in the day and leaving old or dead pieces of chrysanthemum plant in the area will make leaf and flower diseases more likely.

Do not use dimethoate (Rogor®) for pest control on chrysanthemums. It will damage the plant.

White rust of chrysanthemum is caused by a fungus, *Puccinia horiana.* This is a misleading common name as this fungus is not related to the fungi causing other diseases usually called white rusts.

Symptoms first appear on the upper leaf surfaces as slightly sunken pale green to yellow spots that brown with age. On the under leaf surfaces below each spot buff to pink pustules form. These gradually grow to about 4 mm and become white. Badly infected leaves may wither. The fungus may be dormant in the plant in hot dry weather but the symptoms only occur in humid cooler conditions.

Inspect the plants regularly. If the symptoms are noticed early it may be worthwhile to spray with chlorothalonil. Infected plants should be removed or cut off at ground level and all plant parts should be destroyed. Wash hands and tools thoroughly after handling infected plants. Plant only resistant varieties.

Cineraria
ANNUAL

Senecio × hybridus

This plant is not suitable for outdoor growth in a hot dry climate or in a very cold one. It should be protected from frost, strong sun and drying winds.

The most common problems are aphids (P), cineraria leafminer (P), earwigs (P), and powdery mildew (D). Rust (D)—the one that attacks English marigolds—is also a possibility.

Daffodil and jonquil
BULBOUS

Narcissus spp.

These bulbs tolerate both cold and hot conditions. They are usually left undisturbed for several years and lifted only when the flower size and number decreases. However, if basal rot (D) has been detected, they should be lifted, inspected and planted in a new position each year. Basal rot may be associated

with the use of hormone preparations and with heavy applications of nitrogenous fertiliser.

The leaves should be inspected regularly for signs of virus disease. These include indistinct mottling; yellow, brown or purplish streaks; and twisting. Dig up and burn any infected plants. Control of aphids (P) will help to stop spread of these virus diseases from plant to plant.

If the leaves are twisted with irregular ridges running along them, bulb nematode (D) may be the cause. The hot-water treatment of bulbs recommended for this problem must be timed correctly, or

subsequent growth and flowering will be adversely affected.

Scorched leaf tips and reddish-brown spots indicate leaf scorch (D).

The larvae of the lesser bulb fly (P) may burrow inside the bulb and cause serious injury. Bulb mite (P) and tulip bulb aphid (*Dysaphis tulipae*) may also cause damage.

Dahlia
BULBOUS

A well-drained soil and a sunny position are necessary for successful dahlia growth. Extra staking will be necessary unless wind protection is provided.

The plants should be provided with regular water during the summer, but overwatering or a poorly drained soil are likely to encourage tuber rots, particularly in the time between tuber planting and appearance of first shoots.

An oversupply of nitrogen will probably lead to a profusion of soft weak leaves and stems unable to adequately support the flowers. Flower production will be reduced.

Tubers should be dug for storage after the plant dies down and planted out again, after division, from mid-spring to early summer. If plants are grown for garden display and soil drainage is good, it is not necessary to dig them every year. If they are grown for showing, however, it is usual to dig them each year.

Light pruning as the plant grows will help to provide a stronger, bushier structure for flower bearing, and removal of some flower buds will produce fewer but bigger flowers.

Distortion of new growth may be caused by the broad mite (P) or the cyclamen mite (P). Flowers may be torn by small beetles called nectar scarabs (P); or chewed by earwigs (P), grasshoppers or redshouldered leaf beetles (P). The latter also attack leaves. Distorted or green flowers may indicate big bud (D).

Leaves with ragged edges may have been chewed by Fuller's rose weevil (P); and leaves with a dull, yellowish appearance attacked by two-spotted mite (P). Leaves will show wavy yellow patterns if affected by spotted wilt (D); a white surface if affected by powdery mildew (D); and small brown spots if affected by leaf spot (D). Grey mould (D) is characterised by a grey furry growth on buds, flowers, leaves or stems.

Dahlia 'stem rot' is referred to as sclerotinia rot (D) on many other plants; and 'collar rot' as sclerotium stem rot (D). Dahlias may also suffer from crown gall (D).

Stunting and yellowing of the plants may indicate attack from root knot nematode (D), and stunting combined with an excessive production of small shoots is probably the virus disease, stunt. Wilting and sudden death of the whole plant may be the disease verticillium wilt (D).

Delphinium ANNUAL
Delphinium spp.

Delphiniums are not suitable for tropical or hot dry climates. If grown in areas with cool summers, they perform well for several years, but in warmer areas they are best used as annuals. They need a fertile soil in a sunny position and a regular water and fertiliser supply. Wind protection (or staking) is necessary for the tall types.

Aphids (P), two-spotted mites (P) and powdery mildew (D) may be problems.

Black leaf spot is caused by the bacterium *Pseudomonas syringae* pv. *delphinii*. On the upper leaf surface these spots appear black, shiny and irregular in shape and size. The spots are brown on the underside of the leaf. The symptoms, which also occur on stems, leafstalks and flowers, begin on the lower part of the plant. Collect and destroy diseased plant material. Practise crop rotation.

English daisy ANNUAL
Bellis perennis

English daisies are not suitable for tropical or hot dry climates but in other areas will tolerate poor conditions. They prefer sun but perform quite well in semi-shade. Weed control is important when the plants are small.

Rust (D) — the one that attacks English marigolds — can be a problem.

In some regions this plant becomes a weed in lawns and open spaces.

English marigold ANNUAL
Calendula officinalis

These perform reasonably well in any soil with good drainage, but full sun is essential. Remove self-sown plants unless they are cared for with the rest of the crop.

Rust (D) is a serious problem, and uncared-for self-sown plants are a source of reinfection. Powdery mildew (D) is a common disease. Aphids (P), and earth mites (P) may also cause trouble.

Floss flower ANNUAL
Ageratum houstonianum

Hot-weather crops will grow quite well in light shade, but full sun is required at other times. Frost tolerance is very low, and a warm position protected from cold winds is to be preferred. They are drought resistant but respond to regular watering.

Earth mites (P), aphids (P) and whiteflies (P) are common problems.

Gerbera PERENNIAL
Gerbera jamesonii

These thrive only in an open sunny position. Very good drainage is essential, and the plants should be positioned with their crowns above the soil surface so that root and crown rots can be avoided.

The 'crown rot' of gerberas is caused by the same fungus as the sclerotium stem rot (D) of many other plants. And 'root rot' is the same as phytophthora root rot (D).

Water infrequently in autumn and winter. The leaves may show symptoms of leaf spot (D) and white rust (D). The flowers may be distorted and/or green as a result of big bud (D).

Gladiolus BULBOUS
Gladiolus hybrids

Gladioli can be grown successfully in a wide range of soil types, but the pH should be slightly acid and the drainage must be good. A friable soil makes digging and cleaning the corms an easier job. Choose an open sunny position with shelter from strong winds.

Low temperatures result in flower failure for some varieties, and plants may be damaged by severe frost. A poor water supply during flower formation will reduce stem length and number of florets per spike.

Be careful to plant only healthy corms, as many serious diseases can be introduced to a new area on corms. Once in

the soil these diseases are difficult to eradicate. The corms should be bright in colour, firm, and free of dark spots or patches.

Crop rotation and good sanitation are important in gladiolus growing. Do not use the same soil year after year. Ideally gladioli should only be grown in an area once every four years.

Plants that turn yellow during the growing season are probably suffering from fusarium yellows (D) and should be removed with the corm and burnt. Plants with streaked or mottled flowers and foliage may have a virus disease and should be destroyed together with their corms. Check first that these symptoms are not caused by gladiolus thrips (P).

Individual plants growing at random and by accident in the garden can harbour pests and diseases and should be removed. All plant debris such as mouldy flower heads and pieces of leaf and stem should be removed from the garden area and destroyed.

If leaves are removed or damaged during flower collecting, the new corms and cormlets will be smaller and therefore less vigorous.

Continue to care for the plants for about five weeks after flowering, and then lift the corms, preferably when the soil is hot and dry. Thrips will migrate from dying leaves to corms, where they lay eggs, if digging is left too long. The husks, which provide protection for thrips, should be removed.

Gladioli suffer from a number of fungal leaf spots such as botrytis leaf and flower spot (D). The control recommended for this disease should control the other leaf-spotting diseases as well.

Insect pests of the growing plant include mealybugs (P) and budworms (P), and caterpillars of moths such as painted apple moth (P) and cluster caterpillar (P). Bulb mites (P), gladiolus thrips (P) and mealybugs (P) are also possible problems on the corms in storage.

Iceland poppy   ANNUAL
Papaver nudicaule

These annuals are not suitable for tropical climates; and if grown in hot dry areas, careful attention to watering is necessary. Grow in full sun in a rich, well-drained soil with a high level of organic matter. Avoid root disturbance when weeding. Mulch would be a good idea, but avoid covering the crown with mulch or soil.

Poppies may be infected with spotted wilt (D); and a 'bud and neck blight' caused by the fungus responsible for grey mould (D) on many other plants.

Iris   BULBOUS
Iris spp.

It is a good idea to have irises correctly identified, because cultural practices and the incidence of pests and diseases vary according to type.

Japanese iris (*I. kaempferi*) grow from rhizomes, which should be positioned at ground level. They need plenty of water and can even be submerged for a while during spring and summer but should be kept dry in winter when the leaves will die down.

The tall-bearded iris also grows from rhizomes, which should be planted very near the soil surface. The rhizomes of both these groups should be left undisturbed for two to three years for best flower performance.

Rhizomatous irises with rusty-red powdery spots on the leaves are probably suffering from rust (D). Brown spots that enlarge and eventually develop into large dead patches are characteristic of leaf spot (D); and light, yellow-green streaks on the leaves indicate mosaic (D).

Rotting of leaf bases and rhizome may be bacterial soft rot (D) or sclerotium stem rot (D). The latter is usually referred to as 'crown rot' when irises are attacked. It is characterised by dieback of leaf tips and rotting at the base of leaves and flower stalks, followed by a gradual rotting of the rhizome.

Bulbous irises need a sunny, well-drained situation and regular water during the period of active growth. They can be left undisturbed for three to five years. They can suffer from sclerotium stem rot (D) and occasionally the other diseases mentioned above, but mosaic (D) is the most common problem.

The lesser bulb fly (P) and the tulip bulb aphid (*Dysaphis tulipae*) feed on both bulbs and rhizomes in storage.

Joseph's coat   ANNUAL
Amaranthus spp.

These plants are not a good choice for cold climates. They need a sunny position with good drainage and protection from strong winds. They will tolerate dry conditions. Use a mulch to reduce soil temperature.

Beet webworm (P) and cluster caterpillars (P) may chew the leaves.

Kaffir lily   PERENNIAL
Clivea miniata

This plant requires a well-drained soil with plenty of organic matter. It needs a position shaded from summer sun and will perform well in full shade. Mulch the soil and water well in spring and summer. Regular small applications of fertiliser will improve flower production.

It has very few problems but occasionally is attacked by the yellow and black striped, lily caterpillar (P) which can cause considerable damage.

Leaves with reddish-brown tips or brown spots may be suffering from leaf scorch (D). Irregular yellowish patterns on the leaves may indicate a viral disease.

Kangaroo paw   PERENNIAL
Anigozanthos spp.

In general, these plants need a well-drained, acid, sandy soil for best growth. The common red and green paw (*A. manglesii*) and the green paw (*A. viridis*), however, can be grown in heavier soils.

Root-rotting fungi will cause problems unless the drainage is good. Rhizomes may die if soil temperatures become very high, so in hot areas the plants should be watered or shaded in summer.

Kangaroo paws grown in areas with high humidity or high rainfall are likely to suffer badly from a disease called 'inkspot' or ink disease (D). Overhead watering will also encourage the disease, which is particularly bad on the common red and green paw. There is also a rust (D) that attacks these plants.

Aphids (P), snails and slugs (P), budworms (P) and leafminers (P) are among the pests that can be troublesome.

Lily
BULBOUS

Lilium spp.

These plants continue growth of the root system even when the tops have died down. If they are lifted, they should be replanted as soon as possible or stored in slightly damp peat or other similar material so that they do not dry out.

Good drainage is essential, and overwatering should be avoided. The many different types of lilies may not be equally susceptible to the pests and diseases mentioned below.

Yellowish-brown or reddish-brown spots on the leaves indicate grey mould (D). Bulb rots include bacterial soft rot (D) and fusarium bulb rot (D). Bulbs may also be damaged by the root lesion nematode (*Pratylenchus penetrans*).

Plant growth may be weakened and flower quality reduced by the presence of viruses such as cucumber mosaic virus, lily symptomless virus, spotted wilt (D) virus, and tulip breaking (D) virus.

Lobelia
ANNUAL

Lobelia erinus

For best performance these annuals need plenty of sun and shelter from strong winds; this is particularly important in cold climates. They prefer a light soil with plenty of organic matter. If cut back after flowering, a second crop of flowers will be produced.

Earth mites (P) can cause grey mottling of the leaves.

Lupin
ANNUAL & PERENNIAL

Lupinus spp.

Russell lupins and other short-lived perennial types prefer cool climates and will stand severe frosts. In temperate climates, annual varieties are to be preferred. Choose a warm sunny position and keep the soil moist.

Lupin seeds may be slow to germinate, and the seedlings do not transplant readily. A very fertile soil and a heavy fertiliser supply will encourage foliage growth at the expense of flowers.

Earth mites (P), such as blue oat mites, attack lupins, and broad bean wilt (D) may also be a problem.

Orchid
BULBOUS

Cymbidium spp.

The cultural requirements of orchids vary from type to type and area to area, but the following general remarks should enable a beginner to grow a range of common orchids successfully. The conditions described can be adapted for particular species as experience is gained.

Many of the orchids cultivated in gardens are epiphytes and can be grown attached to pieces of bark or wood, or to living trees.

If grown in garden beds or rockeries, or in pots and baskets, they usually need a very open, free-draining soil or potting mix. This can be purchased ready-prepared or mixed at home from equal parts of coarse sand and a material such as leaf litter, peat moss, charcoal, pine bark or rice hulls, or a combination of these materials.

Semi-shade is necessary for the culture of most orchids. This may be outside, perhaps under trees, or in a structure covered with wooden slats or shade-cloth. In warm temperate areas 30–50 per cent shade is necessary, but in hotter areas more shade may be required. Long exposure to sun may cause the leaves to scorch. Some cymbidiums can be successfully grown in full sun provided they are well watered in summer. After the

buds have formed, varieties with green flowers need more shade than varieties with flowers of other colours.

Protect the plants from strong prevailing winds, but note that orchids grow best with good air circulation. Pots in a shade house should be spaced at least one pot width apart, and special ventilation arrangements may be necessary.

The high humidity required for orchids can be achieved by hosing nearby paths, fences or similar areas once a day or more frequently during very hot, dry weather conditions.

The roots should be kept damp at all times but not kept wet. Baskets and pots crowded with pseudo-bulbs tend to dry out quickly.

In summer, daily watering may be necessary, whereas in winter weekly watering will probably be sufficient unless the plants are in a heated house. Alkaline water is not suitable. Avoid wetting buds or flowers. In summer, misting the undersides of the leaves with water may decrease problems with two-spotted mite (P).

Different types of orchids require different temperature conditions for best growth. Cymbidiums for example, grow best in warm or cool temperate areas with temperatures of 16–27°C. Fluctuating temperatures are undesirable. Frost will damage flowers, most of which are produced in winter and spring.

Flower initiation is influenced by temperature. For example, cymbidiums will not flower unless night temperatures drop below 13°C in late summer and autumn. If necessary, night temperatures can be reduced by watering plants during the evening.

Cymbidiums need a high-nitrogen fertiliser after flowering — that is, throughout spring and summer. Do not supply large quantities of nitrogen in autumn when flower initiation is taking place.

Cymbidiums and most other cultivated orchids grow from pseudo-bulbs, each of which produces thick, white fleshy roots, and one set of leaves. If the leaves are damaged or removed, the plant does not grow replacements.

In every growing season one or more new bulbs develop on the side of the first. The original pseudo-bulb will flower only after two or three new bulbs have been produced at its side.

The flower spike, which grows from the base of the pseudo-bulb below soil level, takes up to six months to develop.

Hereafter the leaves on this pseudo-bulb gradually deteriorate, although it will usually flower again. Once the leaves have died and fallen, this pseudo-bulb is referred to as a 'back-bulb'.

If back-bulbs are individually repotted, each will produce a shoot from the base. This takes from one to twelve months.' The base of this shoot is the part that eventually develops into a pseudo-bulb which later flowers. This process may take three to five years. Some cymbidiums flower only when the pot is crowded with bulbs.

Dividing is carried out about every three or four years when the pot is very crowded. Repot and divide immediately after flowering. If this is not done between mid-spring and late summer, plant growth will be retarded and flowers may not appear in the next flowering season.

The pseudo-bulbs sometimes rot. This may be black pseudo-bulb rot (D) and probably means that the drainage should be improved.

Hard scales (P) such as orchid scale (P) and oleander scale (P), and soft scales (P) such as hemispherical scale (P) and soft brown scale (P) can be found on orchids. Two-spotted mite (P) can cause considerable damage. The first sign of attack on cymbidiums is a slight silvering under the leaves. Try to control this pest before the buds appear, because flowers can also be damaged. Remove from the area old pieces of leaf and other plant parts, and weeds which are alternative hosts of this mite. Orchid beetle (P) attacks dendrobiums, particularly *Dendrobium speciosum* in preference to other orchids. The larvae tunnel in the pseudo-bulb, and adults and larvae may damage young foliage, buds and flowers.

Orchid flowers and buds can also be damaged by plague thrips (P), loopers (P), aphids (P), and snails and slugs (P).

Grey mould (D) may cause flower spotting if conditions are damp, and trans-lucent spots may result if buds or flowers are wet with rain or irrigation water. Ant (P) control may be necessary because these insects often remove pollen caps from the flowers; this causes withering and browning of the flower.

Mealybugs (P), slaters such as the common slater (P), and the very similar common pillbug may also cause trouble on occasions.

Elongated pale-green or yellow flecks on the leaves or dark-brown to black, roughly circular, concentric markings probably indicate one or more of the orchid virus problems, which will be discussed under cymbidium virus (D).

Other leaf spots may be caused by fungi and can be controlled by the application of a fungicide such as zineb or mancozeb.

Excessive use of fungicides on orchids may upset the symbiotic relationship they have with mycorrhizal fungi. These fungi help the orchid to take up nutrients from the potting mix. If the process is interfered with, the leaves may gradually go yellow and plant growth will be slow.

Pelargonium PERENNIAL
Pelargonium spp.

These plants can be grown successfully in a wide range of climates, but in areas where heavy frosts occur grow them in containers and move them to a frost-free place in winter or strike new cuttings each year.

Regal pelargoniums (*Pelargonium × domesticum*) need wind protection and perform best if they receive only morning sun or if the sun is filtered. Ivy pelargoniums (*Pelargonium peltatum*) require full sun for best flowering performance. Zonal pelargoniums (*Pelargonium × hortorum*) need at least half a day full sun.

Overcrowding of plants and poor air circulation will make leaf, stem and flower diseases such as grey mould (D), rust (D), black stem rot (D) and bacterial leaf spot (D) more likely. These diseases would also be encouraged by a poorly drained soil, overwatering or watering late in the day so that leaves remain wet for a long time.

Leaves may be chewed by caterpillars such as loopers (P) and painted apple moth (P). New shoots may be distorted by aphids (P), broad mite (P) and cyclamen mite (P). Whitefly (P) under the leaves, mealybugs (P) on the stems, and black scale (P) on stems or leaves are other pests. Two-spotted mite (P) also attacks the plants.

Stunting of the plant and yellowing of the leaves may indicate attack by root knot nematode (D).

Yellowing and curling leaves may be pelargonium leaf curl virus; and leaves mottled with light and dark green may indicate pelargonium mosaic virus. Plants with these virus diseases should be destroyed.

Green flowers may be a big bud (D) symptom, and a lump at the base of the stem, crown gall (D).

Petunia ANNUAL
Petunia × hybrida

Petunias can be grown in a wide range of areas and withstand hot dry conditions very well. Plant in a sunny position and protect from wind because the stems are weak. The seed may be very slow to germinate.

Provide a well-drained loam with plenty of organic matter if possible. Encourage bushy growth by pinching out the top of the plant. Prune back when the flowers are almost finished, as this will encourage more flower production.

Petunias may suffer from cyclamen mite (P) attack.

Portulaca ANNUAL

Portulaca grandiflora

Portulaca grows well in all but cold climates. It will thrive in any soil with good drainage and needs full sun and a dry position for best performance. Overwatering will encourage collar rots.

Beet webworm (P) can be a problem with this plant.

Snapdragon ANNUAL

Antirrhinum majus

Snapdragons require a well-drained, nearly neutral soil and a sheltered position in full sun for best performance.

Sowing time is not critical, but it is important to use seed from healthy plants and to sow them thinly to avoid overcrowding of seedlings. Downy mildew (D)

can be a serious problem in an overcrowded seed bed and causes the tips and edges of leaves to curl downwards. Overwet conditions may encourage seedling blight—a rotting of leaves and stems of young seedlings which is caused by a bacterium (*Pseudomonas syringae* pv. *antirrhini*). This disease has also been recorded on other members of the plant family Scrophulariaceae such as *Calceolaria* and *Penstemon*.

Snapdragons may be affected by a number of other diseases. Rust (D), the most common and serious, shows up as reddish-brown dusty spots under the leaves. Discoloured patches and death of young shoots may be attributable to shot hole blight (D) which may also cause pale yellowish spots on leaves and stems. Anthracnose may produce similar spots but occurs under different weather conditions. Cream or light-brown circular spots on leaves and grey spots on stems may be leaf and stem spot. These two diseases can both be controlled by following the programme suggested for shot hole blight (D).

Pests of snapdragons include cyclamen mite (P) and earth mites (P).

Stock ANNUAL

Matthiola incana

These are not suitable for the tropics. They prefer neutral to slightly acid soil with plenty of organic matter, and a sheltered position in full sun. Good drainage is essential if root rots are to be avoided. Soil should be kept moist for best plant growth, but avoid overwatering.

Do not plant them where stocks (or related plants such as cabbages) have been growing in the previous two years. (See the 'Vegetables' section for more information about crop rotation.)

The disease black rot (D) is carried on the seed and is likely to affect more and more plants in each successive crop if stock seed is saved by home-gardeners.

Other diseases are downy mildew (D), mosaic turnip (D), collar rot (D), and stem rot which is often referred to as sclerotinia rot (D).

Aphids (P) and earth mites (P), such as redlegged earth mites, attack stocks.

Tulip BULBOUS

Tulipa spp.

Tulips are native to areas with a long cold winter and a hot dry summer. The bulbs do not perform well for more than one season in warm-winter areas. Buy new ones each year and induce flowering by storing them in a refrigerator for five or six weeks before planting. Bulbs smaller than 30–40 mm in diameter will not flower.

They prefer a slightly more alkaline soil than most other bulbs.

Tulips are subject to a number of viral diseases including tulip breaking virus (D), which causes streaks or blotches on the petals and leaves.

Spots and dead areas in flowers and leaves may be fire (D), a fungal disease which also damages the bulbs. Basal rot (D) is another bulb problem.

The tulip bulb aphid (*Dysaphis tulipae*), the bulb mite (P), the lesser bulb fly (P) and the bulb nematode (D) may all damage the bulbs.

Violet PERENNIAL

Viola odorata

These are not suitable for hot moist areas. They should be sheltered from hot summer sun and drying winds, and planted in well-drained, slightly acid, medium to sandy loam with plenty of organic matter. The crowns should be set just above the soil surface.

Water well during spring and summer to discourage two-spotted mite (P) which causes fine yellow mottling on the leaves. The leaves may be damaged by leaf spot (D) and violet scab (D).

Zinnia ANNUAL

Zinnia elegans

Zinnias are best grown in a very warm sunny position in a rich soil with a good water supply. They will, however, tolerate drought. They should have protection from wind and must have protection from frost.

Flowers and leaves may be chewed by various caterpillars including the cluster caterpillar (P).

The plants frequently suffer from powdery mildew (D) and two-spotted mite (P) attack. Angular leaf spot (D) may also be a problem.

CACTI AND OTHER SUCCULENTS

These plants have evolved in situations where water is not available on a regular basis, and the fleshy leaves and stems are designed to store water for use during dry periods. Some are able to reach water far down in the soil, while others have a wide-spreading but shallow root system which can quickly absorb moisture from dew or occasional showers.

Some are epiphytes, and others naturally grow in rock crevices where water is in short supply.

Most succulents, therefore, are able to withstand periods of drought, and almost all require very good drainage. In heavy, poorly drained soils they will rot.

They can be grown successfully in a mixture made up of equal parts of coarse sand, loam and organic matter. The pH should be moderately acid.

Keep the soil barely moist in warm weather but reduce watering as the weather gets cooler.

Most of these plants require a very bright, warm position and will not grow successfully indoors unless placed on a sunny window-sill.

Others, such as the crab cactus (*Zygocactus* sp.), are epiphytes and need a warm position but more humidity and semi-shade.

Some succulents come from mountainous or other regions with severe winters and are able to withstand frost and even snow.

Pests and diseases
The sea fig (*Carpobrotus* sp.) is often attacked by a scale (*Pulvinariella mesembryanthemi*) which does not feed on other succulents. There are some scales, however, which attack a wide range of succulents; and aphids (P), mealybugs (P), thrips (P) and two-spotted mite (P) are also common problems.

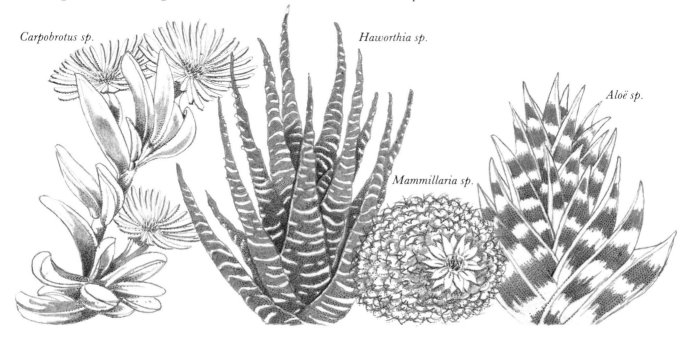

Carpobrotus sp.

Haworthia sp.

Aloë sp.

Mammillaria sp.

CLIMBING PLANTS

Climbing plants seem to suffer from very few pests and diseases. Their usually vigorous growth can readily compensate for some leaf and stem loss, and their informal shape often means that removal of affected sections is not noticeable.

Pests and diseases
They can be attacked by a wide range of leaf-chewing insects such as green looper (P), wingless grasshopper (P), redshouldered leaf beetle (P), painted apple moth (P) and grapevine moth (P).

Sap-sucking insects such as aphids (P), Rutherglen bug (P), whitefly (P), passionvine hopper (P) and green vegetable bug (P) could all cause trouble on occasions.

Scale insects such as soft brown scale (P), pink wax scale (P), black scale (P) and California red scale (P) can also infest climbing plants. The latter may cause yellow spotting on the leaves.

Boston ivy
Parthenocissus tricuspidata

Boston ivy is relatively free of pest and disease problems, but the leaves are often chewed by the caterpillars of the grapevine moth (P), the painted vine moth (P) and a variety of hawk moths (P). Only undamaged leaves can produce good autumn colour.

The virginia creeper (*P. quinquefolia*) suffers from similar problems.

Grape
Vitis spp.

The ornamental grape is best grown in cool dry climates in full sun and in moderately fertile soil. In humid climates, leaf diseases are more common and only leaves undamaged by pests and diseases can produce good autumn colour.

The leaves may be chewed by the caterpillars of the grapevine moth (P), the painted vine moth (P) and various hawk moths (P). Leaf spots may be caused by downy mildew (D) and black spot (D).

Other pests and diseases listed for fruiting grapes (see the section 'Fruits') can also cause problems on ornamental grapevines.

Ivy
Hedera spp.

Scale insects such as soft brown scale (P), pink wax scale (P) and California red scale (P) are sometimes a problem.

Bacterial leaf spot, caused by *Xanthomonas campestris* pv. *hederae*, starts as small, round, light-green spots which

gradually enlarge and become more angular. The edges change to reddish-brown and the centre darkens to brown or black. Leaves yellow and fall. There is also a fungal leaf spot (D) of ivy.

Ivy grown as a ground cover is frequently a home for snails and slugs (P).

Jasmine
Jasminum polyanthum

This climber does well under a wide range of conditions and commonly becomes a weed because of its ability to produce suckers.

Aphids (P) and the caterpillars of various hawk moths (P) such as the Australian privet hawk moth (P) may be troublesome occasionally.

Wisteria
Wisteria spp.

This can be grown successfully in all but tropical and hot dry areas. Place in a sunny position in moderately fertile soil and protect from wind if possible. It will tolerate heavy pruning and is very long lived. The stems may be attacked by longicorn beetle (P) larvae.

FERNS

Most ferns need a moist atmosphere and a moist, but well-drained, slightly acid soil or potting mix with a high proportion of organic matter. The roots should be kept cool. Outdoors, semi-shade is suitable for the growth of a wide range of fern species but some do like more light than others.

Some ferns thrive only in situations that receive more sun. The common maidenhair (*Adiantum aethiopicum*) is one example. Very few ferns tolerate deep shade. If light intensity is too low, the fronds will be pale and grow long and spindly.

Indoors, ferns should not be placed where they will receive sunlight through windows. This will scorch the leaves. However, some, such as common maidenhair, require very bright light for successful growth. Avoid windy or draughty areas, and pay attention to humidity.

If the atmosphere is too dry the fronds will gradually dry out and brown. This often happens with ferns grown indoors, where the air is dry because of airconditioning or central heating. A couple of hints on the adjustment of humidity indoors are mentioned in the section on 'Houseplants'. Outdoors, the humidity can be increased by hosing paths, fences, or the ground.

Most ferns need a good water supply. In summer, daily watering may be necessary, but be careful not to overwater in winter when growth has stopped. The soil or potting mix should be kept moist but not wet. The water must drain freely from potted ferns.

Temperatures of 15–25°C are suitable for a wide variety of fern species although some will grow well at higher or lower temperatures. Blackening and collapse of young fronds may indicate frost damage.

Ferns respond to regular applications of liquid fertiliser in the growing season. Some growers recommend that such fertilisers be used at half the rate suggested on the label.

New fern plants grow from spores which are produced under the fronds. Areas of spore production are different shapes on different ferns. They may completely cover an area near the tip of the frond as in elkhorns; or they may be smaller areas of regular shape, arranged in patterns or rows. In some species, the spore-bearing or fertile fronds are a different shape from the other fronds and should not be mistaken for deformed or damaged fronds.

Young fronds are sometimes pink or extremely pale in colour, but this is perfectly normal. When the fronds first appear they are curled up very tightly and are often referred to as 'fiddle heads' or 'crosiers'. At this stage it is important to make sure that they are not attacked by aphids (P), which could cause deformed fronds.

Fern fronds are often damaged by pests such as mealybugs.

Pests and diseases
Ferns can be damaged by aphids such as the bracken aphid (*Shinjia orientalis*) and the maidenhair fern aphid (*Idiopterus nephrelepidis*). The latter is dark green or almost black in colour with white legs. It feeds on a wide range of different fern species, causing the fronds to curl up and turn black. It has also been known to feed on cyclamen and on the Cape primrose (*Streptocarpus* sp.).

Ferns may be attacked by a variety of scale insects including hemispherical scale (P). Young scales may be found in the groove of stems and are very difficult to see.

More mature scales may look like lumps on stems or under leaves, and if they are squashed a sticky or watery substance exudes.

It is important to search the rhizomes, particularly if these are very hairy ones, for insects such as aphids or scales which can easily be hidden among the hairs and cause considerable damage. A group of pests overlooked on a rhizome can later reinfest the fronds.

Mites (P) such as two-spotted mite (P) can seriously damage ferns if these pests remain unnoticed for a period of time.

Mealybugs (P) also often go unnoticed until a large population has built up. These are very difficult to bring under control and are the most common and troublesome pests encountered indoors.

Outdoors, pests such as whitefly (P), thrips (P), common slaters (P), millipedes (P), snails and slugs (P), earwigs (P) and black field crickets (P) are likely as well.

Brown or black stripes or angular marks on the fronds may be caused by the leaf nematode (D) which, once introduced into an area, thrives in the damp conditions usually provided for ferns.

Loopers (P) and other caterpillars such as those of painted apple moth (P) and light brown apple moth (P) chew fern fronds and crosiers.

If fronds wilt and die back, it is possible that they have been attacked by weevils. The larvae of the large fern weevil (*Syagrius fulvitarsus*) tunnel in the stems of the ferns including tree ferns and braken. The maidenhair fern weevil (*Neosyagrius cordipennis*) does similar damage.

Many ferns, including *Pteris* spp. and *Hyolepis* spp., are damaged by the feeding of the bug *Felisacus glabratus*, which is green, narrow and about 4 mm long. Both antennae and legs are long and thin. The antennae and eyes are dark brown, and the legs and head are shining, pale yellowish-brown. The head may have small red markings. The fronds are damaged by the injection of saliva and the sucking of sap.

Planthoppers such as passionvine hopper (P) also suck sap and may produce honeydew.

Staghorn

Platycerium superbum

In nature this plant generally occurs in rainforests growing on rocks or old logs or high in trees. In a garden situation, however, it is generally not a good idea to attach staghorns or elkhorns directly to the trunks of trees. Plant in a basket or use a backing board. Suspend in a shady situation and keep the plant moist in hot weather. They will tolerate quite cold conditions.

Do not remove any fallen bark or leaves from the centre of the plant, and even add to the nutrient supply there with the occasional addition of a handful of decayed leaves or well rotted animal manure.

Small dark pits in the fronds indicate the presence of the staghorn fern beetle (P). If the areas of velvety spores under the fronds are roughened and the fronds are browning and shrivelling on the tips, this may be caused by the feeding of the elkhorn spore caterpillar which is the larva of a moth.

Elkhorns are attacked by the same pests as staghorns.

Tree fern

The soft tree fern (*Dicksonia antarctica*) is the most commonly sold species. It is usually sawn off at ground level and sold without a root system.

Choose a shady site protected from hot winds, and plant so that about a third of the stump is below ground level. Water from the top, so that the whole hairy stump is kept moist. After the roots have begun to develop, fronds appear at the top. The first fronds may be damaged by winds but those produced later usually remain green and healthy.

The rough tree fern (*Cyathea australis*) is sold with roots and soil attached. Keep the root system moist during the establishment period.

Hard scales (P) and soft scales (P) may be found on tree fern fronds, and possums may eat young crosiers.

FRUITS

The term 'fruit' covers a wide range of plant types, from climbers such as passionfruit to trees such as the apple and to quite different plants such as bananas or pineapples. Others, such as feijoa, which are often considered to be ornamentals, can also be used to produce a fruit crop.

Fruit-growing in a home garden can be an extremely rewarding exercise, but most of these plants need care on a regular basis if their crops are to be worthwhile. Fruit trees should not be planted unless time to care for them properly is available.

Choose the type of fruit and the variety carefully, taking account of whether or not cross-pollination is necessary, and how much continuous cold weather occurs in winter in your area. Satisfactory flowering and fruiting will not occur unless chilling requirements are met.

Also consider the amount of space available and soil type, drainage and aspect.

Climate and position

Cool autumn weather causes deciduous fruit plants to go into a resting state which continues until a certain amount of cold weather has occurred. The length of the cold period required is different for each type of fruit. For example, Chinese gooseberries need 300–500 hours of temperatures below 7°C before they will respond to warm weather and begin to grow again, and European plums need 800–1200 hours below 7°C. Unless these 'chilling requirements' are met, flower and leaf formation will be erratic and the fruit crop will be small or non-existent.

Some types of fruit have varieties that require fewer hours of chilling than others. These low-chill varieties should be chosen for coastal areas with mild winters.

No fruit tree can be expected to produce well in complete shade. Less than half the day in sun is not adequate. Full sun is to be preferred.

Warm sunny situations are essential for Mediterranean fruit such as figs, olives, grapes, apricots, peaches and almonds, whereas fruits that have evolved in cooler climates such as apples, pears, plums and quinces can be grown in situations that are a little colder and shadier.

Low temperatures in winter do not damage deciduous fruit plants as long as the weather has become gradually colder through autumn to winter. However, sudden and unseasonable cold snaps may cause problems.

Once the chilling requirements have been met and the tree is responding to the increased warmth of spring, frosts may cause serious damage to buds, flowers, young fruit or new shoots. Damaged flowers will not develop fruit, and the skin of young fruit may crack.

The later a plant flowers in spring the less likely it is to be damaged by frost. Flowering time varies from fruit to fruit and variety to variety. Stonefruit, for example, is more susceptible to frost damage than apples and pears because stonefruit flowers earlier. (See the reference to frost on page 20.)

The summer temperatures of an area should also be considered. In some inland areas, winter temperatures are low enough for cool-climate fruits but the extremely hot summers cause leaves and fruit to be scorched. Such

Feijoa, a very attractive fruiting plant

fruit is not fit for consumption. Trunks and branches may also be sunburnt.

Other fruits such as olives, figs and almonds require hot summers to produce good crops.

Wind may be very damaging to young growth and to fruit. A north-facing slope will be protected from southerly winds. A windbreak of some sort should be provided in very windswept areas. Do not plant shelter trees on which pests of the fruit crop can feed.

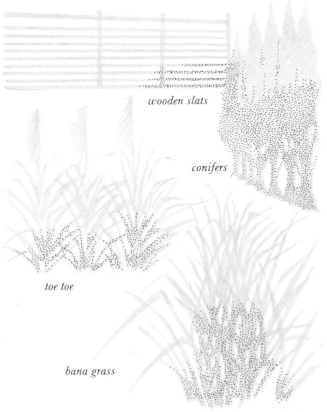

wooden slats

conifers

toe toe

bana grass

Windbreaks can be formed from living plants or constructed of materials such as shade cloth.

Rain when the fruit is mature or nearly mature can be a serious problem for fruit such as cherries, grapes and figs. They are prone to fungal diseases at this time and may split.

Pollination

Pollination, which is necessary for the production of most fruit, involves the transfer of pollen from the anthers (the male parts of the flower) to the stigma (the female part of the flower).

If a fruit variety produces a reasonable crop when pollinated with its own pollen, it is referred to as 'self-fruitful'.

Many fruits, however, must be pollinated by pollen from a different variety of the same species if a good crop of fruit is to be produced. For example, more 'Granny Smith' apples will be produced if 'Jonathan' pollen has been transferred to the 'Granny Smith' flowers than if the 'Granny Smith' pollen alone was involved.

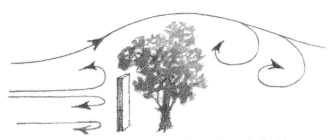

Solid walls and dense trees cause winds to eddy on both sides.

More open windbreaks slow the wind down and provide protection without creating unpleasant turbulence.

Most pollen is moved from flower to flower on the bodies of honeybees as they search for nectar. Low bee activity may account for poor fruit set.

Bees usually stay in the hive if temperatures drop below 13°C or if it is raining. In showery weather they fly only between showers and only for short distances. They are most active at 16–21°C. Bees do not like to fly in a strong wind.

These problems may be overcome in an orchard situation by providing at least three strong colonies of bees per hectare. It is said that bees will be attracted if the tree is sprayed with a sugar solution (200 g of sugar in 1 L of water).

The two varieties must flower at the same time, their pollen must be compatible and they must be planted fairly close together.

If there is room in a garden for only one tree, then order a 'multi-graft' from your nurseryman. These are also referred to as 2-in-1 or 3-in-1 fruit trees and have one or two pollinating varieties grafted on to the main tree. That is, the tree will develop with branches of other varieties. (It is also possible to plant two varieties in the one hole and prune them as though they were the two halves of a single tree.)

The 'pollinating' branches should not be allowed to bear too much fruit. This will help to ensure that they carry many flowers in the following season. They should be permanently labelled so their whereabouts is not forgotten at pruning time. If they are damaged or pruned off by mistake, fruit will not be formed.

Initial preparation and planting

Most fruit-bearing plants take years to come into full production but continue to bear good fruit crops for many years. It is therefore not sensible to skimp on preparation of the soil, or to buy an inferior plant.

Fruit trees are almost always grafted—that is, the roots of one variety have the shoots of another grafted on to them. In these 'combination' trees the roots and lower trunk are referred to as the 'stock', 'rootstock' or 'understock', and the upper trunk and foliage as the 'scion' (pron. sigh-on). The ultimate tree is greatly influenced by the type of rootstock used, and in each situation there may be a *best* rootstock.

Rootstocks may be resistant to particular pests and diseases common in the area; and they may cause reduction in tree size. This factor may be an advantage in a home garden or orchard. In addition, some rootstocks perform better than others in damp or alkaline conditions or in soil with high salt levels. (See citrus fruit.)

Seedling trees are cheaper to buy than grafted trees but may never perform well even if an effort is made to maintain them properly. They may take longer to produce a first good crop, and it may be irregular in size each year. This can be a great disappointment. It is far better to buy a proven variety in the first place. It is good fun to germinate the seeds of fruit such as apples, citrus and avocados, but don't think of these plants as suitable for fruit-bearing. Use them instead as background greenery for patio or verandah, and throw the plants away if they begin to look unhealthy.

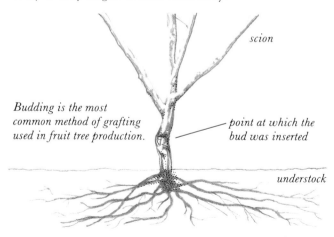

Budding is the most common method of grafting used in fruit tree production.

scion

point at which the bud was inserted

understock

If a number of trees are to be planted, preparation of the soil in the total 'orchard' area is preferable to preparation of individual spots. Install subsurface drainage if natural drainage is inadequate.

The soil should be a deep loam but other soil types can be managed successfully. Increase the organic matter content of the soil by adding compost or by growing a crop such as beans in the area and digging in the plant remains. The topsoil should be at least 600 mm deep.

If a garden or orchard is to be planted in an area of virgin bush, make sure that all stumps and tree roots are cleared from the area. The disease armillaria root rot (D) can be spread to the new trees from such sources.

In the case of fruit trees it is particularly important to keep the graft union well above ground level. This junction is about 150 mm above the soil mark on the stem, and the stem curves slightly outward at this point. It is wise to plant the tree to the same depth as it was planted in the nursery.

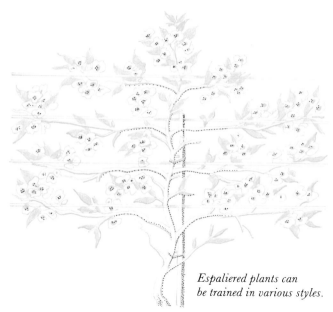

Espaliered plants can be trained in various styles.

Further information on planting is given in the section on 'Trees and shrubs'.

Plants should be spaced so that they receive maximum sunlight. If space is limited it may be preferable to train trees into flat shapes either free-standing or against a wall (espalier). Dwarf varieties may also be available. If the trees are to be free-standing and 'spherical' in shape, then they should not be planted closer than 3–4 m apart.

Training and pruning

The plant must be well cared for from the beginning. The early years are important in the development of a strong, healthy framework for later fruit bearing. The tree must be healthy enough to form the fruit and strong enough to bear its weight.

If the tree is to be trained with a central leader—that is, one main trunk—make sure that it does not develop a 'rival' trunk as well. If it is to be trained in a 'vase' shape, make sure that the 'V' angle between the branches is wide enough to accommodate growth. If the angle is too acute, the branches will soon rub together as they increase in girth. This will always be a weak area and the tree will be likely to split at this point. Note that it is now considered unwise to prune too heavily a non-bearing tree.

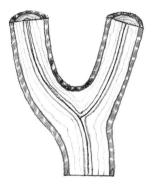

Angle between branches allows room for growth.

Branches will soon grow together, creating a weak point.

Enough fruit for a family can probably be produced for a few years without knowledge of pruning techniques, but these trees will not continue to bear satisfactory fruit crops unless pruning procedures are correct. Consult your local Department of Agriculture about the methods suitable for the type of tree you own. There are books about pruning included in the bibliography.

It is important to remove and destroy dead or diseased wood and diseased or fallen fruit,

Severely cut back citrus trees will bear good crops again in two or three years.

Rejuvenation of old trees: It is possible to put new life into an old neglected tree such as an apple by cutting it back and grafting new shoots on to it. The tree will bear good crops again in a relatively short time because the root system is already well established. Citrus trees are rejuvenated by cutting them back and allowing new shoots to grow.

Care of young trees

Weed control is particularly important in the early stages of growth. Mulch around the tree or remove the weeds by hoeing. Take care not to damage the shallow root system. Mulch will also help water conservation. The roots should not be allowed to dry out in the establishment period.

Young trees have no canopy of foliage to shade the trunk, which may be seriously damaged if sunburnt. In hot areas the trunk can be protected by painting it with flat white plastic housepaint or loosely wrapping aluminium foil or Sisalation ® around it to reflect the sun.

Do not allow the tree to bear any fruit in the first two years or until it is about 2 m high.

Maintenance of established trees

The type and amount of fertiliser required depends on the type of fruit and the district; seek information from your local Department of Agriculture. Applications of large quantities of fertiliser will encourage vigorous growth, and a large tree will result. This may be undesirable in a home garden.

Most of a fruit tree's root system is found in the top 300–500 mm of soil and within the spread of the canopy. Some roots spread further than this. When watering, at least one-quarter of this zone should be thoroughly wetted. Watering to far greater depths is wasteful. Soaking with a slowly-running hose for two or three hour-long periods once a week would be suitable in many circumstances. Watering should be more frequent in hot weather or if soils are sandy.

It is not always possible to provide enough water for optimum plant growth. If water is in short supply, concentrate on timing the applications correctly: water just after flowering to help ensure a good fruit set; in early summer while next year's buds are forming; and in the three to four weeks before harvest to increase fruit size. In general pomefruits (apples, pears) will tolerate periods without water better than stonefruits will.

Removal of weeds, which use water, and application of a mulch will increase the amount of water available to the tree. (See also the notes on watering on page 20.)

Optimum weather and cultural conditions often mean that a fruit tree will set large quantities of fruit. Some may drop naturally but it may be necessary to remove some more. Thinning will increase the size of remaining fruit and will reduce the chance of limbs breaking under the weight of the fruit. A tree that is allowed to bear a very heavy crop one year is likely to bear a very light one the next year.

Thinning is done by hand in a home garden and should be carried out when the fruit is about marble-size — that is, within six weeks of full bloom. If the procedure is left too late, fruit on the tree will get bigger but next year's crop will not be influenced.

The flowers and leaves for next season are beginning to develop when this year's fruits are still very small. If there is a large number of fruit this year, the formation

Suckers growing from the understock should be removed promptly. They are often vigorous, but do not produce satisfactory fruit.

of flower buds for next year will be suppressed by substances formed in the seeds of the developing fruit.

It is also a good idea to thin (or remove all) the fruit if the tree has suffered root damage. The sugars that would have gone into the fruit can then be used by the tree for new root growth. The long-term good health of the roots is of more importance than one fruit crop.

Causes of a small fruit crop

Some fruit trees have a natural tendency to bear a light crop one year and a heavy crop the next. This is termed 'alternate cropping'. Some other trees occasionally set a very heavy crop, but if the tree is allowed to bear all this fruit the crop in the following year will usually be much smaller.

Attack from mites (P) such as two-spotted mite (P) is also likely to reduce fruit size and number in the following season.

Diseases including brown spot (D) of stonefruit and citrus scab (D) can reduce the crop. And insects can also destroy flowers or cause fruit fall; these insects include plague thrips (P) and spined citrus bug (P).

The number of fruit produced may be small if pollination was inadequate; if the necessary chilling did not occur; if frost damaged the flowers; if the supply of nitrogen to the tree was too low; if the tree suffered water stress while fruit was forming; or if the tree was incorrectly pruned.

Pests and diseases

Pests and diseases must be controlled to some extent if a crop, the most important reason for having the tree in the first place, is to be harvested. Some pests are considered to be so serious that their control is required by law. For example, in areas where Queensland and Mediterranean fruit flies occur, well-organised spray programmes are necessary if a crop is to be harvested, and if legal obligations are to be met.

You should be familiar with the legal requirements of your area. Sometimes dates are specified for the completion of tasks — for example, all quinces must be removed from trees by 30 April each year in all areas of New South Wales.

The movement from place to place of some fruit and fruit-producing plants is restricted by quarantine laws which aim to reduce the spread of pests and diseases.

The constant schedule of sprays necessary to produce perfect fruit may prove too time-consuming for a home-gardener, and some level of fruit damage may be tolerated. Fruit intended for storage, however, should be produced on well cared for trees and should have an undamaged skin.

Good garden hygiene and cultural methods can markedly lessen pest and disease problems. These methods are very important to a home-gardener and are discussed in connection with each fruit plant or each pest and disease if applicable.

Wilting and dieback of branches may indicate some root problem such as armillaria root rot (D), phytophthora root rot (D), nematodes such as root knot nematodes (D), elephant weevil (P) or fruit-tree root

Brackets such as these protruding from branches indicate a long-standing fungal infection.

weevil (P). Dead branches may also be caused by various woodrots (D).

In some areas twigs damaged by egg-laying of cicadas may snap under the weight of ripening fruit.

Never buy a tree with an irregular lump on one side of the stem near ground level. This is likely to be crown gall (D).

A great variety of hard scales (P) and soft scales (P) can be found on fruit-bearing crops.

Leaves may be chewed by many different insects such as light brown apple moth (P), Fuller's rose weevil (P), wingless grasshoppers (P), apple weevil and locusts.

Aphids (P) can cause leaves to curl and wilt. Leaves with a 'silver' appearance are probably affected by the disease silver leaf (D). Yellowing of leaves may be due to mites (P) such as two-spotted mite (P), European red mite (P) and bryobia mite (P).

Rabbits, hares, wallabies and kangaroos all chew young bark and may ringbark young trees. Birds frequently destroy ripening fruit.

Lichens (D) may be found growing on trunks of old trees but are usually considered to be harmless.

The presence of oozing gum on the trunk and branches may be the result of attack from fruit-tree borer (P) or bacterial canker (D).

Premature browning and falling of petals may be caused by plague thrips (P), while other thrips may damage foliage. See also western flower thrips page 51.

Fruit is commonly attacked by various fruit flies (P) and by bugs such as coon bugs, Rutherglen bugs (P) and fruitspotting bugs (P). Other fruit attacking insects are the citrus katydid (P), the inland katydid (P), driedfruit beetles (P) and fruitpiercing moths (P).

The bronze beetle (*Eucolapsis brunneas*), which chews holes in leaves and young fruit, can be controlled with carbaryl. Long grass should be removed from tree butts.

There are many fungal and other diseases which attack fruit but these tend to be specific to particular types.

Almond
Prunus amygdalus

These trees have a beautiful shape and beautiful fragrant blossom, so are often grown purely as ornamentals.

Cross-pollination is necessary for production of nuts, and these can only mature satisfactorily (without constant disease problems) in areas of long, hot dry summers. Areas where cool, showery weather prevails during flowering (July/August) are unsuitable because pollination is interfered with and nut set is therefore reduced. Frosts damage the flowers and, because almonds bloom early, this may be a serious problem.

Almonds will grow well in a wide range of soil types but need a deep soil with very good drainage. Suspect poor drainage if the tree dies in the spring or early summer after coming into leaf, and the dead foliage remains on the tree. Keep the soil moist during the time the nuts are maturing.

Bryobia mite (P), shot hole (D), rust (D) and brown rot (D) are the most common problems. Birds may also cause trouble. Carob moth larvae damage the nuts in some areas.

(See also the entry on stonefruit.)

Apple
Malus domestica

The most suitable areas for apple growth have mild summers and cool to cold winters. There are, however, some varieties that can be grown successfully in hot inland areas. Winter cold is the most important factor, because unless chilling requirements are met, growth will be slow and fruit production erratic. If you wish to try apples where the winter is warmer, choose a variety whose chilling requirements are as low as possible.

The soil should be deep, well-drained and slightly acidic. Problems with nutrient deficiencies are likely to occur in alkaline soils. Boron deficiency (D), or corking, which shows up more in dry seasons, causes brown corky areas inside the fruit and sometimes cracks in the surface. This should not be confused with bitter pit (D), a physiological disorder associated with calcium supply and causing small discoloured spots under the skin particularly near the calyx end.

Warm sunny weather and plenty of bee activity at flowering time usually ensure enough fruit set for a home garden. Check that this is possible for the variety you intend to buy. For optimum production, however, apples require cross-pollination. It is therefore necessary either to plant two different varieties that flower at the same time, or to plant a tree with more than one variety grafted on to the rootstock.

Some drop of almost mature fruit is not uncommon with early varieties such as 'Jonathan' and 'Gravenstein'. Commercial growers spray with a growth regulator such as NAA to prevent this fruit loss. In home-garden situations the crop that remains will probably be sufficient for family needs.

Apples have many pest and disease problems. Look on the stems for woolly aphid (P); scales such as San José scale (P); and the red eggs of bryobia mite (P) and European red mite (P). The flowers may be attacked by plague thrips (P); and the fruit by apple dimpling bug (P), codling moth (P) larvae, light brown apple moth (P) larvae, oriental fruit moth (P) larvae, and fruit fly (P) larvae. The fruit also shows symptoms of the diseases: apple scab (D) also known as black spot; bitter rot (D); sooty blotch (D); and fly speck. The last two are commonly found together on the same fruit.

Powdery mildew (D) can be a serious apple disease and affects 'Jonathan', 'Rome Beauty' and 'Gravenstein' more seriously than other varieties.

Virus-tested trees should be bought if they are available. This should mean freedom from the diseases 'twist' in 'Gravenstein' and 'green crinkle' in 'Granny Smith'. There are also many other virus diseases of apples.

Other pests and diseases include apple leafhopper (P), two-spotted mite (P), painted apple moth (P), fruit-tree root weevil (P), elephant weevil (P), apple weevil, apple mosaic (D), silver leaf (D) and fireblight. Fireblight is a bacterial disease not yet found in Australia. Small fruits die soon after petal-fall, and affected leaves go brown and remain attached to the tree.

Apricot
Prunus armeniaca

Apricot trees grow best in areas of hot dry summers and cold winters, although by careful choice of variety it is possible to produce crops in a range of different climates. They will not tolerate saline or waterlogged soils. Most varieties blossom early, so site to avoid frosts. The flowers may also be destroyed by blossom-blight (brown rot (D)).

Most apricots are self-fertile so usually only one tree is necessary.

Some varieties tend to crop heavily in one year and lightly in the next. This alternate cropping can be reduced by thinning a very heavy crop.

Do not plant apricot trees in land that has previously grown strawberries, potatoes or tomatoes because of the danger of 'black heart of apricots'. This disease causes wilting and death and is discussed more fully in the stonefruit entry.

Apricots are highly susceptible to a disease called bacterial canker (D). Shot hole (D) and freckle (D) are also common. Leaf curl (D) and rust (D) occur occasionally.

Excessive gumming, wilting, and dieback or brittleness of branches can indicate 'dead arm disease'. Contact your local Department of Agriculture for a positive diagnosis. The fungus responsible (*Eutypa* sp.) gains entry to the tree through pruning cuts. Prune off and burn dead, infected wood from which

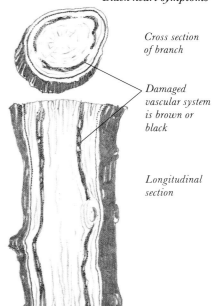

Black heart symptoms

Cross section of branch

Damaged vascular system is brown or black

Longitudinal section

spores can be spread . Carry out annual pruning when a growth has started, and avoid making large wounds. Any large wounds that are made should be coated immediately with a water-based paint. (For further information, see the entry on stonefruit page 83.)

Avocado

Persea americana

The avocado is basically a subtropical plant but will also grow in temperate and Mediterranean climates. Unless a frost-free site is available, choose a frost-tolerant variety such as 'Bacon' or 'Fuerte'. Provide a warm sunny position with shelter from strong winds which may damage fruit and slow down the growth of the tree.

Allow sufficient space for the mature tree. Size and shape depend upon variety, but some avocados may grow to 12 m high and spread about the same distance. 'Wurtz' and 'Rincon' are dwarf varieties which grow only 3–4 m high by 3–4 m wide.

Choice of variety is also influenced by pollination requirements. These are different in different areas, so check for suitable variety combinations with your local Department of Agriculture. 'Fuerte' is a self-pollinating variety.

If phytophthora root rot (D) is to be avoided the planting site must have good subsurface drainage. Also provide good surface drainage by planting the tree on a mound from which water will run quickly. Mulch with well-rotted material, but do not allow it to build up in contact with the trunk.

The soil should contain a high proportion of organic matter, be moderately acid to neutral (pH 7 or less) and be free of salt. Avoid using irrigation water high in salts.

Regular fertilising is necessary, but application during flowering may cause flower fall and reduced fruit set. Avoid fertiliser in the chloride form.

Zinc deficiency, likely on alkaline soils, shows up as yellowing between the veins and small leaves crowded together on terminal growth. In this case spray with a solution of 23% zinc sulphate (10 g in 10 L of water) in spring.

Although the avocado is evergreen, heavy leaf fall is common when the tree is flowering.

Fruit, which should be clipped (not torn) from the tree, will not ripen until harvested and may be 'stored' on the tree for some time. Note that although they are dearer to buy than seedlings, grafted avocado trees are quicker to produce the first fruit, and the size of the crop and the

quality of the fruit are more uniform from year to year.

Watch for the damage of fruit flies (P), banana spotting bugs (P) and fruitspotting bugs (P) on fruit. Diseases such as anthracnose (D), stem-end rot (D) and sun-blotch also affect the fruit. Sun-blotch symptoms include pink, white or yellow leaf variegations, yellow streaks on bark, and yellow or red streaks on fruit; the latter usually start near the stem end. The fruit may also be small and deformed. This virus-like disease can be avoided if the tree is bought from a nurseryman who has used virus-free propagating material. It has no cure. Other problems are redshouldered leaf beetle (P), latania scale (P), white wax scale (P) and orange fruitborer.

Banana

Musa x paradisiaca

These require a tropical or subtropical climate for best growth but can be grown in a cool temperate climate if given a very warm position. The site should be frost-free and sheltered from winds, particularly cold ones. Cold weather may cause the leaves to yellow, and weaken the plants. 'Williams' tolerates cold better than some other varieties. Wind tears the leaves, thus reducing food-manufacturing capacity and ornamental value. Strong winds may blow the plant over because the root system is in the top 500 mm of soil and cannot anchor the plant firmly. Even in sheltered situations it may be necessary to provide stout stakes as the fruit develops.

The soil should be deep and well-drained, with plenty of organic matter.

The planting material is likely to rot unless watered sparingly or not at all in

the first few weeks. Once established, bananas need a good regular water supply and heavy fertiliser applications for best performances.

Weed control is important, and in some areas the law demands that no weeds be allowed to grow within 2 m of a banana plant. Use old plant parts for mulch (if they are healthy), but keep them away from the base of the plant. These measures help control the banana weevil borer (P).

The time between planting and harvesting a bunch of fruit is about 15 months in warm conditions and about 20 months in cooler conditions.

The young bunches can be covered to protect them from birds, wind and sun. White or green plastic bags (such as those used in kitchen waste bins) are suitable. Tie them at the top and leave the bottom open. Harvest when the ribs on the fruit are no longer prominent.

Each stem will produce only one bunch and it should be cut off at ground level after harvesting.

Quarantine regulations restrict the movement of banana plants or parts of banana plants in some areas of Australia. It is important to check with your local Department of Agriculture on this point.

Growth of choko and passionfruit vines amongst bananas will increase problems with banana-silvering thrips (*Hercinothrips bicinctus*) which feed on these two plants as well as on weeds. The adults are about

1.5 mm long. They are black and appear to have a pale yellow line down the centre of the body. Nymphs are yellowish. These thrips may feed anywhere on the fruit and attack fruit of all sizes. They cause silvery patches which turn brown later. Shiny black dots of excrement will be present where feeding has occurred. Cracks may appear along the skin if feeding starts when the fruit is very small. Look for these thrips in spring and early summer, and control with the programme suggested for banana rust thrips (P) which also attack the fruit.

Fruit can also be damaged by fruit-spotting bugs (P), banana-spotting bugs (P), banana fruit caterpillar (P), fruit flies (P) and strawberry spider mite (P).

Scale insects such as latania scale (P) are not usually serious on bananas although they can occur.

The banana aphid (*Pentalonia nigronervosa*) congregates under leaves, on emerging suckers, around the bases of pseudo-stems in the soil, and under leaf bases. They produce vast quantities of honeydew which attracts ants and in which yeasts may grow to produce a white paste-like material. Sooty moulds also grow on the honeydew. Apart from direct damage, this aphid spreads the serious virus disease 'bunchy top', and aphid control is obligatory in areas where bunchy top is present . Use dimethoate (30%) at the rate of 1mL per litre of water. Allow some of the spray to run down around the plant base and into the soil.

Bunchy top is characterised by broken, dark-green streaks along leaf veins. The leaves are held very upright. They are narrow, brittle, shorter than normal and have wavy margins. Your local Department of Agriculture must be notified if you suspect that this disease is present. The plants will be destroyed following a particular procedure.

Root knot nematodes (D) and burrowing nematodes may damage the roots. The latter enter the roots and cause large hollows. Soil-inhabiting fungi subsequently gain entry and extensive rotting may occur. The plants may fall over, particularly in wet windy weather. Bunches are small and fruit is undersized. Take care to obtain clean healthy sets, and plant in clean soil or soil treated with fenamiphos granules as directed on the label.

Dead leaves hanging down around the plant may be an indication of 'Panama wilt' which is a fungal disease and begins as yellowing along older leaf edges. If the pseudo-stem is cut through at ground level, a brown to black discoloration of the water-conducting tissues will be seen. This fungus remains in the soil for many years once established. It affects only the tall-growing varieties, such as 'Gros Michel', 'Lady Finger' and 'Sugar'.

Leaf yellowing may indicate 'corm rot' which is caused by the same fungus as armillaria root rot (D) in other plants.

Leaf spot (D) and leaf speckle (D) are the most common leaf diseases. Snails (P) may cause problems on occasions.

Blackcurrant
Ribes nigrum

Blackcurrant bushes produce a good crop only if temperatures are low for long periods in winter. They should be planted in a sunny area free of late spring frosts. New growth will be damaged unless the bushes are sheltered from strong winds in early summer. Berries dry out rapidly if exposed to hot winds.

They grow in a wide range of soils but prefer medium to light loam high in organic matter and only very slightly acid. They will tolerate slightly wetter soil than other berries, but drainage should be good. They must not be allowed to dry out in the growing season.

Prune to encourage new growth each season. This wood will bear fruit in the next year.

Watch for bud damage from the currant bud mite (P) and the leaf nematode (D); the stems may be damaged by currant borer moth (P) and the black vine weevil (P); and the leaves by leaf spot (D) and by two-spotted mite (P) which causes bronzing. Light brown apple moth (P) larvae may roll leaves up and chew leaves and fruit clusters.

Blueberry
Vaccinium corymbosum

There are now varieties of blueberry suitable for quite warm areas, but in general, moist cool conditions are preferable so avoid situations with hot afternoon sun and hot dry winds. Do not crowd blueberries with other shrubs because good air circulation helps to reduce the incidence of problems such as grey mould (D) which may affect the ripe berries in humid conditions.

The soil should be well drained, acid and contain a high proportion of organic matter. Blueberries do not require as much fertiliser as most other fruit crops but they do require a good water supply. Mulch the soil surface and keep the soil moist in the growing season.

Fruit is produced on one-year-old wood so, after the plant has been allowed a year to establish, carry out pruning during winter.

Birds are a problem, as are light brown apple moth (P) caterpillars and looper (P) caterpillars. Various fungi may cause leafspotting, and phytophthora root rot (D) may also be a problem.

Cherry
Prunus avium

These trees need a cold winter and will not grow and fruit satisfactorily in hot or semi-tropical climates. They will not tolerate shallow, waterlogged or saline soils. Choose a position sheltered from strong winds and frost-free in spring.

A pollinating variety nearby is necessary for fruit set. The fruit is likely to split if rainy weather prevails at ripening time.

Cherry trees are often seriously damaged by a disease called bacterial canker (D) which can attack the flowers and, more importantly, the trunk and branches. Early symptoms include sunken areas of bark and exudation of gum. Prune as little as possible and *never* in winter. The cultivars 'Florence', 'Napoleon', 'St Margaret' and 'William Favourite' are highly susceptible; whereas 'Ron's Seedling' and 'Van' are more tolerant. It is important to obtain trees from a reputable nurseryman, because this disease can be introduced into an orchard on nursery stock.

Trees allowed to suffer water stress during the summer are more likely to be troubled by bacterial canker.

Excess gum oozing from branches or trunk should be investigated. It may be the result of prolonged waterlogging, water deficiency, heavy pruning, intense heat, or attack from pests and diseases such as fruit-tree borer (P) or bacterial canker.

Birds and cherry aphids (P) can be serious problems. (See also the entry on stonefruit.)

Chinese gooseberry

Actinidia chinensis

These very vigorous vines need a strong supporting structure of considerable length—they may grow more than 10 m. Choose a warm position sheltered from strong winds, hot drying winds and late spring frosts. The vines will tolerate temperatures of 40°C, and down to –9°C while dormant.

The soil should be well-drained, slightly acid and contain a high proportion of organic matter. The shallow root system must not be allowed to dry

out or be disturbed by cultivation, so mulching is a good practice.

Both male and female vines are necessary for fruit production. Each female plant should be close to a male. Do not allow them to become intertwined, or pruning would be difficult. If space is restricted, a male vine may be grafted on to the female but it must be cut back hard after flowering to keep its vigorous growth under control and labelled so that its location is not forgotten. Bees are the most important pollinating agent.

It may be 4-5 years before fruit is produced in any quantity. Correct pruning and heavy fertiliser applications are necessary if crops are to be worthwhile. Fruit is produced only on current season's growth arising from older wood.

Problems include passionvine hopper (P), lightbrown apple moth (P), root knot nematode (D), phytophthora root rot (D), grey mould (D), and scales such as greedy scale (*Hemiberlesia rapax*). Large numbers of greenhouse thrips (P) may occur on the flowers but do not appear to damage them; later they may cause silvering of leaves but this is not important.

Applying oil sprays to Chinese gooseberry vines is likely to injure them.

Citrus

Citrus spp. — *Fortunella* spp.

Citrus trees are best grown in warm to hot climates where a mild winter occurs. In colder climates some citrus can be successfully grown if careful attention is paid to choice of variety and planting site. Lemons, cumquats and 'Wheeny' grapefruit can be grown in colder areas, but other grapefruit, oranges and mandarins do not ripen well without a long warm summer. Mature trees will tolerate some frost when fully dormant in winter, but even light frosts in late winter or spring or in early autumn will kill young growth. Lemons and limes suffer more from frost than other citrus. 'Lisbon' lemon variety is more suitable than 'Eureka' for cold climates, and the 'Meyer' lemon is less frost susceptible than either 'Lisbon' or 'Eureka'.

Choose a position that receives more than half a day of sun and is protected from strong wind.

Citrus trees exposed to wind will grow more slowly than sheltered trees, and their leaves and fruit will be damaged when rubbed against thorns, dead twigs and branches. Symptoms of wind injury (D) include puckered, split and misshapen leaves and fruit with irregular brown marks on the rind. The first spring leaves on 'Wheeny' grapefruit are often crinkled, but this should be ignored as

Valencia

Navels can be distinguished from other oranges by the indentation at the end opposite the stalk.

Navel

leaves produced later when the weather is warmer are normal.

Frost will damage trees suffering from lack of water more than those adequately supplied with water. Cold winds and frosts may cause foliage to curl up. The exposed undersides of the leaves are bleached by the sun and develop reddish-brown spots and patches. This can be termed sunblotch (D) or tar spotting.

In late winter and early spring, leaf yellowing is common. This is usually caused by nitrogen deficiency which is the result of cold soils. The leaves will go green again as the weather warms up and the roots begin to operate actively.

Trees in shaded or very sheltered situations where the foliage dries slowly after rain, and where air circulation is poor, are highly susceptible to brown spot (D) which occurs mainly on mandarins.

The soil should be deep, well-drained sandy loam of slightly acid to slightly alkaline pH. The level of soil salts (and irrigation water salts) should be low.

If the soil is shallow or heavy, special attention should be given to drainage and choice of rootstock. Some rootstocks such as 'Trifoliata' are not affected by phytophthora root rot and are therefore a good choice in areas where drainage may be a problem. Note that 'Eureka' lemons are not compatible with 'Trifoliata' rootstocks and usually have rough lemon (citronelle) roots.

If irrigation water is high in salt, consideration should be given to the use of rough lemon rootstock, which takes up less salt than other rootstocks. It is, however, highly susceptible to phytophthora root rot (D). All the different rootstocks have advantages and disadvantages, so you should consult your local Department of Agriculture or a specialist citrus grower about the rootstocks most suitable for the soil conditions you are able to provide. This is of paramount importance if a citrus orchard is being planned.

Plant the tree to about the same depth as it was in the nursery. Never bury the bud union, and keep the trunk clear of mulch and weeds. Do not grow vegetables or other plants under a citrus tree. If the tree is in a lawn, it will need extra water and fertiliser.

Citrus trees usually produce many more flowers than are necessary for a good crop of fruit and most, except some mandarin varieties, shed the surplus. Fruit drop occurs at the end of flowering or when the fruit is about pea-size and again when the fruit is about 20 mm in diameter. By three months after flowering, the size of the crop is established.

Fruit may also fall when it is almost mature. Navel oranges, grapefruit and 'Ellendale' are the types that most commonly have this problem. In a commercial orchard it is possible to spray to prevent this drop, but in a home garden try to minimise its effects by paying special attention to watering, fertilising and control of pests and diseases.

It may be almost impossible to grow a good-sized fruit crop in areas where hot dry winds are common from blossom to late January.

Citrus scab (D) causes shedding of young fruit, as does the feeding of spined citrus bug (P) and bronze orange bug (P). An inadequate supply of copper will also cause young fruit to drop.

A good water and fertiliser programme will help reduce problems with black spot, as will picking the fruit from the warmest (northern) side of the tree first.

Citrus trees require a lot of water, especially in summer. Avoid wetting the trunk. Keep the roots moist in dry hot weather or they may drop too many flowers and fruit as mentioned above.

Remember that overwatering and/or poor drainage will increase the likelihood of phytophthora root rot (D) and collar rot (D).

If large areas of the pulp are dry, excess water loss is indicated. Hot drying winds, for example, may cause water to be removed from the fruit and taken back to the leaves. This condition may be referred to as 'internal decline'.

Smaller dry patches inside the fruit may be the result of the feeding of spined citrus bug (P); and gum inside the fruit can result from spined citrus bug (P) attack or from exanthema (copper deficiency). The latter may also cause exudations of gum on the outside of the fruit and on shoots; dense bushy growth; and dieback of terminal twigs. Copper deficiency will probably not occur if copper oxychloride is used occasionally in the disease-control programme.

If deficiencies are suspected, first apply a complete fertiliser (unless this has already been done). The best times are July and November. Watch the results. The symptoms often disappear.

Citrus trees use comparatively large amounts of nitrogen, so apply a mixed fertiliser with about 10% nitrogen, 4% phosphorus and 6% potassium at the rate of 500 g per year of tree age up to five years. Mature trees can receive more fertiliser, but remember that overfertilising can kill a tree.

There are various soil additives or foliage sprays that supply other nutrients and which can be used if necessary. Do not apply these mixtures unless you are sure that deficiency problems do exist. It may be wise to seek more information from your Department of Agriculture.

Citrus may suffer from various deficiency problems. Magnesium deficiency (D) causes the leaves to yellow from the edges; the base of the leaf near the

stalk usually remains green. Zinc deficiency (D) causes small narrow leaves crowded on the stems; the leaves go yellow between the veins. Manganese deficiency (D) shows up first on young leaves as light-green or yellowish-green areas between the veins; the leaves are a normal size. Iron deficiency (D) causes leaves to gradually lose their green colour; the veins remain green the longest, but the leaves may end up completely white.

Deficiency in boron, although often spoken about, is very unlikely. In fact, boron toxicity is more common. This is indicated if leaf tips yellow and then go brown, and if the areas between the veins

Nagami cumquat

go yellow first near the leaf tip and then towards the leaf base. The drainage system and water quality should be investigated. Heavy watering with good-quality water will wash excess boron down below the reach of plant roots.

Pruning of citrus trees is normally restricted to removal of dead wood and crossing branches. Suckers from the rootstock should be removed also.

Citrus trees often grow branches very close to the ground. Sometimes these are pruned off to keep fruit off the ground and to let air circulate. This practice is referred to as 'skirting'. It helps to control brown rot (D), but will allow more light under the tree and therefore weed growth will increase.

If trees are old and neglected and do not respond to applications of water and fertiliser, they may be 'skeletonised'—that is, cut back to the branches. This should not be attempted until all danger of frost is passed. The bare trunk and branches should be protected from sunburn by painting with white plastic housepaint. The tree will not bear fruit for two years, but if cared for correctly it should resume vigorous growth and production.

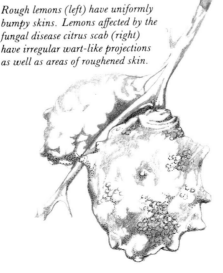

Rough lemons (left) have uniformly bumpy skins. Lemons affected by the fungal disease citrus scab (right) have irregular wart-like projections as well as areas of roughened skin.

Occasionally fruit, leaves or branches in a small area develop in an abnormal way. This is usually the result of a mutation, an accidental change in the genetic make-up. Examples include crinkled or variegated leaves; corrugated, striped or elongated fruit; and rough bark on branches. Small sections of the tree can simply be pruned off and the problem will probably not recur. Some trees, however, have been propagated from unstable budwood and tend to keep on producing peculiar parts. These trees should be cut back and regrafted or removed altogether.

Citrus suffer from some virus diseases which cannot be controlled once they appear. The symptoms include flaking bark, indentations in the trunk, and yellow mottling on leaves. It is possible to mistake the symptoms of deficiency and some other diseases for viral diseases.

When buying a new tree, buy from a reputable nurseryman and make sure the label states that it has been propagated from virus-tested or 'approved' material.

Fruit splitting, particularly of navel oranges, may occur in autumn. This may be associated with severe copper deficiency which hardens the rind and prevents normal expansion, but climatic factors seem to be more commonly implicated. It may help if the water supply to the tree is kept constant.

Fruit picked so that the rind is damaged is very likely to develop storage rots such as blue and green mould. Do not pick fruit wet with rain or dew. Always remove and destroy diseased fruit.

It is possible to store some types of citrus on the tree for long periods in a home garden, although this means longer exposure to some pests and diseases and the quality may decline after a few months. Mandarins should be picked within a few weeks after ripening.

If lemons are to be stored, they must be picked when the dark-green colour is beginning to lighten or when no more than slightly yellow. Clip them from the tree right next to the 'button' at the end of the stalk near the fruit. They must be undamaged, healthy, and quite dry. Wrap each one in a sheet of crumpled newspaper, and place loosely in a container such as a box or large brown paper bag, not in a lidded plastic container or sealed plastic bag. Store in a cool, dark, well-ventilated place.

Apart from pests and diseases already mentioned, fruit may be damaged by greenhouse thrips (P), orange fruitborer, fruit flies (P), citrus katydid (P), melanose (D), septoria spot, mealybugs (P), sooty blotch (D) and fly speck.

Leaves are likely to be damaged by snails (P), the bacterial disease citrus

blast, citrus leafminer (P), whiteflies (P), passionvine hopper (P), Fuller's rose weevil (P); and the caterpillars of the small citrus butterfly (P) and the large citrus butterfly (P).

Small stems may have the swellings of the citrus gall wasp (P) which is a serious pest and must be controlled.

Roots and branches may be damaged by fruit-tree root weevil (P), elephant weevil (P), and longicorns (P) such as the citrus branchborer.

Various mites may also cause problems: broad mite (P), citrus bud mite (P), citrus rust mite and citrus red mite. Rind injury is a common result of their feeding. Scale insects which attack citrus include cottonycushion scale (P), soft brown scale (P), black scale (P), white wax scale (P), pink wax scale (P), white louse scale (P), California red scale (P) and purple scale. Yellow scale (*Aonidiella citrina*) is similar in appearance to California red scale and is often found on the same tree in the more shaded places such as under leaves on lower and inner branches. It causes bright yellow marks on the leaves. It is not as serious a pest as California red scale and can be controlled by the same programme.

Custard apple
Annona cherimola

This tree requires a position sheltered from wind, and from frost which will damage the fruit. It performs best in a warm climate with high humidity in summer. Rainfall or high humidity during the flowering period is necessary for a good fruit set. Hand pollination can be carried out if necessary.

The variety 'African Pride' would be a good home-garden tree. Compared to 'Pink's Mammoth' it starts to bear fruit sooner, yields better, is more tolerant of cold weather, and does not grow as tall.

In order to reduce the likelihood of phytophthora root rot (D), plant in well-drained soil at the same depth as in the pot and spaced about 6 m apart. Keep mulch back from the stem.

Young fruit will fall if attacked by fruitspotting bug (P). Fruit can also be damaged by fruit flies (P) and yellow peach moth (P) larvae. The latter usually enter the fruit near the stalk or where two fruits are touching.

The foliage can be eaten by various caterpillars.

Mealybugs (P), probably the most serious problem, gather on the fruit usually near the stalk. It is a good idea to rely on natural enemies such as ladybirds for control. Stop ants gaining access to the fruit. Do this by using tree bands or

chemicals around the butt or trunk of the tree and by trimming branches so that they do not touch the ground or nearby small plants. Spray as little as possible.

Scales such as black scale (P) should be similarly dealt with. See black canker symptoms photo page 26.

Removal of mummified fruit and dead twigs and branches will help control the disease, black canker, which shows up as purple spots or blotches, and diplodia rot which is similar but causes dieback of young twigs as well as deeper rotting of the fruit.

Slow decline of the whole tree may indicate armillaria root rot (D).

Feijoa
Feijoa sellowiana

This evergreen tree grows about 4 m high and has a similar spread. It is grown for the red flowers as well as for fruit and tolerates a wide range of conditions. For a home garden, choose a grafted variety such as 'Mammoth' which is self-fertile.

Although the plant is drought resistant, a good fruit crop will be produced only if summer water is supplied and a fertiliser programme followed.

Fruit collected from the ground will have a far better flavour than that picked from the tree.

Plan control of fruit flies (P); light brown apple moth (P); and soft scales (P) including Chinese wax scale (P)

Fig
Ficus carica

Fig trees tolerate a wide range of climates but are most successful in a warm dry climate in a sandy loam of neutral pH. They will not grow satisfactorily in an

acid soil or in a poorly drained one. A frost-free position is desirable, but where this cannot be provided young trees must be protected.

Plant 6–8 m from other trees, and water well in summer. The shallow root system may be damaged by cultivation and must not be allowed to dry out.

Failure to produce a crop may mean that cross-pollination, necessary for some fig types, has not occurred. Choose a self-fertile variety such as 'Brown Turkey', 'Black Genoa', 'White Adriatic' or 'Cape White' when buying a new tree.

A small crop may be the result of slow tree growth. Most fruit develops on new wood, so unless the tree produces new growth each year the crop will be small. Old trees do not grow actively and can be encouraged to make new growth by cutting them back in winter. Seek advice about correct pruning techniques from your local Department of Agriculture.

Splitting and rotting of fruit may be the result of a sudden increase in water supply when the fruit is near maturity, or the result of high humidity.

Large dark-brown spots on the leaves are probably caused by brown leaf spot; and smaller spots by rust (D). The leaves may be attacked by a number of pests, including fig blister mite, figleaf beetle (P) and the similar fig beetle. Fig leafhoppers cause leaves to curl and develop brown patches. Cottonycushion scale (P) may be found on the stems; the larvae of fig longicorn bore into the stems; and the larvae of the fig bark beetle damage shoots. Plan control of fruit fly (P) larvae and birds which attack the fruit. More mature fruit is often attacked by driedfruit beetle (P).

Grape
Vitis vinifera

Grapes grow best in areas where warm to hot, long summers and cool winters are the norm.

In areas of high summer rainfall there are usually serious problems with berry-splitting, fungal fruit rots and downy mildew (D), and in these circumstances 'Golden Muscat' and 'Isabella' which are varieties of the American grape, *Vitis labrusca*, should be chosen.

Grapes can be successfully grown in cold highland areas but should be sited to avoid early spring frosts which will kill new growth and reduce fruit set.

They grow well in a wide range of soils, but good drainage is essential.

Optimum fruit production will be achieved only if the vine is grown in full sun and correctly pruned each year. Small, malformed and unevenly ripening bunches with sour fruit are usually the result of inadequate pruning. Consult your local Department of Agriculture or pruning texts about suitable methods.

In hot, dry, windy weather, excessive water loss from the plant may mean that water is withdrawn from the fruit and it shrivels. This is termed 'wind-suck'.

A grapevine will not fruit successfully at different levels above the ground. Therefore, if you want to grow grapes on a structure like a pergola, you will need two or three vines for each side. Divide the distance from the ground to the top roughly into three, and train one vine to grow to the top before branching. Allow one of the others to branch at about two-thirds of the distance from the ground, and train the last with all its branches about one-third of the way up.

Vines are subject to many pests and diseases. The most serious is grape phyl-loxera (P), an aphid which can cause root or leaf galls. Quarantine measures are in force to stop the spread of this pest. Consult your local Department of Agriculture if you wish to move plants or cuttings from one area to another.

Webbing on the leaves and bunches indicates light brown apple moth (P). Leaves may be chewed by redshouldered leaf beetles (P) and by the larvae of a variety of moths, including grapevine moth (P), painted vine moth (P) and hawk moths (P) such as the grapevine hawk moth (P).

Look in or on stems for grapevine scale (P), black vine weevil (P) and elephant weevil (P). Apple weevil larvae attack the root system. Other pests of grapevines are plague thrips (P), bunch mites (P), grapeleaf rust mite (P), grapeleaf blister mite (P) (bud mite), passionvine hopper (P), mealybugs (P), such as the longtailed mealybug, and fruit flies (P).

Diseases of grapes include powdery mildew (D), downy mildew (D), grey mould (D) and black spot (D).

There are also a number of virus diseases such as leafroll and fanleaf.

The symptoms of fanleaf are more pronounced in cool weather and include yellow mottling, zigzag growth of canes, and shortened internodes. Growth of vine is slow and fruit bunches often straggly.

The symptoms of leafroll may include pronounced rolling under of leaf margins, thickening of leaf blades, and unusual autumn colouring of leaves—for example, black- or red-fruited varieties may develop purplish or reddish blotches between the large veins. Growth is slow and yields reduced.

There is no cure for either of these diseases. Remove the vine and make sure replacement planting material comes from healthy vines.

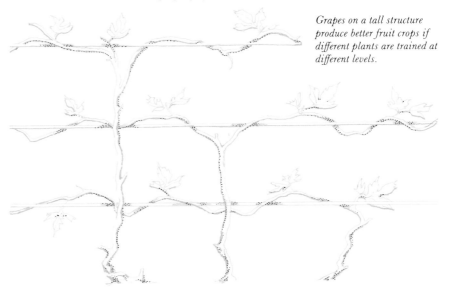

Grapes on a tall structure produce better fruit crops if different plants are trained at different levels.

Guava

Psidium spp.

These plants need a warm temperate to subtropical climate. They will not tolerate frost, and young trees should be sheltered from strong winds.

Guavas will grow in a wide range of soils and need heavy fertiliser applications to produce a worthwhile crop.

Immature fruit will fall if the plant suffers water stress. Fruit should be ripened on the bush; it will not ripen properly if picked green.

Fruit flies (P) are a serious pest of guavas because the fruit is on the tree in late summer when the fly numbers are high. Do not use dimethoate for control because it may harm the leaves.

Greenhouse thrips (P) may damage fruit or foliage, and the larvae of the guava moth (*Coscinoptycha improbana*) feed

in the ripening fruit. Guava moth larvae are similar to those of yellow peach moth (P) and the pest could probably be controlled in the same way.

Guavas do not have serious disease problems as a general rule.

Loquat

Eriobotrya japonica

This tree is of subtropical origin but will grow satisfactorily in a wide range of climates. Although an established tree will withstand winter frost, blossoming occurs early and flowers will be damaged by frost. Excessively hot and humid climates will make diseases more likely. Plant in a sunny position, and protect from wind so that the fruit will not be abraded.

Loquats will grow in a wide variety of soils. They need large quantities of

fertiliser. Water supply should be regular and continue through the summer.

A grafted plant will perform better than a seedling. The choice of an early-maturing variety such as 'Herd's Mammoth' will minimise problems with fruit flies (P) such as Queensland fruit fly. Unless this pest is controlled in loquats, it multiplies and attacks other later-maturing fruit. Note that spraying may be difficult, as a mature tree could be 7–8 m high.

Lightbrown apple moth (P) caterpillars may also attack loquats. And the disease fleck (D) is sometimes a problem.

Lychee

Litchi chinensis

These trees will succeed only in areas of humid, warm to hot weather in spring and summer and cool weather in winter. Periods of cold are required to induce flowering, but young trees may be killed by frost and older trees tolerate only light frosts. Growth will be poor if the trees are planted on windy sites.

The soil must be deep and well drained, preferably slightly acid, and rich in organic matter.

Lychees grow slowly in the first few years, but after 15–20 years reach a size of about 12 m high by 12 m wide and are very long-lived. They begin bearing after three to five years, and the crop increases in size as the tree gets older.

A smaller crop than usual may result from low humidity or dry soils during flowering or during the following few weeks. Rain during this time may adversely affect fruit set.

Cracks in the fruit skin may be caused by drying winds and low humidity while the fruit is maturing.

The fruit usually ripens over a few days. It should taste pleasant when picked, as it does not continue to ripen after picking. Cut only the fruit bunch. New growth, on which the next crop will be borne, will then develop on the outside of the tree. Avoid picking fruit wet with rain or dew because it will not store well.

The most serious pest of lychees is probably the fruit bat (P); these animals can eat large quantities of fruit in one night. They may fly considerable distances to do so. Fruit flies (P) and green vegetable bugs (P) also damage fruit. Flower and fruit drop can be caused by the erinose mite (P).

Other pests include scales and various beetles and caterpillars such as redshouldered leaf beetle (P), and the macadamia nutborer (P).

Macadamia

Macadamia tetraphylla and
M. integrifolia

Macadamias will grow well in a variety of soils, but good drainage is essential. Best results will be obtained if the pH is moderately acid and the position is frost-free and sheltered from strong winds. Rain (or irrigation) in spring and summer is essential for a good crop.

Macadamia tetraphylla is the most suitable species for fresh nuts. Home-gardeners should note that it may grow to 15 m high and 12 m across in good conditions and is not normally pruned. It has a shallow root system which should not be disturbed, and mulching is therefore a good idea. Keep young trees shaded and do not allow grass or other plants to grow closer than 1 m from the stem.

The tree should be encouraged to grow quickly, but do not use a fertiliser high in phosphorus.

Trunk canker or phytophthora root rot (D), armillaria root rot (D) and nut anthracnose (D) are among the very few macadamia diseases.

Pests that attack flowers or buds include macadamia flower caterpillar (P), loopers (P), redshouldered leaf beetle (P) and the hairy lineblue butterfly.

Pests that cause most of their damage on nuts include fruitspotting bug (P), banana-spotting bug (P), macadamia nutborer (P) and yellow peach moth (P).

Predominantly foliage pests include macadamia felted coccid (P), macadamia leafminer (P), macadamia cup moth (P), and orange fruitborer.

Hard scales (P) that attack the macadamia include latania scale (P), macadamia white scale and macadamia mussel scale. The latter occurs mostly on leaves. It is light brown and about 2–3 mm long. The scale coverings are curved and wider at one end than the other, giving the appearance of the shellfish mussel. The leaves yellow in the area immediately around each scale, and

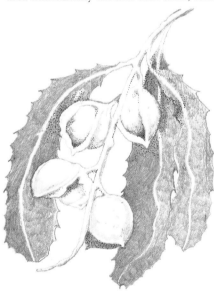

if the infestation is heavy, leaf fall may occur. This reduces tree vigour if no control measures are undertaken.

The small stems may be attacked by macadamia twig-girdler (P).

There are many other insects that feed on macadamia trees, but control is not usually necessary.

Mango
Mangifera indica

This attractive tree has a wide spread, and it should be planted at least 10–12 m from buildings or other trees.

The soil type is not critical but drainage must be good. The mango, which grows best in the tropics, requires a warm climate with dry conditions during flowering and the early stages of fruit development. A fungal disease called

anthracnose (D) can seriously affect fruit set if conditions are wet during this time.

The flowers may be attacked by redshouldered leaf beetles (P) and the small fruit by the fruitspotting bug (P).

Thrips (P), such as the redbanded thrips, cause a fine mottling on the upper leaf surface.

Hard scales (P), such as oriental scale and mango scale, may be found on the fruit and stems; whereas pink wax scale (P) is more common on the leaves, and white wax scale (P) on stems.

The mango seed weevil (*Sternochetus mangiferae*), which is dark brown and about 10 mm long, sometimes bores its way out of a mango of good eating quality. The eggs are deposited on the fruit, and the tiny tunnel made by the larva on its way to the seed is not usually noticed. The larva feeds in the seed and pupates there. By this time the fruit is ripe. The adults may remain in the seed for weeks before chewing their way to the outside of the fruit.

Other pests and diseases are the fruit flies (P): Queensland fruit fly, Jarvis's fruit fly and mango fly; the large mango tipborer (P); fruitsucking moth (P); powdery mildew (D); bacterial black spot (D); and stem-end rot.

Mulberry
Morus spp.

This large spreading deciduous tree may grow up to 10 m tall.

It will thrive in many different soils and climates, but it does need an open sunny position and a good regular water supply, especially in summer.

Mulberries suffer from two diseases: bacterial blight (D) and leaf spot (D). Redshouldered leaf beetle (P), fruit flies (P), and scales such as cottonycushion scale (P) are also problems sometimes.

Olive
Olea europaea

Olives will grow in a wide range of soil types. They will tolerate fairly high levels of alkalinity and salinity but they will not tolerate waterlogging. They are drought resistant although the roots are shallow.

Cold winters and long hot summers are necessary for good fruit production, as is good water supply during fruit formation. The trees tend to bear heavier crops every second year.

Black scale (P), soft brown scale (P) and oleander scale (P) infest leaves and twigs. The leaves may also be attacked by the olive lace bug (P) which causes yellow dots on the upper leaf surfaces.

Olive trees may be damaged by excessive use of oil sprays. Scale control should be carried out with a combination spray such as 10 mL of white oil plus 2 mL of 50% maldison per litre of water.

Papaw
Carica papaya

Papaws are of tropical origin and therefore grow best in areas of high temperature, high humidity and high rainfall. They can be grown satisfactorily in temperate-zone home gardens if given a warm position. Exposure to cold winds slows growth and reduces fruit production. Light frosts damage leaves, and continuation of frosty conditions may kill established trees. A problem called 'star spot' may occur on the exposed sides of green fruit after frosts and very cold winds. These greyish star-shaped spots are about 6 mm in diameter and only on the surface.

In cooler areas it is probably more sensible to grow the mountain papaw (*Carica candamarcensis*) which is frost-hardy once established and fruits well in cool climates. The fruit is usually smaller than a tennis ball.

A soil with a high organic matter level is the most suitable. It must not be strongly acid, and there is some evidence to suggest that a slightly alkaline pH will decrease trouble with the disease dieback. Good drainage is essential, but the soil should not dry out too rapidly as the root system is shallow. Mulching with organic matter is a good practice. Papaw trees planted in areas of poor drainage will almost certainly die from root rots.

The plants bear male flowers only, female flowers only, or both male and female flowers. (The latter are referred to as bisexual or hermaphrodite plants.)

A bisexual plant would be a good choice for a home garden in the warm subtropics, but in colder areas such a plant is likely to change to the male form. It is therefore necessary to have female plants to bear the fruit and male plants to produce the pollen.

Unfortunately it is not possible to tell male from female plants until they flower. Female flowers are large, fleshy, and close to the trunk; whereas the funnel-shaped male flowers are borne on branched stalks.

Plant three or four seedlings about 250 mm apart in a group, and about 1.5 m away plant another group of three or four. After flowering, remove all plants except one female in one group and one male in the other. In situations where more plants are required, plant more groups and retain one male for every ten females.

The first fruit should be ready for harvest between 18 months and two years after planting. Replacement trees should be planned because bearing continues for only about five years.

Fruit is susceptible to a number of different rots. Some of these are caused by fungi which spread to the fruit when it is green and remain dormant until ripening begins. Fruit on trees planted in cold exposed places is more likely to be affected than that on trees in warm sheltered areas.

Note that the milky sap of papaw trees will irritate human skin and eyes.

Remove any plants that develop mottled narrow leaves, many short side-shoots, and dark-green or olive water-soaked streaks on the leafstalk and upper stem. These symptoms characterise 'mosaic', the cause of which is not yet established. This problem could be confused with two-spotted mite (P) damage if only leaf symptoms were considered.

Yellowing of young leaves and death of the stem tip may indicate dieback. A good supply of potassium to the plant will help to avoid this.

Yellowing of older leaves and the development of claw-like young leaves is probably yellow crinkle (D), but all the symptoms discussed should be noted so that confusion with broad mite (P) damage does not arise.

White powdery areas on leaves, stems or fruit are powdery mildew (D). Brown, rounded spots up to 5 mm across are symptomatic of a disease called 'brown spot'. This also causes elliptical brown spots on the stems but is not considered serious enough to warrant control.

Pawpaws can be attacked by insects such as fruitspotting bugs (P) which can cause the fall of young fruit, banana-spotting bug (P), fruit flies (P) including cucumber fly, yellow peach moth (P) and fruitpiercing moths (P).

Passionfruit
Passiflora spp.

Passionfruit vines require a warm, almost frost-free position and shelter from strong winds. The purple or black passionfruit (*Passiflora edulis*) is the best choice for temperate areas, whereas the golden passionfruit (*P. edulis* f. *flavicarpa*) is used in subtropical areas. The latter is not self-fertile, so it is necessary to plant two vines.

The soil should be very slightly acid to slightly alkaline and contain a high proportion of organic matter.

Vines will not tolerate poor drainage and may suffer from root and collar rots.

Another soil-associated disease is fusarium wilt which is characterised by wilting of shoots and plant collapse. When examined, the wood under the bark of the stem will appear brown or reddish-brown instead of white. In areas where fusarium is known to exist in the soil, buy resistant golden passionfruit seedlings or a vine that is grafted on to resistant golden passionfruit roots. Where this problem does not exist, seedling passionfruit will usually grow and fruit just as well as grafted passionfruit.

Poor air circulation caused by weed growth, crowding with other plants and lack of pruning will increase problems with the disease brown spot (D). Other leaf- and fruit-spotting diseases are septoria leaf spot (D) and 'grease spot'. The latter is a bacterial disease caused by *Pseudomonas syringae* pv. *passiflorae*. It is characterised by roughly circular dark-green greasy blotches on the fruit and brown spots with a wide pale-yellow halo on the leaves. Spray with copper oxychloride, following the programme suggested for brown spot (D).

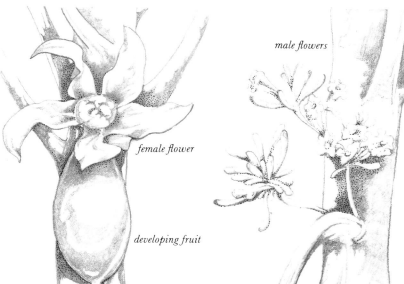

female flower

developing fruit

male flowers

Blackening of young tip growth is caused by phytophthora blight (D). It is important to remove and destroy all dead and diseased material.

As the vines age the problem of woodiness (D), or 'bullet', increases and is characterised by thick rinds and leaves mottled with yellow. A good water and fertiliser supply and warmth will minimise the effects of woodiness. Avoid any practice that would encourage new growth during cold weather. Time the annual pruning with this in mind. Vines resistant to this disease may soon be available to home-gardeners.

Pruning is important on established vines. Fruit is produced only on the current season's growth, so removal of old wood and excessive end growth not only keeps the vine within bounds — often necessary in a home garden — but also encourages growth that will bear fruit.

Fruit set is likely to be poor if the weather is very hot, very cold, or showery at flowering time. Vines do not come into full production for 18 months to two years after planting.

The root system is extensive and shallow. Do not allow it to dry out or damage it by cultivation or uneven application of fertiliser. Mulching is a good idea. Young fruit is likely to fall if the water supply is inadequate.

Pests include California red scale (P), soft brown scale (P), black scale (P), fruit flies (P), mealybugs (P), passionvine hopper (P), and passionvine mite.

Various bugs such as green vegetable bug (P) and fruitspotting bugs (P) may suck sap from flowers or young fruit. Any fruit produced from damaged flowers will probably be deformed.

It is not wise to apply maldison–protein hydrolysate bait sprays to the vine itself, because leaf and flower drop may result. Apply to the trellis posts or similar structure in the area.

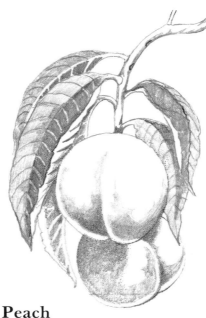

Peach

Prunus persica

Peaches and nectarines do best in areas with warm summers and low winter temperatures. Avoid positions where spring frosts may damage flowers. Humid summers mean more trouble with brown rot (D). Unless winter chilling requirements are met, shedding of buds often occurs; new 'low-chill' varieties are successful in coastal areas.

Most varieties are self-fertile but 'J. H. Hale' needs a pollinating variety such as 'Blackburn' nearby. A useful fruit crop should be produced in the third year after planting.

Fruit production will be maximised if pruning is carried out in winter. This timing however, is likely to cause problems with a serious disease, bacterial canker (D), and a spray programme should be organised. Leaf curl (D), freckle (D) and rust (D) are also common diseases. Green peach aphid (P), black peach aphid and the inland katydid (P) are common pests.

(See also the entry on stonefruit.)

Pear

Pyrus communis

Pears do best in a cool climate, but there are varieties such as 'Williams' (also referred to as 'Williams's Bon Chrétien' or 'Bartlett') which will tolerate warm to hot summers. However, growth will be poor and the fruit crop irregular unless winters are cold enough for chilling requirements. Frost will damage pear blossoms.

The trees prefer deep, moist soils and will tolerate wetter soil conditions than many other fruit trees. In acid soil conditions, some varieties suffer from the excessive amount of manganese available; while in alkaline soils, deficiency of available manganese or iron can cause problems. Boron deficiency leads to rough skin and cracks in the fruit, and twig dieback. 'Williams' variety suffers badly if conditions are saline.

Pear trees are slower to start producing a crop but they keep bearing fruit longer than many other fruit trees. Heavy pruning in early years lengthens the time from planting to first crop and subsequently reduces fruit production. Prune only lightly until the tree has filled the space provided for it. Seek advice on modern pruning techniques.

Most varieties — except 'Williams' — need cross-pollination and unless there is another pear variety growing within 7–8 m will not produce fruit.

Home-grown pears should be picked before the green base colour becomes yellowish. The best flavour will develop if pears are ripened at a temperature of about 20°C.

If conditions are wet and cool at blossoming, a bacterium called *Pseudomonas syringae* pv. *syringae*, which occurs naturally on the plant surface, may cause a blossom blight. In this case the crop will be greatly reduced.

Fireblight, another bacterial problem, is one of the most serious diseases in the world but is not yet in Australia.

Black spots on the leaves and rough black scabs on the fruit probably indicate pear scab, which is a fungal disease very like apple scab (D). Fruit blemishes are also caused by sooty blotch (D) and the associated fly speck. Stony pit (D) is a virus disease characterised by extremely malformed fruit; at the base of each de-

Boron deficiency may result in depressions and cracks in the skin.

pression in the fruit there are small areas of very hard flesh.

Blister-like galls under the leaves probably result from attack by pearleaf blister mite (P); and leaves with the upper surface removed indicate attack from pear and cherry slug (P).

Flowers can be attacked by plague thrips (P), and the leaves by two-spotted mite (P) and bryobia mite (P) which both cause fine yellow mottling.

Look for grey flaky San José scales (P) on twigs, branches and fruit. The fruit can also be damaged by the larvae of codling moth (P), lightbrown apple moth (P), and fruit flies (P) such as Queensland fruit fly and Mediterranean fruit fly.

Persimmon
Diospyros kaki

These trees will grow well in subtropical to cool temperate climates. They are very tolerant of frost while dormant. They prefer deep, acid soils but can be grown in other soil types provided the drainage is good. Poor drainage is likely to lead to problems with phytophthora root rot (D) which is referred to also as 'cinnamon fungus'.

They are deciduous and colour well in autumn even in warm temperate climates. They grow to about 5 m and have a spreading habit, so plant at least 6 m from other trees.

A grafted tree is to be preferred to a seedling and should begin to bear after three years. Fertilise, and water well in summer for good fruit production.

Prune lightly only. Hard pruning will encourage excessively leafy growth and premature fruit drop. The fruit crop is carried on the current season's growth and may be heavier every second year.

A black coating on the leaves and white fluffy areas on stems may indicate mealybug (P). Curled and chewed leaves are characteristic of lightbrown apple moth (P). Fruit is attacked by fruit flies (P). Two-spotted mite (P) and greenhouse thrips (P) cause leaf fall, and a woody lump at ground level is probably crown gall (D).

The scales (P) that may be found on this tree include white wax scale (P) and oleander scale (P).

Pineapple
Ananas comosus

Pineapples will grow in a wide range of soils but prefer one rich in organic matter and acidic (pH 4.5 to 5). Good drainage is essential, as is a warm frost-free position sheltered from cold winds. It takes 18 months to 2 years from planting to harvest. The growth is slower in colder situations.

Tops are excellent planting material. Remove the flesh and the bottom leaves. Allow them to dry out for a few days. Plant them shallowly (about 50 mm deep) and keep the soil just moist. Root rot may occur if the soil is too wet at planting or at any time during growth.

Slips, which grow from the fruit stalk, and suckers, which grow from the base of the plant, can also be used to start new plants. Slips should be planted at the same depth as tops, and suckers a little deeper. Space plants about 250 mm apart in rows about 1 m apart. It may take a month or more for production of the first new leaves.

Close planting may make problems with pineapple scale (P) and pineapple mealybugs (P) more serious. Mealybugs (P) on pineapple can be controlled if necessary by spraying thoroughly with maldison (50%) at the rate of 1 mL per litre of water. Add 10 mL of white oil per litre. Pay special attention to the lower leaves of the plant.

Mealybugs are thought to spread a disease referred to as 'mealybug wilt'. Inner leaves remain normal but outer leaves may fade to pale green or yellow. They die back from the tip. There is no chemical control.

White curl grubs (P) chew roots and gouge furrows in the butts of the plants; plants may be yellow and stunted. Similar symptoms may result from root knot nematode (D) attack.

Top and root rot (D) may be indicated if heart leaves change to yellow or lightbrown with a reddish tinge. There are other rotting diseases associated with poor drainage or overwatering.

Maximum production will be achieved only if the plant is fertilised regularly. Once the fruit has formed, stop fertilising until after harvest. Do not drop solid fertiliser into the growing top.

After harvest remove all slips, and all suckers except one which will grow to produce another pineapple during the next 18 months.

Each plant may produce for many years, but as the fruit gradually decreases in size, replacements should be planted. Each stem produces only one fruit.

Vigorous plants about 15 months old can be induced to set fruit by applying 50 mL of NAA (10 ppm a.i.) to the leaves. The fruit should be ready to harvest about 10 months later. If NAA is not applied, this may take longer.

Plum
Prunus domestica and *P. salicina*

Japanese plums (*P. salicina*) can be grown in warm temperate areas, but European plums (*P. domestica*) need cold winters for good fruit production. Choose a site not subject to frost, and provide protection from hot winds.

If water lost from the leaves during hot dry periods cannot quickly be replaced, water is moved from the fruit to the leaves and the fruit shrivels. This is referred to as 'crinkle of plums'.

Plums do best in a deep, well-drained soil but will tolerate heavier soils and more soil moisture than peaches, apricots and almonds.

If only one tree is to be planted, choose the variety carefully and find out about pollinating requirements in your area.

Japanese plums such as 'Santa Rosa' and 'Satsuma' and European plums such as 'Black Diamond' and 'Angelina' usually set sufficient fruit for home consumption without the presence of a pollinating variety in the vicinity.

They produce better, however, if a pollinating variety is nearby. Japanese and European plums will not pollinate each other because they don't flower at the same time.

A heavy fruit crop should be thinned. This will increase fruit size and discourage biennial bearing. Remove some of the small fruit by hand until Japanese plums are about 10 cm apart and European plums about 5 cm apart.

Japanese plum trees are very vigorous and regular hard pruning is necessary. European plum trees need less pruning.

The most troublesome diseases of plums are silver leaf (D), brown rot (D) and rust (D). Bacterial leaf spot (*Xanthomonas campestris* pv. *pruni*) occurs on some varieties. Bladder plum (*Taphrina pruni*) occurs in some areas; this shows up as swollen distorted fruit. The disease-causing organism is closely related to the one causing leaf curl of peach (D) and the leaf symptoms are similar.

(See also the entry on stonefruit.)

Quince
Cydonia oblonga

This tree will perform best in temperate climates and is not suitable for growth in the tropics.

The soil should be acid, because quince trees commonly suffer from iron deficiency in alkaline conditions. The soil should also have a high moisture-holding capacity and therefore light sandy soils are not suitable.

The fruit may be bumped and rubbed against branches in windy conditions, so some shelter is desirable.

The quince is a late-maturing fruit; and in areas where the fruit flies (P)

(Queensland fruit fly or Mediterranean fruit fly) occur, a rigorous spraying schedule will be necessary. The fruit may also be attacked by lightbrown apple moth (P) larvae, codling moth (P) larvae, and oriental fruit moth (P) larvae. Note that carbaryl is not a suitable insecticide for use on quinces, because the leaves will be seriously damaged.

Fleck (D) is the most serious quince disease and causes spots on leaves and fruit.

Raspberry
Ribes idaeus

These are best suited to cool moist climates and grow well in areas where apples can be successfully produced. A cool to cold winter is the most important factor, but avoid sites where mid- to late-spring frosts are likely because young growth will be damaged.

Raspberries need a sunny position but protect them from hot afternoon sun. This is very important if they are being grown in a warmer climate. Ensure that they receive a good water supply in summer. If temperatures are very high, overhead watering can be used in order to cool the fruit.

They should be protected from strong winds, particularly hot winds which will snap fruit-bearing side-shoots and dry out the berries.

The soil should be slightly acid to neutral and have a high proportion of organic matter. Good drainage is essential. It is important to eradicate perennial weeds before the canes are planted.

Raspberries are sensitive to build up of salt in the soil, so when potassium is being applied use the sulphate rather than the chloride form.

Leaves may be chewed by raspberry sawfly (P) larvae, or show symptoms of rust (D). The buds and berries may be damaged by spur blight (D) and grey mould (D) and by the larvae of the raspberry bud moth (*Carposina adreptella*). Minimise the damage of the latter by pruning as early in autumn as possible and burning the prunings.

Grey or purplish spots on the canes indicate cane spot (D). White flaky areas on the stem indicate rose scale (D).

Cut off at ground level the canes that have fruited and burn them. This will improve fruit production and eliminate possible sources of fungal infection.

Other berry fruits such as lawtonberries, boysenberries, youngberries, loganberries, and kroonberries (or Scoresby selection) have very similar cultural requirements to raspberries. They will, however, tolerate more heat. Recommended spacing of plants, pruning and trellising differ from type to type, and it is worthwhile knowing their requirements before planting.

Pest and disease problems are similar to those of raspberries. Look also for the larvae of the bramble sawfly (P) and lightbrown apple moth (P).

The problem 'dryberry' is a downy mildew (D). Infected berries are dry and hard and may split. Infected leaves have pink to wine-red blotches commonly bounded by veins and next to the main vein. Remove suckers, including root suckers, regularly. Overhead irrigation encourages this disease. A spray programme is also necessary.

Rhubarb

Rheum rhabarbarum

The soil for rhubarb must be well drained. A slightly acid pH and large quantities of organic matter are necessary for optimum growth.

A planting can last for three or four years and should therefore be separate from vegetables planted annually. Do not begin harvesting until a strong crown has developed.

Water well in hot weather and pinch out any flower heads that appear. Vigorous growth will help overcome disease problems, so apply fertiliser regularly. Use complete fertiliser. Do not apply extra nitrogen.

Badly drained soil or overwatering will encourage crown rot, a firm brown to black rot at the base of the plant. Bacterial soft rot (D) may also attack the crown. A fluctuating water supply will make an attack of sclerotium stem rot (D) more likely; this causes wilting and death. Rhubarb also suffers from leaf diseases such as rust (D), leaf spot (D) and downy mildew (D). The passionvine hopper (P) may feed on the leaves.

Stonefruit

Prunus spp.

This group comprises almonds, apricots, cherries, nectarines, peaches and plums. They all need regular maintenance to produce good fruit crops, and this maintenance includes correct pruning.

Pruning instructions, however, often fail to comment on procedures necessary for disease control. For example, trees pruned in autumn–winter will be more prone to bacterial canker (D) or bacterial gummosis. This is a disease that can attack all the stonefruits, but cherries and apricots are particularly susceptible.

It is unwise to plant potatoes, tomatoes, strawberries, raspberries or gooseberries between stonefruit trees or to grow stonefruit in land that has previously grown any of these plants, because of the risk of 'black heart of apricots'. This disease is caused by the same fungus as verticillium wilt (D). Apricots and almonds are most likely to be infected, but the disease has also been known on peaches and plums. Weeds such as fat hen (*Chenopodium* sp.) may also act as disease hosts.

Slight wilting of leaves on the tips of the branches is an early sign of infection. Wilting gradually spreads and leaves fall. If infected branches, twigs or roots are cut through, they show characteristic brown to black spots which may form a ring towards the edge. If longitudinal cuts are made, discoloured stripes will be seen. There is no cure for this disease. Land to be replanted would have to be fumigated.

A large number of other pests and diseases can cause problems with stonefruit.

Yellow spots or patches on the leaves may be an indication of rust (D) which is more common on peaches, nectarines and plums than on other stonefruit.

Pink, puckered leaves are caused by leaf curl (D) which may occur on almonds and apricots but is more common on peaches and nectarines.

Blossom blight may rot the flowers, and the associated disease brown rot (D), can cause serious losses of fruit particularly in humid areas. Fruit and leaves may show symptoms of shot hole (D), freckle (D), and bacterial leafspot (*Xanthomonas campestris* pv. *pruni*).

The latter attacks only some varieties of peach, plum and cherry. It shows up on peach leaves as pale angular spots. On plum trees a yellow halo usually occurs around each spot and the centre may fall out. The disease is usually characterised by an oily sheen on the spots. Exudations produced during wet weather dry out later and may flake off like pieces of tissue paper. Dieback of twigs also occurs. The maintenance of vigorous growth is the best defence against this disease.

There are a number of virus diseases that affect stonefruit. In general, careful selection of propagating material by nurserymen will minimise the occurrence of virus affected trees.

Look on the stems or leaves for scales such as San José scale (P), frosted scale (P) and soft brown scale (P).

The fruit may be attacked by fruit flies (P) such as Queensland fruit fly and

mid bud-swell

late bud-swell

early bloom

full bloom

petal fall

Stages of flowering — peach

Mediterranean fruit fly, Rutherglen bug (P), green vegetable bug (P), fruitspotting bugs (P), coon bug, and driedfruit beetles (P). The latter may spread brown rot (D).

Insects such as green peach aphid (P), black peach aphid, cherry aphid (P), passionvine hopper (P), and mealybugs (P) suck sap from leaves and stems.

Leaves may be chewed by painted apple moth (P) larvae, by pear and cherry slugs (P), by redshouldered leaf beetle (P), and by lightbrown apple moth (P) larvae. Leaves with a silver appearance are probably showing symptoms of silver leaf (D).

The many other pests of stonefruit include yellow peach moth (P), oriental fruit moth (P), plague thrips (P), greenhouse thrips (P), fruit-tree borer (P), elephant weevil (P), fruit-tree root weevil (P), European red mite (P), two-spotted mite (P), wingless grasshopper (P), citrus katydid (P) and inland katydid (P).

Note that copper sprays used after the trees come into leaf are likely to cause severe leaf burn and defoliation.

Strawberry

Fragaria × *ananassa*

Strawberries need a sunny position, but in very hot districts a summer fruit crop is very likely to be sunburnt and therefore shade or evaporative cooling in the form of a fine mist of water should be provided.

Fruit rots will be more prevalent in areas of high humidity. The plants should be protected from early spring frosts and hot drying winds.

Strawberries can be grown in a wide range of soil types, but good drainage is essential. High organic matter content and a slightly acid pH are desirable.

Planting in soil that has previously grown capsicums, potatoes or tomatoes increases the chance of problems with verticillium wilt (D).

Sclerotinia rot (D), which is also known as 'sclerotinia crown rot', may be a problem if strawberries follow some other crop that has had this disease.

Replant every two or three years using only runners certified as tested for virus disease. These runners can be purchased at nurseries. Virus diseases such as crinkle-yellow edge are spread by the strawberry aphid (*Chaetosiphon fragaefolii*) and have no cure. They are characterised by symptoms such as stunting, uneven leaflet size, reduced leaf size and small, misshapen fruit.

New runners formed as the plants grow should be removed and destroyed. Allowing them to remain decreases fruit production.

Plant so that the crown rests on the soil. If buried too deeply the crown may rot. A mulch of straw, shredded newspaper or black polythene controls weed growth, keeps berries clean and conserves soil moisture. It may also help to reduce the incidence of grey mould (D).

The beds should be well prepared before planting, especially if polythene mulch is to be used. Make holes with a garden fork down the centre of the plastic. The soil should be moist before plastic is laid, and subsequent watering should be slow, to allow penetration through the holes and to avoid the problem of excessive runoff.

Water supply must be regular for good berry formation.

Avoid overhead watering; or if this cannot be avoided, water at a time of day that allows quick drying of leaves and fruit. Remove weeds so that moist air is not held around the plants.

Poor drainage and overwatering lead to poor root formation and therefore weak plants. Some browning of leaf edges may occur.

The first spring fruit of some varieties has small leafy outgrowths from the seeds on the surface of the fruit. This is a physiological abnormality and usually does not occur in fruit produced later.

The fruit is subject to a number of different rots such as gnomonia fruit rot (D), black spot (D), grey mould (D) and leak. They are generally more serious in warm, humid conditions.

Leaf diseases include leaf spot (D), and leaf blight (D).

Removal of dead and diseased leaves and other plant parts will help to control diseases. Weeds around the strawberry plants may harbour disease and should be removed.

Other possible problems are armillaria root rot (D), root knot nematode (D), slime mould (D), sclerotium stem rot (D) and powdery mildew (D). This disease shows up as purplish blotches on strawberry. The typical white powdery growth may not be seen. The leaves are brittle and curl upwards at the edge.

Serious damage may be caused by the strawberry weevil, the thin strawberry weevil, and the black vine weevil (P). These pests tunnel in the crown and the stems of larger leaves. Roots, leaves, flowers and fruit may be chewed. They are difficult to control.

Other pests of strawberries include: birds, snails and slugs (P), black field crickets (P), cluster caterpillar (P), cutworm (P), corn earth worm (P), lightbrown apple moth (P), white curl grub (P), Rutherglen bug (P), reshouldered leaf beetle (P), two-spotted mite (P) and cyclamen mite (P).

Attack on flowers by thrips (P) such as plague thrips (P) or strawberry thrips may cause uneven pollination and misshapen berries.

Walnut

Juglans regia

Walnut trees may spread 15–18 m when they mature after 20–25 years.

They cannot be grown successfully in a warm coastal district because chilling requirements will not be met. Traditional apple-growing areas are usually suitable. The site must be free from frosts, particularly late spring frosts which can damage or destroy flowers and young shoots.

Soil must not be allowed to dry out while the nuts are maturing, but unless drainage is good, problems may arise with crown rots or root rots such as phytophthora root rot (D). Armillaria root rot (D) is another serious root problem in some areas.

Walnut trees are self-fertile, but because the male and female flowers mature at slightly different times it is necessary to plant more than one variety if the crop is to be maximised. They are wind pollinated, and dry weather during flowering time is necessary for successful nut production.

It would be worthwhile to choose the varieties carefully as each has different characteristics. For example, the variety 'Franquette' apparently shows some resistance to the widespread and serious walnut blight (D) and may also escape damage from spring frosts because it flowers and comes into leaf late. Pests include codling moth (P), walnut blister mite (P), two-spotted mite (P) and vegetable weevil (P). Attacks from animals such as birds and 'possums can be serious.

HOUSEPLANTS

The first step towards a good indoor display involves choosing a suitable and healthy plant at the nursery. If you require a plant for a certain situation, discuss the possibilities with your nurseryman and consult gardening books. Remember that most of the flowering pot plants such as poinsettias and chrysanthemums are not usually suitable for continuous indoor use.

Try to buy from a nursery or shop where the plants are cared for, and avoid plants that have had many leaves removed or stems cut off at soil level. Make plant purchases last in a shopping expedition and take them straight home. Plants left in a hot car for an hour or two may be seriously damaged.

Growing plants indoors will provide many challenges as obviously the plants are far from their natural environment and it is not surprising that many failures occur. The time necessary to care for indoor plants is often underestimated.

Give some thought to the proposition that indoor plants past their prime should be thrown away. Buy new ones instead of spending a lot of time with their care. After all, although an indoor plant costs two or three times as much as a bunch of flowers, it lasts much longer. No one worries about throwing out a bunch of dead flowers. So, why not throw away a dreary, unhealthy indoor plant.

If time available for care of indoor plants is limited, choose some of the tougher types. These include *Aglaonema, Aspidistra, Philodendron, Spathiphyllum* and *Syngonium*, which are all plants that will tolerate dry conditions for a week or two.

Sensible placement will also help in the maintenance of a good display. The plants should be as accessible as possible. You should not need the help of an extension ladder and Samson to get them down to water, prune, or search for pests. Avoid areas where smoke, fumes, dust or fluff from clothes dryers occur.

Hallways are probably the most difficult place for successful plant growth — they tend to be draughty and are often darker than other rooms.

Most houseplant problems arise through lack of light, temperatures that are too high, too low or fluctuating and humidity that is too low, or a combination of these factors. If these points are taken into account, successful indoor plants can be grown.

This pulley system is one way of making plants easily accessible for watering and other maintenance.

Plants which receive inadequate light grow long and spindly like the syngonium on the right.

Light

Light is necessary for normal plant growth and development. The combination of light intensity and duration of exposure is important. Deprived of sufficient light, a plant will grow long and spindly, its leaves will become paler, and brown spots may develop. Growth may cease altogether and the plant may eventually die.

Different plants require different light levels for optimum growth. Flowering plants usually need to be placed on a sunny windowsill, and variegated or coloured-leaf plants generally need to be in a more lighted situation than fully green-leafed plants. Many of these green-leafed plants come from tropical forests where they grow on the forest floor and receive very little light. These can be placed in the interior of the room and will be reasonably successful.

Most plants tolerate light levels higher than their optimum better than lower levels. Plants growing near a definite light source tend to grow towards that light. They should be regularly turned so that their growth will be uniform.

It is rarely possible to make up for generally low light levels by exposing a plant to full sun for part of the day. Sudden exposure to more light than usual may cause leaves to bleach or burn.

Light reaching the inside of a room can be increased by using mirrors or by painting the walls in white or pastel shades. Consider installation of extra lights which can also, of course, enhance the decorative quality of a plant display.

If artificial light is to be used, a combination of cool, white fluorescent and incandescent sources is the best for plant growth. Plants should be about 350 mm away from fluorescent light sources and about twice as far from incandescent sources because the latter give out heat which may adversely affect the plants. There are also special horticultural 'growing' lights available. Consult books on indoor gardening for more details.

Humidity

The atmosphere inside houses is usually fairly dry, especially when airconditioning or heaters are in use. Many of the plants commonly used indoors originate in areas of high humidity. They do not perform well in a dry atmosphere and their leaves may gradually go yellow or brown.

It is possible to make the air around the plants themselves a little moister by spraying the foliage with a fine mist of water, by grouping plants together, or by placing saucers of water underneath or nearby. Do not allow the pots to stand in water; raise them above water level on pebbles.

If a plant is prone to leaf- or flower-spotting diseases such as grey mould (D), a very high humidity will increase the likelihood of damage.

Temperature

Indoor plants in general resent sudden fluctuations in temperature. Try for somewhere between 15°C and 20°C during the day and no colder than 7°C at night. They will probably get too hot if positioned near heaters, or near windows in full afternoon sun; and too cold in unheated rooms or near windows at night in winter.

Watering

As well as a suitable environment, indoor plants also need correct watering and fertilising practices. If you own numerous potted plants it is a good idea to develop a set procedure. This will help avoid watering plants twice in quick succession or overlooking some plants for long periods of time.

Frequency of watering depends on the season, the type of plant, the potting mix, the type of pot and the position in which the plant is growing.

If the plant is in very bright light and warm conditions, it will need more water than it would if kept in darker and cooler conditions. Plants that are in small pots and in need of repotting often require more water than those newly repotted or those with plenty of room for the roots in the pot. There are exceptions to this. For example, some plants evolved in situations where very little soil or other matter surrounded the root system.

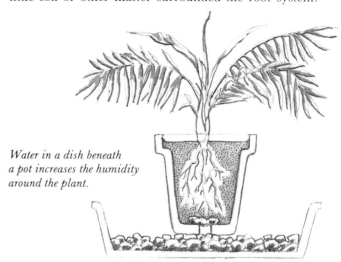

Water in a dish beneath a pot increases the humidity around the plant.

Hoya flowers should not be picked, as flowers are produced on the same small stalk year after year.

The wax plant (*Hoya carnosa*) is one of these. It grows naturally in the forks of trees, with very little covering for the roots and very good drainage. These plants thrive in situations where there is not much room for the root system and must be watered sparingly.

In general, ferns must be watered more frequently than other indoor plants, and fleshy-leaved plants such as succulents should be watered less. Any plant over-watered by mistake should be placed in a bright, airy position for a few days.

Nurserymen use many differing potting mixes. Some of these will need watering more frequently than others, and some are very hard to wet again once they dry out. If this occurs, give the pot a long thorough soaking in water with a few teaspoons of detergent added.

Do not be misled by the colour of the potting mix — some appear very dark even when they are dry. Feel the contents of the pot carefully and water when the layer 10–20 mm below the surface is dry. This will usually be about once a week in summer, but in winter the plants are usually not growing vigorously and the water supply should be less.

The type of pot will also influence the frequency of watering. Evaporation occurs from the sides of terracotta or clay pots, and plants in them are likely to need watering more frequently than plants in plastic pots.

Remember that a pot with wet contents will be heavier than a pot with dry contents. If the pot is tapped, wet potting mix will produce a dull thud.

It is generally a bad practice to water with cold water — tepid water would be more suitable.

Watering from below is a good idea. Stand the pots in a sink, tub or bucket of water, and allow the water to seep up from beneath until the potting mix is fully moistened. Allow them to drain thoroughly before replacing them in their usual positions.

Some indoor plants develop marks on their leaves if watered from above. For example, the African violet develops small yellow rings. Gloxinia and cyclamen may also resent this type of watering.

Never let the plants stand in saucers of water for a long time. The soil or potting mix needs to be moist, but it should not be saturated, because the roots need oxygen for continued health and growth.

Overwatering favours the development of root, crown and lower stem rots, and the leaves will probably darken and collapse.

In general squat pots do not drain as well as taller ones with the same volume, and overwatering is therefore more likely.

Fertilising

Many indoor plants can be satisfactorily maintained for long periods without the use of fertiliser. If, however, an increase in leaf number and size is required, fertiliser is usually necessary.

Delay the first application for two or three weeks after purchase while the plant adapts to its new position.

Never exceed the manufacturer's recommendations. Overfeeding may lead to the production of soft leaves, which are easily damaged and more prone to disease. It may also cause leaf burn (usually around the edges or at the tips), or even plant death. Fertilising when the potting mix is dry may also cause damage.

Overfertilising often results in burnt leaf tips and edges.

After repotting, allow several weeks to elapse before fertilising, and never fertilise in seasons when growth does not occur. Most plants grow very little in cool weather and roots may be damaged by excess fertiliser.

The leaves of plants which are receiving insufficient nutrients may be abnormally pale. Growth will be slow and the lower leaves may die although younger ones are still being formed.

Do not fertilise an unhealthy plant until all other possible reasons for the symptoms have been investigated. Symptoms can have more than one cause, and lack of nutrients is usually the least likely explanation for the poor growth of indoor plants.

Pests such as scales and mealybugs often build up into large populations where leaves sheathe the stem.

Repotting

Repotting is necessary from time to time. If potting into the same-sized container, cut off any old and very thick roots and remove about one-third of the potting mix. Replace this with fresh mix.

If a new container is required, use one only slightly larger than the original.

Water the plant well immediately after repotting, but water sparingly for the following week or two until the roots again grow actively. Do not apply fertilisers during this period.

Pests and diseases

Indoor plants suffer from a restricted range of problems but infestations can be serious. People are often puzzled about how insect pests get to plants indoors. This can happen in a number of ways.

Firstly, ants (P) that have access to plants can carry scales, mites and mealybugs from outdoors. These pests can also be moved on the clothing of gardeners.

Secondly, because many of the insects concerned are very small, they can be brought into the house on the plant at the time of the original purchase and remain undetected for a considerable period. By the time noticeable damage is present, the pest population will have increased markedly.

Thirdly, if moths are able to fly indoors at night they may lay eggs on house plants. These hatch into caterpillars which can cause serious damage before their presence is detected. Even when damage has been noticed the caterpillars themselves are not easy to find. They are often green, feed from the underside of leaves at night, and remain still during the day. They are virtually in-

visible among the stalks and leaves. A sheet of white paper positioned under the leaves should collect the insect's droppings and indicate its exact whereabouts. The green looper (P) is one of these caterpillars.

Mealybugs (P), which are characterised by white cottony areas, are probably the most common and serious problem indoors. On plants with leaves that sheathe the stem, infestations often go unnoticed until the damage is extensive and very difficult to control. Mealybugs infest a wide range of plant species and can walk from plant to plant in a room. They spread quickly if plants are touching one another and they thrive in warm humid conditions. They infest the roots as well as the above-ground parts of the plant.

Two-spotted mite (P) is also troublesome indoors and usually causes leaf yellowing. Misting under the leaves with water may reduce their numbers.

Sticky leaves or furniture indicate insects such as aphids (P), whiteflies (P) or scales. Soft brown scale (P) and hemispherical scale (P) are both common indoors.

Tiny dark-coloured flies flitting around the plants are probably fungus gnats (P).

Wedge-shaped or straight-sided brown patches particularly on ferns, begonias, gloxinias or African violets are likely to be caused by the leaf nematode (D).

If plants are inspected once a week for signs of pest and disease, action can be taken before much damage is done. Regular leaf washing will help to remove insect pests. Use water with a small quantity of detergent and then rinse with clean water; or gloss the leaves with water and white oil.

Prompt removal of dead flowers and leaves will help control diseases such as grey mould (D).

The damage of leaf nematodes often has an angular appearance.

Terrariums

The atmosphere inside a terrarium is ideally suited to the growth of many fungal diseases. It is important to choose only plants that are perfectly healthy for use in such a position.

Remove any brown, spotty or dead leaves. Inspect the plants carefully and do not use plants that have any sign of mealybugs or scales. Remove any caterpillars from the plants.

The potting mix should be suitable for indoor plants, and preferably treated for destruction of pests, disease, and weed seeds. Buy a bag from your local nursery, or treat some in a domestic oven for 30 minutes at 100°C. Wash the glass container thoroughly with hot soapy water and rinse with hot water so that it dries quickly. Place a layer of coarse material, such as gravel, in the bottom. This helps keep plant roots out of any water that drains through the potting mix.

Do not overwater. As long as some water condenses on the sides and top of the container each day, the terrarium does not need water. Overwatering may lead to fungal diseases such as grey mould (D).

The completed terrarium should be well lit but not in direct sun.

If pest and disease problems do occur, it is best to throw away the entire contents of the terrarium and begin another one.

Once established, terrariums need very little care.

African violet

Saintpaulia ionantha

A warm, humid situation is usually considered best for these plants.

Keep the potting mix moist but not wet. If the crown of the plant is too wet, the leafstalks will rot; and where the leaves are splashed with water, small yellow rings or patches develop. Water the pots from below or with a narrow-spouted watering can.

These plants should be kept in fairly bright light but not in the sun. The use of artificial light to extend the hours of exposure is said to markedly increase their flowering performance.

Cyclamen mite (P) and mealybugs (P) may cause serious problems.

Cyclamen

Cyclamen persicum

The corms should be planted in a potting mix with plenty of organic matter so that water can drain freely. Each corm should be placed so that about half of it projects above the soil surface. This, and avoiding too much water, will reduce the likelihood of root, crown and leafstalk rots.

Keep the plants out of strong sun and in hot dry conditions mist the foliage with water. As potplants, they seem to do well if they are kept in very bright light during the day and put into a cool place at night.

The leaves and buds may be attacked by aphids (P) and mealybugs (P), but the most serious pest is the cyclamen mite (P) which is one of the causes of deformed foliage and flowers.

Leaf nematode (D) also attacks cyclamen. Removal of dead and damaged leaves will help in control of grey mould (D) which produces a furry growth on leaves, flowers or stems.

Plants bought in flower for indoor decoration should be discarded when the display is finished. Attempting to make them flower for a second year is probably not worth the effort.

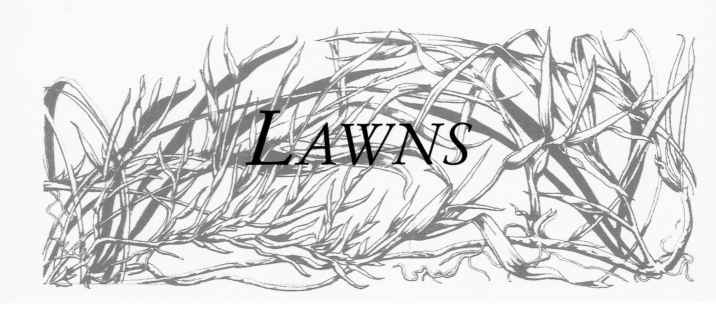

LAWNS

Most lawn problems can be avoided by selecting a grass type suitable for the climate and situation. Buying the cheapest available grass without regard to its suitability will make growing a beautiful lawn very difficult.

Choice of grass

The choice of grasses for lawns is dictated by local climate. There are two distinct groups of grasses: one group does well in cool climates, and the other in hot climates.

COOL-CLIMATE GRASSES	WARM-CLIMATE GRASSES
Fine-textured	
Bent (*Agrostis* sp.) Fescue (*Festuca rubra*) Wintergrass (*Poa annua*)	Couch (*Cynodon* sp.)
Medium-textured	
Rye (*Lolium perenne*) Kentucky blue (*Poa pratensis*)	Queensland blue couch (*Digitaria* sp.) Zoysia (*Zoysia* sp.)
Coarse-textured	
Tall fescue (*Festuca arundinacea*)	Buffalo (*Stenotaphrum* sp.) Durban (*Dactyloctenium australe*) Carpet (*Axonopus* sp.) Kikuyu (*Pennisetum* sp.)

When an area combines the extremes of both cool and warm climates, cool-climate grasses are the best choice if the atmosphere is dry and if plenty of water is available in the hot period. Heat coupled with high humidity is disastrous for cool-climate grasses.

In general, warm-climate grasses do not retain a good green colour in cool winters but some cultivars provide better winter colour than others. The lawn may be oversown with cool-climate grasses to keep it green for longer periods.

Very few grasses are adapted to heavy shade, as most originated in open areas with few trees. Planning a lawn for a heavily shaded area is asking for trouble. Satisfactory lawns can be grown in areas of medium to light shade if the type of grass and its care are correct.

Cool-climate grasses that show good shade tolerance are the fine fescues, bents and rough blue grass (*Poa trivialis*). The latter, a medium-textured grass, is not commonly grown except in the shade. Durban has the best shade tolerance of the warm-climate grasses. Buffalo, Queensland blue couch and zoysia have moderate tolerance. Couch grass has the poorest tolerance of all cultivated lawn grasses.

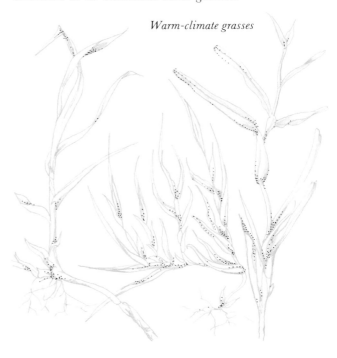

Warm-climate grasses

A good fertilising and watering programme, and frequent *but not low* mowing are essential if lawns in shade are to succeed. Diseases may cause more problems in shady damp areas than out in the sun.

Most grasses grow best in slightly acid soil, but there are exceptions. For example, carpet grass will thrive in very acid conditions.

In alkaline soils most grasses will quickly go yellow (chlorotic) and will need supplementary fertilising with iron sulphate. Buffalo survives better than most grasses in alkaline conditions.

Few grasses tolerate high levels of salt. However, one very salt-tolerant lawn grass has been developed for use in South Australia and Western Australia; this is *Paspalum distichum*. Some zoysias are also very salt tolerant. Buffalo has a fair tolerance of salt.

Mowing

Lawn care should not be equated to the rotary mowing of a green patch as low and as infrequently as possible. Together with excessive wear, this is the most damaging programme possible.

Infrequent lawn mowing is bad for grass. It causes the sward to open out, thus allowing easy weed invasion. The more frequent the cut and the less growth removed per cut the happier the grass will be. Any cutting that removes more than one-third of the leaf canopy at one time will cause damage.

Different grasses should be cut at different heights. Normal domestic lawns of couch or bent should not be cut lower than 15 mm.

Kikuyu should be cut at least weekly in the growing season at a height of 20 mm. If cut more frequently, it will have a finer finish with more leaf and less stalk. If cut higher, it will rapidly become spongy.

Rye grass, Kentucky blue and most coarser warm-season grasses should be cut at 30–40 mm.

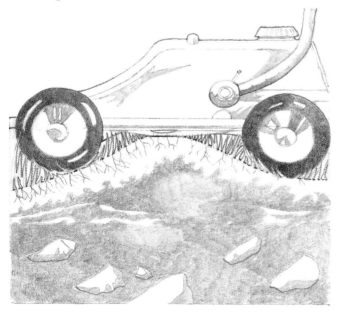

Small high areas in a lawn may be left bare after mowing. This is called 'scalping'.

Cylinder mowers not only give a finer finish but they also damage the grass much less than rotary mowers.

Watering and drainage

Good surface and subsoil drains are essential for top-quality lawns. Grasses do not like very wet or very dry conditions, but excessively wet soils are often the worst.

The more traffic there is on an area, the more critical it becomes to manage the watering well. Generous watering once a week is generally better than a little each day. However, when cool-season grasses are being grown in hot dry climates, a little watering each day may be essential.

A green algal slime may grow on the lawn in poorly drained areas particularly if shade is excessive.

A mechanical spreader helps to distribute fertiliser evenly.

Fertilising

The amount of fertiliser, and the frequency of application, both influence the quality of the lawn. Many people fertilise lawns only once a year but they really need to be fertilised once a month in the growing season. The equivalent of 2 kg of sulphate of ammonia per 100 m² (about 1000 sq. ft) per month is a useful guide for a high-care lawn. An even distribution of fertiliser is important; the grass will 'burn' wherever excessive amounts are applied.

Established lawns need little phosphate in comparison to nitrogen and potash, but when sowing a new lawn high levels of phosphate are required. A heavy dressing of superphosphate at 6 kg/100 m² or a proprietary 'starter' fertiliser is advisable.

Fertilisers are often used to burn out weeds. This is a poor practice, because the excessive salt levels created destroy soil structure and also harm soil microbes and chemical balance.

Pests

Damage from insect pests is normally irregular. Pest problems vary greatly from district to district and what may be a major problem in one area will be a minor problem in others. Most areas will have some form of beetle grub that damages roots. These attacks will vary in severity from season to season and may be severe in older lawns. African black beetle (P) and the many other

Corbie moth (Oncopera intricata) *can be a serious pest in cool temperate areas. Wing span 37 mm.*

cockchafers, such as blackheaded pasture cockchafer (P), all cause very similar damage which is often not evident until heat stress begins and the damaged roots fail to supply enough water to the leaves. These beetles have larvae called white curl grubs (P).

Lawn armyworms (P) and cutworms (P) generally cause trouble only when they reach plague proportions, but in some areas this may be a problem that needs control each year.

Corbies (P) and sod webworms (*Herpetogramma licarsisalis*) are bad pests in some geographic areas and may need to be kept in check on a yearly basis.

The adult of the latter is a moth and the damage is done by the larvae which chew the grass roots.

Argentine stem weevil (P), which is also called ryegrass weevil, should be watched for in bent and ryegrass areas because its damage is severe and sudden and the grass is slow to recover.

Grass-crown mealybug (P) or felted grass coccids cause general unthriftiness in a wide number of lawn species. This occurs mostly in warmer areas.

Grasswebbing mite (P) and other mites are more likely to cause problems in warm dry weather than cool damp weather. Couchgrass mite (P) causes 'witches' broom', a shortening and bunching together of shoots. Tarsonemid mites, which cannot be seen with the unaided eye, build up in numbers on kikuyu during prolonged dry spells and cause thinning of the sward as well as witches' broom.

Couch that fails to grow vigorously may be under attack from couchtip maggot (P).

Grass is usually quick to recover from the damage of most pests once treatment has been carried out. There are very few lawns on which regular preventive treatments are required.

Diseases

Most diseases have a distinctly circular pattern, although kikuyu yellows (D), which is water-borne, has more irregular symptoms.

There are few diseases in Australia which require regular preventive treatment. Some diseases such as fusarium patch (D) have a cold requirement and are a regular feature of winter in southern states. If this disease is severe in your area, a preventive programme may be worthwhile.

Damping-off (D), which kills seedlings during the establishment of seeded lawns, may also require control.

Some diseases, especially rust (D) and red thread (D), can be more readily treated by keeping the grass growing vigorously with a good fertiliser programme than with any other treatment.

Many diseases become a problem because people try to grow unsuitable grasses for the situation. It is often better to change the grass than to treat the disease. Dollar spot (D), leaf spot (D) and brown patch (D) are all normally associated with high humidity. Dollar spot is more common at colder temperatures than either of the other diseases.

The root rot disease, spring dead spot (D), is specific to couch and is especially severe in South African couch (*Cynodon transvaalensis*) and some of the hybrid types derived from it, such as 'Tifdwarf' and 'Santa Ana'.

Ophiobolus patch (D) is more severe on cool-climate grasses in hot areas. The root injury becomes more obvious under hot conditions.

Some non-pathogenic problems can be confused with disease. This is most common with the urinary patches of female dogs which are often quite circular and appear on the lawn suddenly.

Grass will not thrive where there are areas of dry water-repellant soil.

Dry patch (D) is a condition that occurs where the soil repels water. It is a common problem on sandy soils but may also be found on clay. The waterproofing of the soil makes it both difficult to wet and also hard.

In many places salt levels in the water supply are a problem and it is better to use slow-release fertilisers and organic fertilisers, which are naturally slow-release materials, than to use totally soluble fertilisers.

Turf nematodes (D) cause serious damage in a few areas but in general are not a major problem. Slime moulds (D) may occur in warm humid conditions and may kill grass by blocking out the light.

PALMS

In general, palms are slow growers and, unlike other trees, grow only at the top of the stem. This means that those that form a single trunk will die if the growing point is destroyed. Thus, palms cannot be lopped to reduce their height. Less severe damage may slow growth and spoil appearance for many years.

The trunks of palms are tough and not easily damaged but any damage that does occur cannot be repaired by the plant. Trunks do not thicken with age in the way that the trunks of other trees do.

The leaves produced when the plant is young may differ in appearance from those produced when the plant is mature. Some species take many years to reach the stage of maturity.

The number of leaves on most mature palms remains constant—that is, as an old leaf dies a new one unfolds.

It may take years for a leaf to grow to its full size and eventually die. Damaged fronds, therefore, detract from the plant's appearance for a long time. The removal of leaves before they die naturally may adversely affect the health of the plant.

Some palms drop their dead leaves promptly and are often referred to as 'self-cleaning palms'. Other species retain their dead leaves indefinitely.

The root system of a palm is usually less extensive than that of other trees. It causes fewer problems with drains or structures because palm roots do not increase in thickness and only branch to a limited extent. New

Many palms are slow to produce a trunk, and increase in height until a certain stage of maturation has been reached.

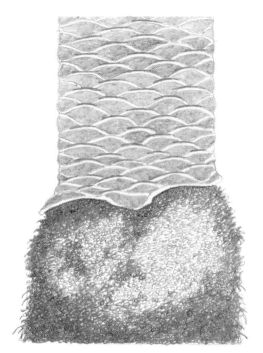

Formation of adventitious roots above ground level is a common sight on Canary Island date palms (Phoenix canariensis).

roots are produced regularly, and on mature plants they may develop above ground. Vigorous potted specimens may be pushed up out of the pot by these roots. The roots should never be allowed to dry out. The watering programme necessary varies from situation to situation but may involve a thorough soaking of the roots twice a week in summer.

In general, palms growing outdoors tolerate over-watering better than underwatering, but good drainage is essential.

Do not allow saucers beneath potted palms to remain full of water. Avoid the use of pots much larger than the root system. The increased available water may lead to root rots, and the increased amounts of nutrients available in the extra soil will encourage rapid growth.

Most palms of rainforest origin require an acid soil, but palms from dryland areas can be cultivated in many different soils. A high level of organic matter will promote healthy growth.

Outdoor palms will receive most benefit from fertiliser if it is applied to the upper layer of the soil. Liquid fertiliser preparations are suitable for potted palms, but remember that frequent application may hasten the day when the specimen is too large for indoor use.

Outdoors many palms need shade and high humidity and protection from wind. The fronds of young palms will go brown if regularly exposed to wind.

Humidity can be increased by hosing the fronds or by misting them with water. If either the soil or the atmosphere is too dry, the leaves are likely to dry out and brown on the tips. Problems with two-spotted mite (P) attack are also more likely under dry conditions. Damaged fronds may appear dull and lifeless or have a faint white or yellowish mottle.

Although large numbers of palm species require a warm moist climate, there are some that grow well in other situations. Jelly palms (*Butia* spp.) and fan palms of the genus *Chamaerops*, for example, will thrive in dry temperate climates and it is even possible to find a few, such as the fan palms of genus *Trachycarpus*, which will withstand severe frosts.

Note that palms available for sale in a district are not always suitable for that district. For example, the Alexandra palm (*Archontophoenix alexandrae*) does not grow well in Adelaide or in Sydney (indoors or outdoors) although offered for sale. It needs a moist, tropical climate for successful growth.

Indoor pots

Careful choice of palms for indoor use is important. Many palms will deteriorate rapidly when taken indoors, and ideally all palms used for indoor decoration should be alternated with a second set kept in a shade house or other suitable outdoor location. Some palms such as the walking-stick palm (*Linospadix monostachya*) need regular periods of time outdoors because the leaves may be seriously damaged by low humidity indoors.

On the other hand, palms such as kentia palm, parlour palm and lady palm can be successfully maintained indoors for long periods of time. Others suitable for indoor use are the pygmy date palm (*Phoenix roebelenii*), the fishtail palm (*Caryota* spp.) and the golden palm (*Chrysalidocarpus lutescens*).

Well-lit and well-ventilated situations are best, but direct sun and draughts are to be avoided. The leaves of palms positioned near heaters and airconditioners usually brown at the tips unless efforts are made to increase the humidity. (See also the notes on humidity in the 'Houseplants' section.)

If possible clean the leaves about once a month. Start with a teaspoon or two of detergent in half a bucket of water and then rinse the leaves with clean water. This treatment not only removes dust but also reduces the likelihood of serious infestations of mealybugs, scales and two-spotted mites.

Pests and diseases

White cottony areas on the fronds may be mealybugs (P) and should be dealt with promptly. They are particularly serious on palms with persistent, long, sheathing leaf bases. Mealybugs can build up into large numbers in these sheltered areas and it is almost impossible to eradicate them.

The bamboo palm (*Chamaedorea erumpens*) is one plant that suffers seriously from mealybug attack.

The fact that the leaves are long-lived enables hard scales (P) such as California red scale (P) and white palm scale (P) to become established. Soft scales (P) such as pink wax scale (P) also attack palms.

Caterpillars of insects such as yellow palmdart, which is found only in the northern areas of Australia, and the orange palmdart (P), which is found further south, chew palm fronds and produce a very tattered look. Search for caterpillars in parts of fronds that are folded over and webbed together.

In northern areas of Australia coconut palms and a few others such as the royal palm are attacked by the palm leaf beetle (*Brontispa longissima*). Very young palms are more seriously damaged than older palms because their leaves open much more slowly. The tightly folded youngest leaves may be so badly damaged that the plant is killed. Leaves that have had their surfaces chewed by the larvae are brown and scorched when they open.

The beetles are about 10 mm long and black with a wide yellowish-brown band near the head. The larvae are white at first but gradually yellow. They have two spines on the end of the body.

Spray with carbaryl (80%) at the rate of 1.25 g per litre of water. Add a few drops of wetting agent. Apply to youngest leaves only. If the leaves are very tightly folded, separate them by gentle bending and twisting. Leaves that are fully open will not be attacked by this pest so should not be sprayed.

Palm leaf beetles chew the leaf tissue in thin lines parallel to the mid-rib.

Bangalow palm
Archontophoenix cunninghamiana

This palm originates in warm areas of high rainfall and moist soils. It should be well watered at all times and protected from sun and wind in the early stages of growth. The leaves will develop brown tips if the atmosphere is dry.

It is less suitable for indoor use than a number of other palms, but is, however, more successful indoors than the Alexandra palm (*A. alexandrae*).

Jelly palm
Butia capitata

The jelly palm will tolerate dry conditions, full sun from an early age and even frost. It can be grown in tubs outdoors and will succeed in seaside gardens. It will not grow well in deep shade and is not a suitable indoor palm.

Kentia palm
Howea forsteriana

Outdoors this palm needs a moist situation. It should be protected from sun when very young but will tolerate full sun and windy conditions at later stages of growth. It will not grow well in the tropics or in hot dry climates. It will tolerate light frosts, and has been grown successfully in seaside gardens.

As indoor specimens kentia palms tolerate lower temperatures, drier air and lower light levels than many other palms. They will perform better, however, if placed in bright light with warmth and a moist atmosphere.

Lady palm
Rhapis spp.

These palms thrive in warm shaded situations with high humidity. They should be well watered. They will tolerate low temperatures and poor light, and can be successfully grown indoors. Pots should be large enough to allow room for the production of new stems.

Indoors, the slender lady palm (*R. humilis*) seems more susceptible to attack from two-spotted mite (P) than does the broad lady palm (*R. excelsa*).

Mediterranean fan palm
Chamaerops humilis

This palm grows in hot dry conditions and tolerates full sun from an early age. It will also survive very cold conditions and is frost and wind tolerant. It can be grown at the seaside.

It is a suitable choice for growing indoors in a very bright position.

Parlour palm
Chamaedorea elegans

Outdoors, the parlour palm needs a warm moist shaded situation. Indoors it should be positioned so that it is never in

the sun. It will tolerate fairly low light levels but low humidity will cause the tips of the leaves to brown.

The summer water supply should be good, but the palm will survive if the soil dries out occasionally.

Queen palm
Syagrus romanzoffianum

Outdoors this palm will thrive in full sun if well watered, although shade during the establishment stages is desirable. It will also tolerate deep shade and cool conditions. It can be successfully grown in seaside gardens.

It is suitable for growth indoors but becomes tall very quickly.

TREES AND SHRUBS

Planting

Container-grown specimens can be planted at any time with success, but autumn and spring are preferred. The soil in autumn is warm enough to enable the roots to make some growth before winter and establish the plant so that in spring it can make early top growth. Planting in spring enables establishment before the heat of summer. Frost-tender plants should be planted in mid- to late-spring when danger of frosts is over.

Deciduous plants such as roses and stonefruit are frequently offered for sale in winter when they are dormant. The roots may be free of soil and wrapped in a material such as damp straw or have the attached soil wrapped in hessian or sacking. The latter is often termed 'balled' or 'burlapped'.

Plastic pots, plastic bags, and plastic or metal tubes as well as geotextile root control bags must be completely removed before planting. Sacking may be left in place but it must be loosened and pulled away from the stem. All ties must be removed.

The soil or mix around the roots should be moist at planting time so that it clings more firmly to the roots. Plant the whole soil ball with minimum disturbance unless the roots are very matted. In this case it may be desirable to make several vertical cuts around the outside of the root ball or gently roughen the outside of the root ball. Remove any extensive mat of roots from the bottom.

Do not allow the roots to dry out at any time. Any roots that have begun to grow in a circle around the pot should be untangled and directed downwards. Prune off damaged roots. A recently purchased badly root-bound plant should be returned to the seller and a replacement requested. The growth of such a plant will be slow and it will never look really healthy. Do not plant potbound plants.

The size of the prepared planting hole depends on the size of the plant but should be as deep as and at least 500 mm wide for a plant in a container 250 mm in diameter. The wider the better. This should allow room for trial positioning and for root spread if necessary.

If this depth of topsoil is not available, do not dig down into clay subsoil to form a hole as this will hold water around the roots in wet weather. In this case some extra topsoil should be provided on top of that already present and the hole dug in this, without disturbing the underlying clay. Otherwise, plant smaller plants. The plant roots are able to penetrate subsoils when they reach them later.

Do not allow the root system to come into direct contact with freshly applied fertiliser.

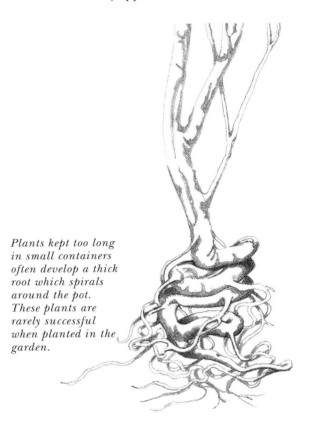

Plants kept too long in small containers often develop a thick root which spirals around the pot. These plants are rarely successful when planted in the garden.

If the plant is grafted, do not bury the graft union. The final soil level should be the same as it was when the plant was growing in the nursery.

It has long been the practice to add soil amendments such as sand and peat to the soil from the planting hole before replacing it around the plant. There is now doubt about the value of this practice. Some experiments have shown that this encourages prolific root growth in the hole but that the roots do not grow beyond it into the surrounding soil. More study of this problem is needed before definitive statements can be made. It is probably wise, however, to avoid creating a mixture which is very different from the soil in the general area.

During the establishment period, keep the area immediately beyond the 'hole' moist as well as the area within the 'hole'.

In areas where a regular water supply will not reach the plant, the use of a high proportion of peat is undesirable. Peat, once dry, is very hard to re-wet. This may add to the problems of a water-stressed plant.

After the hole is filled in, press the soil down around the plant firmly with a foot, and water thoroughly so that pockets of air are removed. Stamping and jumping around the plant may damage the root/stem junction.

Guard stakes can prevent damage from lawnmowers.

Staking

If the plant needs support — as it may if it has a very thin stem topped by a lot of foliage — drive the stakes in carefully, avoiding the root ball, before the hole is refilled. Use at least two stakes. Do not stake conifers.

If the wind generally comes from the same direction, position the stakes so that the wind blows the tree away from the stakes. Tie high enough to stabilise the root ball in the soil and prevent excessive movement but low enough to allow some trunk movement. This allows the trunk to strengthen gradually. Bark injuries sustained when trees bang into or rub against a stake are possible attack sites for pests or diseases. Ties should be soft, and checked on a regular basis. Trunk or branches can be constricted if they grow too big to fit within the tie. The same applies to strings or wires attaching labels.

Spacing

Trees and shrubs intended to be a permanent part of the garden should be given enough space to reach their full size without restriction from buildings, powerlines, sewers and other plants.

The comparative bareness of the garden in early stages can be relieved by the growth of annuals or soft-wooded perennials.

Sometimes fast-growers, such as most wattles, are planted with more slow-growing but long-living plants, such as conifers. As the conifers get bigger, some of the wattles are removed. Do not allow the trees or shrubs to grow into one another because leaves within the foliage of another shrub are heavily shaded and often die.

Pruning

Pruning should not be considered a routine annual event for every garden plant. Many plants perform very well without pruning, and some others can be damaged by it. Sometimes it has a result opposite to the one intended. For example, pruning a tree such as a jacaranda or a brush box often encourages a number of shoots to grow from near the cut end of the branch. These vigorous shoots grow straight upwards, thus completely spoiling the tree shape and increasing the height of the tree, whereas the original intention was probably to reduce the height of the tree.

If the intention is to train the tree to avoid obstructing a driveway, the position of the cut must be carefully considered and the resultant growth monitored.

Plain green shoots should be pruned off a variegated plant, and suckers growing from an understock should be removed.

Pruning procedures may vary from area to area. For example, in places with a hot dry summer, trees are often pruned so that leaves are in the correct position to shade the trunk and branches. This prevents sunburn which may lead to wood rots (D).

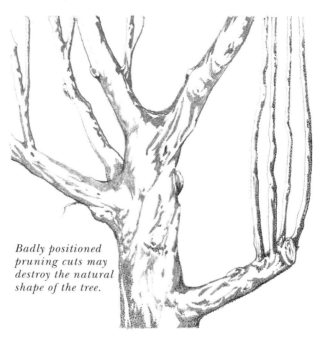

Badly positioned pruning cuts may destroy the natural shape of the tree.

Pruning cuts

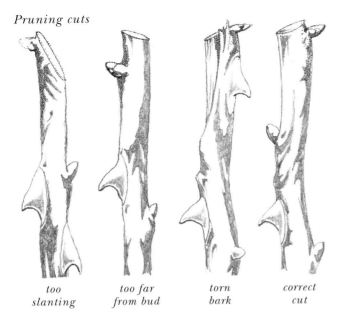

| *too slanting* | *too far from bud* | *torn bark* | *correct cut* |

Never break branches or flowers off a tree or shrub. Always use sharp secateurs. Jagged edges or torn bark are excellent places for the development of fungal diseases or the laying of insect eggs.

The shoots that grow from buds grow in the direction in which the bud is pointing. Always prune so that the last bud on a branch will produce a new shoot growing up, out and away from the centre of the tree or shrub. Cut so that there is a bud or node near the end of the branch or twig. If the last bud is far from the cut, the end of the twig will die. Fungal diseases may begin in such a dead area.

Trees and shrubs that should be pruned are pruned for a number of different reasons. In early years this may be to improve their shape. This should be done to enhance the natural shape, not to change it markedly.

Pruning a tree or shrub to make it fit into a space too small for it is rarely successful; and considering the variety of shapes and sizes available, it seems particularly foolish to try forcing a plant into an unsuitable place. Topiary, espalier and bonsai are exceptions to these remarks. Plants thus treated require fairly constant care and attention and are trained to grow in these ways from the beginning.

Very careful and considered pruning is needed for the formation of an espalier — a tree or shrub trained into a flat shape rather than letting it grow into its own natural more bushy rounded form. Espaliers are often trained against a wall in a cold climate because the wall stores heat during the day and keeps the plant warm at night. This heat also promotes early flowering and fruit maturity — a factor that may help avoid pest and disease problems in some seasons.

There are detailed instructions available to explain the formation of espaliers. They may be formal or informal but both require considerable and constant attention. Trees and shrubs that flower on spurs such as apples, flowering quince (Chaenomeles), cotoneaster and pyracantha lend themselves most to formal espalier, for example where the branches are trained to grow horizontally from the trunk in opposing pairs. The branches can be trained gradually along parallel wires which support them. The wires should be 20 cm from the wall to allow for some air circulation and decrease the possibility of fungal diseases.

Where birds are a garden problem, fruit trees trained flat are much easier to protect with bird netting.

Many trees grow naturally with one main stem or 'leader'. If this leader is damaged, the branches on each side of it at the top will become dominant and begin strong growth. Gradually that tree will develop with growth in two halves and with a shape nothing like the natural one.

Prune off rival leaders. Allowing more than one leader to develop will produce a weak junction between them, and part of the tree may blow off in a storm. It is also an excellent site for rots and insect damage.

Pruning may be carried out so that flower and fruit production can be increased. Trees grown mainly for fruit need special attention if crops are to be maximised. Detailed instructions are usually available from local Departments of Agriculture.

Ornamental trees usually flower adequately without pruning and in any case are often too tall for this to be carried out in a home garden.

Consult gardening books to find out whether or not each of your shrubs should be pruned to improve flowering. It is necessary to know the type or age of the stems on which the flowers are borne. If a shrub fails to flower this may be because badly timed pruning has removed all the flowering wood.

Shrubs and trees that flower in summer and autumn produce flowers on new or current season's wood and should generally be pruned in winter. In spring new shoots are produced, and these grow and become mature enough to bear flowers in summer and autumn. The crepe myrtle (*Lagerstroemia* sp.) is one of these.

Topiary

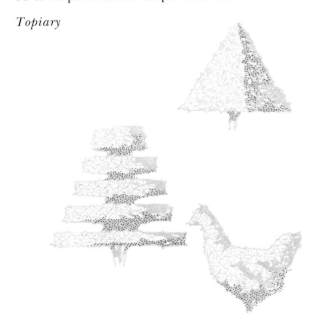

Some plants, such as box or yew, can be cut into fancy shapes.

Other trees and shrubs, such as the spring-flowering peach, produce flowers in spring on wood that is one year old. This is called 'the previous season's wood'. These plants should be pruned during or immediately after flowering. After pruning they produce new shoots which grow into branches through the rest of spring and summer and gradually mature through autumn/winter and flower in spring.

Still other plants flower on older wood and are infrequently pruned.

If shrubs are to be pruned to keep them bushy, this procedure should be started as soon as they are established, and continued on a regular basis.

Pruning should be carried out to remove dead branches or twigs. These areas are often infected with fungi and constitute a source of reinfection for the actively growing parts of the tree. In some cases dead and dying flowers are sources of fungal infection. Their removal may decrease fungal problems and should also encourage the development of more buds.

Branches growing inwards and crossing over other branches or rubbing against other branches should be removed. They spoil the shape of the tree and ultimately provide sites for insects to lay eggs.

Any shrub that is vulnerable to leaf diseases which are aggravated by humid conditions should probably have the centre branches thinned out so that improved air circulation will decrease humidity.

Fertiliser should be applied below the outer edge of the foliage in slanting holes made with a crowbar. The total quantity of fertiliser required should be divided evenly between the holes.

Fertilising

Many trees will grow reasonably well without added fertiliser and most problems arise from other factors such as drought and compaction. However, maintained tree health and vigour will lower pest and disease problems.

In nature, fallen leaves eventually decay and return some nutrients to the soil for re-use by the tree. If you do rake up fallen leaves, do not burn them, it adds to air pollution and destroys possible nutrients. Instead, make a compost or mulch for flower beds, shrubs and trees.

Often inorganic fertiliser is necessary as well as organic soil mulches. Have the soil pH level checked as this could be the reason for nutrient problems. A light dose in early summer and in mid-to-late summer will enable the tree to use the extra nutrients while actively growing.

Placement is important. Most active roots — ones that will absorb nutrients — are very close to the surface and from just inside the outer edge of the canopy 'drip-zone' to many metres beyond. In cultivated soil, fertiliser can be spread evenly around this area and lightly forked in.

If the tree is growing in a lawn there are two methods of fertilising it. The first is the easiest and probably the most efficient. Complete fertiliser or blood and bone should be broadcast over the entire area in which the tree is growing. The lawn will also benefit from some fertiliser. If you usually fertilise the lawn each year then you will not need to provide more for the tree.

The second method involves making a series of slanting holes into the soil. These should be in circles around the tree at 1 m spacings; that is, 1 m between rows and 1 m between holes in the rows. Start the holes a metre or so inside the canopy and keep going to several metres beyond the dripzone. The holes should be 100-150 mm deep. Into each hole carefully pour no more than 20 g (half a matchbox full) of fertiliser. All fertiliser applications should be watered in.

Areas where branches rub against one another are likely sites for insect infestation.

Weeding

Do not allow lawn grasses or weeds to grow close to the trunk of a small tree. Hand weeding and mulching are the safest ways to keep the area clean.

Herbicides may be used but it is better to use granules or a 'wipe-on' application than to spray. Sprays are harder to keep off the easily damaged green bark. Herbicides such as glyphosate (Roundup® or Zero®) which has little soil residue should be used in preference to other types.

Environmental problems

Browning or death of the leaf tip and leaf edge may be caused by a number of factors including hot dry winds. These remove water from the leaves faster than it can be replaced by the roots. Trees, as well as shrubs, should be watered in hot dry weather. If the leaves of a tree or shrub brown every year, it may be that the particular type of plant is unsuited to that position in the garden or to the overall climate.

Air pollution badly affects some trees and shrubs. Edge-browning of leaves is one symptom but there are others. Damage depends on local weather conditions as well as on the exact nature of the pollutant. This problem is more likely in inner city areas, near busy roads or parking lots, and in or near industrial suburbs.

Excessive applications of fertiliser or high levels of salt in soil, water or air can also cause leaf scorch. This may be referred to as salt toxicity. In areas where salt is a problem, choice of plants that will tolerate such conditions as well as suitable management of watering are vitally important. (See the notes on watering in the section 'Planning and Maintaining Your Garden'.)

Apart from stripping leaves from trees and shrubs, hail can also bruise or split branches so that attack from insects such as longicorns (P), moth borers (oecophorid) (P), and moth borers (cossid) (P) is more likely. Hail may also predispose leaves to diseases. For example, a disease of *Pinus radiata*, called shoot blight (D), commonly occurs after a hailstorm.

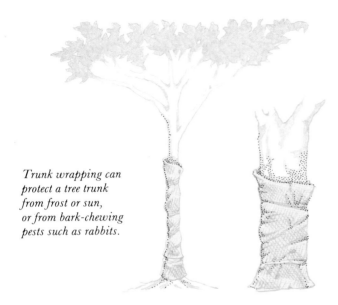

Trunk wrapping can protect a tree trunk from frost or sun, or from bark-chewing pests such as rabbits.

Damage such as this may result from lightning strike.

Lightning can cause serious tree damage. Sometimes this is a spectacular splintering of wood or a dead strip of bark right down the trunk, but sometimes the damage is internal and the tree later mysteriously dies. Damaged branches that endanger life and property must be removed immediately; but otherwise, delay repairs for some months until it is clear that the tree will recover.

Splits running up and down the trunk of a tree may be the result of rapid growth. The internal tissues seem to grow faster than the bark which splits open under the strain. This problem is common on smooth-barked eucalypts, particularly if a period of dry weather is followed by good rains.

In areas with cold winters, similar splits can be caused by low temperatures, and patches of damaged bark may result from rapid changes in temperature. These changes may occur on bark that has been warmed by the sun during the afternoon and is then subjected to sudden cooling when night falls.

In hotter weather the sun can burn young trunks. It may be wise to position a wide stake so that the trunk is shaded during the afternoon, to paint the trunk white or wrap the trunk loosely with materials such as hessian or Sisalation. Trunk-wrapping will also discourage rabbits and other animals, as well as providing protection in times of low temperature if necessary.

Sun injury also occurs on older trees particularly if, for some reason such as the removal of another nearby tree or shrub, the trunk and branches suddenly receive more sun than they are accustomed to. Wood rots (D) are likely in these circumstances.

Pests and diseases

Trees and shrubs are subject to many pests and diseases. Buds and new shoots may be attacked by aphids (P), and whiteflies (P) may suck sap from leaves.

Flowers can be damaged by insects such as thrips (P) and nectar scarabs (P). Flattened stems with tiny leaves are characteristic of a condition called fasciation (D).

Leaf chewers include Fuller's rose weevil (P), metallic flea beetles (P), redshouldered leaf beetles (P) and various caterpillars. Case moth (P) larvae chew the leaves of plants from the protection of a sack-like structure covered with twigs or leaf pieces.

Fruit on ornamental trees and shrubs such as flowering quince (*Chaenomeles* spp.) and crabapple (*Malus* spp.) can be attacked by fruit flies (P) and constitute a source of infection for fruit trees.

Grey, meandering lines or bubbles on the leaf surface are probably the damage of leafminers (P).

Silver or silver-grey leaves may indicate silver leaf (D); greyish or dirty-looking leaves have probably been attacked by thrips (P); and yellowish leaves by mites (P) such as two-spotted mite (P). More distinct yellow patterns may appear if the plant is not receiving an adequate nutrient supply.

Yellowing and browning of leaves may indicate damage to the root system or to a branch. Remember that the leaves of evergreen trees and shrubs do not last forever but yellow and fall after a certain time. These leaves are usually scattered over the plant, not grouped together in the one place.

Various soft scales (P) and hard scales (P) can attack leaves and stems. One such hard scale is the apple mussel scale (*Lepidosaphes ulmi*) which can infest a wide range of ornamentals as well as apples and pears. These include ash, cotoneaster, elm, lilac, maple, poplar and viburnum. The scale tends to build into large numbers on one or two branches, and these may be killed. The adult females are about 3 mm long, brown, slightly curved, and wider at one end than the other. The name describes this 'mussel' shape.

There are many different species of mistletoe that parasitise ornamental and forest trees.

The parasitic plants mistletoe (D) and dodder (D) should be removed as soon as they are observed. Mistletoe can kill trees; and the thin winding stems of dodder, which may be found on shrubs and smaller plants, are also parasitic.

The trunks and branches of trees and shrubs can be attacked by fruit-tree moth borer (P) and termites (P), as well as by wood-rotting fungi of various types. The latter are all discussed together as wood rots (D). Lichens (D) grow on the bark but do not harm the tree.

Lichen does not usually cause tree damage.

Root systems may be damaged by armillaria root rot (D), phytophthora root rot (D), nematodes such as root knot nematode (D), and weevils such as black vine weevil (P) and fruit-tree root weevil (P). A lump near ground level may be crown gall (D). This should not be confused with the lignotuber that occurs on plants such as some species of eucalypts.

Trees growing in lawns are commonly attacked by longicorns (P). Adult beetles lay eggs in the bark in cracks such as those caused by lawnmowers. It is better to mulch the area directly around the trunk, but if grass must be grown there, it should be clipped by hand. Herbicides used to control weeds in lawns may damage and even kill trees of all sizes. Check the label and take particular care if using any preparation containing the chemical 'dicamba'.

If the leaves die and continue to hang on the tree then a toxic substance in the soil is a likely cause. Death from lightning strike may also produce this effect.

Young bark may be chewed by rabbits or other larger animals such as kangaroos, wallabies and deer. Possums often chew young shoots, flowers, and fruit. Birds may cause similar problems. Fruit bats (P) are serious fruit attackers in some areas.

Snails (P) may also feed on the leaves of young shrubs and small trees.

Care of established trees

People neglect and damage established trees because the trees seem sturdy and because they seem always to have been there. Trees need care just as much as other garden plants and are worth caring for, not only because of their shade and beauty, but because the cost of removal and repair is high.

Climbers such as wisteria may also cause problems by growing around the trunk or branches. The tree keeps growing and is constricted by the loop of climber, which remains the same size. Climbers also compete for light, water and nutrients and may hide problems such as borer damage and decay. The additional weight may break branches.

Attached structures such as swings and letterboxes damage a tree and may lead to infestation of borers such as longicorns (P). If you must use trees in this way, watch for the first signs of damage and repair it promptly. Water and fertilise the tree regularly.

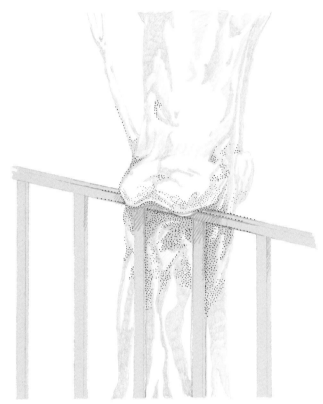

Areas where the bark has grown around obstructions such as this are likely sites for the start of insect damage.

Trees that have grown up in a certain environment usually resent disturbance of the root system. This commonly occurs when new buildings are being erected in an area. The root system which extends further than the foliage spreads, has developed over the years in harmony with its environment, the soil. That is, it is adapted to the aeration, water supply and drainage in a certain area.

The installation of swimming pools or large areas of paving may remove parts of the root system. New areas of paving stop rain falling on the soil where tree roots may previously have used the water; and may also divert the water collected on the surface to another tree unused to that amount.

Building up soil around a tree to form a rockery or garden bed usually means that the water supply to the roots is increased and that the air supply is decreased.

The general changes of soil level and the compaction of soil by heavy machinery (common during building) both decrease the air supply to the roots. Trees thus disturbed often die, although it may take five or more years for them to do so.

If established trees are to be retained on a building site, barriers must be erected so that construction machinery cannot bump into trunk or branches, or compact the soil. Enclose an area at least 1 m beyond the edge of the foliage with the trunk in the centre.

If grades are to be changed or drains installed near a tree seek advice from well-qualified arborists or other persons skilled in tree care. The construction of a simple brick 'wishing-well' around the base of a tree will only prolong its life, not save it. Rescue operations can be complicated and expensive. It can be argued that all trees that would be affected by alterations to grades or drains should be removed, and that a replanting programme should take place after the changes have been made. There are quick-growing trees available, and these would grow up adapted to the new environment and be more successful in the long run.

Note that many local councils enforce tree preservation orders, which may prohibit the heaping up of soil around the base of an established tree and the growing of vines on it, as well as prohibiting tree removal or lopping without permission.

Bonsai
This art involves dwarfing a tree, shrub or climber by judicious root pruning and training of the above-ground parts of the plant.

Appropriate cultural practices and prompt attention to pest and disease problems are essential because every leaf and stem is important in the design.

Plants treated in this way are not intended for continuous indoor display and are best kept outdoors in a sheltered position.

They dry out quickly because there is little soil to retain moisture, and regular attention to watering is of the utmost importance.

Misting the leaves with water in hot, dry weather will help avoid leaf browning.

Bonsai may suffer from the same pests and diseases as their large, naturally growing counterparts.

Bonsai specimens should not be kept indoors permanently. Pests and diseases should be controlled promptly.

NATIVE PLANTS OF AUSTRALIA AND NEW ZEALAND

In Australia there is a widespread notion that there is something mysterious and particularly difficult about growing Australian native plants. A similar phenomenon occurs in New Zealand.

It is thought that these plants should not be pruned and that fertiliser is unnecessary or harmful. There are some species which are difficult but the majority of Australian native plants and New Zealand native plants benefit from pruning and fertilising. As with any other plant, care should be taken to select species suitable for the site.

Banksia, boronia, bottlebrush, eucalypt and grevillea are all-Australian groups. Kaka beak is from New Zealand only and some of the most commonly grown cabbage tree, kowhai, lacebark, olearia and pittosporum species are also from New Zealand.

Climate

Australia is a large continent with different climates in different areas. A plant that has evolved in one part of Australia is not necessarily suitable for growth in another. For example, plants native to Perth are used to a dry summer and may be difficult to grow in Sydney with its wet summer. Sydney is also generally 'wetter' than Perth. It has half as much rain again per year and a higher humidity.

In New Zealand the most important factor is probably the low winter temperatures which occur in many areas. Plants which have evolved in more temperate North Island areas may not survive being frozen in the south.

Choose a plant suitable for your area by consulting a reference book (see Bibliography) or discuss your choice with your local nurseryman.

Drainage

Plants are more likely to survive very cold temperatures if they are in a well-drained soil. Poorly drained soils are relatively common in New Zealand.

Australian plants too need good drainage to grow well, and many will die unless it is provided. This can often be achieved by planting into raised beds.

If drainage cannot be improved, the range of plants likely to be successful is considerably reduced. Root rots, such as phytophthora root rot (D), are a serious problem under wet conditions.

Soil

It seems that Australian natives in general grow best in an acid soil. Most Australian plants *are* acid, so unless lime has been recently added, any well-drained garden soil should be suitable for most species.

Do not plant natives near new concrete paths. Do not add lime, dolomite or ashes unless you are sure the species requires an alkaline soil.

Fertiliser

Native plants from both countries respond well if provided with additional nutrients. Fertiliser should be applied when new growth is being made. The application of two or three small doses, say three weeks apart, is preferable to one large dose.

Water the garden before and after it is spread. Watch the plant response on each occasion, and remember that overfertilising can easily kill a plant, whereas underfertilising simply means it grows more slowly.

Australian soils are commonly low in phosphorus, and native plants are adapted to this. Unless you have positive advice to the contrary for a particular species, choose a mixed fertiliser which has a balance of nitrogen/phosphorus/potassium close to 10:4:6. Do not use superphosphate.

Members of the family Proteaceae (e.g. grevillea, banksia and isopogon-drumsticks) seem particularly sensitive to an overdose of phosphorus.

Pests and diseases

Native trees and shrubs often seem to be attacked by pests and diseases more than exotics. This is because native insects have evolved to feed on native trees and shrubs, and most of the natural pests and diseases of exotics are back in their homeland.

Many Australian native plants are short-lived. When they have reached their full stature and are no longer actively growing, they are more prone to attack from pests and diseases.

Repair the damage of insects and wind promptly so that other pests do not find easy access. Plan replacement plants.

The trees and shrubs discussed in more detail below have been chosen on the basis that they are commonly grown or that they suffer from specific pests or diseases. (Fruit² and nut-bearing plants are listed in the section commencing on page 65.)

Athel tree

Tamarix aphylla

This tree will grow in a variety of harsh conditions. It tolerates hot, dry conditions, moderately saline soils, severe pruning and salt-laden winds, but it should be protected from frost while young. It has a very deep and spreading root system.

Severely stressed specimens are likely to die back. The large auger beetle (P) attacks dead and dying trees.

Azalea

Rhododendron spp.

Azaleas and rhododendrons generally grow best in semi-shade or in a situation where they receive morning sun but are protected from the heat of the afternoon sun and hot winds. Some varieties can be successfully grown in full sun if the soil is kept moist.

The soil should be well drained and friable with plenty of organic matter. It should be moderately acid and generally this means that lime should not be applied. Problems may arise if concrete pots are used or if azaleas are planted where mortar from new brick work has fallen on garden areas.

The root system develops close to the soil surface and should be kept cool, moist and undisturbed. A mulch is desirable to decrease temperature and moisture fluctuations, and to discourage weed growth in the area.

Azaleas suffer from a number of pests and diseases which can be controlled only if spray programmes are carried out. Damaged leaves remain on the plant looking ugly for quite a long time.

The many cultivars have various different features. For example, 'Schryderi' and 'Mauve Schryderi' both have sticky foliage.

Brown spots or patches on leaves may be a fungal leaf spot or may be caused by azalea leafminer (P). White circular areas may be powdery mildew (D).

Fine white, yellow or grey mottling may be caused by azalea lace bug (P); greenhouse thrips (P); whiteflies (P) or by two-spotted mite (P).

Thick, fleshy leaves are characteristic of a disease called leaf gall (D) which is more likely to occur on some cultivars than others.

Rotted petals may be the result of petal blight (D) or of grey mould (D).

Scattered yellow leaves are probably those that have finished their useful life, but a more general yellowing, particularly of young leaves, is likely to be chlorosis (D). If the yellowing occurs on one branch first and is associated with leaf drop and dieback, it may be phytophthora root rot (D).

The azaleas 'Pink Dream' and 'Dr Arnold' seem particularly prone to attack from leaf-chewing caterpillars.

Rhododendrons do not suffer from these pests and diseases as often as azaleas. The most likely problems are petal blight, leaf spot, azalea lace bug and two-spotted mite. They may also become sunburnt if exposed to too much sun and not adequately watered.

The one spray programme should control two-spotted mite, greenhouse thrips, lace bug and whitefly.

Banksia

Banksia spp.

Most banksias need a sunny position and grow best in slightly acid, sandy or gravelly soils which provide excellent drainage. They should, however, be watered in dry weather for best performance.

A few species tolerate or prefer different conditions. For example, the swamp banksia (*B. robur*) needs a moister soil for optimum performance.

Mature specimens of old man banksia (*B. serrata*) are particularly prone to attack by longicorn (P) larvae.

Banksia leaves may be chewed by the larvae of moths such as the banksia moth, the grevillea looper (P) and the doubleheaded hawk moth (P); and webbed together by the macadamia twiggirdler (P).

The larvae of moth borers (oecophorid) (P) such as fruit-tree borer (P) attack the bark, and some of the others bore in the flower spikes or the cones.

Banksias may yellow and die because of phytophthora root rot (D). Experiments at the Victorian Plant Research Institute, Burnley, have shown that some species are more resistant than others to this disease. Two that showed strong resistance were *B. caleyi* and *B. collina*, the hill banksia. Less resistance was shown by *B. media*; *B. marginata*, the silver banksia; and *B. grandis*, the bull banksia. Susceptible species included *B. lehmanniana*, *B. coccinea* and *B. brownii*.

Barberry

Berberis spp.

These shrubs are best suited to cool and temperate districts. They should be grown in full sun and watered in dry weather.

White wax scale (P) and pink wax scale (P) are the only common problems. Look for these on the stems and along the midribs of the leaves.

Bay tree

Laurus nobilis

A temperate to warm climate is the most suitable for the bay tree. It needs a position in full sun and a good water supply in hot weather. The soil or potting mix should be well drained. When the plant is established, many leaves may be removed without harm to the plant.

Waxy lumps on the stems may be white wax scale (P), and on leaves and stems pink wax scale (P).

Beech

Fagus sylvatica

This tree is not suitable for tropical or subtropical climates and in warm temperate areas only at high altitudes. Provide a deep soil with a high proportion of organic matter and good drainage.

Oak leafminer (P) is sometimes a pest of the beech and causes brown blisters on the leaves.

Boronia

Boronia spp.

These shrubs are not suitable for tropical or highland areas. Most need a light well-drained soil, and if this is not provided they may succumb to root rots such as phytophthora root rot (D). The roots, however, should not be allowed to dry out or get very hot. Mulching will help to protect the root system, but remember that organic material placed close to the stem will hold moisture and collar rot may result. Protection from hot drying winds is necessary.

Bottlebrush

Callistemon spp.

Most of these shrubs are native to areas of damp soils. They will tolerate light frosts once established and can be grown in a wide range of climates. A position in full sun is necessary for maximum flower production.

The larvae of callistemon sawfly (P) can cause serious foliage damage. Swellings on the stems are probably wasp galls (P). Wilting and death of young shoots may be caused by the feeding of an insect

which can be referred to as callistemon tip bug.

Leaves with edges curled under have probably been attacked by thrips (P).

Moth borers (oecophorid) (P) also attack these plants.

Small purplish spots on the leaves are probably fungal leaf spots. These do not usually cause serious damage.

Box

Buxus spp.

These shrubs and small trees grow best in cool to temperate areas although they will tolerate high temperatures. They have few pest and disease problems.

If leaves yellow and twigs die back, check for a hard scale (P) such as purple scale, and apply a recommended control.

Brush box

Lophostemon confertus

This tree survives almost any condition once it is established. It will look its best if grown in a warm situation on fertile soil with good drainage and a regular summer water supply. Protect from frost until established. It will survive occasional inundation.

These trees have few problems. A white powdery substance on new leaves may indicate psyllids (free-living) (P), and large yellowish spots are probably a fungal leaf spot (D). Galls on buds or leaves are probably wasp galls (P).

The leaves may be chewed by larvae of cup moths (P), case moths (P), white stemmed gum moth (P), gumleaf skeletonizer moth (P) and leafblister sawflies (P).

Cabbage tree

Cordyline australis

This plant tolerates wind, and drought or wet soil. Almost any soil is suitable.

The larvae of the cabbage tree moth (*Epiphryne verriculata*) feed at the centre of the plant and damage young leaves. Inspect this area regularly and remove the caterpillars. Dead leaves on which the moths themselves rest undetected should be cut off and burned.

The leaves may be attacked by a variety of different scales (P).

Camellia

Camellia spp.

These plants grow well in a wide range of situations but they are not suitable for tropical climates. Many camellias are unsuitable for seaside planting, and in hot dry areas they must be given a protected shady position.

Sasanquas will grow well in full sun (or shade) if the climate is temperate, but Reticulatas and Japonicas may be damaged unless they are shaded for at least half of the day in summer.

Sunburn shows up as brown patches on the leaves. These damaged areas are often colonised by the fungus *Pestalotiopsis* (D). The sun may also damage buds or flowers in the morning if they are wet with frost or dew.

Camellias will grow in a range of soils but perform best in slightly acid soils high in organic matter. They must not be planted too deeply. The drainage must be good but the shallow roots should not be allowed to dry out completely in summer. *Camellia japonica* may suffer from phytophthora root rot (D) in poorly drained soils, but *C. sasanqua* is rarely affected. This is the reason that most

nurseries sell *C. japonica* plants which are grafted on to *C. sasanqua* roots.

Problems such as bud drop or flowers failing to open may be environmental problems. The plant may have produced too many flowers or been damaged by the sun, overwatering, underwatering, poor drainage or lack of nutrients. The camellia bud mite (*Cosetacus camelliae*) may also cause premature bud drop.

Dark-grey rough corky areas on the leaves are probably oedema (D).

The camellia rust mite (*Acaphylla steinwedeni*) may cause discoloration of leaves, and the ribbed tea mite (*Calacarus carinatus*) may cause badly infected leaves to take on a bronze colour and dusty appearance.

Dead shoots with a curled tip are characteristic of dieback (D), and thick white or pink leaves are probably leaf gall (D) symptoms.

Pieces of regular shape removed from leaf edges indicate the presence of leafcutting bees (P). More irregular edge-chewing may be the work of Fuller's rose weevil (P). Aphids (P) and thrips (P) may attack camellia foliage. Mealybugs (P) are sometimes found in the junctions of leaves and stems, and broad mite (P) may distort new growth. A number of scale insects attack camellias including purple scale, fiorinia scale, greedy scale, soft brown scale (P) and hydrangea scale (P).

Faint green rings on the leaves are ringspot (D); and small yellow marks, irregular in size and occurrence, characterise infectious variegation (D).

Leaves mottled with fine yellow flecks have probably been attacked by two-spotted mite (P).

Cassia
Cassia and Senna spp.

Shrubs such as *Senna artemisioides* and *S.glutinosa* will not succeed unless grown with very good drainage in coarse soils. They tolerate moderately low temperatures and are not well suited to the heavy rainfall and high humidity of the tropics.

Trees and shrubs such as *Cassia fistula*, *S.bicapsularis* and *S.didymobotrya* are best suited to tropical or warm temperate climates. Flattened and curled stems with tiny stunted leaves indicate a condition called fasciation (D).

Bugs such as crusader bugs (P) may suck the sap from young shoots, and the catepillars of cassia butterfly may chew the leaves.

Christmas bush
Ceratopetalum gummiferum

This tree (usually pruned to a shrub in gardens) grows well in a range of climates but would not be a good choice for the tropics or in an area of heavy frost. A light well-drained soil mulched regularly with compost will produce good results. Protect the tree from strong, hot or salty winds.

Flower and branch production will be improved if the plant is well watered in spring. Pruning at or soon after 'flowering' will keep the bush dense, but severe cutting back on a regular basis will weaken the plant and predispose it to attack from longicorns (P). Webbing and 'sawdust' at the junctions of twigs or branches is produced by larvae of moth borers (oecophorid) (P).

The flowers may be damaged by thrips, possibly plague thrips (P), and new leaves damaged by psyllids (P). Scale

insects such as soft brown scale (P) and white palm scale (P) may be found on the leaves and stems of the bush. Dieback of branches may be caused by phytophthora root rot (D).

Conifers

Conifers can be grown successfully in a range of different climates, but most look their best in cool temperate and highland areas. In tropical or subtropical climates the number of species that grow well is considerably reduced.

In general, they require good fertile soils with a high proportion of organic matter and good drainage.

If the roots are allowed to become hot and dry or if hot drying winds prevail, the foliage may appear dull and lifeless or brown on the tips.

Areas with salt-laden winds, shallow sandy soils and air pollution are not suitable for many conifers.

There are some exceptions to these remarks. For example, the swamp cypress (*Taxodium distichum*) will thrive in areas with waterlogged soil, and cypress pines (*Callitris* spp.) can grow well in sandy soil and in dry areas.

Although full sun is generally recommended for conifers, avoid positions that are very hot. For example, a conifer, particularly a cultivar flecked with white or yellow, is very likely to develop dry, brown needles if planted against a western wall.

Some of the 'book-leaf' conifers naturally develop dead foliage in the centre of the plant. This can be removed with a gloved hand if desired.

Browning or blackening of foliage may also result from aphid (P) or spruce spider mite (P) attack. Foliage chewers include the larvae of case moths (P), painted apple moths (P) and loopers (P).

Foliage may also be damaged by beetles such as bronze beetle (*Eucolaspis brunnea*) which is found throughout New Zealand. These shiny brown beetles are oval and about 5 × 3 mm. They jump when disturbed. They cause withering and browning of conifer needles and attack a wide range of other plants.

Other problems are greenhouse thrips (P), cypress bark weevil (P), cypress bark beetle (P), pine adelgid (P), sirex wasp (P), cypress pine sawfly (P), cypress canker (D) and orange fruitborer.

Jewel beetles (P) and longicorns (P) are not common conifer pests but do attack weakened maidenhair trees (*Ginkgo biloba*) and older dawn redwoods (*Metasequoia glyptostroboides*), particularly in coastal areas.

Phytophthora root rot (D) can be a serious problem, but conifers grafted onto rot resistant roots are now being produced.

Conifer pests and diseases should be taken seriously and controlled, because if part of the plant has to be removed the elegant formal shape may be destroyed.

Coral tree
Erythrina spp.

These trees grow well in all but the coldest areas. They tolerate salt-laden winds and, once established, both dry and wet soil conditions.

They have few pest and disease problems, but in late summer and autumn the leaves are commonly attacked by leafhoppers which cause leaf yellowing. Old trees may be attacked by longicorn beetle (P) larvae.

Crabapple
Malus spp.

These small trees perform best in a moist climate with several months of cold weather during the year and will tolerate quite low temperatures. Full sun and shelter from wind are necessary for an optimum flower display. They prefer a loamy soil with good drainage.

Crabapples are problem-free in most years but may be attacked by pests and diseases of apples grown only for fruit, including apple leafhopper (P), two-spotted mite (P) and lightbrown apple moth (P).

Many established crabapples show the symptoms of apple mosaic (D) on their leaves. This disease is not serious, but if a new tree is to be bought ensure that it is labelled to show that it was propagated from virus-tested material. Long white threads on stems or around the base of the tree indicate the presence of woolly aphid (P).

Crepe myrtle
Lagerstroemia indica

This plant grows well under almost any conditions, but the soil should be well drained. It will stand light frost.

In humid areas powdery mildew (D) may cover new leaves with a white growth and cause them to curl up. It causes more damage on some cultivars than others.

The trunk and branches may be attacked by fruit-tree borer (P) which produces an area of sawdust and webbing usually near branch junctions. Crepe myrtles usually recover very well after treatment.

Cypress
Cupressus spp.

Most of these trees grow well only in deep moist soils. In and around Sydney and in similar coastal areas, a number of cypresses including the Bhutan cypress (*C. torulosa*) and Brunning's golden cypress (*C. macrocarpa* 'Brunniana Aurea') are regularly attacked by cypress bark weevil (P) which can kill branches or the whole tree. A regular watering and fertilising programme would help the trees to resist attack, but it is probably more sensible to plant other species more suited to the area.

A well-drained site will make phytophthora root rot (D) less likely. The Bhutan cypress (*C. torulosa*) seems to be resistant to this disease, but other cypresses may not be resistant.

Monterey cypress (*C. macrocarpa*) is one of the species very susceptible to cypress canker (D) and also to the cypress bark beetle (P).

Aphids (P) may cause browning and blackening on foliage.

The foliage on Brunning's golden cypress may be chewed by cypress pine sawfly (P) larvae. The larvae of the moth called the orange fruitborer (*Isotenes miserana*) feed on young foliage. They begin green but change to cream with reddish-brown bands along the body. The head is dark brown.

Cypress pine
Callitris spp.

These trees withstand strong wind, frost and dry conditions. They should be planted in well-drained soil in a sunny position.

Cypress pine sawfly (P) larvae may cause serious foliage damage and spoil the formal shape of the tree.

Aphids (P) can also attack these trees.

Daphne
Daphne spp.

Daphnes grow best in cool areas. The soil should be rich in organic matter, well drained and slightly acid. Do not lime. Grow in semi-shade and mulch the surrounding soil. Keep the mulch from direct stem contact or diseases such as sclerotinia rot (D) will be encouraged.

Daphne odora, the most common species, suffers from a number of virus diseases. The symptoms are variable and on the leaves include yellow blotches, irregular streaks, dead flecks and twisting and puckering. Flowers are often small, distorted and green. They may fail to open. Flower buds may blacken and fall off. The whole plant may be stunted. There is no cure for these problems.

Daphnes with fewer viruses have been developed and will become increasingly available to the public. They will be labelled to indicate this and may be termed 'High Health' plants.

Fasciation (D) sometimes occurs on the stems. Look on the stems and leaves for scales (P). The flowers may be rotted by grey mould (D), and the plant may die suddenly if affected by phytophthora root rot (D).

Eucalyptus
Eucalyptus spp.

Gum trees, or eucalypts, have evolved to suit a wide range of climates and soil types. Choose one suitable for your situation with the help of gardening books, your local nurseryman or the State Forestry Commission.

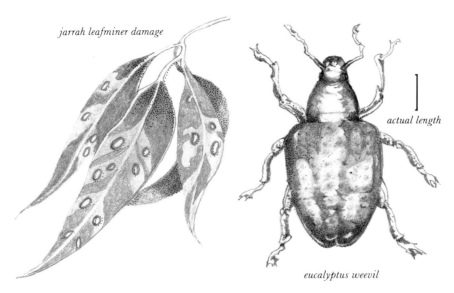

jarrah leafminer damage

actual length

eucalyptus weevil

Planting a species unsuitable for the site is likely to involve added pest and disease problems.

There are a number of leafminers (P) that attack gums—for example, the blackbutt leafminer (*Acrocercops laciniella*) and the jarrah leafminer (*Perthida glyphopa*). The latter causes reddish-brown blotches, and when the larvae make cases in which to pupate, oval holes are cut in the leaves. In areas where this insect is prevalent, the jarrah (*Eucalyptus marginata*) is an unsuitable choice unless constant chemical control is undertaken.

Blisters on the leaves indicate the damage of leafblister sawflies (P). Various scarab beetles attack gums. These include the Christmas beetle (P) which often chews leaves in a saw-tooth pattern.

There are also a number of small weevils that chew gum leaves. These include the eucalyptus weevil (*Gonipterus scutellatus*) and the redlegged weevil (*Catasarcus impressipennis*). Adults of the former, which are brown and about 10 mm long, chew around the leaf edges. Their larvae feed all over the leaf surface. They are usually kept under control by a wasp which parasitises the eggs.

The redlegged weevil, which is grey-green and 10–15 mm long, can cause serious damage in summer, particularly to the tuart (*Eucalyptus gomphocephala*). Feeding generally occurs around the edges of the leaves.

Other leaf-chewers are steelblue sawfly (P) larvae; larvae and adults of leaf beetles (P) such as the eucalyptus tortoise beetle (*Paropsis atomaria*); and the larvae of cup moths (P), gumleaf skeletonizer moth (P), autumn gum moth (P), emperor gum moth (P), whitestemmed-gum moth (P), and case moths (P). These pests occur more commonly in some areas than others.

A bug sometimes referred to as the eucalyptus tip bug causes wilting of young shoots.

Lumps on leaves or stems may be wasp galls (P), coccid galls (P) or the result of interaction between small flies and certain nematodes.

Gumtree scale (P) and gumtree hoppers (P) are sometimes found on twigs and small branches, which are also occasionally damaged by the egg-laying of cicadas.

There are numerous psyllids (P) such as the brown basket lerp (P) which suck sap and are usually found under leaves.

Trunk and branch damage may result from the activities of longicorns (P), jewel beetles (P) moth borers (oecophorid) (P) moth borers (cossid) (P), and by wood rots (P). The scribbly gum and similar trees have brown wandering lines on the trunk; these are caused by the scribbly gum moth which is an interesting insect but not a pest (illustrated page 23).

The most common root problems are armillaria root rot (D) and phytophthora root rot (D).

There are numerous fungi that cause spots and flecks on gum leaves. The leaf spot (D) on eurabbie and Tasmanian blue gum is one of the more common.

Young eucalypts in damp situations may show symptoms of a disease called shoot blight (D).

Mistletoe (D) is a common problem on eucalypts and should be removed.

False cypress
Chamaecyparis lawsoniana

This tree must have a moist atmosphere and deep moist soils for most successful growth.

It may be attacked by aphids (P) and is also highly susceptible to the disease cypress canker (D).

A well-drained position will reduce the possibility of phytophthora root rot (D). Experiments have shown several cultivars, including 'Filiformis', and 'Allumii', to be susceptible to this disease.

Fig
Ficus spp.

These trees prefer well-drained open soils and a warm climate. They will tolerate salty winds. Their large mature size and invasive root system make them unsuitable for most home gardens.

They may be attacked by a number of pests including figleaf beetle (P) and fig psyllid (P).

Larvae of the oleander butterfly (P) and the native fig moth (P) may chew the leaves and cause serious damage.

Firethorn
Pyracantha spp.

These shrubs perform best in full sun or in a cool moist environment. They are not a good choice for tropical areas but tolerate harsh conditions such as poor water supply and frosts. They have few problems. Look for white wax scale (P) and pink wax scale (P) which appear as waxy lumps on the stems or on the midribs of leaves. They are occasionally affected by the same diseases as their relatives—these being apples, pears, quinces and loquats.

Flowering peach
Prunus persica

This tree is one of a large group of 'flowering' stonefruits grown purely for ornamental purposes. There is a great variety of these — cherries, plums, almonds, peaches and apricots — which produce beautiful crops of flowers but few, if any, fruit. They are, however,

often subject to the same pests and diseases as the 'fruiting' varieties.

They are not suitable for tropical or subtropical climates, and some such as *Prunus serrulata* look their best only in a cool area. Others, such as the purple-leafed cherry-plum (*P. cerasifera* 'Nigra'), will tolerate hot dry conditions.

Flowering stonefruits will grow in moderately fertile soil but most of them perform better in rich, deep soil. They require good drainage, but the roots should not be allowed to dry out.

A sunny position is necessary for healthy growth and flowering, and the display of blossoms will last longer if the plant is protected from strong winds.

Pruning in winter will remove much of the flower crop soon to appear in spring. Pruning treatment varies from type to type. *Prunus × blireana* and the cherry-plum (*P. cerasifera*) flower well without pruning and should not have all the branches shortened. Instead, completely remove several of the interior branches at the base each year. If this is not done, these branches eventually grow big enough to rub against one another and provide excellent sites for attack from fruit-tree borer (P). Watch also for suckers from the understock. These have green leaves, unlike the other purple-leafed branches, and should be removed.

The flowering peach (*Prunus persica*) and the Chinese bush cherry (*P. glandulosa*) should be pruned hard during or immediately after flowering.

The most common disease problems on flowering stonefruits are shot hole (D), rust (D) and leaf curl (D). Do not buy a tree with a lump near ground level because this indicates crown gall (D).

Pests include fruit-tree borer (P), pear and cherry slug (P), two-spotted mite (P), light brown apple moth (P), green peach aphid (P), black peach aphid and cherry aphid (P).

(See also the entry on stonefruit in the 'Fruits' section, page 83.)

Frangipani
Plumeria rubra

This plant prefers a warm humid situation. Grow in full sun and protect the brittle branches from strong winds.

A coarse-textured soil with plenty of organic matter is best. Root rots may result from poor drainage and/or the application of excessive water.

The fleshy stems sometimes become hollow, papery, and dark brown on the ends. This dieback seems to occur where temperatures drop too low. These damaged areas are often invaded by insects such as little beetles.

Small brown to black oval lumps scattered on the stems are probably hemispherical scales (P).

Fuchsia
Fuchsia × hybrida

Grow fuchsias in partial shade, and water well in hot weather. This will help avoid sunburn. Protection from strong winds is important because the branches are brittle. Frosts may kill the uppermost

parts of the plant but new shoots appear in spring. Encouraging new growth, by a weekly application of liquid fertiliser, will help overcome the problem of rust (D), which produces brown patches on the upper leaf surface with orange dust beneath each patch.

Fuchsias are intolerant of salt in soil and need a water supply low in salt.

Dull, unhealthy leaves with fine mottling may be caused by the feeding of whiteflies (P), greenhouse thrips (P) or two-spotted mite (P).

Holes in the leaves may have been chewed by grapevine moth (P) larvae.

Small, distorted new shoots may result from cyclamen mite (P) damage; and white fluffy areas on the stems are probably mealybug (P).

Gardenia
Gardenia spp.

Warm-temperate to subtropical climates are the most suitable for these shrubs. Choose a semi-shaded position with a slightly acid soil. Gardenias will not grow well in an alkaline soil, and in full sun the flowers burn quickly. Fertilise and water regularly in summer. Inadequate soil moisture may cause buds to fall off.

Plants that, despite care and attention, do not grow and tend to wilt quickly in dry weather may have roots infested with root knot nematode (D).

Minerals such as iron or magnesium may be in short supply if the foliage is generally pale green or yellowing, but a few yellow or yellowing leaves scattered over the plant are merely those at the end of their useful life.

The leaves may be chewed by larvae of the bee hawk moth or by Fuller's rose weevils (P). Flowers with moving black specks are probably infested with thrips (P). Look on stems and leaves for mealybugs (P), white wax scale (P) and soft brown scale (P).

Geebung
Persoonia spp.

These plants need a well-drained sandy or gravelly soil. Optimum growth will be achieved in a temperate climate.

Leaves may be chewed by various caterpillars such as the macadamia twig-girdler (P) and the doubleheaded hawk moth (P); and disfigured by a black fungal leaf spot.

Geraldton wax
Chamaelaucium uncinatum

This plant must have a very well drained soil, and a sandy one is probably best. Position the plant where it will receive no more than light shade and where the roots will not be disturbed.

The flowers are useful for indoor decoration. Once the plant is established stems of about 300 mm could be cut. This will keep the plant bushy.

Do not allow mulch or other plants to keep the main trunk damp near ground level, and keep the soil fairly dry. The most likely problem is phytophthora root rot (D).

Grevillea
Grevillea spp.

Various species of grevillea are suitable for different climatic zones. In general they need an acid soil, good drainage and

full sun, but careful selection of species can produce good results in some other situations.

They are commonly attacked by moth borer (oecophorid) (P). The leaves may be chewed by the grevillea looper (P), doubleheaded hawk moth (P) larvae and banksia moth larvae (illustrated page 30).

Scale insects found on grevilleas include latania scale (P); and bugs such as the crusader bug (P) may suck sap from young shoots.

The leaves of the silky oak (*G. robusta*) and of *G. banksii* may be attacked by the grevillea leafminer (P). *G. rosmarinifolia* often has its new growth and flowers attacked by psyllids (P).

Grevillea 'Robyn Gordon' commonly suffers from a leaf spot (D) in humid weather. Fasciation (D) is quite frequent on *G.* 'Sandra Gordon'.

A number of insects, including the macadamia flower caterpillar (P), attack the flowers.

Hakea
Hakea spp.

Most of these plants should be grown in a well-drained sandy or gravelly soil.

The leaves may be attacked by caterpillars of insects such as grevillea looper (P) and macadamia twig-girdler (P). Black spots on the leaves detract from the plant's appearance. This fungal leaf spot (D) also occurs on grevilleas.

Hawthorn
Crataegus spp.

These trees are not suitable for tropical or subtropical areas and grow best in cool temperate climates with deep, fertile, well-drained soils with good watering programmes. Occasional pruning to remove crossing branches may be required.

New growth may be attacked by powdery mildew (D) or infested with aphids (P). Leaf surfaces may be removed by the slug-like grubs of the pear and cherry slug (P). Apple mussel scale, which is a hard scale (P), may infest the branches and twigs, giving them an excessively rough appearance.

Purple scale may cause problems in some situations.

Hebe
Hebe spp.

These can be grown successfully in a wide range of climates, although hot, very dry areas would be least suitable. Most species tolerate cold conditions but some may be damaged by severe frosts. Hebes tolerate exposed sites near the sea.

It is advisable to prune lightly after flowering to keep the plants bushy.

White waxy lumps on the stems are white wax scale (P) or Chinese wax scale (P), and in humid conditions the leaves may develop fungal leaf spots.

Distorted young shoots which then turn black and die may indicate downy mildew (D).

Wandering lines on the leaves are caused by leafminers (P).

Hibiscus
Hibiscus spp.

These shrubs require a regular watering and fertilising programme to look their best. They need a well-drained soil and a position in full sun.

Chinese hibiscus (*H. rosa-sinensis*), confederate rose (*H. mutabilis*) and *H. schizopetalus* grow best in warm temperate and tropical climates. Shrub althea (*H. syriacus*) thrives in cooler areas.

Different pruning practices are necessary for the different types. For example, *H. syriacus* should be cut back severely in the first few years to encourage a bushy framework; some *H. rosa-sinensis* cultivars require harder pruning than others, but none should be touched until all danger of frost has passed.

The following problems may occur on the Chinese lanterns (*Abutilon* spp.) as well as on hibiscus.

Small black insects clustered on buds and new shoots are probably aphids (P) or cottonseed bugs (P). White areas or lumps on the stems may be white wax scale (P) or mealybugs (P).

Holes in leaves and flowers probably result from metallic flea beetle (P) attack. Hibiscus flower beetle (P) is commonly found in the flowers.

Black dots on the leaves may indicate

fly speck (D); and larger purplish spots, bacterial leaf spot. The latter is most common on *H. rosa-sinensis* 'Apple Blossom'.

Many specimens of *H. rosa-sinensis* suffer from a virus disease. This shows up as yellow flecks on the leaves and translucent areas along the veins. The flowers, however, seem unaffected. When cuttings for propagation are taken from a diseased plant, all the new plants produced will also have the disease.

In some areas hibiscus can be killed by 'collar rot' (*Phytophthora nicotianae* var. *parasitica*). This is most likely on *H. rosa-sinensis* 'Apple Blossom' and *H. r.* 'Wilder's White'. The leaves go pale green, and the plant soon wilts and dies. On closer examination a soft brown area can be found near ground level. Later this dries out and the outer layers of bark peel off, giving the area a stringy appearance. Remove the plant and replace with a different type of shrub. Read the notes on phytophthora root rot (D).

Holly
Ilex spp.

Holly will grow best in a cool climate in full sun. The organic matter level in the soil should be high and water should be applied in hot, dry weather.

Look for scale insects on stems and leaves. Grey-pink waxy lumps on leaf midribs are probably pink wax scale (P); and brown or grey lumps may be greedy scale, soft brown scale (P) or black scale (P). Purple scale is also found on holly.

Hop-bush
Dodonaea viscosa

Hop-bush can be grown successfully in a wide range of situations. It will tolerate salt-laden winds, soils of low fertility, and heavy frosts once it is established. The purple-foliaged *D. viscosa* 'Purpurea' needs full sun for optimum development of foliage colour.

White waxy blobs on the stems are probably Indian white wax scale (P) but may be white wax scale (P).

Deformed shoots and lumps on the leaves are probably the result of attack by gall-forming flies and should be pruned off the plant and destroyed.

Hydrangea
Hydrangea spp.

Hydrangeas are best suited to cool moist climates. If grown in cold areas, protect from frost. Strong dry winds or hot sun will cause burning of the foliage. Water well in hot weather.

The colour of the flowers, in all except the white cultivars, is influenced by the pH of the soil. If the soil is strongly acid the flowers will be deep-blue, and if it is slightly alkaline they will be clear-pink or rosy-red. There is a range of pale-blues, mauves and pale-pinks in between. It is possible to alter soil pH, but this will also influence the availability of nutrients such as iron. Leaf yellowing, chlorosis (D), may be caused by iron deficiency. (See the notes on soil pH in 'Planning and Maintaining Your Garden'.)

White felt-like oval lumps on stems or under leaves are hydrangea scale (P). White powdery spots on leaves indicate powdery mildew (D). If the foliage and/or flowers are mottled, and cup-like blisters appear on young leaves, the plant has been attacked by the hydrangea spider mite.

The underside of leaf with pockets caused by the hydrangea spider mite

Indian hawthorn
Raphiolepis sp.

These shrubs are best suited to cool temperate climates and well-drained soils. They will tolerate neglect but should be well watered during summer and lightly trimmed after flowering for their best performance.

Pest and disease problems are few but include a fungal leaf spot (D).

Kaka beak
Clianthus puniceus

This spreading shrub will thrive in any well-drained soil. It will withstand frost and drought once established. Avoid excess fertiliser.

Wandering white lines on the leaf indicate a leafminer (P). A mass of small leaves on small stems growing close together is referred to as a 'witches' broom'; it is probably caused by mites (P). Mottled leaves may have been caused by the feeding of mites such as two-spotted mite (P).

The hairy caterpillars of the kowhai moth (*Uresiphitz polygonalis maorialis*) may chew the foliage.

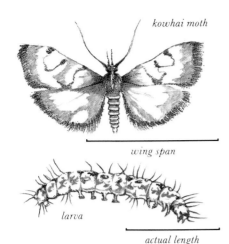

kowhai moth

wing span

larva

actual length

Kowhai

Sophora spp.

The kowhai (*S. microphylla*) should be grown in a cool moist climate with good soils. The Japanese pagoda tree (*S. japonica*), on the other hand, will tolerate more exposed and drier situations and almost any soil.

The hairy larvae of the kowhai moth (*Uresiphitz polygonalis maorialis*) may defoliate these trees. Scales may also be a serious problem.

Kurrajong

Brachychiton populneus

The kurrajong requires a well-drained sandy or light loam. It will withstand drought and frost once established.

Damaged or dying branches may be attacked by the kurrajong weevil (*Axionicus insignis*) whose larvae tunnel in the wood. Remove or repair damaged limbs promptly.

There are several insects that feed on the seeds and at least two different psyllids (P) that attack the young growth.

The flame tree (*B. acerifolius*) is best grown in a deep, well-drained loam. Keep it well watered. Grow in a sunny position, but avoid areas of strong, hot or salty winds. This tree may drop all or only some of its leaves in spring and produce flowers on the bare branches.

Both the kurrajong and the flame tree are attacked by the larvae of the kurrajong leaf-tier (P) moth.

Lacebark

Hoheria spp.

These flowering trees will grow in any well-drained soil and survive frost and heavy pruning.

Wilting of foliage and death of shoots and small branches may be a condition called 'dieback of lacebarks'. Try to stop the problem by pruning out dead wood.

Trees under stress are likely to be attacked by mites (P) which cause woody galls on the small branches. Prune to remove as many as possible.

The disease 'rust of lacebark' is characterised by yellow or brown patches on leaves, and stems may be disfigured by irregular distorted areas. Control would be difficult on a tree, but see note on rusts (D) for possible control methods.

Lilac

Syringa vulgaris

This shrub flowers well only in cool areas and needs two or three years to establish itself first. It should be in a sunny position with some wind protection, and it prefers a slightly alkaline, moist loam rich in organic matter.

Mulch the soil and do not allow the root system to dry out in summer.

Spots or large blackened areas on the leaves may be bacterial leaf spot (D).

Lillypilly

Acmena spp. and *Syzygium* spp.

These trees grow best in well-drained loam in a warm frost-free position. They should be well-watered in summer.

A number of scale insects can occur on leaves or stems and may be associated with a black sooty covering on the leaves. White wax scale (P), pink wax scale (P) or soft brown scale (P) are all possibilities.

Small bubbles on new leaves are usually caused by psyllids (P).

Liquidambar

Liquidambar styraciflua

This tree will grow reasonably well in most climates except tropical. Autumn colour, however, will be more spectacular and reliable in cooler areas. It has few serious pest and disease problems but is attacked often by thrips (P) which give the leaves a silver-grey or dirty appearance. Longicorn beetle (P) larvae may attack old, damaged or weakened trees.

Note that the production of corky flanges is a natural feature of the liquidambar bark even on young twigs. This is termed 'corking'.

Magnolia

Magnolia spp.

Deciduous members of this group usually grow best in a cool moist climate with full sun or light shade. The soil should be rich in organic matter and have a slightly acid pH. Their root systems are close to the soil surface and should neither be disturbed by cultivation nor allowed to dry out. Mulching could solve this problem.

Hot or salty winds will cause the leaves to brown, and this will also occur in hot weather or in hot areas if watering has been neglected.

Thrips (P) cause the leaves to look grey or dull in colour, and birds often peck holes in the flowers.

Note that on the evergreen species, white or southern magnolia (*Magnolia grandiflora*), the undersurfaces of the leaves are naturally a rusty colour.

Magnolia × *soulangiana* 'Lennei' and *M.* × *s.* 'Alexandrina' suffer from a bacterial leaf spot caused by *Pseudomonas syringae* pv. *syringae*. The symptoms seem

to be variable but include small brown spots with yellow haloes. If these spots grow together, splits may develop in the infected leaves.

Maidenhair tree
Ginkgo biloba

This tree performs well over a long period of time only in cool areas in full sun and with deep fertile soils. It is under stress in warm temperate areas and often subject to longicorn beetle (P) attack.

Maple
Acer spp.

Cool moist climates are the most suitable for these trees. The soil should be loam with a high proportion of organic matter. Make sure that the root system does not dry out. Hot dry winds and atmospheric pollutants will cause browning around leaf edges. Leaf damage of any type will detract from autumn colour.

Dry papery leaves may be the result of insufficient water supply or two-spotted mite (P) attack. Thrips (P) sometimes feed on the leaves, producing small sticky brown spots and a greyish appearance. The trunk may be attacked by longicorn beetle (P) larvae, which tunnel under the bark and cause it to crack.

Melaleuca
Melaleuca spp.

These trees and shrubs are tolerant of a wide range of conditions. Check the requirements of individual species with your nurseryman. Many melaleucas thrive in a constantly damp soil.

The paperbark sawfly (P) commonly chews the leaves and pupates in the bark of these plants. The Chinese wax scale (P) is often found on the twigs.

The young growth on *M. bracteata* cultivars, particularly 'Revolution Gold', sometimes dies back. This may be a fungal disease and seems to be associated with cool, shady conditions.

Mint bush
Prostanthera spp.

A very well drained sandy or gravelly soil with added organic matter is necessary for these plants. Position in no more than light shade, protect from hot dry winds, and water regularly in spring and summer. Mulch will help to keep the root system cool and prevent drying out, but it must be kept back from the stem.

The plant will become spindly unless tip-pruned for the first few years and then annually after flowering.

Phytophthora root rot (D) is the most common problem and is associated with wet soil. Buy a mint bush grafted on to the roots of the coast rosemary (*Westringia fruticosa*) which is resistant to this disease.

Monterey pine
Pinus radiata

This tree should be planted in well-drained soil and does best in highland areas. Loopers (P) (*Chlenias* spp. and *Boarmia lyciaria*) and the larvae of painted apple moth (P) and case moth (P) are among the foliage chewers which may cause problems.

Sirex wasp (P) is most likely to successfully attack trees that are in a weakened condition, such as those planted in unsuitable areas with poor soils and low or erratic rainfall.

A white woolly substance at the base of the needles may indicate pine adelgids (P) (*Pineus pini*) which are brown and about 1 mm long. These insects are similar to aphids and cause the death of terminal shoots. Small plants may be killed and older ones stunted.

Cypress bark weevil (P) sometimes causes problems.

Shoot blight (D) is most likely to occur on trees that have suffered water stress or been damaged by an occurrence such as a hail storm or attack from leaf chewers.

Monterey pine seems to be resistant to phytophthora root rot (D).

New Zealand flax
Phormium spp.

These plants will grow well in a wide range of soils and climates. They tolerate salt spray, and wet soils. A sunny position is best.

Caterpillar damage

They may be attacked by hard scales (P) or soft scales (P); by the larvae of the flax moth (*Orthoclydon praefectata*) which chew furrows along the leaves; and by the larvae of the edge-cutting flax moth (*Melanchra steropastis*) which chew V- or U-shaped holes in the edges of the leaves. If necessary, spray these larvae as suggested for loopers (P). Add some wetting agent so that the spray adheres to the flax more efficiently.

Brownish or greyish patches on the leaves near the tips or edges may indicate fungal leaf spots. Badly infected leaves should be cut and burnt. Spray the rest of the plant with copper oxychloride (50%) at the rate of 5 g per litre of water.

Norfolk Island hibiscus
Lagunaria patersonia

This tree grows best in warm areas although it will survive mild frosts when established. It prefers a well-drained, fertile soil and a sunny position; and tolerates winds laden with salt or atmospheric pollutants.

The leaves may be attacked by a metallic flea beetles (P) and stems by the cotton harlequin bug (P).

Norfolk Island pine
Araucaria heterophylla

This large tree will grow in most soils and will withstand frost and salt spray.

The death of these trees on some beachfronts is thought to be related to their proximity to sewerage outlets. Sewage contains surfactants from domestic and commercial detergents, and these are blown on to the trees with the salt spray. In other areas near the sea, these trees can grow well.

The golden mealybug (P) can cause problems with this tree.

Oak

Quercus spp.

Most oaks need a cool moist climate and a deep fertile soil for best growth.

The following common pests and disease problems of oaks produce leaf damage: oak blotch miner (P) causes brown blisters; powdery mildew (D), white spots; aphids (P), a black covering; and thrips (P), a grey or dirty appearance.

In many areas golden oak scale (*Asterodiaspis variolosa*) is kept under control by natural enemies.

Oleander

Nerium oleander

This shrub will grow satisfactorily under harsh conditions and withstand low temperatures. Water in hot dry conditions will improve its performance.

Woody lumps on stems, midribs, flowers or pods indicate a disease called bacterial gall (D).

Oleander is attacked by a number of scale insects: pale-brown to black lumps on stems or leaves, or removable whitish spots on leaves, may be scales such as soft brown scale (P) or oleander scale (P). Control may be necessary.

Caterpillars of the oleander butterfly (P) sometimes chew the leaves.

Olearia

Olearia spp.

Most of these trees and shrubs are tolerant of salt-laden winds, drought and poor sandy soil. The mountain holly or New Zealand holly (*O. ilicifolius*), however, re-

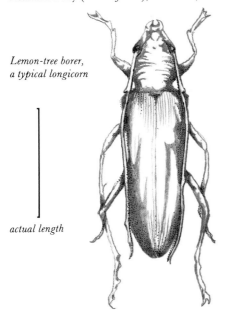

Lemon-tree borer, a typical longicorn

actual length

quires a cool, moist and partly shaded location. Mulch spread beneath the plant will control weeds without disturbance of the shallow root system. Prune the shrubs regularly so that they remain bushy.

The larvae of the lemon-tree borer (*Oemona hirta*), which is a longicorn (P), tunnel in the branches, and Chinese wax scale (P) can be found on twigs.

The olearia gall midge (*Oligotrophus oleariae*) attacks new shoots which develop roughly spherical, tightly-packed groups of distorted and stunted leaves. Prune off these 'galls' and burn them as soon as they are noticed.

The olearia leafminer (*Nepticula ogygia*), the adult of which is a fly, is an occasional pest and similar to many other leafminers (P).

Rust on olearia can be controlled by measures discussed under rusts (D).

Olive

Olea africana

This tree prefers a sandy or gravelly soil in an area with hot summers and cool winters. It will tolerate drought and frost once established.

Black scale (P) and soft brown scale (P) infest leaves and twigs. The leaves may be attacked by the olive lace bug (P) which causes yellow mottling.

(The species *Olea europaea* is listed in the 'Fruit and nuts' section.)

Pepper tree

Schinus areira

This tree tolerates harsh conditions including poor soils, and drought. It should be grown in full sun and in a well-drained soil.

Leaf chewers such as the larvae of emperor gum moth (P), and redshouldered leaf beetles (P), seem to be the only problems of the pepper tree.

Photinia

Photinia spp.

These plants are tolerant of a wide range of conditions, but tropical and subtropical environments would be the least suitable. They will stand frost. They are grown principally for their red new foliage, which can be maintained by regular trimming, watering and fertilising.

Watch for aphids (P) and the fungal disease, powdery mildew (D), both of which may attack new shoots. Look on the leaves and stems for hard scales (P) and soft scales (P).

Pittosporum

Pittosporum spp.

These trees succeed in a wide range of climates from tropical to highland but generally withstand only light frosts. They like a deep well-drained fertile loam with a good summer water supply, but they will tolerate drought.

Native daphne or sweet pittosporum (*P. undulatum*) is commonly attacked by the pittosporum leafminer (P) in certain areas. Both this species and the variegated pittosporum (*P. eugenioides* 'Variegatum') are attacked by longicorns (P), such as the pittosporum longicorn, if they are in a weakened condition.

Scales including soft scales (P) are common on pittosporum.

Young leaves are frequently curled under at the edges by thrips (P). Various bugs suck sap, including the pittosporum bug (*Pseudapines geminata*) which is oval in outline, about 8 mm long, and black with light markings.

The pittosporum chermid or psyllid (*Trioza vitreoradiata*) causes small lumps on the leaves like those on lillypilly damaged by psyllids (P).

Poplar

Populus spp.

Poplars are not suitable for tropical areas. They are best grown in temperate climates in deep, fertile soils, well-drained but with a good water supply. They will tolerate occasional flooding and temperatures below 0°C.

Yellow blisters on the leaves are caused by leaf blister, and brown patches may indicate anthracnose (D).

Browning around leaf edges is likely to be caused by salt toxicity or by potassium deficiency. For the latter, apply complete fertiliser in the way described in the introduction to the tree and shrub section.

Rust (D), which causes yellow flecks on the leaves, is difficult to control. It is probably unwise to plant *P. nigra* 'Italica' or *P. deltoides* until resistant clones are readily available.

Lumps on the leafstalks are caused by poplar gall aphid (P).

Port-wine magnolia
Michelia figo

This shrub should not be chosen for areas where frost or salt-laden winds occur.

It has few pest and disease problems but can be killed by hard scales (P) such as (*Pseudaulacaspis* sp.) if action is not taken. Yellow patches on the leaves with white flakes beneath some of them indicate this problem.

Rose
Rosa spp.

Roses can be grown in both hot and cold climates but are not suitable for tropical areas. They need an open sunny position without competition from other large trees and shrubs. Shade, and the growth of annual flowers or other small plants in the same bed, will increase humidity and encourage black spot (D) on the leaves.

Protect the plants from strong winds which will damage flowers and new growth. The leaves will have a tattered look if they are bashed on to the thorns.

Roses may be grown successfully in a wide range of soil types. Good drainage

is essential and the pH should be neutral or no more than slightly acid. Sandy soils should be improved by the addition of well-rotted organic matter.

Do not plant the bushes too close together. The growth habit of the particular roses concerned should dictate how far apart they should be. Consult your nurseryman on this matter, but miniatures are usually planted about 600 mm apart and larger growers about 1.2 m apart. Correct spacing enables work on the plants to be carried out more easily and improves air circulation.

Be careful not to allow the roots to dry out at planting time. Do not buy a rose plant with an irregular gall near the junction of stems and roots. This indicates a disease called crown gall (D).

Mulch the soil but keep the mulching material away from the stems. Water and fertilise regularly.

Correct pruning and flower-gathering procedures will not only ensure a good flower supply but also reduce the incidence of rose canker (D), a gradual browning and death of stems from the cut end downwards. This disease can also cause splits in the stem.

The prompt removal of spent flowers and dead leaves from the area will help control diseases.

Rose stems may be infested with scale insects such as cottonycushion scale (P), California red scale (P), and rose scale (P), which can form a thick layer.

Rose leaves may be attacked by the painted apple moth (P) caterpillar; by Fuller's rose weevil (P) which chews the edges ragged; or by the leafcutting bee (P) which chews neat oval or circular pieces from the edges.

The leaves may also show the irregular yellow patterns of mosaic (D) and the spots of anthracnose (D), downy mildew (D) or rust (D).

Dry, papery leaves are probably the result of two-spotted mite (P) attack, and silvering of leaves may be due to silver leaf (D).

Leaves and flowers may be damaged by the redshouldered leaf beetle (P) and metallic flea beetles (P).

Flowers with brown petals and tiny brown dots have probably been attacked by plague thrips (P). Nectar scarabs (P), small brown beetles, also move around between petals. Pinkish rings or grey furry growth on the buds or petals indicate grey mould (D).

New shoots and buds are the most likely place for aphids (P) and powdery mildew (D).

New leaves that are curled under or brittle may indicate rose wilt (D). Verticillium wilt (D) of roses is indicated by wilting of leaves at the tips of young canes and by yellowing of older canes. Dieback may occur.

Yellowing associated with general poor growth may be root knot nematode (D).

Apart from rose wilt (D) and rose mosaic (D) there are other viral diseases of roses. These are of more importance in commercial production of roses than in home garden cultivation.

Sacred bamboo
Nandina domestica

There are few problems connected with the culture of this plant, but occasionally white waxy lumps are found on the stems. These are probably white wax scale (P) or cottonycushion scale (P).

She-oak
Casuarina and Allocasuarina spp.

These plants thrive in full sun with well-drained soil and constant water supply. They will, however, tolerate a wide range of conditions and are troubled by very few serious pests or diseases.

Moth borers (oecophorid) (P) may attack the trunk. Spittlebugs (P), various plant hoppers, and coccid galls (P) may be found on the twigs.

Silk tree
Albizia spp.

Silk trees grow well in a wide range of climates. They tolerate light frosts and short-term dry conditions. The soil should be well-drained and they seem to grow best if it is light and not rich in organic matter. They need a warm, sunny position.

They are subject to longicorn beetle (P) attack. This should be treated promptly.

Smooth-barked apple
Angophora costata

This tree is not one for the tropics or for very dry or cold areas.

It requires good drainage and grows to about 20 m in fertile soil. If the soil is poorer the tree will take on a more contorted shape and remain smaller. Protection from salt-laden winds is necessary.

These trees are noted for the deep red kino gum which oozes from the trunk. Changes in the environment and mechanical damage frequently predispose the trunk to attack from longicorn beetle (P) and moth borers (cossid) (P). Various caterpillars such as those of the cup moth (P) chew the leaves.

Spindle tree
Euonymus spp.

These shrubs do best in full sun in a cool temperate climate but will tolerate hot dry conditions.

Powdery mildew (D) appears as whitish spots on the leaves of the tree, and California red scale (P) appears as orange-red spots on stems and leaves. White (waxy) lumps on the stems are white wax scale (P), and brown lumps may be another soft scale (P).

Tea-tree
Leptospermum spp.

These small trees and shrubs are generally not suitable for the tropics but they will withstand almost any other conditions. Some tolerate salty winds.

The cultivars of *L. scoparium* must be provided with good soil, water in dry weather, and be tip-pruned regularly if they are to look their best.

Pest and disease problems are often serious, and control procedures must be carried out.

Leaves and twigs are frequently attacked by the larvae of the tea-tree web moth (P) and the tea-tree moth.

Other problems may include moth borer (oecophorid) (P); reshouldered leaf beatle (P); and scales such as white palm scale (P) and manuka blight (P).

If stems and leaves appear black, they are probably covered with sooty mould (D) which is associated with scales, particularly manuka blight (P).

The flowers are attractive to insects such as soldier beetles (P), which do very little damage to the plant.

Tupelo
Nyssa sylvatica

This deciduous tree will grow well in a wide range of climates but is not a good choice for tropical or subtropical areas. It should be positioned in full sun for best autumn colour and watered well in summer. A deep fertile loam will produce the best growth. It would be suitable for an area of continually damp soil.

Thrips (P) sometimes cause the leaves to look grey or dirty, but the tupelo is free of serious problems.

Turpentine
Syncarpia glomulifera

This grows best in warm humid areas in fertile soil. It should be sheltered from frost and well watered to avoid browning of leaf edges.

Turpentine has very few pests and disease problems, but the hairy lumps that are commonly found under the leaves are very noticeable; these are wasp galls (P). Control is not really necessary.

Umbrella tree
Schefflera spp.

This plant will grow well in sun or shade in a frost-free position. It needs good drainage and a plentiful water supply in the growing season. It can be cut back severely and will develop a more bushy shape if this is done.

It makes a very successful long-term pot plant and is suitable for indoors.

Blackened or sticky leaves probably indicate mealybugs (P); or scales such as pink wax scale (P), hemispherical scale

(P) or soft brown scale (P). Two-spotted mite (P) may be a problem.

Brown marks on the leaves may indicate leaf blight (D).

Viburnum
Viburnum spp.

These plants have few serious problems. Leaves dull and mottled with grey or yellow may indicate greenhouse thrips (P) or two-spotted mite (P). White, round, detachable spots on the leaves are probably white palm scale (P).

Waratah
Telopea spp.

These grow best on acid, well-drained sandy loam of low fertility. Mulch with leaf litter or similar materials, and water

the plants when they are young. The position should be sunny or slightly shaded.

The flowers are borne on the ends of the main stems. If the plant is pruned or the flowers cut, more terminal shoots and therefore more flowers will be produced in the next year.

Waratahs may be attacked by moth borers (oecophorid) (P) and macadamia cup moth (P). Scales such as white palm scale (P), also known as 'waratah scale', may also occur on the plant.

Water gum
Tristaniopsis laurina

This tree should be protected from frost while young and watered well in summer for optimum growth.

It frequently develops reddish, cupped leaf tips. The cause of this distortion is

not clear but may result from the feeding activities of psyllids (free-living) (P) which also produce a covering of white powdery wax on new shoots.

It is also a host for the woolly giant mealybug (P) which is an interesting insect but not a pest.

Wattle
Acacia spp.

There are more than 600 native Australian wattles. Choose one suitable for the situation to be provided, with the help of your local nurseryman or forestry authority. Note that some wattles are naturally longer-lived than others, but the longest possible pest- and disease-free life will only be obtained by careful choice of species.

Many wattles are attacked by longicorns (P), moth borers (cossid) (P), and moth borers (oecophorid) (P) such as the fruit-tree borer (P), particularly as the trees age or if they are neglected.

They are also host to a number of weevils such as the elephant weevil (P), which can cause serious damage, and the diamond beetle (P), which generally does very little damage.

The plants may be chewed by redshouldered leaf beetles (P) and by the larvae of moths such as the painted apple moth (P) and of the common imperial blue and the tailed emperor butterflies.

The Queensland silver wattle (*A. podalyriifolia*) and some other phyllodinous wattles are attacked by the wattle leafminer (P).

The weeping myall or boree (*A. pendula*) and one or two other wattles can be attacked by the larvae of the bagshelter moth (P) in some areas.

The Cootamundra wattle (*A. baileyana*) and others are hosts for sap-suckers such

as the crusader bug (P), the green treehopper (P), and scales such as cottony-cushion scale (P). The twigs may be infested with the wattle mealybug (P), wattle tick scale (P) and spittlebugs (P).

In some areas the acacia spotting bug (P) causes elongated rusty-brown patches on wattle phyllodes.

Various galls are also found on flowers, leaves or stems. These include fungal galls such as rust gall (D) and insect galls such as the wasp galls (P) found on the Sydney golden wattle (*A. longifolia*). Rough, discoloured stems on Cootamundra wattle are probably a fungal stem gall (D).

Waxflower
Eriostemon myoporoides

This shrub will grow well in most climates but is not a good choice for the tropics. A position with sandy loam, shelter from wind, and semi-shade will produce the best results. Water in summer is essential, but drainage must be good.

White wax scale (P) is one of the few pests that attack this shrub. Look for white waxy lumps on the stems and black powdery covering on stems and leaves.

White cedar
Melia azedarach

This tree will grow in a wide range of climates and in almost any well-drained soil. It tolerates very dry conditions. Severe frosts may cause leaf fall but the tree usually recovers.

White cedar moth (P) caterpillars commonly defoliate the tree.

Willow
Salix spp.

These trees will grow well in most climates except very dry ones. A very good water supply is necessary, but consistently waterlogged soils are not suitable. Willows tolerate quite cold conditions.

Yellow flecks on the leaves indicate rust (D). Pale-green or reddish lumps about 8 × 4 mm on the leaves are probably caused by the willow gall sawfly (*Pontania proxima*). The galls spoil the appearance of the tree but do not cause serious damage. A systemic insecticide may protect young growth.

The leaves and stems may become infested with San José scale (P) and California red scale (P).

Longicorn beetle (P) larvae may be found feeding in the trunks and branches of weakened trees.

VEGETABLES

Satisfactory quality and quantity of production in a home garden depends on good planning, soil preparation and maintenance. Time spent on preparation before seeds or seedlings are planted is well worthwhile. Attention should be given to the following factors.

Placement

A vegetable garden should be situated so that it is in full sun all day or almost all day. A north or north-easterly aspect is ideal because plants receive morning sun but are protected from very hot afternoon sun in summer. They are also protected from south-westerly winter winds.

Shelter the garden from strong or salty winds, and avoid siting it near trees and shrubs. These compete for water and nutrients intended for the vegetables.

The area should be well drained. If the drainage is poor, the installation of subsoil drains is the best course of action. The problem, however, can be partially overcome by building the beds up above the level of the existing ground.

Soil

Successful production cannot be achieved with less than 200 mm of topsoil, and 300 mm is desirable.

A neutral to slightly acid pH is desirable for good growth of a wide range of vegetables. The soil should not be markedly acid or alkaline.

A high proportion of organic matter is desirable to help retain soil moisture and provide plant nutrients. The soil should be well dug, with clods and stones removed, and raked to produce an even fine surface. Prepare the beds several weeks before planting is intended to allow germination and removal of any weeds present in the soil.

In recent years, methods of growing vegetables and other plants without soil have been developed. Systems using water and added nutrients are referred to as 'hydroponics' or 'soilless gardening'. More details can be obtained from the many books on the subject.

Gardens constructed on top of lawns, concrete paths or bare soil with layers of newspaper, hay, straw and compost can produce large crops of good-quality vegetables. Such a system is referred to as a 'no-dig garden'.

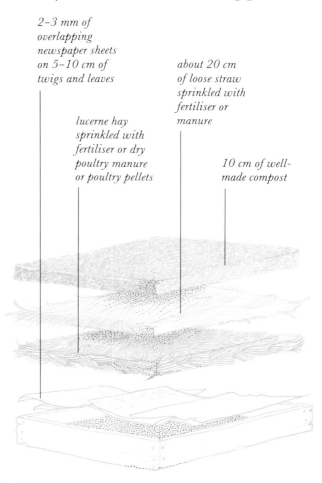

2–3 mm of overlapping newspaper sheets on 5–10 cm of twigs and leaves

about 20 cm of loose straw sprinkled with fertiliser or manure

lucerne hay sprinkled with fertiliser or dry poultry manure or poultry pellets

10 cm of well-made compost

On a concrete path, 'no-dig' gardens should begin with planks, rows of bricks, or any other material that will contain the layers.

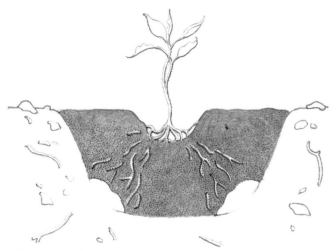

Dig a trench about 100 mm deep and 150 mm wide and place a band of fertiliser 25–50 mm wide along each side. Fill in the trench and plant seedlings or seeds.

Fertilising

It is often necessary to fertilise the soil before the crop is planted. Make sure that fertiliser is placed to avoid contact with seed or seedling roots at sowing or planting time. In addition, crops with a high nitrogen requirement usually have more fertiliser placed along the sides of the rows later. If spilled fertiliser is allowed to remain on the leaves, burnt spots and patches may result.

Watering

Frequency of water application is influenced by soil type, weather, the vegetable being grown and stage of growth. Hot weather and strong winds increase the evaporation rate of water from leaves and soil and water must be applied more frequently.

Young seedlings need constant moisture for survival, but the soil should not be too wet. The time between waterings can be lengthened as root systems develop.

Some vegetables such as cabbage, lettuce and onion grow only a shallow root system and can only obtain water from close to the soil surface. This area dries out rather quickly, and these plants need watering more frequently than do deep-rooted plants such as pumpkin or tomato, which can obtain water from lower down.

Frequent shallow watering of naturally deep-rooted plants will result in proliferation of roots in the moist area and little root development further down. Consequently the plants will not perform as well as they should and will continue to require frequent watering. Taller plants which have a poorly developed root system will fall over easily.

Leafy vegetables nearing maturity have a high water requirement.

Vegetables grown for their pods or fruits are very sensitive to drying out at flowering and while further development takes place. Water stress may lead to flower drop or smaller-than-normal fruit.

If water is applied after puddles have formed around the plants, this causes soil compaction and wastes the water which runs away.

Mulching and weeding

Mulching helps to prevent the formation of a surface crust impervious to water; reduces soil temperature fluctuations; discourages weed growth; aids moisture retention; keeps fruit such as cucumbers clean; and helps to stop splash of disease spores from the soil on to the plants.

Mulches in close contact with plant stems may encourage stem rots because high moisture levels are maintained in the soil.

Note that thick mulches of fresh grass clippings may form an impervious layer which water cannot penetrate.

Remove weeds as soon as they appear. They are using water and nutrients intended for the vegetables and may also be shading them. They are often a source of pest and disease.

Mulching or light cultivation when weeds are small are the most suitable methods for a home garden.

Seeds and seedlings

Seeds and seedlings should be purchased from a reputable source so that seed-borne diseases are less likely to be present.

Failure to establish healthy plants from seed may be caused by a variety of factors. First, make sure that the seed is not too old. Seed remains viable for varying periods of time depending on the type. For example, onion, radish and sweet corn seeds last for only one or two years, whereas rockmelon, tomato or cucumber seed may last for more than five years. Check the expiry date on the seed packet.

Some seed suffers mechanical damage if the packet is dropped. Peas and beans are easily damaged in this way and will not subsequently germinate.

Seeds may also be attacked by small pests which chew out the embryo. Any seed with holes in it will probably not germinate.

These bean seedlings have grown from damaged seed. Note the lack of terminal shoots and the production of side-shoots.

After the seed is sown other factors may stop the appearance of seedlings above ground. Pests such as springtails (P) and false wireworms (P) may chew the seed, or ants (P) may carry it away for food.

If the soil is allowed to dry out after germination has started, death will probably occur. On the other hand, overwet soil conditions favour damping-off (D), a disease that causes the seed (or seedlings) to rot. There are also several common seed-borne diseases that destroy the seed or first shoot or root.

Sowing too deep may also cause failure. In general, seeds should be sown at a depth of twice their diameter. In warm weather, or in light sandy soils, seeds should be sown slightly deeper; and in cool weather, or in heavy clay-loam soils, slightly shallower.

If soil temperatures are low, germination will be slow. At least 18°C (65°F) is desirable for most summer crops. Some seeds such as those of lettuce and celery will not germinate at temperatures above 24°C (75°F). This problem can be overcome by germinating the seeds in the refrigerator in moist kitchen paper. Treat them very gently when planting into soil.

The seedlings of some plants—for example, carrots and onions—are not capable of pushing up through a crusted soil surface.

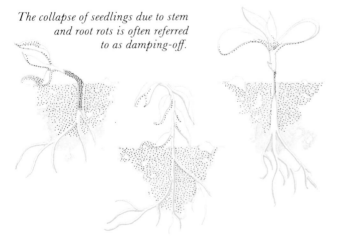

The collapse of seedlings due to stem and root rots is often referred to as damping-off.

Other problems occur after seedlings have appeared above ground. Damping-off (D) is common in seedlings because the fungi concerned are favoured by the moist crowded conditions. Seedlings rot off at ground level and fall over. This may happen quite suddenly.

If transplanting the seedlings, do it as soon as they are large enough. Delay may mean they will be slow to recover from the move.

Do not, however, plant out on a very hot day or before 'hardening off' the seedlings. This involves watering them less and getting them used to brighter, hotter conditions by exposing them to the sun for longer periods each day.

Beans, peas, cucumbers, pumpkins, melons, root crops and sweet corn do not transplant well and should be sown direct.

Lettuce, onions and silver beet can be transplanted but grow much better if sown in permanent positions.

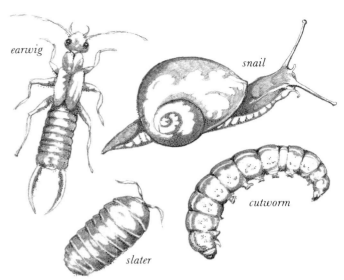

Seedlings are attacked by a number of chewing pests.

Seedlings may be chewed above or below ground by pests such as the common slater (P), and the very similar common pillbug, cutworms (P) and earwigs (P). Snails and slugs (P) also attack seedlings.

Collecting seed

Saving your own seed is fun and cheaper than buying new seed each year. There are, however, some points to keep in mind:

Seed may carry disease organisms inside or on the outside of the seed coat. It is very important to save seed from healthy plants only. If there is any doubt about this, seed can be treated in hot water or dusted with a fungicide. The recommended treatment differs from one type of seed to another. Suitable treatments for a range of different seeds are described on page 38, and further advice can be sought from your local Department of Agriculture.

Many vegetable varieties now grown are hybrids whose seed will not produce similar plants. In fact, the resulting plants may differ widely from the parents and from one another. Such vegetables include tomato, sweet corn and zucchini.

Cross-pollination can occur within some vegetable groups (e.g. cabbages and cauliflowers, or beetroot and

Members of the Family Chenopodiaceae

silver beet). This also means that resulting seed will produce plants of varying characteristics.

Store seed for a month or two after harvest because the seed of some plants will not germinate immediately.

Crop rotation

It is generally a bad practice to grow the same type of plant or closely related ones in the same place each year. Diseases, and sometimes even pests, may remain dormant on plant debris in the soil and readily attack the next season's crop.

Closely related plants also tend to use soil nutrients in the same proportions. Better use can be made of fertilisers if different types of plants are grown in succession. Groups of related plants are listed below. Some examples of annual flowers* and weeds† have been included. The weeds in each group tend to harbour pests and diseases for that group. Weed control is most important.

1 Tomato, potato, capsicum, egg plant, petunia*, thornapple†, nightshade†.
2 Pumpkin, zucchini, squash, cucumber, marrow, melons, paddy melon†.
3 Beans, broad beans, peas, lupins*, hairy vetch†.
4 Cabbage, cauliflower, Brussels sprouts, broccoli, turnip, swede, radish, kohl rabi, horseradish, wallflower*, stock*, wild turnip†, shepherd's purse†.
5 Onion, garlic, leek, shallot, chives.
6 Beetroot, silver beet, spinach, fat hen†.
7 Lettuce, endive, artichoke, China aster*, cineraria*, zinnia*, cape weed†, thistles†.
8 Carrot, parsley, parsnip, celery.

Members of the Family Apiaceae

Caterpillars of Spilosoma glatygni *are often referred to as 'woolly bears'. They feed on many plants including vegetables.*

Pests and diseases

There are many pests and diseases which attack a wide range of vegetables under some circumstances. Their damage can be reduced in extent and severity if the crop is inspected regularly and control is prompt.

Leaves and stems may be chewed by various caterpillars including the green looper (P), bogong moth (P) caterpillars, cluster caterpillars (P) and woolly bears (P).

Whitefringed weevil (P), vegetable weevil (P), African black beetle (P) and redshouldered leaf beetles (P) also chew various plant parts. Snails and slugs (P) attack most vegetables particularly in moist weather. Sap-suckers such as aphids (P), passionvine hopper (P), whiteflies (P), horehound bug (P), green vegetable bug (P), Rutherglen bug (P), harlequin bug (P) and vegetable jassid also have a wide host range.

Thrips (P), earth mites (P), such as blue oat mite and redlegged earth mite, and spider mites such as the two-spotted mite (P) and the bean spider mite, are common pests of vegetables and produce grey, white or yellow areas on the leaves. Thrips may also attack the flowers.

Root systems may be damaged by black field crickets (P), mole crickets (P) and false wireworms (P).

Common vegetable diseases showing symptoms on leaves are downy mildew (D) and powdery mildew (D).

Wilting and death may be caused by fusarium wilt (D) and verticillium wilt (D). Root knot nematodes (D) also cause wilting of above-ground plant parts. Bacterial soft rots (D) damage fleshy organs; and collar rot (D), sclerotium stem rot (D) and sclerotinia rot (D) attack a wide range of vegetable plants. Grey mould (D) sometimes damages pumpkins and other flowers.

The vegetables chosen for further discussion are those most commonly grown and those with most specific pest and disease problems.

Bean

Beans grow well in a wide range of soil types, but the pH must not be highly acid. Manganese toxicity is one problem likely to occur in acid soils. This is characterised by stunting, lack of flowers, and leaves with scorched edges or yellow-brown areas between the veins. If this occurs the soil should be limed. Beans do not tolerate waterlogging or salt in soil or irrigation water.

The plants are seriously injured by frost, and need protection from strong winds because the stems are brittle. Take care not to break off parts of the plant when picking the beans.

Poor germination can be caused by: allowing fertiliser to come into direct contact with the seed; planting too early when the soil is too cold; 'crusting' at the soil surface; overwatering the seeds; and damaging the seed before planting (by dropping the seed packet).

Mechanical injury to the seed may result in a condition called 'baldhead'. In this case the plant has no terminal growing point, produces only small side shoots, and may die.

The soil directly under the seeds should be firm. Cover the seed with 30 mm of soil and then apply a light mulch to stop the formation of a surface crust through which the seedlings cannot push. The seeds should be sown into moist soil; and unless the weather is hot, do not water again until the seedlings have appeared.

The plants should be hilled about a fortnight after the seedlings emerge and again when they are larger. This helps to support the plant; brings more soil and therefore more nutrients into the root zone; and may help to overcome any damage to the lower stem caused by bean fly (P).

Do not disturb the shallow roots when weeding, and make sure the plants do not suffer from lack of water, particularly from flowering onwards.

If very hot weather occurs at flowering time, pod set may be poor. Overhead watering may be used to increase humidity in this case.

If successive sowings are being made, try to plant them in different parts of the garden. The older plants are likely to be infested with bean spider mite and two-spotted mite (P) which cause fine yellow mottling of the leaves and can easily spread to a nearby young crop. Mottled leaves can also be the result of whitefly (P) attack. There are a number of caterpillars that may chew leaves; these include green looper (P).

Stunted plants with greyish leaves may have been damaged by the vegetable leafhopper (*Austroasca viridigrisea*).

Diseases that cause leaf spots include rust (D), halo blight (D), angular leaf spot (D), bacterial brown spot (D) and anthracnose (D). Pods also may show spots if these diseases are present. Pod spots on one side of the pod only are probably caused by the sun. Check for red, slightly sunken streaks on the pods in summer. This is termed 'sunscald'.

Pods can be attacked by sap-suckers such as harlequin bug (P), Rutherglen bug (P), green vegetable bug (P), and the podsucking bug (*Riptortus serripes*) which is dark brown with a yellow stripe on each side; it has spines on its thorax and hind legs. Other pod-attackers are bean podborer (P), corn earworm (P), grass blue butterfly (P), and pea blue butterfly larvae. Twisted pods may be produced if bean blossom thrips (P) have attacked the flowers and by the bacterial disease, pod twist. Onion thrips (P) and the onion maggot (P) may also damage bean plants.

If the whole plant is yellowing and wilting, check for clover stunt (D), and summer death (D).

Beans may be attacked by collar rot and stem rots like other vegetables. They should be grown in the same ground only once in three years.

Bean plants are best sprayed early in the day when the leaves are horizontal rather than later when they are held in a vertical position.

The use of carbaryl and some other insecticides to kill leaf- and pod-attacking caterpillars will also kill predators of spider mites (red spider). This may mean a rapid build-up of mite numbers and serious damage may result. Watch carefully for bean spider mite and two-spotted mite (P) damage, and act to control these pests promptly.

Beetroot

Beetroot can be grown successfully in most areas and throughout the entire year, except when the growing conditions are hot.

Soak the seed in water overnight (*not* for days and days), and sow direct into a well-drained and well-prepared soil. As soon as the seedlings are established, thin them out to about 100 mm apart. If thinning is left till much later, this will result in a high proportion of deformed and small roots.

Do not 'hill' beetroot.

Beetroot grown slowly will be tough, so make sure they do not suffer from water stress or competition from weeds.

Beetroot does not thrive in acid soils; and in excessively alkaline soils boron deficiency (D) will occur. This is characterised by death of young leaves and scorched, wilted older leaves. Many small new leaves may start to grow.

Remove any spotted or dead leaves from the plants and burn them. This will help to control cercospora leaf spot (D) and beet rust (D).

Ideally, beetroot should not be grown in the same soil more than once every four years.

Leaves may be attacked by the beet webworm (P), earth mites (P) and beet leafminer (P). Hollows in the beet may be caused by vegetable weevil (P); and lumps by common scab (D) or root knot nematode (D). Plants that grow slowly, wilt quickly in hot weather and have prolific growth of secondary roots may have been attacked by the beet nematode. These nematodes occur only in certain areas, so if they are suspected seek positive identification from your local Department of Agriculture.

Beet nematode causes the growth of a mass of fine roots.

Broad bean

Broad beans are not suitable for the tropics. They prefer cool growing conditions and can withstand severe frost. Unfortunately symptoms of a common and serious disease, broad bean wilt (D), are more pronounced under cold to cool conditions. Adjust the time of seed planting so that as much as possible of the life of the crop, 18 to 20 weeks, occurs at temperatures a little over 20°C. Temperature seems to be particularly important towards the end of growth.

Broad beans will grow in a wide range of soils, but they perform best in heavy but well-drained soil of neutral to slightly alkaline pH.

They should be sown directly into their permanent positions. Germination will be poor if the seed is allowed to come into

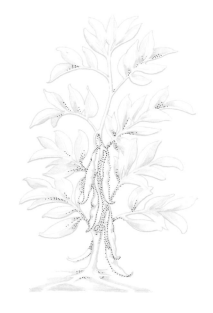

direct contact with fertiliser; or if it is sown in very wet soil or watered too heavily.

High levels of nitrogenous fertiliser will favour production of leaf at the expense of flowers (and pods). Pod set will also be adversely affected by wind, heavy rain or extremes of temperature at flowering time.

Supports of twine and stakes are necessary for taller varieties.

Broad beans are legumes and are a valuable source of nitrogen if the plants are dug into the soil when the crop is finished.

Plants with distorted leaves, dead growing points, or stiff stunted growth, probably have a virus disease such as broad bean wilt (D), spotted wilt (D), or 'leafroll'. 'Leafroll' is also known as

clover stunt (D). The leaf spotting caused by aphid honeydew is referred to as chocolate spot.

Brown leaf spots with small black dots on them are probably caused by the fungus *Ascochyta fabae*. This disease, which is favoured by moist weather, begins on lower leaves and spreads up. Stems may crack open and collapse. Crop rotation and use of disease-free seed will help to avoid this problem.

Note that the soft, tender leaves and stems of these plants are easily damaged during cultural operations or by chemicals, and this damage may show up as leaf and stem spots.

Capsicum

Capsicums grow best in warm weather and are susceptible to frost at all stages of growth. The soil must be well drained, and should have a high level of organic matter and a slightly acid pH.

In very hot weather, exposed fruit may be sunburnt. This will show up as grey to white slightly sunken patches.

Irregular watering is likely to lead to blossom-end rot (D), a sunken area at the end of the fruit. Fruit may also be attacked by budworms (P), green vegetable bug (P), and fruit fly (P) larvae. Leaves may also show symptoms of diseases such as spotted wilt (D), powdery mildew (D) and target spot (D).

Pests and diseases of tomato are likely to affect capsicums because the two plants are closely related.

Carrot

Carrots prefer cool growing conditions but are susceptible to frost.

They grow in a wide range of well-drained soils, but one of open texture is the best. Carrots tolerate moderately acid soils. A stony, cloddy or shallow soil is unsuitable; applications of fresh animal manure, green manure or other fertiliser later than three weeks before sowing are likely to cause forked or hairy carrots.

Seedlings cannot be transplanted and seed must be sown into permanent positions. Sow thickly, cover by no more than 5 mm, and add a thin mulch on top. Keep the soil damp at all times, because the seedlings cannot push up through a crusted surface. If the seed is sown thinly the individual seedlings will probably not be able to push through the surface by themselves. High temperatures during germination can cause poor results. A regular water supply is necessary for the production of high-quality carrots.

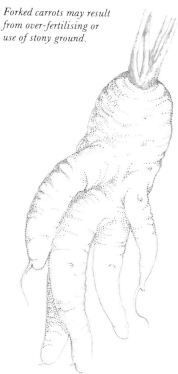

Forked carrots may result from over-fertilising or use of stony ground.

It is important to control weeds from the beginning. Remove them carefully by hand. Carrots should not be 'hilled'.

The springtail (P) called lucerne flea may skeletonise the leaves. Carrot aphids (*Caraviella aegopodii*) feed from beneath the leaves and cause them to twist and buckle. The leaves go yellow with a reddish tinge and the plants remain small. Carrot aphids also feed on other plants (including the willow) and carry a virus disease, carrot motley dwarf, which causes yellowing and stunting.

Symptoms of leaf spot (*Cercospora carotae*) and leaf blight (D) can be confused but the control is the same.

The roots may be attacked by vegetable weevil (P), root knot nematode (D), spotted vegetable weevil and carrot rust fly larvae. Rotting can be caused by bacterial soft rots (D) or sclerotinia rot (D).

Celery

Celery needs more care than many other vegetables. It requires about four months of mild cool weather for best results. Temperatures should range between 13 and 24°C and humidity should be high. Once established, the crop will tolerate higher temperatures in the first month or two but not later. Celery will stand light frost, but exposure to temperatures of 4–13°C for ten days or more induces the plant to go to seed. This is often termed 'bolting'. Heavy frosts near harvest cause blistering on the stems.

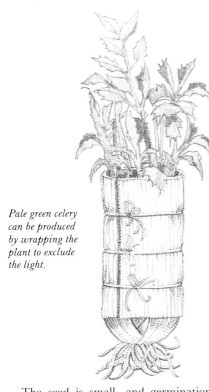

Pale green celery can be produced by wrapping the plant to exclude the light.

The seed is small, and germinations may be erratic and take two weeks or more. Plant no more than 3 mm deep, and use a light mulch to prevent surface crusting.

When the seedlings are about 100 mm high, they are ready to transplant.

When transplanting, keep as much soil as possible around each root system; and position so that the crowns are at, not below, the soil surface. Space the plants from 250 mm to 400 mm apart and water promptly.

The soil must be neutral to only slightly acid, high in organic matter and well drained. Celery does not tolerate waterlogging.

The plants must be well supplied with water especially in the last six weeks. Water stress checks growth and can cause 'black heart' — a gradual browning and then blackening of the young centre leaves. This indicates that insufficient calcium is reaching the plant. The use of sodium nitrate as a nitrogenous fertiliser makes the problem worse.

If the soil is light it may be necessary to water every day in hot weather. However, constantly wet leaves may make problems with fungal diseases more likely to occur.

Celery also has a high fertiliser requirement and needs a good supply of nitrogen. Unless it is grown quickly the stalks become tough and stringy.

Celery cannot compete with weeds, but do not disturb the shallow root system when removing them.

If pale stems are required, exclude the light for the last three or four weeks by covering them with several layers of paper (preferably waterproof) tied top and bottom. The leaves should be left exposed to the sun.

Cracked stems indicate boron deficiency (D) which is often described as 'cat scratch'. Late blight of celery (D) causes spots on the leaves. Bacterial soft rot (D) first appears on the leaf stalks as small water-soaked spots. Sclerotinia rot (D) can affect celery and is often known as 'pink rot'.

The plants may be attacked by the general range of pests, including the vegetable weevil (P) and aphids (P).

Crucifers

The crucifer or brassica group includes cabbages, cauliflowers, broccoli, Brussels sprouts and kohl rabi, which are basically cool-climate plants. Radish, turnip, swede and a number of weeds are also crucifers.

Cabbages are the most adaptable as far as climate is concerned but choose a variety suitable for the planting time. Broccoli grows best in cool to cold conditions.

Brussels sprouts give best results when growth begins in warm conditions and ends in cool to cold conditions. Loose, open sprouts may result if the soil is too rich in nitrogen.

Cauliflowers are the most demanding, and good heads will not form unless the weather is cool and humid with medium to short day-lengths. They should also be kept growing steadily.

Cabbages and kohl rabi should be grown quickly, so generous supplies of nitrogen are needed.

All these plants grow in a wide range of soils but the drainage must be good. A high level of organic matter is definitely an advantage.

The soil should be neutral to only slightly alkaline. In acid soils the disease club root (D) and the disorder whiptail (D) are likely to occur; whereas in alkaline soils boron deficiency (D) may develop, particularly in cauliflowers, and manganese also may become unavailable to the plant under these conditions.

Rotting may indicate sclerotinia rot (D) or bacterial soft rot (D).

Leaf-spotting diseases include mosaic — turnip (D), downy mildew (D), and white rust (D). Alternaria leaf spot, which causes dark spots up to 10 mm, can usually be avoided by following the cultural practices outlined here.

Crop rotation is important in the control of diseases such as black rot (D), black leg (D) and black root of radish (D).

Disease-free seed and removal of cruciferous weeds are also very important in the control of crucifer diseases.

Leaves may be chewed by various larvae including those of cabbage white butterfly (P), cabbage moth (P), cluster caterpillar (P) and the corn earworm (P). Aphids (P), and earth mites (P), can also cause problems.

Fine, meandering lines on the leaves are probably caused by cabbage leaf-miner (*Liriomyza brassicae*). These would cause most problems in seedlings and should be controlled by programmes aimed at other pests.

Crucifer leaves are covered with wax, and sprays tend to run off. To overcome this problem, add a small quantity of wetting agent when sprays are being prepared. Household washing-up detergent can be used for this purpose.

Cucurbits

Cucurbits such as pumpkin, marrow, squash, cucumber, zucchini, watermelons and rockmelons all have similar cultural requirements, and similar pest and disease problems.

They can be grown successfully on a wide range of soils but they must have good drainage.

Large amounts of organic matter greatly improve performance, and the soil should be slightly acid. Molybdenum deficiency will probably occur if the soil is highly acid. In this case, growth will be slow. The leaves become mottled and go yellow around the edges, which roll up. The problem can be overcome by watering the leaves with 7 g of sodium molybdate in 10 L of water. Seek the advice of your local Department of Agriculture.

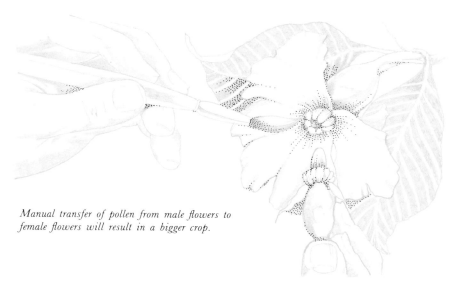

Manual transfer of pollen from male flowers to female flowers will result in a bigger crop.

Cucurbits grow best in hot weather. They are frost sensitive, and cool winds or low temperatures retard growth.

Seed germination is greatly influenced by soil temperature. Best results are obtained above 20°C. At soil temperatures below 16°C, the seeds will not germinate satisfactorily.

The plants need a lot of water and the soil should not be allowed to dry out. On very hot days the leaves are likely to wilt but recover in the evening if soil moisture is adequate. Regular watering will help avoid blossom-end rot (D), a problem that occurs commonly on watermelons. Moisture stress may cause some immature fruit to drop from the vine.

Fruit may also fall off if the vine has produced more than it can mature.

Weeding is necessary when the plants are young, but take care not to damage the shallow root system.

Generally these plants bear both male and female flowers, and bees are the usual pollinators. A poor fruit crop may be the result of adverse weather conditions, lack of male or female flowers, or absence of bees. If there are no bees, the flowers can be hand pollinated (preferably in the early morning). Pick a male flower, remove the petals and rub the pollen into a female flower. Male flowers are borne on a long spindly stem. Female flowers have a bulge between the petals and the stalk.

Cucurbit leaves may be attacked by various pests including pumpkin beetle (P), redshouldered leaf beetle (P), leafeating ladybird (P), two-spotted mite (P) and whitefly (P). Large plants can tolerate quite high populations of whitefly, so control may be unnecessary.

Leaves may show symptoms of mosaic (D), downy mildew (D), anthracnose (D) and fusarium wilt (D). The latter may cause death of seedlings also.

Powdery mildew (D) is a common cucurbit disease which usually shows up first in the centre of the vine as a white powdery coating on leaves. If this problem is serious in your area, choose varieties that are resistant to the disease. This is usually mentioned on the seed packet.

Other diseases include bacterial leaf spot (D); angular leaf spot (D) which is most common on cucumbers; and gummy stem blight (D), most common on watermelons.

The use of the fungicide, copper oxychloride, on cucurbits before they begin to run may cause injury. Sulphur dust and wettable sulphur should be used with great care on cucumbers and rockmelons, particularly in hot weather. They can cause severe leaf scorching.

Flowers and small fruit may be rotted by grey mould (D) in cool humid conditions. Flattening of stems is fasciation (D), which occurs more on apple cucumbers than on other cucurbits.

Lettuce

There is a range of lettuce varieties. Choose a variety suitable for the area and the season. Cos and butterhead lettuce have fewer pests and disease problems than crisphead lettuce. Lettuces tolerate light frosts.

They will grow in most soils as long as drainage is good and the pH slightly acid to slightly alkaline. They will not tolerate very acid soils. Uneven germination is likely to result if seed is sown deeper than 10 mm.

Unless growth is continuous, the leaves may be coarse and bitter and the plant may 'go to seed' — that is, it may stop producing leaves and start producing flowers and seed. An even growth depends on a regular heavy watering programme and a good supply of fertiliser high in nitrogen. As a general rule, apply fertiliser along the side of the rows one week after thinning and thereafter fortnightly. The root system is small so place the fertiliser fairly close to the plants and do not dig in deeply. Water afterwards to wash fertiliser, which will cause marks, off the leaves.

Excessive applications of fertiliser may lead to browning of the edges of inner leaves. This browning is called 'tip burn' and indicates that the proportion of sodium, potassium or magnesium salts is too high compared with the proportion of calcium salts available to the plant. Additions of lime will probably be beneficial in this case.

Thin the seedlings to spacings of about 500 × 300 mm. Closer plantings encourage fungal diseases such as downy mildew (D) and grey mould (D).

Yellowing and wilting indicate a viral disease called lettuce necrotic yellows (D); and thickened leaves with transparent veins are the result of infection by lettuce big vein virus (D). Diseases that cause spots on leaves include bacterial leaf spot (D) and anthracnose (D). Lettuces are commonly attacked by bacterial soft rots (D) which cause brown slimy patches. A brown rot is also produced by sclerotinia rot (D) or 'lettuce drop'.

Pests that commonly attack lettuce leaves include Rutherglen bug (P), earth mites (P) and cineraria leafminer (P).

Onion

Onions grow best as a cool-weather crop because they require a gradually increasing temperature for proper formation of the bulbs.

The soil should be well drained and slightly acid to slightly alkaline. Onions will not tolerate highly acidic soils. Added compost or animal manure must be well rotted, especially in areas where onion maggot (P) occurs. Onions should not be grown in the same soil more than once in three years.

An over-rich soil will produce prolific foliage growth at the expense of bulb formation. It may also encourage the formation of thick, open necks which allow easy entry of fungi. Split or double bulbs may be the result of an uneven water supply.

Dead, twisted leaves and distorted bulbs may indicate onion bloat, caused by nematodes.

Choose a variety suitable for the time of sowing. If early varieties are sown late, or late varieties are sown early, there will be little bulb formation.

The seed bed should have a firm base with about 25 mm of fine loose soil on top. The seed, which must be fresh, takes 10–21 days to germinate. The seedlings will not push through the surface if it is allowed to form a crust.

Onions cannot compete with weeds, so control is important especially when the plants are small.

Some of the diseases mentioned below can be identified on onions purchased from the greengrocer.

Bulb rots such as neck rot (D) and other diseases such as smudge (D) are likely to occur unless dry weather prevails at harvest time. Do not water at this time. Unless onions to be stored are dry, and the storage area is dry and well ventilated, black mould (D) may also develop. Yellow and dying leaves may indicate white rot (D), downy mildew (D) or

a soil that is too acid. If leaves die from the tips, suspect fusarium basal rot which produces a white fungal growth at the base of the bulb. Practise a long crop rotation, ensure good drainage, and avoid bulb damage at harvest.

Leaf twisting and bending on seedlings, together with dark-brown to black powdery masses within leaf tissues, may indicate onion smut, a very serious disease. Report this to your local Department of Agriculture.

Misshapen seedlings and distorted bulbs may indicate onion bloat which is a nematode problem. Always remove all bulbs from the area at harvest time.

The most important onion pests are onion thrips (P), the springtail (P) called lucerne flea and onion maggot (P). Aphids (P) are a problem occasionally.

Plants such as garlic, leeks, shallots and chives have similar cultural requirements and pest and disease problems.

Parsnip

Most of the remarks made about carrots also apply to parsnips. The latter, however, will not tolerate acid soil and need a greater depth of open-textured soil than carrots. The seed, which must be fresh, needs a very fine-textured soil in which to germinate and should not be covered by more than 12 mm. Germination, which is most efficient at about 18°C, may take from two to three weeks. Thin to about 100–150 mm apart.

A white powdery growth on the leaves is powdery mildew (D). Leaf spots and crown rot are usually parsnip canker (D). Lumps on the root are probably caused by root knot nematode (D).

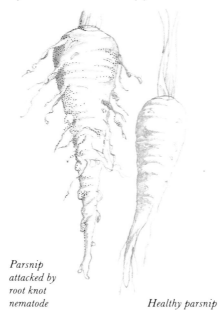

Parsnip attacked by root knot nematode   *Healthy parsnip*

lucerne flea
Sminthurus viridis

actual length 3 mm

Pea

Peas cannot be grown in the tropics. Temperatures over 30°C cause serious reduction in yield. Peas need a cool moist growing period but note that frost damages flowers and pods.

The soil must be well drained, preferably high in organic matter, and slightly acid to slightly alkaline. It must not be highly acid.

Seed should be sown in moist soil and watered sparingly or not at all until plants appear above ground. Overwatering in early stages encourages seed and seedling rots.

Poor germination will result if fertiliser is allowed to come into direct contact with the seed. Nitrogenous fertiliser is rarely needed because peas are legumes and can make use of the nitrogen in the atmosphere.

Some reduction of disease problems can be achieved by growing the peas on a trellis. The plants do not compete well with weeds.

Yellow stunted plants may be suffering from clover stunt (D), which is sometimes referred to as 'top yellows'. Plants with black spots may have leaf and pod spot (D). Downy mildew (D) and powdery mildew (D) both attack pea crops. Papery areas on leaves and stipules may indicate bacterial blight (D).

Pods may be attacked by the pea weevil, budworms (P) and green vegetable bug (P). Leaves are damaged by earth mites (P), and the lucerne flea which is a springtail (P).

The problem called 'foot rot' is associated with leaf and pod spot (D).

Chemical controls can be difficult with peas because they have a very waxy surface which sheds water, and because the plants are usually very tangled and quite dense.

Potato

Potatoes can be grown in a wide range of climates and soils. Note, however, that the plants are damaged by frost (a severe frost will kill them) and that they need good soil drainage. The soil should have a high proportion of organic matter and be free of clods.

Do not plant potatoes in soil that has been recently limed or had wood ashes added. Tubers are likely to develop rough spots on the skin in alkaline soils. This is a disease called common scab (D) which may be confused with root knot nematode (D) attack.

It is important to plant disease-free seed tubers. Buy certified seed tubers from nurseries, or save small healthy potatoes from a home-grown crop. Whole small tubers are preferable, but if large tubers are to be used cut them into pieces weighing about 50 g with at least two 'eyes'. Do not plant before the cut surfaces dry out. If wet and cold conditions prevail, planting should be delayed.

Ideally the cut or whole seed potatoes should have sprouts appearing before they are planted. Spread the tubers out in a well-lit warm place and leave for about a month. The sprouts should be short and thick. Any seed potatoes that have long thin sprouts should be destroyed, because they are infected with the virus, leafroll (D).

Overwatering before the plants have appeared will encourage the development of black leg (D), and wet conditions during growth make bacterial soft rots (D) (also called 'tuber soft rots') more likely.

When the plants are about 150 mm high, carefully hoe out the weeds and begin to hill the soil up around the plants. Further hilling at flowering time is important to ensure that the tubers are always well covered and therefore not exposed to light which will make them turn green. Maintenance of the hills until harvest, and regular watering to prevent soil

cracks, will help avoid attack from the tunnel-eating potato moth (P) larvae.

Potatoes have a high fertiliser requirement, but too much nitrogen will encourage the growth of tops at the expense of tuber production. Fertiliser should always be mixed and distributed evenly and water should be applied evenly and regularly. If care is taken in this regard and wide plant spacing is avoided, then 'hollow heart' (cracks and hollows in the centre of tubers) will probably not occur. Dry soil conditions especially from flowering onwards are thought to be the cause of 'brown fleck' (irregular brown spots and blotches through the tuber). On the other hand, excessively wet conditions cause the lenticels to enlarge and develop into corky spots. These are similar to common scab (D) spots but are more evenly distributed over the surface of the tuber.

Try not to plant potatoes in the same soil more frequently than every four or five years. Sweet corn and lawn grasses would be suitable for rotation with potatoes to reduce problems such as rhizoctonia (D) and common scab (D).

Potatoes should be harvested carefully to help avoid problems with gangrene (D) or phoma. Tubers may also be damaged by late blight (D), powdery scab (D) and rhizoctonia (D).

Brown spots on the leaves may be caused by early blight, also known as target spot (D); and yellow mottling and crinkling of leaves by mosaics (D).

If leaves are rolled up and/or purple, check for leafroll (D) and purple top wilt (D). A bronze or black discoloration may indicate spotted wilt (D). Leaves can be attacked by the vegetable leafhopper which produces yellow stippling; and leafeating ladybird (P) which removes the surface in patches.

The tubers and root system may be attacked by African black beetle (P), black field cricket (P) and the vegetable weevil (P).

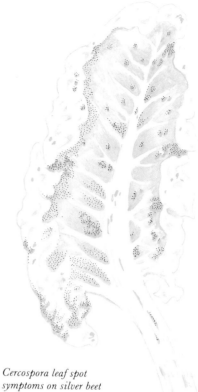

Cercospora leaf spot symptoms on silver beet

Silver beet

This plant, also known as Swiss chard, needs an open, well-drained soil with plenty of organic matter. Unless grown quickly the leaves may be bitter. It should therefore be well supplied with nitrogen and water.

Extremely hot or extremely cold conditions are not suitable for successful growth of this plant.

Do not harvest until the plant is well-established and remove any flower stalks that appear.

Apart from general pests and diseases, silver beet can be attacked by beet leafminer (P), earth mites (P), beet rust (D) and cercospora leaf spot (D).

Sweet corn

Sweet corn, or maize, needs a fertile, well-drained soil and a constant good water supply. Its fertiliser requirements are high, and some nitrogen should be applied at planting time, particularly if the crop is sown early in the season.

The soil should be slightly acid to neutral for best results. In highly alkaline soils corn is likely to develop zinc deficiency, which may cause stunting and death of young seedlings or broad creamy-yellow stripes on the leaves. If this is known to occur in the district, dust

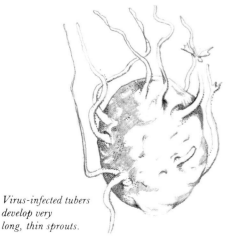

Virus-infected tubers develop very long, thin sprouts.

Healthy tubers produce thicker sprouts.

the seed with colloidal zinc before sowing. It will also be necessary to spray with zinc sulphate, 5 g in 10 L of water per 10 m², when the plants are about 250 mm high and again when about 500 mm high. Manganese deficiency is also likely in alkaline soils.

Sweet corn is a warm-weather crop and requires full sun; optimum growth occurs when the temperature is 24–27°C. Germination is usually poor if the soil is cold and the plants are severely damaged by frost at any stage of growth.

Pollination, which is by wind, will be most uniform if the plants are arranged in a block rather than in a long row. Heatwave conditions at tasselling will interfere with pollination, and unless pollination occurs the grains will not become plump and juicy.

Weed control is important, but the shallow roots should not be disturbed. The practice of hilling-up soil around the plants does little to help them remain upright and may damage the roots.

The roots may be attacked by African black beetle (P), earwigs (P) and false wireworms (P). Cobs are commonly chewed by caterpillars of the corn earworm (P) and also by redshouldered leaf beetles (P). The stem may be chewed at the nodes by caterpillars of the yellow peach moth (P); or rotted below ground by bacterial soft rots (D).

Patterns of light green and dark green on the leaves are probably caused by maize dwarf virus; dark-green upward-pointing leaves are characteristic of a virus disease called 'wallaby ear'; and long, light-brown leaf spots indicate leaf blight (D). Many other diseases affect sweet corn occasionally.

Tomato

Tomatoes can be grown successfully in many different areas but they must be protected from frost and strong winds.

Choose a variety suitable for the situation; for example, some types of tomato, such as 'Rouge De Marmande', will set fruit in cool conditions. There are also varieties resistant to verticillium wilt (D), fusarium wilt (D) and root knot nematode (D), all problems in certain areas. In very hot districts the sun may burn the fruit. This is termed sunscald and may be largely overcome by planting varieties that produce abundant leaf growth and shade the fruit. Almost any soil type will produce reasonable crops, but drainage must be good and high organic matter levels are desirable. Tomatoes are tolerant of acid soils.

Pest and disease problems will increase year by year if tomatoes or related crops

Spots on leaves and fruit may be caused by a variety of fungi, bacteria or viruses. An accurate diagnosis is necessary if control is to be efficient.

are planted continuously in the same place. A four-year interval is a good idea.

Tomatoes need a good fertiliser supply but excessive amounts of nitrogen will encourage foliage rather than fruit production.

The water supply should be even and regular in an attempt to avoid problems such as blossom-end rot (D), dark sunken areas at the ends opposite the stalks; and sclerotium stem rot (D), white fungal threads on the stem at ground level. Watering or rain when the fruit is mature may cause the skin to split near the stem. This fruit should be used quickly.

Poor pollination and fruit set are often the result of temperatures less than 15°C at flowering. Temperatures more than 38°C have a similar effect.

Tomato fruit is subject to a number of different rots. If the plants are staked, anthracnose (D) and soil rots are far less likely to appear.

Tomatoes are affected by a number of virus diseases including mosaic, yellow top and spotted wilt (D). Mosaic symptoms include mottling of green on the leaves, streaks of varying lengths on the stems and sunken brown patches under the skin of the fruit. It is spread during operations such as pruning and also on smokers' fingers because most cigarette and pipe tobacco contains this virus. Smokers should wash thoroughly before touching the plants.

Yellow top infected plants are stiff and upright. The leaf edges are yellow and tend to curl downwards. Control of weeds and aphids (P) will reduce problems with this disease.

Control of onion thrips (P) will reduce the spread of spotted wilt (D).

If you grow tomatoes from seed, seek advice about the various different seed-treatments which can be carried out to

reduce losses from mosaic, and from bacterial canker (D), bacterial spot, bacterial speck and bacterial wilt.

Bacterial wilt may be involved if rapid wilting and death occur. This disease should be identified accurately. The disease-causing organisms survive between crops in weeds such as blackberry nightshade and cobbler's-pegs.

Fungal leaf spots which cause problems include target spot (D). It is sensible to seek advice about their identity because the one fungicide will not control all these diseases.

The disease, big bud (D), is spread by the common brown leafhopper (*Orosius argentatus*). This insect is active, about 3 mm long, and speckled brown. It moves on to tomatoes in hot weather when weeds dry off.

Bronzing of the foliage may be the result of tomato russet mite (P) attack. Leaves and shoots of the plant may also be attacked by whiteflies (P) and leafeating ladybirds (P).

The fruit may be damaged by bugs such as green vegetable bug (P) and Rutherglen bug (P); and by fruit flies (P) including metallic-green tomato fly (*Lamprolonchaea brouniana*) which attacks only injured or split fruit. This is likely in a home garden where the fruit is ripened on the bush. The flies are about 6 mm long, stout and bright green. The maggots are similar to those of other fruit flies. Spray programmes for other tomato pests will control this too.

Other tomato pests include African black beetle (P); corn earworm (P) which is often referred to as 'tomato grub'; and tomato stemborer (*Symmetrischema tangolias*). The larvae of this moth occasionally tunnel in stems within 200 mm of ground level. By the time damage is noticed, control is difficult.

A–Z of
PESTS

An alphabetical listing of more than two hundred insects and their relatives, with notes on their recognition and control

Control recommendations

The pest control programs in this section are divided for the most part into Organic/Non-chemical and Chemical.

Organic/Non-chemical methods are vital for those who want to use only 'organic' procedures. They are recommended to all gardeners in the interests of efficient control and reduction in pesticide usage.

The use of pesticides is sometimes unavoidable. All gardeners can choose products that are organically acceptable if they wish. These are usually to be found under organic control in this section.

Acacia spotting bug *Rayieria tumidiceps*

This bug, which is about 10 mm long, is elongate in outline and has long slender legs and antennae. The body is yellowish-brown and the wings brown with paler areas near the point of attachment.

The damage caused by injection of saliva and sucking of sap is common in some areas, but the bugs themselves are not often seen. The plants are disfigured by the brown spotting, and leaves die and fall if the attack is severe.

PLANTS ATTACKED Wattles, including Sydney golden wattle (*Acacia longifolia*), Flinders Range wattle (*A. iteaphylla*) and fringed wattle (*A. fimbriata*).

CONTROL Difficult because the bugs are rarely seen feeding on the plant.
• Organic/non-chemical: Supply water and nutrients to keep the plant actively growing.
• Chemical: If spraying is to be attempted, try omethoate and follow label directions.

African black beetle *Heteronychus arator*

These shiny black beetles are about 12 mm long. They chew stems just below ground level, leaving a frayed edge. Plants may wilt and fall over. Holes may be chewed in potatoes, and the eyes of seed potatoes may be damaged. Strawberries may be hollowed out from beneath.

Adults become active in spring, and mating occurs. Eggs are laid in areas of soft soil. The mating and egg-laying period may extend over about three months, which is why larvae and adults can both be found in the soil at any one time.

Young larvae feed on dead organic matter in the soil, but older larvae feed on grass roots. Most damage to lawns and other turf is caused by the last larval stage. Heavily damaged grass appears to need watering and can easily be pulled up. Brown patches may appear. The larvae are typical white curl grubs (P) and grow to about 25 mm. They pupate in the soil and emerge as adults from mid-January to late February/early March. These adults feed until the weather gets cold, then burrow into the soil and become semi-dormant. Pest numbers are high after prolonged dry weather.

PLANTS ATTACKED A wide range, including lawn grasses, sweet corn, potatoes, tomatoes, beetroot, bananas, grapevines, cabbages, cauliflowers, dahlias and petunias. They do not feed on legumes.

CONTROL Treat for black beetle in the spring because the very young larvae are near the soil surface and are easier to kill.
• Organic/non-chemical: Fork over garden beds and expose any larvae to birds. Avoid garden lights. They attract beetles.
• Chemical: Apply fenamiphos granules to lawn areas as directed on the label. Water the lawn thoroughly after application. There is no home-garden chemical suitable for control in other plants. However, if black beetle is controlled in the lawn, damage to other garden plants should be minimal.

Ants Order Hymenoptera: Family Formicidae

Ants live in colonies. Most have underground nests but some species choose logs, wall cavities or the bases of potted plants.

Workers forage for food and take some back to the nest to feed the legless larvae. Different species feed on different substances: dead animal material, other insects, seeds, fungi and honeydew from insects such as scales and aphids.

The Argentine ant (*Linepithema humilis*), which is brown and about 3 mm long, feeds on a wide range of different materials and is considered a major pest. It travels along well-defined trails and does not smell 'anty' when crushed.

CONTROL
• Organic/non-chemical: Ants tend to nest in dry areas. A change of cultural practices may stop them nesting in garden pots. Increase the water-holding capacity of the potting mix by increasing organic matter content, and ensure that when the pots are watered the water penetrates all parts of the mix and flows out of the drainage hole.

Argentine ant cannot be controlled by individuals. Report its suspected presence to your local Department of Agriculture.
• Chemical: Follow ant trails to the nest and treat it with chlorpyrifos or with diazinon. Ants can be discouraged from coming indoors by spraying areas such as doorsteps and window-frames with household aerosol preparations that kill ants. The bases of pots and the trunks of trees could also be sprayed.

Aphids   Order Hemiptera: Family Aphididae

These small insects, which are sometimes referred to as plant lice or blackfly or greenfly, are usually 1 to 2 mm long, although some, such as the conifer aphids, may be 4 or 5 mm long. Different species are different colours — ranging from green to pink, bright deep yellow, black and grey.

They have generally rounded bodies, but the winged forms appear to be elongated. On most aphids it is possible to see two tubes projecting from near the end of the body. These are called 'cornicles' and are found only on aphids.

Aphids are capable of giving birth to living young, and large populations build up relatively quickly. When the colony increases in numbers and the shoot or bud becomes crowded, some winged forms develop and these aphids can fly to other plants or other parts of the same plant.

Aphids have piercing and sucking mouthparts with which they withdraw sap from plants. They prefer new shoots and buds, and if they feed on older leaves they are usually found underneath. Buds fed on by aphids may not open at all or may produce distorted flowers.

Leaves and shoots fed on by aphids may wilt and become twisted and curled. Some aphids, such as grape phylloxera (P), cause plant galls. This species and some others also attack plant root-systems.

Aphids also produce honeydew, a sticky substance which falls from the end of the aphid digestive tract on to anything beneath. This usually makes leaves and fruit sticky and provides a food supply for fungi called sooty moulds (D), which develops into a black coating over leaves, stems and fruit. Honeydew droplets produced by cabbage aphids become coated with a thin layer of wax and roll off the plant.

As each aphid feeds and grows bigger, it discards outgrown skins at regular intervals. These are white and papery and can be found among the aphids in the colony or beneath it. If cut flowers infested with aphids are arranged inside the house, honeydew and old aphid skins will fall on furniture.

To begin with, the rate of increase in a colony depends on temperature. For example, each female cabbage aphid (*Brevicoryne brassicae*) can produce about three young per day at 16°C and up to six at 25°C. However, as the number of aphids in an area increases, the food reaching each aphid decreases and their individual growth becomes much slower, and therefore the rate of increase in the colony is reduced.

Aphids do not thrive in very hot, dry conditions or in very cold ones. Heavy rain decreases aphid populations.

In areas where the winter is cold, eggs are laid in autumn, perhaps around buds or in crevices on the bark of trees, and nymphs and adults present at that time usually die. In the spring the eggs hatch to start a new colony. The young aphids feed on the new growth produced by the plant at that time.

In milder climates and with some species, adults and nymphs are found throughout the year, feeding on various plants. Their numbers, however, are usually reduced in winter, because of the lack of soft food material and because of lower temperatures.

Apart from the curling and wilting and the effects of honeydew, aphids are a serious pest because they carry many virus diseases from plant to plant. Ants and other insects are attracted by the honeydew.

One of the most serious aphid pests is black peach aphid (*Brachycaudus persicae*). This infests the roots as well as the above-ground parts of peach and other stonefruit. Infestations are likely to occur on some parts of the tree and not others. If dormant buds are attacked they open early. In late spring buds and blossoms wither as aphids feed on them, and very small fruit falls. These aphids produce a lot of honeydew.

PLANTS ATTACKED   Some species of aphid breed and feed on several or many different plants and this may follow a particular sequence.

CONTROL
• Organic/non-chemical: Control weeds. Aphids can be removed from plants by hosing them off, but those remaining may produce another colony. If aphids are left undisturbed, they are often attacked by wasps, ladybirds, hoverflies and lacewings, and thus their numbers are reduced. Research on a parasitic wasp (*Aphidius rosae*) that attacks rose aphid (*Macrosiphum rosae*) is in progress and appears promising. A closely related wasp attacks lucerne aphid.

The activities of ants running up and down twigs and through the colonies greatly discourages such parasites and predators. Ant control therefore, must be considered part of aphid control. Read the entry on ants (P) and tree-trunk banding on page 38.
• Chemical: If spraying the aphids is considered necessary, a spray such as dimethoate that enters the plant and moves in the sap is most suitable. Be careful to observe withholding periods on edible plants.

Citrus aphids on lemon

Black peach aphids

Cabbage aphids

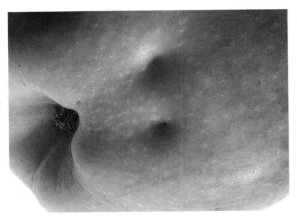

Apple dimpling bug

Campylomma liebknechti

The adult bug is pale green and about 2 mm long. It is a very active insect and flies off the plant quickly if disturbed. The bugs suck sap from around the flowers and the young fruit. This feeding damages groups of cells in the fruit and these subsequently stop growing. The undamaged parts grow normally, thus the indentations are produced.

This attack is similar to damage caused by boron deficiency, but in this case there are no corky areas inside underneath the indentation.

The insect is not a serious pest every year. It depends on climatic conditions and whether or not the blossom is prolific. If there are many insects and very few blossoms then damage is likely to be severe.

PLANTS ATTACKED This insect may attack all apple varieties but is more serious on 'Granny Smith' and 'Delicious'.

CONTROL Some damage is acceptable in a home garden. These bugs also attack aphids. Infestation may not occur till full-bloom or later but watch from the time buds start to show pink colour.
• Organic/non-chemical: Try using yellow sticky traps and shaking branches to disturb the insects and make them fly about.
• Chemical: As soon as they are present spray with omethoate. After 3–4 days check for reinfestation and spray again if necessary. Apply this chemical only in the early morning or the evening to avoid damage to bees.

Apple leafhopper   *Edwardsiana australis*

The adult leafhoppers are about 4 mm long and greenish-yellow with red eyes. The nymphs are similar in appearance. They look a little like tiny cicadas and jump and fly readily. They are usually found congregated underneath the leaf, where they suck sap and generally cause the leaves to turn yellow and fall.

When the infestation is just beginning, the leaves may become mottled with grey. Fruit may also be affected, particularly by the sticky brown droppings of the insect, which are difficult to remove. The winter is spent in the egg stage and these are deposited on young twigs underneath the bark; they hatch in spring, and new leaves are attacked. In warm weather the population gradually increases in size.

PLANTS ATTACKED In commercial orchards, particularly on trees bearing fruit, this insect is not usually a problem because it is killed when the trees are sprayed for other pests. It is a common problem on neglected trees, ornamental crabapples or trees that have not yet begun to bear fruit. Prune trees may also be attacked.

CONTROL
• Organic/non-chemical: Use sticky yellow traps as for whiteflies and shake small branches occasionally to disturb the insects. Try a soap spray such as Natrasoap®.
• Chemical: Spray with carbaryl or dimethoate following label directions for bugs.

This insect is known as canary fly in Tasmania.

There are two weevils near the upper edge of the pile of sand.

Argentine stem weevil   *Listronotus bonariensis*

The adult of this pest is very difficult to detect, as it is very small (3 mm long) and is a dark grey-brown. The weevils can be seen as they move, but if there is disturbance in their environment they feign death. Adults can fly from area to area. Both larvae and adults cause damage. The lawn looks very dry but does not respond to water. This is because the leaves have been severed from the roots, and if the surface is rubbed the grass will come away easily like fluff from a new carpet. Attacks may come any time between September and April, depending on climate. In warmer areas there are many generations per season.

PLANTS ATTACKED A range of grasses including bent and rye (in both lawns and pastures). Also wheat, maize and barley.

CONTROL
• Organic/non-chemical: Change to a less susceptible lawn grass.
• Chemical: Spray with diazinon following label directions. Use a wetting agent. Lightly water-in after application.

This insect was formerly named *Hyperodes bonariensis*.

Australian privet hawk moth
Psilogramma menephron menephron

The light-green caterpillars of this moth are large and fleshy, with diagonal lilac and white stripes. Their most outstanding feature is the long stiff spine on the end of the body. (This is present on the larvae of almost all species of hawk moths.) They are often difficult to see among the leaves.

Pupation takes place in the soil or leaf litter under the plant. The adults have a wingspan of about 100 mm and are mottled in shades of grey.

PLANTS ATTACKED These include jasmine, privet, lilac, golden ash, claret ash, wonga wonga vine and bower plant (*Pandorea* spp.).

CONTROL The caterpillars are not found in big numbers.
• Organic/non-chemical: Pick off by hand.
• Chemical: This is not usually necessary.

Autumn gum moth   *Mnesampela privata*

This dark brown moth is about 40 mm across its outstretched wings. The damage is done by the caterpillars, which often feed in groups of two or three. They attack the juvenile leaves and web several together into a bag in which they shelter. They skeletonise the leaves and chew the edges.

PLANTS ATTACKED Tasmanian blue gum (*Eucalyptus globulus* subsp. *globulus*), the blue gum or eurabbie (E. g. subsp. *bicostata)*, Argyle apple (*E. cinerea*) and some other eucalypts.

CONTROL As the eucalypts become mature attacks are fewer because the larvae do not favour adult leaves.
• Organic/non-chemical: Prune off the groups of webbed leaves and burn them.
• Chemical: Spray with maldison. Add wetting agent.

Azalea lace bug   *Stephanitis pyrioides*

The adult bugs are about 4 mm long and shiny black with lace-like mottled wings. Most eggs are laid in the midrib or larger veins or cemented to the leaf surface. The nymphs have numerous dark-brown spines projecting from the sides of the body. They congregate on the undersurfaces of the leaves and damage the plant by sucking sap.

The upper surfaces of the leaves become finely mottled in white or grey, and the lower surfaces dotted with brown sticky spots of excreta. Damage occurs in spring and summer. These pests should be controlled because damaged leaves look ugly for a long time.

PLANTS ATTACKED Azaleas and rhododendrons.

CONTROL
• Organic/non-chemical: There are no specific non-chemical controls. Try a soap spray or sticky yellow traps and shake the branches.
• Chemical: Spray with a penetrant or systemic insecticide, such as dimethoate, following label instructions.

Azalea leafminer *Caloptilia azaleella*

The adult is a small moth, 6 mm long with a wingspan of 11 mm. Eggs are deposited singly near the midrib of the leaf. The caterpillars begin by feeding between the leaf surfaces near the midrib. Their damage appears first as thin white streaks which can be seen only from the underside of the leaf, and gradually develops into brown patches or blisters about 10 mm long. Gradually, as they continue to feed, each caterpillar causes a brown, wedge-shaped patch about 5 mm long.

The half-grown larvae move to the leaf tip, curl it over and web it in place. They continue feeding here in this shelter and then either pupate within the curled tip or near the edge.

PLANTS ATTACKED Azaleas are the main host of this pest. Attack on other *Rhododendron* spp. is rare.

CONTROL The control programme should begin about the middle of September.
• Organic/non-chemical: If only one or two plants are involved, manual removal and destruction of larvae or pupae in damaged leaves may be successful. Squash the brown areas between thumb and forefinger.
• Chemical: Good control can be achieved in large plantings only by use of a systemic or penetrant chemical such as dimethoate (Rogor®) according to the label directions.

Bag-shelter moth *Ochrogaster lunifer*

The eggs are deposited in masses and covered with scales and hairs from the moth's body. There may be about two hundred eggs in each group and the whole mass resembles a yellowish ball about 20 mm in diameter.

The small larvae shelter here at first but later move to a branch fork where they construct a large, strong bag out of twigs, leaves and masses of webbing. They shelter in this during the day and spread out to feed on the leaves at night. The trees can be completely defoliated and look very ugly with 'bags' hanging in the branches. The 'bags' may end up about 250 mm long because they are enlarged as the larvae grow.

Fully fed larvae leave the tree and seek some loose soil, or leaves and debris on the ground, in which to pupate. The caterpillars in each group follow one another in single file and are often referred to as 'processionary caterpillars'.

The larvae may reach 50 mm in length and are thickly covered with long reddish-brown hairs which can produce very painful and serious rashes if touched.

PLANTS ATTACKED Wattles, particularly the weeping myall or boree (*Acacia pendula*). In the eastern states they are most common in drier western areas.

CONTROL
• Organic/non-chemical: Look for and destroy egg masses in December or remove 'bags' when they are only about golfball size. Wear gloves and handle them very carefully. Keep them away from children, pets and other animals.
• Chemical: Spray with maldison with the addition of wetting agent.

Fully grown larvae leave the tree to pupate.

Groups of caterpillars shelter in bags during the day and feed on leaves during the night.

Adults have a wingspan of approximately 50 mm. This is a pinned specimen.

Banana fruit caterpillar *Tiracola plagiata*

These khaki-coloured caterpillars may migrate in groups from weeds to banana plants. They feed on both foliage and fruit. Small caterpillars chew the fruit skin, but larger caterpillars chew down into the flesh.

They are about 60 mm long when fully grown.

PLANTS ATTACKED Bananas

CONTROL
• Organic/non-chemical: Keep close watch on young fruit and remove caterpillars by hand. Control weeds.
• Chemical: Spray with carbaryl following label directions. Remove nearby weeds or spray them as well.

Banana rust thrips

Chaetanaphothrips signipennis

The adult thrips are yellow and about 1.5 mm long. The nymphs are smaller and may be paler in colour.

They usually feed in sheltered situations such as between fruit and under leaf sheaths. Feeding on leaves causes reddish areas to develop, but fruit damage is more serious. The skin becomes rough and is coloured dull grey flecked with red in the areas where feeding has occurred. Later the skin appears red or reddish-brown and usually has superficial cracks. If the fruit is attacked when very small, the disruption to skin growth may cause the skin to split as the pulp increases in size. The eating quality of the fruit is not affected by the skin damage if the fruit is larger when attacked.

These insects are most numerous from January to March, but look for them on pseudo-stems and bunches from October.

PLANTS ATTACKED Bananas. Sometimes citrus, and cunjevoi (*Alocasia macrorrhiza*).

CONTROL
• Organic/non-chemical: Try a soap spray.
• Chemical: Use maldison. Spray about every six weeks and apply to the soil around the plant as well as the bases of the plants, suckers, stems and bunches. Spray application should be thorough.

Banana-spotting bug *Amblypelta lutescens lutescens*

The adult bug is about 15 mm long and elongated in shape. It is very similar to the fruitspotting bug (P) but is usually a slightly lighter green. The nymphs are a lighter red than fruitspotting bug nymphs and have light-red stippling around the black spots on their abdomens.

If disturbed, both nymphs and adults move quickly to seek shelter. They attack fruit and may also feed on young shoots, causing severe damage. Even a few can cause considerable damage.

On avocados, damage first appears as a watersoaked area from which sap exudes and dries white. This is hard to tell from fruit fly damage. Later these areas dry out and appear plateau-shaped with narrow cracks around them. Internal discolouration may extend to about 15 mm.

On bananas, the fruit skin is sunken and dark where bugs have been feeding. These areas are about 7 mm across and generally rounded with raised centres.

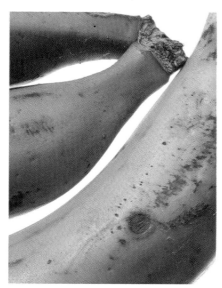

PLANTS ATTACKED Bananas, avocados, papaws, custard apples, passionfruit, guavas, lychees, pecans and citrus. It is native to Queensland, and its wild hosts include white cedars, rough-leafed figs, umbrella trees, coffee apples and corky passionvines. Cultivated plants near areas of bushland are more likely to be attacked than those far removed from bushland.

CONTROL Check regularly for bugs during flowering and fruit development. Spray if unavoidable, non-chemical methods are to be preferred. See fruitspotting bug (P).

Banana weevil borer   *Cosmopolites sordidus*

Eggs are laid in the bases of pseudo-stems or on sheaths of old leaves. The larvae tunnel in the corm and in the pseudo-stem. Rotting often follows. Young leaves may wilt and die. Plants may break and fall over. Fruit production is reduced.

The larvae, when fully grown, are about 12 mm long and creamy-white with a brown head. They are curved, fat and legless. They pupate near the outside of the corm. The adults are black for most of their long life, and oval in outline and about 12 mm long. During the day, they hide in leaf sheaths or around the base of the plant.

PLANTS ATTACKED Bananas and other members of the genus Musa, such as plantain, and Manila hemp. Sugarcane is also attacked.

CONTROL   This is compulsory in many areas. Consult your local Department of Agriculture for details. Quarantine regulations are in force to prevent the spread of this pest. Obtain planting material only from a reliable source, and examine it carefully by removing roots, soil and leaf bases. Also cut a thin slice or two from the outside. If larvae or pupae are discovered, the corm must be destroyed.

Also known as banana root borer.

Bean blossom thrips

Megalurothrips usitatis

These thrips thrive in warmth and humidity and are unlikely in dry inland areas.

They feed on the internal parts of flowers and cause twisted and distorted beans. The beans may also be lumpy and have rusty marks near the stalk end. Attack on young leaves may cause puckering, and down-turning of edges.

The adult thrips are dark brown and about 1.5 mm long. Immature stages are smaller and pale yellow or orange-red.

PLANTS ATTACKED Dwarf French beans, climbing beans.

CONTROL
• Organic/non-chemical: Plant new crops as far as possible from old ones or better still if thrips are troublesome plant only one bean crop each season. Destroy bean plants as soon as they have finished bearing.
• Chemical: If thrips are present at blossoming, spray with dimethoate or maldison. Dusting with 5% maldison dust is also effective. Aim to apply these to the flowers where the thrips are. Unfortunately, both these insecticides are highly toxic to bees. Sprays aimed at bean fly (P) control will control thrips.

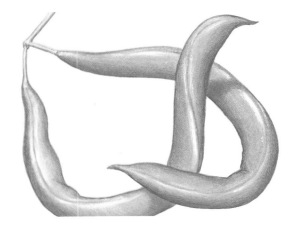

A yellow mark develops wherever eggs are laid.

Bean fly   *Ophiomyia phaseoli*

These glossy black flies are stout and 2–3 mm long. They are most troublesome in warm humid seasons and areas.

The eggs are usually laid in the leaves, and small yellow spots develop wherever this occurs. The damage is done by the larvae, which tunnel in the main stem and leaf-stalks and therefore cannot be seen from the outside of the plant. The stems and stalks become swollen and cracked and reddish in colour. Young plants wilt, yellow and fall over after the larvae have tunnelled in the stem near ground level. Parts of older plants break off easily when beans are picked, or in windy conditions. Crops are reduced in quality and quantity.

PLANTS ATTACKED All French and climbing beans. Broad beans undamaged.

CONTROL   The aim is to kill the adults, or the larvae while they are still in the leaf. Once they reach the stems, control is almost impossible.
• Organic/non-chemical: Plant as soon as danger of frost is over. Watch for the first signs of attack and destroy damaged leaves. Not planting beans every year may help. If the main stem has been attacked, hill the plants to encourage new root growth above the damaged area and ensure that the plant is never short of water.
• Chemical: Weekly application of insecticide may be necessary in areas where the bean fly occurs. Start when the plants are about three days old and continue till blossoming. Dimethoate is suitable.

Bean podborer *Maruca testulalis*

The caterpillars of this moth grow up to 25 mm long. They are greenish-yellow to bright green, with two rows of dark-brown to black spots close together along their backs and other rows further down on the sides.

They feed on flowers and stems and within pods. Webbing and excreta are often seen where flowers and pods join stalks or where pods touch each other.

The adults have a wingspan of about 30 mm. The forewings are smoky brown with translucent patches, and the hindwings are largely translucent with a brown band at the tip.

PLANTS ATTACKED Most types of bean (but not soy beans). Also some other legumes. Worst in warm humid areas.

CONTROL
• Organic/non-chemical: Plant crops as early in the season as possible. Hang sticky traps among the plants when flowering starts — these may capture the moths which usually shelter in the foliage.
• Chemical: This can be difficult because the larvae are well protected if inside pods. Spray with carbaryl, or trichlorfon. Weekly applications are probably necessary if this pest is active in an area.

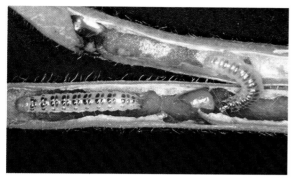

Beet leafminer *Liriomyza chenopodii*

The adult, which is a grey and yellow fly about 1 mm long, lays eggs in leaf-stalks. The white larvae (maggots) tunnel in stalks and leaves, producing white lines which will increase in width as the larvae grow. The leaves are not pleasant to eat and may wither and die. Pupation occurs within the leaf.

PLANTS ATTACKED Beetroot, silver beet and various weeds.

CONTROL
• Organic/non-chemical: Watch for the first fine whitish lines. Squash the young larvae in the leaf or remove the leaf entirely.
• Chemical: Spray weekly with dimethoate following label directions.
  This insect is related to bean fly.

Beet webworm *Hymenia recurvalis*

When young, these caterpillars usually feed under the leaves, removing patches of tissue but leaving the upper leaf surface undamaged to form 'windows'. Webbing is produced and sometimes leaves are joined together. Later, holes are chewed through leaves. Beetroot are sometimes chewed where they protrude from the soil.

The caterpillars begin cream-coloured but develop dark markings and end up predominantly green. They may reach nearly 20 mm in length.

After feeding for about two weeks, they pupate in soil under the plants and later the moths emerge. These adults, which have a wingspan of about 25 mm, are brown with white bands on the wings. If disturbed, moths take flight and settle again under leaves. Eggs are deposited in groups under leaves and take about five days to hatch.

PLANTS ATTACKED Members of the plant family Chenopodiaceae including beetroot, silver beet and weeds such as saltbush and fat hen; the flowering annual Joseph's coat as well as other *Amaranthus* spp.; also pigweed and other *Portulaca* spp. such as the flowering annual.

CONTROL Remove weeds in the area.
• Organic/non-chemical: Avoid growing related plants in the same season. Check under leaves and remove groups of larvae. Spray with Dipel®. More than one application may be necessary.
• Chemical: Spray or dust with carbaryl.

Black field cricket *Teleogryllus commodus*

Both nymhs and adults of this pest chew leaves and may cause serious damage by removing the growing point. Plants may be chewed off at ground level. They also chew fruit such as strawberries.

They usually shelter in cracks or under clods of earth or leaves during the day and feed at night.

Adults are black or dark brown and about 25 mm long. They have long antennae and strong back legs for jumping. Damage is most likely in autumn.

These insects are attracted to light and may enter houses and chew curtains or similar household items.

PLANTS ATTACKED Most young plants, even young trees. In some areas they are principally pasture pests. Wet seasons favour crickets.

CONTROL Manage the soil to reduce cracking.

• Organic/non-chemical: Search for adults and nymphs and squash them.

• Chemical: If chemical control is necessary use fenthion according to label directions.

Black scale *Saissetia oleae*

Black scale on oleander

This soft scale — which is also known as brown olive scale — can be found on both twigs and foliage. It is approximately 3 mm in diameter, with ridges on the back in the form of an H. This marking is not always clearly seen until several scales have been inspected.

Young scales produce vast quantities of honeydew, and plants infested with black scale are usually covered with sooty mould (D). Each female is capable of laying up to 2000 eggs and these eggs hatch over several weeks. This occurs in early summer and another generation may hatch in autumn. Ant activity is very common where this scale occurs and increases when eggs are hatching.

PLANTS ATTACKED These include olives, passionvines, oleanders, geraniums, hollies, citrus and a range of houseplants.

CONTROL

• Organic: Spray, preferably when the eggs are hatching, with white oil at the rate of 20 mL per litre of water. Rub scales carefully off stems by hand.

• Chemical: Spray with 10 mL of white oil and 2 mL of maldison per litre of water.

Black vine weevil *Otiorhynchus sulcatus*

These flightless weevils are 10-12 mm long and brownish-black with faint yellow spots. They feed actively at night but during the day remain in hiding under clods of earth or surface debris, or rest on the plant in dark protected places. If disturbed during the day, they usually drop to the ground as if dead. They chew notches from leaf edges. They may eat the whole leaf but usually leave the midrib. They may also feed on the fruit stalks of grapes.

All adults are female and each is capable of laying hundreds of eggs, which are usually deposited in the soil near the base of a plant. The white larvae are curved and legless and about 10 mm long when fully grown. They usually have an orange, or orange and brown, head. They feed on the root system and may be found from 20 to 400 mm down in the soil near the roots. They remove small roots and ringbark the larger ones. On some plants they chew bark from the lower stems. Corms may have hollows chewed in them. It is common for smaller plants to suddenly wilt and die.

PLANTS ATTACKED These pests can feed on a wide range of different plants: many woody ornamentals; strawberries, blackcurrants, raspberries, blackberries, gooseberries, grapes, hops and apples; vegetable seedlings; and plants such as cyclamen, polyanthus, fuchsias and rhododendrons.

CONTROL This is difficult.

• Organic/non-chemical: Potted plants can have the soil (and larvae) removed from the root system and be repotted in clean soil. Make sure that infested soil is not spread about. Search for the adults at night with a torch and squash them. See Manual Removal page 37. A preparation containing nematodes which kill the larvae is available commercially (Otinem®).

Typical damage on olive

Blackheaded pasture cockchafer
Aphodius tasmaniae

These beetles mate in summer, and eggs are laid in the soil usually in areas without a thick grass cover.

Young larvae feed on organic matter in the soil. Older larvae form a tunnel to the surface and emerge at night to feed on leaves which they chew off at ground level. Some leaf pieces are taken into the tunnel and eaten later. The tunnels do not have webbing as the corbie (P) tunnel does, but there is a mound of fine soil at the entrance. Feeding continues through summer, autumn and winter. In late spring, the larvae pupate and the next generation of adults emerges in summer.

PLANTS ATTACKED Grasses, particularly rye and also clovers.

CONTROL
• Organic/non-chemical: Collect and destroy larvae and adults whenever they are seen.
• Chemical: Spray with carbaryl. Add wetting agent. Use 5 L over every 100 square metres. Do not water in.

Bogong moth *Agrotis infusa*

The wings of the bogong moth span up to 50 mm. The forewings have a row of three light-brown spots on the brown to black background. The hindwings are brownish-white.

These moths fly at dusk in spring to feed on nectar. They build up considerable reserves of body fat and migrate in large numbers to peaks such as Mt Kosciusko, Mt Hotham and Mt Bogong. There they spend the summer resting in caves and rock crevices.

In late summer the moths fly north again, mate and lay eggs. The caterpillars that hatch from these eggs feed on the lush growth of broad-leafed plants encouraged by autumn rain. Expect damage in autumn, winter and early spring.

PLANTS ATTACKED A wide range of weeds, pasture plants, vegetables and ornamentals.

CONTROL Practise weed control.
• Organic/non-chemical: Search for caterpillars under fallen leaves and clods of earth. Most likely to be found in or near weedy areas. Larger plants can probably tolerate some damage while natural predators build up in numbers.
• Chemical: Spray or dust plants and surrounding soil with carbaryl.
  See also cutworms (P).
  Agrotis infusa is also known as the common cutworm.

Bramble sawfly *Philomastix macleaii*

The yellowish-brown adults of this species are 10–15 mm long and have smoky-yellow wings each with a dark band across it.

The eggs are laid in the leaf tissue. The larvae have large heads and two long thin structures projecting from the end of the body. They can defoliate plants.

PLANTS ATTACKED Loganberries and blackberries (both cultivated and wild) are the main hosts.

CONTROL
• Organic/non-chemical: Keep a close watch on plants and remove leaves with groups of young larvae before they have spread out over the plant.
• Chemical: Spray with maldison following label directions.

Broad mite *Polyphagotarsonemus latus*

These mites cannot be seen with the unaided eye. They feed on the lower surfaces of young, soft leaves which become bronze in colour. The leaf edges curl in and the leaves remain narrow. The leaves may also be brittle, puckered and curled.

Growth is stunted and attacked buds often fall. Flowers may be deformed and discoloured. Lemon fruit, if attacked when very young, may develop a silver or grey surface discolouration.

PLANTS ATTACKED A wide range, including dahlias, camellias, zinnias, gerberas, chrysanthemums, fatsia, fatshedera, ivies, begonias, fuchsias, hibiscus, stocks, silver beet, French beans, peppers, eggplants, lemons and mandarins.

CONTROL

• Organic: Spray with wettable sulphur. Sulphur dust also kills these mites. Do not use sulphur in very hot weather. Remove and destroy the newest, tiny shoots continually over a period of 3 weeks.

• Chemical: Use sulphur as described above or spray with dicofol.

Typical broad mite damage on young dahlia shoots.

Bronze orange bug *Musgraveia sulciventris*

This pest can cause serious damage to citrus trees. Eggs are laid mid-summer to autumn. They are deposited under leaves in groups of up to fourteen, arranged in four rows. They are spherical and about 3 mm in diameter. In winter, early stages of nymphs are found under the leaves. They are green, about 6 mm long, oval in shape and extremely flat. They would be easily overlooked except for their strong smell.

The colour of later nymphal stages varies considerably: green, grey-green, orange or orangy-pink. They are often clustered in groups around new shoots. Adults, which are about 25 mm long, are brown with a metallic sheen when young and gradually change to almost black as they age.

Both adults and nymphs cause flower and fruit fall by sucking on the stalks. New shoots wilt and brown. The foul-smelling secretions produced by both adults and nymphs are said to scorch the leaves they fall on.

These bugs die if temperatures are high and humidity is low. They often cluster around the base of the tree on hot days.

PLANTS ATTACKED Various native citrus species such as finger lime (*Microcitrus australasica*) and all cultivated citrus. They prefer vigorous, heavily foliaged trees.

CONTROL

• Organic/non-chemical: Best controlled in winter when small nymphs can easily be killed with a soap spray. Pay particular attention to the undersides of leaves in the lower part of the tree. Control by hand when larger. The smell they produce may make the job unpleasant. See also Manual removal of pests section page 37.

• Chemical: Spray with maldison or with dimethoate. Add white oil at the rate of 1 mL per L. Do not use dimethoate on Seville oranges, cumquats, or Meyer lemons. Spray the foliage, or the butt of the tree if they are clustered there.

Bronze orange bug nymphs

Brown basket lerp *Cardiaspina fiscella*

This is probably the most damaging of the group called psyllids. The insects feed under the leaves and produce small open-weave coverings for themselves , see photograph. They suck sap, and gradually the upper leaf surface becomes marked with reddish or yellowish blotches. Eventually the leaves turn brown, and the tree looks as if it has been damaged in a bushfire. A tree that is attacked repeatedly may die.

PLANTS ATTACKED The swamp mahogany (*Eucalyptus robusta*) and other eucalypts.

CONTROL

• Organic/non-chemical: Choose other eucalypt species to plant. Water and fertilise so that new growth is encouraged.

• Chemical: Ensure that the insects are still feeding before carrying out control procedures. Spray small trees with maldison and wetting agent.

Masses of eggs on the bark.

Bryobia mite *Bryobia rubrioculus*

This mite overwinters as eggs on the bark or branches and twigs. If many of these are grouped together, as is often the case, the bark has a reddish tinge. Branch junctions and cracks are common egg-laying sites.

The young mites, which are bright red to begin with, hatch from the eggs in spring and feed on the new leaves. Their feeding produces a faint, fine whitish mottling and the leaves eventually become pale all over. The bronze colouration, typical of European red mite (P), does not develop on trees attacked by bryobia mites. Tree vigour, and fruit size and number, are reduced because the leaves cannot function properly.

During the day they often congregate on twigs, and at night spread out on the leaves to feed. A period of frequent rain will markedly decrease mite numbers.

The adults are nearly 1 mm long and vary in colour from purplish-brown to greenish-grey. They have four pairs of legs; the front pair is very long. This species of mite does not produce webbing.

PLANTS ATTACKED The range includes apples, pears, almonds and prunes. Hawthorns (*Crataegus* spp.) are also attacked.

CONTROL Kill the overwintering eggs by spraying with white oil at early green-tip stage for apples and pears, and at late bud-swell for stonefruit. Pay special attention to branch junctions and bark crevices. If the oil spray is not applied, the mites become active about late October.

Spray at the first signs of damage with dicofol (non-organic) or wettable sulphur (organic).

Budworms *Helicoverpa* spp.

Budworms are the larvae of some members of the moth family Noctuidae. This group feed mainly on flowers, flower buds and developing fruits and seeds. They can cause serious damage to a wide range of crops. They are known by different names including corn earworm (P), tobacco budworm, tomato caterpillar, and native budworm.

The moths, which have a wingspan of about 40 mm, have grey-brown to reddish-brown forewings with darker markings. The hindwings are pale at the base and dark at the tips. Moths remain inactive during the day but fly at night to lay eggs and feed on nectar. Each female may lay up to 1000 eggs which are deposited singly on young growth. The small caterpillars may feed on soft young foliage but soon attack the blossoms and fruit. The entry holes of tiny caterpillars are easily overlooked, but as the caterpillars grow, entry holes are bigger and more easily seen.

Each caterpillar feeds for two or three weeks in warm weather. When fully developed, they are approximately 40 mm long and yellow-green, buff or red-brown in general colour, with some darker markings or stripes along their body.

When they have eaten enough they leave the plant and burrow down into the soil about 100 mm where they pupate.

Rainfall or irrigation stimulates the emergence of the next generation of moths. If the weather is dry or cool, four or five months may elapse before another generation of moths appears. If summer rainfall is good, then food plants are usually plentiful and so are budworms.

PLANTS ATTACKED A wide range, including tomatoes, sweet corn, peas, beans and strawberries. Sometimes, young apples, pears or stonefruit may be attacked. These caterpillars also feed on cotton, lucerne, tobacco and maize and a variety of weeds. Hearting lettuces and cabbages are sometimes attacked; larvae bore into the heart after feeding on outer leaves for a while. These caterpillars bore into a wide range of flower buds, including those of roses, gardenias and carnations.

CONTROL This is difficult because once the caterpillars have entered the fruit they cannot be reached with insecticide. You must kill them before they enter. Several applications 7–10 days apart may be required.

• Organic/non-chemical: Use Dipel®. Spraying is usually necessary because although this insect has a number of natural enemies they do not work fast enough to prevent serious damage.

• Chemical: Use carbaryl as directed on the label.

Budworms on dianthus

Budworm on geranium

Bulb mite *Rhizoglyphus echinopus*

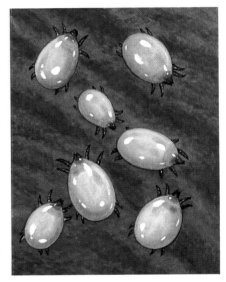

These pests are globular and a yellow-white with brownish legs. They are a little more than 0.5 mm long and easy to see because they glisten. They move slowly.

Infested bulbs produce stunted plants with yellow and distorted leaves. Because of their open structure, lily bulbs are easily attacked by these mites, which at first feed around the basal plate and destroy the roots. Bulb scales and stems are attacked later.

After they have become established, the damaged area is extended and the bulb may be completely destroyed. This is due partly to the feeding of the mites and partly to micro-organisms that they have introduced.

The mites build up into large populations rapidly if humidity and temperature are high (optimum temperature: 23–26°C).

Mites move in the soil or in storage from rotting bulbs to firm bulbs. Attack is most likely on bulbs that are already damaged. (Damage may occur during digging or be caused by other pests such as bulb flies.)

One of the bulb mite stages is capable of attaching itself to other pests such as flies, and is spread in this way to other areas. Movement of infested bulbs also spreads bulb mites from place to place.

PLANTS ATTACKED These mites are most common in daffodil and jonquil bulbs but also attack hyacinth, tulip, amaryllis, and lily bulbs. Onions, shallots, chives, garlic, potatoes, beetroot, dahlia 'tubers', and freesia and gladiolus corms may also be damaged.

CONTROL
• Organic/non-chemical: Destroy badly damaged propagating material. These mites will be killed if bulbs are treated in hot water as explained in the section Planning and Maintaining Your Garden page 39; this procedure should be carried out soon after the bulbs are lifted. Damage may occur if it is left until near planting time.
• Chemical: Plantings of chives may be drenched with dimethoate (30%) at the rate of 1 mL per litre of water. Observe the withholding period.

These mites damage fruit stalks and cause fruit to shrivel.

Bunch mite *Brevipalpus californicus*

These mites are microscopic and are found on the undersides of the leaves close to the bunch of grapes or on the bunches themselves.

Leaf damage is usually not important, but the leaves may have a brown and rough appearance. Damage to the bunch and berry stalks may interfere with the water supply to the fruit and this may cause berries to drop or to shrivel. Sometimes the mites feed on the berry surfaces and this results in a brown, thick 'skin' which may develop a network of cracks.

The mites spend the winter in colonies in cracks in the bark of stems.

PLANTS ATTACKED Grapes. Most damage is done to the woolly-leafed varieties.

CONTROL Spray with wettable sulphur but not on hot days. Next year spray the vines thoroughly just before bud burst with lime-sulphur.

Cabbage moth *Plutella xylostella*

This pest causes more damage in hot, dry districts than in coastal areas, and its numbers are highest in summer. The larvae of this moth initially tunnel in the leaves but soon begin chewing holes which do not go right through the leaf. This produces the so-called 'window-pane' effect. Many small holes scattered over the leaves characterises later stages of attack. As the plant ages, the larvae move to younger leaves in the centre and may foul the heart with webbing and droppings.

The larvae are green and grow to about 12 mm long. The small moths are greyish-brown with a wingspan of about 10 mm. When at rest the folded wings form a row of very roughly diamond-shaped marks where they join.

PLANTS ATTACKED Cabbages and other cruciferous vegetables, annual flowers and weeds are all susceptible.

CONTROL Be sure to cover the lower surfaces of the leaves thoroughly with spray.
• Organic/non-chemical: Use Dipel® or derris dust, following the directions on the label.
• Chemical: Use carbaryl dust, or spray with carbaryl.

Cabbage white butterfly *Pieris rapae*

This is a serious pest of cruciferous plants such as cabbages. The larvae, which grow to about 30 mm, are green with a faint yellow line along the top of the body and on each side. When young they feed from underneath the leaves, but later they may be found on both sides. They generally feed at night and remain still during the day, perhaps along the main leaf vein. Most damage occurs on the outer leaves.

The butterfly forewings span 40-50 mm and are creamy-yellow with black tips. The hindwings each have one black spot at the front edge. The female has two black spots on the forewings and the male one spot.

If the larvae have a group of small yellowish cocoons on them, they have been parasitised by a wasp and will soon die.

PLANTS ATTACKED These include cultivated vegetables, such as cabbages, cauliflowers, broccoli, turnips, and radishes. Also nasturtiums, mignonette, spider flowers (*Cleome* spp.), stocks and wallflowers. Weed hosts include wild mustard, shepherd's purse and peppercress.

CONTROL It is more important to protect the young plants from this pest than the older plants.

• Organic/non-chemical: Use Dipel®. After a week or so natural enemies should be reducing pest numbers. Ensure thorough application to the lower leaf surfaces.

• Chemical: Use carbaryl or maldison dust or spray.

California red scale *Aonidiella aurantii*

This hard scale — which is also known as 'red scale' — is more orange or orange-pink in colour than red. The adult female scale covering is about 1.5 mm across.

All above-ground parts of the plant can be infested, but this scale is found most on the outer parts of the canopy of a mature tree because it is a 'light-lover'. High populations may develop on small trees because their foliage receives a lot of light. Small trees can be seriously damaged or killed. Infestation causes leaf yellowing, leaf fall, and twig and branch dieback. Fruit infested when young will develop a small pit wherever a scale has been feeding. The bark on stems may crack.

The scale numbers build up quickly in dry dusty areas or dry seasons.

PLANTS ATTACKED This is a serious pest of citrus and also infests a wide range of ornamentals including hollies, ivies, mangos, mulberries, olives, passionfruit, roses, wattles and willows.

CONTROL Spray with white oil at the rate of 20 mL per litre of water. If the infestation is serious, spray twice; once in December and once in about mid-February. If the infestation is light, spray only in December. It is important to cover all parts of the tree thoroughly with spray.

In some areas this scale is kept under control by parasitic wasps. These are not damaged by oil sprays.

California red scale on ivy.

Callistemon sawfly *Lophyrotoma* sp.

Larvae of this sawfly can defoliate shrubs and small trees. They may also skeletonise leaves, as shown in the photograph. They are typical sawfly larvae: bulging behind the head and tapering towards the end of the body.

PLANTS ATTACKED Bottlebrushes.

CONTROL

• Organic/non-chemical: Prune off the damaged and infested parts.

• Chemical: Spray with maldison following label directions.

Case moths Order Lepidoptera: Family Psychidae

The larvae of the moths in this family group make bag-like structures to protect themselves while they feed. Some species leave the silken bag bare, some cover it with grains of sand, and yet others cover it with pieces of twig or leaf in patterns characteristic of the particular species. If the larva is feeding on a conifer, for example, the case may be covered with pieces of conifer and therefore is very well camouflaged until the pieces begin to go brown. The larva stays inside the bag except that when chewing leaves its head protrudes. The bag is increased in size as the larva grows.

When fully fed, pupation occurs inside the case. The female moths are wingless and after fertilisation they lay eggs inside the case. The larvae that emerge will disperse, and begin to make their own cases.

PLANTS ATTACKED Different case moths may attack different plants, but between them they feed on a wide range.

CONTROL This is not usually necessary.

• Organic/non-chemical: Hand removal in a home garden is quite easy and an adequate control. Early detection of a large infestation would be important.

Cherry aphid *Myzus cerasi*

Young aphids are brown, and adults are black. In spring large numbers of them may be found under young leaves and on young twigs. The new growth yellows and curls. Honeydew and then sooty mould (D) disfigure leaves and fruit. When the growth on the trees matures and is therefore harder, aphid numbers decrease. Some move to softer growth on suckers and seedlings, where colonies exist throughout summer and autumn.

In late autumn, overwintering eggs are laid around buds on the trees. A few adults and nymphs may survive low temperatures and feed on buds which then open prematurely.

PLANTS ATTACKED Fruiting and ornamental cherry trees.

CONTROL

• Organic/non-chemical: Remove suckers and small unwanted cherry tree seedlings. Do not spray if there are numerous ladybirds present. These insects should to reduce the aphid population to an acceptable level.

If the season is damp, the aphid population may build up very quickly and spraying may be necessary. Use a soap spray like Natrasoap®.

• Chemical: Use dimethoate. Close to harvest take extra care with the withholding period.

Cherry aphids usually congregate under the leaves and may cause this severe curling and twisting.

Chinese wax scale *Ceroplastes sinensis*

The young scales feed on the leaves of the host, and in the early stages of wax production look like tiny white daisies or stars along the midrib of the leaf. As they get older and produce more wax for protection, this wax is usually pink but in some cases may be red. Later still, as the wax ages, it fades to white or brownish-white.

The young adults move from the leaves and settle on the stems, where they continue to suck sap and produce honeydew. Mature females with their waxy covering may be 7 mm long by 5 mm wide and 3 mm high. There are seven dark spots around the edge of the wax and one in the centre. The female produces approximately 2000 eggs.

PLANTS ATTACKED   Lillypillies, bottlebrushes, citrus, diosmas, hop-bushes, hollies, bracelet honey myrtles, pomegranates, rondeletias, turpentines, brush boxes, feijoas, tamarillos and many others.

CONTROL   This scale does not seem to have become a serious pest of citrus, or of ornamentals, either exotic or native, and chemical control does not seem warranted. If it is considered necessary, use white oil at the rate of 10 mL per litre of water. Spray when the scales are on the midribs of the leaves, about the end of March.

Christmas beetles *Anoplognathus* spp.

The adult beetles are found from November to January and feed on eucalypt leaves. They produce at first the characteristic saw-tooth pattern of damage shown in the photograph. If feeding continues on the leaf, this pattern may be destroyed. Individual trees by roadsides or in large areas of grass are damaged more than trees growing together in big groups. It is uncommon for trees growing in forest conditions and below 2.5 m to 3 m high to be attacked.

The larvae — referred to as white curl grubs — are found in the soil feeding on the roots of grasses and other small plants.

PLANTS ATTACKED   Many species of eucalypts.

CONTROL

• Organic/non-chemical: Tree injection, whilst effective because the chemical remains active for a longer period of time, causes significant damage to the tree. It is not recommended. Beetles can cause serious damage quickly, and by the time spraying is carried out it may be too late. Hose or knock off the tree and destroy.

The grass grub (*Costelytra zealandica*) of New Zealand is similar to Christmas beetle.

Chrysanthemum gall midge

Rhopalomyia chrysanthemi

The adult fly is reddish-brown and about 2.5 mm long. Eggs are deposited on any young growth. The tiny larvae burrow in the leaf tissues and after about a week, minute light patches indicate their presence. Gradually cone-shaped galls develop. These are about 2 mm long and project at an angle from the leaf surface.

Warm, moist conditions favour this pest and lead to severe infestations which produce twisted stems and deformed leaves and flowers. Spread from area to area occurs through the introduction of infested plants or cuttings. In winter it is not possible to detect their presence in the plant.
PLANTS ATTACKED *Dendranthema* x *morifolium* only.
CONTROL Plan to look for infestation earlier the following year.
• Organic/non-chemical: Remove and destroy infested plant parts.
• Chemical: Spray with a systemic or penetrant chemical such as fenthion. Apply as soon as the infestation is detected. Do not use dimethoate on chrysanthemums.

Cineraria leafminer   *Chromatomyia syngenesiae*

The adult of this pest is a very small black fly (about 2 mm long) which usually goes unnoticed. It inserts its eggs into the undersides of the leaves and when the larvae hatch out, they tunnel inside the leaf. A grey or silverish wandering line is produced on the leaf. This gradually increases in width as the larvae grow bigger. These lines make the leaves very ugly and may cause wilting and death in extreme cases. Very often, however, the plant will still produce a good crop of flowers.
PLANTS ATTACKED Cinerarias, chrysanthemums, mist flowers and nasturtiums. Lettuces and the weeds sow thistle, capeweed and prickly lettuce are also hosts for this insect.
CONTROL Control weeds.
• Organic/non-chemical: Remove and destroy first infected leaves. Fertilise and water.
• Chemical: Spray with a penetrant or systemic chemical such as dimethoate at the first sign of attack. Spraying at weekly intervals until late September may be necessary. Make sure that the larvae are still active to justify the spraying programme. If most of the insects have pupated, it is too late to spray. Hold several leaves up to the light; if most tunnels have small round hard lumps at the end, then pupation has occurred, and spraying will be ineffectual.

Citrus bud mite   *Eriophyes sheldoni*

This mite cannot be seen with the unaided eye. It may be found on the plant throughout the year, but its numbers will decrease markedly if conditions are extremely hot and dry. Lemons are the most common host.

The mites feed mainly in unopened flower and leaf buds, although they may also be found in other situations such as where fruits touch one another or under the calyx lobes (that is, near where the stalk joins the fruit). If the mites have fed in these areas, the skin of the fruit will go black. Buds also blacken and may be completely destroyed.

The leaves that develop from infested buds will be distorted. They often have an irregular margin and may also be cupped.

The most characteristic feature of this attack is the rosetting of leaves at the tips of shoots. A number of the leaves are deformed in different ways and grow from almost the same point. Deformed flowers are produced from infested buds, and any fruit set will grow into peculiar distorted shapes, perhaps with several lobes or fingers.

Symptoms on orange trees are similar but less pronounced. Badly deformed fruit usually falls at an early stage, but some may develop with ridges in the rind.
PLANTS ATTACKED All citrus may be attacked, but the most commonly and seriously infested are 'Eureka' lemons and 'Washington Navel' oranges.
CONTROL Spray in mid-winter and again in summer or early autumn.
• Organic: Use wettable sulphur.
• Chemical: Use dicofol.

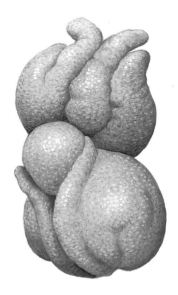

Citrus gall wasp *Bruchophagus fellis*

In about September this extremely small black wasp lays groups of eggs in young soft twigs, thorns, fruit stalks or main veins on leaves. As the larvae of the wasp develop, the plant is stimulated to produce extra cells. Galls are obvious by December or January and gradually increase in size as the wasps develop. The galls are full-sized by autumn.

In September or October adult wasps emerge through the outside of the gall and leave it 'peppered' with small holes. The wasps are poor fliers and tend to reinfest the same tree. They may, however, be blown to other areas by wind or transported on infested nursery stock.

If a tree continues to be attacked it will be weakened and become unproductive.
PLANTS ATTACKED All citrus, but rough lemons and grapefruits suffer most. This insect is native to coastal New South Wales and Queensland where it develops in the finger lime *Microcitrus australasica.*
CONTROL
• Organic/non-chemical: Cut off the galls and burn them by the end of August. This date is a legal requirement in some areas where this pest is termed a 'proclaimed pest' and must be controlled or a fine may be imposed. This cut-off time is set so that the galls will be removed before the adult wasps emerge and lay eggs in new shoots.

Citrus katydid *Caedicia strenua*

These insects are found in coastal districts. They are green, about 45 mm long and resemble grasshoppers as adults, but when they are in the nymphal stage they look rather like large ants with long antennae. They feed on very small soft leaves at first, producing a lace-like effect; and then move on to the upper surfaces of older leaves, where they chew holes. Leaf edges are rarely eaten.

They also feed on young citrus fruit, gouging hollows and removing the surface. They do not feed on fruit of more than golfball size. The patches are white initially and show up clearly on the green fruit. As the fruit grows, the spots become flatter and greyish in colour.
PLANTS ATTACKED Citrus, some types more than others. Lemons are not as often attacked as 'Washington Navel' and 'Valencia' oranges. Injury is more common on heavily foliaged trees.
CONTROL In a home garden, these insects could be tolerated because internal fruit quality is not affected unless secondary fungi begin rots in the damaged area.
• Chemical: If spraying is required use carbaryl or fenthion.

Citrus leafminer *Phyllocnistis citrella*

The adult of this pest is a tiny moth with a wingspan of about 5 mm. It is silvery-white with yellowish markings, and there is a black spot on the tip of each forewing. It moves around only at night.

The eggs are usually deposited along the midrib of young leaves. When the larvae hatch out, they tunnel in the leaf for 5–6 days. The silvery lines produced stand out against the green of the rest of the leaf. The leaves often become severely distorted. When the larva is fully grown, it curls the edge of the leaf into a shelter and pupates within. The whole cycle takes 2–3 weeks in good conditions.
PLANTS ATTACKED All cultivated citrus and probably native citrus species as well. Mature trees can usually survive attacks.
CONTROL
Limit water and fertiliser in summer/autumn to avoid a growth flush when the pest population is highest. Fertilise in winter.

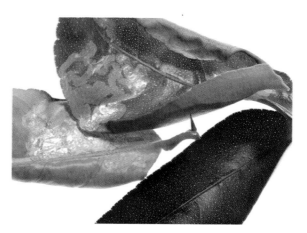

If summer/autumn protection of young growth is required use white oil. Apply thoroughly till the spray runs off the leaves. Don't spray the rest of the tree unless aiming at scales as well.

Cluster caterpillar *Spodoptera litura*

The adult moth has dark forewings with silvery-white markings and pearly-white hindwings; wingspan is about 40 mm. Eggs are laid in groups of several hundred covered with a brown 'fur' from the body of the female.

The small larvae usually feed in a group under the leaves and remove patches of the epidermis or skeletonise them. Later, as they get bigger, they spread out and feed by themselves. At this stage they may be found on any part of the plant including the flowers, particularly where the flowers join the stem. In the case of strawberries, the fruit is also damaged.

Mature larvae, which are about 45 mm long, are green to brownish with two rows of black triangles along the back.

PLANTS ATTACKED A wide range of annual flowers, vegetables and weeds.

CONTROL

• Organic/non-chemical: Look for groups of eggs and small larvae and remove the leaves they are under. Take particular care when late summer rainfall is above average. Larger larvae feed during the day so can easily be seen and handpicked. Spray with Dipel® if necessary.

• Chemical: Dust with carbaryl dust, or spray with carbaryl. It is important to cover the undersides of the leaves as well as the tops.

Coccid galls—eucalypts

Order Hemiptera: Superfamily Coccoidea

These galls are found on small stems and leaves. There are a number of species of sap-sucking insects whose feeding stimulates the plant cells to produce a gall. This eventually completely surrounds the adults. The female remains inside her gall but the male, a tiny winged insect, emerges through a hole. The galls formed are characteristic of the species and may be different shapes for males and females.

PLANTS ATTACKED Eucalypts. Young trees seem to be attacked much more than established trees.

CONTROL

• Organic/non-chemical: Spraying is not sensible. It will not make the galls go away and can rarely be timed accurately enough to stop their formation. Water and fertilise the tree so that it grows vigorously. Damage is then less obvious.

Coccid galls—she-oak *Cylindrococcus spiniferus*

These galls are characteristic of small sap-sucking insects. As they feed on the plant, their saliva stimulates plant cells to grow in such a way as to form galls that look rather like the fruit of she-oaks to those unfamiliar with the plant.

Inside each gall there is a reddish-brown female. Her young will move out through an opening, start feeding on another part of the plant and in turn produce other galls.

PLANTS ATTACKED She-oaks (*Casuarina* and *Allocasuarina* spp.).

CONTROL Usually unnecessary, but removing young galls from the plant may reduce future infestations.

Codling moth *Cydia pomonella*

Pinned specimen of codling moth

The adults have a wingspan of about 20 mm. Near the tip of each greyish-brown forewing, there is a circular area with a metallic sheen.

Eggs are laid at dusk on or near small fruit when the temperature is 15°C or higher. The larva chews its way into the fruit core, where it feeds and produces webbing and droppings. One larva may feed in the centre of more than one apple.

The first entrance hole begins very small and often goes unnoticed. The caterpillar feeds in the core and surrounding areas for three to five weeks and gradually enlarges the entrance hole through which it pushes its sawdust-like excreta. It chews another tunnel to the outside when it leaves the fruit. Damaged fruit often drops prematurely.

Once the larva is fully fed it leaves the fruit, and walks down the branches and trunk searching for a suitable place to pupate. This might be a small piece of loose bark or a crevice in the branch or trunk.

There may be up to three generations during the warm weather, but as the weather begins to cool the last larvae do not pupate immediately and remain in their cocoons in the bark crevices for some months. In spring, pupation occurs and the moths emerge in spring and summer.

PLANTS ATTACKED Apples, pears, quinces and crabapples. Hawthorn fruit, walnuts, stonefruit and some others may be attacked.

CONTROL This insect is considered to be a very serious pest. In some areas there are laws that demand adequate control measures and these include spraying. Quarantine restrictions are also in force to stop its spread to uninfested areas.

• Organic/non-chemical: Remove and destroy infested fruit from the ground and the tree. Remove pieces of flaking bark, broken branches, and litter from the crotch of the tree. Avoid leaving branch props, or packing cases or other solid shelter near the tree. Squash pupae — slim and about 10 mm long.

The larvae can be trapped during their search for a suitable pupation site. See page 38 — tree banding. Traps with pheromones to attract the moths will soon be more widely available. Using several per one or two trees may provide adequate control but unless the gardener is prepared to make strenuous efforts to control this pest then susceptible fruit trees should not be grown.

• Chemical: Spray programmes are also necessary. If this pest was a serious problem in the last apple crop, apply the first spray at petal-fall and then every 14 days until about late December; spray at 21 day intervals after this time. If the pest was not serious in the last crop, apply the first spray within 14 days of petal-fall and thereafter every 21 days. Spray thoroughly. Use fenthion or carbaryl. Do not use carbaryl within 30 days after full bloom because it causes fruit fall.

Common slater *Porcellio scaber*

The adults are 9–15 mm, oval in shape and fairly flat. They may be grey or brown, or yellowish-orange speckled with black. These are not insects but crustaceans and related to prawns and lobsters. The common pillbug (*Armadillidium vulgare*) is a similar animal and also a crustacean.

They are found in damp dark situations, where they feed on decaying organic matter. Seedlings are sometimes chewed near ground level. They are likely to be a problem in old shaded gardens or conservatories. They may be found in the back of staghorn ferns and in orchid pots where they may chew young roots.

PLANTS ATTACKED Small soft plants in damp situations. Plants already damaged by some other factor.

CONTROL

• Organic/non-chemical: Remove breeding sites such as piles of rotting timber, rock heaps, rotten timber garden edges, and heaps of decaying vegetable matter.

• Chemical: Methiocarb (Baysol®), sold to control snails, will also control slaters. Diazinon could be sprayed over breeding sites.

Corbie *Oncopera intricata*

This insect is in the family Hepialidae (swift moths).

The eggs are deposited in a loose mass on the ground (other, related species scatter their eggs over a large area). The larvae make vertical tunnels in the soil and emerge at night to feed on the leaves of the surrounding grass. The tunnels are lined with webbing ('silk'), with a small mound of fine soil particles and webbing usually evident at the entrance.

A severe infestation can lead to large bare areas which become invaded by weeds. Damage is most severe in autumn and winter when the larvae are almost fully grown and the grass growth is slow.

The porina caterpillars of New Zealand, such as *Wiseana cervinata*, are very similar to corbies.

PLANTS ATTACKED Lawn and pasture grasses.

CONTROL

• Organic/non-chemical: Search at night, collect and destroy.

• Chemical: Spray with carbaryl. Add wetting agent. Use 5 L over 100 square metres. Do not water in.

Corn earworm *Helicoverpa armigera*

The larvae, which grow to about 40 mm, show great colour variations. They may be various shades of green, fawn, yellow, or reddish-brown, with brown or black stripes running along the body.

Young tomatoes may be destroyed as soon as the caterpillar enters, or they may continue to grow with the developing caterpillar inside.

Sweet corn is usually damaged at the ends of the cobs. Eggs are laid on the silks or at the tip of the cob. Once the caterpillar has moved inside the sheath, control is difficult. Damaged cobs can still be eaten, but are prone to rotting and attack from other insects.

Flowers and pods of beans are attacked. The larvae make large holes in the pods when they tunnel into them and may also feed from the outside. There is no webbing associated with these larvae.

PLANTS ATTACKED A range, including tomatoes, beans, strawberries, and sweet corn.

CONTROL This is difficult. Once the pest enters the fruit, it may not be worth saving.

• Organic/non-chemical: Attack on corn cobs can be prevented by cutting off the tips of the husks and the silks after most of the latter are brown and beginning to dry out. Cut about halfway between the end of the husk and the forming cob.

• Chemical: In a home garden, carbaryl dust applied to vulnerable areas such as the tips of corn cobs and the stalk area of tomatoes, as well as to young growth, may reduce damage.

See also budworms (P).

Cotton harlequin bug

Tectocoris diophthalmus

The adult bugs are about 20 mm long. The females range in colour from yellow to orange-yellow with black patches. The males are often red with dark metallic blue or green patches.

The female guards the eggs and the very young nymphs. The adults and nymphs all suck sap but on ornamentals the damage is rarely serious.

PLANTS ATTACKED Hibiscus, both native and exotic, Norfolk Island hibiscus, and other members of the plant family Malvaceae, such as cotton.

CONTROL Not necessary on ornamentals. Tolerate the slight damage so that the extremely beautiful bugs can be observed and enjoyed.

Female

Male

Cottonseed bug *Oxycarenus luctuosus*

The adult bug, as shown in the photograph, is about 3 mm long and basically black and grey. With the nymphs, they tend to congregate in and around buds, flowers and fruit. They suck sap and may cause distortion and wilting or discoloured patches on ripening fruit.

PLANTS ATTACKED Members of the family Malvaceae are favourite hosts. These include Norfolk Island hibiscus (*Lagunaria patersonia*) and *Hibiscus rosa-sinensis*.

CONTROL
• Organic/non-chemical: If necessary use a soap spray such as Natrasoap®.
• Chemical: Spray with dimethoate or fenthion. Add some wetting agent.

Cottonycushion scale *Icerya purchasi*

This scale infests twigs and branches. The mature female is oval in shape, reddish-brown with black hairs, and about 5 mm long. When fully mature, she settles in the one spot and an egg-sac of white grooved wax is gradually extruded from a series of holes in the body to encase the hundreds of bright red eggs. Each female can be seen at the end of the sac she has produced.

The sap-sucking activities of this scale do not usually cause serious damage to the plant, but the honeydew and consequent sooty mould (D) may do so.

PLANTS ATTACKED *Pittosporum* spp., various wattles, grevilleas, roses, climbing figs, laburnums, magnolias, willows, liquidambars, flowering quinces, fruit trees including citrus, fig, mulberry, and some other plants.

CONTROL These insects are usually kept under control by a ladybird (*Rodolia cardinalis*), the larvae and adults of which eat cottonycushion scales.

If spraying is really necessary, use white oil at the rate of 20 mL per litre of water in late summer to early autumn when a high proportion of young stages will be present. If this time is missed, spray when the colony is seen; but note that this will not kill eggs in ovisacs, so a second spray a few weeks later is necessary to kill the new crawlers. For this spraying use white oil (10 mL per L). Do not use 20 mL of white oil per litre of water for both sprayings because the plant is likely to be damaged.

Couchgrass mite *Dolichotetranychus australianus*

There are several different mites that cause the symptoms called witches' broom on couch grass. This is a shortening of internodes so that the leaves at the top of the shoot have a bunchy appearance.

These mites favour dry sites, especially the dry edges and corners of a lawn, and are often a problem at the base of retaining walls or buildings where heat build-up occurs. The injured areas will be straw-coloured.

PLANTS ATTACKED Couch grasses.

CONTROL Improve watering techniques. These mites are almost totally protected by sheathing leaf bases and are difficult to treat.
• Organic: Try wettable sulphur.
• Chemical: Try dicofol.

Couchtip maggot *Delia urbana*

Eggs laid in the growing point of the grass allow the larvae to eat out the growing tip of the plant. The grass fails to develop strong runners and to cover the ground. It never appears vigorous. The tips can be pulled out from the plant with very little effort. The pest often goes completely unrecognised because damage is not severe enough to kill the grass. Clouds of small flies may be seen moving away if the grass is walked on.

PLANTS ATTACKED Couch grasses.

CONTROL
- Organic/non-chemical: Fertilise and water to keep the grass growing.
- Chemical: Spray with dimethoate. Add wetting agent. Do not water in, the aim is to allow the inseticide to stay on the leaves, near the pest.

Damaged shoot on right, undamaged shoot on left.

Crusader bug *Mictis profana*

These bugs are light brown and about 20 mm long in the adult stage. They are referred to as 'crusader' bugs because of the pale yellow cross on the back of the adult. The nymphs have no cross but two dots of a similar colour, one beneath the other. They are not a pest in every season and in every area but occasionally sap-sucking causes wilting and death of young shoots and flower heads.

PLANTS ATTACKED This bug attacks a wide range of plants including grapes and citrus, but is most commonly found on wattles and cassias.

CONTROL   This will be easier if attempted when the bugs are still nymphs.
- Organic/non-chemical: The bugs may alternatively be removed by hand and dropped into a container of water with some kerosene added. Wear gloves so that the foul-smelling fluid the bugs produce when disturbed does not get on your hands. A few bugs on a large shrub can be ignored. Later, prune off damaged shoots.
- Chemical: Spray with dimethoate or fenthion. Add wetting agent at the rate of 1 mL per litre of water.

Cup moths *Doratifera* spp.

Cup moth pupa

The larvae of most of these moths are basically rectangular in shape with a saw-tooth edge. They sit very flat on the plant surface and appear to glide along. Most are green with bright patterns in colours such as red, yellow and blue. They are about 25 mm long when mature. The spines they carry can inflict a painful sting and cause some local inflammation.

When they are small they feed in a group and remove the leaf surface. Later they feed individually and chew the edges from the leaves. The fully-fed larvae construct cup-shaped cocoons stuck to twigs or under loose bark. The moths emerge after pushing up a small lid at the top of the cocoon.

Eggs are laid in groups on the leaves and covered with hairs from the female moth's body. This looks like a roughly circular patch of light brown fur about 10 mm across.

PLANTS ATTACKED Most attacks occur on eucalypts, brush boxes, water gums, and smooth-barked apples (*Angophora costata*), but damage has been recorded on others such as apricots and guavas.

CONTROL   Consult a trained arborist if attack is severe.
- Organic/non-chemical: Remove eggs and other stages by hand. Take care not to touch the larvae. Dipel® can be tried on small trees. Apply water and fertiliser to keep the tree actively growing.
- Chemical: Spray with maldison if the tree is small enough. Look for fresh insect droppings, as they indicate that damage is still occurring.

Cup moth larva

Currant borer moth *Synanthedon tipuliformis*

This moth has clear wings and a black body with yellow stripes aross it. It is about 12 mm long, with a wingspan of about 18 mm. Eggs are deposited on the stems in late November or December. The larvae get into the stems by chewing through new buds or by crawling through holes left by emerging adults. Once in the stems the larvae feed on the pith which is part of the plant's carbohydrate store. This damage greatly reduces the plant's capacity to produce fruit, and the yield is lowered. Stems break easily in strong winds or when work is being carried out on the plants. Wilting may also occur.

Before they pupate, the larvae chew a circular hole almost through the woody stem. The moths can easily push out through the remaining thin layer after they emerge.
PLANTS ATTACKED Currants (*Ribes* spp.), particularly blackcurrants; gooseberries; and raspberries. Persimmons, hazels, elders and junipers are sometimes attacked.
CONTROL
• Organic/non-chemical: Remove and burn infested stems. Infested stems produce only small yellowish leaves in spring and eventually die. Later, when the adults emerge, they leave the empty pupal cases protruding from the damaged stems. These stems are then easy to identify. Control in newly established commercial plantings has been achieved by use of cuttings sprayed with a solution containing a particular nematode which destroys the larvae.
• Chemical: Chemical control is not very effective because the larvae are well protected inside the stems. Use of chemicals also kills the predators of the two-spotted mite (P), another pest of blackcurrants.

Healthy buds

Damaged buds

Currant bud mite *Cecidophyopsis ribis*

This pest produces a condition that is sometimes referred to as 'big bud'. The buds are about twice the size of normal buds and very rounded. They usually dry out and may produce small distorted leaves. Infested canes may die or develop abnormally. The mites spend the winter inside buds and move out to feed on growing leaves and flowers about mid-September.

These mites are spread from plant to plant in wind.
PLANTS ATTACKED Blackcurrants (those varieties with hairiest leaves are least affected).
CONTROL
• Chemical: Prune off swollen buds. Spray with lime-sulphur (50 mL per litre of water) just before the buds burst.

Cutworms Order Lepidoptera: Family Noctuidae

These caterpillars are the larvae of members of the moth group Noctuidae. Young larvae feed on the lower surfaces of leaves, and older larvae chew through plant stems near ground level. Hence the name 'cutworm'. Sometimes they chew on only one side of the stem but the plant probably still falls over. Seedlings and soft plants are preferred, and fruits such as strawberries are also attacked.

The caterpillars, which curl up into a flat coil if disturbed, feed at night and hide under clods of earth or leaves during the day.

They may grow to 30–40 mm long and about 5 mm thick. Cutworms are usually smooth-bodied and of uniform colour. Colour may vary considerably from pinkish-brown or olive-green to dark grey or almost black.

Different cutworms do damage in different seasons and the life cycle is greatly influenced by rainfall and temperature. In the case of the brown cutworm (*Agrotis munda*) pupation occurs in the soil in early or mid-summer. The moths may not emerge until the following spring if the summer is dry, but if rain falls they do emerge and lay eggs. Good rains produce lush foliage for a new generation of caterpillars to eat. The bogong moth (P) is another cutworm.
PLANTS ATTACKED A very wide range including vegetable seedlings, annual flower seedlings and strawberries.
CONTROL Weed control will help to reduce the cutworm population.
• Organic/non-chemical: Protect each seedling by pushing a sturdy plastic drink cup with the bottom removed into the soil around it, leaving at least 60 mm above ground.
• Chemical: Spray with carbaryl. Apply in the late afternoon because the caterpillars emerge during the dark to feed.

Cyclamen mite *Phytonemus pallidus*

This very small mite (0.2 mm) usually congregates inside leaf and flower buds. If mite numbers are relatively low, the flowers may be flecked with dark spots or discoloured, but if the infestation is more serious the flower buds will probably wither and die. The leaves on which the mites have fed end up curled, twisted and brittle. As the leaves unfold and get larger, the atmosphere around them becomes drier. Most of the mites will then move into new buds where the atmosphere is more humid.

Sometimes more developed leaves are attacked and in this case the mites feed on the lower surfaces and cause the leaf to curl. Pockets in which the mites shelter may develop in the leaf. The mites feed on cyclamen corms in storage and from them have access to the newly growing plant. It is likely that these mites damage plants by injecting toxins during the feeding process.

PLANTS ATTACKED Include azaleas, ivies, begonias, chrysanthemums, fuchsias, gerberas, gloxinias, busy lizzies (*Impatiens*), pelargoniums, petunias, African violets, dieffenbachias, columneas, umbrella trees, cyclamen and many others.

CONTROL Control is difficult because the mites are well protected inside buds.
• Organic/non-chemical: Remove newest leaves regularly during 3–4 weeks.
• Chemical: Try spraying with dicofol or omethoate. Use additional wetting agent so that the chemical will spread thoroughly around buds and small leaves.

These anthurium leaves were damaged when very small.

Cypress bark beetle *Phloeosinus cupressi*

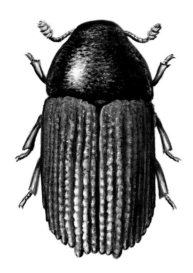

The dark brown to black adults are about 3 mm long and 1.5 mm wide. The white and legless larvae are 3–4 mm long.

The female lays eggs at intervals along a tunnel under the bark of the tree. When the larvae hatch out, each one chews a tunnel more or less at right angles to the one where the eggs were laid. Pupation occurs at the end of the tunnel and the adults emerge to the outside of the tree through circular holes about 2 mm in diameter. There are usually many holes near one another.

The first sign of attack is usually the death of the top branch. The side branches die later. Small areas of wilting or reddish-brown foliage may also occur. This is caused by the adult beetles which bore down small twigs (up to 4 mm in diameter). These may break off completely or hang by threads of bark.

PLANTS ATTACKED Cypresses such as *Cupressus macrocarpa*, *C. arizonica*, and *C. torulosa*; also Lawson cypress, *Chamaecyparis lawsoniana*, and some other conifers. Trees attacked are often dying from another cause.

CONTROL   If the tree is only slightly damaged, remove the affected branch. Fertilise and water regularly. Change other factors that may be stressing the tree.

The tree may need to be removed. Any replacement should be chosen carefully for the site and well cared for.

Cypress bark weevil *Aesiotes leucurus*

The first signs of attack from this pest are loss of colour from the foliage and dieback of branches.

The white, legless larvae, which grow to 20 mm long, feed under the bark in the phloem-cambial region. If they feed right around a branch (or the trunk), it will be ringbarked and eventually die. Each fully grown larva pupates in a hollow in the sapwood covered with shredded wood. When the adult emerges, it chews a round hole (6 mm) through the bark. Adults may be seen on the tree in spring and summer. They are about 20 mm long and dull, dark grey to dark brown with a dirty white area on the end of the wing-covers and white 'knees'. They cause the death of branchlet tips by feeding on the young bark. Damage is more likely to be serious in times of drought or if the tree is growing in poor soil.

PLANTS ATTACKED Attack is common on stressed and older conifers. Ornamental cypresses such as the Monterey cypress (*Cupressus macrocarpa*) and the Bhutan cypress (*C. torulosa*) are the most commonly attacked. Monterey pine (*Pinus radiata*) and other *Pinus* spp. are sometimes attacked.

The pine bark weevil (*Aesiotes notabilis*) attacks the hoop pine (*Araucaria cunninghamii*) and the bunya pine (*A. bidwillii*) in a similar fashion.

CONTROL Remove dead branches. Water and fertilise the tree on a regular basis.

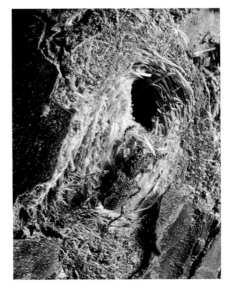

Cypress pine sawfly *Zenarge turneri*

This pest is most common in dry inland areas but it can be found on the coast.

The larvae are a translucent green and difficult to see on the branchlets. They can defoliate a tree in a short time. The tips of the shoots wither and may fall to the ground. When fully grown, the larvae (which are then about 25 mm long) leave the tree and pupate in the soil.

PLANTS ATTACKED Cypress pines (*Callitris* spp.) and cypress (*Cupressus* spp.).
CONTROL
• Organic/non-chemical: Prune off infested or damaged branchlets.
• Chemical: Spray with maldison.

Diamond beetle *Chrysolopus spectabilis*

This insect causes very little damage but is one of the few brightly coloured weevils. It is also known as the Botany Bay weevil and was one of the first insects to be collected by Sir Joseph Banks.

The larvae tunnel in the roots and stems of wattles, and the adults may chew new shoots. The mostly black adult beetle has patches of colour which are sometimes metallic green or metallic blue.
PLANTS ATTACKED Wattles.
CONTROL Unnecessary.

Doubleheaded hawk moth

Coequosa triangularis

The large green caterpillar of this moth appears to have a head at each end of the body. It lacks the abdominal spine characteristic of most hawk moth larvae and is covered with very short stiff 'bristles'.

The moth is usually deep yellow and brown, with a dark-brown triangle on the front edge of each forewing. The wingspan is about 150 mm.
PLANTS ATTACKED Banksias, persoonias, grevilleas, hakeas and other members of the family Proteaceae.
CONTROL Rarely necessary. The moths are so beautiful that they make up for a few eaten leaves.
• Organic/non-chemical: Larvae could be removed from the plant by hand.

Driedfruit beetles *Carpophilus* spp.

The beetles in this group are dark brown and only about 3 mm long. The wing covers, which do not quite cover the body, have yellowish patches in some species.

The adults can fly very well so they can easily move to areas where there is ripe fruit. The eggs are deposited in decaying fruit on the tree or on the ground. As the beetles move from fruit to fruit, they spread the spores of the fungal disease brown rot (D).

The larvae, which are about 1.5 mm long, are white with a brown section at each end. They develop in the fruit, and when fully fed pupate in the soil. In winter, adults may be found sheltering under bark or in crevices in the tree, and larvae may be found in fallen fruit. Both adults and larvae can move quickly when disturbed.

These beetles also cause serious problems in dried fruit.

PLANTS ATTACKED Arrange of fruit including stonefruit and tomatoes.

CONTROL

• Organic/non-chemical: Destroy unwanted fruit. Do not leave it on the ground. In future, techniques for using pheromones to mass trap these insects may be available.

• Chemical: If beetles are active, spray the tree with maldison every few days.

These little beetles also attack ripe fruit including tomatoes.

Carpophilus hemipterus
Length 3 mm.

Earth mites

Order Acarina: Family Penthaleidae

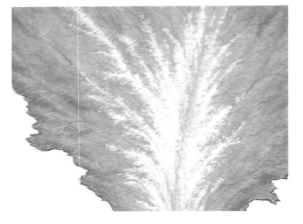

Earth mites are autumn, winter and spring pests, and their activity ceases for the year when hot weather begins. They feed at night, in the early morning or evening, or on dull days. On hot days they shelter under leaves resting on the soil or burrow into the soil.

The two species are about 1 mm long. Both have pink or red legs. The redlegged earth mite (*Halotydeus destructor*) has a velvety black body; and the blue oat mite (*Penthaleus major*) has a purple-blue or blue-black body and a red 'spot' towards the end of the body.

Feeding of both young and adult mites produces a mottled effect, which often begins near the main veins and then gradually spreads until the whole leaf has a grey or whitish appearance. If feeding continues and mite numbers build up, leaf tips turn brown and die. Small plants may die.

Damage is likely to be most severe if an autumn with good rains precedes a dry winter.

PLANTS ATTACKED The redlegged earth mite is mainly a pest of broad-leafed plants. The blue oat mite prefers to feed on cereals and other grasses. Both can damage peas, lupins, lettuces, stocks, snapdragons, lobelia, beetroot, silver beet, and crucifers. Weeds that provide an alternative food supply and are a source of crop infestation include capeweed, pigweed, shepherd's purse, Paterson's curse, skeleton weed and variegated thistle.

CONTROL

• Organic/non-chemical: Control should include removal of weeds which are important breeding and feeding sites. Those with a rosette habit such as capeweed and thistles are particularly important.

• Chemical: Spray with dimethoate. Treat surrounding grasses also if they are to be retained. Be careful to observe the withholding period on edible crops.

Earwigs Order Dermaptera

These insects are shades of brown or black, and all have the characteristic thick curved pincers or forceps at the end of their bodies. The adults of one species, the European earwig (*Forficula auricularia*), are reddish-brown and about 20 mm long. Young earwigs are generally paler in colour than the adults.

Earwigs congregate in leaf litter and other debris on the ground, under loose bark and in piles of rocks or timber. They like to creep into very small places where their bodies are touched by the surroundings.

They feed on a wide range of living or dead plant and animal material. They chew flowers, buds and fruit. Some species of earwig invade houses if they are present in large numbers.

Earwigs lay their whitish oval eggs in batches of 20–50 at the bottom of a burrow in the top 50 mm of soil. The female stays with and protects the eggs until they hatch and for about two weeks afterwards.

PLANTS ATTACKED Lettuces and other vegetables. Many ornamentals, including dahlias and chrysanthemums.

CONTROL

• Organic/non-chemical: Clean up breeding and hiding sites. Trapping is also possible. Traps can be made from pieces of crumpled newspaper stuffed inside a flower pot; the paper can be destroyed with the insects inside it.

Another type of trap can be made from grooved boards. The grooves should be about 6 mm wide and 6 mm deep, running the length of the board. Make two of these and then join the boards together so that the two sets of grooves are matching. Tie them together with pieces of string and stand them on end in places where earwigs are known to congregate. Check about twice a week, and remove and destroy the earwigs by dropping them into a bucket of soapy water.

• Chemical: If chemical control is necessary, carbaryl will protect plants. Carbaryl can be sprayed also on paths and wall and fence bases to stop earwigs moving from place to place.

Pinned adult

Pinned adult

Male and female of European earwig (Forficula auricularia) *and a specimen of black field earwig* (Nala lividipes).

Elephant weevil *Orthorhinus cylindrirostris*

These weevils vary in size from about 10 to 20 mm long and in colour from grey to black. They are so called because the head has a pronounced elongation like an elephant's trunk.

The adults chew buds and green bark, but the larvae tunnel in trunks and roots and cause more serious damage. The tunnels are tightly packed with frass (excrement, etc.) and round in cross-section.

Eggs are laid beneath the bark of trees/vines that are not growing vigorously. The larvae bore downwards for a period and then turn and come up again. Pupation occurs in the trunk between a few centimetres and a metre above ground level. The emerging adult chews a round hole to the surface. Adults are strong fliers and can move to weakened trees to lay eggs.

PLANTS ATTACKED Grapevines, all cultivated citrus, apples, apricots, peaches, gums (*Eucalyptus* spp.) and many others.

CONTROL

• Organic/non-chemical: Keep plants growing vigorously.

• Chemical: If this insect proves a pest in your area, spray the butts and trunks of trees several times in spring with carbaryl.

Emperor gum moth

Opodiphthera eucalypti

The caterpillars of this moth are light bright green with small red and blue lumps topped with blue spines. They are thick and fleshy and may be 120 mm long when fully grown. The caterpillars normally hang upside down on twigs and feed from that position. Damage is not usually severe. The tough brown egg-shaped cocoon is usually attached to a twig or small branch.

PLANTS ATTACKED The most common hosts are eucalypts and the pepper tree (*Schinus areira*), but the larvae are occasionally seen feeding on other plants including liquidambars, apricots, silver birches and Monterey pines (*Pinus radiata*).

CONTROL This is rarely necessary.

• Organic/non-chemical: Birds break open the pupal cases and eat the contents. Pupae may also be parasitised.

• Chemical: If spraying is to be carried out use maldison following the label directions.

Erinose mite—lychee *Eriophyes litchii*

These microscopic mites attack young leaves, shoots, flower buds and fruit. The leaf damage is quite spectacular. The eggs may be laid on leaves while they are still in the bud. The feeding of young mites on the surface cells stimulates the production of millions of 'hairs' which gives the damaged area a velvety appearance. The leaves develop blisters on the upper surface and may twist and curl. The velvety growth changes from yellowish to reddish-brown and then black. Mites move on to young leaves as soon as they appear.

PLANTS ATTACKED Lychees.

CONTROL Dip the above-ground parts of a newly bought tree in a wettable sulphur solution (4.5 g per litre of water) before planting; add some wetting agent. Spray wettable sulphur at the same rate 10–14 days later. This treatment should kill any mites present on the tree, and future problems are unlikely.

If the tree is already infested, spray with wettable sulphur just before a new flush of leaves is to occur and monthly thereafter until new growth develops without symptoms. Always add wetting agent and spray thoroughly.

European red mite *Panonychus ulmi*

These mites are up to 0.5 mm long and brownish-red with white spots. They cause fine yellow mottling on the leaves, which gradually become pale all over and develop a bronze colour. If the infestation is heavy, the leaves will brown and fall. Damage is most serious if it occurs early in the season because tree vigour and crop size will be adversely affected. Depletion of food reserves in the tree makes it more susceptible to injury from low winter temperatures.

These mites do not produce webbing on the leaves, but if an attack has been severe adult females often suspend themselves on web and may then be blown to nearby trees.

As the weather cools down in autumn, overwintering eggs, which are a bright red, are laid on the bark of the tree at a junction of two branches or perhaps on the fruit at the end of the stalk, or on small stems.

PLANTS ATTACKED Apples, pears, quinces, stonefruit, grapes, raspberries, hawthorns, elms, roses and others.

CONTROL Spray in late winter to kill eggs on the bark. Use an oil spray. If the mites are a problem later in the season, then spray with wettable sulphur. Do not apply when temperature is over 24°C. An application in the middle of December is usually very effective.

False wireworms
Order Coleoptera: Family Tenebrionidae

False wireworms and wireworms (family Elateridae — click beetles) are the larvae of two different groups of beetles. Their appearance and damage, however, are similar. They are slim, roughly cylindrical and usually brown or yellow, smooth and shiny. The legs are near the head. When fully grown they are 20–35 mm long.

They chew roots, and stems at or below ground level. They bore straight through fleshy organs such as potatoes, and tunnel in fleshy stalks at the base. Plants, particularly small ones, may wilt and die.

PLANTS ATTACKED Carrots, potatoes, cabbages, grasses etc.

CONTROL

• Organic/non-chemical: Control weeds. Keep plants growing vigorously. Prepare the ground thoroughly before planting. The adults may seek the shelter of weeds and vegetable litter on the soil surface. They are likely to collect under a bag or piece of wood on the soil and can be removed and destroyed.

• Chemical: In lawns the treatment recommended for African black beetle (P) would kill these pests too.

Fig psyllid *Mycopsylla fici*

This small insect is a sap-sucker. It feeds on the undersurfaces of the leaves but does not produce its own covering as other psyllids do. It becomes covered with the white sap oozing from the punctured areas and as this congeals a blob (much like old chewing gum) develops. Leaves attacked by these pests often fall and can then easily become attached to the feet of passers-by or to picnic rugs.

PLANTS ATTACKED Figs (*Ficus* spp.) particularly the Moreton Bay fig.

CONTROL This is quite difficult.

• Organic/non-chemical: Try to ensure that the tree is watered in dry periods and lightly fertilised to help maintain vigour.

• Chemical: Small trees may be sprayed with maldison but its effect would be limited.

Figleaf beetle *Poneridia semipullata*

This Australian native beetle (and the very similar *Poneridia australis*) belongs to the Family Chrysomelidae. Its eggs are laid on the leaves in groups of about 50. The spiny larvae, which begin yellowish, later become dark brown to black and grow to about 12 mm long.

They feed in groups and skeletonise the leaves, which usually fall. The skin of the fruit may also be damaged. When they have eaten enough they crawl down the trunk of the tree and pupate in the soil or in leaf litter or other rubbish around the base of the tree.

Adult beetles, which are about 10 mm long, and a dull brown on the main part of the body graduating into reddish-brown on the thorax and head, emerge about two weeks later and return to the trees to feed on leaves and fruit and lay eggs. During the warm summer weather there may be several generations.

PLANTS ATTACKED Figs grown for ornament or for fruit.

CONTROL

• Organic/non-chemical: On a small tree it may be possible to avoid serious damage by squashing the groups of pale yellow eggs.

• Chemical: Look for these beetles and their larvae in the early summer and undertake spray programmes quickly. Use carbaryl.

Frosted scale *Eulecanium pruinosum*

In September and October, the adult scales may be found concentrated on the undersides of small twigs. They have a tough brown skin and a thin covering of white powdery wax. They are oval in shape, and about 5 mm long and 3 mm wide.

The eggs begin hatching in late November, and the crawlers walk on to the leaves where they settle on the undersides to feed. Before the leaves fall in autumn, the young scales move back onto the twigs where they finish their development.

Frosted scales produce honeydew in large quantities, and sooty mould (D) grows wherever it has fallen on the plant. This detracts from the appearance of an ornamental and lowers the value of the fruit.

PLANTS ATTACKED These include a wide range of ornamentals, and plum, prune, apricot, nectarine and peach trees.

CONTROL Spray late in the dormant period. Use white oil (or a similar product). Apply to undersides of the laterals with particular care.

Fruit bats *Dobsonia* spp. and *Pteropus* spp.

These animals, which are in sub-order Megachiroptera, are mammals and related to the insectivorous bats. They are also known as flying foxes because of their long, fox-like muzzles. They live in colonies in trees where during the day they hang upside down from the branches. At dusk they leave to look for food and they can often be seen flying just above the treetops and all travelling in the one direction. Later in the night, after feeding, the fruit bats return to the same trees, their camp, and remain there until the next evening when they become active again. They are very noisy and a disturbance to any nearby residents.

They are native Australian animals and prefer the fruits and blossoms of native trees if they are available. They are known to fly many miles in search of food and do feed on soft cultivated fruit, particularly as more areas of natural vegetation are destroyed.

Fruit bats are most often seen in subtropical and tropical climates but there are several colonies of them in Sydney suburbs.

PLANTS ATTACKED Native trees such as the Moreton Bay fig. Also bananas, mangos, guavas and lychees.

CONTROL This is extremely difficult, particularly in large trees. The production of high-frequency sound or loud noises may deter them for a while. Netting placed over trees can protect the fruit, but the animals get caught in it and then must be released. Strong-smelling substances such as naphthalene (in mothballs) hung in the tree may keep them away from the area.

Fruit bats are often referred to as flying foxes because of their long, fox-like muzzles.

Native flowers form part of their diet.

Fruit bats rest in groups during the day.

Fruit flies   Order Diptera: Family Tephritidae

These flies lay their eggs in small groups just beneath the skin of the fruit. When the larvae hatch, they often make their way to the centre of the fruit. Their feeding and the action of rotting organisms introduced when the eggs are deposited soon destroy the fruit. Fruit fly larvae are often referred to as 'maggots' and are typically creamy-white and taper towards the head.

Queensland fruit fly (*Dacus tryoni*) is reddish-brown with yellow markings and about 7 mm long.

Mediterranean fruit fly (*Ceratitis capitata*) is smaller. It is usually yellow, and the wings have noticeable brown bands.

These two fruit flies have similar life cycles. They are considered serious pests, and their control is compulsory in some areas. The larvae of both these species are 7–9 mm long when fully grown. They leave the fruit at this stage and burrow down into the soil, where they pupate. The brown pupal cases are about 5 mm long and look like somewhat elongated hens' eggs.

Females are capable of laying eggs about one week after emergence. Adults live many weeks and feed on sweet liquids such as honeydew from aphids and similar insects.

Flies commonly overwinter in the adult form. They become active when warm weather begins in August and lay eggs in citrus fruits. Loquats are infested soon after and gradually the population builds to a peak in late summer.

Infested fruit may ripen early and fall. On tomatoes, sites where the ovipositor was inserted may remain as pinprick spots of green when the rest of the fruit ripens. In passionfruit, eggs deposited in immature fruit are enveloped in woody tissue and do not hatch. However, if the fruit is ripe when the eggs are laid, woody tissue will not be formed and larvae may hatch.

The sites of egg-laying in avocados develop into star or T-shaped cracks 3–7 mm across, often with raised edges. The damage is shallower than that caused by fruitspotting bug (P). If eggs are laid in immature avocados, they are surrounded by woody tissue and no further damage occurs.

PLANTS ATTACKED   Queensland fruit fly and Mediterranean fruit fly have similar host ranges. Fruit attacked includes avocados (particularly 'Fuerte' and 'Rincon' varieties), bananas, citrus, figs, stonefruit, pomefruit, grapes, persimmons, quinces, loquats, passionfruit, olives, walnuts, guavas, feijoas, tomatoes, eggfruit, and capsicum. Queensland fruit fly attacks fruits of rainforest trees also.

Other fruit flies may attack some of the same fruits, as well as some different ones. For example, the cucumber fly (*Dacus cucumis*) lays eggs in cucurbit fruit of all types, tomatoes, and papaws allowed to ripen on the tree.

CONTROL
• Organic/non-chemical: Control is obligatory for some species. Infested fruit must be removed from the ground or from the tree and destroyed by burning or boiling. Or it may be immersed for at least three days in water with a layer of kerosene on the surface. Maggots will also be killed if the fruit is sealed in a plastic bag and left in the sun for several days. It must not be buried as this simply continues the normal life cycle of the insect. A trap such as Dakpot® will give some idea of the presence of flies, but in itself is not a sufficient control, and chemical sprays and/or baits are also necessary.
• Chemical: Begin to take action when stonefruit and pomefruit are about half-size and citrus fruit is beginning to colour.

In urban areas spraying is almost always necessary. This will kill eggs and larvae in the fruit. Fenthion and dimethoate area suitable chemicals. Follow label directions. Note that dimethoate may cause leaf and fruit drop in apricots and early peaches, and that fenthion is particularly toxic to poultry and other birds.

In more isolated areas baiting may be sufficient. This method kills the adult flies but cannot affect larvae in fruit.

A suitable bait would be 7 mL of maldison (50%) and 50 g of sugar dissolved in a litre of water (dissolve the sugar before adding the maldison). Splash the mixture with a paintbrush on to leaves, smooth tree trunks or other non-absorbent objects in the area. The fly is attracted more to bait applied in large drops than to bait sprayed on. This should be applied at least every seven days during the ripening period and for two weeks after all fruit is harvested.

Larvae in peach

Adult fly

Adult fly on tomato

Fruitspotting bug *Amblypelta nitida*

This is an Australian native bug, and cultivated trees near areas of bushland are most likely to be attacked. Even the adult bugs do not move readily from tree to tree, so that it is common to find large populations on one tree but very few on adjacent trees. When disturbed they move quickly to seek shelter.

The adult bugs are green, elongated in shape and about 15 mm long. Each female may lay many eggs during warm weather, and bug numbers can build up quite quickly in these conditions.

The nymphs have reddish-black legs, and a dark, reddish abdomen with two black spots. Both adults and nymphs suck sap, and even a few of them can cause serious damage to macadamia nuts. The symptoms vary, but often include nut fall which may be the first indication of an infestation. When these green nuts are examined, if the fruit fall has been because of fruitspotting bug attack, the nuts will have small slightly sunken dark spots. There may also be small brown areas where the husk joins the nut. Attack may also result in deformed kernels or translucent kernels.

On papaws the bugs suck sap from the growing point, leafstalks and young fruit; the fruit usually falls. Peaches that have been attacked exude gum, and contain gum pockets; again, the fruit usually falls. On avocados the damage of this pest is very like the damage caused by banana-spotting bug (P).

These insects are very like banana-spotting bugs and may be found in association with them.

PLANTS ATTACKED Macadamias, avocados, pecans, custard apples, guavas, lychees, passionfruit, plums, peaches, nectarines, persimons, mangos, papaws, citrus, and others.

CONTROL   Check regularly for bugs at flowering and during fruit development.
• Organic/non-chemical: Spray only when and where symptoms of attack are serious. Try a soap spray. Early detection is important. Another related species, *Dasynus fuscescens*, is also known as fruitspotting bug.
• Chemical: Spray the bugs with trichlorfon only if absolutely necessary.

Damage on avocados

Adult and young nymph on a damaged avocado.

Othreis *sp.*

Fruitpiercing moths

Othreis spp. and *Eudocima* sp.

The larvae of these moths feed on vegetation in areas of rainforest or along creek banks. It is the adults that do damage to cultivated fruit. The skin of the ripe fruit is pierced with the proboscis and the juice is sucked out.

The moths fly and feed at night. They have a wingspan of about 100 mm. The feeding holes are larger than the marks made by an egg-laying fruit fly, and in some fruits there is a soft sunken area around a small hole. In other fruits the area under the hole is dry and pithy. Fungi that cause rotting can gain entry to the fruit in damaged areas.

PLANTS ATTACKED   Citrus, bananas, guavas, mangos, papaws, tomatoes, and others.

CONTROL
• Organic/non-chemical: Pick fruit before it is fully ripe if problems occur on a regular basis. Overripe fruit (or sweet sherry or mashed ripe bananas) could be used in a home-made trap constructed so that once the moths entered (attracted by the fruit inside) they could not escape. However, the effectiveness of such a trap is not established.
• Chemical: Chemical control is not satisfactory for this pest, because the moths feed for only a short time and it is not always possible to know when they will arrive.

Damage on lychees

Fruit-tree borer *Maroga melanostigma*

These moths are in family Oecophoridae. They usually lay their eggs singly at branch junctions — which may be almost any combination of trunk, branch and twig. Each larva makes a daytime shelter for itself by tunnelling down into the wood. The tunnels end up about 60 mm deep.

The larva comes out during the night to feed on the bark surrounding its hole and sometimes drags leaves down into the hole. Damaged areas are neatly covered with chewed wood, bark, webbing and droppings. This covering helps to protect the larvae from predators such as ants. Sometimes branches are ringbarked. Some trees such as cherries produce quantities of gum which ooze out of the damaged area.

PLANTS ATTACKED These caterpillars attack a wide variety of different plants, including ornamentals such as acacias, crepe myrtles, jacarandas; and fruiting and flowering stonefruit.

CONTROL
• Organic/non-chemical: If only one or two trees are attacked, remove the webbing from the entrances and poke a piece of wire down the tunnel or inject a few drops of kerosene. If old wattles are badly damaged remove the whole tree and replace. Maintain vigorous trees by watering and lightly fertilising.
• Chemical: Spray with carbaryl following label directions. Make sure that trunks and branches are sprayed as well as the leaves. Non-chemical controls are to be preferred.

Fruit-tree root weevil *Leptopius squalidus*

The larvae of this weevil chew on the roots of trees and large shrubs and gouge furrows out of them. This may seriously weaken the tree. When the larvae have eaten enough, they pupate in the soil. The adult pushes up through the soil and climbs the trunk or overhanging branches to reach the top of the tree. The adults may chew new leaves and young stems, and later lay eggs in a folded-up leaf.

PLANTS ATTACKED This weevil feeds on a wide range of fruit trees including apples, pears, figs and citrus. It also attacks ornamental shrubs and trees.

CONTROL Control involves stopping the adult getting up to the top of the tree. This can be achieved by placing around the trunk a wide band of material which the weevil cannot negotiate (see page 38).

Ensure that surrounding plants and overhanging branches do not meet. Spraying is not warranted in a home garden, because the weevils are rarely found more than one or two at a time.

Fuller's rose weevil *Asynonychus cervinus*

These weevils are greyish-brown and about 7 mm long. They can be found in summer and autumn and may live for several months. All the individuals are females and they have a small, faint, white, saucer-shaped mark on each side of the 'body'. The adults chew ragged holes around the edges of leaves and also attack buds and young shoots.

The eggs are laid in various locations, such as underneath loose bark, in curled dead leaves or on the ground. They are usually in groups of about 30, and each individual may lay about ten such groups of eggs.

When the larvae hatch from the eggs they make their way into the soil, where they feed on the roots of a number of different plants. The damage is not very great unless the plant is a small one such as tomato. When fully grown, the stout larvae are about 6 mm long and greyish-white. The underground phase of the life cycle lasts about nine months. Adults push up to the surface of the soil and make their way to the top of a nearby plant.

PLANTS ATTACKED These insects feed on a wide variety of plants, almost any broadleaf plant in fact. The young adults prefer tender foliage, but as they get older they move to tougher, more fibrous tissue. Citrus, passionfruit, blackberries, camellias, gardenias, peaches, roses, dahlias, cherries and blackcurrants are all known to be attacked. Weeds such as fat hen and stinking roger can also be hosts.

CONTROL
• Organic/non-chemical: See note on manual removal page 37.
• Chemical: When the first adults are seen feeding on the leaves spray with carbaryl. Cover leaves, trunk and surrounding soil with the solution.

Fungus gnats

Family Mycetophilidae and Family Sciaridae

Adult

Pupa on the left.
Larva on the right.

These insects are associated with decaying organic matter, and many of them feed only on fungi. However, some damage small soft plants and seedlings. The adults are small grey and black flies about 3 mm long. They hover in groups around plants or run over the surface of pots. They can be a nuisance indoors around potted plants.

The thin legless larvae, which grow to about 5 mm long, are a translucent white and have black heads. They feed on the root hairs of seedlings and cause wilting or slow growth. They can sometimes be located by looking for a tiny slimy trail glistening on the surface of the soil or potting mix.

PLANTS ATTACKED   A wide range of seedlings, cuttings and other small plants.

CONTROL   Dry out affected soil or potting mix. Take care not to overwater potted plants. Repot using a mix with less organic matter.

Garden soldier fly   *Exaireta spinigera*

This insect is also known as a garden maggot. The adults are long and narrow (12 mm) and black with smoky brown at the ends of the wings. They are often found indoors on the windows.

The larvae of these flies are about 15 mm long when fully grown and have leathery brown skins. Their bodies are flattened and bear some 'hairs'. They may be found in large numbers in moist areas of soil particularly where there is a lot of rotting organic matter.

PLANTS ATTACKED   These insects do not usually feed on living plants. They feed on decaying leaves or fruit.

CONTROL   This is not really necessary. Bury decaying fruit and vegetables deeply. Masses of larvae could be killed by putting them in a bucket of water with some kerosene added.

Gladiolus thrips   *Thrips simplex*

These thrips feed on the leaves, causing silver streaks, and on buds, causing deformed flowers. The buds may not open at all. If open dark-coloured flowers are attacked, patches of colour will be removed and even a few of these whitish flecks considerably reduce the value of the flower. On light-coloured varieties damage is not so noticeable.

The young nymphs are found inside the leaf tubes and flower buds, whereas the adults are usually found feeding in the open on the leaves. The resting stage may be found either on the plant or in the soil beneath the plant. If the plants are left for a long time in the field after flowering, the thrips will migrate to the corms as the leaves die, and continue feeding. Damage also occurs while corms are in storage. In this case they become sticky, and later hard and scabby. When the corms are planted again the thrips may feed on young roots and cause serious injury.

Hot dry conditions favour this insect, and if heavy rain or cool and wet weather occurs, their numbers will be very much reduced. Wind may blow the thrips from one group of plants to another.

PLANTS ATTACKED   This thrips feeds on a relatively restricted range of plants. It seems to prefer the gladiolus, but may also feed on carnations, irises, calla lilies, red hot pokers (*Kniphofia* sp.), montbretias (*Crocosmia* sp.), and tiger flowers (*Tigridia pavonia*).

CONTROL

• Organic/non-chemical: New plantings of gladiolus should be positioned as far as possible from old plantings, and any odd gladiolus plants that have grown up around the garden should be removed. Overhead watering will considerably reduce numbers of thrips.

• Chemical: Spray plants with dimethoate or with maldison. Before storage dust corms with 5% maldison dust.

Golden mealybug *Nipaecoccus aurilanatus*

These mealybugs are black and produce a band of bright yellow wax along their bodies and around the edge. They suck sap from stems and occasionally from pine needles. Eggs are deposited in a white, nearly oval sac. After the infestation has been on the plant for a period of time, the mealybug bodies are not easy to see because they have become covered with mealy white wax and egg-sacs are interspersed throughout the population.

The mealybugs produce honeydew, so the tree may also look dirty because of the sooty mould (D) that is growing there. A reduction in the tree's growth rate and discolouration of needles is also common.

Most damage is done in the spring, because later in the season the population of mealybugs is reduced when they are attacked by a small ladybird and its larvae. The ladybird larvae look a little like large mealybugs and are covered with white wax. They are, however, much more agile and move quickly up and down the stem.

PLANTS ATTACKED Norfolk Island pines and bunya pines.

CONTROL Even if damage is being done in the spring and no ladybirds or their larvae are present, it is still best to wait for natural predators. On a small tree mealybug numbers can be reduced by gently rubbing them off. Be sure not to kill the ladybird larvae. See page 30 for photograph.

Grape phylloxera *Daktulosphaira vitifolii*

This extremely serious pest is an aphid that can live on the root system of the plant as well as on the above-ground parts. Root systems that have been attacked have fleshy yellow galls on the fine roots. These are about 10 mm across and may be curved into an S-shape. If they are cut open, one or two greenish-yellow aphids may be seen. Once a gall forms, that root stops growing. Infected vines have weak growth and will never produce properly. Sometimes the leaves are also attacked, and in this case, fleshy yellowish irregular swellings occur on the lower surface.

PLANTS ATTACKED Grapevines grown in heavy soils will be more seriously affected than those grown in very sandy soil.

CONTROL There is no chemical control for this pest and no economic means of removing it from the soil once it is established. It is therefore extremely important to obey the quarantine regulations which exist regarding the movement of grape cuttings and other plant parts. Find out what these regulations are for your district. Spreading phylloxera to a new area would cause great disruption (your own supply of table grapes, dried grapes such as sultanas, and wine may also be seriously affected). In areas where the pest is known to exist, grapes are usually grown on resistant rootstocks. This means that the root system is not suitable for the development of these aphids and very few galls will be formed.

Grapeleaf blister mite *Colomerus vitis*

Upper surface

Lower surface

This mite is extremely small and cannot be seen with the unaided eye. It spends the winter sheltering in the buds and attacks the new leaves in the spring. The mites congregate on the undersurface of the leaves where a felt-like patch develops. This is a creamy colour to begin with but later goes brown. Corresponding to these areas but on the upper surface of the leaf, bubbled patches appear. These may be 10 mm across and are sometimes referred to as 'erinose'.

The mites are more active if the spring is wet or if the vine is growing in a moist area. The mite can move from old to new leaves, and moves into buds as the weather gets cooler. This pest may concentrate its feeding on tiny leaves in the buds. This results in dead buds or thick canes with short internodes and short spindly branches.

PLANTS ATTACKED Grapes, some varieties more than others.

CONTROL There may be some value in collecting and destroying old leaves that have been attacked. This is not a serious pest, but if it is considered that the blistered or bubbled leaves are ugly then spray with lime-sulphur just before the buds burst. Use 50 mL per litre of water. Do not use lime-sulphur after the leaves have appeared. At this stage or later, wettable sulphur should be used at the rate of 2 g per litre of water. If spraying is carried out on a very hot day, leaf burn will result. Cover the vine thoroughly with spray.

Grapeleaf rust mite *Calepitrimerus vitis*

It is not possible to see these mites with the unaided eye, although they are often present in large numbers particularly on the upper surfaces of the leaf. Their feeding gives the leaf a reddish-brown or rusty appearance particularly along the main vein.

The vines, however, appear to produce well even if most of the leaves show this discolouration. The leaves usually fall a little before they would normally have fallen in the autumn.

PLANTS ATTACKED Grapes.

CONTROL Spraying before bud-swell with lime-sulphur (20%) at the rate of 50 mL per litre of water should give good control of all vine mites. Cover all parts of the vine and make sure that the spray gets into crevices around the buds. If control is necessary during the growing season, wettable sulphur should be used. Do not use lime-sulphur.

Grapevine hawk moth

Hippotion celerio

The caterpillar of this moth may be green or brownish-black and grows about 75 mm long. It has the typical stiff spine of hawk moth larvae. The larvae chew leaves, and if occasionally present in large numbers may defoliate sections of vines or other plants.

The adult has a pointed abdomen and light brown forewings with black and silver lines, one of which extends from wingtips to the base. The hindwings are deep pink with black markings. The wingspan is about 75 mm.

PLANTS ATTACKED The larvae of this moth are known to feed on a wide variety of plants, including calla lilies, balsam, sweet potatoes, golden guinea vines, rhubarb, Virginia creeper, Boston ivy, and both fruiting and ornamental grapes.

CONTROL
• Organic/non-chemical: Handpick. The presence of fresh insect droppings will help locate the larvae.
• Chemical: This is occasionally necessary, and carbaryl is suitable. Follow label directions.

Grapevine moth *Phalaenoides glycinae*

The black moth has yellow markings and a wingspan of about 50 mm. There is a tuft of orange hairs on the end of the body.

The caterpillars, which may grow to 50 mm, are black and marked with white and fuchsia-pink. They usually feed from the underside of the leaf. A few larvae can defoliate a vine. They may also attack developing bunches of grapes. Pupation takes place in soil or leaf litter underneath the plant or in crevices in fences or posts.

PLANTS ATTACKED Fuchsias, grapevines (both fruiting and ornamental), Boston ivy. It also feeds on some Australian native plants such as *Hibbertia* sp.

CONTROL
• Organic/non-chemical: Predators are often successful in keeping this pest in check. A range of different insects such as beetles and wasps attack grapevine moth larvae and pupae. A predatory shield bug (*Oechalia schellembergii*) kills by sucking out the body fluids. It is dull brown, up to 13 mm long and 5 mm wide. Birds also attack this pest. Spray with Dipel® only if the infestation is severe.
• Chemical: Only spray severe infestations. Use carbaryl and follow the label directions.

Grapevine scale *Parthenolecanium persicae*

These scales are in the adult stage in the winter and are found on old parts of the vine in rough bark. They produce eggs beneath the scale cover. When these eggs hatch in the late spring, the crawlers, which are yellowish, move out and settle on the leaves to feed. In autumn they move back on to the canes of the plant and then on to the older wood where they finally mature.

The mature scales are a rather shiny dark brown, oval, and 7 mm long by 4 mm wide. They have a hard, convex exterior. They produce honeydew, and the sooty mould (D) that grows in honeydew can be a help in locating infestations. The scales do not cause serious damage unless honeydew falls on to the fruit, where the sooty mould makes the bunches unpalatable and unmarketable. The vine would be weakened if infestations were really severe.

Grapevine scales occur in both coastal and inland areas. They are spread from place to place on cuttings. They are more likely to be found in large numbers in a home garden than in a commercial orchard.
PLANTS ATTACKED Grapes.
CONTROL   At pruning time some infested canes will be removed. Spraying can then be carried out with oil at the rate of 30 mL per litre of water. Summer spraying, if necessary, should thoroughly cover the lower leaf surfaces; use 10 mL of white oil per litre. Spot spraying of infested areas is usually sufficient.

Grass blue butterfly *Zizina labradus labradus*

This common butterfly is a minor pest of garden peas and beans. It is an Australian insect and is found in all states — in dry inland areas as well as on the coast and in the mountains. Although areas of its natural habitat have been destroyed the cultivation of extensive leguminous pastures has provided a constant food supply and its numbers have probably increased. The larvae, which may be attended by a few small black ants, feed on small leaves, flower buds and seed pods. They are most likely to be seen in summer. The white or pale blue mandarin-shaped eggs are laid singly on leaves, stems and flowering heads. The youngest larvae are white but when fully grown, the larvae are green, pink or brown with a white stripe down each side of the body. They are about 10 mm long and have brown heads and a very fine covering of small pale brown hairs. The pupae are pink or pale green to grey with darker markings.
PLANTS ATTACKED Members of the plant family Papilionaceae including garden peas and beans, plants such as clovers and medics, trees such as virgilia (*Virgilia capensis*) and Australian native plants such as Darling pea (*Swainsona greyana*) and indigo (*Indigofera* spp.).
CONTROL
• Organic/non-chemical: Check around the youngest leaves, flowers and tiny pods of the plant — remove larvae by hand.
• Chemical: If necessary, spray with carbaryl.

Grass-crown mealybug
Antonina graminis

This insect — which is also known as 'felted grass coccid' — is a common cause of lack of vigour in grasses and makes them look thin and straggly with few leaves and exposed runners. The damage is done when the insect sucks sap from the plants. Checking the nodes on the stems and the crowns will show clumps of the small 'mealy' coated insects. The female produces many hundreds of eggs. The crawlers move a short distance away and settle to feed.
PLANTS ATTACKED Many warm-climate grasses.
CONTROL
• Organic/non-chemical: Try a soap or oil spray.
• Chemical: Use a penetrant such as dimethoate. Add wetting agent and follow directions on label. Once the protective waxy coat has developed, contact insecticides are ineffective.

Grasswebbing mites

Oligonychus araneum and *O. digitatus*

The presence of these pests is not usually noticed until large bleached circular patches occur on an area of grass. Normally there is fine white webbing in the patch. However, it is only in very heavy infestations that this becomes so obvious that it cannot be missed. The mites are quite small but may just be seen with the naked eye, moving on the web. Leaves show a distinctly silvered and rubbed look, and the patch itself may look dry.

PLANTS ATTACKED Grasses, particularly warm-climate species.

CONTROL
• Organic: Wettable sulphur; use 2 g per litre of water.
• Chemical: Spray dicofol. Add wetting agent.

Green looper *Chrysodeixis* sp.

These slim green caterpillars hide on foliage during the day and feed mostly at night. They are extremely difficult to see, and considerable quantities of foliage may be eaten before their exact whereabouts is discovered. Look for their small dry brown droppings on leaves or on surfaces beneath potted plants. They move with a looping motion.

After growing to about 40 mm long, they pupate in a flimsy cocoon under a leaf. The copper-brown adult moth has a wingspan of about 30–40 mm and some silver markings on the forewings.

PLANTS ATTACKED A wide range of vegetables, annual flowers and soft-wooded perennials. Attacks may occur indoors as well as outside.

CONTROL Spray both leaf surfaces.
• Organic/non-chemical: Handpick or spray with Dipel®.
• Chemical: Spray with carbaryl at the rate suggested on the label.
  The scientific name of this moth was formerly *Plusia chacites*.

Pictured: *Chrysodeixis argentifera*

Green peach aphid *Myzus persicae*

This aphid is extremely common and is a serious pest because, apart from direct feeding damage, it carries a number of serious viruses from plant to plant. It can be found as adults and nymphs throughout the year in warm coastal areas, and wherever there is a mild winter. In areas with a more severe winter, this aphid passes the winter in the egg stage on peach trees.

Eggs are usually laid around the bases of buds and hatch out when the buds are plump. Feeding continues on these buds, but the population does not increase rapidly until the buds have burst. Early and uneven opening of flower buds indicates attack.

Many flowers fail to set fruit, and young fruits that do develop may fall early. The aphids feed on new leaves, which become twisted and distorted. Older leaves may shrivel, and blacken with sooty mould (D), and may fall. As the leaves become tougher and less palatable in the summer, this aphid develops winged forms which usually move to smaller plants. When the weather gets colder in the autumn, the aphids migrate back to the peach trees and lay eggs.

If this pest is not controlled serious dieback and loss of fruiting capacity will result.

PLANTS ATTACKED A wide range, including peaches, nectarines, plums, almonds, capeweed, dock, sow thistle, dahlias, Iceland poppies, roses, peas, potatoes, spinach, tomatoes, cabbages, cauliflowers, radishes, lettuces and beans.

CONTROL
• Organic/non-chemical: Watch for first aphids. Hose or rub off until natural enemies build up their numbers. Spray deciduous fruit trees in winter with oil.
• Chemical: In areas with a cold winter where the aphid overwinters as eggs, spray with oil. If this spray is missed or in areas with a milder winter, wait till some leaves are on the trees and spray with dimethoate. Do not use dimethoate on early varieties of peach.

Dimethoate is suitable for use on most shrubs. On vegetables, it is important to observe the withholding period.

Green planthopper

Siphanta acuta

This sap-sucker is light green and about 10 mm long. It can jump actively if disturbed. The nymphs have a tuft of white threads at the end of the body. These may become detached and stick on the plant. The honeydew produced may also disfigure the plant.
PLANTS ATTACKED A wide range of plants; mainly trees and shrubs, including native and exotic.
CONTROL   Is usually unnecessary.

Green treehopper   *Sextius virescens*

These small green insects are about 9 mm long and usually found together in a group. Their heads are tucked down beneath the body (typical of the group) and they have a horn-like projection on each side of the head.

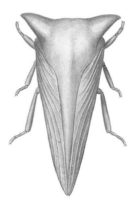

The horns on the body resemble parts of the plant on which treehoppers usually feed.

They produce large quantities of honeydew and therefore ants (P) and sooty mould (D) are associated with them. Terminal shoots may be killed by their sucking, and slits are cut in twigs when eggs are laid. As the plant grows, these slits may become more noticeable.
PLANTS ATTACKED Wattles, particularly the black wattle, are likely to be attacked.
CONTROL
• Organic/non-chemical: Prune off damaged twigs.
• Chemical: Spraying is not usually necessary, but a penetrant or systemic insecticide such as dimethoate with added wetting agent would kill them.

Green vegetable bug   *Nezara viridula*

The adults of this bug are approximately 15 mm long and are usually green. They can be distinguished from similar bugs by the top edge of the triangle on their back: it has a black spot in each corner and three small yellow spots between them. The adults shelter in plant litter and perhaps under the bark of trees during the winter. At this time they are brownish in colour. In the spring they begin egg-laying. The eggs are deposited in groups of 40–80, usually in a neat hexagonal shape. The nymphs are marked in yellow, red, orange, green and black.

The young nymphs feed in the same way as the adults — that is, they suck sap. New shoots are a favoured part of the plant for nymphs, but older bugs feed on fruit and seeds in preference to leaves. Their predominant colour may be green or black. On bean plants young pods which are often attacked become dried out and distorted. More mature pods become pale and blotched in appearance. Tomato fruit when attacked develops mottled areas.
PLANTS ATTACKED Many, including pumpkins, capsicum, potatoes, spinach, oranges, peas, passionfruit and many garden plants and weeds. Beans and tomatoes are attacked regularly in some areas.
CONTROL
• Organic/non-chemical: Handpick. Control weeds and remove plants which have finished bearing.
• Chemical: Use an insecticide such as fenthion or dimethoate. Take care to observe withholding period.

Greenhouse thrips *Heliothrips haemorrhoidalis*

Despite the name, this insect commonly occurs outdoors. In warmer climates it attacks only plants growing in shady, cool and relatively moist conditions. The dark brown to black adults are nearly 1.5 mm long, and the young thrips are smaller and paler than this.

These thrips usually feed under the leaves and produce dark brown blobs of excrement. The upper leaf surface becomes dull grey or silver. Feeding may take place between two overlapping leaves or even on the upper surface — in this case the leaves may appear to be dusty and dull. Leaves may brown and fall.

Persimmon fruit may be blemished by spots of thrip excrement, and leaf fall may weaken the tree. On 'Valencia' oranges, fruit left hanging on the tree until late summer may be damaged by thrips. The rind may develop grey patches speckled with dark droppings.

PLANTS ATTACKED A wide range, including azaleas, rhododendrons, fuchsias, viburnums, passionfruit and grapes.

CONTROL On many trees and shrubs a small infestation can be ignored.

• Organic/non-chemical: A small wasp parasite (*Ceranisus* sp.) helps to reduce thrips numbers. A soap spray may help.

• Chemical: If spraying is necessary use maldison. Pay special attention to the undersurfaces of leaves.

Grevillea leafminer

Peraglyphis atimana

The adult of this pest is a moth in the family Tortricidae.

The larvae, which may grow to about 10 mm long, feed between the leaf surfaces and cause brown blisters. Attack year after year may seriously weaken the plants.

PLANTS ATTACKED Silky oaks (*Grevillea robusta*) and Banks' grevilleas (*G. banksii*).

CONTROL

• Organic/non-chemical: Water and lightly fertilise the tree to increase vigour.

• Chemical: Spray small trees with fenthion.

Grevillea looper *Oenochroma vinaria*

These caterpillars are smooth and slender and taper slightly towards the head. They are green with many small spots and two small fleshy projections towards the head. They move with a looping action. In some areas shrubs can be defoliated.

The moths have wings which spread about 50 mm and are usually rosy-purple on top with a purplish spot on the underside of the forewing, as shown in the photograph.

PLANTS ATTACKED Grevilleas, banksias, hakeas and others. Two similar species feed on geebungs (*Persoonia* sp.).

CONTROL

• Organic/non-chemical: Remove by hand.

• Chemical: If spraying is necessary, use carbaryl following label directions.

Gumleaf skeletoniser   *Uraba lugens*

This moth lays eggs in groups of 100-200 or more. When the caterpillars are young, they feed in a group and remove the surface from the leaves so that only the veins remain. As they get older, they feed individually and chew pieces from the leaf.

These caterpillars are conspicuous because of the 'horn' they carry on their heads. This is made up of the head capsules from skins which they have outgrown. As they moult and discard each skin, the head section is retained and each one is pushed further into the air at the next moult until a horn-like projection is produced.

Hairs from the caterpillars, which grow to about 25 mm long, can produce a severe itch. The moth has a wingspan of 25 mm.

PLANTS ATTACKED These caterpillars prefer to feed on the blackbutt (*Eucalyptus pilularis*), the Sydney blue gum (*E. saligna*), the narrow-leafed peppermint (*E. robertsonii*), the river red gum (*E. camaldulensis*), the snow gum (*E. pauciflora*), the mountain gum (*E. dalrympleana*), and the brush box (*Lophostemon confertus*).

CONTROL   Control is not usually necessary.

• Organic/non-chemical: Prune off groups of leaves with eggs or small larvae on them.

• Chemical: Spray with maldison; add a wetting agent to the spray so that the long fine hairs of the larvae can be penetrated.

Gumtree hoppers   *Eurymela* spp.

The adults of insects in this group are about 10 mm long. Different species have different colours and markings.

They suck sap from young twigs and branchlets and may cause malformation. They produce large quantities of honeydew, so ants (P) and sooty mould (D) are associated with them.

The eggs are laid in twigs. The nymphs feed together in a group and move quickly around to the other side of the twig if disturbed. Adults can hop and fly.

PLANTS ATTACKED Eucalypts, she-oaks and wattles.

CONTROL

• Organic/non-chemical: Try knocking groups off the tree into soapy water. Prepare well beforehand and move quickly.

• Chemical: Spray with dimethoate or omethoate. Add some wetting agent.

Gumtree scale   *Eriococcus coriaceus*

This pest is not usually noticed until the female scales have formed egg-sacs. These are about 3 mm long and roughly the same shape as hens' eggs and a similar colour to begin with. If they are crowded together, this shape is not so easily seen. As they age, they get darker until they are a reddish-brown colour. When the eggs hatch, the crawlers escape through a small hole in one end of the egg-sac. The females settle on stems, petioles and leaf veins.

The male scale coverings are much smaller and usually clustered together, often on leaves or above the females on the stem.

This insect produces vast quantities of honeydew which falls on to the leaves beneath, making them very sticky. If the infestation has been on the tree for some time, sooty mould (D) will grow on the honeydew. Attacks on young trees can cause branches to die.

PLANTS ATTACKED   Some gums are more prone than others. Scribbly gum (*Eucalyptus haemastoma*), spinning-top gum (*E. perriniana*), silver-leafed gum (*E. pulverulenta*), ironbark peppermint (*E. smithii*), tingiringi gum (*E. glaucescens*), and white peppermint (E. linearis) can all be severely affected.

CONTROL

• Organic/non-chemical: Much of the infestation can be removed by hand by rubbing the branches and breaking all the scales. Spray with oil.

• Chemical: Use dimethoate. Apply in early or mid-spring when the eggs have hatched.

Pseudaulacaspis *sp. on port-wine magnolia*

Hard scales   Order Hemiptera: Family Diaspididae

These scales are also referred to as armoured scales. Even small populations can cause serious damage, which includes yellow blotches on leaves, leaf fall, and dieback of twigs and even branches. Fruit can be disfigured and distorted. Serious damage and even death of the plant can result if control measures are not carried out.

Female scales typically produce living young, called 'crawlers', a few every day over several months. The crawlers settle near the older scales and begin to suck sap. Each young insect produces a protective covering from wax and cast-off skins. This covering is made bigger as the insect grows. The mature females remain beneath the covering, but the males (minute insects with two wings) do emerge and are sometimes noticed flying around a group of scale coverings.

Hard scales do not produce honeydew.

PLANTS ATTACKED Many plants have hard scales associated with them. Some species of hard scale attack a wide range of plants, but others attack only a few plants.

CONTROL   Plants such as citrus which are attacked by a number of different hard scales should be given a routine annual spray to keep populations at low levels. However, scales on most ornamentals can be controlled satisfactorily by spraying whenever scales are noticed; this may be once every few years.

Use white oil at the rate of 20 mL per litre of water, or use 10 mL of white oil per litre of water on plants considered to be delicate. Spraying should be thorough. Cover all surfaces and apply till the spray runs off the plant. Keep the spray mixture well stirred during application. Deciduous trees and shrubs can be sprayed in winter if good coverage of trunk and branches is the aim.

See also California red scale (P), rose scale (P), San José scale (P), white louse scale (P), and apple mussel scale (page 101).

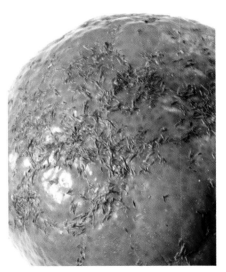
Lepidosaphes gloverii *on orange*

Fiorinia *sp. on camellia*

Harlequin bug   *Dindymus versicolor*

This bug is about 12 mm long, and black and red or black and reddish-orange. Swarms of these insects often move to cultivated plants from native trees, shrubs, and weeds along roadsides when these dry out in the summertime. The plants are damaged when the insects suck sap from young tissues, and may eventually wilt and die. Fruit may be blemished by insect excrement.

These bugs often cluster on fences, wood heaps, tree trunks and similar places, and move on to nearby plants to feed during the day. In winter they may hibernate in the same sorts of places or under the bark of trees.

PLANTS ATTACKED A wide range, including trees such as apples, figs and oranges; and smaller plants such as grapes, rhubarb, melons, pumpkins, tomatoes, dahlias, violets and a variety of weeds.

CONTROL   Treat bugs on garden structures as well as those on the plants. Control weeds.

• Organic/non-chemical: Knock groups of bugs into soapy water or try spraying with pyrethrins.

• Chemical: Spray with dimethoate, carbaryl or maldison.

Hawk moths

Order Lepidoptera: Family Sphingidae

The moths in this group generally have bodies that taper towards the end. While at rest their wings are swept back, delta-fashion. Most of them are fast fliers and have a long proboscis with which they suck the nectar from flowers as they hover.

The larvae of almost all hawk moths are fleshy and have a stiff spine on the end of the body (the doubleheaded hawk moth (P) larva is one exception). These larvae can be confused with some of the larvae from the family Notodontidae (the prominents), which have a shorter, more fleshy projection at the end of the body.

These larvae are not usually found in big numbers and most are not serious pests, although they feed on a wide range of plant material and occasionally need to be controlled.

PLANTS ATTACKED A wide range of plants, including ornamental and fruiting grapes.

CONTROL
• Organic/non-chemical: Hand removal would usually be adequate.
• Chemical: If spraying is necessary, carbaryl would be suitable.

See also Australian privet hawk moth (P), doubleheaded hawk moth (P) and grapevine hawk moth (P).

Hemispherical scale *Saissetia coffeae*

This scale is very similar to black scale (P) except that it lacks the mark on the back. It produces large quantities of honeydew.

PLANTS ATTACKED A wide range of houseplants including ferns and many shrubs including frangipanis (*Plumeria* sp.).

CONTROL   Use white oil at the rate of 20 mL per litre of water on shrubs. Ferns may be sensitive to white oil, so try 10 mL per litre of water.

Pictured: *Saissetia oleae*, black scale.

Hibiscus flower beetle

Aethina (Olliffura) concolor

This beetle is dull black, oval in shape and about 3 mm long. It belongs to a family of beetles called Nitidulidae — as do the driedfruit beetles (P).

It is often found in large numbers in hibiscus flowers. It is predominantly a pollen-feeder, and although it may chew holes in petals it is unlikely to be responsible for holes in hibiscus leaves.

Bud drop, often attributed solely to this beetle, is more likely to be caused by overdry soil or sudden cold spells after an early warm spring.

PLANTS ATTACKED Hibiscus, particularly *Hibiscus rosa-sinensis*, and magnolias.

CONTROL
- Organic/non-chemical: Collect and destroy any fallen buds and flowers.
- Chemical: If necessary this beetle could be killed by spraying with carbaryl or diazinon. Do not apply when bees are present.

See also metallic flea beetles (P).

Horehound bug *Agonoscelis rutila*

These bugs suck sap and may cause wilting of new shoots. They develop through five nymphal stages.

PLANTS ATTACKED Usually horehound (*Marrubium vulgare*), but may swarm on to a variety of ornamental and fruiting trees and shrubs.

CONTROL
- Organic/non-chemical: Knock the swarm into soapy water or try spraying with pyrethrins.
- Chemical: Spray the swarm with dimethoate or maldison.

Hydrangea scale *Pulvinaria hydrangeae*

The adult female scale is oval and about 3 mm long. Towards the end of spring the females begin to produce ovisacs — structures of soft, white wax to hold the eggs. These usually end up about 10 mm long but may be as long as 16 mm. The dead female scale can be seen at one end of the ovisacs.

When the eggs hatch, the young scales or crawlers settle under leaves and on stems, sucking sap. When winter arrives they enter a resting stage and only become active again in the spring when they feed and finally reach the adult stage.

PLANTS ATTACKED Hydrangeas, camellias and some other plants.

CONTROL   Infestations may be noticed only when the ovisacs are produced. Control is difficult at this stage because of the quantities of wax present. It would be better to wait until most of the eggs have hatched in the early summer and then spray with white oil at the rate of 25 mL per litre of water. If the plants are in flower use only 15 mL per litre of water. It is necessary to thoroughly cover the undersides of the leaves and the stems.

About four weeks after spraying, inspect the plant to see how successful the operation has been. Dead scales will be dry or produce a thick liquid if squashed. Living scales produce a watery liquid, and if many of these occur spraying should be undertaken again.

Indian white wax scale *Ceroplastes ceriferus*

This scale is very like white wax scale (P)) except it is a little smaller. The wax covering is smoother and has a small curved projection at the head end. The life cycles of the two insects are very similar.

PLANTS ATTACKED A range of different plants including many ornamentals such as chrysanthemums, Michaelmas daisies, perennial phlox, hop-bushes, lillypillies, gardenias, sacred bamboos, pyracanthas, waxflowers and barberries.

CONTROL   Remove by hand. Or spray with white oil at the rate of 20 mL per litre of water. See also the control procedures for white wax scale.

Indian white wax scale on Camellia sasanqua.

Inland katydid *Caedicia simplex*

The adult insect looks much like a grasshopper and is about 50 mm long, including the wings. The top edge of the wings has a narrow yellowish band running along it and continuing on to the thorax.

Eggs are usually deposited on the soil surface in groups of about twelve with soil attached. This makes them look like small clods of earth. Look for plant damage in early spring when the nymphs skeletonise the foliage of suckers or low branches. They do not usually feed on the edges of leaves. Later they move upwards to chew holes in higher leaves. Fruit may be badly damaged when adults gnaw on the surface, producing irregular indentations which may be up to 12 mm deep.

The adults feed mostly at night. They are very active insects, and each individual can attack many fruit.

PLANTS ATTACKED Peaches are the most commonly attacked. Also other plants such as apples, pears and grapes.

CONTROL
• Organic/non-chemical: Try catching them — not an easy task!
• Chemical: Spraying for other pests such as oriental fruit moth (P) and lightbrown apple moth (P) would usually keep this insect under control. If spraying is necessary, try carbaryl.

Jewel beetles Order Coleoptera: Family Buprestidae

The beetles in this group are often shiny or metallic and patterned in bright colours including green, purple and orange. The hundreds of different species come in different sizes but are the same basic shape. They are usually elongated, flattened, and taper towards the end. They have short antennae.

The adults chew leaves and are often found around nectar-bearing flowers. They are active on hot nights.

Their larvae, which are creamy-white and legless, look like tiny cobras (snakes) and feed under the bark of trees. They produce tunnels which are oval in cross-section and packed with chewed wood. They pupate in the sapwood, and the adults emerge to the outside of the tree through oval holes. Attacks occur on trees that are damaged or very unhealthy and dying.

PLANTS ATTACKED Various different trees including eucalypts. Some species are associated with particular hosts: for example, the small cypress jewel beetle (*Diadoxus erythrurus*) attacks *Callitris* spp.

CONTROL   Check that the tree is not dying from some other cause. See also longicorns (P). Damage can be assessed by removing damaged bark until live tissue is found. If the damage extends more than half the way around, consult a qualified arborist. The tree may have to be removed.

Tunnels packed with frass are exposed when the bark is removed.

Kurrajong leaf-tier   *Lygropia clytusalis*

The light green, agile larvae of this moth always feed in a group and web a number of leaves together to form a shelter. They do some feeding within this shelter, but also come out at night to feed on other leaves of the tree. They pupate inside the shelter, and the moths that emerge have a wingspan of about 25 mm and are pale orange with irregular wavy black bands across them.

These bags or rolled-up leaves on the trees can give it an ugly appearance.

PLANTS ATTACKED Kurrajong (*Brachychiton populneus*) and Illawarra flame tree (*Brachychiton acerifolius*).

CONTROL Because all of the caterpillars are in the bags during the day, they can be controlled by cutting off the bags and burning them. The caterpillars are often attacked by predators. Water and fertilise the trees to maintain vigour.

Large auger beetle   *Bostrychopsis jesuita*

The creamish-white larvae of this beetle tunnel in the sapwood of trees that are already dead or dying. The tunnels are vertical and tightly packed with frass. Pupation occurs at the end of the tunnel. The adults bore their way to the exterior and emerge through round holes about 9 mm in diameter.

The black adults are 12–18 mm long and cylindrical in general shape. The head is turned down beneath the body.

PLANTS ATTACKED A range of trees, including citrus and other fruit trees, wattles, athel trees, silky oaks, white cedars, eucalypts and the kurrajong.

CONTROL These beetles hasten the death of an already-dying tree. Plan a replacement tree. Choose a species suitable for the site, and water and fertilise it adequately.

Large citrus butterfly   *Princeps aegeus*

This butterfly usually lays its eggs singly on citrus branches. Each larva, in its early stages, looks like a bird-dropping but later grows fat and fleshy and is olive green with three brown diagonal stripes edged in white. If disturbed, the larva throws two fuchsia-pink horns out of its head. These structures produce a foul smell which is meant to drive away predators. The caterpillars eat leaves and can consume a considerable amount, so it is particularly serious on small ornamental trees such as the cumquat where the removal of leaves from one branch may completely spoil the shape of the tree.

The male butterflies have a wingspan of about 120 mm. They are black, with a pale yellow irregular band near the tip of the forewing and a wider band on the hindwing with a red spot at one end of it.

The female is brown-black, with large pale areas on the outer half of the forewings. The hindwings have a curved row of red/orange crescent-shaped marks and two similar blue marks.

PLANTS ATTACKED Citrus, both cultivated and native. Also other members of the plant family Rutaceae such as Mexican orange blossom (*Choisya ternata*) and waxflower (*Eriostemon myoporoides*). Occasionally plants from some other families are attacked.

CONTROL
• Organic/non-chemical: Remove by hand.
• Chemical: If spraying is necessary, use carbaryl following label directions.

See also small citrus butterfly (P).

Large mango tipborer *Penicillaria jocosatrix*

The eggs of this moth are laid near the new growth. Initially the larvae feed on small and young leaves, but later they bore into the twigs from the tips. This causes the leaves to go pale and die, and the shoot may die back from the tip. The larvae are yellowish-green with rows of tiny red dots along the body.

PLANTS ATTACKED Mangos and also cashews.
CONTROL Prune off damaged tips. Spray with Dipel®. Control can probably be achieved on young plants, but it would be very difficult on a large, fully grown tree. Fertilise and water adequately to maintain tree vigour.

Latania scale *Hemiberlesia lataniae*

This hard scale is found throughout the world and has a very wide host range. The female scale covering is about 2 mm across and is pale grey with a light brown centre. The male covering is smaller. In warm areas several generations are completed in a year. On avocados, slight pitting may occur if young fruit is infected and even a few scales are noticeable on the dark fruit; infestation may also restrict areas to which the fruit can be marketed. On macadamias, it is common on branches and nuts, and heavy infestations may cause leaf fall.
PLANTS ATTACKED These include brush boxes, bangalow palms, avocados and macadamias.
CONTROL Spray in early summer with white oil (summer oil) at the rate of 20 mL per litre of water.

Heavy infestation on twig

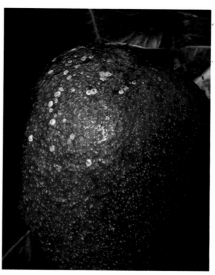

Latania scales on avocado

Lawn armyworm *Spodoptera mauritia*

Armyworms are the caterpillars of members of the moth family Noctuidae. They feed mostly on lawn and other grasses including weeds. They can cause serious damage to cereal crops such as barley and oats.

They attack leaves and stems and seedheads. Their name refers to the fact that they tend to occur in large numbers and, when they have eaten all the available food in one area, they move off to look for more in a group, rather like an army on the march. They leave nothing but bare stems behind.

Their bodies are smooth and usually dark in colour: brown, greenish-brown or almost black. They may have stripes along the body or lines of markings such as triangles. Fully grown they may be up to 45 mm long and 7 mm wide. They have a rather inflated appearance, and the body is wider than the head.
PLANTS ATTACKED Paspalum, kikuyu and couch, although Queensland blue couch is not as favoured as a food plant. Other plants attacked include sweet corn.
CONTROL
• Organic/non-chemical: Rake up and put in a bucket of soapy water.
• Chemical: Spray with carbaryl, chlorpyrifos, diazinon or cyfluthrin. Add wetting agent. Five litres of made-up spray is necessary to cover 100 square metres. Do not water in.

Leaf beetles   Order Coleoptera: Family Chrysomelidae

This family includes the pumpkin beetle (P), the leafeating ladybirds (P), redshouldered leaf beetle (P), metallic flea beetle (P), figleaf beetle (P) and orchid beetle (P). The eucalyptus tortoise beetle (*Paropsis atomaria*) is one of many that attack eucalypts.

Those that feed on eucalypts often lay their eggs on small stems or leafstalks, in a circular arrangement which produces a structure like a cob of corn or a rosette. The larvae tend to feed in a group on new leaves. The upper, outer parts of a small tree may be completely stripped of leaves. When fully grown, the larvae pupate in the soil.

The adults feed on older foliage as well as young growth, and the leaves may have scalloped edges. Adults vary in size and colour according to species but are about 10 mm long. They are hemispherical and have big feet.

PLANTS ATTACKED   Eucalyptus tortoise beetle (*P. atomaria*) attacks many species of eucalypt including *Eucalyptus globulus*, *E. viminalis* and *E. macarthurii*. Wattles are also leaf beetle hosts.

CONTROL
• Organic/non-chemical: Birds commonly attack this insect in its larval stage in Australia and it rarely needs to be sprayed.
• Chemical: If infestation of beetles is severe, spray with maldison or use omethoate in aerosol form.

Adult female and rosette of eggs

Larvae and the eggs from which they hatched.

Typical damage of adult beetles

Damage and pupae of leafblister sawfly

Leafblister sawflies   *Phylacteophaga* spp.

The larvae of this sawfly feed (or 'mine') inside leaves. A blister-like patch develops where each larva is feeding, and the leaf surface there becomes brown and papery. The problem can be severe on small trees, but as the adults do not seem to lay eggs in leaves at heights above four metres, larger trees usually escape serious attack. If hard, oval lumps (pupae) can be seen in most blisters then spraying has been left too late. The following year check the trees for signs of attack earlier in the season.

PLANTS ATTACKED   A wide range of eucalypts, and the brush box. Street trees and trees in exposed situations are attacked more frequently than others.

CONTROL
• Organic/non-chemical: Prune off and destroy branchlets with many active larvae.
• Chemical: Spray with a systemic insecticide such as dimethoate or fenthion.

Leafcutting bees *Megachile* spp.

These bees are 6–16 mm long and mostly black with bands of light-coloured hair. They resemble the honey bee in general appearance but are stouter.

They chew pieces from the edges of leaves. The pieces are regular in shape, some circular and some oval, about 10 mm across. They hold the leaf with their legs and cut with their jaws. The leaf pieces are used to make nests, which are cigar-shaped and in situations such as cracks in fence posts or between two bricks where the mortar has fallen out.

These bees can be important pollinators of some plants including lucerne.

PLANTS ATTACKED Roses, camellias, cherries, lilacs and many others.

CONTROL Control is not necessary.

Leafeating ladybird larvae

Leafeating ladybirds *Epilachna* spp.

The larvae, which grow to about 6 mm, are greenish-yellow and covered with branched black spines. They usually feed on the undersurface of the leaves and skeletonise rounded patches. They may pupate under the leaves or move onto leaf litter nearby.

The beetles are oval in outline, about 6 mm long and more or less hemispherical. They are orange-yellow with 26 or 28 spots, and tend to feed on the upper surfaces of leaves. The leaves may become brown and papery.

Do not confuse these pests with the common spotted ladybird (*Harmonia conformis*) which has only 18 spots and eats aphids and other small plant pests.

PLANTS ATTACKED All cucurbits, including pumpkins, zucchini and rockmelons. (The latter are favoured food plants.) Many other plants such as beans, potatoes and tomatoes. Also solanaceous weeds such as the nightshades (*Solanum* spp.).

CONTROL
• Organic: Removal by hand may be possible in home gardens or use derris dust.
• Chemical: Apply maldison or carbaryl dust, or spray with carbaryl.

Leafminers

There are a number of different insects whose larvae feed inside leaves. These can be referred to as 'leafminers'. Adults may be beetles, wasps, sawflies, moths or flies. They lay their eggs on or in the leaf.

Each species always produces the same shape and size of 'mine'. Some look like blisters, and some are thin meandering lines. Others may be a combination of both.

Some insects mine in the leaves and attack another part of the plant as well. Bean fly (P) and potato moth (P) are examples.

Pupation may occur inside the leaf or elsewhere.

PLANTS ATTACKED A wide range. Each leafmining species may attack only one plant or it may attack a number of plants.

CONTROL
• Organic/non-chemical: Remove leaves promptly when first mines appear or ignore.
• Chemical: Choose a penetrant or systemic chemical such as dimethoate.

Damage on nasturtium

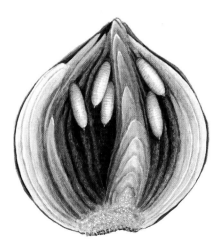

Lesser bulb fly *Eumerus tuberculatus*

These flies are approximately 8 mm long and generally black in appearance, with three pairs of white crescent-shaped marks on the body and white lines on the thorax.

The females most often lay their eggs on damaged bulbs near the neck, in folds of the coat or on the ground near the bulb. The yellowish larvae when fully grown are 8 mm long. They are rather transparent in appearance and are found mostly in the neck of the bulb, although the whole bulb may eventually be rotted. There may be many larvae in the one bulb.

The fly usually gains access to the bulbs at the end of the season when the foliage has died down. This attack can be lessened if the holes where the dead leaves were are filled up with soil. Bulbs that have been partially destroyed by the larvae will either not grow at all or will produce only grass-like foliage and poor (if any) flowers.

PLANTS ATTACKED Daffodils are the most commonly attacked. Hyacinths are sometimes attacked and also bulbous irises, jonquils, amaryllis, and onions.

CONTROL Hot water treatment, as recommended for bulb nematode control (page 39), will control this pest also.

Lightbrown apple moth *Epiphyas postvittana*

The larvae of this moth are slender and green. They grow to nearly 20 mm long and if disturbed, wriggle and drop down on a thread of webbing. They always feed under cover and may web two leaves together or roll one into a tunnel for shelter.

Young larvae graze on leaf surfaces, and older larvae chew holes. Fruit such as apples or peaches may have furrows gouged in the surface. Apples are commonly damaged at the stem end.

If young grape bunches are chewed, the bunch develops with few fruit. Later the grapes may be rendered inedible by webbing and droppings. This pest is more likely to cause damage in cooler areas than in hot dry areas.

PLANTS ATTACKED This native Australian insect attacks a very wide range of plants including ornamentals, fruit such as grapes, citrus and pomefruit, and weeds. It is more likely to cause damage on short-stemmed clustered apples such as 'Jonathan' than on longer-stemmed varieties such as 'Granny Smith'.

CONTROL
• Organic/non-chemical: Remove weeds. Spray with Dipel®. Natural enemies may keep this pest under control.
• Chemical: Use carbaryl.

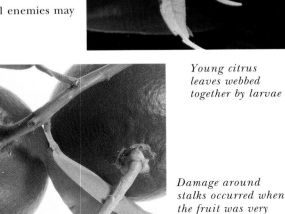

Young citrus leaves webbed together by larvae

Damage around stalks occurred when the fruit was very young.

Lightbrown apple moth larva

Lily caterpillar *Spodoptera picta*

These black and yellow caterpillars chew away the leaf surfaces and seriously disfigure the plants they feed on.

The moth has a wingspan of about 50 mm and has forewings patterned in red and black. It is a member of the family Noctuidae and is therefore related to the cutworms.

PLANTS ATTACKED Kaffir lilies (*Clivea*) and similar plants.

CONTROL
• Organic/non-chemical: Prune off the damaged leaves together with the caterpillars or use Dipel®.
• Chemical: In a large group of plants spraying may be necessary. Use carbaryl and add some wetting agent.

Longicorns or long horn beetles

Order Coleoptera: family Cerambycidae

Tiger longicorn Aridaeus thoracicus

These beetles vary in size from 5 to 60 mm. Most are patterned in brown or grey, and all have the same basic shape: the sides of these beetles are fairly straight, they appear to have square 'shoulders', and their antennae are extremely long. The beetles themselves do very little damage, perhaps chewing on a few new shoots or young bark, but the larvae can do considerable damage to a variety of trees, shrubs and even climbers.

The larvae of most species tunnel in an area just under the bark, referred to as the phloem-cambial region. This area contains the cells in which water and food supplies are moved around the plant and also cells that create new food-conducting cells or new water-conducting cells. If the tunnels are extensive, they may girdle the tree, and the tree will eventually die.

Eggs are laid in cracks in the bark. The larvae are cream-coloured and fleshy and have no obvious legs; they are wider at the front than the rear. The tunnels created are usually oval in shape and tightly packed with sawdusty material. This material is usually referred to as 'frass'. Trees are commonly attacked near the base of the trunk where damage from lawnmowers and backing cars is frequent. Considerable damage may be done before cracking bark indicates their presence. Damage is more noticeable on smooth-barked trees.

PLANTS ATTACKED There are hundreds of species of longicorn. Most attack only branches that are already dead, or newly felled trees. Those that do attack living plants may attack one type of plant only or a few different types.

CONTROL These beetles are usually able to succeed only in plants that are stressed for some reason. Action should involve discovering why the plants are not growing vigorously and rectifying this problem. The trees may be short of water or very old. Improve the care of the tree by watering and fertilising, and use tree surgery techniques on the damaged part of the trunk. There is no useful chemical control.

Typical larva

Loopers and Semi-loopers

Order Lepidoptera: Family Geometridae and Family Noctuidae

Caterpillars of many members of these moth families move with a looping action. They arch up the middle part of the body to an inverted U-shape or a loop.

Family Noctuidae (semi-loopers): If they are disturbed, they remain attached with the rear part of the body and wave the front section about. They have a number of thin white lines along their bodies.

Each of these moths may live for up to three weeks and lay up to 1000 eggs, which are usually deposited singly on the undersurfaces of lower leaves. The caterpillars, which hatch from the eggs, are only about 3 mm long and graze on the undersurfaces of the leaves. This produces a window-like effect, because the upper leaf surface (the epidermis) remains intact. As they grow, the caterpillars move up the plant and chew holes in the foliage. Flowers may also be attacked.

Family Geometridae (loopers): When disturbed these caterpillars remain attached to a branch by the hind end and project stiffly outwards, like a small twig.

Autumn gum moth (P) and grevillea looper (P) are both in Family Geometridae.

PLANTS ATTACKED Fam. Noct.: A wide range, especially broad-leafed plants such as potatoes, beans, tomatoes, and soft-leafed indoor plants. Fam. Geom.: Many native plants including wattles and banksias.

CONTROL
• Organic/non-chemical: Look for their droppings on the leaves beneath them or on the floor under potted plants. Remove by hand.
• Chemical: If spraying is necessary, use carbaryl. If vegetables have been sprayed, do not harvest until three days have elapsed.

Family Noctuidae (top) and Family Geometridae (bottom)

Macadamia cup moth *Mecytha fasciata*

The moth is black and white, with a wingspan of 40 mm. The larvae are oval in outline, green and flat, and there is a distinct yellow stripe along the back. These larvae may grow up to 35 mm long and 20 mm wide. They often rest so that the stripe lies along the main vein of the leaf. They feed mainly on mature leaves and could defoliate a young tree.

When they have eaten enough they move to the bottom of the tree where they pupate among the debris on the soil surface. The cocoon is cuplike.

PLANTS ATTACKED Members of the plant family Proteaceae, including macadamias and waratahs.

CONTROL
• Organic/non-chemical: Search for and handpick these caterpillars or prune off small branches where they occur in large numbers.
• Chemical: Spray with maldison or cabaryl

Macadamia felted coccid

Eriococcus ironsidei

This Australian native insect may be found on all above-ground parts of the tree. It causes distortion and stunting of young growth. Young trees can be killed if the infestation is severe. Yellow spotting on older leaves and reduction in nut yields also occurs.

The adult insects are about 1 mm long and white to yellow-brown. They are often found in protected places such as at leaf axils, in bark crevices, between buds and along the main vein under leaves. They are usually introduced to an area on infested plant material, but they may be spread on birds, insects or human clothing.

PLANTS ATTACKED *Macadamia integrifolia* and *M. tetraphylla.*

CONTROL The many natural enemies of the felted coccid include ladybirds and wasps. They seem to be successful in keeping populations at an acceptable level except when the coccid is first introduced into an orchard.

If spraying is considered necessary, white oil (or summer oil) at the rate of 10 mL per litre of water is a suitable spray. Ensure that the spray reaches all plant parts.

Macadamia flower caterpillar

Cryptoblabes hemigypsa

The young larvae feed inside the buds, and the entry hole often has a drop of sap exuding from it. Older larvae feed mainly on the outside of the buds and on flowers. Excrement and chewed pieces of bud become attached to the damaged area in masses of webbing. If the infestation is heavy, very few nuts will be set. When fully grown the larvae are about 12 mm long and vary in colour from light green to grey to reddish-brown, with some longitudinal stripes. They usually pupate in a silken cocoon in leaf litter on the ground.

The adult that emerges is grey, about 6 mm long, and has a wingspan of 15 mm. When at rest, the wings are folded to cover the body and three wavy, darker grey stripes near the tip of each forewing join to form inverted V-shaped marks.

PLANTS ATTACKED All known hosts belong to the family Proteaceae and include wild and cultivated macadamias, grevilleas such as silky oak (*Grevillea robusta*), and Banks' red grevillea (*G. banksii*); and woody pears (*Xylomelum pyriforme*).

CONTROL Keep a close watch on damage levels and pest numbers. There are a number of wasps and bugs that attack this insect, so spraying should not be carried out unless damage is increasing in severity.
• Organic/non-chemical: Plant varieties that flower early and for a limited period.
• Chemical: Carbaryl is a suitable insecticide.

Undamaged flowers on the left

Macadamia leafminer *Acrocercops chionosema*

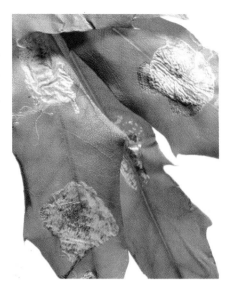

The adult of this pest is a small moth which is only 8 mm across the outstretched wings. The front wings are banded in brown and a silvery white. Most eggs are laid on the upper surface of the young leaves. The larvae hatch from the underside of the egg straight into the leaf, and begin feeding between the two leaf surfaces.

The first sign of their presence is a fine whitish line on the leaf, and this is gradually enlarged until a blister appears. If infestation is heavy, the whole of the leaf surface may be covered with papery-looking blisters and the trees look as though they have been fire scorched. When the larvae have eaten enough, they make their way to the ground and pupate in debris on the surface.

These pests can be active throughout the year, but their life cycle progresses more quickly in warm weather.

Tree growth will be slowed because of the dieback of new leaves. The problem will be worse near high-altitude rainforest areas (where some other native plants are hosts to this pest), and if the plantings are protected from wind.

PLANTS ATTACKED Macadamias (both wild and cultivated) and some of their relations such as hakeas and buckinghamias.

CONTROL
• Organic/non-chemical: In a home garden, on small trees remove leaves as soon as the first white lines are seen. Avoid heavy pruning which will encourage a flush of new growth and provide a good food supply for this pest.
• Chemical: No appropriate recommendation for home gardens.

Macadamia nutborer

Cryptophlebia ombrodelta

The larvae of this moth are active in the December-February period and may cause nut fall if they attack immature nuts. Initially, the larvae are able to penetrate the shell and feed on the kernel. Later, when the shell has hardened they can only get through if it is thin or weakened by attacks from other insects such as fruitspotting bugs (P). They tend to feed mostly in the husk at this stage. Infested nuts may have sawdust and webbing on the surface.

The fully grown larvae may be 20 mm long and are pinkish with dark-green spots in rows along the body. The adult female moth has a wingspan of about 25 mm and is reddish-brown with a black triangular mark on the hind edge of each forewing.

PLANTS ATTACKED Macadamias, lychees, and ornamentals like poincianas, golden raintrees, bauhinias and bird of paradise trees.

CONTROL
• Organic/non-chemical: Save some of the crop by regularly squashing eggs (white, 1 mm long) on soft, immature nuts.
• Chemical: Spray during the fruit-setting period with carbaryl. Two or three applications of pesticide may be required.

Macadamia twig-girdler *Xylorycta luteotactella*

This pest is found most on young trees and can stop growth or even kill the tree. The problem is worst in summer and autumn and in elevated areas.

The larvae, about 23 mm long when fully fed, have dark brown heads and paler, mottled brown bodies with rows of black dots along them. They shelter in tunnels of webbing and eat the bark from twigs near forks or where leaf whorls occur. They also web leaves together and skeletonise them. The damage caused if they tunnel in nuts is similar to macadamia nutborer (P)) damage. Young trees may be defoliated, and the damaged twigs snap off in wind or die back. The webs usually have sawdust-like excrement stuck on them.

The satiny white moths, which have a wingspan of about 25 mm, lay their eggs on young leaves and nuts. They are active at night.

PLANTS ATTACKED Macadamias and many other members of the plant family Proteaceae such as banksias, buckinghamias, grevilleas, hakeas, geebungs (*Persoonia* spp.), and the Queensland firewheel tree and other species of *Stenocarpus*.

CONTROL
• Organic/non-chemical: There are more than 20 native insects that attack the twig-girdler. Most are wasps. They may be successful in keeping numbers down.
• Chemical: Spray with carbaryl if necessary.

Manuka blight *Eriococcus orariensis*

This problem is the result of the feeding of scale insects (P). They establish themselves in bark crevices and under loose bark.

The sap-sucking of large populations causes serious damage; and because the insects produce large quantities of honeydew, the plants become thickly covered with sooty mould (D). The dead twigs and blackened trunks make it seem that they have suffered fire damage. The white pupal cases of the males may be seen on the blackened surfaces.

PLANTS ATTACKED Only tea-trees. Manuka (*Leptospermum scoparium*) can be seriously weakened or killed, but kanuka (*L. ericoides*) on the other hand, is hardly affected.

CONTROL White oil sprayed at the rate of 20 mL per litre of water. This Australian insect is kept to very low numbers in Australia by natural enemies and is not known to cause damage. In New Zealand, however, it has few successful natural competitors and the damage can be severe.

Mealybugs Order Hemiptera: Family Pseudococcidae

Mealybugs on custard apple

These insects are oval in outline and divided across into many sections. They usually have a fringe of short waxy threads around their bodies. Some also have several long filaments of wax on the end of the body. Their pale pink, yellow or grey bodies are covered with white, powdery wax.

Some mealybugs lay eggs in large masses of wax (egg-sacs), while others lay eggs singly. Sometimes five to six hundred eggs are laid in a batch. In an established colony the mealybug bodies may be difficult to distinguish because of the accumulation of egg-sacs and other wax. Sometimes a colony is mistaken for fungal growth. They feed by sucking sap and may cause wilting, and distortion of new leaves. Sooty mould (D) may grow in the honeydew they produce.

Mealybugs thrive in warm, moist conditions and tend to congregate in protected places. They may be found where leafstalks join the plant or where leaves sheathe around the stem. They congregate around buds, where two pieces of fruit touch or where leaves overlap. They are also found below ground. They can move about to seek better feeding sites, although they crawl only slowly.

They are also moved from place to place unnoticed on plant material or by ants. Ants are attracted to the honeydew and move mealybugs from plant to plant. Underground, the tunnels made by ants are easy passageways along which the mealybugs can move to a new part of the root system.

PLANTS ATTACKED A wide variety of plants, including ferns, palms and other plants kept indoors, cacti and other succulents, and many trees and shrubs, both fruiting and ornamental.

CONTROL

• Organic/non-chemical: Mealybugs are worse on plants grown in homes and glasshouses, and on plants sprayed regularly for other pests — sprays used for other pests kill insects such as ladybirds and lacewings, which usually attack mealybugs and keep their numbers under control. These sprays, however, do not kill many mealybugs because they are in protected places and covered with a water-repellent wax.

Outdoors, avoid spraying mealybug-prone plants for other pests and diseases. Control ants (P). If action is necessary, consider spot spraying, or pruning off badly affected sections of the plant. Spray with white oil at the rate of 20 mL per litre of water. Application should be thorough.

Indoors, mealybugs have often built up into large numbers before their presence is noticed. The method using cottonwool wrapped around a match to dab methylated spirits on to mealybugs does kill them, but is extremely tedious and time-consuming; in the process, stems and leaves are easily broken, particularly on fine-foliaged plants such as ferns.

• Chemical: A badly infested fern should probably be thrown away, or perhaps much of the foliage should be cut off before any chemical control is attempted. Use fenthion or omethoate from an aerosol can and be sure to hold the can 25–30 cm from the plant as suggested.

Chemical control mixtures should be applied to the soil or potting mix as well as to the foliage and stems. Disulfoton (Disyston®) granules applied to the soil for aphid control will probably kill mealybugs as well.

Metallic flea beetles *Altica* spp.

These small shiny and metallic-looking beetles are in family Chrysomelidae. Their hindlegs are thickened and adapted for jumping, hence the reference to 'fleas' in their name. They are about 3 mm long.

They chew tiny holes of irregular shapes in young leaves and buds. As the leaves grow, the holes enlarge.

Larvae of most species feed in stems but seem to do little damage.

PLANTS ATTACKED A range of plants, including hibiscus, Norfolk Island hibiscus, dahlias, grapevines, avocados, rhubarb, lettuces, sweet potatoes, potatoes and various weeds including the mallows.

CONTROL
• Organic/non-chemical: Sticky traps may be successful.
• Chemical: Use carbaryl on edible crops. Be sure to adhere to the withholding period. Do not apply when bees are present.

Damage on hibiscus

Millipedes Class Diplopoda

Millipedes are segmented, long and thin and have a hard external covering and many legs in pairs. They usually curl up in a flat spiral if disturbed. Many are brown in colour.

Most species do very little garden damage unless they are able to build up into large numbers in moist conditions with high levels of organic matter. They may attack young roots, seeds and seedlings and soft ripe fruit such as strawberries, but usually do not damage tougher plant parts. Once these are damaged by other factors, however, millipedes will start feeding.

The black Portuguese millipede (*Ommatoiulus moreletii*) does not attack plants but builds up into huge populations and may invade houses.

CONTROL
• Organic/non-chemical: Reduce the amount of organic matter in the soil. Reduce areas of organic mulch. In some areas, physical barriers are required to keep millipedes out of houses. Seek advice on this from your local Department of Agriculture.
• Chemical: Methiocarb (Baysol®), spread as directed on the label, will protect plants.

Mites Class Arachnida

Other animals in Class Arachnida include ticks, spiders and scorpions. The groups of mites which cause plant damage include the eriophyid mites such as grapeleaf blister mite (P) and citrus bud mite (P); the tarsonemid mites such as cyclamen mite (P) and the spider mites such as two-spotted mite (P).

They feed on a variety of plant and animal materials, living and dead. Some mites are just visible with the unaided eye, although the majority are too small. Most adult mites and their immature stages have four pairs of legs. However, the first immature stage has only three pairs of legs and all active stages of eriophyid mites have only two pairs of legs. Plant-feeding mites deposit eggs singly or in groups on the plant surface. They may be structured or placed so as to withstand adverse conditions.

Some mites, such as two-spotted mite (P), cause only physical injury and move to different leaves when those they are on dry out.

Some other mites secrete saliva containing growth regulators. These sustances cause changes in plant growth. For example, there may be production of galls characteristic of the species and masses of short hairs which look rather like felt. Witches' brooms can also result from the feeding of some mites.

Some viruses are transmitted by particular mites.

CONTROL This can prove very difficult. Specific miticides can be used but mites seem to develop resistance to pesticides very rapidly and it has been necessary to introduce biological control programmes such as the one developed for two-spotted mite (P). As well, they often escape notice until large populations have developed.

Citrus rust mite damage

Mole crickets *Gryllotalpa* spp.

These insects are brown and up to 45 mm long in the adult stage. They have wings and do fly to lights, but they spend most of their time underground where they construct a deep permanent burrow as well as others nearer the surface as they search for food. The eggs are laid in an underground chamber and the female stands guard over them. Crickets are often heard chirruping at the entrance to their burrow particularly after rain. They have strong, flattened forelegs which are suitable for digging, and their front feet have a scissor-like mechanism for cutting through plant roots.

They eat plant roots and also other insects and worms. They chew holes or furrows in potatoes. Their tunnelling may push seedlings out of the ground.

PLANTS ATTACKED A range of vegetable and flower crops and lawn grasses.

CONTROL
- Organic/non-chemical: Search for and destroy.
- Chemical: This pest is only an occasional one, so action may be unnecessary. In lawns they can be controlled with the application of diazinon or fenthion. This should be applied in approximately 200 L of water over 100 square metres.

Moth borers   Order Lepidoptera: Family Cossidae

Many of the moths in this group are very large, with wingspans of up to 250 mm. They are generally patterned in grey or brown, and lay eggs on the bark, usually at the site of some injury. The larvae chew a tunnel into the wood and may proceed upwards or downwards. They feed in the tree for many months or even years. Damaged branches may be weakened and fall in a storm. Small trees may be blown over.

The larvae of the Australian goat moth (*Culama caliginosa*) feed in a group of up to about ten under the bark of angop horas and sugar gums (*Eucalyptus cladocalyx*). They may ringbark the tree.

The witjuti, or witchetty (*Xyleutes leucomochla*), has larvae that feed on the roots of a native South Australian wattle (*Acacia ligulata*).

PLANTS ATTACKED Eucalypts, wattles, smooth-barked apples (*Angophora costata*).

CONTROL This problem cannot be controlled by spraying or tree injection. Remove badly damaged trees. Cut away any damaged bark, so that the extent of the damage can be assessed. Improve tree vigour by fertilising lightly and watering.

Moth borers   Order Lepidoptera: Family Oecophoridae

The most damaging members of this family are probably those that feed on bark, such as the fruit-tree borer (P) and the macadamia twig-girdler (P).

The larvae of *Uzucha humeralis* feed on the bark surface of smooth-barked eucalypts and angophoras. They have no tunnel but protect themselves with a gallery of silk and bark particles.

The larvae of some species chew very little bark but feed on leaves which they drag to the entrance of their tunnels.

Other species tunnel in the flower spikes of banksias.

PLANTS ATTACKED A wide range, including New South Wales Christmas bush (*Ceratopetalum gummiferum*), hakeas, grevilleas, and banksias.

CONTROL
- Organic/non-chemical: Remove any webbing and damaged areas of bark. Kill larvae down tunnels with a few drops of kerosene or poke them with a piece of wire. Fertilise the tree. If infestation is severe, particularly on older trees and shrubs, remove and replace them.

If small twiggy growth on shrubs or trees has been attacked, prune it off.
- Chemical: Spray with carbaryl. Add wetting agent. Apply to the branch junctions as well as to the leaves.

Typical damage on a shrub

Native fig moth *Lactura caminaea*

The larvae of this moth skeletonise the leaves at first but later chew pieces from them and may defoliate a tree.

They grow 15–20 mm. Damage usually occurs in late winter or spring.

PLANTS ATTACKED Most commonly Moreton Bay figs and Port Jackson figs.

CONTROL
• Organic/non-chemical: Fertilise and water young trees to maintain vigour of the plant.
• Chemical: Spray with maldison. Add wetting agent. Tree injection would damage the tree.

Nectar scarabs *Phyllotocus* spp.

This is a group of small native beetles, which measure approximately 6 mm long. One of the species is light brown with darker brown tips to the wing covers, and hind legs that are much longer than the other legs.

These beetles usually occur in large swarms on flowers such as roses or dahlias and cause considerable damage by pushing around among the petals with their spiny legs.

The eggs are laid in the soil in areas of grassland, lawns or other turf. The larvae which hatch out are tiny grubs called white curl grubs (P). These feed mostly on decaying organic matter and sometimes on roots, but this causes very little damage to the plants.

PLANTS ATTACKED The flowers of a wide variety of plants.

CONTROL
• Organic/non-chemical: Ignore the presence of these insects.
• Chemical: Spray the whole swarm with carbaryl but not when bees are present.

Oak leafminer

Phyllonorycter messaniella

The adult of this pest is an extremely small moth which lays eggs on the undersides of oak leaves near the midrib or perhaps near the margin. The larvae feed inside the leaf and initially produce fine lines. As they continue to feed, blisters develop. The area later becomes brown and papery. Oak leaves with a number of these blisters look almost as if they had been burnt, and even from a distance the tree looks ugly.

PLANTS ATTACKED Oak trees, both deciduous and evergreen. (It may spend the winter on evergreen oaks.) The beech is another common host, and in some areas liquidambars, apples, stonefruit, feijoas, and Spanish chestnuts are attacked.

CONTROL
• Organic/non-chemical: This is an annual pest in many areas. Do not plant oak trees.
• Chemical: Control on large trees is a serious problem and can usually only be achieved by using the technique called tree injection. However, injection will cause considerable long-term damage. On smaller trees a spray programme is possible. Begin in November when the very smallest lines are first seen. Several applications may be necessary. If the damage were noticed only towards the end of summer, spraying would be a waste of time and money because the leaves will fall in autumn. Dimethoate will kill this pest.

Oleander butterfly *Euploea core corinna*

The caterpillars of this butterfly are reddish-brown with thin black and white bands around the body. They also have a white band along each side towards the bottom, and four pairs of long black fleshy 'tentacles' on the upper surface. They feed on the leaves of various milky-sapped plants and grow up to 50 mm long.

The pupae, which are attached to the plant, are about 25 mm long and extremely beautiful because of their silver or golden metallic sheen.

The adult's wings span about 75 mm and are very dark brown to black with white spots around the edge.

PLANTS ATTACKED These include oleanders (*Nerium oleander*), Madagascar jasmines (*Stephanotis floribunda*), Chilean jasmines (*Mandevilla laxa*), star jasmines (*Trachelospermum jasminoides*) and various native figs (*Ficus* spp.).

CONTROL This would rarely be necessary. In any case, the beauty of the pupae compensates for the leaves that are chewed.

Also known as the Australian crow butterfly.

Oleander scale on Dendrobium kingianum

Oleander scale *Aspidiotus nerii*

The female scales are 1–2 mm in diameter and roughly circular. They are white to brownish in colour and attack bark, leaves and fruit. If they occur on fruit, it may be downgraded and therefore return much less to the grower.

PLANTS ATTACKED A wide range of host plants, including wattles, gold dust trees, Boston ivy, camellias, azaleas, daphnes, ivies, ferns, grapes, hollies, persimmons, hakeas, magnolias, maples, mulberries, olives, roses, umbrella trees, viburnums, buddleias, guavas, poinsettias and orchids.

CONTROL Spray with white oil at the rate of 20 mL per litre of water.

See also Hard scales (P).

Also known as ivy scale.

Olive lace bug

Froggattia olivinia

These bugs are about 3 mm long and brown with lacy wings. Both adults and nymphs feed on the underside of the leaf. They suck sap and cause yellow mottling of the leaves, which then go brown and fall. Trees can be defoliated if the bug population is large.

PLANTS ATTACKED The native olive (*Notelaea longifolia*) and cultivated olives.

CONTROL
• Organic/non-chemical: Use a soap spray or try sticky traps.
• Chemical: Spray thoroughly with dimethoate or with maldison.

Onion maggot *Delia platura*

The adults of this species are greyish-brown hairy flies about 5 mm long. The eggs are laid in soil wherever there is a lot of decaying plant material or on seeds or seedlings. The legless larvae are yellowish-white and grow to about 7 mm long. They are tapered towards the head and have a tough skin.

The maggots feed on decaying organic matter until they encounter seedling stems. They may burrow into stems and hollow them out. Seedlings wilt and die.

Pupation occurs in the soil. Pupal cases are brown and about 5 mm long.

This pest is more likely to attack crops in sandy soils. Applications of blood and bone or animal manure near planting time make attack more likely.

PLANTS ATTACKED Onions, beans, crucifers, cucurbits and some others.
CONTROL
• Organic/non-chemical: Note the problem with organic fertilisers — delay addition until plants are bigger.
• Chemical: Use inorganic fertilisers near planting time in areas where this fly occurs. In onions, spray with diazinon just after the seedlings come up and again about ten days later.

Damaged leaves with typical tiny white flecks.

Onion thrips *Thrips tabaci*

These thrips, which feed on onions and a wide range of other plants, are most common in dry weather. On onion plants, the young thrips, which are cream to yellow, congregate at the base of the central leaves. Here they feed on the leaf surfaces and attack new leaves as they emerge. The adults, yellowish-grey to brownish-grey in colour and about 1.5 mm long, feed further up the leaves. Damaged foliage is blotched with silver, grey or white, and will be twisted and bent if the thrips population is high. Small plants may be killed, but if larger plants are well-watered, populations of thrips up to about 50 will not reduce bulb size.

Onion thrips carry the disease spotted wilt which infects many plants including tomatoes, potatoes, and numerous ornamentals.

Under lettuce and cabbage leaves, the areas where feeding has occurred are shiny with a grey or brown appearance.

PLANTS ATTACKED A wide range, including onions, lettuces, tomatoes, beans, crucifers, peas, potatoes, dahlias and Iceland poppies.
CONTROL
• Organic/non-chemical: Control weeds. Keep the plants well watered. Inspect the throat of onion plants regularly.
• Chemical: If necessary spray with dimethoate. The undersurfaces of broad-leafed plants should be sprayed. See also thrips (P).

Orange palmdart

Cephrenes augiades sperthias

The adult palmdarts are orange and brown and are members of a group referred to as 'skippers' because of the way they dart about.

The caterpillars have a very distinctive appearance. They are a pale blue-green, smooth and translucent. Their head is very distinct, and appears to be attached to the body by a very narrow neck. Each caterpillar folds a section of frond around itself and secures it in place with some webbing. After they have been feeding in their sheltered positions and therefore going unnoticed for a while, the leaves of the palm appear very tattered. This shelter, which is usually coated inside with fine white powdery wax, is also the pupation site.

PLANTS ATTACKED Palms, particularly the bangalow palm (*Archontophoenix cunninghamiana*) and the cabbage tree palm (*Livistona australis*).
CONTROL
• Organic/non-chemical: Keep watch for tattered leaves. Unfold them and remove larvae. Spray with Dipel®.
• Chemical: Spray with carbaryl. Add wetting agent.

Orchid beetle *Stethopachys formosa*

This insect is sometimes called the dendrobium beetle. The stout, cream-coloured larvae tunnel in the top of the pseudobulb and in new shoots. They may chew cavities in fleshy leaf bases and may feed on petals and the throat of the flower. They are covered with a slimy material.

The pupae are covered with a white foam-like material and are usually found around the base of the plant.

The adults are about 12 mm long and orange with black spots. They feed on buds, flowers and leaves.

PLANTS ATTACKED This beetle will attack cymbidiums and cattleyas but prefers dendrobiums. *Dendrobium speciosum* is the most commonly attacked.

CONTROL This is difficult. There is no suitable chemical for home-garden use. Search for the beetles in the evening and early morning and remove them manually. Hold a folded newspaper or similar item under the plants before moving the leaves because the beetles drop off the plant and hide very quickly if disturbed.

Orchid scale *Diaspis boisduvalii*

The female scale is roughly circular. The male scales are smaller, more elongated and have three ridges along them.

These scales can build up into large populations before being noticed because they tend to congregate under sheathing leaves around the base of the plant. The leaves go yellow and the plant stops growing.

PLANTS ATTACKED A range of orchids and others such as palms.

CONTROL Watch carefully for scale build-up. It may be possible to remove small infestations manually. Spray with white oil, 10 mL per litre of water. Apply thoroughly using plenty of spray mixture. Keep the mixture well stirred.

Oriental fruit moth *Grapholita molesta*

This moth, which rarely flies about during the day, lays its eggs on the undersurface of leaves or on stems near young shoots or fruit. The larvae tunnel down new shoots which they usually enter near the tip, at the junction of a leafstalk. Each caterpillar feeds on up to five shoots. The leaves on these twigs die and go brown. Gum is produced around the twig, particularly on stonefruit trees.

Fruit may also be attacked. The larvae enter near the stalk, or where a leaf or small branch touches the fruit, and tunnel to the stone or core.

Fully fed larvae leave the twigs and fruits to pupate. If the weather is still warm, this occurs high in the tree; but later, more protected places such as under loose bark on the trunk or in soil crevices around the base of the tree are chosen.

If new shoots on a young tree are attacked year after year, the training of the tree into a satisfactory long-term shape may be seriously jeopardised.

PLANTS ATTACKED Principally nectarines and peaches (both fruiting and ornamental). Other stonefruit, apples, pears and quinces may also be attacked.

CONTROL
• Organic/non-chemical: Cut off and burn any infested twigs early in the season. Do this as soon as wilting of the leaves occurs and remove about 200 mm. Wrap corrugated cardboard or hessian around the trunk by about the end of December. Inspect regularly and kill any larvae or pupae within. Remove and destroy infested fruit every few days. Remove loose bark and rubbish from near the base of the tree.
• Chemical: If spraying is necessary, use carbaryl or fenthion. Make the first application when moth activity is first observed (about early October). Repeat every three weeks until harvest is about three weeks away.

Painted apple moth   *Teia anartoides*

Larva

The caterpillars have four tufts of hair on the back (much like tufts of bristles in a toothbrush) and a pair of thinner longer tufts of black hairs projecting forward like horns. They chew leaves and when fully fed are about 30 mm long. They pupate in a very flimsy cocoon with some of the hairs from the body of the larvae webbed into it.

The male moth (wingspan 25 mm) has mottled brown forewings and deep yellow hindwings with a broad black outer band. The fat wingless female is thickly covered with fawn hairs. The eggs are laid on the outside of the cocoon.

Because the female is wingless, this species can only spread from place to place if the larvae walk there. Infestations are therefore fairly localised and they may occur in the same place year after year if no control measures are taken.

PLANTS ATTACKED This moth is a native Australian insect. Its original food source was the wattle (it used to be referred to as the 'painted wattle moth'), but it soon adapted itself to feed on apple orchards and now attacks a very wide range of native and exotic plants.

CONTROL
• Organic/non-chemical: Control can probably be achieved by hand-picking the cocoons and larvae and destroying them. Spray with Dipel® if necessary.
• Chemical: If a spray programme is necessary, use carbaryl.

Damage, coocoon eggs

Painted vine moth   *Agarista agricola*

This moth has a wingspan of about 65 mm and is basically black. The forewings are marked with a pattern of pale blue, deep yellow, cream and red. The hindwings are black with a white edge. The larvae have black, orange and cream stripes and a number of slender black projections from the body.

PLANTS ATTACKED Native grape or kangaroo vine (*Cissus* spp.); grapevine (*Vitis* spp.), both ornamental and fruiting; and Boston ivy and Virginia creeper (*Parthenocissus* spp.).

CONTROL
• Organic/non-chemical: These caterpillars are not usually found in large numbers so they may be removed by hand quite easily. Spray with Dipel®, following the packet directions.
• Chemical: Spray with carbaryl.

Paperbark sawfly   *Pterygophorus* sp.

The larvae of these sawflies can defoliate trees but cause most permanent damage when they pupate in the bark of the trunk. If large numbers of larvae burrow into the bark, the tree may be ringbarked. They also pupate in soft timbers such as those found in a western red cedar fence and in soft pine weatherboards.

PLANTS ATTACKED Tea-trees (*Leptospermum* spp.) and a number of different paperbarks (*Melaleuca* spp.) but mostly the bracelet honey myrtle, *M. armillaris*.

CONTROL
• Organic/non-chemical: Prune off the small branches on which the larvae occur. This removes not only the larvae but also the damaged areas, and helps to keep the plant bushy.
• Chemical: Spray with maldison.

Passionvine hopper   *Scolypopa australis*

This insect is brown and resembles a small moth. It can fly or hop when disturbed and is about 8 mm long. The wings are transparent and mottled with brown. Eggs are laid in twigs and young shoots or even within tendrils of passionvine. The young leafhoppers (or nymphs), which hop actively when disturbed, are greenish in colour and have a group of long white filaments at the end of the body.

Both the adult and immature forms of this insect damage the plant by sucking sap. The leaves wilt, young fruit shrivels, and leaf and fruit fall may occur. The insect also produces honeydew in which sooty mould (D) often grows.

PLANTS ATTACKED A wide range, including passionfruit, grapes, citrus, peaches, rhubarb, beans, hydrangeas, dahlias, kiwifruit and many others.

CONTROL

• Organic: Use pyrethrin spray.

• Chemical: Control is best undertaken when the insect is still young. Spray with maldison and add wetting agent (1 mL per L). Alternatively, use dimethoate. Apply to the plant and the ground beneath in an attempt to kill individuals that have jumped off the plant.

Pear and cherry slug   *Caliroa cerasi*

This insect is so called because the larvae are very dark green and slimy in appearance. They feed on the upper surfaces of leaves until only a network of veins remains. From a distance this damage gives the plants a white or brownish appearance which may completely destroy their ornamental value.

When the larvae have eaten enough, they drop to the ground and dig down into the soil, where they later pupate. The adults push their way to the surface and fly to the leaves. Here the female lays eggs inside the leaf and later the slug-like larvae hatch out. The larvae may be 10 mm long when fully fed. The adult is a glossy black sawfly which is about 8 mm long.

PLANTS ATTACKED Hawthorns, crabapples, apples, quinces and both fruit-bearing and flowering pears, cherries and plums.

CONTROL

• Organic/non-chemical: Hose them off the leaves.

• Chemical: Spray the leaves with carbaryl.

Pearleaf blister mite   *Eriophyes pyri*

The adult mites spend the winter inside the buds. Eggs deposited in this area hatch in spring and the small mites begin to feed on the undersides of the new leaves. The feeding causes small yellow or reddish pustules on the upper leaf surfaces. These blisters eventually contain colonies of young mites which are well protected and may move in and out of the blister through a small central opening on the underside of the leaf. A number of generations may occur each year.

Activity usually decreases in the very hot summer months, but sometimes fresh blisters are produced in the late summer. Blisters are up to 3 mm across and turn brown or black as they age. The mites migrate to the buds before leaf fall in autumn. Damaged buds are brown. The tree is weakened and the crop reduced.

The mites also attack the fruit and cause depressed spots and malformation in severe cases. In some areas, these mites live freely on the tree without forming blisters, and as soon as next season's buds are formed they move into them.

PLANTS ATTACKED Pears, apples, quinces, rowans, hawthorns, and cotoneasters.

CONTROL

• Organic: Spray with a soap preparation or wettable sulphur.

• Chemical: Spray in spring with carbaryl. Or spray at green-tip stage with lime-sulphur.

Pine adelgid *Pineus pini*

This pest, which is related to the aphids, sucks sap. It is commonly found on trees that are under stress such as those with a low water supply or those planted too close together.

The insect gathers on new shoots, and a white woolly secretion at the base of the needles indicates its presence. White waxy threads may be seen also on branches and on the trunk. Shoots may die back.

PLANTS ATTACKED *Pinus* spp.

CONTROL   There are a number of insects that attack the pine adelgid. If possible delay spraying in the hope that they will control the pest.

• Organic/non-chemical: Rely on natural enemies, or try soap spray. Take care not to exceed label recommendations and do not apply on a hot day.

• Chemical: If necessary spray small trees with dimethoate. Add wetting agent.

Also known as woolly pine aphid in Queensland.

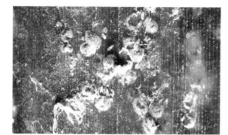

Pineapple scale *Diaspis bromeliae*

This scale causes yellow spots on the foliage and, if present in large numbers, forms a light grey, scurfy covering on leaves and sometimes fruit. Heavily infested plants may become stunted and are not capable of producing good-quality fruit.

The adult female scale covering is about 2 mm across and dirty white. The scales are usually found on shaded parts of the plant. Check leaf bases for early signs of infestation.

PLANTS ATTACKED These include pineapples, *Agave* spp., *Billbergia* spp. and *Bromelia* spp.

CONTROL   Take care to use only uninfested planting material. Remove and burn badly infested leaves or whole plants. Natural enemies should keep small infestations under control.

Pink wax scale *Ceroplastes rubens*

These scales are found on the midribs of leaves and on young twigs. They produce large quantities of honeydew, and plant health declines if the infestation is heavy. In areas where summer is very hot and dry, this scale would not be a serious pest. The adults are covered with hard, pink or greyish-pink wax about 3 mm long.

PLANTS ATTACKED All citrus (mandarins most likely to be attacked; lemons and grapefruit least likely), umbrella trees, custard apples, avocados, mangos, *Ficus* spp., lillypillies, hollies, magnolias, *Pittosporum* spp., ivies and others.

CONTROL   Mature scales are very difficult to kill. Spray before the young scales have grown to about 1 mm long.

• Organic/non-chemical: It may be better to remove as many scales as possible by hand and arrange to spray at the correct time the following year. Use white oil.

• Chemical: Use carbaryl plus 10 mL of white oil per litre of water. (Note that some mandarin varieties are damaged by oil sprays.)

If this time is missed, some success is possible if you spray with the following mixture: 25 g of fresh washing soda crystals plus 5 mL of white oil per litre of water. Expect some fruit marking, leaf fall and fruit fall, particularly in hot weather.

Pink wax scale on ivy (Hedera canariensis)

Pittosporum leafminer
Phytoliriomyza pittosporphylli

The adult of this insect is a small fly (3 mm) from the family Agromyzidae. Each circular area of damage shown in the photograph is caused by one fly larva. Although most leaves are attacked, the plant is not seriously affected.

PLANTS ATTACKED Sweet pittosporum or native daphne (*Pittosporum undulatum*).

CONTROL It would be almost impossible to prevent attack by this insect. Spraying the new growth regularly enough is too hard. If the damaged leaves are considered ugly, it would be sensible to position the tree away from thoroughfares so that the perfumed flowers can be appreciated without a close-up view of the leaves.

Plague thrips   *Thrips imaginis*

Plague thrips, which are about 1 mm long and less than 0.5 mm wide, damage flowers and fruit and occasionally leaves.

The relatively large, kidney-shaped eggs are usually deposited in slits made by the ovipositor in the more permanent parts of the flower such as the stalk. Occasionally eggs may be laid in young leaves near the flowers. The tissue at these sites may fall from the leaf and produce a series of small holes. The females lay more eggs per day in warmer weather than cool weather (about nine per day at 23°C but only one per day at 10°C). The eggs hatch after a few days.

Young thrips, which are almost colourless at first and later go yellow, may begin by feeding on the leaves, but soon congregate inside the blossom. After feeding for a while they leave the plant and enter a resting period in the soil or in leaf litter around the base of the plant. During this time the thrips need humid conditions. Very dry or very wet soil or leaf litter will result in a high mortality rate.

When the adults have developed they fly back to the flowers and begin feeding again. The eggs will not mature unless the female is able to feed on pollen.

Feeding in apple blossom reduces fruit set because reproductive parts are attacked. On nectarines, however, fruit set is not interfered with but feeding on the surface of the young fruit causes a network of brown marks to develop.

Garden flowers such as roses can seriously be damaged; the petals turn brown and fall early, and the sticky brown blobs of excrement are very noticeable on pale-coloured blooms. Thrips are a nuisance inside cut flowers.

The thrips population is usually very much reduced in winter, because of the scarcity of flowers and because low temperatures slow their development. Plague thrips will be very numerous in spring if there were good autumn rains and a mild winter. Warm, calm days are favoured for adults to leave the soil and fly to flowers. This sometimes results in plagues of the tiny insects flying on to damp washing as well as into flowers.

PLANTS ATTACKED The flowers of almost any plant, including apples and pears, citrus, stonefruit, grapes, strawberries, raspberries, weeds and even grasses.

CONTROL This can be difficult if the thrips are deep inside flowers. Anyway, it is not always necessary. For example, damage on grapes, citrus, plums and pears is slight, and control is not warranted.

• Organic: Spray with soap spray or pyrethrins.

• Chemical: Damage is more serious on strawberries, raspberries and other berry fruit, so control should be attempted. Spray as soon as the thrips are noticed. Use maldison or dimethoate. It may be necessary to spray a second time, 10–14 days later. The second spray will kill newly hatched nymphs and adults which were in the resting stage in the soil at the time of the first spray. If possible, avoid spraying when the plants are in full bloom and being worked by bees. Losses can be minimised by spraying late in the day when the bees have returned to the hive.

Damaged apple petals shrivel and go brown.

Poplar gall aphid *Pemphigus bursarius*

These aphids cause galls on the leafstalks of the Lombardy poplar. The galls are curved and 25–30 mm long. If a gall were cut open, a group of wingless aphids and their woolly wax would be found. In summer and autumn some winged aphids develop, and these leave the gall by an opening at the end. They emigrate to weeds such as curled dock (*Rumex crispus*) and dandelion (*Taraxacum officinale*), where they establish colonies on the roots for the winter. In spring there is a move back to the poplar.
PLANTS ATTACKED Lombardy poplars.
CONTROL Unnecessary.

Potato moth *Phthorimaea operculella*

The moths of this species are rarely noticed because of their small size and the fact that they fly mostly at dusk.

The larvae mine in the leaves, producing brown blisters. Later they move into leafstalks and stems and cause the death of plant parts above. The larvae also tunnel in tubers, at first near the surface but later more deeply. The tunnels are about 1 mm across. When tomato plants are attacked, the larvae may bore into fruit at the stalk ends or where fruits touch one another. Fruit often rots later.
PLANTS ATTACKED Potatoes, tomatoes and weeds in the same plant family, such as thornapple and nightshades.
CONTROL
• Organic/non-chemical: Problems with this pest are less likely if the soil has a high organic matter content and is well watered. Hill the potatoes. Control weeds, particularly those related to potatoes. Remove and destroy infested potatoes promptly. Harvest as soon as the crop is mature.

Stored potatoes can be protected by dusting with derris dust and by keeping temperatures as low as possible.
• Chemical: Spray infected plants with dimethoate.

Psyllids Order Hemiptera: Family Psyllidae

This family of about 80 species of small insects is related to the aphids, whiteflies, mealybugs and some other similar sap-suckers. Many species of psyllid produce protective coverings (lerps) in a shape and colour characteristic of that species.

The eggs are deposited on the leaf surface. The nymphs, which are commonly orange in colour, build lerps and shelter beneath them while they feed. The winged adults are about 5 mm. Some psyllids cause bumps to develop in leaves.
PLANTS ATTACKED A wide range of eucalypts and related trees.
CONTROL Birds and some insects often eat psyllids, so human intervention may not be necessary.
• Chemical: If spraying is to be carried out, use maldison or dimethoate.

See also fig psyllid (P) and brown lace lerp (P).

Psyllids — free-living

These small insects do not produce the coverings common in this group but instead protect themselves by the production of masses of white powdery wax. They suck sap and may distort new growth. They look a little like tiny cicadas and move around quite freely.

PLANTS ATTACKED   Water gums, brush boxes, and a range of other plants.
CONTROL   Not usually necessary.
Chemical: If severe, spray with a systemic such as dimethoate. Add some wetting agent.

Psyllids on brush box

Psyllids — grevillea

These tiny insects damage both flowers and new growth. Flower spikes may be small, and buds may fail to open. Buds at the end may shrivel and fall, leaving the main flower stalk curled and brown.

Damage to new growth is variable. The leaves may be yellow and distorted. The shoots do not elongate normally, and the leaves are small and sparse. The whole plant is stunted and woody.

It is thought that these insects — which are sometimes called 'grevillea bud-drop psyllids' — inject a toxic saliva into the plant when they suck the sap.

It is possible that this type of damage is also caused by other pests such as mites.
PLANTS ATTACKED   Grevilleas.
CONTROL
• Organic: Pyrethrin or soap sprays may be successful.
• Chemical: Spray with fenthion. Apply just before a flush of new growth is expected.

*Damage on
Grevillea rosmarinifolia*

Psyllids — lillypilly   *Trioza eugeniae*

This small insect is sometimes referred to as the 'pimple psyllid'. The first-stage nymphs move about for a time but soon settle, usually under the leaves, and begin sucking sap from new leaves. This feeding causes the plant to develop oval lumps on the upper surface of the leaves and corresponding depressions on the lower surface, with the now scale-like insect inside. The new growth can be completely covered with lumps and looks rather ugly.

PLANTS ATTACKED   This insect attacks a range of different lillypillies but affects some more than others. The most damaged seems to be blue lillypilly (*Syzygium coolminianum*). Brush cherry (*S. australe*) is badly affected also.
CONTROL   This is difficult. By the time the damage is noticed it is too late to spray.
• Organic: A soap spray may be successful.
• Chemical: Next year, watch for the formation of new growth on small plants and spray with a penetrant such as dimethoate as soon as the tiny insects are sighted.

Pumpkin beetle *Aulacophora hilaris*

This native beetle, which is a yellowish-orange with four black spots, is approximately 6 mm long. The adults chew the flowers and the leaves. The larvae feed on the root system or stem bases but seem to do very little damage. They may also chew the surface of fruit in contact with the ground.

Pumpkin beetles thrive in warm dry conditions and are most common in inland areas. They are most likely to attack in late spring, summer and early autumn.

PLANTS ATTACKED All cucurbits. Other plants are damaged occasionally.

CONTROL If young plants are attacked, they can be easily destroyed, but once the plants are older and have begun running, the amount of material eaten by these beetles may be less significant and control, therefore, unnecessary.
- Organic: Use derris dust.
- Chemical: Dust young plants with maldison dust. This may be continued on older plants, or they may be sprayed with carbaryl.

Raspberry sawfly *Priophorus morio*

The adults of this insect are about 6 mm long and black with whitish legs. The eggs are laid in the canes or the leafstalks. When the larvae hatch, they move to the undersides of the foliage where they chew holes between the main veins. The larvae are about 12 mm long when fully grown. They are yellowish and have a broad band of dark brown down the back with a fine white line along the middle. The pupae are papery and are found between leaves or in the soil.

PLANTS ATTACKED Raspberries and blackberries.

CONTROL
- Organic/non-chemical: Remove larvae when small.
- Chemical: Spray with carbaryl. Cover the undersides of the leaves thoroughly with spray.

Redshouldered leaf beetle

Monolepta australis

This small native beetle — which is also known as the monolepta beetle — is about 6 mm long, and yellow with a cherry-red band across the top of the wingcovers, and one red spot on each wingcover towards the back. It always occurs in large swarms, which are most common in spring and late summer. These insects are gregarious and tend to remain in the swarms on one or two plants instead of spreading out through a garden or orchard.

Damaged flowers have a scorched appearance and will probably not set fruit. The beetles chew on the skin of the fruit and, as it grows further, this injury becomes a depressed scar which may develop cracks. If many beetles feed on a piece of fruit they will completely remove the skin and destroy the pulp.

They feed on both upper and lower surfaces of the foliage and chew ragged holes in it. Once leaves are destroyed, the twigs thus exposed to the sun may become sunburnt and die back.

This pest often attacks sweet corn. If this happens before pollination takes place and swarms of beetles feed on the silks, then no cobs of corn will eventuate. Cobs on which the grain has set may be exposed at the tips and thus be more susceptible to fungal diseases or attack from caterpillars or weevils.

PLANTS ATTACKED An extremely wide range, including avocados, macadamias, mangos, citrus, strawberries, mulberries, figs, peaches, plums, grapes, beans, pumpkins, sweet corn, dahlias, roses and other shrubs. The pepper tree, wattle and tea-tree are also attacked.

CONTROL This insect is very difficult to control.
- Organic/non-chemical: On small plants try knocking the beetles into soapy water.
- Chemical: Spray the beetle swarm with carbaryl.

Rose scale *Aulacaspis rosae*

This scale is found mostly on the stems and branches of the host, but if control procedures are not carried out it will gradually spread on to old flower stalks and on to leafstalks. By this stage the plant would be spindly and stunted, with a white flaky crust of scales on the bark. The females are flat, white, rounded and about 2.5 mm across. The male scale is much smaller, and long and narrow. Each female lays about 40 eggs and perhaps a second batch after that. The young scales or crawlers are pale red. They soon settle down to feed near the adults.

The females may remain alive for almost a year, and several overlapping generations can be found on the one plant. Sometimes stems are seen covered entirely with females and very few males; other stems may have many males and very few females.

PLANTS ATTACKED Roses, raspberries, loganberries, blackberries.

CONTROL Prune off badly affected stems and burn them. Spray with white oil at the rate of 25 mL per litre of water when the plants are dormant. In the growing season, an application of 10 mL of white oil per litre of water will help keep scale populations low and kill any aphids on the plant.

Rutherglen bug *Nysius vinitor*

This grey-brown bug has silvery wings and is approximately 5 mm long. It generally feeds on weeds and grasses in wastelands or along roadsides and will move from those situations on to cultivated crops only in hot weather when the unwatered plants have dried off. When they arrive in crops such as lettuce or cherries in huge numbers and begin sucking sap, they can cause considerable damage. Leaves wilt, stonefruit is pitted, and beans wither. Grey dots of excrement also blemish fruit and leaves. If green peaches are attacked, long threads of clear gum will exude from the punctures caused by feeding.

PLANTS ATTACKED Grapes, beans, stonefruit, lettuces, onions, strawberries, tomatoes, potatoes, carrots and others.

CONTROL Control should be undertaken quickly to minimise losses.
• Organic: Spray with pyrethrins.
• Chemical: Use dimethoate, carbaryl or maldison. Be careful to observe withholding periods on edible plant parts near to harvest.

Damage on young peach

Adult bugs

San José scale *Quadraspidiotus perniciosus*

This scale insect is found principally on the trunk, branches and twigs of deciduous trees. The scale itself is difficult to see because its purplish-grey colour is similar to the colour of the branches. The latter, however, develop a very rough texture, which indicates the presence of the scales.

Fruit may also be infested, mostly at the calyx end. A reddish ring or halo develops around each grey scale, and even if the scales themselves are removed, this reddish ring remains. Reddish discolouration also occurs around the scales of the bark, but this is not so obvious. This insect can build up into big numbers very quickly and spread throughout the tree, which shows a general loss of vigour and may die if the infestation is not dealt with. This scale is considered to be so serious that it is termed a 'proclaimed pest' in some areas and its control is required by law.

The female adult scale is about the size of a pinhead. Each female is capable of producing up to 400 young and there may be several generations each year. The female scale gives birth to living young which leave the mother scale, settle down and begin to suck sap. Gradually the scale covering is built up.

PLANTS ATTACKED Apricots, almonds, peaches, plums, apples, pears, firethorns, cotoneasters, japonicas, hawthorns, tree lucerne, osage oranges, willows and many others.

CONTROL Apply sprays thoroughly to trunks, branches and twigs. Pay special attention to cracks in the bark, and spray right to ground level. Treat ornamentals as well as fruiting trees and shrubs.

If the infestation is serious on deciduous plants, spray twice: once in winter, with winter spraying oil, and once in spring, with white oil. Leave an interval of at least four weeks between sprays.

If the infestation is light on a deciduous tree, application of the winter spray only is sufficient.

Evergreens should have only the spring spray, applied towards the end of October.

Scales Order Hemiptera

These insects suck sap and can cause serious plant damage. They do not look like typical insects because most of them form a protective covering over themselves and do not move about after they reach a certain stage.

There are many hundreds of different species in Australia and New Zealand. Some are native to these countries, but others have been accidentally introduced. Those that attack fruit trees have been most studied, but there are many others about which little is known. They feed on trees and shrubs and smaller perennials.

Some scales, such as cottony pigface scale (*Pulvinariella mesembryanthemi*), have only one known host. This scale has been found only on the succulent *Carpobrotus edulis*. It is an example of a scale that produces a waxy sac to protect the eggs. These coverings are often considerably larger than the female body.

The scales are divided into two main groups: hard scales (P), and soft scales (P).

PLANTS ATTACKED A wide range. Different scales feed on different plants. Some scales have a wide host range.

CONTROL White oil at the rate of 20 mL per litre of water should control most scales but check that the hosts will not be damaged. Timing is often very important.

A soft scale on camellia (Pulvinaria *sp.*)

Fern scale
(Pinnaspis caricis)

Sirex wasp *Sirex noctilio*

The adult wasps vary greatly in length (10-14 mm). The females are a metallic blue with a pointed projection at the end of the body. The male is a similar colour but has a broad orange band on the body.

When eggs are laid in the tree trunk, spores of a particular fungus and a mucous secretion are inserted as well. The mucus predisposes the wood to infection by the fungus. The fungus grows in the wood and renders it suitable for use as food by sirex larvae. It is actually the fungus that kills the tree, not the tunnelling of the larvae.

The larvae are creamy-white with a distinct head and a short dark spine on the end of the body. Their tunnels are circular in cross-section and packed with chewed wood. Most are vertical and in the sapwood at first. Later the heartwood is also attacked.

There are several indicators of sirex attack. Beads of resin appear on the trunk wherever the ovipositor has been inserted. The needles of attacked trees wilt, and change from green to yellow then reddish-brown. Browning of tree tops and circular holes 3–7 mm in diameter in the trunks may be an indication of sirex attack.

PLANTS ATTACKED Monterey pines (*Pinus radiata*) and a few other *Pinus* spp. Dying larches (*Larix* spp.) or spruces (*Picea* spp.) may also be attacked.

CONTROL
Plant Monterey pines in a suitable site. Keep them growing vigorously and control leaf-feeding insects. If you suspect an infestation of sirex, you should inform your local forestry office.

Small citrus butterfly *Eleppone anactus*

The caterpillars of this species grow to about 45 mm long and can consume considerable amounts of foliage. Like large citrus butterfly larvae, when disturbed they produce a strong smell from a forked pink scent organ (osmeterium) which protrudes from the head.

Both male and female adults have a wingspan of about 75 mm and similar markings; the forewings are black with grey and white, and the hindwings are marked in white, orange-red and blue. Like the large citrus butterflies, these adults feed on the nectar of various plants but they lay eggs only on citrus and related plants. The pale yellow, almost spherical eggs are deposited singly.

This species is sometimes also known as the dingy swallowtail. In some areas a different citrus butterfly (*P. canopus*) is more common than *P. anactus* or *P. aegeus*. It does similar damage.

PLANTS ATTACKED Citrus, both cultivated species and native species such as *Microcitrus australasica* and *Eremocitrus glauca*. Also other members of the plant family Rutaceae such as Mexican orange blossom (*Choisya ternata*) and waxflower (*Eriostemon myoporoides*). Occasionally plants from some other families are attacked.

CONTROL
• Organic/non-chemical: Remove by hand.
• Chemical: If spraying is necessary, use carbaryl following label directions.

Snails and slugs *Class Gastropoda*

These animals chew holes in leaves and may completely remove seedlings and other small plants. They leave a slimy trail of mucus wherever they move.

Snail eggs are laid in moist soil at a depth of 20-40 mm. They are white, spherical and about 3 mm in diameter. The young snails feed in a group for a few months and then disperse.

Snails may move up trunks of trees such as citrus to feed on the foliage. Most feeding occurs at night, particularly after rain or hosing. During the day they are found in cool moist situations such as leaves of broad-leaved low-growing plants and under rocks and boards.

In dry weather snails seal themselves inside the shell and may remain dormant for up to three years. Slugs congregate in as damp a place as possible such as under stones or logs.

PLANTS ATTACKED A wide range including seedlings, leafy vegetables and citrus.

CONTROL
• Organic: Remove hiding places. Bait with metaldehyde. Do not put pellets in heaps; avoid sites accessible to dogs (which can be poisoned). Khaki Campbell and Indian runner ducks can be used to eat snails.

Snails that have a flattened shell are probably the cannibal or carnivorous snail (*Strangesta* sp.). These eat slugs and snails that damage plants but may not be an efficient controlling agent.
• Chemical: Bait with methiocarb pellets. Keep away from dogs. Spray snails in trees with methiocarb.

Damage on citrus

Snails and their damage on zinnia

Soft brown scale *Coccus hesperidum*

The mature female is 3-5 mm long. It is soft, and roughly oval in outline, although all the scales are not exactly the same shape. It is a pale yellowish-brown and sometimes tinged with green or mottled with dark brown. These scales concentrate on midribs and leafstalks but are also found on stems and fruit stalks. Infestations are usually worse in warm, dry climates. Distribution on a plant or within a group of plants is often irregular. For example, on older citrus trees, scale colonies may occur in some parts of a tree but not others.

On a leaf the scale seems very flat, but if small twigs are infested, the scales appear to be folded around the twig. They suck sap, but the most serious damage occurs because of the vast quantities of honeydew produced. This means that sooty mould (D) will cover leaves, fruit and stems, and ant populations will be high wherever this scale is found.

Each female produces one or two eggs each day over a period of up to two months. The small insects crawl out from beneath the parents and settle on other parts of the plant. They are yellowish and about 0.5 mm long. They can easily be overlooked, particularly on finely divided leaves such as fern fronds or if the plants are situated indoors in dim light.

PLANTS ATTACKED A wide range, including citrus, grapes, figs, passionfruit, peaches, pears, palms, ferns, oleanders, olives, daphnes and camellias.

CONTROL
The natural enemies of these scales will often keep them under good control. Assist by controlling ants. Spray the butt of the tree and a small area of surrounding soil regularly with a household ant spray (chemical) or band the trunk (organic).

If spraying the scales is necessary, this should be done in summer when most of the scales will be young (on plants outdoors, this is indicated by intense ant activity). Use white oil.

On ferns and soft-foliaged plants, use a low rate of white oil. This rate is also suggested for daphne. Do not apply oil sprays on hot days. Badly affected ferns should be thrown away or cut back.

Cottony pigface scale
(Pulvinariella mesembryanthemi)

Soft scales Order Hemiptera: Family Coccidae

The insects in this group protect themselves by developing a tough outer skin or by producing large quantities of wax over their bodies.

Many species in this group have no males. The females lay large batches of eggs, which hatch into crawlers. These are just visible to the unaided eye. They may wander about for a while and then settle down in permanent positions.

These insects suck sap but this does little damage. However, they produce honeydew, a sugary solution, which falls on to leaves and other plant parts beneath the scales. This makes the leaves sticky and they often become black with sooty mould (D), a fungus that feeds on the honeydew. Some species produce much more honeydew than others. Blackened leaves are ugly and have reduced capacity for photosynthesis.

White wax scale (P) and black scale (P) are typical members of this group. See also pink wax scale (P), soft brown scale (P), Chinese wax scale (P), and Indian white wax scale (P).

PLANTS ATTACKED Many. Different scale species attack different plants.

CONTROL These are best controlled soon after the eggs have hatched and before the protective waxy covering is formed. This tends to occur at the same time each year in a certain location. Look for crawlers between mid-December and mid-January. Increased ant activity often indicates hatching periods. Ant control is vital in keeping scale populations low. Ants frighten away the natural enemies of scales and also move crawlers from one plant to another.

Application of spray should be thorough. Concentrate on areas where the scales are. Use white oil at the rate of 20 mL per litre of water. Scales can be removed with a brush or gloved fingers if numbers are small.

Soldier beetles *Chauliognathus lugubris*

These beetles feed on soft-bodied insects and often gather in large swarms on flowering trees and shrubs waiting to attack insects that are attracted to the nectar. Large swarms may weigh down and break thin branches, and occasionally they have been known to damage ripe cherries or newly-set fruit. They may interfere with pollination.

Soldier beetles are about 13 mm long, with dull blue-green wingcovers and a yellow band near the black head. The yellow end of the abdomen can also be seen from above.

PLANTS ATTACKED Any flowering plant may attract these beetles.

CONTROL Usually unnecessary.

• Chemical: If spraying must be carried out, spray late in the day when bees have returned to the hive. Maldison will kill the beetles. Apply it to the swarm rather than to all the surrounding flowers.

Spined citrus bug *Biprorulus bibax*

Spined citrus bug is green with a prominent horn or spine on each of the front corners near the head. It is approximately 20 mm long, but quite difficult to see among the green leaves. The nymphs are yellow and black, or orange and black, with more and more green as they grow to adults. They do not feed on the leaves but attack the fruit. Sap is sucked from the interior of the fruit, causing dry patches inside and a flat patch of skin on the outside where they have been feeding. Gumming and browning also occur inside attacked fruit and some fruit may fall. Even just a few of these bugs on a tree can cause serious damage. Individuals may live nearly two years.

PLANTS ATTACKED Mandarins and lemons are commonly attacked. Its native hosts are desert lime (*Eremocitrus glauca*) and finger lime (*Microcitrus australasica*).

CONTROL

• Organic/non-chemical: Control methods using pheromones and assassin bugs are being researched. Remove by hand.

• Chemical: Spray with maldison or dimethoate. To each add 10 mL of white oil per litre of water. Note that either insecticide would also control scale insects and dimethoate would help to control fruit flies. However, dimethoate can injure cumquats, Meyer lemons and Seville oranges. Do not pick the fruit until seven days have elapsed after spraying

Spittlebugs
Order Hemiptera: Superfamily Cercopoidea

The nymphs of these sap-sucking insects protect themselves from drying out by producing wet, frothy material around themselves.

The adults (about 10 mm long) are referred to as 'froghoppers' and are capable of jumping vigorously.

PLANTS ATTACKED Eucalypts, wattles, she-oaks, bottlebrushes and a range of other plants including exotics.

CONTROL   Unnecessary, but they could be removed from plants by hosing.

Springtails   Class/Order Collembola

These soft-bodied small insects occur most commonly in moist situations where there is a high proportion of organic matter, such as around the edges of compost heaps, under small plants in a rockery, or in leafy mulch.

The most commonly seen species are white or grey and less than 2 mm long. When disturbed they run about or jump up and down.

The lucerne flea (*Sminthurus viridis*) is green or fawn with dark patches. It is a cool-weather problem. It attacks a range of vegetables and gradually eats away the leaf surfaces.

PLANTS ATTACKED They do not usually damage large plants, but if present in high numbers seeds and seedlings may be chewed. They may feed on already-damaged roots or fruit such as strawberries. Springtails can seriously damage mushrooms.

CONTROL   If control in mushroom beds is required, seek advice.

• Organic/non-chemical: Numbers can be reduced by forking over the soil and drying it out, or by liming if this is possible.

• Chemical: Spray with dimethoate or with maldison. Add wetting agent.

Spruce spider mite *Oligonychus ununguis*

These mites attack only conifers. The nymphs are pale green, and the adult females are orange to greenish-black but because they are very small and cannot be seen with the naked eye, large populations can build up before the problem is noticed.

They feed on conifer needles and may turn them yellow, grey, brown, or nearly white. The plant may take on a bronze colour and the needles are often shed. Foliage eventually dies. If the infestation is severe, a very fine webbing will be formed between leaves and branches. Large trees are damaged more on lower branches, and seedlings and small trees may be killed if infestation is allowed to continue.

Winter is probably passed in the egg stage on the twigs. Most damage is done by this pest in hot dry seasons.

PLANTS ATTACKED Spruces, firs, junipers, pines and some other coniferous plants.

CONTROL

• Organic: Be cautious. Spray with wettable sulphur in cool weather. Do not exceed the recommended rate. Make sure the tree is well watered.

• Chemical: Spray with dicofol as soon as the infestation is seen.

Staghorn fern beetle

Halticorcus platycerii

These tiny (3 mm) rounded beetles are a bluish-black with four orange-red spots. They chew small 'craters' into the fleshy fronds, and the brown, scattered marks spoil the appearance of the frond.

The eggs are deposited near the tips of fronds where new growth will occur. The larvae tunnel inside the tips.

PLANTS ATTACKED Staghorns and elkhorns.

CONTROL

Clip off and destroy tips of fronds as soon as damage is noticed. Search for the adults and remove them by hand. Early morning is a good time. See notes on manual removal on page 37.

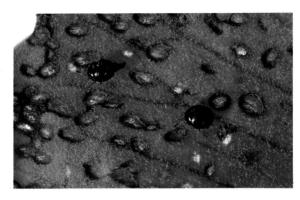

Steelblue sawflies *Perga* spp.

The eggs of this sawfly are deposited in slits in the leaves. After hatching, the larvae remain together in the same group during the day, spread out over the tree to feed at night, re-assemble for the next day, and so on. A small tree with several larval groups may be seriously damaged. They leave the tree when fully fed and pupate in the soil.

If the clusters of larvae are disturbed, they wave their bodies up and down and exude a thick yellowish fluid. The larvae are brownish to begin with but darken to black as they age.

PLANTS ATTACKED Eucalypts.

CONTROL

• Organic/non-chemical: If possible, prune off a small branch with the group of larvae attached.

• Chemical: Spray the group and surrounding leaves with maldison.

Strawberry spider mite *Tetranychus lambi*

On bananas these mites congregate on the undersurfaces of leaves. Look for them along the main leaf vein. Their feeding causes a gradual yellowing of leaves, and the leaves dry out and fall. The mites produce a very fine webbing.

They also attack the fruit, particularly under covers, and cause an overall reddening of the skin. The damage tends to be worse at the stalk end.

Damage is most serious in dry weather, particularly if the plant does not receive an adequate water supply.

PLANTS ATTACKED A wide range, including bananas, strawberries, beans and broad-leafed weeds.

CONTROL

• Organic/non-chemical: Control weeds.

• Chemical: Spray banana leaves and small plants with dicofol.

Teatree web moth *Catamola thyrisalis*

The larvae of these moths feed together in a group. They shelter during the day in a mass of webbing and come out at night to feed on surrounding leaves.

If the webbing is disturbed they may quickly drop down on silken threads and disappear into leaf litter around the base of the plant.

PLANTS ATTACKED Tea-trees (*Leptospermum* spp.).

CONTROL

• Organic/non-chemical: Prune off the mass of webbing.

• Chemical: Spray with carbaryl. Add wetting agent.

Termites Order Isoptera

These insects — which are sometimes referred to as 'woodmen' or 'white ants' — live in colonies. Each colony has a king and queen, workers, soldiers and some other forms (or castes). The soldiers have dark-coloured large heads, sometimes with a point at the front; they are used for identification of the species. Most termites are 4–10 mm long, white or cream, and soft-bodied.

Nests are constructed in various places depending on the species. They may be underground, on tree branches, in the base of trees, or in mounds above ground. Most termites chew wood in living trees, fallen logs, or timber in houses or fences. Attack in standing trees often goes unnoticed until a damaged branch blows off in a storm. The termites may enter from underground and chew the heartwood, thus structurally weakening the tree. Termites in trees do not necessarily attack houses.

PLANTS ATTACKED A range of trees.

CONTROL   It is a good idea to have termites positively identified by an expert before control procedures are undertaken. Collect several soldiers and put them in a small quantity of methylated spirits in a jar. Take them to your local forestry office and ask about suitable treatment or employ a pest control operator.

Thrips Order Thysanoptera

Thrips damage on apple leaves

Thrips in gardenia flower

*A native thrips species
and its damage on
Ficus sp.*

A number of thrips are serious plant pests. Some do not attack living plants at all but feed on decaying organic matter such as dead leaves, old wood or fungi. Others are predaceous and feed on aphids or mites.

Thrips are often overlooked because of their small size and the fact that they tend to feed in protected places such as under leaves, where leaves overlap, or deep in the flowers.

Some thrips feed on leaves only, and others on flowers only. They attack a very wide range of plants, from fruit trees and ornamental shrubs, to annual flowers, weeds, or vegetables. They have mouthparts that are described as 'rasping and sucking'. With these they damage the surface of the leaf or flower and then suck the sap which oozes out. They may also carry viruses from plant to plant.

Most plant damage involves distortion of young leaves or a silver or grey appearance on older leaves. Some thrips cause leaf edges or whole leaves to roll up, and still others cause the plant to produce characteristic galls.

Thrips droppings, which are large compared to their body size, show up as little brown tar-like blobs. This is ugly on the leaves of shrubs and on flowers such as roses which are cut for indoor display.

Feeding in flowers often involves damage to the reproductive organs and results in fewer or deformed or blemished fruit. Petals go brown and wither quickly.

Most thrips are from 1–2 mm long and about 0.5 mm wide. They come in a number of different colours — mostly yellow, cream, white, brown or black — but there are a few that are red. The narrow, fringed wings of the adults may look like one or two stripes down the centre of the body. Young thrips (nymphs) do not have wings and are usually paler than the adults.

The adult females commonly lay their eggs in slits in plant tissue. The first two nymphal stages (that is, the very young thrips) feed on the plant, but the next two stages are usually found in leaf litter or perhaps in the soil at the base of the plant. These nymphs do not feed, although they will move if disturbed. When the adults have developed, they move back on to the plant and begin feeding again. Soon after, the females lay a batch of eggs.

Thrips have few insect enemies to keep their numbers down. They are, however, greatly influenced by weather conditions. Heavy rain and very hot, dry weather reduces thrips populations. Thrips do not fly if conditions are cool and windy.

PLANTS ATTACKED A wide range.

CONTROL   This can be difficult. Read the entries for banana rust thrips (P), bean blossom thrips (P), gladiolus thrips (P), onion thrips (P), and plague thrips (P).

Also see western flower thrips, page 51.

Tomato russet mite *Aculops lycopersici*

This pest is extremely small and in the field can be seen only with a magnifying glass or hand lens. Look for long yellowish bodies, which may be present in large numbers, feeding underneath the leaves, on stems and on fruit.

The first signs of infestation usually occur on the lower leaves, which become a dull grey and smooth underneath. They hang down and become brown and papery. The stems also become smooth with a brownish surface and may eventually become rough and corky or crack longitudinally. The mites gradually move upwards, and if the infestation continues and numbers build up, blossom and fruit drop may occur. Fruit that does not fall may have a corky surface or become sunburnt because the leaves are no longer shading them.

PLANTS ATTACKED Tomatoes, eggplants, peppers, potatoes, petunias; and related weeds, such as nightshade.

CONTROL   This is difficult. Do not plant tomatoes continually in the same place because mites can move from old leaves on the ground on to new plants.

Spray as soon as the first symptoms are observed.

• Organic: Wettable sulphur and sulphur dusts control this pest but will damage plants if used in very hot weather.

• Chemical: Use dimethoate or maldison.

Two-spotted mite *Tetranychus urticae*

This mite has been known in the past as 'red spider'. Look for these pests on the undersides of leaves. They are just visible to the unaided eye. The females, which are more numerous than the males, are pale green or yellowish-green with a dark mark on each side of the body. In winter the adult females may become orange-red in colour and congregate in protected places such as under bark, at the bases of trees or in branch junctions. They produce quantities of fine webbing. In early spring these overwintering forms usually move on to small plants at the base of trees and begin to feed. They change back to green with dark spots. Later they move up into the trees again.

Aggregations of overwintering mites may also be found on the tips of leaves of old bean plants left in the field. Mites may be moved from place to place on dead leaves or in webbing stuck to insects or birds. They are more damaging in hot dry weather. Long periods of rain decrease their numbers.

Feeding on fruit trees first causes a faint yellow mottling on the upper leaf surface. As they continue to feed, the leaves yellow all over and may become thin and papery. Fine webbing is produced at the feeding site. Premature leaf-fall weakens the tree and reduces quantity and quality of future crops.

On orchids a faint silvering of the leaf is the first sign of attack. The leaves later yellow and fall. Dark mottling or translucent spots on the flowers may indicate that they have been damaged by mites.

On strawberries the leaves may first look dull and then show yellow speckles. Underneath the leaves a silver or brownish area develops, and the mites and their eggs and webbing can be seen.

On bean leaves the mottling may look greyish, and the leaves later yellow and fall.

PLANTS ATTACKED A wide range, including fruit trees and vegetables, annual flowers, ornamental trees and shrubs.

CONTROL

• Organic/non-chemical: In a home garden the following cultural control measures may be adequate: water the affected plants from above, remove and destroy badly infested leaves or whole plants promptly, and control weeds.

Two-spotted mites have many natural enemies, including tiny ladybirds (*Stethorus* spp.), lacewing larvae, and predaceous thrips. It is possible to buy predator mites (*Phytoseiulus persimilis*) — look for advertisements in gardening magazines — and distribute them in the garden, but this is unlikely to be successful in a mixed planting. The predators need a constant supply of two-spotted mites to eat, or their population dies out. They are killed by some chemicals used in the control of diseases or pests such as caterpillars or aphids. If you wish to try their establishment in a home orchard or large rose garden, seek further advice from your predator suppliers.

• Chemical: Spraying with dimethoate or dicofol may reduce numbers. Add some wetting agent, and cover the undersurfaces of leaves thoroughly. However, this pest is resistant to these chemicals in many areas. Dusting sulphur and wettable sulphur are also possibilities but should not be used in hot weather.

Dots on the webbing are two-spotted mites

Typical fine yellow mottling on bean leaves.

Vegetable weevil *Listroderes difficilis*

Most damage by this pest occurs in cool weather — that is, in autumn through the winter and in spring. The larvae, which grow to about 12 mm, are cream-coloured at first but become greener as they age. They attack in late autumn and winter, sheltering in the soil and under the base of the plants during the day and feeding from below the leaves at night. At first they concentrate around the base of the plant, and small irregular holes appear. Later the feeding may be more extensive and whole leaves may be removed. Hollows may be chewed in fleshy stems and around the crown of the plant.

When the larvae have eaten enough, they pupate in the soil. The adults that emerge are approximately 10 mm long, and brown with a faint white V-shaped mark and two faint white lumps towards the end of the 'body'. During spring they feed on leaves at night and hide in the soil nearby during the day.

PLANTS ATTACKED A wide range of vegetable crops, annual flowers and weeds. They particularly favour fleshy-rooted vegetables such as beetroot, carrots and parsnip. Cabbages, lettuces, and silver beet are also attacked. They do not attack beans and peas, and pumpkin and squash, so these could be used in a crop rotation programme if chemical control was considered undesirable.

CONTROL
• Organic/non-chemical: Removal of weeds, particularly marshmallow and capeweed, will help to keep the numbers of this pest down. Crop rotation will help.
• Chemical: Spray the plants with carbaryl and/or spray freshly chopped weeds and distribute them between the plants in the evening.

Pinned specimen showing typically elongated weevil head.

Walnut blister mite *Eriophyes tristriatus*

The feeding of these mites produces blister-like swellings on the upper leaf surfaces mostly near the main vein. Heavily infested leaves may be badly distorted.

PLANTS ATTACKED Walnuts.

CONTROL This is not usually necessary. Spray just before bud-burst with lime-sulphur at the rate of 50 mL per litre of water.

Another species, *Eriophyes erineus*, is also known as the walnut blister mite.

Wasp galls Order Hymenoptera: Family Eurytomidae

Most of these gall-forming wasps are only a few millimetres long and are usually not noticed. They lay eggs into very young plant tissue, and the plant is stimulated to produce extra cells so a gall develops.

The larvae feed on the plant tissue and pupate inside the gall. The adults emerge through holes they make in the outside of the gall.

PLANTS ATTACKED Eucalypts, wattles, bottlebrushes and a number of other Australian native trees.

CONTROL Chemical control is not possible. Prune the affected twigs or leaves off the plant if you wish. Fertilise the plant.

See also citrus gall wasp (P).

Wasp galls—turpentine   *Epimegastigmus* sp.

These tiny wasps are only 1.5 mm long and would rarely be noticed. The feeding of their larvae results in the gradual production by the plant of rounded lumps covered with thick hairs. The tree is not seriously damaged.

PLANTS ATTACKED   These galls are very common on turpentines.

CONTROL   Once the galls are noticed, it is too late for control.

Wattle leafminer   *Acrocercops plebeia*

The adult of this pest is an extremely small moth which usually goes unnoticed. The larvae tunnel inside the leaves, first making a very fine line, but very soon producing a pinkish blister. The leaf epidermis dries out, goes brown and eventually flakes off.

The larvae pupate inside the blisters, and by the time the moth is ready to emerge the blister is papery and the moths can easily escape. There are some areas where the damage is so severe and so regular that unless a spray programme is carried out the tree looks extremely ugly.

PLANTS ATTACKED   This pest does considerable damage to phyllodinous wattles such as the Mount Morgan wattle (*Acacia podalyriifolia*).

CONTROL
• Organic/non-chemical: Prune off the blisters before they become papery and burn them. Better still, plant a different wattle.
• Chemical: A spray programme can be carried out with a penetrant such as fenthion.

Ants often cluster around these mealybugs to feed on the honeydew they produce.

Wattle mealybug   *Melanococcus albizziae*

These insects are oval in shape, 3–4 mm long, and very dark purple or black. They produce bands of white wax across their bodies.

They are quite spectacular gathered in groups on stems or feeding on the soft new growth, but do not cause serious damage.

PLANTS ATTACKED   These include a range of wattles and a few others such as the silk tree (*Albizia* sp.).

CONTROL   Prune off the infested twigs.

Wattle tick scale *Cryptes baccatus*

This scale, which is comparatively large (about 5 mm across), begins light bluish-grey and ages to light or dark brown. It is quite spectacular and tends to be seen in a group of about 30 or 40 on a small branch or twig. They resemble berries and are quite shiny to begin with.

PLANTS ATTACKED Wattles, including the early black or green wattle (*Acacia decurrens*), Sydney golden wattle (*A. longifolia*), and the blackwood (*A. melanoxylon*).

CONTROL They are usually not present in sufficient numbers to warrant control. If necessary, prune them off the plant.

White cedar moth *Leptocneria reducta*

The larvae of this moth grow to about 45 mm long. They are dark brown with yellow heads and masses of long grey and black hairs. The hairs cause skin irritation.

The caterpillars gather at or near the base of the tree during the day and spread out to feed on the foliage at night. When they have defoliated one tree, they walk in single file to another white cedar tree and are consequently sometimes referred to as 'processionary caterpillars'. Occasionally they stray into buildings. Pupation occurs in debris near the tree.

There are two generations in a year, one in spring and one in autumn.

PLANTS ATTACKED White cedars (*Melia azedarach*).

CONTROL
• Organic/non-chemical: A sack or piece of hessian tied around the tree provides a place for the larvae to congregate during the day. Examine the band each day and destroy the larvae. Banding is usually a very successful procedure.
• Chemical: Spray the trunk and lower leaves with maldison.

White curl grubs

Order Coleoptera: Family Scarabaeidae

These are the larvae of scarab or cockchafer beetles. They vary in size according to the age of the larva and the size of the adult beetle.

They are whitish, or blue-white, with an orange-brown distinct head and long jointed legs. They usually rest curled into a semi-circle and are referred to as C-shaped or U-shaped.

Most of these larvae feed on plant roots, but some feed around the bases of low-growing plants. Various white curl grubs chew furrows in the butts of pineapple plants, and blackheaded pasture cockchafer (P) larvae chew grass leaves. Strawberry plants may have their roots eaten right to the crown. White curl grubs can be a serious problem in potted plants.

PLANTS ATTACKED A wide range.

CONTROL
• Organic/non-chemical: Birds, fungal and viral diseases, and predaceous insects such as ground beetles may all attack these grubs.
• Chemical: In lawns and in potted ornamentals they can be controlled with fenamiphos (Lawn Beetle Killer®) granules applied as directed on the label. Seek advice about control in other situations.

See also Christmas beetle (P) and African black beetle (P).

Whiteflies   Order Hemiptera: Family Aleyrodidae

There are about 20 species of whitefly known in Australia. The adults have a wingspan of about 3 mm and are covered with a powdery wax; they look like tiny white moths. They congregate on the undersides of leaves to suck sap from the plant, which results in a fine yellow mottling on the upper surface. They also produce honeydew in which sooty mould (D) grows. When disturbed, the adults fly quickly from the plant but soon settle again.

Each female may lay about 200 eggs. These are usually deposited on the undersides of leaves, sometimes in a special pattern characteristic of the species or just singly at random. The tiny crawling insects which hatch from the eggs settle after two or three days in the position where the rest of their development will take place.

The oval-shaped immature forms often look like scale insects. Some species produce very long, thick waxy threads, which look like white hairs.

PLANTS ATTACKED   A wide range. The greenhouse whitefly (*Trialeurodes vaporariorum*) has the largest host range including tomatoes and beans. The azalea whitefly (*Pealius azaleae*) is found on rhododendron species; the sugarcane whitefly (*Neomaskellia bergii*) on sugar cane and various grasses; and the Australian citrus whitefly (*Orchamoplatus citri*) on various citrus. There are also whiteflies that live on ferns.

CONTROL   Small populations of whitefly can usually be ignored, particularly if they are on ornamentals in a garden.

• Organic/non-chemical: If day temperatures are at least 23°C and night temperatures at least 20°C, the numbers of greenhouse whitefly (*Trialeurodes vaporariorum*) may be reduced by a parasitic wasp (*Encarsia formosa*).Parasitised nymphs (the scalelike structures) are black. (Whitefly traps are useful — see page 39.)

• Chemical: If chemical control is necessary, use dimethoate. Observe withholding periods.

Adults and nymphs. Black nymphs have been parasitised.

Whitefringed weevil

Graphognathus leucoloma

These insects are long-lived and can cause considerable damage in an area once they have become established. The adults chew the edges of leaves, but the larvae cause much more serious damage by chewing pits and furrows in tap roots and other underground plant parts such as potato tubers.

The legless larvae are whitish grubs with brown heads and curved bodies. They begin about 1 mm long and are about 12 mm when fully grown. Many larvae are seen in spring at depths of from 50-150 mm. They pupate in the soil, and the weevils push their way to the surface and feed on nearby plants.

The adults, which are about 12 mm long and dark grey to brownish-black in colour with a white band along each side of the body, can be seen throughout summer and autumn. They are not able to fly but can walk for considerable distances.

PLANTS ATTACKED The larvae may feed on the root systems of fruit trees, ornamental trees and shrubs, and weeds. Many vegetables are attacked, particularly fleshy-rooted ones such as carrots and turnips. Potatoes, tomatoes, beans, cabbages, broccoli, strawberries, carnations and chrysanthemums are also attacked.

CONTROL

• Organic/non-chemical: Leaving the soil completely bare for a period of time may reduce infestation. This could include forking the soil over at regular intervals so that any larvae present are turned up to the surface and perhaps eaten by birds. If more than one or two adults are discovered they should be destroyed. Remove weeds, particularly those with tap roots.

• Chemical: There is no chemical recommended for control in a home garden.

White louse scale *Unaspis citri*

The infestation begins on the trunk and may not be noticed for a considerable period of time. The male scale covers are white and only about 1 mm long. A few scattered on the trunk would go unnoticed. The female scale covers are brown and, although longer (2 mm), are even harder to see on the bark.

As the infestation builds up, however, the trunk develops a white, almost powdery look, which is partly fine white webbing produced by the small predatory larvae of a moth. The scales gradually spread to the branches and twigs. A tree with scales on small twigs leaves and fruit has been neglected for a number of years.

This scale can cause serious weakening of the tree, including dieback of branches, and predisposes the tree to attack by other pests such as longicorns (P). Leaves may develop yellow spots and fall.

PLANTS ATTACKED Citrus.

CONTROL Parasites and predators help to keep this scale under control but an annual or biennial application of wettable sulphur at the rate of 5 g per litre of water is necessary to keep the tree in good health. Apply to the trunk and branches in late autumn, winter or spring.

An application of lime-sulphur every second year also controls this pest. Apply only in winter according to label directions.

Serious infestation of white louse scale

White palm scale *Phenacaspis eugeniae*

These hard scales are found most commonly under the leaves of the plant, but if a large population develops, they may also be found on upper leaf surfaces. Like other scales, these insects suck sap and the upper leaf surfaces develop yellow blotches wherever they are feeding. Eventually, if no control measures are adopted, the leaves wither and die as the population of scales increases.

The female scale is white, pear-shaped and about 2.5 mm long. The male scales are smaller and covered with a white cottony substance which obscures their outline. They are often found in groups. There may be several generations in one year.

PLANTS ATTACKED Palms, magnolias, New South Wales Christmas bushes, geebungs, lillypillies, viburnums and others.

CONTROL Spray with 10 mL of white oil per litre of water on hardy shrubs. On palms and soft-foliaged plants, reduce the concentration of white oil. Do not apply on hot days. Do not allow excess spray to run into pots when treating potted plants.

Whitestemmed gum moth *Chelepteryx collesi*

This large moth has a pattern of wavy grey-brown lines on the wings, which spread to about 150 mm. The body is covered thickly with off-white hairs. There is one generation per year. The eggs hatch in the wintertime, and the larvae are fully fed and ready to pupate by the middle of summer.

The larvae grow to about 110 mm long and are covered with tufts of sharp spines or hairs, which can easily break off if they are handled. This is like having a number of very fine splinters in the skin. The larvae are very efficient feeders, and do little damage compared to the size to which they grow. They usually rest in cracks in the bark during the day and feed at night. They roam about from tree to tree, causing slight damage to a number of trees rather than serious damage to one.

Pupation occurs in a tough, dark-grey cocoon covered with the hairs that protected them as larvae. These cocoons and larvae should be handled very carefully (wear gloves) as they cause serious skin reactions in some people .

PLANTS ATTACKED Scribbly gums (*Eucalyptus haemastoma*) and brush boxes (*Lophostemon confertus*).

CONTROL

• Organic/non-chemical: A band of sacking around the tree high on the trunk may be useful when the larvae are young; they are likely to gather here during the day and can be removed.

• Chemical: Spray with maldison.

Pupal case attached to bark

White wax scale

Ceroplastes destructor

The mature scales, which are found on the twigs, are all females and their protective white or greyish-white waxy coverings may reach 10 mm long by 7 mm high. Each is capable of laying approximately 1000 eggs, which look like grains of very fine sand and are easily seen because they are bright pink.

When they hatch the young scales or crawlers move out on to the leaves to feed for five to six weeks. Here they settle down along the main veins of the leaf and begin to produce their waxy covering which makes them look rather like small white stars. Later on, they move back to the twigs and produce more wax. The shape of this wax is reminiscent of a mountain peak, and the insect is referred to as being at the 'peak' stage. As they get older, more wax is produced until a lump of more rounded shape develops. This is termed the 'dome' stage. All this takes approximately one year.

The sap-sucking of these insects does not cause a great deal of damage. However, the honeydew they produce attracts ants and makes the plant sticky wherever it falls. The sooty mould (D) which grows on the honeydew disfigures the plant and may reduce photosynthesis.

PLANTS ATTACKED A range of plants including citrus, gardenias, waxflowers, barberries, bay trees and firethorns.

CONTROL

A neglected citrus tree may be covered with white wax scales. Many of these will be dead and it is probably a good idea to remove a lot of this material manually with a small stiff brush such as a toothbrush.

Spraying must occur when the young are on the leaves for easiest control (mid-December to mid-January). At this stage it is possible to spray with white oil (at the rate of 20 mL per litre of water), and achieve a good kill. The white oil and water spray will cause little mortality among other insects such as parasitic wasps.

Control is much more difficult if the scales are in the 'peak' or 'dome' stage because they are well protected. In the past, washing soda has been suggested for removal of scales at this stage. This treatment may cause leaf fall, however, and the damage to the plant caused by the treatment is probably just as bad as the damage to the plant caused by the scales. It is probably far better to remember to treat the scales in the following summer at the right time.

Wingless grasshopper

Phaulacridium vittatum

Eggs are laid in the soil, usually in small bare areas, and hatch in spring. The young nymphs feed on very low-growing plants and do not move far, but older nymphs feed on a wider variety of plants.

By summer there are many adults present. In hot weather when pastures dry off there may be movement of large numbers of adults into nearby orchards or gardens. Attack on fruit trees usually begins in the lower branches. Surfaces may be chewed from the fruit and the edges from the leaves.

The adults are greyish-brown and often paler on the top than at the sides. They may have white stripes at the side. If the population is large, they may be very dark brown. They are never green. Adult females are 12–18 mm long, but the males are smaller. The wings are usually short and pointed and cannot be used for flying, but there are some winged forms.

PLANTS ATTACKED Many broad-leafed plants including fruit trees, vegetables, ornamentals and weeds.

CONTROL

• Organic/non-chemical: There are no satisfactory non-chemical control methods.

• Chemical: Spray with dimethoate, carbaryl or fenthion. Follow label directions.

Woolly aphid *Eriosoma lanigerum*

These aphids feed on the root system and the woody above-ground parts of the tree. They are also found around the fruit stalks on apples and at the calyx end. The aphids are purple-brown, but as they develop they gradually cover themselves with masses of white waxy threads. Look for them in cracks in the bark, in pruning scars or on new growth. They are able to attack only where the bark is still thin on new growth or because it has been damaged.

Their feeding stimulates the production of woody galls. Heavily infested trees become very open and twisted in appearance because lateral growth is distorted and buds are destroyed. Sooty mould (D) grows in honeydew produced by the aphids, and their sticky white wax is a great disadvantage when fruit picking. Fruit may also fall before ripening.

The aphids feed on the root system throughout the year. Above ground, however, the population decreases in autumn as aphids migrate to the root system and increases again as the weather warms up in spring and they move up on to the new growth. This pest prefers shaded situations and is most likely to be found on inside parts of dense trees or those shaded by nearby windbreaks or other trees. It is more likely to be a problem in cool, moist areas.

PLANTS ATTACKED A serious pest of apple trees, it also attacks crabapples, hawthorns, firethorns, cotoneasters and very occasionally pears.

CONTROL

• Organic/non-chemical: On ornamental trees and shrubs, this aphid is usually kept under control by a small black wasp (*Aphelinus mali*) which lays its eggs in aphid bodies. The wasp eggs hatch and the wasp larvae develop inside the aphids and destroy them. Parasitised aphids lose their wax and turn black. Apple trees on 'Northern Spy' or Malling-Merton rootstocks, however, are not seriously attacked because the aphids cannot successfully feed on the roots.

• Chemical: On apple trees which are being sprayed for other pests, these wasps are often killed. Spraying for woolly aphid then becomes necessary. Use dimethoate. Spray thoroughly into cracks and crevices and branch junctions. Control may be difficult, because the aphid population on the roots is hard to contact.

Woolly giant mealybug

Monophlebulus pilosior

This native Australian insect sucks sap but is never present in sufficient numbers to cause damage. It is oval in shape and orange or pinkish-orange with black markings. It develops a mass of very long thin white waxy threads over the body as it matures. It is related to the cottony-cushion scale (P).

PLANTS ATTACKED This insect is often found on wattles and on the water gum (*Tristaniopsis laurina*).

CONTROL Not necessary.

Woollybear caterpillar

Spilosoma glatignyi

These are the larvae of some of the moths in family Arctiidae. They are thickly covered with bands of black and brown hairs which may cause rashes if they come into contact with human skin.

The moths are very variable in colour and have a wingspan of about 50 mm. In one colour form the abdomen is red, and the white wings are patterned in reddish-brown to almost black.

PLANTS ATTACKED A wide range of herbaceous plants in wasteland, native bush and in gardens.

CONTROL

• Organic/non-chemical: Handpick larvae. Be sure to wear gloves.

• Chemical: Spray the caterpillars with carbaryl. Add wetting agent.

Yellow peach moth   *Conogethes punctiferalis*

The caterpillars are pinkish with darker oval spots and may grow up to 35 mm long. They are fully grown in about three weeks in summer. On macadamias the insects bore into nuts that occur in clusters, where they can shelter. This space may be filled with webbing and sawdusty material called 'frass'.

On sweet corn plants, the larvae tunnel in the nodes of the stem. This causes the plant to grow less vigorously and weakens it so that it may fall over later when the cobs are heavy. The holes where the caterpillars have entered the stalk are usually covered with frass.

On papaws the caterpillars often feed in the main growing point, and this may cause dieback. Branches further down may start growing more vigorously. The larvae may also tunnel into the fruit, usually where one fruit touches another.

Caterpillars feed around the stones of peaches. Gum may exude from the surface if the fruit is green.

The moth's wings, which span about 25 mm, are bright yellow or orange with some black spots in irregular rows.

PLANTS ATTACKED   These include peaches, macadamias, papaws, guavas and sweet corn. Also crops such as sorghum and cotton.

CONTROL   Not easy if infestation is well established.

• Organic/non-chemical: Remove and destroy infested fruit. Try Dipel®.

• Chemical: Spray with carbaryl. Begin within two weeks of petal fall on stonefruit and repeat every two or three weeks.

Pinned specimens. Adult moth has a wingspan of approximately 25 mm.

Larva and damage on custard apple

A-Z of
DISEASES

An alphabetical listing of more than two hundred plant diseases and related problems, with notes on their recognition and control

Control recommendations

The disease control programs are divided, for the most part, into Organic/Non-chemical and Chemical.

Organic/Non-chemical methods are vital for those who want to employ only procedures known as 'organic'. Non-chemical controls are also an important part of control for all gardeners.

Also, in the Chemical suggestions there is usually a chemical solution that conforms to organic requirements. Mostly, the pesticides available for home gardeners for disease control are, in fact, products acceptable to 'organic' gardeners.

Angular leaf spot — bean

Phaeoisariopsis griseola

This fungal disease causes rounded spots of about 10 mm in diameter on the primary leaves. Much smaller spots, say 2–3 mm across, occur on the trifoliolate leaves. These spots have an angular appearance because they are usually bounded by veins. Sometimes small, black, bristle-like structures are visible on the lower surfaces of the spots. Symptoms on the pods are dark sunken patches. Because the pods are attacked, the seed inside can be infected and so carry the disease to a new crop, perhaps in a new area. The seed can also be contaminated at harvest when plant debris attacked by the fungus comes in contact with it. The disease is favoured by cool showery weather and it can be spread quite rapidly through a patch of beans by wind-driven rain.
PLANTS AFFECTED French beans. The variety called 'Redlands Greenleaf' is resistant to this disease.
CONTROL
• Organic/non-chemical: Destroy plant debris as soon as harvesting is finished. Use disease-free seed. Plant a resistant variety. This disease may not be a problem where plants are being sprayed for other fungal diseases such as rust (D).

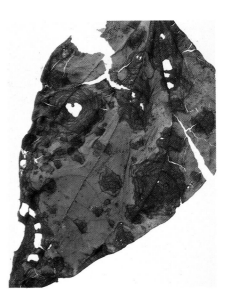

Angular leaf spot on pumpkin

Angular leaf spot — cucurbits

Pseudomonas syringae pv. *lachrymans*

The bacteria that cause this disease are spread by splashing or running water and on the hands or the clothing of people who work on the plants. They enter the plant through wounds, stomates or hydathodes. This disease is more likely to occur in warm humid conditions.

Look for small watersoaked spots on the leaves. These grow to about 3 mm in diameter. They are angular and appear brown on the upper surface of the leaf, and shiny or white underneath. The spot centres may dry and crack and fall away. Spots can occur on leafstalks, stems and fruit. Immature fruit may fall. Fruit may develop brown rot under the spot, and the bacterial ooze may dry to form a white crusty material.
PLANTS AFFECTED Cucumbers, particularly those termed 'Lebanese cucumbers', and also rockmelons, watermelons and squash.
CONTROL
• Organic/non-chemical: Crop rotation is important. Destroy diseased plant material as soon as possible. Do not work on these plants when they are wet, and plant only seed that has come from healthy crops.
• Chemical: Spray with copper oxychloride or copper hydroxide.

Angular leaf spot — zinnia

Xanthomonas campestris pv. *zinniae*

This disease is seed-borne. In the damp conditions necessary for seedling growth, leaf spots enlarge rapidly and the growing tips may be killed. Losses may be great.

On older leaves, spots are usually angular but they may be circular. They are reddish to dark brown, 1–4 mm across and often surrounded by a yellow ring or 'halo'.

Leaf-spotting can severely disfigure the foliage and adversely affect plant vigour.
PLANTS AFFECTED Zinnias (*Z. elegans*).
CONTROL
• Organic/non-chemical: Remove infected plants and destroy them as soon as they are observed. Check the source of the seed.

Mature leaves

Seedling leaves

Anthracnose — avocado

Glomerella cingulata var. *minor*

The fungus that causes this disease can live in dead twigs on the plant as well as in leaves and fruit. Spores from these areas are spread about in warm wet weather. Those that reach the fruit begin growth but very soon go into a state of dormancy. The fungus begins growing actively only if the fruit is damaged or when it begins to ripen. The first symptoms to be seen are small, light-brown, circular spots, which quickly get bigger and darker. The centres of the spots may be slightly sunken, and if the fruit is cut through the spread of the rot into the flesh appears semi-circular.

Masses of pink powdery spores are produced on the outside of the skin if conditions are moist.

PLANTS AFFECTED This is a disease of avocados, but some cultivars are more susceptible than others. 'Fuerte', 'Nabal' and 'Rincon' are frequently attacked.

CONTROL
• Organic/non-chemical: Clip the fruit from the tree and handle it carefully to avoid damage. Store it in a cool well-ventilated area. Prune out dead twigs.
• Chemical: Spray with copper oxychloride. Begin this programme at flowering time and continue until harvest, approximately once a month. If the weather conditions are wet and showery, the tree may need to be sprayed more often. Wetting agent is not necessary.

Anthracnose — bean *Colletotrichum lindemuthianum*

On small plants this fungal disease causes dark-brown marks about 12 mm long on the stems. It is most obvious, however, on larger plants, where spots may appear on leaves, stems and pods. Leaf veins become black. This is clear from the lower surface. On the pods, small reddish-brown spots develop into large black sunken craters up to 12 mm across. In moist conditions a pink colour may appear on these spots. This is masses of spores. Once the pods are infected, the seeds within can easily become infected and thus the disease can be transferred to another crop if these seeds are used. Long black sunken marks may appear on the stems and leafstalks.

PLANTS AFFECTED A variety of legumes including French beans, mung beans and lima beans.

CONTROL
• Organic/non-chemical: Use disease-free seed. If you save your own seed, ensure that it comes from disease-free plants. Do not plant beans for at least two years in an area where this disease has occurred. Plant resistant varieties of beans if possible.

Do not pick or cultivate in a crop when it is wet, because this will quickly spread the spores from plant to plant. Remove diseased plants and destroy them.
• Chemical: Spray with mancozeb or zineb. Wet the undersides of the leaves as well as the tops.

Anthracnose — cucurbits

Colletotrichum orbiculare

Reddish-brown to black spots appear on the leaves. These spots are roughly circular and have a watersoaked edge. On the stems the spots are sunken and elongated. If conditions continue to be suitable for the fungus (moist), these spots may spread around the stem, and the runner will wilt and die.

Sometimes masses of pink spores appear on the round sunken fruit spots. Even if fruit from an infected crop appears normal at harvest, it will probably develop symptoms during transit or storage.

The plants may be initially infected from diseased crop trash or infected seed. Once there are a few plants in a crop that are diseased, it is spread throughout the crop by wind-blown rain, animals (including humans) and implements.

PLANTS AFFECTED This fungal disease is most common on watermelons, but it may attack rockmelons and cucumbers.

CONTROL
• Organic/non-chemical: Crop rotation is important. Removing diseased leaves promptly may help. Do not grow cucurbits in the same soil more than once every four years or save seed from infected crops.
• Chemical: Spray with mancozeb if necessary.

Well developed spots on pumpkin

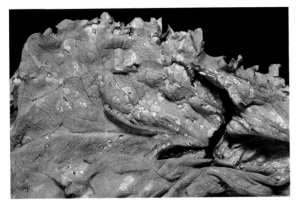

Anthracnose — lettuce

Marssonina panattoniana

The first sign of this fungal disease is tiny spots on the leaves. The spots enlarge to about 4 mm in diameter and change colour from yellow to brown with a reddish margin. The centres may dry and fall out. If the plants are heavily infected, they may be stunted.

This disease is favoured by cool wet weather. In wet weather, spores produced on the sunken spots have a pinkish colour.

PLANTS AFFECTED Lettuces.

CONTROL

• Organic/non-chemical: Use only disease-free seed, practise crop rotation, improve air circulation, improve drainage. Remove old lettuce plants and pieces of lettuce from the area and destroy.

• Chemical: If spraying is necessary, use mancozeb.

Anthracnose — macadamia nut

Colletotrichum gloeosporioides var. *minor*

This fungus produces different symptoms on different macadamias. On *Macadamia integrifolia* the first symptom usually noticed is a soft brown spot about 10 mm across; this enlarges until the whole husk is rotted, but the shell and kernel are not affected. On hybrids of *Macadamia integrifolia* and *Macadamia tetraphylla* many small brown spots about 4 mm in diameter occur on the husk but the kernel is unaffected.

This fungus lives in dead twigs and leaves and is spread about by water splash.

PLANTS AFFECTED Macadamias.

CONTROL   This has not been found necessary.

Spots on nut from hybrid tree

Anthracnose — mango

Colletotrichum gloeosporioides var. *minor*

On the leaves this fungus causes small black spots which may enlarge to form large dry areas that often crack. Pieces of the leaf then fall out. Sometimes spots are more common along the margins or along the main vein. If flowers are affected, small black spots spread out, and the flowers die and fall.

If young fruit is infected, it may fall. On older fruit, small black spots grow into dark-brown or black irregular patches. In humid conditions pink spores often appear in the centres of the discoloured areas. If green fruit is infected, the fungus may remain dormant until the fruit ripens.

The fungus lives in dead parts of the plant, and spores are spread from these areas to leaves and fruit, flowers by water splash.

PLANTS AFFECTED Mangos.

CONTROL

• Organic/non-chemical: Prune off all dead plant parts.

• Chemical: Spray with mancozeb every week while the blossoms are on the tree, then every four weeks until harvest. If weather is dry when the plant blossoms, fewer sprays may be required.

Anthracnose — poplar *Sphaceloma populi*

This fungus causes leaf spots 3–4 mm across, which may coalesce into larger damaged areas. The spots tend to be concentrated along the veins. They may also occur on petioles (leafstalks).
PLANTS AFFECTED Lombardy poplars (*Populus nigra* 'Italica').
CONTROL   This may be unnecessary on a large tree.
• Organic/non-chemical: Treat young plants by pruning off badly affected stems.
• Chemical: Try an application of zineb following label directions.

Anthracnose — rose *Sphaceloma rosarum*

The spots caused by this fungus may be watersoaked at first, but by the time they are noticed they are probably black with a very distinct and clear-cut edge. They are small and circular. As they enlarge the centre dries out and becomes grey. The edge of the spot goes purple and the centre may fall out to give a shot-hole appearance. The leaves go yellow but not to the same extent as with black spot (D) disease. Defoliation is not as serious either. Spots may occur on stems and flowers, but not very often.
   Spores of this fungus are spread by wind and it is worse in cool humid weather. It is not common in warm coastal areas.
PLANTS AFFECTED Roses, some varieties more than others. The common rose rootstock, *Rosa multiflora*, is very susceptible.
CONTROL
• Organic/non-chemical: Lower humidity by improving air circulation around the plants. Ensure the plants are in the sun almost all day.
• Chemical: Spray with copper oxychloride. If the plants are being sprayed for black spot, that spray programme will control this disease as well.

Anthracnose — tomato

Colletotrichum gloeosporioides

This is principally a disease of ripe or ripening fruit. The first symptoms on tomato are small, round, watersoaked and slightly depressed spots. Later these develop into saucer-shaped depressions about 12 mm across with concentric rings. Dark specks on the tan-coloured centre are fungal fruiting bodies and contain spores. There may be so many that the centre of the depression is black.
   If the weather is about 25°C and very humid, the spots will continue to spread and the whole fruit will be rotted. Seed in diseased fruit will become infected. Pieces of diseased fruit left in the soil will be a source of infection for other crops.
   The problem occurs most on fruit near or on the soil and is spread about by splashing water.
PLANTS AFFECTED A wide range.
CONTROL
• Organic/non-chemical: Use only healthy seed. Practise crop rotation. Harvest fruit before it ripens.
• Chemical: Spray with zineb or copper hydroxide. Start when fruit begins to ripen.

Apple mosaic

The symptoms of this virus disease are varied and appear only on some leaves of the plant. They may be light or dark-green mottles or various patterns of yellow or creamy-yellow. They may consist of flecks or patches, and different patterns may be seen on the one tree. Symptoms do not usually occur on leaves that grow while temperatures are above 27°C.

The leaves thus affected are very susceptible to sunburn and may fall early. There are no fruit symptoms, although it has been shown that the fruit crop is reduced on infected trees. Trees that have the disease are not sources of infection for others nearby, because the virus is only transmitted during the propagation process. It is not transmitted by insects.

PLANTS AFFECTED Commonly seen on older apples and crabapples. 'Jonathan' is a variety that is commonly infected.

CONTROL When buying an apple or crabapple, ensure that it is propagated from virus-tested stock and the tree will be free of this disease for its lifetime. A virus, once inside an individual plant, cannot be got out again.

No amount of spraying, organic or otherwise, will rid the plant of the virus.

Apple scab *Venturia inaequalis*

Apple scab symptoms on leaves

The symptoms of this disease — which is also known as black spot — are usually seen first on the leaves. Look for spots about 3 mm in diameter that are a different green. The spots gradually darken and become black. The spots may grow into one another to form large patches. In severe cases, small distorted leaves may result.

The fruit develops black spots which age to brown and go corky in the centre, with irregular margins. Fruit infected when small develops deep cracks and becomes misshapen. Fruit infected when it is more or less fully formed will have only surface blemishes and will be quite edible.

Spores that grow on the surface of the spots are splashed from leaf to leaf and fruit to fruit in showery weather and produce new infections. The fungus continues to develop in fallen leaves in winter, and in spring spores are released to infect the new leaves and flowers. If the weather is such that the leaves remain wet for ten hours at a temperature of 14.5°C, for longer at lower temperatures or a shorter time at higher temperatures, infection will probably occur. In some regions, warnings to growers are broadcast when these conditions have occurred so that spray programmes can be timed accurately.

PLANTS AFFECTED 'Granny Smith' and 'Delicious' are the most susceptible varieties. 'Jonathan', 'Gravenstein' and others are infected occasionally. This disease is very like pear scab, although the fungus causing apple scab cannot attack pears, and vice versa.

CONTROL
• Organic/non-chemical: Rake up and bury all leaves in the autumn.
• Chemical: Regular applications of fungicides are necessary. Spray with copper oxychloride or copper hydroxide, at greentip stage (early to mid-September), and again 14 days later. Then spray every 14 days with mancozeb. Stop about the end of October unless the weather is wet.

Apple scab symptoms on crabapple

Apple scab symptoms on 'Granny Smith'

Armillaria root rot   *Armillaria* spp.

Leaves on affected plants may brown around the edges. On some plant species the leaves yellow and fall. Wilting and dieback are common. Citrus trees may set a very heavy fruit crop in spring but collapse and die when the weather gets hot in summer and the soil dries out.

The roots of affected trees may have a white sheath of fungal hyphae in or under the bark. It has a strong mushroomy smell. The wood may be dry and powdery or wet and jelly-like. Long thin black structures (which look a little like shoe-laces) are characteristic of this fungus and can spread the infection from root to root and plant to plant by growing through the soil. The fungus that causes the problem is a weak parasite on native trees and can also grow on old roots and stumps. It spreads from these to newly planted trees and shrubs.

In humid autumn weather if the soil is moist, yellowish-brown toadstools grow up from the rotted roots and appear on the soil surface.

PLANTS AFFECTED A wide range of woody ornamentals and other smaller plants such as strawberries. Fruit trees are commonly attacked.

CONTROL
• Organic/non-chemical: Clear bushland thoroughly, preferably a year or two before establishing an orchard or garden. Remove and burn all large roots. Trees that are in the early stages of attack can be treated by exposing the roots to air to a distance of about 600 mm around the butt. Cut off and burn damaged roots. Do not replace the soil for several years. Treat surrounding trees in the same way even if they do not yet exhibit symptoms.

Remove and burn badly affected trees, including the roots. If replanting in the area is necessary, fumigate the soil. Consult your local Department of Agriculture.

Fungal fruiting bodies

Bacterial black spot — mango

Xanthomonas campestris pv. *mangiferaeindicae*

The symptoms of this disease on the fruit are black oval raised spots with a gummy exudate. On the leaves, the disease first shows up as greasy areas, which darken and develop into black angular raised areas. These small patches often have a narrow yellow edge and one or two straight sides, because they tend to be restricted by the veins of the leaf. If the leaf spots grow together, then black areas extending from the midrib to the margin may occur. On the stems there are black cankers filled with gum.

The disease may occur in combination with a fungal disease called anthracnose (D) which is also very common. The fungal disease has circular spots on leaves and fruit and often masks the bacterial disease.

PLANTS AFFECTED Mangos.

CONTROL
• Organic/non-chemical: This is difficult. Consult your local Department of Agriculture for a positive diagnosis and advice about a control programme. Avoid exposed areas when planting. Outbreaks of this disease may be associated with low soil nutrient levels.

Bacterial blight — mulberry

Pseudomonas syringae pv. *mori*

This disease first attacks young leaves as they burst from the bud and may cause them to blacken. Leaves that are infected later develop small brown or black angular spots, which are often surrounded by a yellow area. The leaves may become severely distorted if they are rapidly growing when infected, because growth stops wherever bacteria are present, but the rest of the leaf keeps growing.

Cankers may develop on young shoots and they may be killed. Millions of bacteria ooze out of such cankers when the weather is wet and are spread by rain to other leaves and shoots. The twigs die back on an infected tree, and consequently young trees do not grow well.

PLANTS AFFECTED Mulberries.

CONTROL
• Organic/non-chemical: This is difficult. Prune out and burn all dead shoots in the autumn. Prune off and destroy blighted shoots as soon as they are noticed.
• Chemical: Try spraying with copper oxychloride when the buds are swelling, and again two weeks later. Further applications may be necessary.

Bacterial blight — pea

Pseudomonas syringae pv. *pisi*

These bacteria enter the plant through stomates and through wounds. Symptoms may appear on all above-ground parts and are more likely in cool to warm damp weather. Frost damage may initiate this and a few related diseases.

The disease is introduced into an area on infected seed. Plants growing from this seed are likely to develop watersoaked spots on the stem near ground level. These spots darken to purplish-brown, and the stem may be shrivelled and thin. Bacteria spread from these plants to produce symptoms on others.

On leaflets and stipules, lesions often fan out from the base. They are watersoaked at first and then change colour through yellow to brown. They dry out and become papery.

On pods, the spots are dark green and watersoaked at first but go dark brown. They are most common along the edges of the pods. In wet conditions a cream-coloured slimy exudate may be seen on these spots. Young infected pods shrivel.

PLANTS AFFECTED Peas, sweet peas and a few related plants.

CONTROL

• Organic/non-chemical: Use disease-free seed. Do not save seeds from diseased plants. Practise a three-year crop rotation. Remove 'volunteer' plants promptly. Do not work on a wet crop.

Bacterial brown spot — bean

Pseudomonas syringae pv. *syringae*

Small rounded reddish-brown spots on the leaves are characteristic of this disease. They may be bounded by veins and are often surrounded by a pale green area. The leaf may become tattered as the centres of the spots dry out and tear.

Spots on the stems are about 10 mm across with reddish-brown margins. Sunken brown watersoaked spots appear on the pods, and the bacteria can enter seed that is forming there.

Infection often occurs in areas where rust (D) has already damaged the plants. Plants damaged by blowing sand or by frost are also more susceptible to this disease. Cool showery weather creates more problems, because bacteria are easily spread from plant to plant in wind-driven rain.

PLANTS AFFECTED Beans: French beans and kidney beans.

CONTROL

• Organic/non-chemical: It is important to use only disease-free seed. Plant resistant varieties if possible. Do not work on diseased plants when they are wet with rain or dew. Remove and destroy diseased plants and those nearby. Crop rotation is recommended, because the bacteria can survive for more than a year in pieces of old bean plant that are left from a previous crop.

• Chemical: Spray with copper hydroxide if necessary.

The leaf tears as the damaged areas dry out.

Bacterial canker — stonefruit

Pseudomonas syringae pv. *syringae*

The bacteria responsible for this disease are always present on the leaves of stonefruit and a wide range of other plants. They are able to enter the plant and cause disease if the plant is injured during autumn, winter or early spring. Actively growing trees are resistant to infection. Natural occurrences such as wind-driven rain or hailstorms damage the bark and tear leaves from the tree. The bacteria may also enter the plant through leaf scars in autumn when the leaves fall. Entry is more likely if conditions are wet and windy. Pruning wounds and storm damage to branches are also possible areas of infection.

The problem is worst on young trees. Severe infection causes wilting and death of branches. Gum exudes from trunk and branches, and cankers are produced. New shoots may wilt and die back. Buds may die and leaves show brown spots. Fruit develops dark sunken spots.

PLANTS AFFECTED All stonefruit. Apricots are highly susceptible, as are cherries. The cherry cultivars 'Florence', 'Napoleon', 'William's Favourite' and 'St Margaret' are highly susceptible; least-susceptible cultivars are Merton types 'Ron's Seedling' and 'Van'. Nectarines, peaches and plums are generally less susceptible than apricots and cherries.

CONTROL
• Organic/non-chemical: Consult your local Department of Agriculture. In general, control involves the following procedures: prune only when trees are actively growing (generally late summer before autumn leaf-fall) so that wounds can heal over before rain splashes spores on to the cut surface. Avoid damage to the trunk and branches from mowers and other machinery. Prune out and burn infected limbs during summer. Disinfect saws and secateurs frequently. Avoid overhead watering. Badly infected small trees should be replaced because they will never produce well.
• Chemical: Spray programmes involve application of Bordeaux mixture, or copper oxychloride, particularly at leaf-fall. Copper sprays can damage and defoliate trees in leaf. Commercial growers often find it necessary to apply up to six sprays from early leaf-fall to bud-swell.

Bacterial canker — tomato

Clavibacter michiganensis subsp. *michiganensis*

Plants may become diseased because they have been grown from infected seed or because the soil in which they are planted contains pieces of infected plant debris. Diseased seed usually produces plants that look healthy even until they are nearing maturity, but then the disease progresses rapidly.

The first symptom is wilting of lower leaves, often on one side only. Wilting progresses up the plant. Affected plants are stunted and develop yellow to brown streaks on stems and leafstalks which may later crack open. If the stems were cut open, cavities would be seen and brown streaks would indicate the damaged vascular system.

In damp weather bacteria splashed from leaves and stems cause spots about 3 mm across on the fruit. These begin slightly raised and white, then develop a light-brown rough centre. The white colour around the edge remains.

PLANTS AFFECTED Tomatoes and solanaceous weeds such as nightshades (*Solanum* spp.) and thornapples (*Datura* spp.).

CONTROL
• Organic/non-chemical: Practise crop rotation: 4–5 years between tomato crops is desirable. Ensure that seed is free from disease by treating it before planting. (Seek advice from your local Department of Agriculture.) Remove weeds, particularly those related to tomatoes. Remove and burn diseased plants. Wash hands and tools in warm soapy water after touching diseased plants. Avoid overhead watering.
• Chemical: Spray with copper hydroxide.

Infected leaf from young plant curls to one side and the leaflets begin to shrivel.

Bacterial gall — oleander

Pseudomonas syringae pv. *savastanoi* (oleander strain)

These bacteria seem to gain entry to the plant through wounds caused by pruning or insects.

Symptoms can occur on all above-ground plant parts. On younger shoots, longitudinal swellings split open and develop into rough irregular cankers as the plant continues growth. Rough woody galls may appear on midribs, or seed pods. Leaves infected early in their development may become twisted, and seed pods infected early are shorter and thicker. Flowers may also be attacked.

PLANTS AFFECTED Oleanders.

CONTROL Prune off all galls and destroy them. Repeat if more galls appear. Disinfect secateurs between cuts. Keep the plant growing vigorously by fertilising and watering.

Bacterial leaf spot — cucurbits

Xanthomonas campestris pv. *cucurbitae*

Symptoms on zucchini

This bacterial disease causes spots on the leaf. Look first for small water-soaked areas under the leaves, and corresponding faint yellow areas on the upper surface of the leaf. After a few days, these spots are more defined and may be round to angular, with brown translucent centres and with a wide yellow area around them. These spots may be up to 7 mm in diameter and may grow together to form large dead areas. The spots do not tear as in angular leaf spot (D).

Sometimes spots appear on the young stems and petioles, which may subsequently crack. Spots on young pumpkin fruit look watersoaked with a light-brown 'ooze' on the surface. Later the centre of the spot dries rough and pale yellow. On mature fruit, the spots may be 10 mm or more across, with a dark-green greasy margin. The flesh beneath the spots is often affected and the seeds contaminated with bacteria.

The disease is worse in warm humid conditions and spreads in a way common for bacterial diseases: splashing rain or irrigation water, and on tools or clothing or hands.

PLANTS AFFECTED Cucumbers, marrows, pumpkins, and squash.

CONTROL
• Organic/non-chemical: Use disease-free seed. Obtain it from a reputable source or save it from pumpkins completely free from spots. Practise crop rotation, because the bacteria can survive on pieces of plant in the soil. Destroy self-sown plants. Crops with bacterial diseases should not have work done on them in wet weather.
• Chemical: Use copper oxychloride if spraying is necessary.

Bacterial leaf spot — lettuce

Xanthomonas campestris pv. *vitians*

This disease is spread by water splash and is most common in cool wet winters. It is first noticed as translucent spots which are 5–10 mm across. Veins may be blackened. The spots may grow into one another to cause complete leaf collapse. If young plants are infected and prolonged damp weather occurs, then the whole plant may rot. The bacteria do not survive long in the soil once the leaves rot.

PLANTS AFFECTED Lettuces.

CONTROL
• Organic/non-chemical: Use seed from healthy crops. Avoid overhead irrigation. Provide good drainage.

Bacterial leaf spot — lilac

Pseudomonas syringae pv. *syringae*

This disease appears first in early spring as brown watersoaked spots on leaves and very young stems. If the weather is wet, these blacken and enlarge quickly. Young leaves and shoots may be killed. The stems bend where they have been girdled and wither and die.

The spots enlarge more slowly on older stems and leaves. Black sunken areas develop on stems. Blackened, dead buds may remain on the plant for some time.

PLANTS AFFECTED Lilacs (*Syringa vulgaris*), particularly white-flowered varieties.

CONTROL
• Organic/non-chemical: Prune off affected branches and destroy. Avoid excessive nitrogenous fertiliser.
• Chemical: Spray with copper oxychloride.

Bacterial leaf spot — pelargoniums

Xanthomonas campestris pv. *pelargonii*

The leaf symptoms of this disease begin as pinhead-size brown sunken spots which increase in size and large areas may be affected. Leaves go yellow and fall from plant.

The same organism can cause a brown to brownish-black rotting on the stems. This often begins at the top of the stem but may start at the base.

The stem rot caused by the fungus *Pythium* is darker in colour (blackish-green to coal black) and develops more rapidly.

This disease is favoured by warm wet weather.

PLANTS AFFECTED Pelargoniums (geraniums). Seen most on ivy geraniums.

CONTROL
• Organic/non-chemical: Remove and burn infected leaves promptly. Affected branches can be pruned off; make the cut 30–40 mm below the damaged area.

If the base of the stem is rotted, the plant should be removed and burnt. Do not take cuttings from infected plants. Regular spraying may be necessary in warm wet weather.

Avoid overhead watering. Increased spacings between plants may lower humidity and reduce problems with this disease.
• Chemical: Spray with copper oxychloride (50%) at the rate of 2.5 g per litre of water as soon as affected parts have been removed and again a week later.

Bacterial soft rot *Erwinia carotovora* subsp. *carotovora*

The bacteria that cause this disease are common in soil and on plant surfaces. They attack a wide range of succulent plants. They are more likely to cause trouble in damp conditions and if the plant has been damaged by insects or by another disease.

The rot is soft, and usually evil-smelling. It is often slimy. There is no furry growth because this is associated with fungal not bacterial disease.

On potatoes the first symptoms are soft depressed areas around lenticels. On calla lilies the disease starts below ground level and is first seen as watersoaked areas at the bottom of the flower and leafstalks; these rot and fall over. If sweet corn plants are attacked, the stem section just above soil level becomes dark brown, watersoaked and slimy; it eventually collapses. Sometimes vegetables such as carrots and potatoes are contaminated with bacteria at harvest time and rot later in storage. This is one reason for removing such vegetables from the plastic bags they are sold in as soon as possible.

PLANTS AFFECTED This disease affects the more fleshy parts of a wide range of plants. Roots, tubers, fleshy leaf bases, fruit, buds and stems can all be attacked. Vegetables such as crucifers, potatoes, celery and lettuces, and ornamentals such as irises, dahlias and calla lilies.

CONTROL
• Organic/non-chemical: Do not overwater. Do not dig up tubers and other storage organs if the soil is wet: avoid damage at harvest time and store in dry conditions.

Basal rot — daffodil *Fusarium* sp.

This fungal disease starts at the bottom of the bulb, the small hard part where the roots appear. From there the rot spreads up into the scale leaves. If these bulbs are planted, they rot in the soil or produce a few narrow yellowish leaves. The plant usually dies. This rot can occur while the bulbs are being stored and will be worse if the temperature is allowed to rise too high in the storage area.

Before planting the bulbs should be inspected very carefully, although it is not always easy to pick out those that are only slightly damaged. Look around the edge of the base plate where the new roots will emerge. If there is any brown discolouration, investigate further. Remove the outer scales and see if the rot is very extensive. Badly infected bulbs must be destroyed. Sometimes white or faintly pink fungal growth is seen between the inner scales or occasionally outside the bulb at the base.

PLANTS AFFECTED Daffodils.
CONTROL
• Organic/non-chemical: If an area of garden has been planted with bulbs that have basal rot, no further daffodil crops should be grown there for five years and each year the bulbs should be lifted and inspected for this disease. Then plant healthy bulbs in a new area of soil. Fumigation of the soil would be the only thing that would make it ready for replanting daffodils within five years.

The bulbs should be stored in a cool dry place preferably in wire baskets or slatted wooden trays.

It is possible to spread this disease from bulb to bulb during the hot-water treatment recommended for bulb nematode control, so inspect carefully for basal rot before the hot-water treatment.

Do not apply excessive amounts of nitrogenous fertiliser.

Beet rust *Uromyces betae*

This fungal disease appears first on the older leaves and is spread from them to the younger ones growing up in the centre of the plant. It is characterised by rusty-brown, small, dusty spots scattered over the leaf.

PLANTS AFFECTED Silver beet and beet.
CONTROL
• Organic/non-chemical: Plant only disease-free seed. Remove any diseased leaves from the crop and destroy them.
• Chemical: If necessary, spray with zineb or wettable sulphur. Pay particular attention to the underside of the leaf.

Symptoms on aster

Big bud

This disease is caused by a mycoplasma and is spread from plant to plant by the common brown leafhopper (*Orosius argentatus*). It is known also as 'greening' or 'virescence'. Some or all of the petals are green instead of their usual colour. There may be a proliferation of shoots, which gives the plant a very bushy appearance.

In tomatoes the stems are thick and the plant is stiff and upright. Fruit production is greatly reduced.

PLANTS AFFECTED A very wide range, including vegetables such as tomatoes, potatoes, and lettuces; ornamentals including asters, chrysanthemums, geraniums, gerberas, dahlias and zinnias, and weeds such as dock, lamb's-tongue and sow thistle.

CONTROL
- Organic/non-chemical: Remove weeds.
- Chemical: Control leafhoppers with dimethoate or soap sprays.

Bitter pit — apple

This problem is connected with the supply of calcium to the fruit and generally occurs more on young trees, mature trees with small crops, and in larger fruit. Apples towards the outside of the tree are also more susceptible, and heavy pruning seems to make bitter pit more likely.

This condition is characterised by round, usually brown sunken spots on the skin of the fruit, mostly at the end opposite the stalk. They are 3–6 mm in diameter, and if the apple is cut through, cone-shaped areas of dried-out cells are seen beneath the spots. Small spots of similar cells are usually scattered through the flesh of the rest of the fruit. Affected fruit can be stored but often has a bitter flavour.

This problem is more prevalent under particular weather conditions, especially if the fruit is nearing maturity. In heatwaves when the soil is very dry and water is withdrawn from the fruit, symptoms may occur. If heavy rain or irrigation follows a drought period and causes sudden increase in fruit size, then the disease is likely.

PLANTS AFFECTED 'Gravenstein', 'Granny Smith', 'Abas', 'Delicious' and 'Golden Delicious' seem most susceptible, but this may vary from area to area.

CONTROL Time applications of water and fertiliser so that tree growth is even.
- Organic: Use rock phosphate or dolomite in the fertiliser programme.
- Non-organic: Use calcium chloride or calcium nitrate at the rate of 50 g in 10 L of water. Calcium nitrate is better on green varieties. Start in late November and apply three sprays. The last should be a few weeks before harvest. Do not apply if temperature is above 34°C.

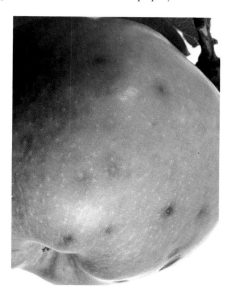

Bitter rot — apple *Glomerella cingulata*

The first signs of infection are small brown spots which usually appear when the fruit is almost fully grown. The rot spreads rapidly and may cover a large part of the fruit in a few days. If conditions continue to be humid, masses of pink spores are formed on the surface of the spot in concentric circles, giving it a target-like appearance. These spores can be splashed to other fruit.

As the spots enlarge they become more and more sunken and the whole piece of fruit may become wrinkled and dried out. It is in this 'mummy' that the fungus can survive and produce spores to reinfect the new fruit in the following season. This would usually occur when temperatures are below 20°C and the fruit is wet.

PLANTS AFFECTED The most serious losses with this disease occur usually on 'Willy Sharp', 'Gravenstein' and 'Granny Smith', although it can attack all varieties.

CONTROL
- Organic/non-chemical: This largely depends on orchard or garden hygiene. Collect and burn all mummified fruit and dead wood. Any fruit that has failed to develop should be removed from the trees. Watch for diseased fruit and remove it quickly. Reduce the humidity in the area by removing long grass. Prune so that the centre of the tree is not dense and bushy. Try to improve the air circulation around a tree, perhaps by removing nearby unwanted trees and shrubs. The fruit will dry more quickly after rain or dew and infection will be less likely.
- Chemical: Spray with zineb, following label directions. Apply the first spray at the beginning of November and spray every two weeks while warm humid weather continues.

Black leg — crucifers *Leptosphaeria maculans*

If this fungus attacks seedlings, a light-brown sunken area develops near ground level and gradually blackens and spreads until the stem is girdled. This causes the death of the seedling.

The first signs of the disease may be wilting. Leaf edges may be slightly red in colour. Plants fall over, and closer inspection will reveal the brown sunken area at ground level.

The stem may appear cracked and corky. Small black dots on this brown area are the fruiting bodies of the fungus, and from here spores can be spread to other plants. Round brown spots with fruiting bodies may also develop on leaves and stems. On fleshy roots such as turnips and swedes, a dry brownish rot develops; this area may have cracks in it and the black fruiting bodies may develop.

This disease is most serious in wet weather because the spores can be spread around in water droplets. The disease is introduced into a crop on infected seed and can remain in the soil on pieces of old plant material for a long time.

PLANTS AFFECTED Crucifers.

CONTROL

• Organic/non-chemical: Use disease-free seed or treat with hot water as described in the section Planning and Maintaining Your Garden. Practise crop rotation, and remove and destroy all pieces of plant material when the crop is harvested.

Symptoms on mature cabbage

Black leg — potato

Erwinia carotovora subsp. *atroseptica*

The bacteria that cause this disease are soil inhabitants and usually attack only if conditions are wet. This could be caused by overwatering or rain after planting. Damage (such as that caused by insects) to the underground parts of the plant would also predispose the plant to infection.

The stem becomes black near ground level, and the rot may proceed rapidly up the stem. The plant may become stiff and the leaves rolled and yellow. The seed tuber usually rots and because the root system has been attacked, the plants are easy to pull out of the ground.

PLANTS AFFECTED Potatoes and a few other plants. 'Sebago' is a highly susceptible variety.

CONTROL

• Organic/non-chemical: Use disease-free (certified) seed potatoes. Use whole seed tubers instead of cut ones. Do not plant in wet soil and do not water until the shoots have appeared above ground level. Avoid mechanical injury to underground parts of plants. If infections have occurred do not use that ground for potatoes for at least one season.

Black mould — onion *Aspergillus niger*

The fungus that causes this problem attacks a wide range of plant material and can live for long periods of time on pieces of any plant material in the soil.

In onions it usually develops only in storage and appears as black powdery masses on the outside of the bulb. As the disease progresses, this black powder is seen between the sections of the onion. These sections, or scales, wither and eventually dry out and become brittle. The black powdery masses can easily be rubbed off, and this distinguishes black mould from some other onion problems.

PLANTS AFFECTED Brown onions are slightly more likely to suffer from this problem than white onions.

CONTROL

• Organic/non-chemical: Depends on harvesting at the correct time and correct storage in a dry well-ventilated situation.

Black pseudo-bulb rot *Pythium ultimum*

The pseudo-bulb may be infected with this fungus at either the base or the top. The roots are not usually damaged.

The rotted tissue is dark brown to very black. (A pinkish look indicates that the fungus responsible is probably *Fusarium*.)

If the infection is progressing from the base, the leaves gradually yellow and wilt.

PLANTS AFFECTED Orchids, particularly cymbidiums.

CONTROL

• Organic/non-chemical: Avoid overwatering. Improve drainage. Discard badly affected plants.

• Chemical: Drench the pots with furalaxyl (Fongarid®) at the rate of 1 g per litre of water. One litre is sufficient for either six 150 mm pots or one 250 mm pot.

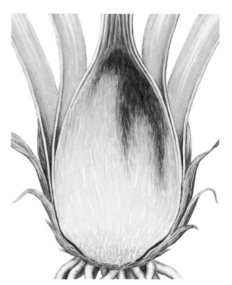

Black root — radish

Aphanomyces raphani

This fungal disease is characterised by irregular black patches on the root. These areas may become sunken, and the root may split. The tissue remains firm unless secondary bacteria or fungi invade the root.

The disease is more common in warm weather and if the soil is moist. Spores can be spread by rain or running water and the fungus can survive for several years in the soil.

PLANTS AFFECTED Radishes. It is more likely to attack long thin radishes than the round radishes.

CONTROL

• Organic/non-chemical: Improve soil drainage. Practise crop rotation, and use round varieties if the soil is known to be infected.

Black rot — cruciferous vegetables

Xanthomonas campestris pv. *campestris*

Leaves of seedlings infected, because of diseased seed or plant debris in the soil, turn pale yellow and go papery. The seedlings may wilt and die. This disease, which is caused by bacteria, can be spread through the crop by splashing water, by insects or by drainage water and even on dust. It is a relatively common disease.

On larger plants it commonly starts around the edge of the leaf, where the bacteria can gain entry to the plant more easily. It may also occur on other parts of the leaf, particularly if the leaf is wounded. V-shaped yellowish-brown areas develop around the margins. These patches increase in size, and areas of leaf that are affected become thin and papery and tear easily. The leaf veins in affected areas become black and eventually the entire area turns orange to dark-brown. If the veins or the stem are cut through, a black or dark brown ring will be seen towards the outside.

Another type of black rot begins as small greasy-looking spots scattered over the leaf. These become pale brown and enlarge. The leaf may become completely tattered as these areas dry out and tear.

PLANTS AFFECTED Crucifers. These bacteria may also cross-infect stocks (*Matthiola incana*) and cause mild symptoms of black rot of stocks (D).

CONTROL

• Organic/non-chemical: Practise crop rotation. Use disease-free seed. Remove and burn all diseased plant material or dig it in and ensure that it is completely decomposed before replanting with crucifers. Control cruciferous weeds such as wild radish (*Raphanus raphanistrum*) and shepherd's purse (*Capsella bursa-pastoris*). Control insects. Avoid overhead irrigation. Avoid overcrowding of seedlings. Seed may be heat-treated as described in the section Planning and Maintaining Your Garden.

Black rot — stock

Xanthomonas campestris pv. *incanae*

This bacterial disease is introduced into a planting with infected seed. Young plants grow slowly and may wilt and die. Lower leaves yellow and fall. Spores can be splashed from these infected plants to others nearby. Plants affected when they are more established may survive to flower, but will probably be stunted. Lower leaves will yellow and fall. Closer examination will reveal black sunken areas where branches and leaves have joined the stem. If the stem is split open, black streaks will be found inside. The disease is worse in warm humid weather.

PLANTS AFFECTED Only stocks.

CONTROL

• Organic/non-chemical: Use seed only from disease-free plants. Even proprietary lines of seed may contain a small proportion of infected seed. Watch seedlings for symptoms, and remove any affected ones together with a small quantity of soil. Burn them promptly. If you save your own seed, it may be advisable to treat it with hot water as described in the section Planning and Maintaining Your Garden.

Practise a two-year crop rotation if the disease has occurred in an area. Although these bacteria affect only stocks to any great extent, it is unwise to plant other crucifers such as cabbages, turnips or wallflowers in the same ground after stocks.

Symptoms on a mature plant

Black spot — grape *Elsinoe ampelina*

This fungal disease is most likely to occur if conditions are damp and temperatures low in the spring. The first symptoms usually appear on the young canes. Brownish-black spots tend to increase in size along the cane rather than around it and develop a sunken centre with a raised margin. Flowers and young fruit will wither and fall if flower stems are attacked.

Spots on the leaves begin grey with a reddish-brown edge but age to black. The centre may fall out of leaf spots, giving the leaf a shot-hole appearance. Fruit spots develop into areas with a grey centre. These also have an associated red band.

PLANTS AFFECTED Sultana grapes more than other grapes.

CONTROL

• Organic/non-chemical: Remove infected canes and young shoots promptly.

• Chemical: Control can be achieved by spraying with mancozeb at bud burst and again 10–14 days later. If the weather continues to be favourable to the fungus — that is, cool and damp — it may be necessary to apply a third spray 14 days after the second spraying.

Black spot — rose *Marssonina rosae*

This fungus causes black spots on the leaves. The spots, which may end up about 12 mm across, are more or less circular and have an irregular or fringed edge. Leaves frequently turn yellow and fall early. Sometimes new leaves are produced, and these may also become infected.

If the plant is continually defoliated in this way it will be weakened. Dieback and death may follow. In very susceptible varieties, young stems are also attacked by this fungus and there will be a reduction in the size and number of flowers as well as dieback of stems.

The problem is worse in humid weather, at temperatures between 13–24°C.

PLANTS AFFECTED Roses. Some cultivars are more susceptible than others.

CONTROL

• Organic/non-chemical: Discard cultivars that become badly affected. Control involves cultural procedures as well as a spray programme. It is important to decrease the humidity around the plants as much as possible. This can be done in various ways. Space the plants correctly at planting time. Do not grow smaller plants such as flowering annuals underneath rose bushes. Do not plant roses in a very sheltered area where air circulation is minimal. Prune so that the centre of the bush is not overgrown. Do not water the plants late in the day so that the leaves remain wet for a long period of time. Do not plant roses in a shady situation. Pick up and burn diseased fallen leaves.

• Chemical: The spray programme should be started when the weather becomes warm and humid and continue on a regular basis if conditions remain the same. Use zineb or triforine. This will control anthracnose (D) of rose also.

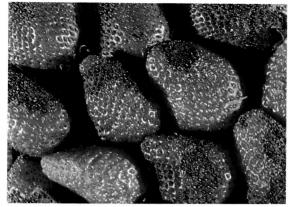

Black spot — strawberry
Colletotrichum acutatum

This fungus infects leaves and green fruit but remains dormant until leaves age and fruit ripens. Circular black spots about 3 mm in diameter appear on ripe or nearly ripe fruit. These spots enlarge to about 20 mm and become sunken. In humid weather white fungal growth and masses of pink spores can be seen on the spots.

Dead leaves and rotting berries can be sources of infection and spores are splashed from them to other plants.

PLANTS AFFECTED Strawberries and other soft fruits grown in warm temperate subtropical or tropical areas. Spores may also be spread during picking. Disease symptoms may develop during storage.

CONTROL
• Organic/non-chemical: Water the plants at a time of day that will allow quick drying of leaves and fruit. Pick thoroughly — never leave any ripe strawberries among the plants.

Black stem rot — pelargonium
Pythium sp.

The fungus that causes this disease is a soil inhabitant, and the symptoms appear first at the base of the stem and then progress upwards. The stem generally blackens and withers, and because the water-conducting cells have been interfered with the plants wilt and die.

This fungus is moved from place to place in water and in soil. The disease is most likely if soil conditions are wet.

PLANTS AFFECTED Regal, ivy and zonal pelargoniums (geraniums).

CONTROL
• Organic/non-chemical: Pull out and burn infected plants. Any replacement cuttings should be taken from branches as far from the soil as possible.
• Chemical: Spray the soil with Fongarid®. Two litres of spray is enough for 0.5–1 square metre of soil. Water the soil after application.

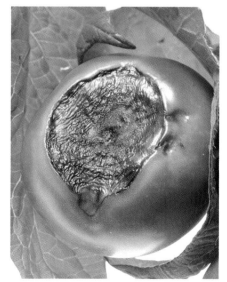

Blossom-end rot

The symptoms of this problem occur only on the fruit at the blossom end, the opposite end to the stalk. The area becomes brown, tough and sunken. Secondary fungal growths may develop in the area. Sometimes in egg tomatoes, this affected tissue might be completely internal and appear as a dark-brown area. This problem is commonly noticed when the fruit is about half-grown.

These symptoms indicate that the supply of the nutrient calcium is not adequate to form the fruit properly. This can arise for several reasons. Firstly, there may not be enough total calcium in the soil. Secondly, the level of other nutrients, which the plant takes up before calcium, may be too high. These problems are made worse if the water supply to the plant fluctuates. Dry conditions and overwatering can both cause problems. Thirdly, if many leaves are forming at the same time as the fruit, the available calcium is usually used for the formation of leaves and is not available to the fruit.

PLANTS AFFECTED Tomatoes and capsicums.

CONTROL The aim is to keep the calcium supply to the fruit even. The soil can be limed or have superphosphate added before the seedlings are planted out. This will supply calcium. Avoid using excessive amounts of fertilisers containing sodium, potassium and ammonium. Organise the drainage so that waterlogging does not occur, and water the plants on a regular basis. Improve soil water-holding capacity by addition of organic matter. In areas where hot dry winds occur, windbreaks should be provided so that the plants do not lose too much water through the leaves.

Boron deficiency

Boron is required in only very small quantities by most plants.

Beetroot, however, needs more boron than many others. In young plants, a deficiency shows up when young leaves die in the centre and many small misshapen leaves grow in their place. If the plant is older, the leaves will develop scorched areas and the stems seem unable to hold them up. Beetroot themselves will develop rough and perhaps black areas at the top or bottom or around the sides. The roots may be hollow with brown areas inside. Black spots are also common.

Boron deficiency in celery is also referred to as 'cat scratch' or 'cracked stem'. The outside stems may crack across, and streaks may appear along the ribs. The stem may be pithy, and tips and edges of young leaves go brown. Older leaves may be mottled.

Cauliflower leaves, in severe cases, will be distorted, and the head will not develop. If some boron has been available to the plant, the head or curd will develop a hollow stem and the surface of the head may go brown. The hollow stem may be brown inside. The curds are bitter to eat, and rough lumpy areas may occur on the midribs of the leaves.

In swedes and turnips, brown hollows may develop inside the root, and the outside may crack and develop a rough leathery surface. Cabbages are not as severely affected as cauliflowers and may show only a hollow section in the main part of the stem.

Application of lime may induce this deficiency disease.

PLANTS AFFECTED A range of plants, particularly vegetable crops.

CONTROL   A deficiency can be corrected by the application of borax to the soil at or just before planting time. The correct amount to apply is approximately 2 g per square metre; but it varies from area to area, so consult your local Department of Agriculture. Mix it thoroughly with some sand or soil, and distribute evenly. Take extra care if celery, cucumber, rockmelon, squash, peas, potato, tomato, watermelon, French beans or strawberries are to follow in that area. These crops are sensitive to too much boron in the soil.

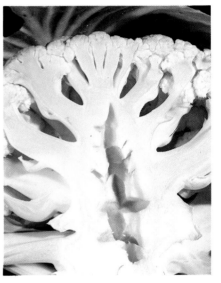

In areas of alkaline soils, higher rates may be necessary. Consult your local Department of Agriculture. This one application should last for three or four years.

A foliar spray can be used. This involves dissolving 1–3 g of borax in 5 L of water and spraying it on to the plants before they are half-grown. Try the lower rate first. Needs vary from area to area. Fowl manure contains some boron.

It is very important not to overdo applications of borax in an attempt to solve this problem. The plants use a very small amount.

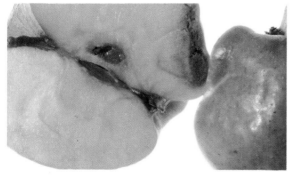

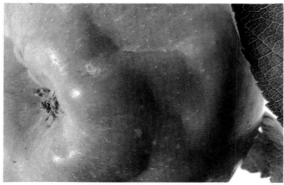

Boron deficiency — apple

There are a number of different symptoms in the fruit: cracking, rough, brown skin; dark, spongy areas in the flesh; browning of the core; and irregular depressions in the skin. These may not occur together.

In late summer, leaves on current-season's twigs may become distorted and turn yellow, with red veins. Dead areas may appear at the leaf tips and edges. Twigs may die. Leaves may develop too close together; they may be small and thick.

This problem is more likely to occur when there are fluctuations in soil moisture and on granite soils.

PLANTS AFFECTED Apples and pears.

CONTROL   Apply borax (46% granular preparation) to the soil in winter or early spring. It should be spread evenly around the tree, and reapplied every fourth or fifth year or when symptoms reappear. About 100–300 g is necessary, depending on the size of the tree. The suggested rates must not be exceeded — too much boron is harmful.

Seek the advice of your local Department of Agriculture if in any doubt, or if non-bearing trees seem to show symptoms.

Botrytis leaf and flower spot — gladiolus

Botrytis gladiolorum

This fungus can attack one plant part or several. Flower spots are small and water-soaked and usually near the edges of the petals. They vary in colour from white to brown and may be white with a brown border. The spots enlarge quickly in humid weather. The petals become rather slimy, and masses of spores develop on them.

The leafspots are small and reddish-brown to begin with, but the centres may go grey and the whole spot may enlarge into a more irregular shape with a brown centre and a darker brown edge. In humid conditions, spots may become covered with a furry grey growth and the leaves may be killed.

If the plant leaves are infected near ground level the fungus may grow from them through into the stem to which they are closely attached, and the stem may be rotted. This condition is referred to as 'neck rot'. The plant yellows and falls over. A grey furry growth with masses of spores may appear on this area, and black sclerotia, the resting bodies of the fungus, may be produced.

Corms are usually infected at digging time when spores from leaf and flower infections come into contact with them. Spores on the husk germinate and grow through to the corm. The rot spreads in wide bands from the outside down into the corm and then spreads throughout. The rotted areas dry out and shrivel. Sometimes the rot spreads from the top of the corm directly down through the centre without the rest of the corm being rotted to any great extent. This disease is favoured by rainy and misty weather.

PLANTS AFFECTED Gladioli. Some varieties suffer more than others.

CONTROL

• Organic/non-chemical: Any diseased plants and spent flowers and crops should be removed and destroyed promptly. Dig the corms in dry weather as early as possible and cure them well (35°C for about a week). Store in a well-ventilated dry situation. Crop rotation is recommended.

• Chemical: Spray weekly with mancozeb. Allow some spray to run down around the neck of the plant into the soil. Add 1 mL of wetting agent per litre.

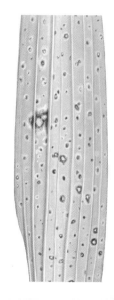

In humid conditions spots such as these may enlarge and become covered with a grey furry growth.

Watersoaked spots spread rapidly in humid weather and the petals are destroyed.

Broad bean wilt   Broad bean wilt virus

The growing tip of the plant becomes black and dies. Later the whole plant may wilt and die. These plants often have blackened areas on the stem near ground level, and roots may be rotted. If the stem is split open, the vascular tissue is brown. Plants that do not die produce mottled leaves with wavy, curled-up edges. The plants are stiff and straight.

The symptoms are most severe in cool to cold conditions. If the temperature rises above 20°C the plants may recover. The disease is spread from plant to plant by several species of aphid including the green peach aphid (*Myzus persicae*).

PLANTS AFFECTED

Broad beans and a wide range of other legumes such as sweet peas (*Lathyrus odoratus*), lupins (*Lupinus* spp.), medics (*Medicago* spp.), and vetches (*Vicia* spp.). Also China asters (*Callistephus chinensis*) and weeds such as lamb's-tongue (*Plantago lanceolata*) and pitchforks or cobbler's pegs (*Bidens pilosa*).

CONTROL

• Organic/non-chemical: Remove and burn diseased plants as soon as they are noticed. Time plantings so that cool conditions are avoided. Control aphids with soap sprays.

• Chemical: Spraying for aphid control with dimethoate may stop the spread in a crop.

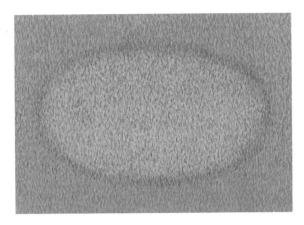

Brown patch   *Rhizoctonia* spp.

This disease assumes many forms depending on the climate and time of year of attack. There are many strains of Rhizoctonia, and while damage is normally associated with hot humid conditions, it also occurs at times in cooler weather.

The most common symptom is a large (up to 1 metre), brownish, more or less circular patch. The patches often have a black or 'smoking' edge, particularly in the early stages of infection. The damage spreads quickly and the turf thins out dramatically.

In cooler climates the edge of the ring is often depressed while the grass in the centre recovers quickly. In warmer climates the grass in the centre often stays thin for some time and algae may become associated with the patch.

PLANTS AFFECTED All lawn grasses. Damage is more severe on cooler climate grasses than on warm-climate types.

CONTROL

• Organic/non-chemical: Reduce application of nitrogenous fertiliser. Improve surface and subsurface drainage. Selectively prune surrounding trees and shrubs to increase light accesss and air circulation.

• Chemical: Use chlorothalonil (Daconil®) at the rate of 125 g in 5 L of water sprayed over 100 square metres.

Brown rot — citrus   *Phytophthora* spp.

These soil-inhabiting fungi produce, on the soil surface, spores that are splashed up on to the lower parts of the plant. The disease is common in autumn in many districts but may occur in some areas for much of the year.

Leaves and fruit may show symptoms. A greyish-brown firm rot develops on oranges and mandarins, and they usually fall. On lemons and grapefruit the rot is yellowish-brown. This disease has a characteristic smell. The leaves are commonly infected near the tips or at the margins, and the infected areas turn greyish-brown or dark brown.

If the weather is wet and therefore favourable to the growth of the fungus, whole shoots may be destroyed. The infected leaves will fall even if they remain green over most of their surface.

PLANTS AFFECTED All commercial varieties of citrus may suffer from this disease, but 'Washington Navel' and lemons are the most commonly attacked. Grapefruit are only occasionally affected.

CONTROL

• Organic/non-chemical: Prune so that the lowest branches are at least 300 mm above the soil even when weighed down with fruit. Remove weeds and other tall plants that keep the area humid. Mulching beneath the tree would be a good idea.

• Chemical: Preventive spraying should occur before or immediately after the first autumn rains; and in years of above-average rainfall, again in late winter or spring. If this spray has not been applied and the tree shows symptoms, then spray immediately. In all cases it is important to apply the spray to the butt of the tree, to the ground around and to the foliage to a height of 1.5 m. Use copper oxychloride.

Brown rot — stonefruit

Sclerotinia fructicola and *S. laxa*

These fungi infect blossoms, which die and turn brown. The fungus grows from the blossoms into the flower stalks and then into the stem. Shoots may be killed if the fungal growth girdles the stem.

Humid or showery weather with mild days and cool nights favours blossom blight.

Fruit infection is most likely as the fruit approaches maturity, but it can occur earlier. The initial small brown spot spreads rapidly and within three or four days the fruit may be completely rotted. Infected fruit may fall, or it may remain attached and gradually dry out. These shrivelled pieces of fruit are called 'mummies'.

PLANTS AFFECTED   Most serious problems occur on stonefruit (all species and varieties). Flowering quince (*Chaenomeles speciosa*) may have all the blossoms destroyed. Some other plants, including apples and pears, may be attacked but damage is usually considered insignificant.

CONTROL
• Organic/non-chemical: Remove and destroy fallen and diseased fruit frequently. Prune mummies with their stalks and infected shoots from the trees. Control dried-fruit beetles (P) and other insects which can spread spores. Burn all diseased material.

Prune so that the tree is as open as possible in the centre and therefore easier to spray. This also increases air circulation, and fruit dries more quickly after rain or dew. Avoid overhead watering when flowers and fruits are on the tree.

• Chemical: Spray thoroughly with copper oxychloride following label directions.

Brown spot — mandarin

Alternaria citri

This fungal disease causes brown spots on leaves, fruit and young stems. Young soft leaves may be attacked and leaf fall may occur. Small brown indentations may develop on young stems, which may later blacken and die.

The fruit may be attacked soon after fruit set, and many small black spots may occur. If the fruit is badly affected, it will probably fall; if not, the spots change to light brown and increase in size to about 30 mm as the fruit grows.

This fungus can live in dead twigs and branches and produce spores which are spread about by wind-driven rain. Thus this disease is more common in cool damp weather in early spring, late summer and early autumn. Trees in situations where wet foliage dries very slowly are more likely to be attacked by the disease.

PLANTS AFFECTED   Mandarins, particularly 'Emperor'; some cultivars of tangelo; calamondins; and occasionally 'Wheeny' grapefruit will develop symptoms.

CONTROL
• Organic/non-chemical: Avoid wetting the leaves when watering. Prune off all dead material and burn it. Do not leave prunings lying around, as the spores could still be spread from this material to the tree.

• Chemical: If the disease does appear on a plant, prune the diseased twigs lightly and spray with copper oxychloride. In early December that spray could be repeated. In late January a spray of zineb will control both brown spot and citrus rust mites. If conditions still favour the disease in autumn, spray with copper oxychloride again in early March.

Symptoms on Minneola tangelo

Brown spot — passionfruit

Alternaria passiflorae

This fungus causes brown spots which may be found on all the above-ground parts of the vine. They may be up to 10 mm across and begin brown, but later the centre dries out and becomes paler. If conditions are favourable for the fungus — that is, warm and humid — leaf spots may grow up to 25 mm in size and may end up angular or circular. If new leaf growth is attacked, whole leaves may be killed. Infected leaves fall and whole vines may be defoliated.

The stem spots usually begin where a leaf joins the stem. They are elongated and may be up to about 25 mm long. They gradually grow around the stem and girdle it, thus killing long pieces of vine.

The first sign of the disease on the fruit is dark-green watersoaked spots. These are basically circular, and become light-brown and sunken with a green edge. The fruit shrivels and falls.

PLANTS AFFECTED Passionfruit, granadilla and other Passiflora species, including wild ones.

CONTROL
• Organic/non-chemical: Do not plant vines too close together; avoid crowding them with other plants. Thin out bushy growth, and remove any dead plant parts.
• Chemical: During winter a monthly spray of copper oxychloride will help to control this disease. During spring apply a monthly spray of mancozeb. Spray more frequently if the weather is damp.

Bulb and stem nematode *Ditylenchus dipsaci*

This nematode is introduced into clean soil by planting infested bulbs. If healthy bulbs are planted into infested soil, nematodes move from the soil into the bulbs. They may infest the new leaves that are produced, which become twisted and distorted and often have raised ridges along them. These raised sections are generally full of nematodes. They may be yellow and are known as 'spikkels'.

In the bulb itself, the nematodes feed on the fleshy leaf bases and if the bulb is cut across the rotted sections appear as brown rings. If the bulb is cut lengthwise then these rotted sections appear more like stripes.

On tulip bulbs, slight infestation is very difficult to see; but after the nematodes have been feeding for a while, there may be greyish or brownish spongy patches on the outside of the bulbs. When the plant is growing pale streaks may appear on the upper stem and the flower. The epidermis often blisters and splits. The flower stalk may be bent over, and the petals distorted.

If onions are attacked, the disease is called 'onion bloat'. Seedlings may never emerge from the soil, and those that do have thick malformed leaves. If older plants are attacked, they remain stunted and wilting is common. Shallots, chives, garlic and leeks may be similarly affected.

Inactive nematodes withstand frost, desiccation and hot summer temperatures.

PLANTS AFFECTED Daffodils, jonquils, hyacinths, tulips, and onions and their relatives. Beans, peas, lucerne, clover, oats and strawberries are also attacked. There are a number of different forms of this species: the form that attacks onions does not thrive on daffodils, and so on.

CONTROL
• Organic/non-chemical: Badly damaged bulbs should be burnt. Others in that batch should be treated in hot water using the procedure described in the section Planning and Maintaining Your Garden. Practise crop rotation with non-susceptible plants such as beetroot, spinach, cabbages, cauliflowers or lettuces.

Do not plant treated bulbs back into infested soil.
• Chemical: Use fenamiphos (Nemacur®) granules as directed on the label.

Cane spot — raspberry *Elsinoe veneta*

This fungal disease — which is also referred to as 'anthracnose'— appears on the canes as many grey sunken spots with purple margins. These spots, which are 1.5–3 mm in diameter, sometimes also occur on the leaves. Loganberries, which are also affected, are severely attacked on the leaves as well as on the canes.

Spots may be numerous and grow into one another to kill large areas of bark. The causal fungus overwinters in young canes and fallen leaves, as well as on the old fruited canes. In the spring the fruiting canes are a source of infection for any young developing canes. If infection is at a high level, the crop will be very much reduced.
PLANTS AFFECTED Loganberries, and raspberries, particularly the variety 'Lloyd George'.
CONTROL
• Organic/non-chemical: This involves a hygiene programme as well as spraying. Remove and burn old fruiting canes and severely infected young canes.
• Chemical: Spray at green-tip stage with copper oxychloride and again at white-bud stage. Take care not to exceed label recommendations.

Cercospora leaf spot *Cercospora beticola*

This disease appears first on the oldest leaves of the plant and shows up as light-grey spots with brown margins. Spots may also appear on other parts of the plant. Spores produced on these spots are spread by wind or insects or water splash on to the younger leaves in the middle of the plant or to plants nearby. The disease is worse if temperatures are high (24–30°C) and conditions are damp.
PLANTS AFFECTED Silver beet, beetroot and related weeds.
CONTROL
• Organic/non-chemical: Crop rotation is important in the control of this disease. Susceptible plants should not be grown more than once every three or four years in the same place. Remove and burn affected leaves, and pick silver beet regularly. Regular picking prevents the fungus becoming established.

If starting new crops, position them well away from older crops that are diseased.
• Chemical: Spraying is usually not necessary, but control could be achieved on seedlings with copper oxychloride. Repeat about a week to ten days later. Plants ready to be picked should not be sprayed.

Chlorosis

The word 'chlorosis' means yellowing, and strictly speaking can be used to describe the symptoms of many pests and diseases. The term 'lime-induced chlorosis' is often used and this is the case with hydrangeas, gardenias, camellias and azaleas. It refers to the fact that iron deficiency, which causes the yellowing, occurs in these plants if the soil is alkaline naturally or has had lime added to it. These plants (and some Australian native plants) are not able to obtain iron from the soil unless it is acid.

The disease involves yellowing of the young leaves, although the veins usually remain green. The result is a creamy-yellow leaf criss-crossed with fine green lines. Often symptoms may include scorching of leaf edges, reduction in leaf size, leaf fall and dieback of young growth.

The problem arises when iron supplies available to the plant are insufficient for the production of chlorophyll for new leaves. It is most likely when the soil is alkaline, because iron is bound up in complex compounds and cannot be used by the plant.
PLANTS AFFECTED Azaleas, hydrangeas, gardenias and camellias and many others.
CONTROL Check the soil pH. If it is above 6, consider trying to lower it. This would be a long-term programme.

Lime, superphosphate or ashes should never be used near azaleas or rhododendrons. Use blood and bone, ammonium sulphate or a proprietary 'azalea food'.

Planting azaleas in new concrete tubs or near new paths may cause problems. Mix iron chelate (pronounced 'kee-layt') with sand or water, and distribute evenly around the plant. Apply in spring when new growth is beginning. If the plant is severely affected, apply several small doses spaced out over 2–4 weeks.

Citrus scab *Sphaceloma fawcettii* var. *scabiosa*

This fungal disease produces symptoms on leaves, twigs and fruit, but the symptoms on the fruit are by far the most noticeable. The skin is marked with irregular greyish, scabby areas and wart-like outgrowths may also occur. Although the interior of the fruit is undamaged, this disease should be controlled because twig damage adversely affects the structure of the tree and eventually causes it to become unproductive.

Lemon fruit with citrus scab are often very large. This is because the disease also causes some fruit fall. The remaining lemons have all the energy of the tree directed towards them and thus become larger than they would otherwise have been.

The first signs of infection on a leaf are small rounded areas, raised on one leaf surface and indented on the other. Brownish, greyish or pinkish scabs develop on the protuberances. The leaf may be distorted if many scabs occur close together.

The spores are produced on scabs and spread by wind-driven rain and insects. Cool damp weather, particularly if it follows a dry spell, is favourable to disease development. Fruit is susceptible only up to about ten weeks after half-petal fall.

PLANTS AFFECTED All varieties of lemon and common lemon; 'Rangpur' limes; sour oranges; calamondins; some varieties of tangelo; and 'Unshiu' mandarins. The leaves of other mandarin varieties are susceptible to infection in cool wet spring weather. Sweet orange varieties rarely suffer from this disease.

CONTROL
• Organic/non-chemical: Prune off infected twigs and leaves. Destroy.
• Chemical: Start in spring when about half the petals have fallen from the flowers. Use copper oxychloride and add 6 mL of white oil per litre of water. A second spray should be applied at the beginning of February at half-petal fall. Use zineb.

Clover stunt Clover stunt virus

This disease is caused by the clover stunt virus and occurs mostly in cool spring weather. It may also be seen in autumn. On beans it is characterised by new leaves yellowing, thickening and curling downwards. The shoots will be stunted, and the growing point may die. Other leaves may be puckered and rolled. Pods do not usually develop.

The disease is carried by several species of aphid, including the green peach aphid and the potato aphid. These aphids migrate mainly during September and October.

Pea plants remain small and upright, with an overall yellow appearance. Young leaves are smaller than usual, and older leaves may be thick and brittle.

PLANTS AFFECTED French beans (some varieties are resistant). Also broad beans (referred to as 'leaf roll') and peas ('top yellows').

CONTROL
• Organic/non-chemical: Plant a resistant variety. Use yellow water pan traps. See page 39.
• Chemical: If aphids are seen spray promptly with dimethoate.

Club root — crucifers

Plasmodiophora brassicae

Plants affected by this fungal disease grow very slowly and wilt quickly on hot days. They may eventually collapse altogether. If the root system is inspected, it will be abnormal; the roots are much bigger than they should be, generally thick in the middle and tapering to each end. This should not be confused with symptoms of root knot nematode (D) attack, which are smaller lumps more evenly distributed along the roots.

The disease is introduced into an area in contaminated soil or infected seedlings. Once in an area it can remain there for long periods. The problem will be worse if the soil is acid and very moist, and also at temperatures between 18–25°C.

PLANTS AFFECTED Crucifers. Most severe in swedes.

CONTROL
• Organic/non-chemical: If the infestation is not severe, liming an acid soil may reduce the problem sufficiently. A long crop rotation should be practised so as to reduce losses when crucifers are next planted. Plant disease-free seedlings. Use resistant varieties when available.

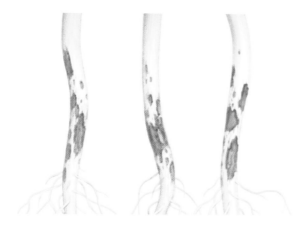

Collar rot *Rhizoctonia solani*

This soil-inhabiting fungus can cause root rots, stem rots, and crown or collar rots. It can attack many different types of plant and usually does so in the early stages of their growth. On bean plants, irregular reddish sunken areas develop just near ground level.

On stocks, wilting foliage and sunken areas at the base of the stem may indicate this disease. Look in the damaged area for soil particles adhering to the fine brown threads characteristic of this fungus.

The disease is most likely in the warm weather of late spring and autumn. It is sometimes referred to as 'rhizoctonia disease'. Other fungi and bacteria also cause collar rots.

PLANTS AFFECTED A wide range. Common on seedlings and vegetables such as French beans. Also annual and perennial flowers.

CONTROL

• Organic-non-chemical: Take care not to overwater. Discard a badly affected batch.

See also damping-off (D).

Collar rot — citrus *Phytophthora citrophthora*

This disease is caused by a soil-inhabiting fungus which can only attack the tree under certain conditions. If the foliage is yellowing and the tree generally looks unhealthy, collar rot may be the cause.

The first symptom is usually seen near ground level where some gum may ooze out from the bark. Later the bark may appear wet in a patch near this gum, and later still it may dry out and become brittle and split. If this disease is not controlled and if conditions for the tree are not improved, the rot will spread right around the trunk and ringbark the tree. This fungus grows well in damp conditions and thrives where weeds have been allowed to grow near the trunk or where vegetables or other small plants have been cultivated near the trunk. It would also be favoured by overwatering.

PLANTS AFFECTED Citrus vary in this regard. The following list begins with the most susceptible and progresses to the least susceptible (resistant): 'Eureka' and 'Lisbon' lemons; grapefruit; 'Washington Navel'; 'Valencia'; rough lemon rootstock; mandarins. Trifoliata and citrange ('Troyer' and 'Carrizo') are completely resistant.

CONTROL

• Organic/non-chemical: If the following measures are taken, this disease is unlikely to occur. Improve the air circulation near the trunk so that humidity is decreased. Avoid wetting the trunk when watering. Do not grow other plants close to the trunk. Prune off low branches. Improve soil drainage.

Citrus trees should always be planted so that the graft union is well above ground level (50–150 mm). Soil should never be built up around the base of the tree nor should mulch be allowed to accumulate there. Trifoliata and citrange rootstocks are resistant to attack, but most scions are not.

Should the disease occur, the damaged area must be repaired. Damaged bark should be cut away with a sharp knife, and the wood beneath smoothed.

Regrowth of bark over a damaged area which has been treated.

Common scab *Streptomyces scabies*

This disease—which is also referred to as 'potato scab' — begins as small brown dots on the tubers. As the tuber grows these increase in size and the damaged areas that result may eventually cover most of the surface. Symptoms vary from raised corky areas to deep pits.

The disease can be introduced to an area on infected tubers and in soil. It is worse in soils that are alkaline, and it is worst in dry seasons.

PLANTS AFFECTED Potatoes, turnips, beetroot.

CONTROL

• Organic/non-chemical: Use disease-free tubers for seed. Do not lime the soil or take any other action that would make the soil more alkaline. Practise crop rotation. Watering procedures that keep the soil moist while the tubers are forming will lower the incidence of the disease.

Crown gall   *Agrobacterium* spp.

This bacterial disease was previously thought to be caused by *Agrobacterium tumefaciens*, which can be obtained from crown galls on any plant but are usually non-pathogenic strains. Crown gall on peaches and roses is now known to be consistently associated with the presence of a tumour-inducing strain of *A. rhizogenes*. On grape, crown gall is most commonly associated with *A. rubi*.

The disease is characterised by large lumps at the base of the stem or on the roots. Galls may appear higher on the stems later. Lumps are relatively soft.

The bacteria are soil inhabitants but can only gain entry to the plant through a wound. This may be caused by cultivation, by insects chewing at the root system or by similar factors. If the plant is infected at an early stage in its growth, the vascular system will be damaged and the plant may never be capable of producing a satisfactory crop of fruit or flowers. The plants wilt readily and grow poorly. As the gall ages, bacteria can be liberated into the soil.

PLANTS AFFECTED Many, including apples, roses, stonefruit and dahlias.

CONTROL
• Organic/non-chemical: Do not buy a tree or a shrub with a lump at the base of the stem (however, don't confuse crown gall symptoms with the lignotubers found on some native Australian plants such as eucalypts).

There is now an easy and cheap control method available for nurserymen, so there is little excuse for the production of diseased plants. The treatment involves dipping cuttings, seedling roots and seeds of susceptible plants in a solution prepared using a non-pathogenic strain of *A. rhizogenes*. The strain may be referred to as Isolate K84 and is sold either in peat or agar. Trade names are No-Gall® and Dygall®. The product is recommended for treatment of stonefruit and roses. Small plants that are already infected should be burnt. Replacement plants should be dipped, if the same area of soil is to be used.

Cymbidium virus

There are a number of viruses that infect orchids. The symptoms are often difficult to distinguish from one another. The leaf may have a mottled appearance with pale-green elongated marks. These are more pronounced in some varieties and usually show up more if the plant is growing in a high light situation. Black spots and streaks may develop on older leaves.

Concentric brown rings also indicate a viral infection. Flowers do not usually develop any marks but may be lower in quality and quantity because of general lack of plant vigour. These diseases are spread from plant to plant in sap on knives or fingers or by aphids.

PLANTS AFFECTED Cymbidiums and other orchids.

CONTROL
• Organic/non-chemical: It is best to destroy infected plants. However, if they are to be retained, position them as far away from healthy plants as possible. Work on plants known to be healthy before those thought to be diseased. Disinfect tools and hands. Control aphids.

Cypress canker   *Seiridium* spp.

This fungal disease is usually noticed only when branches die back. Closer inspection will reveal a brown powdery substance in splits in the bark and resin oozing from the branch.

Splits in the bark or areas damaged by insects or other agency are sites for infection to begin. The area of affected bark gradually spreads to girdle the branch or trunk. The whole tree or branch will then die.

PLANTS AFFECTED Lawson cypress (*Chamaecyparis lawsoniana*), Monterey cypress (*Cupressus macrocarpa*) and Roman cypress (*C. sempervirens*) are very susceptible to this disease and probably should not be planted. Lambert's cypress (*C. lambertiana*) is also susceptible. Arizona cypress (*C. glabra*), Bhutan cypress (*C. torulosa*) and Mexican cypress (*C. lusitanica*) show resistance to the disease.

CONTROL
• Organic/non-chemical: Remove affected trees and replant with different species.

Damping-off

The term 'damping-off' means death of seeds or seedlings when they are attacked by certain soil-inhabiting fungi or bacteria. If the rotting occurs even before the seedling emerges from the soil, it is referred to as 'pre-emergence damping-off'. If it occurs after the seedling has appeared, then it is 'post-emergence damping-off'.

The rot may occur around the base of the stem only or spread from the roots to the lower stem. The seedlings often fall over. Fungi from the genera *Pythium* and *Phytophthora* are commonly the cause.

Sometimes the outer areas of the stems rot but the inner ones remain and hold the plant upright. This may be called 'sore-shin' or 'wire-stem'. The fungus most often responsible for this is *Rhizoctonia*.

Sometimes fungi grow up the stems of a number of seedlings and then from leaf to leaf through the tops of the seedlings. *Rhizoctonia* can be distinguished by the very fine brownish fungal threads it produces where a leaf touches the soil, for example.

PLANTS AFFECTED Any seeds or seedlings.

CONTROL
• Organic/non-chemical: Do not overwater. Sow seeds thinly so that the seedlings are not too crowded. A batch of badly affected seedlings (and their soil) should be discarded in an area away from other plants.
• Chemical: Spraying the soil with furalaxyl (Fongarid®) immediately before or shortly after planting seeds or seedlings will give protection from *Phytophthora* and *Pythium* but not from *Rhizoctonia*. Furalaxyl will also save plants that are already infected provided they are not seriously damaged. Copper oxychloride is also suitable.

Damping-off — lawns *Pythium* spp.

When this disease occurs, the turf will look pale and in the worst areas plants will collapse in circles about 100 mm across. In new plantings or with overseeding, individual plants will often appear wrinkled, twisted or distorted. Roots appear short and brown.

On mature turf, prolonged hot humid weather will cause thinning and a pale yellowish appearance. The disease is favoured by excessive moisture in the soil.

Heavy use of nitrogenous fertilisers can create 'soft' turf which is more susceptible to attack. Nitrogenous fertiliser applied during the establishment stage leads to sudden collapse of seedlings.

PLANTS AFFECTED All grasses, commonly in the seeding stage.

CONTROL
• Organic/non-chemical: Keep the seed moist but avoid overwatering. Do not use nitrogenous fertiliser at this early stage; instead use one with as high a proportion of phosphorus as possible.
• Chemical: Drench the soil with furalaxyl (Fongarid®) at the rate of 1 g per litre. Use 200 L per 100 square metres. This is expensive.

Dieback — camellia *Glomerella cingulata*

The fungus that causes this disease can only enter the plant through a wound. The 'wound', however, can be a natural opening such as a leaf scar, which is the small area where the leafstalk has been attached to the stem.

Once the fungus gains entry to the plant, it kills the tissue around the leaf scar and if this is allowed to continue the fungus may girdle that particular twig. This shows up as a sunken area in the bark and is referred to as a 'canker'. The new shoot growing just above the leaf scar dies, the leaves remain attached to the shoot but curl and go brown. The tip of the shoot is typically curled over like a shepherd's crook.

PLANTS AFFECTED Camellias. This disease is far more common on cultivars with large leaf scars such as 'Donation' than on cultivars with small leaf scars such as 'Cho Cho San'.

CONTROL
• Organic/non-chemical: The affected parts should be pruned off.

Dodder   *Cuscuta* spp.

This is a parasitic plant. When dodder seed germinates in the soil a small seedling is produced. It elongates very rapidly and as soon as the thread-like stem makes contact with a larger nearby plant it twines around it. The dodder sends sucker-like projections (haustoria) into the plant, and soon after the dodder stem shrivels near ground level. Thereafter it obtains its water and nutrients from the host.

Dodder stems are thread-like and yellow or brown. They twine around and over other plants. The mainly cream or white flowers form small clusters and are produced in warmer months (Sept.-May). The seeds may germinate immediately or remain dormant for 20 years.

Dodder can be introduced into an area on contaminated seed, in running water, or in manure.

PLANTS AFFECTED A wide range, including lucerne, onions and many ornamental plants.

CONTROL
• Organic/non-chemical: Destroy patches of dodder (and the plants they are growing on if necessary) as soon as they are seen. Prune off plant parts with dodder twined around. If this is done before the dodder produces seed this action may eradicate it from the area.
• Chemical: Total herbicides will kill dodder and, of course, the plants on which it is growing. However, they will not kill dodder seed so a follow up treatment will be necessary.

Devil's twine (Cassytha sp.) often mistaken for dodder. It has a similar growth habit.

Dollar spot

A number of different fungi cause the symptoms described as dollar spot. The spots of dead grass rarely exceed 50 mm on low-cut lawns but may spread further on grass which is allowed to grow longer.

The disease is most serious when heavy dews occur and is common in spring, humid summers and in autumn. It may sometimes be seen as a white fluffy fungal growth on dewy turf in the early morning.

PLANTS AFFECTED A wide range of grasses. Damage is worst on bent grasses.

CONTROL
• Organic/non-chemical: Apply nitrogenous fertiliser or poultry manure.
• Chemical: Spray with triadimefon (Bayleton®) at the rate of 60 g in 5 litres of water over 100 square metres of turf if the disease is actually present. Use only 30 g/100 m^2 for prevention.

Downy mildews

The group called 'downy mildews' comprise a number of different fungi which cause similar symptoms on different plants. In general, patches or spots appear on upper leaf surfaces. On the underside of the leaves, under each spot, a furry or downy growth is produced if the conditions are humid. This growth is made up of many branched stalks with spores on the ends. It may be slightly violet in colour. Spores can be blown from plant to plant in wind or splashed by rain or irrigation.

They cannot germinate in dry conditions and need a film of moisture on the leaves or at least high relative humidity. High relative humidity is also necessary for the subsequent growth of this group of fungi. As conditions become dry, they gradually stop growing and may die out altogether.

PLANTS AFFECTED A wide range of vegetables, ornamentals and fruit plants. Different species of downy mildew infect different plants.

CONTROL
• Organic/non-chemical: Cultural controls involve reducing humidity by increasing the space between plants, increasing air circulation, and not overwatering. Burning of diseased plants or plant parts is also important.
• Chemical: Suitable chemical controls include zineb, copper oxychloride and copper hydroxide, and furalaxyl, sold as Fongarid®. The undersurfaces of the leaves should be thoroughly wetted.

Downy mildew — crucifers
Peronospora parasitica

This fungus causes pale green to yellow spots on the upper leaf surface. A furry growth appears on the lower leaf surface under each spot if conditions are humid. Seedlings may be killed. Lower leaves on larger plants may be killed and younger leaves spotted. If conditions become dry, fungal growth ceases and the affected areas dry out to brownish irregular patches. On cauliflower heads, the fungus may cause black discolouration.

PLANTS AFFECTED Crucifers such as cabbages and cauliflowers. The race of the fungus *Peronospora parasitica* that attacks these vegetables is not the same race that attacks the annual flower stock.

CONTROL
• Organic/non-chemical: Sow seed thinly. The rows should be at least 100 mm apart. If possible reduce humidity around seed beds and boxes by increased air circulation. Rotate crops. Destroy diseased plant parts.
• Chemical: A routine spray programme may be necessary if the weather is cool and damp. Spray copper oxychloride or copper hydroxide. Apply to seedlings (after 2.5 cm high) thoroughly every few days and to older plants often enough to protect new growth.

Pay special attention to the undersides of the leaves.

Downy mildew — cucurbits
Pseudoperonospora cubensis

This fungus causes yellow spots about 15 mm across on the upper surface of the leaves. The spots are angular on cucumbers, pumpkins and squashes but more rounded on rockmelon. Some furry, slightly purple growth develops under each spot. The spores from this growth are spread in air currents. In moist conditions, attack may be severe. Leaves with many spots will wither and die.

PLANTS AFFECTED All apple cucumbers are susceptible. The cucumbers 'Early Marketer' and 'Dasher' show tolerance. All rockmelons except 'Gulf Coast' are susceptible. Pumpkins and squashes are only affected in very wet weather. Watch for new resistant varieties.

CONTROL
• Organic/non-chemical: If possible, plant a tolerant cultivar. Remove and destroy infected leaves and old plants as soon as possible.
• Chemical: Spray with mancozeb, zineb, or copper oxychloride after the plants start to run. Apply every 7–14 days depending on the weather.

Downy mildew — grape   *Plasmopara viticola*

This fungal disease is worst in warm humid conditions and common in mid-to-late spring. It first appears on the leaves in the form of oily-looking spots which turn pale yellow and dry out. If humidity is high, a white furry growth appears on the under surface of the leaf under each spot. Later the leaves are patterned in different shades of brown. They fall early, leaving the leafstalk attached to the plant. Severe defoliation reduces the ability of the vine to produce a fruit crop, and fruit already on the vine may be sunburnt.

If the bunches are infected at flowering time, irregular fruit set will result. Grapes infected later become hard and grey and shrivel into reddish-brown mummies. A white furry growth may appear over the bunch. The fruit is susceptible until it changes colour.

The fungus survives the winter in dead leaves on the ground, and the first infection of the next season occurs in damp conditions when the temperature rises above 10°C.

PLANTS AFFECTED Grapes (fruiting and ornamental) and *Parthenocissus* spp.

CONTROL
• Organic/non-chemical: Help to reduce the severity and likelihood of attack by avoiding overhead irrigation and by pruning to minimise shaded moist pockets. Produce an even surface grade on the soil so that puddles cannot form, and burn fallen leaves and prunings.
• Chemical: Begin a spray programme when the new shoots are about 250 mm long. Use mancozeb or copper hydroxide. Spraying must be thorough. Cover both leaf surfaces and the bunches. If the weather is warm and humid, spray every two weeks; but if it is hot and dry, once every four weeks is probably sufficient.

Downy mildew — lettuce

Bremia lactucae

Symptoms of this fungal disease appear mostly on the older leaves — that is, the ones nearest the soil. Pale green or yellow patches on the upper leaf surface are usually bounded by veins and look roughly diamond-shaped. Later the patches go brown, and in humid conditions a white furry growth appears under each. Leaves damaged in this way are often subsequently rotted by bacteria (see bacterial soft rot (D)).

Wind spreads spores of the fungus from plant to plant.

PLANTS AFFECTED Lettuces.

CONTROL

• Organic/non-chemical: Do not grow plants too close together. At harvest destroy any unwanted outer leaves. Spraying is probably only warranted on small plants or in cool moist weather.

• Chemical: Use mancozeb, or copper oxychloride. Cover leaves thoroughly.

Downy mildew — onion   *Peronospora destructor*

This disease usually appears as pale oval spots on the older leaves. These spots increase in size until large yellowish areas develop. In cool humid conditions a purplish, violet or grey furry growth appears on the spots. The fungus can grow into the bulbs or into seed heads, thus contaminating the seed. Seedlings grown from diseased seed become covered in purplish fungal growth, and spores are spread by wind to other plants. Weather with dews, fogs or rain will make this disease more serious. The plant may outgrow the disease if weather conditions become dry.

PLANTS AFFECTED Onions, garlic, shallots and leeks.

CONTROL

• Organic/non-chemical: Improve soil drainage. Improve air circulation. Use disease-free seed. If seed origin is unknown, the seed can be treated in hot water.

• Chemical: Applications of nitrogenous fertiliser will help the plant. Spray with copper hydroxide or zineb; the addition of wetting agent, at the rate of 10 mL per litre, will help the spray to stay on the leaves.

Downy mildew — pea   *Peronospora viciae*

This fungus causes upper leaf surfaces to turn yellow. A thick grey-brown furry growth develops under the leaves in humid conditions. The pods develop irregular cream-coloured patches and the leaves go brown. This disease is worse in damp weather.

PLANTS AFFECTED Peas.

CONTROL

• Organic/non-chemical: Cultural controls are very important because pea plants are difficult to spray satisfactorily. Avoid areas with shade or poor air circulation, and avoid watering leaves late in the day.

• Chemical: Spray with mancozeb. Add 10 mL of wetting agent per litre.

Downy mildew — rhubarb

Peronospora jaapiana

The symptoms of this disease are first seen on the upper leaf surfaces. The light-brown patches that develop are angular at first because they are bounded by veins. If the weather continues cool and wet, however, the patches may continue to spread until large areas of the leaf are brown. Eventually these areas will tear, and pieces will fall out so that the leaves have a tattered appearance. Severe defoliation can occur. Underneath the leaf the furry growth characteristic of downy mildew is produced, and the spores on this furry growth are spread about by the wind to other leaves and to other plants.

PLANTS AFFECTED Rhubarb.

CONTROL   Destroy the affected leaves. Keep growth vigorous. If necessary, spray with copper oxychloride, mancozeb or zineb.

Downy mildew — rose *Peronospora sparsa*

This fungus causes purplish-red to dark-brown spots on the leaves. They are not uniform in shape, but many are angular. In humid weather a furry growth may appear on the underside of the leaf beneath each spot.

Stems and flower stalks may split and may be blotched and streaked with purple. The petals may develop brown areas, and sepals may develop purplish-brown spots. If young growth is attacked, new shoots may die and young leaves droop and fall off. Flowers infected as buds are often deformed when they open.

This disease is favoured by humid weather and is spread from diseased plants to healthy ones by wind.

PLANTS AFFECTED Roses. Some varieties are more susceptible than others.

CONTROL
• Organic/non-chemical: Burn all infected leaves and prunings.
• Chemical: Spray with zineb or copper oxychloride. Cover both sides of the leaf and the stems. Fongarid® at the rate of 1 g per litre of water is also suitable for control of this disease.

Downy mildew — stocks *Peronospora parasitica*

This fungus causes yellow patches on upper leaf surfaces. The whole leaf may become yellow and die. The affected leaves will fall, and if this leaf-fall continues the plant will die.

The disease is most serious on seedlings. It is spread on diseased seedlings and by wind dispersal of the spores, which appear as a furry growth on lower leaf surfaces.

PLANTS AFFECTED Stocks. The race of the fungus *Peronospora parasitica* that attacks stocks is different from the race that attacks vegetables such as cabbages.

CONTROL This is difficult, especially in cool humid weather. The crowded growth of seedlings keeps humidity high and makes it difficult to apply fungicidal sprays thoroughly.
• Chemical: Fongarid® at the rate of 1 g per litre of water would be the most efficient spray in a seed-bed situation. Copper oxychloride or zineb could also be used. Apply to seedlings every few days and to established plants often enough to protect newly formed leaves.

Dry patch

This is a water-repellent condition of the soil which occurs more frequently in older turf. The damage is usually worse on grass growing in sandy soils.

The fungi involved do not attack living grass but break down the dead grass (thatch) as they obtain nourishment from it. These activities result in the production of chemicals which waterproof the soil and make it very difficult to wet. This means that rainwater and irrigation water cannot penetrate and therefore do not reach the plant roots and the plants suffer from water stress. Roughly circular patches of dead grass may occur. The stress placed on the live grass is due directly to lack of moisture.

PLANTS AFFECTED Any lawn grass, but short-rooted species such as bent grass are most damaged.

CONTROL
• Organic/non-chemical: Relief of the symptoms can be gained by forking the area to allow better moisture penetration and by drenching the area with a detergent. This may have to be repeated at intervals in severe cases. Agricultural wetters are less likely to cause damage to plants than domestic detergents.

The soil at the top of this plug is water-repellent. Water has soaked into the lower layers from a nearby area.

Fasciation

This abnormality most commonly involves the flattening of plant stems; instead of the stem being more or less round, it develops into a very much larger, flatter structure, perhaps with small leaves on the surface and a group of leaves at the top. These abnormal pieces of stem vary in width but might even be 100 mm across. The cause is thought to be a mutation.

PLANTS AFFECTED This type of growth is seen on an irregular basis on a wide variety of plants including daphnes, roses, cotoneasters and cassias.

CONTROL   Prune off the affected areas. The condition may or may not recur.

Fasciation of Celosia

Fire *Botrytis tulipae*

This fungus causes small brown spots on the leaves and flowers. The spots are most noticeable on light-coloured flowers. Spots spread to involve large areas. Stems may rot. If the bulb is infected, the plant that grows from it is stunted and pale.

Grey furry growth may occur on the damaged areas in warm moist weather. This fungus produces sclerotia which are capable of remaining alive, in the soil, or stuck to plant material for a long period of time.

PLANTS AFFECTED Tulips.

CONTROL

• Organic/non-chemical: Practise crop rotation. Avoid overhead watering. Do not apply large quantities of nitrogenous fertiliser.

If tulips must be grown in areas where the disease has occurred, the soil must be treated. Consult your local Department of Agriculture.

Discard any diseased bulbs before planting. Remove the papery outer scales so that inspection can be thorough. Remove diseased plants carefully from the area and destroy them. Destroy infected plant parts.

• Chemical: Regular spraying with mancozeb should keep this disease under reasonable control.

Fleck *Diplocarpon mespili*

On pear, the first symptoms, very small reddish dots on the top of the leaf, are seen in early spring. They grow and darken until they are almost black and can be seen on both sides of the leaf. On the fruit, small reddish spots age to reddish-brown with a black centre. If the fruit is heavily infected, cracking occurs.

On quince, the small, slightly raised leaf spots are purple with a white dot in the centre. These spots enlarge and darken to reddish-brown and then change to a dark grey. Sometimes the spots grow together to cover most of the leaf with irregular patches. Leaf-fall is often heavy on a quince because the leafstalks are affected and killed. On the fruit, black and slightly sunken spots develop. If these continue to grow, the fruit will be deformed and cracked. It may also fall.

On loquat leaves, the spots are circular and reddish-brown with a white dot in the centre. The fruit may have dark-brown spots with a central white dot. These spots age to black.

This fungus can survive from season to season on diseased parts of stems and on dead leaves on the ground. These areas produce spores in the spring, which are spread by wind on to the new leaves. Rain and wind also spread spores from tree to tree and from leaf to leaf.

PLANTS AFFECTED Pears, quinces, loquats.

CONTROL

• Organic/non-chemical: Rake up and burn all fallen leaves in the autumn. Prune regularly to remove old dead wood.

• Chemical: If a spray programme is being followed for pear scab, then fleck will also be controlled.

Symptoms on quince

Flyspeck — hibiscus *Microthyriella hibisci*

This fungal disease is more likely in humid areas or if the shrub is in a shady position in the garden.

The leaves gradually yellow and may fall. The black specks shown in the photograph are the fruiting bodies of the fungus, they are not always as clearly visible. Serious damage is uncommon.

PLANTS AFFECTED The Chinese hibiscus (*Hibiscus rosa-sinensis*).

CONTROL
• Organic/non-chemical: Not usually necessary. Prune overhanging larger plants to give the affected shrub more sun.
• Chemical: Zineb may prove to be successful.

Freckle *Fusicladium carpophilum*

This fungal disease is characterised by spots on the fruit and, less frequently, on the leaves. Spots are up to 3 mm in diameter and flat on the surface of the fruit. There are usually more on the top of the fruit near the stalk; the fruit may crack in this area. On other occasions the fruit may gradually shrivel.

On apricots the spots are pale green at first and then darken. On peaches the spots are black; and on nectarines, pale green or cream with the development of a dark centre. The spots are clearly defined.

The infections on the twigs are very important because they provide the source of reinfections for the fruit and the leaves from year to year. Spores produced in these bark lesions are washed on to fruit.

PLANTS AFFECTED This disease may occur on all stonefruit, but it is most common on apricots, peaches and nectarines.

CONTROL
• Organic/non-chemical: Prune off and destroy infected twigs.
• Chemical: Apply the first spray when the flowers begin to open. Use copper oxychloride plus 3 mL of clear white oil for apricots and 5 mL of clear white oil for peaches and nectarines.

Spray again when the brown dried flower-remains fall, and thereafter two or three times at three-weekly intervals if the weather is damp or at four-weekly intervals if it is dry. On peaches and nectarines use zineb for these sprays at the rate of 2 g per litre of water with the addition of 5 mL of clear white oil. On apricots use mancozeb (80%) at the rate of 1.5 g per litre of water with the addition of 5 mL of clear white oil. The final spray can be eight or nine weeks before harvest of peaches and nectarines, but apricots must have more sprays applied.

Fusarium bulb rot — lily *Fusarium oxysporum*

This fungus affects the bottom of the scales. These separate from the base of the bulb. Leaves that grow from infected bulbs may go yellow or purple and die. If flowers are produced, they are small and of poor quality.

This disease is much more likely to occur on damaged bulbs than on healthy, undamaged bulbs.

PLANTS AFFECTED Lilies.

CONTROL
• Organic/non-chemical: Inspect bulbs carefully before purchase. Choose an area of garden where lilies have never grown.

Fusarium patch *Fusarium nivale*

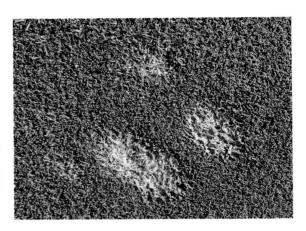

This is a winter disease which attacks grasses in climates where night temperatures are low. When the weather is wet and temperatures are between freezing and 16°C, the fungus spreads rapidly but if the grass dries out and warms up, fungal activity decreases. It also occurs under snow cover. The grass that suffers most is winter grass, which, while often considered a weed, is a common component of lawns in cold climates. Fusarium patch rots the grass to ground level and leaves a slimy look to the yellowed grass. The patch usually develops to about saucer size but may get bigger if the weather is cold and damp.

It is easily spread by mowing. Heavily fertilised grass is more susceptible than lightly fertilised grass. It is important to keep a high potash level to minimise damage.

PLANTS AFFECTED Cool-climate grasses.

CONTROL
• Organic/non-chemical: Choose the least susceptible variety.
• Chemical: Application of a potash fertiliser in autumn will help minimise the disease. The fungicide triadimefon (Bayleton®) will control this disease. If the disease is actually present, apply 60 g in 5 L of water per 100 square metres; but for preventive applications, use only 30 g in 5 L of water per 100 square metres.

Fusarium wilt — carnation

Fusarium oxysporum f. sp. *dianthi*

Carnation plants can be infected at any stage of their development. On older plants, this disease causes a branch here and there to yellow, wilt and die and this gradually progresses until the whole plant is dead. Younger plants may yellow on one side and wilt; the symptoms then spread to the growing point. If the woody tissue on the stem beneath is inspected, it will be found to be discoloured.

Plants may appear bleached and dried out. When the disease is well advanced, the roots rot and the whole plant might be pale green or tan and completely wilted. The bark rots and disintegrates.

This fungus can remain dormant in the soil for a long time and infect cuttings through the cut surface or later through damaged roots. Most infections occur near the soil surface. It can be spread in infected soil on footwear or implements, and in running water such as drainage water. It is commonly brought into an area on infected cuttings. The disease is worse in warm weather.

PLANTS AFFECTED Carnations only.

CONTROL
• Organic/non-chemical: Crop rotation should be practised, and soil that has produced plants with these symptoms should either be fumigated or not used for carnation growing for five to six years.

Burn any plants that have shown these symptoms, but be careful not to spread the fungus around while carrying them. Make sure that cuttings do not come from infected plants or any plants near them. Use pasteurised soil for rooting cuttings. Consult your local Department of Agriculture for more details.

Fusarium wilt — cucurbits

Fusarium oxysporum

This common fungal disease is characterised by slow growth, wilting and death. If the stem is split open near the base of the plant, a reddish-brown discolouration will be seen. Attack on small seedlings may result in damping-off (D). This is most likely in cold weather.

The disease is most likely to occur if rockmelons and watermelons are grown frequently in the same soil.

PLANTS AFFECTED Rockmelons ('Castle King' and 'Early Dawn' are tolerant cultivars) and watermelons ('Colhoun Gray' and 'Warpaint' are tolerant cultivars).

CONTROL
• Organic/non-chemical: Use long crop rotation or grow tolerant varieties.

Mild symptoms on watermelon

Fusarium wilt — tomato

Fusarium oxysporum f. sp. *lycopersici*

This soil-inhabiting fungus enters the plant through the roots and invades the water-conducting tissues. The first sign of damage is usually rapid wilting on hot days. The lower leaves yellow and wilt, and this gradually spreads up the plant. The plant may die. The stem looks normal from the outside, but if it is split open the damaged water-conducting tissues are reddish- or pinkish-brown.

The fungus remains in the soil for years. It may spread in soil on shoes and tools. The disease develops in warm weather (25–32°C).

PLANTS AFFECTED Tomatoes.

CONTROL

• Organic/non-chemical: Practise crop rotation. Use resistant varieties whenever possible. There are chemical treatments that would kill the fungus in the soil. Consult your local Department of Agriculture.

Leaf yellowing and wilting on a group of infected plants.

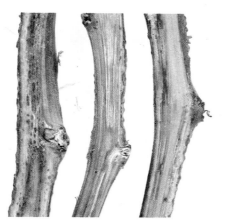

Stems split open to show typical discolouration.

Fusarium yellows

Fusarium oxysporum f. sp. *gladioli*

This fungus is a soil inhabitant and is introduced into the soil in diseased corms which often look healthy from the outside. It can remain capable of infecting gladioli even if a number of years have elapsed since they were last planted in the area.

The fungus enters the plant through roots, leaf bases or old corms. Corms that are severely affected often rot without producing a plant. Less badly damaged corms produce foliage, but the tips of the leaves die and then the leaves yellow all over and die. The disease is favoured by temperatures of 22–25°C and high soil moisture.

A diseased corm may be brown only in the area where it was attached to a rotted mother corm or it may be extensively rotted. Rot often proceeds from the mother corm up the core and then along vascular strands to the outside of the corm where it shows up as small brown patches. Rotting can continue while the corms are being stored.

This fungus also causes a disease known as 'basal brown rot'. This has similar above-ground symptoms to 'fusarium yellows' but rots the corm in a different way. In storage this rot develops in concentric rings and in damp conditions may have a pinkish-white surface when spores are produced.

Try to have this disease properly identified because there are other corm rots caused by different fungi.

PLANTS AFFECTED Some varieties of gladiolus are affected more severely than others.

CONTROL

• Organic/non-chemical: Practise a 3–4-year crop rotation. Examine corms carefully before planting. Burn any with brown dead areas on the basal scar or with internal brown spotting. This can be seen if a small slice is cut from the side of the corm. This does not harm healthy corms.

Control is most efficient if cormlets are treated. Keep them at temperatures of 24–30°C for two months after digging. Then treat them for 30 minutes in water heated to 56–57°C. Drain and cool fairly quickly. After they are dry, cool-store the cormlets for five to six weeks before planting.

Gangrene — potato *Phoma foveata*

This fungus is a soil inhabitant and it infects the tubers at harvest, particularly if they are wounded. The disease then develops during storage. The first signs of the problem are one or two, small, round, dark-brown depressions. These enlarge but remain smooth and firm. They look as if they could have been made with a thumb. Sometimes pinhead-size black fruiting bodies are seen on the surface of these indentations. The tissue beneath the skin rots, and cavities lined with whitish fungal mycelium develop. Fruiting bodies may also develop in these cavities.

PLANTS AFFECTED Potatoes.

CONTROL

• Organic/non-chemical: Avoid introducing this into your growing area by planting only disease-free seed, obtained from a reputable source. Handle all the tubers carefully when digging. Avoid harvesting in cold weather and if the soil is wet. Use clean storage areas. The first week of storage should be at 21°C with high relative humidity, then cooler and drier.

Gnomonia fruit rot — strawberry

Gnomonia fructicola

This fungus can infect the flowers and fruit at any stage. It usually starts on or near the calyx. Flowers and young fruit shrivel, while on larger, riper fruit a firm brown rot slowly spreads through the whole fruit. Old leaves may be infected and develop roughly circular, large brown spots.

Pieces of old infected plant can provide a source of infection, and spores can be splashed about by rain. The disease is usually most prevalent in warm, humid weather.

PLANTS AFFECTED Cultivated strawberries.

CONTROL

• Chemical: Spraying may be necessary in spring and summer. Use copper oxychloride. Apply every two weeks in prolonged periods of warm wet weather.

Typical furry growth on pears

Grey mould *Botrytis cinerea*

This fungus produces sclerotia and may be present all year in pieces of dead plant material. A grey furry growth on the surface indicates spore production. This occurs most in cool humid conditions.

The spores are spread by wind. Fruit and all other above-ground plant parts can be attacked. Those already damaged (perhaps by insects or hail) are most likely to be infected. Pears develop a soft brown rot and then, if conditions are humid, the typical grey powdery spore growth is seen. Dying flowers are often the first to be infected, and the fungus spreads from there.

In cyclamen, attack may begin near soil level. This area is kept humid because of the closed canopy of foliage.

On lily leaves, the fungus causes oval or round yellowish to reddish-brown spots which can be seen from both leaf surfaces. When the spots get bigger, as they do in damp weather, their colour fades. If the spots coalesce, the whole leaf may be destroyed.

Stems may be spotted and break in the damaged area. Affected buds may produce distorted flowers, or wither and brown. Flowers can also be destroyed. In humid conditions, the typical grey furry growth appears. Grey mould on lilies may be caused by *Botrytis elliptica*.

PLANTS AFFECTED A very wide range.

CONTROL

• Organic/non-chemical: Decrease humidity by increasing space between plants. Remove and destroy dead leaves and other plant parts. Prune carefully with sharp tools.

Grey mould — grape *Botrytis cinerea*

This fungus can grow on both living and dead plant material. In cool humid conditions it produces a grey furry growth with masses of spores. These are spread by wind and can begin to grow on damaged fruit. Wind, hail or insect damage may predispose grapes to attack, and the problem is most likely to occur in cool seasons when the bunches are slow to ripen. Infection may also occur at flowering time.

PLANTS AFFECTED Grapes.

CONTROL

• Organic/non-chemical: Organise pruning and trellising so that air circulation and penetration of sunlight are increased. Remove dead or shrivelled bunches and leaves from the growing vine. Pick bunches carefully so that grapes are not damaged, because the disease can develop in storage.

Botrytis cinerea is favoured in some commercial vineyards, because this mould imparts a particular flavour to wine made from affected grapes. Such grapes are used to make sweet white wines—those of the Sauternes region in France being the most famous.

Grey mould — lettuce *Botrytis cinerea*

This fungal disease is most likely to occur when the weather is cool and moist. A soft brown rot develops at ground level or on the lower leafstalks. If conditions continue favourably for the fungus, the stem will be rotted completely and the plant will die. If the stem is only partly rotted, the plant will be stunted. The brown rotted area is sometimes edged in red, and a greyish furry growth may cover the surface. Black seed-like sclerotia or fungal resting bodies then form. These may remain viable in the soil for years.

This fungus usually grows on dead and decaying vegetable material on the soil and usually only infects the plant through a wound or through tissue that is already dead. Spores are spread by wind.

PLANTS AFFECTED Lettuces.

CONTROL

• Organic/non-chemical: Improve the drainage. Improve air circulation by removing weeds and not spacing the plants too close together. Keep them growing vigorously by fertilising and watering adequately.

Botrytis *damage has been followed by bacterial rot*

Grey mould — pelargonium *Botrytis cinerea*

This disease often starts on the flowers. They may fade at first and then fairly quickly wither and brown. In some red varieties the first sign may be a general darkening and deepening of colour. In humid conditions a grey furry growth will develop on the dead petals and they may become matted together.

If these petals fall on to leaves below, these will also be infected. Spores are spread by the wind, and if cool humid conditions prevail, the disease can be quite serious.

PLANTS AFFECTED Regal, ivy and zonal pelargoniums (geraniums).

CONTROL

• Organic/non-chemical: Quickly remove and burn any infected leaves or flowers as these can be a source of infection for other parts of the plant and other plants. Reduce the humidity by spacing the plants well to improve air circulation. Ensure that they receive sun for a greater part of the day.

Grey mould — rose *Botrytis cinerea*

On roses grey mould is principally a disease of flowers and buds. The leaves may be attacked, but this is not common. Infected buds turn brown and decay, and the rot can progress from the bud down the flower stalk to the stem. On flower petals the fungus produces pink rings.

This fungus usually lives on decaying plant material including dead canes and will attack living plant material only if conditions are exactly right for it — that is, cool and humid. If these conditions continue for a period of time, the grey furry growth typical of *Botrytis cinerea* will appear. The spores can be spread by wind to other plants.

PLANTS AFFECTED Roses.

CONTROL

• Organic/non-chemical: Any diseased buds or flowers should be removed from the plant with their stems.

Leaf spots on cucumber

Gummy stem blight — cucurbits *Didymella bryoniae*

Symptoms may appear on the leaves and fruit, but stem symptoms are most common. These occur mostly around the crown of the plant. Watersoaked areas on the stems may develop into light brown or whitish sunken cankers. The fruiting bodies of the fungus may show up as small black dots, and the cankers may split and exude a reddish gum. Any stem girdled by this fungus wilts and dies.

Leaf spots are black, and the fruit may be blemished by firm black sunken spots.

Disease may start in a crop because infected seed was used or because diseased plant material remains from a previous crop. Spores are spread by wind, and attack will be worst in moist conditions.

PLANTS AFFECTED Watermelons are the most commonly attacked cucurbits. Rockmelons may often show slight symptoms, and blemished fruit may occur in the case of cucumbers and pumpkins from time to time if conditions particularly favour the fungus.

CONTROL

• Organic/non-chemical: Crop rotation is important (3–4 years). Seeds should not be saved from an infected crop. If this disease has occurred in a crop, the fruit should be picked very carefully and used quickly.

• Chemical: Spray with copper oxychloride every two weeks if necessary. Do not spray cucurbits with copper oxychloride before they begin to run.

Symptoms on rockmelon

Halo blight of beans

Pseudomonas syringae pv. *phaseolicola*

This bacterial disease is first introduced into a planting through diseased seed. Plants growing from diseased seed are yellow and stunted. Subsequently the disease can spread through the crop. Plants may develop small angular spots with a wide yellowish-green area around them. This 'halo' may be obvious in cool weather but in warmer weather it may not appear.

The bacteria can invade the water-conducting system of the plant and stunting, wilting and death then occur. The leaves may be pale green or yellow, while the veins show up as dark green and circular. Watersoaked or greasy spots occur on the pods and similar long, dark-green spots develop on the stems. If conditions are humid, whitish slime oozes from the spots. Wind, and rainy conditions quickly spread the bacterial cells from plant to plant.

PLANTS AFFECTED French beans and other *Phaseolus* spp. Also some related legumes.

CONTROL

• Organic/non-chemical: Plant only certified or approved seed, or seed that is known to have come from plants that were disease-free. Watch for the first signs of an outbreak, and remove and destroy affected plants, and those around. Do not work on the plants when they are wet. If halo blight has occurred in an area of ground, beans should not be grown there for at least two years because the bacteria can survive on pieces of old plant material.

• Chemical: Spray thoroughly with copper oxychloride or copper hydroxide.

Infectious variegation — camellia

This condition is characterised by variable symptoms which include small yellow marks here and there on the leaves, groups of yellow marks, or yellow leaf margins. It is uncommon for more than a few leaves on a plant to show these symptoms at the same time. The plant grows and produces flowers normally.

The cause may be a virus because it can be transmitted by grafting. There is no evidence of spread from plant to plant by insects or on tools such as budding knives.

PLANTS AFFECTED *Camellia japonica* and *C. reticulata*.

CONTROL

• Organic/non-chemical: Remove leaves showing symptoms if they are considered ugly. Symptoms will develop on other leaves from time to time.

Ink disease — kangaroo paw

Black spots on stems and leaves may indicate a fungal disease. However, note that almost any type of damage causes black marks on these plants.

If a fungus is involved it is likely to be *Alternaria alternata* rather than *Drechslera iridis* as previously thought.

Long periods of damp weather make fungal problems more prevalent and the plant may die if treatment is not carried out.

PLANTS AFFECTED All species of kangaroo paws (*Anigozanthos* spp.) but the red and green paws (*A. manglesii*) seem to be the worst affected. Some newer hybrids are much less affected by this problem.

CONTROL

• Organic/non-chemical: Avoid watering from above. Remove infected plant material from the area.

• Chemical: Mancozeb may control this disease.

Iron deficiency — citrus

When the plant is not able to take in enough iron, the leaves become light green fading to pale yellow or even white. This happens gradually and the veins remain green, almost until the end of the process. Youngest leaves are affected first.

In mild cases the leaf size and new growth appear normal, but if the deficiency is severe, the leaves will be reduced in size and dieback will occur. Fruit crop will be drastically reduced.

PLANTS AFFECTED All citrus.

CONTROL   This problem often occurs on alkaline soils. Some attempt can be made to lower the pH (see the information on pH in the section Planning and Maintaining Your Garden), but this is a slow process.

• Non-organic: Iron can be applied in the form of iron chelates to the soil or to the foliage. Follow label directions. Iron sulphate can be applied near deficient plants. A detailed description of the method can be found in Gardening Down-Under by Kevin Handreck (see Further Reading p. 301).

• Organic: Use a variety of animal manures. Check that poultry manure, mushroom compost and other composts are not alkaline before use in this situation. Be sure to let a few weeks elapse between digging in a green manure crop and planting the next crop.

Kikuyu yellows

Kikuyu yellows is a disease that is favoured by wet soil conditions in hot weather, and is widespread in the north of New South Wales and in Queensland.

The spread of the fungus is aided by water movement over the surface of the soil. The fungus causes extensive root rot and a general thinning and yellowing of the turf. The early stages show in definite circles but later these grow together and spread is more sheet-like.

It should not be confused with the white streaking of the leaves of kikuyu in winter in some areas, which is a physiological phenomenon. The areas affected by yellows become very thin and then die out leaving bare areas which are then quickly colonised by both broad-leafed and grass weeds.

PLANTS AFFECTED Kikuyu.

CONTROL   There is no specific treatment for this disease but improvement of drainage may help.

Late blight — celery *Septoria apiicola*

This fungal disease appears first on the lower outside leaves and then spreads to the rest of the plant, including the edible petioles. The spots are from 0.5 to 2 mm in diameter and brown when first noticed. The disease is favoured by cool moist weather, and if this continues the spots may run together causing whole leaves to wither and die. The development of spore-containing structures, which look like small dots, may give the area a generally black appearance. Late blight damage may be followed by secondary bacterial soft rots (D).

The fungus is generally introduced into an area in diseased seed and can be spread throughout a crop on implements and animals, and by rain and irrigation water. It is not generally spread by wind.

PLANTS AFFECTED Celery.

CONTROL

• Organic/non-chemical: Use disease-free seed or treat the seed with hot water as discussed in the section Planning and Maintaining Your Garden. Seed more than two years old will still germinate but is free of the disease because the fungus dies within this time.

Crop rotation is important, because the fungus can survive for some time on pieces of old plant; celery should not be grown in the same soil more frequently than once every two years.

• Chemical: The plants can be sprayed with a fungicide, but once the disease has started in a crop it is very difficult to control if the weather is suitable for the fungus. Use mancozeb or copper oxychloride. Thorough application is important.

Late blight — potato *Phytophthora infestans*

This disease often begins at the leaf margins as areas of a different colour green which later enlarge and go dark brown. The fungus can spread from the leaves into the stem. Tubers are infected when spores are washed from the top of the plant down into the soil. They develop brown to purplish-black sunken areas on the surface. These areas may be very extensive. If the potato is cut through, there are reddish-brown areas underneath these depressions.

In cool damp conditions, a fine white fungal growth can be seen on the undersides of the leaves, around the edges of the infected areas. The disease is worse in humid weather with cool nights and warm days.

The spores may be spread around by wind or splashed by water from leaf to leaf. Tubers that come into contact with diseased plant parts at harvest may later develop infected areas.

PLANTS AFFECTED Potatoes, tomatoes and some other solanaceous plants. Potato cultivars 'Sebago' and 'Sequoia' are not often attacked.

CONTROL

• Organic/non-chemical: Plant disease-free tubers. If the crop is diseased, cut off the tops and remove from the area before digging. Ensure that all tubers are removed from the ground. Separate diseased from healthy tubers before storage.

• Chemical: Spray with mancozeb or zineb or with copper oxychloride. Start applications as soon as the disease is noticed. Repeat every 7–10 days while the weather favours the disease.

Leaf blight — carrots *Alternaria dauci*

This fungus causes small spots on the leaves. A yellow region develops around each spot, and the leaves take on a general yellow appearance. This disease is worse in periods of rain or if heavy dews occur. The spots may extend on to the leafstalks and the whole foliage can be destroyed if the weather continues to be damp. It is spread from plant to plant by spores carried by air currents and introduced into a crop on diseased seed.

PLANTS AFFECTED Carrots.

CONTROL

• Organic/non-chemical: Seed saved from home-grown plants is likely to carry this disease, whereas commercially produced seed is free from contamination. Always practise crop rotation for carrots, and destroy any diseased plant material quickly.

• Chemical: Spray with copper oxychloride.

Leaf blight — strawberry
Phomopsis obscurans

This fungal disease can attack fruit stalks, leafstalks and stolons but the most obvious symptoms are on the leaves. The spots may be 6–25 mm across, and begin reddish-purple. Later they darken to brown in the centre and develop a reddish margin. The spots are irregular in shape, but are often V-shaped at the leaf edge. They may grow together to cover large areas of the leaf.

The fruiting bodies containing the fungal spores appear on these dead patches as black specks.

PLANTS AFFECTED Strawberries.

CONTROL

• Organic/non-chemical: Do not plant strawberries in shady damp areas. Remove and destroy dead and diseased leaves.

• Chemical: It is a good idea to spray with copper oxychloride when the plants are cut back and again in autumn.

Leaf blight — sweet corn   *Drechslera turcica*

This disease is characterised by long, thin, greyish-green to tan patches. They may reach 30 mm wide by 120 mm long. If a number of patches grow into one another, large areas of leaf can wither and die.

As the patches dry out, the centres become black with fungal spores. If many leaves are destroyed, the cobs will be small.

In coastal areas late-sown sweet corn is very likely to be damaged.

PLANTS AFFECTED Some sweet corn and maize varieties.

CONTROL
• Organic/non-chemical: Practise crop rotation. Use resistant varieties where available. Sow early in areas likely to have a wet autumn.

Leaf blight — umbrella tree
Alternaria panax

This disease is characterised by dark-brown to black patches on the leaves. These may enlarge to involve a quarter or more of the leaf. Leaves fall readily.

On the dwarf umbrella tree (*Schefflera arboricola*) the spots are much smaller and paler. On the underside of leaves the spots may be slightly raised. Young leaves may be distorted. Defoliation is unusual.

PLANTS AFFECTED Umbrella tree (*S. actinophylla*) and the dwarf umbrella tree (*S. arboricola*). Also *Fatshedera* sp. and ivy (*Hedera* sp.). The fungus concerned causes diseases in other members of the plant family Araliaceae such as *Aralia* sp., *Panax* sp., *Polyscias* sp. and *Dizygotheca* sp.

CONTROL
• Organic/non-chemical: Remove and destroy affected leaves promptly.
• Chemical: Try spraying with copper oxychloride.

Leaf curl — peach   *Taphrina deformans*

Look for this fungal disease in spring and early summer. Infected leaves are puckered or curled and much thicker than usual. They begin pale green but develop a deep pink or purplish colouration. Later, a white bloom appears on the surface and the leaves fall and die off. Small infected fruit usually fall also. New leaves form, but the tree will be seriously weakened if this disease is not controlled.

The symptoms on apricot trees are slightly different. In this case whole shoots are affected, with the curled leaves abnormally close together in a 'bunch'.

The leaves are infected when they are bursting from the buds, and by the time the symptoms are noticed it is too late for control measures that year. Make a note to spray earlier in the following year and apply a light dressing of quick-acting fertiliser such as sulphate of ammonia to encourage new leaf production.

This disease could be confused with an attack from the green peach aphid (P) which also results in curled leaves.

PLANTS AFFECTED Mostly peaches and nectarines, but almonds and apricots may be attacked. Some peach varieties are more susceptible than others; for example, 'Blackburn' and 'Elberta' are often attacked. Flowering stonefruit are also affected.

CONTROL
• Chemical: One application of copper oxychloride or copper hydroxide is sufficient but the timing is critical. Spray at or just before early bud-swell — that is, when the buds are beginning to get plumper. Do not apply after buds have burst; it will be too late to control the disease and will burn the young leaves. If in doubt about the state of the buds, spray in late winter and then again at bud-swell.

Leaf gall — azalea *Exobasidium vaccinii*

This fungus may attack leaves, flowers or seed pods, but symptoms are most often seen on the leaves. Whole leaves or parts of leaves may be affected. Affected areas turn pale green and become thick and fleshy. Sometimes the swellings become bladder-like. A white bloom of spores is formed on affected parts in wet weather. Symptoms are on new growth because only immature tissue is open to infection.

PLANTS AFFECTED Blueberries, azaleas and rhododendrons are all affected by this disease but it is most commonly seen on azaleas. Some cultivars are more susceptible than others: 'Hexe', 'Advent Bells' and 'Phoebus' are said to suffer from this problem more commonly than many others.

CONTROL
• Organic/non-chemical: This involves removal and burning of all affected parts. Spray with a fungicide only if new growth is still being formed.
• Chemical: Use copper oxychloride.

Leaf gall — camellia

Exobasidium camelliae

This fungal disease is able to infect the plant only when the leaves are extremely small. The fungus influences some of the cells to grow too large and to divide too much. This means that the leaf becomes extremely thick and much bigger than it would normally be. These infected leaves are usually a light green or white and always on the ends of branches. Sometimes the leaves have a deep pink or reddish appearance, and they are extremely noticeable and very ugly.

PLANTS AFFECTED This disease is common on *Camellia sasanqua* and occasionally attacks *Camellia reticulata.*

CONTROL
• Organic/non-chemical: There is no chemical control for this disease. The leaves should be pruned off and burnt. By the time these symptoms are noticed, the other leaves on the plant will be too old to be infected.

Leaf nematodes *Aphelenchoides* spp.

These nematodes can live on the plant in moist areas around buds or in the junction between leafstalks and stem if the weather is dry. They can also survive in a dried form in dead leaves on the ground.

When the plant is wet by rain or irrigation they move about on the surface and enter the leaves through stomates. Nematodes can be splashed from ground level on to lower leaves where damage will start. This may be a noticeable feature of nematode attack on a tall-growing plant like chrysanthemum.

The nematodes feed within the leaf tissues and cause patches of leaf to yellow and then go brown. The patches are often bounded by veins and appear as stripes (as in the photograph) or triangular areas, depending on the structure of the plant attacked. As feeding continues this pattern becomes less clear.

PLANTS AFFECTED A wide range, including African violets, anemones, begonias, blackcurrants, Cape primroses, coleus, chrysanthemums, cyclamens, ferns, fuchsias, gloxinias, kangaroo paws, ornamental figs and strawberries. Some chrysanthemum cultivars are more susceptible than others.

CONTROL
• Organic/non-chemical: Remove and destroy infested leaves. Avoid overhead watering if possible. Do not take cuttings from infested plants. Chrysanthemum stools can be treated in hot water (45°C for 5 minutes) after cleaning; the temperature must be accurately measured to ensure that the nematodes are killed but the plant is not damaged.
• Chemical: During the growing season the plants may be sprayed with fenthion. Begin the spraying programme as soon as leaf damage is noticed, and repeat once or twice at two-weekly intervals. If the weather is dry, the time between sprays can be increased.

Leaf roll — potato

Plants infected with this virus are usually stunted and have a very stiff, upright appearance. The leaf edges are rolled upwards, and if the plants are shaken, a rattling sound is produced. This disease is carried from plant to plant by aphids, particularly the green peach aphid (P).

Stems are thickened wherever the leaves join on, and tubers will probably be small and produce long thin sprouts.

PLANTS AFFECTED Potatoes.

CONTROL

• Organic/non-chemical: Use only certified seed and control aphids by spraying. Before planting, sprout the seed potatoes, and if any produce long spindly shoots (instead of the short stumpy ones that are normal) they should be destroyed.

Symptoms on clivea

Leaf scorch — bulbous plants

Stagonospora curtisii

Daffodil and jonquil leaves may show symptoms soon after they appear above ground. The leaf tips are reddish-brown and scorched in appearance, and as the leaves grow longer, oval brown spots develop lower down. The leaves go yellow at the tips and around the spots, and this tissue dies.

Belladonna lily leaves and flower stalks are usually bent at the point of infection and red spots appear along the leaf in lines. The bulb scales may develop dark, brownish-red spots.

Note that any injury to the leaves of the belladonna lily, clivea, crinum and hippeastrum, which are all from family Amaryllidaceae, tends to cause reddening.

This disease is most likely to develop in warm humid conditions. The fungus is found at the tops of the bulb scales, and the leaves become infected as they emerge from the bulb.

PLANTS AFFECTED Daffodils, jonquils, belladonna lilies, crinums, African lilies, hippeastrums and Kaffir lilies.

CONTROL

• Organic/non-organic: Regularly remove and burn infected leaves or remove leaf tips. Discard badly affected bulbs.

• Chemical: Try spraying at fortnightly intervals with copper oxychloride. Follow label directions.

Symptoms on agapanthus

Leaf speckle *Mycosphaerella musae*

A smoky discolouration of the undersides of leaves is the first sign of speckle. The leaves yellow in the affected areas, and the characteristic dark-brown to black dots or speckles gradually develop.

Badly affected leaves may yellow all over and hang down around the pseudo-stem. Fruit production will be reduced.

Spores are spread by wind. Germination is more likely on the lower sides of leaves which are shaded and remain moist longer.

PLANTS AFFECTED Bananas.

CONTROL

• Organic/non-chemical: Keep the plants growing vigorously. Remove and destroy diseased plant material.

• Chemical: Spray with mancozeb or with copper oxychloride. Add 1 mL of wetting agent per litre. The first application should be in early December. Repeat every three weeks until March. In tropical areas, spraying may be necessary all year round. Consult your local Department of Agriculture.

Pay special attention to the heart leaves and the undersides of the four youngest leaves. Do not spray plants on which bunches have appeared.

Leaf and pod spot — pea

This problem is caused by several fungi (*Mycosphaerella* sp. and *Ascochyta* spp.) and shows up as brown to black and purple blotches on pods, stems and leaves. The stem may develop a purplish-black rot towards ground level, and the plant may be ringbarked and die. Damage at the base is referred to as 'foot-rot'. Purplish areas may also develop further up the stem where leaves join the stem.

This disease may be introduced on infected seed and spores may be carried in wind. The problem is worst in cool damp weather.

PLANTS AFFECTED Peas.

CONTROL
• Organic/non-chemical: Remove and destroy infected plant material; use a 4–5 year crop rotation; and try to separate new plantings of peas from old ones.
• Chemical: Spray programmes may not be successful. Try mancozeb. Add wetting agent.

Leaf spot — banana *Mycosphaerella musicola*

This fungal leaf spot — which is also known as 'Sigatoka disease' — is widespread and shows up most between May and October. Fruit production is reduced.

The first signs of infection are pale yellow streaks about 10 mm long on the third or fourth youngest leaves. These change to brown, and enlarge to oval spots. Later they develop into grey spots with a thin brown or black border and a yellow halo.

If infection is severe, the leaves become brown with black and grey streaks.

PLANTS AFFECTED Bananas.

CONTROL
• Organic/non-chemical: Keep the plants growing vigorously. Remove and destroy diseased plant material.
• Chemical: Spray with mancozeb or with copper oxychloride. Add 1 mL of wetting agent per litre. The first application should be in early December. Repeat every three weeks until March. In tropical areas, spraying may be necessary all year round.

Pay special attention to the heart leaves and the undersides of the four youngest leaves. Do not spray plants on which bunches have appeared.

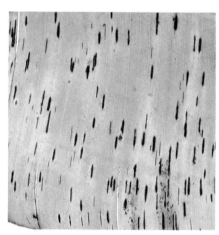

Leaf spot — blackcurrant

Septoria ribis

This fungal disease is common if spring and summer are unusually wet. It shows up on the leaves as light-grey angular spots with purple margins. If many spots are present, the leaves may appear brown and scorched and will fall early. Plant vigour is reduced. The fruit may also become infected and fall. Yields for the current and the next season are reduced. The fungus spends the winter in the fallen leaves and produces spores in the spring. These start a new infection.

PLANTS AFFECTED Currants.

CONTROL
• Chemical: Spray at green-tip stage with copper oxychloride. Follow label directions. When fruit is half-grown, spray again. Take care not to exceed the recommended rate.

Leaf spot — brush box

Elsinoe tristaniae

This fungal disease may be referred to as 'yellow leaf spot'.

The spots, which are a dull fawnish-yellow, may grow to 20 mm or more across. Several may occur on one leaf.

PLANTS AFFECTED Brush boxes (*Lophostemon confertus*). It is common on cultivated trees in some areas.

CONTROL Not usually necessary.

Leaf spot — chrysanthemum   *Septoria* spp.

The first signs of this disease are yellowish areas on the leaves, often near the edges. These become dark-brown circular spots which may continue to grow and run into one another, so that large areas of leaf tissue are browned. The leaves may fall from the plant prematurely.

   Small black dots on dead areas are the fruiting bodies of the fungus. These contain the spores, which can be spread to other leaves or plants by wind or water splash. The disease is worse in wet weather.

PLANTS AFFECTED Chrysanthemums, some varieties more than others.
CONTROL
• Chemical: Spray monthly with zineb or copper oxychloride. Spraying will need to be more frequent if the weather is showery and the plants are growing vigorously.

Leaf spot — dahlia   *Entyloma dahliae*

This fungus causes roundish spots of yellow-green on the leaves. These later go brown and dry out. The spots may be surrounded by a narrow yellowish area. A leaf with many spots may wither and die. Dead tissue in some spots may fall out, thus producing holes in the leaf.

   The disease is worse in cool humid weather, and the spores are spread by wind.
PLANTS AFFECTED Dahlias.
CONTROL
• Chemical: Spray with copper oxychloride when the disease is first seen. Repeat sprays may be necessary if the weather is humid.

Leaf spot — eucalypt   *Mycosphaerella* spp.

There are many different fungal leaf spots of eucalypts, but most are hardly noticed. However, there is a more noticeable leaf spot that infects the juvenile leaves of some eucalypts. In warm humid weather these silvery-blue rounded leaves may become marked with small irregular brown areas. This spotting causes them to look ugly.
PLANTS AFFECTED Eucalypts such as the eurabbie or blue gum (*Eucalyptus globulus* subsp. *bicostata*) and the Tasmanian blue gum (*E. globulus* subsp. *globulus*).
CONTROL   This is not necessary, because the tree is not seriously damaged. Once the adult leaves predominate, the symptoms will not be seen because these leaves are not susceptible to the disease.

Leaf spot — gerbera *Septoria gerberae*

This fungal disease is most likely to be seen in late summer or autumn. The spots begin brown to deep purple but develop grey to brown centres surrounded by a purplish ring. Small black dots on the centre of these spots are the fruiting bodies of the fungus. These contain many spores, which can be spread by wind and rain splash to other plants.

If the weather continues moist, spots (which are usually pinhead-size to 6 mm in diameter) may continue to grow and cause the death of large areas of the leaf.

There are other fungi that cause similar leaf-spotting on gerberas.

PLANTS AFFECTED Gerberas.

CONTROL

• Chemical: Remove as much diseased plant material as possible, and spray with copper oxychloride (50%) at the rate of 2 g per litre of water to protect the new leaves.

Leaf spot — grevillea

Placoasterella baileyi

This disease is characterised by more or less circular black spots on the leaves. It can disfigure the plant but probably does not cause permanent damage. It is found on plants both in the bush and in cultivation.

Reddish-brown leaf spots may be caused by another fungus, *Verrucispora* spp., which is principally a problem of very warm, humid climates or positions.

PLANTS AFFECTED Grevilleas and hakeas.

CONTROL

• Organic/non-chemical: Prune off the affected foliage. Try to improve air circulation in the area.

• Chemical: If necessary spray with mancozeb.

Leaf spot — Indian hawthorn

Entomosporium mespili

This disease is characterised by round spots up to 10 mm across. They develop a light-grey centre and a brown edge. Fungal fruiting bodies may appear as tiny dark-coloured specks. Older affected leaves turn yellow, orange or red, and will fall. Symptoms are most prevalent in winter and early spring.

PLANTS AFFECTED Indian hawthorn (*Raphiolepis indica*) and *R. x delacourii*, particularly mature specimens.

CONTROL

• Organic/non-chemical: Water and fertilise to encourage plant vigour and new growth.

• Chemical: Try spraying with copper oxychloride (50%) at the rate of 5 g per litre of water as soon as the first spots are noticed.

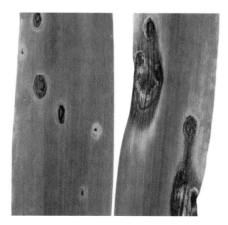

Leaf spot — iris *Cladosporium iridis*

This disease first shows up as tiny brown spots, each with a watersoaked area around it. As these spots enlarge they turn grey and develop brown to red margins. Eventually the spots run together to form large dead areas and the leaves are killed. If this continues the plant is weakened and normal flowering cannot occur.

This disease is worse in warm wet weather. Fungal spores are spread about by wind and by water splash.

PLANTS AFFECTED Irises that grow from rhizomes commonly have this disease, but irises that grow from bulbs are affected less frequently.

CONTROL

• Organic/non-chemical: Remove and burn old infected leaves in autumn.

• Chemical: Spray with copper oxychloride and add a suitable wetting agent at the rate of 1 mL per litre of water so that the spray will stick better to the leaf surface. It may be necessary to repeat this every 10–14 days if the weather continues to be warm and wet.

Leaf spot — ivy *Colletotrichum trichellum*

This fungus is most likely to be damaging in cool spring weather and on ivy plants growing in cool, damp situations or areas.

The leaves yellow and fall from the plant.

PLANTS AFFECTED Ivy (*Hedera helix*).

CONTROL
• Organic/non-chemical: Remove and burn diseased leaves as they are noticed.
• Chemical: If necessary spray with a general purpose fungicide, such as wettable sulphur.

Leaf spot — mulberry *Phloeospora maculans*

In the spring, leaves are infected by spores blown from fallen leaves. Pinhead-size dark-brown spots appear on the leaves. These are usually surrounded by a light green to yellow area. When this part of the leaf dies, the spots are increased in size. Gradually the middle of the irregularly round spot whitens but the edges remain dark brown. Veins near these spots become discoloured also.

The fruiting bodies of the fungus develop on the spots and show up as small, pinpoint black dots. In wet or humid weather these might have a pinkish appearance because of the release of spores. These spores can be splashed to other leaves.

PLANTS AFFECTED Mulberries.

CONTROL
• Organic/non-chemical: Rake up and burn all fallen leaves in autumn.
• Chemical: In spring when young leaves are emerging from the buds, spray thoroughly with lime–sulphur at the rate of 20 mL per litre of water. Two weeks later spray again with lime–sulphur at the rate of 12.5 mL per litre of water. Repeat the last spray after the fruit has set.

Leaf spot — rhubarb *Ascochyta rhei*

This fungal disease begins as small circular brown spots on the leaves. As the spots get bigger, they develop reddish-brown borders and small black dots appear on their surfaces. These black dots are the fruiting bodies of the fungus and contain the spores which can be spread around to other plants by splashing water.

The pieces of affected leaf tissue eventually die and fall out, and if the conditions continue to be wet and therefore favourable to the fungus, the plants may lose most of their leaves. The leafstalks (that is, the part that we wish to eat) can also be affected and small oval reddish-brown spots develop. These increase in size until they are more than 10 mm long.

PLANTS AFFECTED Rhubarb.

CONTROL
• Organic/non-chemical: Affected leaves should be removed and burnt. The plants should be kept growing vigorously by adequate fertiliser and watering programmes.
• Chemical: If spraying is necessary, use copper oxychloride or zineb.

Leaf spot — strawberry *Mycosphaerella fragariae*

The well-defined spots caused by this fungus begin brownish but later change to light grey or white in the centre and purplish or reddish-brown around the edge. They are usually no more than 3 mm in diameter. If large numbers of spots occur, the leaves quickly turn yellow and die. If the disease occurs late in the season, the damage will be minimal, but if it occurs early on poorly cared-for plants, the losses may be serious.

Pieces of old infected plant material in the soil can be a source of infection. The fungal spores are spread by wind or rain splash, and the disease is likely to be more serious in late spring if wet periods prevail.

PLANTS AFFECTED Strawberries.

CONTROL

• Organic/non-chemical: Remove diseased plant parts from the area. Do not plant strawberries in shady damp situations.

• Chemical: It is a good idea to spray with copper oxychloride (50%) when the plants are cut back, and again in autumn. Use a rate of 5 g per litre of water.

Leaf spot — turf *Drechslera* spp.

This disease is characterised by patches which occur in mid- to late summer especially in hot humid weather. They normally grow to about saucer size. The turf turns from black to brown to grey. This colour persists for a long time, possibly months, unless the turf is fertilised generously.

PLANTS AFFECTED Predominantly warm climate grasses.

CONTROL

• Organic/non-chemical: Apply nitrogenous fertiliser.

• Chemical: Spray with mancozeb (80%) at the rate of 120 g in 5 L of water over 100 square metres.

Symptoms on kikuyu

Leaf spot — violet *Cercospora violae*

Violet leaves that are spotted are likely to have been infected by this fungus.

This problem can be serious. If the disease is spreading from leaf to leaf, control measures should be taken.

PLANTS AFFECTED Violets, pansies and violas.

CONTROL

• Organic/non-chemical: Remove and destroy infected leaves as soon as they are seen. Improve air circulation around the plants.

• Chemical: Spray with zineb.

Symptoms on pansy leaves

Lettuce big vein

The symptoms of this viral disease are most pronounced in winter. The problem is most likely to occur if soils are wet and heavy.

The disease is characterised by slow growth of the plant and large transparent bands along the veins. The heart is smaller than normal. The leaves may be yellow or white along the leaf veins and thicker and more crinkled than usual.

PLANTS AFFECTED Lettuces.

CONTROL
• Organic/non-chemical: Crop rotation does not control this disease. Do not plant lettuce in areas where this disease has occurred. There are no suitable chemical controls.

Lettuce necrotic yellows

This viral disease results in stunting and yellowing of the plants and development of one side of the plant more than the other. The leaves may be crinkled. The disease is spread by a particular aphid which feeds on sow thistles and then transmits the disease to lettuce. It is more common in autumn because the aphid population is high at that time.

PLANTS AFFECTED Lettuces.

CONTROL
• Organic/non-chemical: Remove and destroy sow thistles (*Sonchus oleraceus*: also called milk thistle) growing nearby. Chemical controls are not effective.

Diseased plant on the left, healthy plant on the right

Lichens

Each of these plants is a symbiotic association of a fungus and an alga. The fungus shelters the algal cells and the algal cells produce food for the fungal cells.

Some types are flat and grow in a circular fashion while others are more leaf-like. They are typically a greenish-grey colour but some are yellow or orange. Lichens are firmly attached and will remain for a long period unless removed by vigorous brushing.

PLANTS AFFECTED They grow on almost any long-lived plant, on rocks and also on structures such as fences and sheds.

CONTROL
• Chemical: This is not usually necessary, but if required use copper oxychloride. This chemical may harm some building materials.

Magnesium deficiency — citrus

Magnesium deficiency shows up first on older leaves. The leaves begin to yellow near the midrib, and this yellow blotch enlarges until the only green remaining is at the tip of the leaf and near the base in a V-shape. If this problem continues, the entire leaf may yellow.

New growth in mild cases is a normal green, because magnesium, which is a constituent of chlorophyll, is moved from old leaves to new ones. It is also moved to developing fruit particularly in seedy varieties. Leaf fall and a reduction in crop size will follow magnesium deficiency.

This problem is more likely on acid soils but also occurs on alkaline soils.

PLANTS AFFECTED All citrus.

CONTROL This deficiency can be corrected by spreading 500 g to 1 kg of Epsom salts (magnesium sulphate) around under the tree. The area should then be watered. A quicker result will be obtained by dissolving 20 g of magnesium sulphate in every litre of water, and spraying this on to the foliage.

Manganese deficiency — citrus

Manganese deficiency shows up on the younger leaves first as light-green or yellowish-green areas between the main veins. The leaves are a normal size and the veins remain green. If the deficiency is not severe, the leaves go green again as they get older; but if the deficiency is serious, the leaves will remain yellowish-green.

This deficiency occurs in acid soils where manganese is naturally low and in alkaline soils where manganese, if present, is in an insoluble compound and thus unavailable to the plant.

PLANTS AFFECTED All citrus.

CONTROL

• Non-organic: Use a spray of manganese sulphate at the rate of 1 g per litre of water. This should be applied in spring when the leaves are about two-thirds grown. If the plant also shows symptoms of zinc deficiency, add zinc sulphate (1 g per L). Spots of this solution on the fruit would produce dark marks which remain for a long time. Time the spray so that as little fruit as possible is present.

• Organic: Use poultry manure but ensure the soil does not start to become too alkaline.

Melanose — citrus *Diaporthe citri*

This fungus causes reddish-brown to dark-brown tiny dots on the leaves or fruit. If few spores are present the dots will be spaced far apart, but if many spores germinate and begin to grow the dots will be crowded close together and may give an all-over brown appearance in patches on the leaves and fruit.

If the spores are washed by rain or dew so that they run over the surface of the fruit, then they may begin to grow in streaks curving down the side of the fruit. Sometimes so many spores are washed on to a piece of fruit that the skin cracks and what is termed a 'mud-cake' appearance develops. This looks rather like the dried mud on a river-bed. If the fruit is heavily infected it will be slightly deformed or fail to grow to its full size.

This disease occurs more in older trees because there is a greater proportion of dead twigs and branches both on the tree and under the tree. The fungus can live in these areas and produce spores. It grows best at temperatures of about 25°C, and some moisture (rain, heavy dew or fog) is necessary for disease development.

PLANTS AFFECTED 'Washington Navel' oranges, sour oranges, 'Emperor' mandarins and lemons are more susceptible than grapefruit and 'Valencia' oranges. All citrus varieties, however, are sometimes attacked.

CONTROL

• Organic/non-chemical: Prune off dead twigs and remove dead branches. Remove dead material from under the tree.

• Chemical: When about half the petals have fallen, spray with copper oxychloride at the rate of 4 g per litre of water, plus 6 mL of white oil per litre of water. Repeat 6–12 weeks later.

Mistletoes

There are many different species of these parasitic plants. The sticky seeds are spread by birds. When they germinate, root-like growths are sent into the host plant to obtain water and nutrients. The infected trees gradually die.

Mistletoe foliage is generally more fleshy than that of the host and tends to hang down in bunches. It may be a different shade of green.

PLANTS AFFECTED Many different species, both exotic and native. Eucalypts are common hosts. Trees in exposed positions are often parasitised.

CONTROL

• Organic/non-chemical: The mistletoe should be cut out of the branch. It may be necessary to remove the whole branch if damage is severe; merely cutting off the leafy section of the parasite is not sufficient. If the mistletoe is high in a tree, employ a tree surgeon.

Mosaic — cucurbits

This disease is caused by the watermelon mosaic virus. The symptoms are mottling of the leaves in light and dark green. The leaves may become distorted, and the plant may not grow as big as it normally would. The fruit of some cucurbits may have sunken concentric circles, or a raised marble pattern.

The disease is spread by the cotton aphid (*Aphis gossypii*), the green peach aphid (P) (*Myzus persicae*), and other aphids. Weeds such as wild cucumber (*Cucumis trigonis*) may be a source of infection.

PLANTS AFFECTED Most cucurbits are susceptible. Pumpkin and zucchini plants are most often attacked.

CONTROL

• Organic/non-chemical: Affected plants should be removed and destroyed. Once symptoms are noticed in a small planting, spraying to control aphids is useless.

Symptoms on pumpkin

Mosaic — iris

This is a virus disease. On irises that grow from a rhizome, symptoms are light yellow-green streaks on the foliage. These streaks widen and brown and the leaves die. The flowers are normal in appearance but mature earlier than they otherwise would. The disease carries over from season to season in the rhizome and is spread from plant to plant by aphids.

In bulbous irises this disease is very serious. It may prevent flowering or produce flowers with dark streaks on the petals. The leaves are mottled with dark and light green, and this is most evident on young leaves and bud sheaths. In young plants the leaves have yellow streaks along them.

PLANTS AFFECTED Both rhizomatous and bulbous irises.

CONTROL

• Organic/non-chemical: Infected rhizomes and bulbs should be destroyed by burning. Try to control aphids with soap spray.

• Chemical: Use dimethoate as directed on the label.

Mosaic — potato

Several different viruses cause mosaic symptoms on potatoes and other related plants. These viruses are referred to as 'potato viruses X, A and Y'. Symptoms vary from a light mottling of yellow and green on the leaves, to yellow and green spots, or crinkling of leaf tissue. Sometimes leaf veins are blackened. Plants may die early.

PLANTS AFFECTED Potatoes.

CONTROL

• Organic/non-chemical: Control aphids with soap sprays and/or yellow water pan traps. Plant only certified seed.

• Chemical: Spray to control aphids with an insecticide such as dimethoate.

Mosaic — rose

This disease is caused by a complex of viruses and is characterised by yellow patterns on the leaves. These patterns are variable and range from all-over fine blotching to patterns of wavy lines. They may occur on many leaves or only on a few.

The disease is not considered to be serious as it is only introduced into a plant at the time of grafting by the use of diseased understocks or diseased scions.

PLANTS AFFECTED Roses.

CONTROL This disease can safely be ignored as it is not spread by insects. Flower production is normal. Do not use such a plant for propagation.

Mosaic — turnip

On cabbage, cauliflower and broccoli, the first symptoms of this virus disease are yellow rings on the youngest leaves. Later the leaves are mottled with rings and blotches of different greens. These symptoms are most pronounced in warm weather. In colder weather black rings occur on the older leaves.

On turnips and swedes, the youngest leaves show a clearing of the veins and then a coarse mottled and dark-green ring pattern.

On stocks, plants may be stunted, and leaves are distorted, wrinkled and mottled with areas of lighter colour. Flowers are streaked with white or pale colours.

This virus is spread mostly by the green peach aphid (P) (*Myzus persicae*), although a number of other aphids have also been shown to be involved.

PLANTS AFFECTED Cruciferous vegetables such as cabbages, cauliflowers, broccoli, turnips and swedes. Annual flowers in the same family such as stocks, alyssum, wallflowers and honesty. Weeds including shepherd's purse, field cress, wild turnip, mustard and charlock.

CONTROL

• Organic/non-chemical: This is difficult. Insect control is generally of no benefit because aphids can usually transmit the disease before they are killed. The incidence of disease may be reduced if weeds are removed and resistant cultivars are grown. 'Superette' is a resistant cabbage variety. Remove diseased plants and destroy them promptly. Plant only disease-free seedlings.

Neck rot — onion   *Botrytis* spp.

This fungal problem shows up during storage. The top of the bulb around the neck becomes soft and rots. If conditions are humid, a greyish furry growth develops. Resting bodies of the fungus, which are black and up to 5 mm in diameter, sometimes develop beneath the outer skins of the onion.

PLANTS AFFECTED Onions.

CONTROL

• Organic/non-chemical: Allow the onion tops to mature and dry thoroughly before harvesting. Do not cut them off too close to the bulb. Ensure that the onions are not damaged during harvest, and store the bulbs in a cool, dry and well-ventilated situation. Practise crop rotation and remove all old pieces of plant and unwanted bulbs from the growing areas.

Oedema — camellia

'Oedema' is the term used for small corky brown or grey scabby areas on the leaves. The affected tissue is hard and may occur on only a few leaves.

It may be caused by low transpiration rates in humid weather.

PLANTS AFFECTED Most frequently *Camellia japonica*.

CONTROL   Not really necessary. Restriction of water supplies to the plant during cloudy weather may lessen the problem.

Ophiobolus patch

Gaeumannomyces graminis var. *avenae*

This disease of bent grass is caused by the same fungus that causes 'take-all' in wheat. It severely stunts and rots the roots of the plants. This may not be noticed in cool weather while the damage is occurring, but may become obvious with the onset of hot weather. The grass will suddenly show symptoms of browning and yellowing similar to water stress but in definite circles. These may be large: up to several metres in diameter. The grass on the edges is often a fiery orange colour while the grass in the centre recovers poorly and the patch is often invaded by weeds. The disease is more severe in alkaline soils, and outbreaks may follow heavy lime applications. The disease is more likely to occur in soils with low organic matter content and with low or unbalanced nutrient supply.

The fungus responsible for this disease was known formerly as *Ophiobolus graminis* var. *avenae*.

PLANTS AFFECTED Bent grass.

CONTROL   There is no really effective treatment. Ensure that drainage is good and that proper watering practices are followed. If lime is to be applied, use only the coarsest grades. Add poultry manure but check that it is not alkaline. Use acidifying fertiliser such as sulphate of ammonia.

Parsnip canker *Itersonilia perplexans*

Symptoms of this fungal disease appear on the upper widest part of the root as a brown or reddish rough surface. Later, the area might develop large depressions or cankers, and if the infection is severe the entire root may be rotted. This disease is most serious if the season is wet or the soil is poorly drained. It may carry over from crop to crop in infected plant parts in the soil and is also spread by spores in the wind.

Leaf spots have a light brown centre surrounded by a pale yellow area and may be 1–3 mm across. They are commonly bounded by small veins. These affected areas of leaves may become torn. Spots may also occur on the leafstalks. In this case they are elongated, sunken and dark brown.

PLANTS AFFECTED Wild parsnips, wild carrots, chrysanthemums and sunflowers, as well as cultivated parsnips.

CONTROL

• Organic/non-chemical: Quickly collect and destroy all diseased roots and other diseased plant parts. Crop rotation is important; parsnips should be grown in the one area only once every three years. Use disease-free seed. Parsnips are not suitable for storing in the ground after they are mature.

Cracks may develop in the damaged area.

Pestalotiopsis — camellia
Pestalotiopsis sp.

This fungus invades areas of leaf that are already sunburnt or damaged in some other way. The area usually becomes silvery grey and may have the black pinprick-size fruiting bodies of the fungus on it.

PLANTS AFFECTED This seems most common on *Camellia japonica.*

CONTROL   Adjust cultural practices to minimise leaf damage.

Petal blight *Ovulinia azaleae*

The buds and flowers are the only part of the plant affected by this fungal disease. The disease is usually first noticed as circular spots about 2 mm in diameter. The spots are brown on white or other pale-coloured flowers, and white or cream on dark-coloured flowers. These spots enlarge quickly into irregular blotches, and if conditions are humid the whole corolla soon becomes brown and slightly slimy.

Affected flowers dry out until they are brown and papery. They remain stuck on to the plant for some weeks, unlike healthy flowers which fall from the bush once faded.

If humid conditions continue, the fungus produces resting bodies called sclerotia on the dead petals. These resting bodies are seed-like in appearance and become black. They vary in size but many are about 4 mm long. They eventually fall to the ground, and in countries with a severe winter they have been known to be a source of infection for the next flowering season. There is no evidence that this is the case in Australia. If rotted petals only are seen, the problem may be grey mould (D). Failure to diagnose the disease correctly sometimes explains poor results from fungicide applications.

PLANTS AFFECTED   This fungal disease attacks *Rhododendron* spp. including deciduous azaleas such as those in the Mollis group but occurs most on Kurume and Indica azaleas. It also attacks *Kalmia latifolia.*

CONTROL

• Organic/non-chemical: Collecting and destroying dead and diseased flowers will only delay the problem slightly because spores can blow from plants considerable distances away.

• Chemical: This disease cannot be satisfactorily controlled without a spray programme. Begin spraying as soon as the buds show colour, particularly if the weather is humid, and use triadimefon (Bayleton®).

Phytophthora blight — passionfruit

Phytophthora nicotianae var. *parasitica*

The fungus that causes this disease is a soil inhabitant and produces spores on the soil surface in warm wet weather. These spores are then splashed up on to the lower parts of the vine where the infection begins. Wind and driven rain spread spores further up the vine. Mature leaves show large patches which are translucent at first and then turn light brown. Shoots may die from the tip and appear black. On the fruit, large grey-green watersoaked spots enlarge to cover much of the surface. Infected leaves and fruit usually fall from the vine.

The stem may be girdled above the graft. In this case the area appears purple and later brown, and the whole vine wilts and dies.

PLANTS AFFECTED This fungus has a very wide host range. As well as attacking passionfruit, it causes many other diseases including crown rot of rhubarb, and top and root rot of pineapple (D).

CONTROL

• Organic/non-chemical: Plant the vines so that they receive a maximum amount of sunlight and are not too close together. If they become extremely bushy, thin them out by pruning. Avoid leaving areas of bare soil underneath the vine.

• Chemical: Chemical control is difficult but copper oxychloride (50%) at the rate of 2 g per litre of water would be suitable. If conditions are wet and thus favour the fungus, spraying may be necessary every 7–10 days. If the fruit is maturing, copper oxychloride should be avoided because residues may be left on the fruit.

Phytophthora root rot *Phytophthora* spp.

These fungi start by infecting the root hairs and rotting fine roots. Rotting of larger roots and the stem base may follow. Leaves yellow and die, and branches die back from the tips. The plants may die quickly in a period of hot weather or linger for months without putting on any new growth. If only part of the root system is destroyed, one or two branches will die and the rest of the plant may remain alive.

Examination of the root system will show that there are very few small fibrous roots. Those present are dark and brittle instead of whitish.

On avocados pale green wilting foliage may indicate this disease. Leaves fall and branches die back.

The fungus *P. cinnamomi* is apparently unable to infect macadamia roots but does enter the plant through wounds on the trunk around ground level, causing a disease called 'trunk canker'. Discoloured bark and oozing gum probably indicates this disease. The trees are stunted and have yellowish leaves. Unless the disease is treated, the trees may be ringbarked.

The disease develops quickly in moist soils, and spread of the fungi is hastened if there is running water in the area. Spread also occurs on diseased potted plants (before they show symptoms) and in contaminated soil.

PLANTS AFFECTED The fungi that cause this disease can attack a wide range of different trees and shrubs and smaller plants such as strawberries and carnations.

Some plants resist attack. These include Bhutan cypress (*Cupressus torulosa*), Arizona cypress (*C. glabra*), box elder (*Acer negundo*), sweet gum (*Liquidambar styraciflua*), smooth-barked apple (*Angophora costata*), eucalypts (such as *Eucalyptus camaldulensis*, *E. citriodora*, *E. globulus*, *E. maculata*, *E. microcorys*, *E. robusta* and *E. saligna*), purple hopbush (*Dodonaea viscosa 'Purpurea'*), cabbage tree (*Cordyline australis*), spindle tree (*Euonymus japonicus*), New Zealand flax (*Phormium tenax*) and oleander (*Nerium oleander*).

CONTROL

• Organic/non-chemical: Improve drainage. Avoid overwatering. Use organic mulches such as straw around trees but do not allow them to touch the trunk. Use animal manures on a regular basis. If appropriate, apply lime or dolomite. Avoid trunk wounds. Remove and destroy affected plants.

• Chemical: If replanting is to occur, drench the area with furalaxyl (Fongarid®) at the rate of 1 g per litre of water. Apply 2–4 L per square metre of soil and water in. Apply to surrounding shrubs also. Slightly damaged plants can be saved by this treatment. *Trunk canker:* Cut away diseased bark and wood. Paint with copper oxychloride paste.

Affected tree in foreground has pale green sparse foliage. Compare with unaffected tree in background, which has darker leaves.

Powdery mildews

The term 'powdery mildew' applies to a group of related fungi. Some of them can attack a range of different plants, while others attack only one or two. Almost all of them begin as faint white spots on leaves. These spots gradually increase in size if the weather continues favourable for the fungus, until the whole leaf surface is covered in white powder. Buds, stems and fruit may also be infected.

Leaves that are fully formed when the fungus begins to grow are not changed in shape, although they do develop spots which remain even after the powdery substance has disintegrated. But leaves that are young when attacked may be distorted — for example, they may curl up at the edges or become slightly puckered. In the case of powdery mildew on some crepe myrtle (*Lagerstroemia indica*) cultivars, the powdery covering becomes thick and pronounced and the leaves fold up. On pea plants, the leaves and stems may be dwarfed and twisted. Mango fruit develops purplish-brown blotches and immature fruit may fall.

Powdery mildew spores generally require high humidity for germination but they will not germinate in rainy weather. However, once the fungus has started to grow it will continue to do so even if conditions become dry. Most fungi in the powdery mildew group are able to infect plants within a temperature range of 11–28°C.

PLANTS AFFECTED A wide range, including ornamentals such as crepe myrtles, hydrangeas, spindle trees, ajugas, oaks, photinias, sweet peas and zinnias. See also powdery mildew of apples, cucurbits, grapes, papaws and strawberries.

CONTROL
• Organic/non-chemical: Where possible choose the least susceptible varieties.
• Chemical: Spray as soon as the disease is noticed. Use wettable sulphur at the rate of 2–4 g per litre of water. Do not use sulphur in hot weather or if plants are short of water.

Symptoms on crepe myrtle,
Lagerstroemia indica

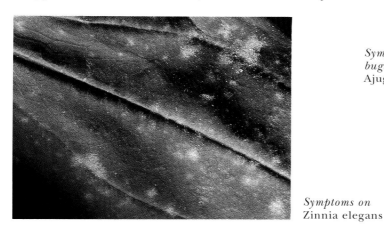

Symptoms on bugle weed, Ajuga reptans

Symptoms on Zinnia elegans

Powdery mildew — apple

Podosphaera leucotricha

This serious disease shows up as a white powdery covering on buds, shoots, leaves and fruit. If buds are affected the leaves may be killed, may develop abnormally or may be brittle and curled. They may also drop prematurely.

If fully formed when attacked by the fungus, leaves usually develop a wavy margin and their edges turn upwards. Fruit symptoms are particularly noticeable on red-skinned varieties, which develop a pattern of fine, yellowish criss-crossing lines.

PLANTS AFFECTED Some varieties such as 'Jonathan' and 'Gravenstein' are more susceptible than others. Quince trees may also be affected.

CONTROL
• Organic/non-chemical: It is possible to recognise powdery mildew-infected shoots in winter. The shoots look thin and slightly dried out, and the buds look dry. Prune off as many of these pieces as possible and remove them from the area. In spring watch for infected shoots and remove them as soon as possible.
• Chemical: The following programme is probably necessary for highly susceptible varieties. Spray with wettable sulphur following label directions. Apply the first spray at blossoming and thereafter at 7–10 day intervals for 4–6 weeks if the weather is favourable to the fungus. On less susceptible varieties, watch for the first signs of the disease and then spray.

See also powdery mildews (D), above.

Powdery mildew — cucurbits *Oidium* sp.

This fungal disease is widespread and worse in warm dry conditions. It is spread from affected plants by spores carried in air currents.

The white spots appear first underneath the older leaves. If conditions that are satisfactory for the fungus continue, these spots may spread to the upper leaf surfaces and gradually, if the fungus continues to grow, both surfaces will be covered with a white powdery growth. The stems may also be affected. The vines will stop growing vigorously and older leaves may yellow and die. The check in growth may reduce fruit size and exposed fruit may be sunburnt.

PLANTS AFFECTED All pumpkins, marrows, squashes and grammas. Watermelons can be seriously damaged, but are rarely affected. The cucumber 'Green Gem' is tolerant of powdery mildew. All apple cucumber cultivars are susceptible. The rock melon cultivars 'Gulf Coast', 'Planter's Jumbo', 'Early Dawn', 'Satacoy' and 'Dixie Jumbo' are tolerant.

CONTROL
• Organic/non-chemical: Plant a resistant cultivar if available. Remove old diseased plant parts as soon as possible.
• Chemical: Spray with wettable sulphur.

Powdery mildew — grape
Oidium sp.

This disease is characterised by greyish-white powdery spots on leaves, shoots and berries. The fungus also damages the flowers and causes poor fruit set. Fruit may split and dry out; dark-coloured varieties may colour unevenly. If the surface-growing fungus is rubbed off, dark web-like markings may be seen. Leaves infected when young may be distorted and eventually shrivel.

This disease is most likely to occur in warm humid weather during the spring and summer.

PLANTS AFFECTED Grapes.

CONTROL
• Chemical: Spray with wettable sulphur at the rate of 4 g per litre of water, or dust with sulphur. Apply when the shoots are 150–250 mm long; and again just before or after flowering. More frequent applications may be necessary if the weather favours fungal growth.

Avoid the use of sulphur in hot weather. If it must be applied, reduce the rate of wettable sulphur to 2 g per litre of water. Apply dusts in the early morning.

If grapes are to be used for wine-making, do not use sulphur within four weeks of harvest.

Powdery mildew — papaw *Oidium* sp.

Damage is most serious on the green fruit. And although many parts of the plant are susceptible, symptoms are most common on older leaves. The fungus can grow on both leaf surfaces but is most likely to be seen on the underside of the leaf. The white powdery growth develops in spots to begin with, but gradually these spread out until they run together and give large areas of the leaf a white powdery appearance. The infected areas go yellow.

The fungus causes light-grey, irregularly shaped areas on the skin of the fruit. Because the growth of the tissue beneath has been interfered with, the fruit will eventually be misshapen. This problem does not affect the flesh of the papaw but would reduce its market value.

The disease is worse in cool weather and is most common in winter. As the weather warms up in the spring, the disease disappears.

PLANTS AFFECTED Papaws.

CONTROL This may be unnecessary in a home garden because the flesh of the fruit is not affected.
• Chemical: Powdery mildew can be controlled by applying wettable sulphur every 2–4 weeks from late autumn to mid-spring. Apply so that both leaf surfaces and the fruit are thoroughly covered. Sulphur should not be used when the temperature is over 24°C.

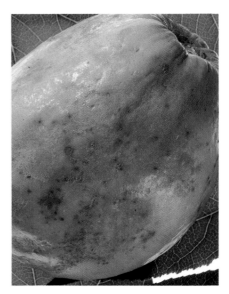

Powdery mildew — rose *Oidium* sp.

This fungal disease produces a fine white coating on the surface of leaves and buds. In severe cases it also infects stems, particularly near thorns. If leaves are attacked while they are young they become distorted and have a wavy appearance. Growth is seriously reduced and flower buds may fail to open.

Flowers which do open are often distorted or discoloured. If fully formed leaves are attacked, their shape is not altered but they do develop a white powdery growth and later blackened areas.

This disease is a problem in hot, humid weather. The fungus survives in dormant buds or on fallen leaves.

PLANTS AFFECTED Roses; some cultivars such as 'Granada' and 'Folklore' are more susceptible than others. 'Dorothy Perkins' and 'Excelsa' are very prone to powdery mildew.

CONTROL
• Organic/non-chemical: Plant the least susceptible varieties.
• Chemical: Control programmes need to start early on susceptible varieties, and spraying should be carried out regularly if the weather continues to be warm and humid. Spray with wettable sulphur at the rate of 2–4 g per litre of water. Triforine is another suitable chemical.

Powdery mildew — strawberry *Oidium* sp.

On strawberries, powdery mildew does not always produce its characteristic greyish-white growth. Usually the first symptoms noticed are upward curling of the leaf margins. Later, purple blotches of irregular shape may appear on the upper surface. These blotches frequently occur along the main veins, and the leaves develop a brittle feel.

Infected plants will bear a poor fruit crop. Flowers die without fruit set. Immature fruit remains hard and small and may not ripen. Fruit that is ripe or nearly ripe at the time of infection develops a dull appearance. The seeds stand out more than usual. Cracks may develop in the fruit particularly near the stem end.

This disease is worse in warm humid conditions, and the spores are spread from place to place by the wind. Strawberry plants in shaded situations are more likely to be affected than those in full sun.

PLANTS AFFECTED Strawberries.

CONTROL
• Chemical: If spraying is necessary, use wettable sulphur.

Powdery scab *Spongospora subterranea*

This disease is characterised by small brown blister-like swellings about 2 mm across on the tubers. The swellings may enlarge to 10 mm or more and are circular or oval.

The brown powdery mass of spores produced inside the gall is exposed when the skin breaks and curls back. Roots may be infected without showing symptoms.

PLANTS AFFECTED Potatoes, tomatoes and some solanaceous weeds.

CONTROL
• Organic/non-chemical: Plant only disease-free tubers. Once this disease is introduced into a soil, potatoes cannot be successfully grown there for very many years. Do not try to grow potatoes in poorly drained land. Do not overwater the soil. This disease is worse if soil moisture is high when infection is likely to take place and at soil temperatures below 18°C.

Purple top wilt — potato

This disease is caused by a mycoplasma which is spread from plant to plant by the common brown leafhopper (Orosius argentatus), a small sap-sucking insect. It is most likely to occur in hot dry weather because the leafhopper moves from weeds that dry off at this time on to cultivated and therefore more succulent crops.

Young leaves curl upwards and leafstalks appear very erect. The leaves of white-flowered potato varieties go yellow, and the leaves of purple-flowered varieties go purple or red at the tips and edges. Eventually the stems collapse, and if they are split a brown discolouration can be seen. Tubers, if formed, are small and flabby. Under irrigation or conditions of high moisture the plants develop a bunched appearance.

PLANTS AFFECTED This organism can exist in a wide variety of different vegetables, ornamentals and weeds.

CONTROL

• Organic/non-chemical: Once a plant has a disease caused by a mycoplasma there is no way it can be cured. Avoid infection by removing weeds from within or around the crop and spraying to control insects.

Ray blight — chrysanthemum

Didymella ligulicola

This disease shows up first as tiny dark-pink spots on the petals. It often starts on one side of the flower, causing the flower to grow in a lopsided fashion if it is in the early stages of development. The fungus spreads quickly from these initial areas of infection and the petals brown and rot.

The fungus may grow from the flower down into the stem and cause the flower stem to weaken and droop. Leaf spots can occur but are not very common. They are large dark-brown spots, often with concentric marks.

The disease is most damaging in early autumn and other times when warm humid weather prevails.

PLANTS AFFECTED Chrysanthemums.

CONTROL

• Organic/non-chemical: Do not overfertilise with nitrogenous fertilisers. Hygiene is important: destroy diseased plants and remove spent flowers with their stalks. Do not take cuttings from infected plants.

• Chemical: Spray every 7–14 days with zineb. Add wetting agent and apply the spray thoroughly. When flower buds start to develop, use 1 g per litre of water and apply at least once per week.

Red thread *Laetisaria fuciformis*

This disease is characterised by mottled patches of grass. Some leaves in the affected area are tan-coloured and dead, while others remain uninfected. The fungus is visible as a broad pink or pale red thread which has a gelatinous appearance; the colour is similar to that of some match heads. Problems usually occur when fertility levels are low. This fungus was formerly known as *Corticium fuciforme*. A similar disease, pink patch, is caused by the fungus, *Limonomyces roseipellis*.

PLANTS AFFECTED Bent and Kentucky bluegrass may be affected, but problems are more common on the fine fescues and rye grass.

CONTROL

• Organic/non-chemical: Nitrogen fertiliser should be applied to the affected area.

Rhizoctonia scab *Rhizoctonia solani*

The disease is worse in cool moist conditions and often attacks in the early stages of plant growth. On potatoes in the initial stages of growth the new shoots may rot before they appear above ground. If the plant is infected later in its growth, red and yellow pigments may develop in the leaves.

The leaves may curl up at the edges, and growth at the top of the plant may have a 'rosetted' appearance—that is, the leaves may be crowded together on the stalk.

The tubers may have cracks or depressions or be malformed. Brownish-black irregular-shaped lumps up to about 8 mm in diameter may form on them. These lumps are sclerotia which are fungal resting bodies and remain in the soil for years.

PLANTS AFFECTED Potatoes. Note that this fungus has many different strains which attack a wide range of vegetables, ornamentals and weeds. Various symptoms are produced. See also collar rot (D).

CONTROL

• Organic/non-chemical: Practise crop rotation, leaving it as long as possible between potato crops (lawn grasses or sweet corn would be the most suitable plants). Plant disease-free tubers.

Ringspot — camellia

This is thought to be caused by a virus but affected plants still grow and produce flowers normally. As the leaves age, the faint green rings develop into bright-green spots with a darker edge and the rest of the leaf goes yellow.

PLANTS AFFECTED *Camellia japonica.*

CONTROL

• Organic/non-chemical: These leaves can look ugly, so remove them from the plant. There is no way of eliminating the disease from the plant, so other leaves will develop this strong colouring in the future.

Root knot nematode *Meloidogyne* spp.

These nematodes — also known as eelworms — seem to cause most problems in light soils and warm climates. They can be serious glasshouse pests.

The nematodes are about 0.5 mm long but cannot be seen with the unaided eye because they are transparent and very thin.

The worm-shaped adult males are found in the soil, but the pear-shaped mature females are embedded in plant roots. Eggs are laid into the soil in a gelatinous mass or get into the soil later as the outer layers of the root disintegrate. One female may produce 2000 eggs.

On hatching the larvae force their way into young roots, usually near the tip. The saliva they inject when feeding stimulates the production of some very large cells and masses of smaller ones, and a lump develops in the root. The root may still continue to grow, or it may branch at this point. The new root tips produced will be attacked by other larvae and so on until the roots have many lumps along them. Potato tubers become lumpy all over (as shown in the photograph).

Such roots may be unable to supply the above-ground plant parts with enough water or nutrients. The result may be a slow-growing, stunted plant which wilts readily in hot weather. Leaves may be a paler green than normal.

These nematodes can be spread about in running water, in soil stuck to shoes or implements, and in infested plants.

PLANTS AFFECTED A wide range. Some species attack particular plants only.

CONTROL

• Organic/non-chemical: Root knot nematodes in young rose plants can be killed by dipping the roots in water at 46°C for 16 minutes, after washing off the soil. Carry out when the plant is dormant. Infected annual plants may survive and produce flowers if they never suffer from water stress.

Practise crop rotation. Sweet corn, onions, cauliflowers and cabbages are tolerant of root knot nematode. A period of completely bare soil will also reduce their numbers. Be sure to cultivate regularly to remove weeds.

Burn diseased plants. Do not compost them. If large areas are involved it would be wise to seek advice from your local Department of Agriculture.

• Chemical: Contaminated soil can be treated with fenamiphos (Nemacur®) as directed on the label.

Chinese Gooseberry

Symptoms on potatoes

Rose canker *Coniothyrium fuckelii*

This fungus is commonly found on the prickles of rose bushes. The pathogen is weak, however, and is not often able to infect a perfectly healthy, undamaged plant. That is, a wound of some kind is necessary before the fungus can enter the plant.

Disease may begin in the ends of stems cut during pruning or flower-gathering operations, particularly if this cut is too flat so that it holds water in which fungal spores can easily germinate, or if it is ragged and torn.

The fungus grows down the stem and causes discolouration. The junction between the dead area of stem and the area yet without symptoms is often a diagonal one and may have a small raised ridge across it. Sometimes the plant is able to combat the fungus and halt this dieback.

Infections can also occur on very bushy plants with criss-crossing branches. When prickles are bashed into stems in windy weather, the fungus is able to enter through the wounds. In this case, pale yellow or reddish spots develop on the bark and as the fungus continues to grow and the plant continues to grow, these areas gradually get bigger and go brown. The bark develops cracks.

On infected areas, many tiny, black, pinpoint-size spots appear. These are the fruiting bodies of the fungus and contain spores. These spores can spread the disease to other parts of the plant, or to other plants.

PLANTS AFFECTED Roses.

CONTROL
• Organic/non-chemical: Prune off diseased canes about 100 mm below the discoloured section. Cut just above a bud, and use sharp secateurs. Make a neat, slanting cut. There is no successful chemical treatment.

Rose wilt

This name is applied to a whole complex of virus diseases and is referred to as 'dieback' in some areas. The symptoms are variable, but it is common in spring to see the young leaves curled downwards until the tip of the leaf almost touches the base of the leaf. They are also very brittle and readily fall from the plant. Bigger leaves, fully formed but fairly young, collapse so that the leaflets are back to back. The terminal leaflet hangs down also.

Defoliated shoots die back. Sometimes the leaflets are crowded together on a leaf-stalk. Leaves may be pale green or yellow before they drop, and their stem begins to die back from the tip. Softer but more mature stems may show purplish blotches. These tend to be in an elongated ring shape — that is, their centres remain the normal stem colour.

The whole plant will be stunted compared to healthy plants, although the flowers will still be produced in reasonable quantity and quality for a home garden. The symptoms will be worse in cool spring or autumn weather. In summer the plant may appear to be normal.

PLANTS AFFECTED Roses.

CONTROL
• Organic/non-chemical: Once a plant has this problem it cannot be cured. It should be removed and burnt. This is important because some of these diseases can be spread by aphids to other plants. Do not use these plants for propagating, and spray rose bushes regularly for aphid control.

Rusts

There are hundreds of different fungi that cause the diseases we call rusts. They generally cause some sort of small yellow patch or spot on the upper surface of the leaf. Under each spot, on the lower surface of the leaf, a powdery pustule appears. This occurs when the fungus within the leaf produces stalks with spores on the end, and the continued growth of these stalks bursts the epidermis of the leaf open in that area. The masses of spores are then blown about by the wind.

Rusts are extremely difficult to control because the millions of spores can start new infections in many plants over a wide area very quickly.

A few rusts stimulate plant cells to grow into a clearly visible structure like a gall. These structures may be very uniform in shape and characteristic of a certain fungus.

Some serious rusts occur in crops such as wheat which cannot economically be sprayed, or on plants such as poplars which are often too tall to spray. Yet some rusts have been used to our advantage. For example, there is a rust that satisfactorily controls skeleton weed, a serious problem in wheat lands.

Each rust has a relatively limited host range so it is not necessary, for example, to worry about rust on peach trees attacking beans or geraniums. These are all quite different fungi and only able to attack a certain plant, or small group of plants.

Some rusts, particularly in areas where a very cold winter prevails, need to grow on two different plants in a certain sequence in order to complete their life cycle and to survive the winter. For example, in Europe, poplar rust spends part of its life cycle on the larch, and wheat rust spends part of its cycle on the shrub barberry. They usually produce very thick-walled spores in autumn. These are capable of living through very cold conditions and causing reinfection of the next plant in the sequence in spring.

It is not possible to generalise about weather conditions favourable for development of rust diseases. Some moisture, however, is necessary for spore germination.

CONTROL
• Organic/non-chemical: The development of rust-resistant varieties of plants is by far the most useful method of control.
• Chemical: Rusts can be controlled using zineb or sulphur.

Salix babylonica

Mint

Salix caprea

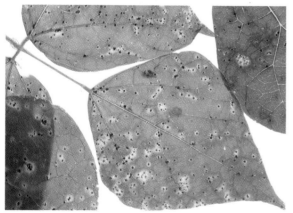

Rust — bean *Uromyces appendiculatus*

The first symptoms of this fungal disease are seen on the leaves. Look for pale yellow spots about 1.5 mm across. On the underside of the leaf corresponding to these spots, small raised blisters develop within two or three days. The thin covering to the blister bursts open and exposes a mass of reddish-brown dust, which is countless fungal spores.

If conditions are suitable for the fungus, hundreds of these pustules develop on the leaves, which yellow and fall. Pustules may also occur on the pods, but the small, almost slimy-looking blisters do not always break open to expose the spores.

The disease is spread from one plant to another by wind-blown spores. Old bean plants may be a source of infection. The disease is worst in cool to warm, damp weather. Heavy dews encourage it.

PLANTS AFFECTED Beans, some varieties are more susceptible than others. Buy resistant varieties. The seed packet should indicate this.

CONTROL
• Organic/non-chemical: If the disease does occur, severely affected plants should be removed and burnt, but a spray programme is probably still necessary.
• Chemical: Use zineb, or wettable sulphur. Wet the undersides of the leaves thoroughly as well as the tops.

Rust—carnation   *Uromyces dianthi*

This fungal disease is very common on carnations. The first symptoms are pale greyish areas which appear anywhere on leaves, stems and sepals. After a period of time, these burst open and a reddish-brown or chocolate-brown powdery mass appears. These pustules are usually 2–6 mm long. Later a ring of secondary pustules may develop around the first.

If the plants are heavily infected, the leaves may be curled and yellow, and the plant stunted. The quantity and quality of flowers will be reduced. It is not uncommon to see this disease on cut flowers bought from a florist. They usually, however, still perform reasonably well in the vase.

The disease is more serious in warm humid weather, and the spores of the fungus are spread from plant to plant by wind.

PLANTS AFFECTED Carnations.

CONTROL

• Chemical: As soon as the first signs of the disease occur, use sulphur dust; or spray with wettable sulphur at the rate of 3 g per litre of water, or spray with zineb at 2 g per litre of water. If the flowers are opening, zineb would be preferable, as sulphur may mark the petals.

Rust — chrysanthemum

Puccinia chrysanthemi

This fungus causes small blister-like swellings, about pinhead size. These are usually seen on the undersides of the leaves. Later they burst open, and dark-brown powdery material is exposed. These are masses of fungal spores which can easily be spread in the wind.

The disease is most prevalent in moist weather — because such conditions favour the growth of the fungus.

If the infection is severe, leaves may wither and plant growth will slow down. The original pustules may each become surrounded by a ring of secondary pustules.

PLANTS AFFECTED Chrysanthemums. Some varieties are more susceptible than others.

CONTROL

• Organic/non-chemical: Remove diseased leaves and destroy them as soon as they are noticed. It is important to begin control as soon as the first signs of the problem occur.

• Chemical: Apply sulphur dust. Or spray with wettable sulphur or zineb.

Rust — English marigold   *Puccinia lagenophorae*

This can be quite a serious disease and appears first as pale yellowish-green spots on the upper surfaces of the leaves. Spots may also occur on stems and flower stalks. The other side of the leaf usually appears orange and powdery.

On closer inspection small cup-like structures will be seen. These contain masses of powdery spores. As the weather gets cooler, the spores produced may be black instead of orange-yellow.

Infected plants and pieces of old leaf lying on the ground are sources of infection. Wind and water splash are the most common methods of disease spread. The disease is worse in warm humid weather.

PLANTS AFFECTED Several native plants in the family Asteraceae, including *Senecio* spp., *Lagenophora* spp. and *Erechtites* spp. Also cineraria, English daisy, and English marigold. The weed groundsel (*Senecio vulgaris*) is another host.

CONTROL

• Organic/non-chemical: Watch the plants carefully and act as soon as symptoms are seen. If the disease is well established, it is very difficult to control. Remove any infected plants quickly and burn them. Do not allow weeds, or any self-sown seedlings, to remain near the crop. Do not plant a new crop near an older crop that has the disease.

• Chemical: Spray with zineb or with wettable sulphur.

Rust — fuchsia *Pucciniastrum epilobii*

This fungus causes purple-red blotches on upper leaf surfaces. These areas die and dry out in the middle, producing brown patches with purple edges. On the lower surface of the leaf, the yellow or orange rust spores may be seen under each patch.

PLANTS AFFECTED Fuchsias. Some cultivars such as 'Orange Drops' and 'Novella' are more likely to be affected than others.

CONTROL
• Organic/non-chemical: The prompt removal of the first-affected leaves may solve the problem.
• Chemical: If spraying is necessary, use zineb or wettable sulphur. Take care not to spray on a hot day.

Rust — iris *Puccinia iridis*

This disease is characterised by rusty-red, powdery spots on both sides of the leaves. The leaf goes yellow around each spot, and this yellowing can become general if the infection is severe. Infected leaves may be killed but the whole plant usually survives.

The spores of this fungus are spread by wind from old infected leaves to new ones. The problem is worse in warm humid weather.

PLANTS AFFECTED Both irises grown from rhizomes and those grown from bulbs may be attacked, but it is more common in rhizomatous irises.

CONTROL
• Organic/non-chemical: Watch for the first pustule or two. Remove affected leaves promptly and carefully. Improve air circulation.
• Chemical: Dust with sulphur. Or spray with wettable sulphur or zineb. If the plants are flowering, use zineb and not sulphur because sulphur may damage the flowers. The addition of a wetting agent at the rate of 1 mL per litre will help the spray to stay on the leaves.

Rust — peach *Tranzschelia discolor*

This disease does occur on twigs and fruit, but the leaf symptoms that can be seen in the late summer and autumn are the most conspicuous. Deep-yellow angular patches about 2 mm across occur on the upper leaf surface. Rusty-red dust, which is masses of spores, appears under each patch. These spores are easily dispersed by the wind. The problem is worst in warm showery weather, and if infection is heavy the leaves will fall early, thus weakening the tree and exposing the trunk and branches to sunburn. If leaf-fall occurs before harvest, the fruit will not mature properly.

PLANTS AFFECTED Peaches, nectarines and plums are most commonly attacked, but rust can occur on other stonefruit.

CONTROL
• Organic/non-chemical: Some rust-infected twigs will be removed at pruning time but others will remain and constitute a source of reinfection for the leaves and fruit. Burning diseased leaves may help slightly.
• Chemical: Spray at early bud-swell with copper oxychloride. Three more sprays may be required: one at petal-fall, one four weeks after petal-fall, and one eight weeks after petal-fall. Use zineb or wettable sulphur at the rate of 2 g per litre of water for these three sprays.

Rust — pelargonium
Puccinia pelargonii-zonalis

This very common fungal disease appears first as small pale green spots on the upper leaf surface. Under each of these spots on the lower leaf surface the small blister soon bursts open to expose a mass of reddish-brown spores. The fungus often continues growing outwards and may produce a ring of secondary pustules around the first. These also burst open and expose spores. The spores are quickly spread in the wind, and in hot humid weather the disease can be quite serious. The infected leaves yellow, but the areas where the pustules occur remain green.

PLANTS AFFECTED Zonal pelargoniums (geraniums) are very commonly attacked, whereas regal and ivy-leaf pelargoniums do not seem to be affected.

CONTROL
• Organic/non-chemical: Remove infected leaves from the area as soon as possible. Do not apply excessive quantities of nitrogenous fertiliser.
• Chemical: Spray with zineb every 7–10 days or use wettable sulphur.

Rust — poplar *Melampsora medusae* and *M. larici-populina*

The symptoms of this disease usually appear in January or February and in a severe case the yellow leaves are spectacular from a distance. On closer inspection the upper leaf surfaces are flecked with yellowish-green. The spores usually develop on the underside of the leaf and appear as yellowish-orange powder. The wind easily spreads the spores from tree to tree and leaf to leaf.

Infected leaves may brown in patches and fall early. New leaves may appear and also become infected and fall early. This sequence seriously weakens or even kills small trees or nursery stock. Larger trees do suffer some dieback, possibly because the disease interferes with the hardening of the shoots which are therefore exposed to damage by low temperatures.

PLANTS AFFECTED Lombardy poplars (*Populus nigra* 'Italica') and cotton-woods (*P. deltoides*) are the most common hosts, but other poplars can be infected.

CONTROL
• Organic/non-chemical: The only long-term solution to this problem is the development of poplars resistant to the disease. Spraying is not possible on large trees, so it may therefore be pointless to protect smaller ones.
• Chemical: However, spraying with wettable sulphur may help.

Rust — raspberry *Phragmidium rubi-idaei*

This fungal disease is first obvious towards the end of December as bright-orange powdery pustules on the upper surface of the young leaves. These spores spread the disease to other leaves, and later in the season on the undersurface of the leaves dull-orange areas appear. As the weather gets colder, areas turn black because black thick-walled spores tolerant of cold conditions are produced.

PLANTS AFFECTED
This rust is only serious on the raspberry varieties 'Lloyd George' and 'Neka'.

CONTROL
• Chemical: Spray with copper oxychloride (50%) at the rate of 4 g per litre of water when the disease is first seen.

Rust — rose   *Phragmidium mucronatum*

This disease occurs in hot humid weather and causes yellow patches or spots on the upper surface of the leaves. Under each spot an orange-yellow dust appears. This is the spores of the fungus and enables it to spread in the wind to other leaves and to other plants.

When the weather becomes colder in autumn, the colour of the pustules of spores changes to dark brown. Leaves affected in this way usually fall before healthy leaves.

PLANTS AFFECTED Roses, although very few varieties are seriously affected. They are usually older varieties.

CONTROL
• Organic/non-chemical: Rake up and burn fallen leaves. Do not water from above, or at least be sure to water early in the day so that leaves can dry quickly.
• Chemical: If control is necessary, spray with sulphur, or zineb.

Rust — snapdragon   *Puccinia antirrhini*

The first signs of this fungal disease are found on the undersurfaces of the leaves in the form of light-coloured raised spots. The epidermis of the leaf splits open after a few days and exposes a mass of reddish-brown spores which look like dust. The first pustule may become surrounded by further rings of pustules.

Pustules may also occur on other above-ground plant parts, and the fungus may spread right around the stem, thus killing the plant.

The disease is spread as spores on seed or blown from diseased plants on to healthy ones. Most problems from this disease will occur during cool humid weather.

PLANTS AFFECTED Snapdragons.

CONTROL
• Organic/non-chemical: Sow only seed collected from disease-free plants. Choose a rust-resistant cultivar.
• Chemical: If a spray programme is necessary use zineb every 7–14 days or wettable sulphur. Do not spray when the temperature is high.

Rusts — turf grasses

Puccinia spp. and *Uromyces* spp.

Rusts will occur on many grass species and can be very destructive. If the attack is very severe, the whole sward will take on an orange-red colour. Individual leaves will be covered in pustules of orange-coloured spores that darken as they age.

PLANTS AFFECTED Rye grass, Kentucky bluegrass, the fine and coarse fescues, winter grass and kikuyu may all be badly affected by rust. Kikuyu and rye will be especially badly affected if the weather is very hot and humid.

CONTROL
• Organic/non-chemical: The best treatment is to keep the grass growing vigorously with high levels of nitrogen fertiliser.

Rust gall — wattle   *Uromycladium* spp.

The fungus *U. tepperianum* most commonly attacks wattles with phyllodes, and *U. notabile* most commonly attacks bipinnate wattles. They both cause the production of large woody rust-coloured galls. Severely affected trees may die.

After the galls have formed they are often invaded by small insects which are sometimes mistakenly thought to be the cause of the galls.

Other species of *Uromycladium* produce different symptoms on wattles, including witches' brooms.

PLANTS AFFECTED Wattles, both in gardens and in the bush.

CONTROL
• Organic/non-chemical: If the tree is severely attacked, it should be removed. It looks ugly and is a source of infection for other wattles. A replacement wattle can be planted, and because most of them are quick growers the garden will soon be restored. Slightly affected trees should be pruned and fertilised.

Sclerotinia rot   *Sclerotinia* spp.

This fungal disease is characterised by a soft, brown, rapidly spreading rot which develops a white fluffy growth on the surface. Hard, fungal resting bodies called sclerotia later develop in this area. They may be up to about 10 mm across and darken to black.

Sclerotia may also be formed inside the stems of infected plants. They remain in the soil or in plant debris and are capable of infecting plants for years.

Particular plants may have slightly different symptoms. For example, lettuce leaves wilt so that the whole plant looks flat and limp. Plant parts (of beans, for example) infected in the field and still healthy-looking when harvested, develop rots in storage. The disease is worse in cool (10–25°C) humid conditions.

PLANTS AFFECTED A wide range of vegetables and flowers, including lettuces (lettuce drop), carrots (pink rot), beans, celery, cabbages, cauliflowers, potatoes, tomatoes and dahlias (stem rot). Also many weeds.

CONTROL

• Organic/non-chemical: Use a combination of methods. Practise crop rotation with plants that are not susceptible, such as grasses, beetroot, spinach, sweet corn and onions. Reduce humidity in the crop by spacing the plants as far apart as possible, removing weeds, and careful timing of watering. Improve drainage. Do not plant susceptible crops in low-lying areas. Remove and burn single infected plants as soon as they are noticed.

Right-hand stem is split open to show sclerotia towards the base.

Sclerotium stem rot   *Sclerotium rolfsii*

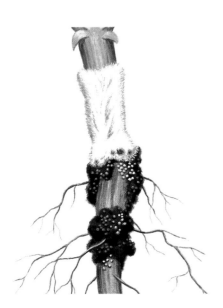

This fungus is a common soil inhabitant. It attacks near ground level and becomes obvious as a white growth, like many cotton threads, on the affected tissues and even on the soil surface. The plant may wilt and die rapidly. Resting bodies (sclerotia) of the fungus develop in the white fluffy growth. They begin white but darken to brown. They are about 2 mm in diameter and more or less spherical. These are capable of reinfecting other plants months or years later.

This fungus causes most trouble when the organic matter content of the soil is high and when temperatures are between about 25 and 30°C. Alternate wetting and drying of the soil surface stimulates sclerotia to start growing.

PLANTS AFFECTED A very wide range, including rhubarb, beetroot and many other vegetables; carnations, dahlias and irises.

CONTROL

• Organic/non-chemical: Remove and destroy infected plants. Do not bury any of the foliage when cultivating around plants. Do not put infected plant parts into a compost heap. If sclerotia can be buried deeper than 150 mm in damp soil, they will die after about six weeks. Adjust the watering programme to avoid fluctuations, and avoid future plantings into areas high in undecayed organic material.

Use only healthy propagating material (e.g. healthy rhubarb crowns). On plants growing from a rhizome, such as iris, the plant can probably be saved by removing the diseased areas with a sharp knife.

Septoria spot — passionfruit

Septoria passifloricola

Leaf and fruit spots are the most common features of this disease. On the fruit, which can be infected at any stage of growth, light brown blotches appear. These may continue growing and run together to cover much of the fruit. Tiny black dots on the fruit surface are the fruiting bodies of the fungus. Although the pulp can still be eaten, the fruit will ripen unevenly and be generally inferior.

The leaf spots are smaller and more numerous than those of the disease brown spot (D) and may readily cause leaf-fall. The fruiting bodies of the fungus appear as dark dots on the leaf spots, and the spores produced in them can be spread about by splashing water. Note that these fruiting bodies are not produced by the fungus that causes brown spot of passionfruit.

PLANTS AFFECTED Passionfruit and granadilla (*Passiflora quadrangularis*).

CONTROL

• Chemical: Spray with mancozeb approximately fortnightly.

Shoot blight — eucalypts *Ramularia pitereka*

Infected young shoots appear shiny white and become twisted and distorted. On the leaves, spots 1–2 mm in diameter develop. These are often along one edge of the leaf and eventually cause twisting and distortion. The spots are brown with a thin reddish-purple edge, and a number of spots may grow together in large irregular patches. Sometimes sunken brown areas occur on petioles and stems.

This is principally a glasshouse disease, but it also occurs outdoors on small trees in areas where shade and poor air circulation keep humidity high. It is most common in spring and autumn and may kill small plants.

PLANTS AFFECTED These include yellow bloodwood (*Eucalyptus eximia*), red-flowering gum (*E. ficifolia*), spotted gum (*E. maculata*) and smooth-barked apple (*Angophora costata*).

CONTROL
• Organic/non-chemical: Try to reduce shade and improve air circulation. Improve greenhouse ventilation.
• Chemical: Spray with copper oxychloride. Repeat treatments may be necessary. Leave an interval of about two weeks between each application.

Shoot blight — pine *Diplodia pinea*

Trees attacked by this fungus have brown areas towards the ends of branches here and there on the tree. Larger areas will be brown if many of these dead tips occur together. The side shoots behind the killed tip may grow abnormally long, thus giving the tree a peculiar appearance.

Fungal spores are found on dead needles, twigs and bud scales, and seem able to attack the new needles only after some sort of damage has occurred. Attack is common, for example, after a hailstorm in hot dry weather. The needles gradually yellow and then brown. The whole shoot dies back.

PLANTS AFFECTED This fungus succeeds on plants that are weakened for some reason, such as water stress. It can attack a wide range of pine species. *Pinus radiata* seems one of the most susceptible. In some areas, this fungus is known to cause a collar rot of nursery stock.

CONTROL
• Organic/non-chemical: Fungicidal treatments are of doubtful benefit and impossible on large trees. Trees should be watered in dry weather and fertilised to keep them growing vigorously; infection will then be less likely and a plant that has been attacked will be encouraged to grow new needles and new shoots.

Shot hole blight *Heteropatella antirrhini*

This fungal disease is favoured by cool moist weather and spreads via spores on infected seed and in wind from other infected plants.

Pale yellowish spots on leaves and stems are symptomatic of a mild attack of this disease. The affected leaf tissue often falls out, leaving holes with purplish borders — hence the name 'shot hole'. A more severe attack may destroy the young shoots. Pale patches on leaves and stems dry out and turn brown, giving the plant a scorched appearance.

If weather conditions become hot and dry, the fungus will not continue to spread and new growth will be healthy.

PLANTS AFFECTED Snapdragons.

CONTROL
• Organic/non-chemical: Do not use seed from infected plants. Watch plants closely. Destroy affected specimens promptly.
• Chemical: Spray with zineb every 7–14 days, or with copper oxychloride every 14 days if necessary.

Symptoms on peaches

Shot hole — stonefruit *Stigmina carpophila*

The first symptoms noticed are small brown spots with reddish edges on the leaves. The centre later falls out, producing holes. Large holes of irregular shape may be produced if groups of spots occur close together.

These spots can be confused with those caused by the bacterium *Xanthomonas campestris* pv. *pruni*. The latter, however, causes spots that are more angular and have an oily sheen.

On apricot fruit, raised brown scabs and exudations of gum appear. These exudations, however, are much more copious on almond fruit. The fruit may crack. On peaches and nectarines, the spots may develop into deep indentations.

On twigs, round or oval brown spots occur. They may be raised all over or depressed in the middle with a raised edge. Exudations of gum occur. Twigs may be girdled and die.

PLANTS AFFECTED Most damage occurs on almonds and early-flowering peaches and apricots, but nectarines, cherries and plums can also be affected.

CONTROL
• Chemical: With the addition of an autumn spray, the programme outlined for freckle (D) would also control shot hole. If shot hole alone is involved, spray, just as the first flowers open, with copper oxychloride with the addition of 5 mL of clear white oil. Apply the same mixture again after leaf-fall and before pruning.

Symptoms on
Prunus serrulata

*Symptoms on
peach leaves*

Silver leaf *Chondrostereum purpureum*

This fungal disease affects a wide range of deciduous fruit trees and woody ornamental shrubs. The appearance of silver-grey leaves in spring is often the first sign that a plant is infected, although this symptom does not occur on every infected plant.

The fungus enters a plant through broken branches or pruning wounds and grows in the wood, gradually causing dieback. Leaves on the infected branches will appear silver because toxins produced by the fungus alter the leaf structure and thus alter light-reflecting quality.

The fungus produces fruiting bodies, called brackets, on recently dead wood. These are 20–30 mm across, brown on top and mauve beneath. The spores, which are leased during or immediately after rain, can infect wounds for only about 24 hours after they occur. This disease is more common in areas with a mild wet winter.

PLANTS AFFECTED These commonly include peaches, apricots, apples, pears, roses, poplars, and willows. Other plants that may be infected include broom, tibouchina, mountain ash and hydrangea.

CONTROL
• Organic/non-chemical: There is no suitable fungicide at present. Try to prune when the weather will be dry for 24 hours afterwards. Paint large cuts with a wound dressing containing fungicide. Burn all prunings. Completely remove stumps of trees that died from the disease.

Fungal fruiting bodies

Slime moulds

These fungi are generally in damp shaded places on the surface of decaying organic matter such as dead leaves or rotting logs. For most of their life cycle they exist as jelly-like blobs which may grow to several centimetres across and move very slowly as they feed on spores, microscopic organisms and small pieces of plant material.

They are noticed occasionally only when they move up on to leaves of grass or other low-growing plants such as strawberries to produce spores. The species most consistently associated with strawberries, *Diachea leucopoda*, is usually seen in late spring or autumn after prolonged wet weather. The fungal mass develops into black spore containers on white stalks. The stalks are 1–2 mm long and the spore containers are less than 1 mm across.

PLANTS AFFECTED Slime moulds could move up on to any low growing plant in a damp place.

CONTROL

This is not usually necessary because these fungi do not feed on living plant material. Hosing would disperse the fungal mass.

Smudge — onion *Colletotrichum circinans*

The first sign of this fungal disease is small, greenish dots on the outside of the onion before harvest. Later these become black, and while the onion is being stored the fungus continues to grow. The bulbs may shrink and sprouting may occur.

The disease is worst if conditions are moist in the field and in storage. It comes into a crop through the presence of already infected crop remains in the soil and through spores spread by wind.

PLANTS AFFECTED White onions are readily attacked by this fungus, but most brown onions are resistant.

CONTROL

• Organic/non-chemical: This depends on cultural practices such as crop rotation, removal of diseased plant parts and unwanted bulbs. These should be destroyed. If the disease is recurrent, plant only brown varieties.

Sooty blotch and fly speck

These two diseases are caused by fungi. Sooty blotch (*Gloeodes pomigena*) is characterised by dark smudges which are seen most commonly on fruit. The smudges begin circular but later may grow into one another so that large areas of the fruit are blackened. Fly speck (*Leptothyrium pomi*) is characterised by small black specks. The spores are splashed about by rain, and so these diseases are more likely in damp weather or in damp situations such as the shady side of trees.

Sooty blotch should not be confused with sooty mould (D), which is generally drier in appearance and associated with honeydew-producing insects.

Fruit infected with these two diseases can still be eaten because the fungi are growing only on the skin of the fruit. The fruit would look unpalatable, however, and would not store well.

PLANTS AFFECTED Apples, pears, and citrus fruit. Sooty blotch may also appear on the young twigs of plants such as peaches, and a number of Australian native plants including wattles.

CONTROL

• Organic/non-chemical: Ignore the problem.

• Chemical: *Apples*: If the trees are being sprayed for black spot control, then additional sprays are not usually necessary. Zineb (65%) at the rate of 2 g per litre of water sprayed every 3–4 weeks would solve the problem. If the disease has been on the trees in the previous season, try to start the spray programme about a month before the disease was first seen in the previous year. *Stonefruit*: Sooty blotch is usually kept under control when other diseases are sprayed. *Citrus*: The melanose control programme would keep sooty blotch under control.

Sooty moulds

These fungi are well named because they are black and dry and look just like soot. Many grow in a substance called 'honeydew' which is produced by insects such as aphids and soft scales. Wherever the honeydew falls sooty moulds can grow.

They do no direct damage to plants but may cause a reduction in photosynthesis if very thick or extensive or if they remain for very long. Fruit quality will be reduced because the appearance is spoiled. On ornamental trees and shrubs the black covering on the leaves makes the plant look very ugly.

PLANTS AFFECTED Any.

CONTROL
• Organic/non-chemical: Sooty moulds can only be removed if the insects producing the honeydew are controlled. Once these insects are gone and the honeydew supply stops, the sooty mould can no longer grow actively. Any already on the plant will gradually dry out and flake off. This process can be assisted by hosing.

Symptoms on dahlia leaves

Spotted wilt Tomato spotted wilt virus

The first symptoms on tomato plants are small brown spots on the smallest leaves. Bronze-coloured spots or rings develop between the veins on older leaves and the stems become streaked with brown. Young plants may be killed. Plants infected when more mature bear fruit that ripens unevenly and is marked with circular blotches.

On young potato leaves, there are brown, dead, angular spots; the ends of shoots may be killed, and on old leaves, brown zoned spots may be visible. On broad bean plants, the main shoot may die, the stems are streaked with brown, and the pods spotted with black; new leaves are mottled. Capsicum leaves show yellowish parallel lines or concentric rings; the fruit is marked with yellow rings and blotches up to 10 mm wide which may not show up till the fruit ripens.

Calla lily leaves develop yellow spots, or streaks parallel to the veins. Chrysanthemum and dahlia leaves are marked with series of irregular wavy lines, one inside the other. The leaves on varieties which are very susceptible go brown and die. Dahlia stems may be streaked with brown or purple.

The disease is carried from plant to plant by onion thrips (*Thrips tabaci*), and tomato thrips (*Frankliniella schultzei*). These insects are more active in hot dry weather, and thus the disease is more prevalent in such conditions. Western flower thrips (*F. occidentalis*), an efficient vector of this disease, is now in Australia. See page 51.

PLANTS AFFECTED A very wide range of vegetables and annual and perennial flowers, including dahlias, chrysanthemums, calla lilies, Iceland poppies, zinnias, capsicums, tomatoes and lettuces. Also weeds.

CONTROL
• Organic/non-chemical: Remove infected plants promptly and destroy them. Control weeds. Spray for thrips control. Rhizomes or tubers from infected plants will also produce infected plants. It is possible to obtain dahlias free of the virus by allowing the swollen rootstocks to shoot and then using these shoots for cuttings. Some of these cuttings will develop into healthy plants. Discard the rootstock.

Spring dead spot

Leptosphaeria narmari and *L. korrae*

The symptoms of this disease show up first in winter as circular patches of dead turf. They are 300–500 mm in diameter and look white compared to the straw colour of the dormant couch. The fungus responsible is a soil inhabitant which damages the roots in late summer and autumn. The name 'spring dead spot' refers to the fact that the grass fails to start growing in spring after winter dormancy.

PLANTS AFFECTED Couch grass, South African couch (*Cynodon transvaalensis*) and many of its hybrids are severely damaged.

CONTROL Choose the least susceptible available variety.

Spur blight — raspberry
Didymella applanata

The symptoms of this fungal disease are most conspicuous in late summer and autumn when reddish-brown shield-shaped areas spread around the base of leaves and buds on first-season canes. These infected areas become silvery-grey as they age and black dots, which are the fruiting bodies of the fungus, appear on their surfaces. The buds that should produce fruiting arms are killed, but the canes normally survive.

PLANTS AFFECTED This fungal disease is common on raspberries and it is sometimes found on loganberries.

CONTROL
• Organic/non-chemical: Remove all infected canes and burn them.
• Chemical: Spray at greentip stage with copper oxychloride (50%) at the rate of 4 g per litre of water, and again at white-bud stage.

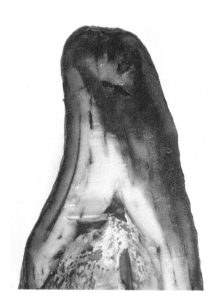

Stem-end rot — avocado *Dothiorella* sp.

The fungus causing this disease lives on any dead twigs and leaves on the plant, and spores are splashed onto the fruit during wet weather. No symptoms appear and the fungus remains dormant until the fruit is mature and begins to ripen.

At this stage a dark-brown to black firm rot begins at the stem end and gradually progresses down the fruit.

PLANTS AFFECTED Avocados.

CONTROL
• Organic/non-chemical: Ensure that the stem end of the fruit is not damaged during harvest by clipping the fruit from the tree. Handle it carefully so that it is not bruised. Prune out any dead twigs or branches on a regular basis and store fruit in cool, well-ventilated places.

Stem gall — wattle *Botryosphaeria acaciae*

This disease can be referred to as Dingley branch gall. Small, cushion-like galls occur on the branches. One gall may be up to 10 mm across, and they may be crowded together, producing a knobbly appearance.

PLANTS AFFECTED A range of wattles, particularly the Cootamundra wattle (*Acacia baileyana*).

CONTROL
• Organic/non-chemical: If the problem is noticed when only a few galls have appeared, prune off the affected twigs. Make the cut about 100 mm from the junction of healthy and diseased wood. Burn the prunings.

If a badly affected plant appears ugly, it should probably be replaced.

Stony pit — pear

This virus disease causes severe malformation of the fruit. Large numbers of pits or depressions in the flesh of the fruit cause it to lose its uniform shape.

A tree that has been infected for some time is likely to have bark with cracks and folds rather than the more smooth bark one would expect on a healthy tree.

If the fruit is cut through, an extremely hard group of cells will be found at the bottom of each pit. These are quite like small stones, and this distinguishes stony pit from other problems such as boron deficiency where brown areas are corky but not really hard. The stony areas may occur throughout the flesh. Sometimes the fruit on one branch is affected and the rest of the fruit is normal.

PLANTS AFFECTED The variety 'Williams' is less likely to be affected by stony pit than other pears such as 'Packham', 'Winter Cole', 'Josephine', and 'Beurre Bosc'.

CONTROL

• Organic/non-chemical: Remove the tree entirely or cut off the top and graft pieces of the variety 'Williams' on to the remaining framework. Seek advice on this procedure. It is referred to as 'reworking'.

Summer death of beans

This is a virus or virus-like disease. It is characterised by the sudden yellowing or death of the plant in hot weather. If the weather is cooler, symptoms are milder. The plant may appear stunted and wilted and the young leaves may curl downwards.

If it is suspected that this disease is present, cut the lower stem through. Some discolouration means the plant is infected. As the disease progresses the discolouration will increase until it is black, and at this stage the roots will rot.

This disease is spread by the common brown leafhopper from weeds to beans and possibly other cultivated crops. The disease is more common in hot weather. This is partly because the insects are more likely to move from weeds that are drying off, on to crops which are more succulent at this time.

PLANTS AFFECTED Not all varieties of French bean are susceptible to this disease. Among those resistant are 'Apollo', 'Cascade', 'Canyon', 'Jackpot', 'Orbit', and 'Burnley Conquest'.

CONTROL

• Organic/non-chemical: Plant a resistant variety.
• Chemical: Spread within a crop can be lessened by spraying with dimethoate or soap sprays to control leafhoppers.

Sunblotch — citrus

Cool winds and frost can both cause citrus leaves to curl upwards. This may happen only on one side of the tree (the coldest side). The exposed undersides of the curled leaves are later bleached by the sun and may develop reddish-brown spots and patches as shown in the photograph.

PLANTS AFFECTED Citrus.

CONTROL

• Organic/non-chemical: Make a careful choice of planting site. Prune the damaged leaves from the tree if they are considered ugly.

Target spot *Alternaria solani*

Dark-brown to black spots develop on the leaves. Spots vary slightly in shape and size depending on which plants the fungus is attacking. They generally have a series of concentric marks on them, hence the name 'target spot'. The lower and therefore older leaves show the symptoms first, and the spots may gradually grow together to kill large areas of the leaf.

On potatoes, the leathery-looking spots are angular and may be up to 20 mm wide. On tomatoes, they are generally oval, 6–12 mm in diameter and surrounded by a yellow halo.

On potato tubers, small round sunken pits develop and these may extend to form whole sunken areas on the potato.

On tomato stems, the marks are more elongated and the series of lines shows very quickly. On tomato fruit, the fungus attacks near the fruit stalk and usually causes rotting on one side. This will be dark brown to black and depressed with the typical concentric marks. The rot extends into the fruit beneath. Tomato seedlings may be killed if the fungus attacks near ground level.

This disease is favoured by warm moist weather and first comes into a planting of tomatoes or other plants on infected seed. Spores produced on leaf spots are spread about by the wind, rain and insects. This fungus can survive on pieces of plant material for a year or more.

PLANTS AFFECTED Potatoes, tomatoes, capsicums, eggplants and solanaceous weeds such as nightshade (*Solanum* sp.).

CONTROL
• Organic/non-chemical: It is important to have disease-free seed and to practise crop rotation. Remove and destroy any diseased parts and remove weeds, particularly solanaceous ones. Keep plants growing vigorously.
• Chemical: Spray seedlings at weekly intervals with copper oxychloride, copper hydroxide, zineb or mancozeb. Continue after transplanting.

Top and root rot — pineapple

Phytophthora spp.

Top rot symptoms occur first on the heart leaves, which go yellow or light brown with a reddish tinge. Leaf edges curl back. The stem and leaf bases are rotted, and leaves are easily pulled from the plant. The plant has an unpleasant smell.

Root rot has similar leaf symptoms. Outer leaves die back from the tips and become limp. The root system is rotted, and the plant can be pulled from the ground easily.

These soil-inhabiting fungi are favoured by wet soil. Spores are spread by running water and water splash. Tops and slips, both of which have more soft tissues than suckers, are more likely to be infected by this fungus.

Green fruit on or near the ground can also be rotted. This is usually referred to as 'green fruit rot' and is kept under control by the same method as 'top and root rot'.

PLANTS AFFECTED Many
CONTROL
• Organic/non-chemical: Do not plant in poorly drained areas. Do not overwater. Plant in raised beds and install drains so that rain water can move away quickly. If the soil is alkaline, take steps to lower the pH.
• Chemical: There is no chemical control for use in a home garden.

Tulip breaking

This is a virus disease which causes a change in the colour of tulip flowers, which is referred to as 'colour-breaking'. In red and orange varieties, streaks of light or dark red, yellow or white appear on the petals. In yellow and white varieties, the streaks are much less obvious; they may be translucent or just a slightly different shade of white or yellow. Sometimes the streaks appear in the unopened bud. The petals may also be serrated on the margin and appear tattered. The leaves may show yellow or light-green streaks, but this symptom is easy to overlook.

There is also a reduction in bulb size associated with this disease. The virus is spread from plant to plant by aphids and particularly the green peach aphid (P). The symptoms will not show up on the flower in the season the infection occurs, but only in the following season. Therefore in areas where warm climates do not allow the use of tulip bulbs in a second season, this disease will be of little concern.

PLANTS AFFECTED These include tulips and liliums.

CONTROL

• Organic/non-chemical: Destroy bulbs from which diseased leaves and flowers grew.

• Chemical: Control aphids by spraying with dimethoate or with a soap spray.

Nematode affected plant on the right shows thin top growth and short-ened root system with multiple branching.

Turf nematodes

Nematodes cause stunting of grass roots and produce a distinctive digitate pattern of branching in the roots. Damaged roots often become heavily infected by fungi and are subject to water stress.

There is only one known major nematode problem in turf in Australia. This is caused by the cyst nematode *Heterodera graminis* and occurs in Newcastle and the Hunter Valley (N.S.W.). Turf from any affected areas should not be moved to other regions.

PLANTS AFFECTED Warm-climate grasses. In particular, couch.

CONTROL

• Organic/non-chemical: Ensure that the grass receives enough fertiliser and water to avoid stress.

• Chemical: Apply fenamiphos (Nemacur®) at the rate of 50 g per square metre if the infestation is heavy; or 15 g per square metre if it is light. Spread as evenly as possible.

Verticillium wilt *Verticillium dahliae*

This soil-inhabiting fungus enters the plant through root hairs and invades the water-conducting tissues. The stem appears normal from the outside, but if split open near ground level a dark-brown to black discolouration will be apparent.

Symptoms vary slightly from plant to plant. On tomatoes the lower leaves wilt and dry out first; the whole plant may die later. On chrysanthemums the leaves on the lower branches develop a pinkish or purplish look and wither. If apricot trees are planted after or interplanted with tomatoes or potatoes, they may be attacked by this fungus and a disease called 'black heart of apricots' develops. The leaves on the ends of the branches wilt and later yellow and fall.

The fungus can remain in the soil for years. It is favoured by cool conditions and spread on implements and in soil washed down slopes.

PLANTS AFFECTED A wide range, including potatoes, tomatoes, strawberries, brambles, perennials such as dahlias and chrysanthemums, and weeds such as nightshade (*Solanum* spp.) and noogoora burr (*Xanthium pungens*). Fruit trees can also be attacked.

CONTROL

• Organic/non-chemical: Improve drainage. Do not plant a series of solanaceous crops in the one area. Control weeds. Use resistant cultivars where possible. Remove and destroy infected plants.

In the case of chrysanthemums, cuttings should not be taken from infected plants unless the variety is particularly rare or important. If this is to be done, take the cuttings when the shoots are about 400 mm high. Use as little of the tips of the stems as is possible. Watch these cuttings carefully as they grow, and destroy those that are infected.

• Chemical: Once this fungus is present, the soil will have to be chemically treated (consult your local Department of Agriculture on this matter) if crops are to be grown in the area.

Affected field spinach plant on the left. Healthy plant on the right.

Violet scab *Sphaceloma violae*

The first symptoms of this fungal disease are tiny watersoaked dots. These enlarge and develop into irregular, grey or fawn scabby patches. They may have a deep green edge. The centres may fall from the affected areas, leaving holes.

The plant may be twisted and distorted. Symptoms may also occur on stems, leaf and flower stalks and on seed capsules. If the fungus grows right around the stem, parts of the plant will die

PLANTS AFFECTED Violets and pansies.

CONTROL

• Organic/non-chemical: Remove badly affected plant parts. Improve air circulation and thus dry the leaves and stems .

• Chemical: Spray with zineb. Repeat sprays 10–14 days apart if necessary.

Badly damaged nuts

Walnut blight *Xanthomonas campestris* pv. *juglandis*

This disease is also referred to as 'walnut black spot'. It is very damaging and difficult to control. The bacteria overwinter in infected buds and twigs and are splashed from these sites to new growth in the spring. Bacteria can survive in dead buds for several seasons. Frequent spring rain and frost or hail damage will make new infections more likely to occur.

The first symptoms seen are very small, round watersoaked spots on leaves and catkins. These enlarge and go brown. On leaves, the spots end up angular in shape and 2–3 mm across. Dark, sunken spots may develop on the veins, midribs and stalks of the leaves. Catkin infection can interfere with pollen production and thus reduce the number of nuts set. Symptoms on nuts depend on how young they are when infection occurs. They may have stained, shrivelled or rotted kernels, the husk may stick to the shell, or the nuts may fall. On shoots, sunken black areas develop. These may girdle the shoot and kill it. Shoots are only susceptible to infection when young. By the end of the first season they are immune.

PLANTS AFFECTED Walnuts. Seedling trees seem worst affected. Try to buy the varieties that are least damaged by the disease.

CONTROL

• Organic/non-organic: In winter, prune out and burn infected shoots.

• Chemical: Spray with Bordeaux mixture (50 g : 50 g : 10 L), or with copper oxychloride (50%) at the rate of 3 g per litre of water. Apply the first spray at bud-burst and thereafter at 10-day intervals if the weather is showery and at 14-day intervals if it is dry. Three to five sprays are necessary. The top of the tree must be thoroughly covered to prevent re-infection of the rest of the tree.

Leaves affected when they are young become distorted

Whiptail

The term 'whiptail' is applied to the symptoms of molybdenum deficiency in crucifers. The symptoms are most pronounced on cauliflowers. The leaf is very much reduced in size and appears as a small ribbon-like piece of leaf along each side of the main vein. This may be very twisted and puckered.

Different symptoms occur on other crucifers. They may have leaves yellowing between the veins and dying around the edges and the plants may also be stunted. On Brussels sprouts older leaves are cupped and young ones strap-like and twisted.

This problem is more common in acid soils than in alkaline soils.

PLANTS AFFECTED Crucifers, especially cauliflowers.

CONTROL
• Organic: Liming the soil may raise the pH sufficiently to prevent molybdenum deficiency occurring.
• Non-organic: Use a complete fertiliser which contains molybdenum. Or water every square metre of soil with the following solution: 3 g of ammonium molybdate *or* 4 g of sodium molybdate in 5 litres of water. This solution could also be sprayed on to half-grown plants showing symptoms. In this case, add wetting agent at the rate of 1 mL per litre.

White rot — onion *Sclerotium cepivorum*

This fungal disease is first noticed when leaves begin yellowing or dying. On closer inspection the base of the onion is found to be rotted, and the root system partly or totally destroyed. The plants are easily dislodged from the soil.

The fungus produces a white fluffy growth and gradually develops a large number of small pinhead-size black sclerotia or resting bodies. It is these resting bodies which make the disease so difficult to cope with once it is introduced into an area because they can start to grow and infect plants for many years afterwards. They can also be easily spread from place to place on footwear or implements.

PLANTS AFFECTED Onions, shallots, leeks.

CONTROL
• Organic/non-chemical: Raise your own onions from seed, unless you can be sure of getting healthy plants. Remove diseased onion parts and burn them. Once this disease has occurred in an area, the area should not be planted with susceptible plants for an indefinite period. Take steps to avoid spread of soil or plant material from this area to clean areas, by washing boots and garden implements. Consult your local Department of Agriculture for more detailed advice.

Symptoms on radish leaves

White rust — crucifers

Albugo candida

This fungal disease is sometimes called 'white blister', and is not related to the group of diseases generally referred to as rusts. It is characterised by small raised yellowish-green spots on the upper surfaces of the leaves. On the undersurface of the leaf, corresponding to these spots, white soft-looking masses of spores appear. These spores can be carried to healthy plants by wind or by insects. Pieces of diseased plant left after a crop is finished can be the source of infection for a new crop. Badly affected leaves will be misshapen. The disease is most serious in cool, moist conditions.

PLANTS AFFECTED Radishes, horseradishes, swedes and turnips are most affected, although it can affect other crucifers occasionally.

CONTROL
• Organic/non-chemical: Crop hygiene is important. Remove any pieces of diseased plant material. Practise a crop rotation of 3–4 years. Weed control is important because this disease can also be found on common cruciferous weeds such as bittercress (*Coronopus didymus*), shepherd's purse (*Capsella bursa-pastoris*), hedge mustard (*Sisymbrium officinale*) and wild radish (*Raphanus raphanistrum*). Spraying is not effective against the disease.

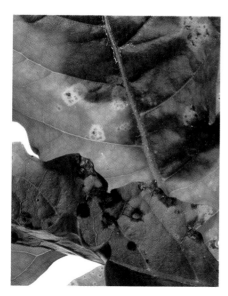

White rust — gerbera   *Albugo tragopogonis*

The fungus that causes this disease is not related to the 'true' rusts (D) and is a different species of *Albugo* from that which attacks radish or mesembryanthemum.

Off-white, soft-looking pustules appear on the lower leaf surfaces. These consist of masses of spores. There is a yellowish-green blotch on the upper leaf surface corresponding to each pustule. These blotches darken with age. The disease may spread rapidly in spring but slows down in hot dry weather.

PLANTS AFFECTED   Gerberas. Some varieties are more seriously and more frequently affected by this disease than others.

CONTROL
• Organic/non-chemical: Do not apply excessive amounts of nitrogenous fertilisers. Remove and burn infected leaves promptly.

• Chemical: In areas where this disease occurs regularly, a spray programme should start in late winter even if symptoms have not appeared. Use zineb and cover both leaf surfaces with spray.

Wind injury — citrus

Citrus trees can be very adversely affected by strong winds. If new leaves are bashed on to branches or thorns, they can have some cells damaged. These cells will stop growing but other undamaged cells on the same leaf will continue to grow. This may result in splits and puckers in the leaf or indentations in the midrib.

This leaf damage means a reduction in leaf area for photosynthesis and therefore a reduction in the amount of sugars produced for the maintenance of the tree and for fruit production. Damage can be particularly serious on a young tree.

PLANTS AFFECTED   All citrus.

CONTROL   Choose a site that is not exposed to strong winds, or provide windbreaks.

Woodiness of passionfruit

Symptoms of this virus disease include fruit that is indented and deformed. If cut through, the fruit is seen to have a very thick rind and a small pulp cavity. The leaves may show a faint yellow mottle, or be a paler green than normal healthy leaves. The internodes may be shortened.

This disease is carried by aphids and most vines will eventually succumb.

PLANTS AFFECTED All *Passiflora* spp. may be affected to some degree but the purple passionfruit (*Passiflora edulis*) suffers most.

CONTROL

• Organic/non-chemical: Virus-resistant plants may soon be available. In the meantime, the best way to overcome this problem is to look after the vine very well. Plant it in as warm a place as possible, and fertilise and water regularly. Never prune when cold weather is approaching. Plan to replace the vine every three or four years. Symptoms show up most clearly on leaves in cool weather, whereas in warmer weather the leaves and fruit that are formed may be perfectly normal. Spraying for insects is not a useful control on a plant expected to live and produce for years.

Wood-rots — eucalypts

Fungal decays are most likely to begin in trees that have been physically damaged and are under stress such as lack of water and nutrients. Fungal spores grow into a network of fine threads which obtain nourishment from the tree. Some fungi attack the heartwood and some the sapwood. After the fungus has been growing in the tree for a considerable period of time, a fruiting body, perhaps a bracket-shaped one, will be formed on the surface of the decayed area.

PLANTS AFFECTED A wide range of eucalypts and many other trees such as smooth-barked apple (*Angophora costata*).

CONTROL

• Organic/non-chemical: Fungicidal sprays will not solve this problem. If fungal brackets are noticed on a tree, seek advice from your local forestry office or employ a qualified arborist. Decayed trees can be extremely dangerous, as they are likely to drop branches or fall over in a storm. Many such trees can be repaired and if also watered and fertilised can be safely retained and regain a beautiful appearance.

Wood-rots — fruit trees

This group of fungi are weak pathogens and unable to attack healthy and undamaged trees. However, factors such as sunburn, drought, broken limbs, root injury, waterlogging and poor nutrition may predispose trees to attack. The fungi grow in damaged branches and obtain nourishment from the wood. This continues for a considerable period of time before the production of the fruiting bodies called 'brackets' on the outside of the affected wood. The brackets vary in colour and size depending on the species of fungus involved. They may be orange-red, grey, pink, brown or white and 10–60 mm across. Symptoms such as staining of the wood, wood rotting, bark cracks, and papery bark are often seen. Even large branches die back.

PLANTS AFFECTED A wide range of fruit, nut and ornamental trees.

CONTROL

• Organic/non-chemical: Dead limbs must be removed following approved tree surgery techniques. Fertilise lightly and water so that new bark will more quickly cover the wound. Sunburn can be minimised by painting the tree trunk and branches with a flat white plastic paint to reflect the sun, and by pruning so that the trunk and branches are shaded as much as possible. Control any diseases that cause leaf-fall in the summer.

Yellow crinkle — papaw

This disease of papaw is caused by the same mycoplasma which causes big bud (D) of a number of plants such as tomatoes, annual flowers and weeds. The first sign of the problem is the yellowing of the older leaves and a slight bending of the stalks at the junction of the trunk. The leaves at the top of the plant develop thin translucent areas around the edges and between the major veins. Sometimes these areas split and pieces fall out, giving the leaf a ragged appearance.

The topmost leaves also develop a claw-like appearance and remain far too small. Young fruit usually fall. Older leaves gradually fall from the plant until all that remains is a bare stem with a few deformed leaves at the top. Trees often do not die immediately but remain in this condition for months and months. They will never recover.

The disease is spread by a small leafhopper and is most common following periods of hot dry weather which cause the leafhopper to move from weeds (where it usually breeds and feeds) on to papaw plants. Do not confuse the damage of this disease with the damage caused by the broad mite (P).

PLANTS AFFECTED Papaws.

CONTROL Remove diseased plants and burn them. Replace with healthy trees.

Early symptoms: yellowing and drooping of leaves.

Zinc deficiency — citrus

If the plant is not able to take in enough zinc, the new growth being produced will have small, narrow leaves growing very close together in what is termed a 'rosette'. The areas between the main veins on the leaf will become whitish-yellow. This will be seen on young growth and will persist even as the leaves get older. In extreme cases the leaves will go completely white or yellow. There will be a dieback of smaller twigs and increased production of small, weak shoots if no measures are taken to combat this problem. Fruit will be reduced in numbers and in size and will appear elongated and pale. Zinc is leached out of light, sandy soils. In soils with a high organic matter or lime content zinc is present but unavailable to the plant.

PLANTS AFFECTED All citrus but only in certain areas.

CONTROL

• Organic: If the soil is alkaline try to make it more acid. This can be done by applying dusting sulphur. See *Gardening Down-under* by Handreck for details. If using poultry manure to supply micronutrients ensure it is not alkaline.

• Non-organic: Spray the leaves with a solution containing zinc. Apply this when the spring leaves are about two-thirds as big as they can become. Dissolve 1 g of zinc sulphate in every litre of water. The addition of urea at the rate of 10 g per litre of water will make the uptake of zinc by the plant more efficient, as well as applying some extra nitrogen. If manganese is also in short supply to the plant, manganese sulphate (1 g per litre of water) can also be added. Hot water will dissolve the zinc sulphate more quickly than cold water. Allow to cool before use. All spraying equipment must be thoroughly washed after use, because zinc corrodes metal. It is best to consult your local Department of Agriculture if deficiency diseases are suspected because different districts may require slightly different dose rates.

ACKNOWLEDGMENTS

I want to thank my mother and father, Elma and Lionel John Baker, for providing me with the education that made writing this book possible; and my family, Peter, Stephen and Julian McMaugh, for their help and forbearance during the four years that it took.

I appreciated greatly the help I received from Peter Fahy, John Walker, and Tony Bertus (Department of Agriculture, New South Wales), Peter McMaugh, Jackie Batten, Graeme Lown and Ray Rowell; and the many other busy people who cheerfully gave their time and knowledge, including Pat Barkley, Murray Fletcher, John Forsyth, Max Hill, David Letham, Ebehard Schicha, Rex Sweedman, Bruce Valentine, John Wilson of the Department of Agriculture, New South Wales; Helen Brookes (then Waite Institute, Adelaide); Bob Price (Department of Agriculture, Victoria); Tom Woodward (University of Queensland); Lynette Queale and Ted Matthews (South Australian Museum), and Phil Hadlington.

Thanks are also due to Betty Willis who typed the manuscript so efficiently; to Beverley Barnes who edited it; and to Anne Wilson, Nola Mallon, Liz Duncan and Dianne Leddy who were always pleasant and supportive.

This book owes a great deal to the artistic and technical ability of the designer, Sarah Laffey, whose hard work and meticulous attention to detail I appreciated greatly.

PHOTOGRAPHS

Reg Morrison and Ray Joyce took most of the photographs in this book. I appreciated their patience when photographing live insects, their care in following instructions so that the major features of the specimens could be emphasised, and their willingness to make themselves available whenever suitable specimens were found.

Most of the specimens used for the photographs were located and collected by the author. However, Graham Brown, Peter Fahy, Ross Fitzell, David Peasley and Bob Wickson, all of the Department of Agriculture, New South Wales, and David Ironside of the Department of Primary Industries, Nambour, Queensland, helped considerably with difficult-to-find or distant specimens, and their assistance was greatly appreciated.

Thanks are also due to John Hamilton and Colin Simson (Department of Agriculture, New South Wales), to Harley Rose (University of Sydney), to Ted Taylor (Forestry Commission, New South Wales), A. R. Paul (Royal Melbourne Institute of Technology) and James Wong (Department of Agriculture, Tasmania), for providing specimens; and to Helen Brookes (then of the Waite Institute, Adelaide), and Julia Humphreys (Department of Agriculture, New South Wales) for assistance with identification.

Judy McMaugh
1985

Contributing photographers and the photographs they supplied are listed below. All other photographs were taken by Reg Morrison and Ray Joyce.

Nan Barbour
p. 221 armillaria root rot

G. Goodyer, Department of Agriculture, New South Wales
p. 139 bogong moth; p. 157 earwigs (2)

A. J. Graham
p. 166 grapevine hawk moth

Anthony Healy
p. 30 bronze orange bug eggs; p. 30 caper white butterfly eggs; p. 31 bee hawk moth; p. 31 emperor gum moth; p. 31 spined citrus bug nymph; p. 133 Australian privet hawk moth (2); p. 188 oleander butterfly (2); p. 247 freckle; p. 259 leaf and pod spot — peas; p. 285 slime mould; p. 289 target spot (leaves)

M. Hill, Department of Agriculture, New South Wales
p. 224 bacterial leaf spot — cucurbits

D. A. Ironside, Department of Primary Industries, Nambour, Queensland
p. 162 fruitpiercing moth; p. 177 large mango tipborer; p. 177 latania scale on macadamia twig; p. 182 macadamia felted coccid; p. 182 macadamia flower caterpillar damage; p. 183 macadamia twig girdler; p. 193 pineapple scale; p. 197 redshouldered leaf beetles

D. Letham, Department of Agriculture, New South Wales
p. 218 anthracnose — lettuce; p. 238 club root — crucifers; p. 243 downy mildew — cucurbits

Julian Matthews
p. 184 Manuka blight

D. A. H. Murray, Department of Primary Industries, Nambour, Queensland
p. 193 pineapple scale

L. J. Penrose, Department of Agriculture, New South Wales
p. 223 bacterial canker — stonefruit

R. A. Peterson, Nambour
p. 287 stem-end rot — avocado

Brian Roberts
p. 18 weeds between wall and path; p. 18 broadleafed weeds.

F. S. Sedun, University of New England
p. 290 verticillium wilt

R. Weir, Department of Agriculture, New South Wales
p. 232 boron deficiency — beetroot; p. 254 iron deficiency — citrus

P. T. W. Wong, Department of Agriculture, New South Wales
p. 254 kikuyu yellows; p. 268 ophiobolus patch

Department of Agriculture, New South Wales
p. 38 V-shaped caterpillars (2)

Department of Agriculture, Tasmania
p. 259 leaf spot — blackcurrant

Department of Primary Industries, Queensland
p. 216 angular leaf spot — cucurbits; p. 217 anthracnose — bean; p. 218 anthracnose — macadamia nut; p. 222 bacterial blight — pea; p. 225 bacterial leaf spot — lettuce; p. 227 bitter rot — apple; p. 228 black leg — crucifers; p. 229 black root — radish; p. 231 black spot — strawberry; p. 239 common scab; p. 243 downy mildew — crucifers; p. 244 downy mildew — lettuce; p. 245 downy mildew — rose; p. 248 fusarium wilt — carnations; p. 248 fusarium wilt — cucurbits; p. 249 fusarium wilt — tomato (2); p. 249 fusarium yellows; p. 250 grey mould; p. 252 gummy stem blight (2); p. 253 halo blight — bean; p. 255 late blight — potato; p. 255 leaf blight — carrot; p. 258 leaf roll — potato; p. 264 lettuce big vein; p. 264 lettuce necrotic yellows; p. 266 mosaic — cucurbits; p. 267 mosaic — potato; p. 267 mosaic — turnip; p. 270 phytophthora blight — passionfruit (leaves); p. 273 powdery mildew — strawberry; p. 274 purple top wilt; p. 288 stony pit — pear; p. 292 white rot — onion; p. 295 yellow crinkle — papaw

Department of Primary Production, Northern Territory
p. 137 bean podborer

Department of Technical and Further Education, New South Wales
p. 227 big bud

APPENDIX I

Chemicals for pest control

® denotes registered trade name. Some common chemicals are sold by some manufacturers without a trade name. These include carbaryl and maldison. Some are sold as mixtures of an insecticide and a fungicide.

This list includes some commonly available products. The omission of some other products is inadvertent and is not meant to imply that they are not satisfactory.

*Chemical names are in alphabetical order.

Common Chemical Name	Trade Name
carbaryl	Carbaryl, Chewing Insect Spray®
chlorpyrifos	Chlorban®
cyfluthrin	Baythroid®
diazinon	Ant Killer Spray®, Grass Grub Killer® Diazamin®
dicofol	Kelthane®
dimethoate	Rogor®, Sucking Insect Killer®
disulfoton	Disyston®
fenamiphos	Nemacur®, Lawn Beetle Killer®
fenthion	Lebaycid®
maldison	Malathion®, Bug-Aphis Killer®, Malathon®
metaldehyde	Defender®, Snail & Slug Killer®
methiocarb	Mesurol®, Baysol®
omethoate	Folimat®
trichlorfon	Lawn Grub Killer®, Caterpillar Killer®

*Trade names are in alphabetical order

Trade Name	Common Chemical Name
Baysol®	methiocarb
Baythroid®	cyfluthrin
Bug-Aphis Killer®	maldison
Carbaryl®	carbaryl
Chlorban®	chlorpyrifos
Defender®	metaldehyde
Diazamin®	diazinon
Disyston®	disulfoton
Grass Grub Killer®	diazinon
Kelthane®	dicofol
Lawn Beetle Killer®	fenamiphos
Lawn Grub Killer®	trichlorfon
Lebaycid®	fenthion
Malathion®	maldison
Malathon®	maldison
Mesurol®	methiocarb
Nemacur®	fenamiphos
Rogor®	dimethoate
Snail & Slug Killer®	metaldehyde

APPENDIX II

Chemicals for disease control

® denotes registered trade name. Some common chemicals are sold by some manufacturers without a trade name. These include copper oxychloride and zineb.

This list includes some commonly available products. The omission of some other products is inadvertent and is not meant to imply that they are not satisfactory.

*Chemical names are in alphabetical order.

Common Chemical Name	Trade Name
chlorothalonil	Bravo®
copper hydroxide	Kocide®, Dry Bordeaux®
copper oxychloride	Bordox®
fenamiphos	Nemacur®
furalaxyl	Fongarid®
mancozeb	mancozeb
triadimefon	Bayleton®
triforine	Saprol®, Rose Spray® (mixture)
zineb	Curit®, zineb

*Trade names are in alphabetical order.

Trade Name	Common Chemical Name
Bayleton®	triadimefon
Bordox®	copper oxychloride
Bravo®	chlorothalonil
Curit®	zineb
Fongarid®	furalaxyl
Nemacur®	fenamiphos
Rose Spray®	triforine (mixture)
Saprol®	triforine

Organically acceptable pesticides

The definition of acceptable chemicals is not straightforward. For example, some of the chemicals that are accepted in small quantities are in fact artificial and some of the chemicals which are natural are processed chemically to extract or concentrate them.

Light mineral oils such as white oil — these are readily available and organically acceptable.

Soap sprays — these are available and have been improved in recent years.

Pyrethrum sprays (preferably without piperonyl butoxide) when the pyrethrum is extracted from *Chrysanthemum* * *cinerariaefolium* are acceptable, but not for constant use. This is a broad spectrum insecticide and so kills beneficial insects as well as pests. While there are a number of products on the market containing pyrethrum they usually also contain piperonyl butoxide which is called a synergist and helps the pyrethrum work more efficiently against insects.

Neem oil and extracts kill insects of various types. They are not yet available to home gardeners but research on their efficacy is well advanced and experiments on refining and extraction are being carried out.

Derris dust or rotenone kills a range of insects and is found in a number of home garden preparations. It is often an ingredient of mixtures aimed at controlling a range of diseases, insects and mites. A mix of sulphur and derris is common.

Sulphur dust, wettable sulphur, lime-sulphur are all acceptable in an organic garden if pesticides must be used. Sulphur preparations can be used to help control some mites, hard scales and fungal diseases.

Of the copper preparations, copper hydroxide is preferred by organic gardeners. Bordeaux mixture and copper oxychloride can also be used to help control some fungal and bacterial diseases.

Where to find organically acceptable methods

The future

In the next few years many more (new) efficient non-chemical control measures will become available. These are usually developed by scientists in universities or in government research institutions. Continued public funding of these bodies will help ensure refinements and additions to these methods.

Be on the lookout for new resistant varieties.

A greater variety of traps for monitoring or controlling insects will be available in the not too distant future and there will be more types of predators and parasites available for sale to individual gardeners.

The following are already available in large quantities for commercial growers and will become increasingly available to home gardeners.

Wasp parasites to control California red scale (p.143)
Ladybirds to control scales and mealybugs.
Wasp parasites to control citrus mealybug (*Planococcus citri*).
Wasp parasites to control greenhouse whitefly (see whiteflies p.210).
Predatory mites to control two-spotted mite (p.206).

Some of these are available in domestic packs for home garden use. These include the mealybug ladybird (*Cryptolaemus montrouzieri*) which eats a number of mealybug species can be obtained from from Bugs for Bugs, Mundubbera, Queensland and the Chilean predatory mite (*Phytoseiulus persimilis*) which attacks two-spotted mite can be obtained from Bio-Protection, Warwick, Queensland. These are sent through the post carefully packed with detailed instructions on how to use them to best effect. Gardening magazines may carry advertisements for these companies from time to time.

*Dendranthema

APPENDIX IV

Measuring chemical concentrates

Care must be taken at all times when pesticides are being used, and it is particularly important to take safety precautions when measuring concentrates. (See page 46.)

Follow label directions and measure accurately.

Some manufacturers provide measuring spoons or other systems specially designed for use with their products. Use these when they are provided.

In some cases measuring is unnecessary because the product is pre-weighted and packed in sachets, each designed for use in a given quantity of water.

In this book when detailed pesticide recommendations appear they are expressed like this:

Apply dimethoate (30%) at the rate of 1 mL per litre of water.

The term dimethoate (30%) means that 30% of the contents in the bottle is active ingredient and the other 70% is made up of other ingredients.

Another way of writing dimethoate (30%) is dimethoate 300 g/L, i.e. each litre of product contains 300 grams of active ingredient. Another example — Maldison (50%) can be expressed as maldison 500 g/L and this means that each litre of product contains 500 grams of active ingredient.

If the amount of active ingredient per unit of product changes, then the rate of use may change. For example, zineb (65%) requires the use of 2% of product per litre of water but zineb (80%) requires the use of only 1.5 g of product per litre because the 80% product has more active ingredient per litre than the 65% product.

The strength or recommended dose rates of products may differ from place to place, so you should follow the directions of your local Department of Agriculture.

It is not usually easy for home gardeners to weigh out small quantities of powdered pesticides.

If the measure provided with the pesticide has been lost it may be convenient to use the information below.

	grams/litre of water	equivalent in level metric teaspoonsful
carbaryl	1.2	1/2
copper oxychloride	2.5	1/2
	5	1
	7.5	1 1/2
mancozeb	1.5	1/2
wettable sulphur	2	1/2
	4	1
zineb	2	1

APPENDIX V

Safe use of pesticides

See also section on chemical controls pp. 41–48

1. Store pesticides in a locked cupboard.
2. Read the label.
3. Wear protective clothing.
4. Measure the concentrate carefully.
5. Spray on a still day.
6. Do not eat or smoke while measuring or spraying.
7. If you live far from medical help, keep a bottle of ipecac syrup (which will induce vomiting) and an emergency supply of 0.6 mg atropine tablets in your medicine cupboard. Atropine is an antidote for some pesticides.
8. Wash thoroughly after spraying and wash the protective clothing as well.
9. Seek medical advice if poisoning is suspected.

FURTHER READING

Baxter, Paul. *Fruit for Australian Gardens*. Pan Macmillan, Sydney, 1991.

Baxter, Paul. *Growing Fruit in Australia*. 4th ed. Nelson, Melbourne, 1990.

Blombery, Alex & Rodd, Tony. *Palms*. Angus & Robertson, Sydney, 1982.

Burke, Don. *Growing Grevilleas in Australia and New Zealand*. Kangaroo Press, Kenthurst, Sydney, 1983.

Chapman, B et al. *Natural Pest Control*. Nelson, Melbourne, 1986.

Common, I. F. B. & Waterhouse, D. F. *Butterflies of Australia*. Rev. ed. Angus & Robertson, Sydney, 1981.

C.S.I.R.O. *The Insects of Australia*. 2nd ed. Melbourne University Press, Melbourne, 1991.

Elliott, W. Rodger. *Pruning: A Practical Guide*. Lothian, Melbourne, 1984.

Fahy, P. C. & Persley, G. J. (editors) *Plant Bacterial Diseases: a diagnostic guide*. Academic, Sydney, 1983.

Forsberg, J. L. *Diseases of Ornamental Plants*. University of Illinois Press, Chicago, 1975.

Glowinski, Louis. *The Complete Book of Fruit Growing in Australia*. Lothian, Melbourne, 1991.

Hadlington, P. W. & Johnston, J. A. *Australian Trees: Their Care and Repair*. 4th ed. NSW University Press, Sydney, 1988.

Hadlington, P. W. & Johnston, J. A. *An Introduction to Australian Insects*. NSW University Press, Sydney, 1982.

Hadlington, P. and Taylor T. *The Native Garden Doctor*. Simon & Schuster (East Roseville, NSW), Australia, 1992.

Haller, John N. *Tree Care*. 2nd ed. Macmillan, N.Y., 1986.

Handreck, K. *Gardening Down-under*. CSIRO, Melbourne, 1993.

Handreck, H.A. & Black, N.D. *Growing Media for Ornamental Plants and Turf*. 2nd ed. NSW University Press, Sydney, 1994.

Harris, Richard W. *Arboriculture — Integrated Management of Landscape Trees, Shrubs and Vines*. 2nd ed. Prentice-Hall, Englewood Cliffs, N. J., 1992.

Hartmann, H. T. et al. *Plant Science*. 2nd ed. Prentice-Hall, Englewood Cliffs, N. J., 1988.

Hely, P. C. et al. *Insect Pests of Fruit and Vegetables in N.S.W.* Inkata Press, Melbourne, 1982.

Horst, R. Kenneth. *Compendium of Rose Diseases*. The American Phytopathological Society, St Paul, Minnesota, 1983.

Hughes, R. D. *Living Insects*. Collins, Sydney, 1975.

Johnson, Warren T. & Lyon, Howard H. *Insects that Feed on Trees and Shrubs*. 2nd ed. Comstock, Ithaca, 1988.

Jones, D. L. & Clemesha, S. C. *Australian Ferns and Fern Allies*. 2nd ed. Reed, Sydney, 1989.

Jones, David. *Palms in Australia*. Rev. ed. Reed, Frenchs Forest, Sydney, 1987.

Jones, David and Elliot, W. Rodger. *Pests, Diseases and Ailments of Australian Plants*. Lothian, Melbourne, 1986.

Kilpatrick, David T. *Pruning for the Australian Gardener*. Rigby, Adelaide, 1968.

Kleinschmidt, H. W. & Johnson, R. W. *Weeds of Queensland*. Government Printer, Brisbane, 1987.

Lewis, T. *Thrips: Their Biology, Ecology and Economic Importance*. Academic, London, 1973.

McCubbin, Charles. *Australian Butterflies*. Nelson Savvas, Adelaide, 1985.

Marks, G. C. et al. *Tree Diseases in Victoria*. Forests Commission, Victoria, Melbourne, 1982.

Metcalf, L. J. *The Cultivation of New Zealand Trees and Shrubs*. 2nd ed. Reed, Wellington, 1975.

Oakman, H. *Tropical and Subtropical Gardening*. 2nd ed. Jacaranda, Brisbane, 1981.

Pirone, P. P. *Diseases and Pests of Ornamental Plants*. 5th ed. Wiley, N. Y., 1978.

Pirone, P. P. *Tree Maintenance*. 6th ed. Oxford University Press, N. Y., 1988.

Raven, Peter H. et al. *Biology of Plants*. 5th ed. Worth, N. Y., 1992.

Rowell, R. J. *Ornamental Flowering Trees in Australia*. 2nd ed. Reed, Sydney, 1991.

Rowell, R. J. *Ornamental Flowering Shrubs in Australia*. 2nd ed. Reed, Sydney 1991.

Rowell, R. J. *Ornamental Plants in Australia*. 4th ed. NSW University Press, Sydney, 1992.

Simpfendorfer, K. J. *An Introduction to Trees for South Eastern Australia*. 2nd ed. Inkata Press, Melbourne, 1993.

Smiley, R. W. *Compendium of Turfgrass Diseases*. 2nd ed. American Phytopathological Society, St Paul, Minnesota, 1992.

Swane, Valerie. *The Australian Gardeners' Catalogue*. Rev. ed. Angus & Robertson, Sydney, 1990.

Tattar, Terry. A. *Diseases of Shade Trees*. Rev. ed. Academic, New York, 1989.

Vock, N. T. A *Handbook of Plant Diseases*. Qld. Department of Primary Industries, Brisbane, 1978.

Weier, T. Elliot. *Botany: An Introduction to Plant Biology*. 6th ed. Wiley, N. Y., 1982.

Westwood, Melvin N. *Temperate-zone Pomology*. Rev. ed. W. H. Freeman, San Francisco, 1988.

Wheeler, B. E. J. *An Introduction to Plant Diseases*. Wiley, London, 1969.

Whitney, P. J. *Microbial Plant Pathology*. Hutchison, London, 1976.

Wrigley, John W. *Australian Native Plants*. 3rd ed. Collins, Sydney, 1988.

Woods, A. *Pest Control: A. Survey*. McGraw-Hill, London, 1974.

Leaflets published by State Departments of Agriculture and Primary Industries.

INDEX